AUTOMOTIVE STEERING, SUSPENSION, AND ALIGNMENT

FOURTH EDITION

James D. Halderman

PEARSON

Prentice
Hall

Upper Saddle River, New Jersey
Columbus, Ohio

Library of Congress Cataloging-in-Publication Data

Halderman, James D.,
   Automotive steering, suspension, and alignment / James D. Halderman.
—4th ed.
      p. cm.
   Includes index.
   ISBN 0-13-222905-6
 1. Automobiles—Steering-gear. 2. Automobiles—Springs and suspension. 3. Automobiles—Wheels—Alignment. I. Title.
   TL259.H35 2008
   629.2'47—dc22   2007013660

Editor in Chief: Vernon Anthony
Associate Managing Editor: Christine Buckendahl
Editorial Assistant: Lara Dimmick
Production Coordination: Judy Ludowitz, Carlisle Publishing Services
Production Editor: Holly Shufeldt
Design Coordinator: Diane Ernsberger
Text and Cover Designer: Candace Rowley
Cover art: Jeff Hinckley
Senior Production Manager: Deidra Schwartz
Director of Marketing: David Gesell
Marketing Assistant: Les Roberts

This book was set in Weidemann by Carlisle Publishing Services. It was printed and bound by Edwards Brothers. The cover was printed by Phoenix Color Corp.

Thanks to Byers Chevrolet, Dublin, Ohio, for allowing us to shoot the cover image in their showroom.

Pearson Education Ltd.   Pearson Education Australia Pty. Limited
Pearson Education Singapore Pte. Ltd.   Pearson Education North Asia Ltd.
Pearson Education Canada, Ltd.   Pearson Educación de Mexico, S.A. de C.V.
Pearson Education—Japan   Pearson Education Malaysia Pte. Ltd.

10 9 8 7 6 5 4 3 2 1
ISBN-13: 978-0-13-222905-0
ISBN-10:   0-13-222905-6

PREFACE

PROFESSIONAL TECHNICIAN SERIES

Part of Prentice Hall Automotive's Professional Technician Series, the fourth edition of *Automotive Steering, Suspension, and Alignment* presents students and instructors with a practical, real-world approach to automotive technology and service. The series includes textbooks that cover all eight ASE certification test areas of automotive service: Engine Repair (A1), Automotive Transmissions/Transaxles (A2), Manual Drive Trains and Axles (A3), Suspension and Steering (A4), Brakes (A5), Electrical/Electronic Systems (A6), Heating and Air Conditioning (A7), and Engine Performance (A8).

Current revisions are written by the experienced author and peer reviewed by automotive instructors and experts in the field to ensure technical accuracy.

UPDATES TO THE FOURTH EDITION INCLUDE:

- All content is correlated to 100% of the ASE and NATEF tasks for the Suspension and Steering (A4) content area.
- Expanded coverage of electronic suspension, including electronic stability control (ESC), is included.
- New content on tire pressure monitoring systems (TPMS) including direct and indirect systems.
- Many new photographs and line drawings help students understand the content material and bring the subject alive.
- Expanded content is presented on suspension and steering details.
- Many new photo sequences help explain service procedures.
- Each technical topic is discussed in one place or chapter. Unlike other textbooks, this book is written so that the theory, construction, diagnosis, and service of a particular component or system is presented in one location. There is no need to search through the entire book for other references to the same topic.

ASE AND NATEF CORRELATED

NATEF-certified programs need to demonstrate that they use course materials that cover NATEF and ASE tasks. This textbook has been correlated to the ASE and NATEF task lists and offers comprehensive coverage of all tasks. An **NATEF TASK CORRELATION CHART** and an **ASE TEST CORRELATION CHART** are included in the appendices to the book.

A COMPLETE INSTRUCTOR AND STUDENT SUPPLEMENTS PACKAGE

This textbook is accompanied by a full package of instructor and student supplements. See page vi for a detailed list of all supplements available with this book.

A FOCUS ON DIAGNOSIS AND PROBLEM SOLVING

The Professional Technician series has been developed to satisfy the need for a greater emphasis on problem diagnosis. Automotive instructors and service managers agree that students and beginning technicians need more training in diagnostic procedures and skill development. To meet this need and demonstrate how real-world problems are solved, the "Real World Fix" features that appear in the textbook are included throughout and highlight how real-life problems are diagnosed and repaired.

The following pages highlight the unique core features that set the Professional Technician series apart from other automotive textbooks.

IN-TEXT FEATURES

OBJECTIVES and **KEY TERMS** appear at the beginning of each chapter to help students and instructors focus on the most important material in each chapter. The chapter objectives are based on specific ASE and NATEF tasks.

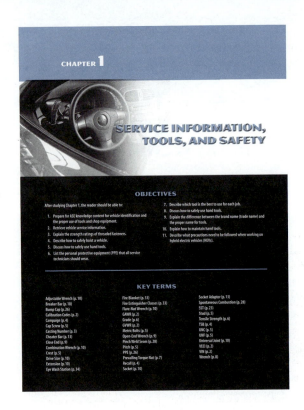

CHAPTER **1**

SERVICE INFORMATION, TOOLS, AND SAFETY

OBJECTIVES

After studying Chapter 1, the reader should be able to:

1. Prepare for ASE knowledge content for vehicle identification and the proper use of tools and shop equipment.
2. Retrieve vehicle service information.
3. Explain the strength ratings of threaded fasteners.
4. Describe how to safely hoist a vehicle.
5. Discuss how to safely use hand tools.
6. List the personal protective equipment (PPE) that all service technicians should wear.
7. Describe which tool is the best to use for each job.
8. Discuss how to safely use hand tools.
9. Explain the difference between the brand name (trade name) and the proper name for tools.
10. Explain how to maintain hand tools.
11. Describe what precautions need to be followed when working on hybrid electric vehicles (HEVs).

KEY TERMS

Adjustable Wrench (p. 10)
Breaker Bar (p. 10)
Bump Cap (p. 26)
Calibration Codes (p. 2)
Campaign (p. 4)
Cap Screw (p. 5)
Casting Number (p. 3)
Cheater Bar (p. 13)
Close End (p. 9)
Combination Wrench (p. 10)
Crest (p. 5)
Drive Size (p. 10)
Extension (p. 10)
Eye Wash Station (p. 34)

Fire Blanket (p. 33)
Fire Extinguisher Classes (p. 33)
Flare-Nut Wrench (p. 10)
GAWR (p. 2)
Grade (p. 6)
GVWR (p. 2)
Metric Bolts (p. 5)
Open-End Wrench (p. 9)
Pinch Weld Seam (p. 28)
Pitch (p. 5)
PPE (p. 26)
Prevailing Torque Nut (p. 7)
Recall (p. 4)
Socket (p. 10)

Socket Adapter (p. 13)
Spontaneous Combustion (p. 28)
SST (p. 23)
Stud (p. 5)
Tensile Strength (p. 6)
TSB (p. 4)
UNC (p. 5)
UNF (p. 5)
Universal Joint (p. 10)
VECI (p. 2)
VIN (p. 2)
Wrench (p. 8)

TECH TIP

RIGHT TO TIGHTEN

It is sometimes confusing to know which way to rotate a wrench or screwdriver, especially when the head of the fastener is pointing away from y
looking at the fastener, say "righ

SAFETY TIP

SHOP CLOTH DISPOSAL

Always dispose of oily shop cloths in an enclosed container to prevent a fire. See Figure 1-72. Whenever oily cloths are thrown together on the floor or workbench, a
ccur that can ignite the cloth even
. This process of ignition without
spontaneous combustion.

REAL WORLD FIX

I THOUGHT THE LUG NUTS WERE TIGHT!

Proper wheel nut torque is critical, as one technician discovered when a customer returned complaining of a lot of noise from the right rear wheel. See Figure 4-14. for a photo of what the technici
(wheel) nuts had loosened and

CAUTION: Most vehicle manufactu
studs/nuts should *not* be lubricated
of a lubricant on the threads could cause

FREQUENTLY ASKED QUESTION

IS IT LB-FT OR FT-LB OF TORQUE?

The unit for torque is expressed as a force times the distance (leverage) from the object. Therefore, the official unit for torque is lb-ft (pound-feet) or Newton-meters (a force times a distance). However, it is commonly expressed in ft-lbs and even some torque wrenches are labeled with this unit.

TECH TIPS feature real-world advice and "tricks of the trade" from ASE-certified master technicians.

SAFETY TIPS alert students to possible hazards on the job and how to avoid them.

REAL WORLD FIXES present students with actual automotive service scenarios and show how these common (and sometimes uncommon) problems were diagnosed and repaired.

FREQUENTLY ASKED QUESTIONS are based on the author's own experience and provide answers to many of the most common questions asked by students and beginning service technicians.

NOTES provide students with additional technical information to give them a greater understanding of a specific task or procedure.

CAUTIONS alert students about potential *damage to the vehicle* that can occur during a specific task or service procedure.

WARNINGS alert students to potential dangers to themselves during a specific task or service procedure.

NOTE: Some power steering pumps are of the slipper or roller design instead of the vane type. When the engine starts, the drive belt rotates the power steering pump pulley and the rotor assembly inside the power steering pump.

CAUTION: When the steering wheel is released, the spring force of the torsion bar returns the two elements to their natural positions. Fluid pressure equalizes throughout the steering gear and re-centers the piston in the middle of the steering gear.

WARNING: When the steering wheel is aimed straight-ahead, the valve is in its neutral position. Fluid enters the valve and flows equally to both sides of the steering gear piston and to the return line.

STEP-BY-STEP photo sequences show in detail the steps involved in performing a specific task or service procedure.

HOISTING THE VEHICLE Step-by-Step

STEP 1 The first step in hoisting a vehicle is to properly align the vehicle in the center of the stall.

STEP 2 Most vehicles will be correctly positioned when the left front tire is centered on the tire pad.
TIRE PAD

STEP 3 Most pads at the end of the hoist arms can be rotated to allow for many different types of vehicle construction.

STEP 4 The arms of the lifts can be retracted or extended to accommodate vehicles of many different lengths.

SUMMARY

1. Bolts, studs, and nuts are commonly used as fasteners in the chassis. The sizes for fractional and metric threads are different and are not interchangeable. The grade is the rating of the strength of a fastener.
2. Whenever a vehicle is raised above the ground, it must be supported at a substantial section of the body or frame.
3. Wrenches are available in open end, box end, and combination open and box end.
4. An adjustable wrench should only be used when the proper-size wrench is not available.
5. Line wrenches are also called flare-nut wrenches, fitting wrenches, or tube-nut wrenches and are used to remove fuel or refrigerant lines.
6. Sockets are rotated by a ratchet or breaker bar, also called a flex handle.
7. Torque wrenches measure the amount of torque applied to a fastener.
8. Screwdriver types include straight blade (flat tip) and Phillips.
9. Hammers and mallets come in a variety of sizes and weights.
10. Pliers are a useful tool and are available in many different types, including slip-joint, multigroove, linesman's, diagonal, needle-nose, and locking pliers.
11. Other common hand tools include snap-ring pliers, files, cutters, punches, chisels, and hacksaws.

REVIEW QUESTIONS

1. List three precautions that must be taken whenever hoisting (lifting) a vehicle.
2. Describe how to determine the grade of a fastener, including how the markings differ between fractional and metric bolts.
3. List four items that are personal protective equipment (PPE).
4. List the types of fire extinguishers and their usage.
5. Why are wrenches offset 15 degrees?
6. What are the other names for a line wrench?
7. What are the standard automotive drive sizes for sockets?
8. Which type of screwdriver requires the use of a hammer or mallet?
9. What is inside a dead-blow hammer?
10. What type of cutter is available in left and right cutters?

CHAPTER QUIZ

1. The correct location for the pads when hoisting or jacking the vehicle can often be found in the _____.
   a. Service manual
   b. Shop manual
   c. Owner's manual
   d. All of the above
2. For the best working position, the work should be _____.
   a. At neck or head level
   b. At knee or ankle level
   c. Overhead by about 1 foot
   d. At chest or elbow level
3. A high-strength bolt is identified by _____.
   a. A UNC symbol
   b. Lines on the head
   c. Strength letter codes
   d. The coarse threads
4. A fastener that uses threads on both ends is called a _____.
   a. Cap screw
   b. Stud
   c. Machine screw
   d. Crest fastener

The **SUMMARY, REVIEW QUESTIONS,** and **CHAPTER QUIZ** at the end of each chapter help students review the material presented in the chapter and test themselves to see how much they've learned.

SUPPLEMENTS

The comprehensive **INSTRUCTOR'S MANUAL** includes chapter outlines, answers to all questions from the book, teaching tips, and additional exercises.

An **INSTRUCTOR'S RESOURCE CD-ROM** features:

- A complete text-specific **TEST BANK WITH TEST CREATION SOFTWARE**
- A comprehensive, text-specific **POWERPOINT PRESENTATION** featuring much of the art from the text as well as video clips and animations
- An **IMAGE LIBRARY** featuring additional images to use for class presentations
- Additional student activities including **CROSSWORD PUZZLES, WORD SEARCHES,** and other worksheets
- A **SAMPLE ASE TEST** as well as the complete **ASE TASK LIST**

Included with every copy of the book, the **STUDENT RESOURCE CD-ROM** features:

- A comprehensive, text-specific **POWERPOINT PRESENTATION** featuring all of the art from the text, as well as video clips and animations
- Additional activities including **CROSSWORD PUZZLES, WORD SEARCHES,** and other worksheets
- **A NATEF TASK CHECK LIST**
- **A SAMPLE ASE TEST** as well as the complete **ASE TASK LIST**

Available to be packaged with the book, the **STUDENT WORKTEXT (NATEF CORRELATED TASK SHEETS)** includes dozens of job sheets tied to specific NATEF tasks. Contact your local Prentice Hall representative for information on ordering the textbook packaged with the student worktext.

ACKNOWLEDGMENTS

A large number of people and organizations have cooperated in providing the reference material and technical information used in this text. The author wishes to express sincere thanks to the following organizations for their special contributions:

Allied Signal Automotive Aftermarket
Arrow Automotive
ASE
Automotion, Inc.
Automotive Parts Rebuilders Association (APRA)
Bear Automotive
Bendix
British Petroleum (BP)
Cooper Automotive Company
CR Services
DaimlerChrysler Corporation
Dana Corporation
Fluke Corporation
FMC Corporation
Ford Motor Company
General Motors Corporation Service Technology Group
Hennessy Industries
Hunter Engineering Company
John Bean Company
Lee Manufacturing Company
Monroe Shock Absorbers
MOOG Automotive Inc.
Northstar Manufacturing Company, Inc.
Perfect Hofmann-USA
Shimco International, Inc.
SKF USA, Inc.
Society of Automotive Engineers (SAE)
Specialty Products Company
Tire and Rim Association, Inc.
Toyota Motor Sales, USA, Inc.
TRW Inc.
Wurth USA, Inc.

Technical and Content Reviewers

The following people reviewed the manuscript before production and checked it for technical accuracy and clarity of presentation. Their suggestions and recommendations were included in the final draft of the manuscript. Their input helped make this textbook clear and technically accurate while maintaining the easy-to-read style that has made other books from the same author so popular.

Jim Anderson
Greenville High School

Victor Bridges
Umpqua Community College

Robert Costanzo
Gateway Community College

Dr. Roger Donovan
Illinois Central College

A. C. Durdin
Moraine Park Technical College

Herbert Ellinger
Western Michigan University

Al Engledahl
College of Dupage

Larry Hagelberger
Upper Valley Joint Vocational School

Oldrick Hajzler
Red River College

Betsy Hoffman
Vermont Technical College

Steve Levin
Columbus State Community College

Steven T. Lee
Lincoln Technical Institute

Carlton H. Mabe, Sr.
Virginia Western Community College

Roy Marks
Owens Community College

James McCormack
American River College

Kerry Meier
San Juan College

Fritz Peacock
Indiana Vocational Technical College

Dennis Peter
NAIT (Canada)

Kenneth Redick
Hudson Valley Community College

Peter Robert
Lansing Community College

Mitchell Walker
St. Louis Community College at Forest Park

Jennifer Wise
Sinclair Community College

Photo Sequences

I wish to thank Chuck Taylor, Mike Garblik, Blaine Heeter, and Frank Clay of Sinclair Community College, Dayton, Ohio, who helped with many of the photos.

Special thanks to Richard Reaves for all of his help. Most of all, I wish to thank Michelle Halderman for her assistance in all phases of manuscript preparation.

James D. Halderman

BRIEF CONTENTS

CONTENTS

SERVICE INFORMATION, TOOLS, AND SAFETY

OBJECTIVES

After studying Chapter 1, the reader should be able to:

1. Prepare for ASE knowledge content for vehicle identification and the proper use of tools and shop equipment.
2. Retrieve vehicle service information.
3. Explain the strength ratings of threaded fasteners.
4. Describe how to safely hoist a vehicle.
5. Discuss how to safely use hand tools.
6. List the personal protective equipment (PPE) that all service technicians should wear.
7. Describe which tool is the best to use for each job.
8. Discuss how to safely use hand tools.
9. Explain the difference between the brand name (trade name) and the proper name for tools.
10. Explain how to maintain hand tools.
11. Describe what precautions need to be followed when working on hybrid electric vehicles (HEVs).

KEY TERMS

VEHICLE IDENTIFICATION

All service work requires that the vehicle, including the engine and accessories, be properly identified. The most common identification is knowing the make, model, and year of the vehicle. For example

> **Make:** Chevrolet
> **Model:** Trailblazer
> **Year:** 2003

The year of the vehicle is often difficult to determine exactly. A model may be introduced as the next year's model as soon as January of the previous year. Typically, a new model year starts in September or October of the year prior to the actual new year, but not always. This is why the **vehicle identification number,** usually abbreviated **VIN,** is so important. See Figure 1-1.

Since 1981 all vehicle manufacturers have used a VIN that is 17 characters long. Although every vehicle manufacturer assigns various letters or numbers within these 17 characters, there are some constants, including:

- The first number or letter designates the country of origin.

1 = United States	6 = Australia	L = China	V = France
2 = Canada	8 = Argentina	R = Taiwan	W = Germany
3 = Mexico	9 = Brazil	S = England	X = Russia
4 = United States	J = Japan	T = Czechoslovakia	Y = Sweden
5 = United States	K = Korea	U = Romania	Z = Italy

- The fourth or fifth character is the vehicle line/series.
- The sixth character is the body style.
- The seventh character is the restraint system.

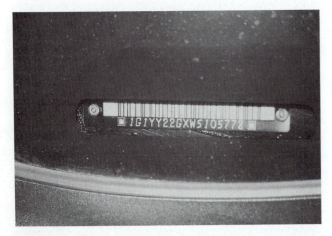

FIGURE 1-1 Typical vehicle identification number (VIN) as viewed through the windshield.

- The eighth character is often the engine code. (Some engines cannot be determined by the VIN number.)
- The tenth character represents the year on all vehicles. See the following chart.

VIN Year Chart			
A = 1980/2010	J = 1988/2018	T = 1996/2026	4 = 2004/2034
B = 1981/2011	K = 1989/2019	V = 1997/2027	5 = 2005/2035
C = 1982/2012	L = 1990/2020	W = 1998/2028	6 = 2006/2036
D = 1983/2013	M = 1991/2021	X = 1999/2029	7 = 2007/2037
E = 1984/2014	N = 1992/2022	Y = 2000/2030	8 = 2008/2038
F = 1985/2015	P = 1993/2023	1 = 2001/2031	9 = 2009/2039
G = 1986/2016	R = 1994/2024	2 = 2002/2032	
H = 1987/2017	S = 1995/2025	3 = 2003/2033	
Note: The pattern repeats every 30 years.			

Vehicle Safety Certification Label

A vehicle safety certification label is attached to the left side pillar post on the rearward-facing section of the left front door. This label indicates the month and year of manufacture as well as the **gross vehicle weight rating (GVWR),** the **gross axle weight rating (GAWR),** and the vehicle identification number (VIN).

VECI Label

The **vehicle emissions control information (VECI)** label under the hood of the vehicle shows informative settings and emission hose routing information. See Figure 1-2.

The VECI label (sticker) can be located on the bottom side of the hood, the radiator fan shroud, the radiator core support, or on the strut towers. The VECI label usually includes the following information:

- Engine identification
- Emissions standard that the vehicle meets
- Vacuum hose routing diagram
- Base ignition timing (if adjustable)
- Spark plug type and gap
- Valve lash
- Emission calibration code

Calibration Codes

Calibration codes are usually located on powertrain control modules (PCMs) or other controllers. When diagnosing an engine operating fault, it is often necessary to know the calibration

FIGURE 1-2   The vehicle emission control information (VECI) sticker is placed under the hood.

code to determine whether the vehicle is the subject of a technical service bulletin or other service procedure. See Figure 1-3.

Casting Numbers

Whenever an engine part such as a block is cast, a number is put into the mold to identify the casting. See Figure 1-4. These **casting numbers** can be used to check dimensions such as the cubic inch displacement and other information such as the year of manufacture. Sometimes changes are made to the mold, yet the casting number is not changed. Most often the casting number is the best piece of identifying information that the service technician can use for identifying an engine.

SERVICE INFORMATION

Service information is needed by the service technician to determine specifications and service procedures, as well as learn about any necessary special tools.

Service Manuals

Factory and aftermarket service manuals contain specifications and service procedures. While factory service manuals cover just one year and one or more models of the same vehicle, most aftermarket service manufacturers cover multiple years and/or models in one manual. See Figure 1-5.

Included in most service manuals are the following:

- Capacities and recommended specifications for all fluids
- Specifications including engine and routine maintenance items

FIGURE 1-3   A typical calibration code sticker on the case of a controller. The information on this sticker is often needed when ordering parts or a replacement controller.

- Testing procedures
- Service procedures including the use of special tools when needed

Electronic Service Information

Electronic service information is available mostly by subscription and provides access to an Internet site where service-manual-type information is available. See Figure 1-6. Most vehicle manufacturers also offer electronic service information to their dealers and to most schools and colleges that offer corporate training programs.

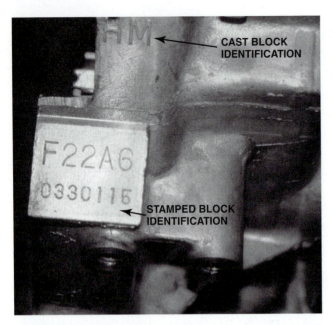

FIGURE 1-4 Engine block identification can be either cast, stamped, or both.

FIGURE 1-5 A factory service manual contains all specifications and procedures for a particular vehicle or model in one or more volumes.

FIGURE 1-6 Electronic service information is available from after-market sources such as All-Data and Mitchell-on-Demand as well as on websites hosted by the vehicle manufacturer.

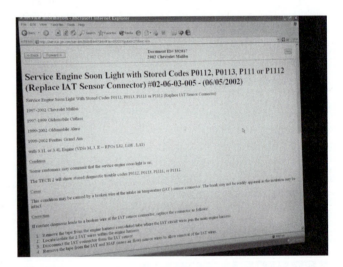

FIGURE 1-7 Technical service bulletins are issued by vehicle manufacturers when a fault occurs that affects many vehicles with the same problem.

Technical Service Bulletins

Technical service bulletins, often abbreviated **TSBs,** are issued by the vehicle manufacturer to notify service technicians of a problem, and they include the necessary corrective action. Technical service bulletins are designed for dealership technicians but are republished by aftermarket companies and made available along with other service information to shops and vehicle repair facilities. See Figure 1-7.

Internet

The Internet has opened the field for information exchange and access to technical advice. One of the most useful websites is the International Automotive Technician's Network at *www.iatn.net*. This is a free site, but service technicians need to register to join. If a small monthly sponsor fee is paid, the shop or service technician can gain access to the archives, which include thousands of successful repairs in the searchable database.

Recalls and Campaigns

A **recall** or **campaign** is issued by a vehicle manufacturer and a notice is sent to all owners in the event of a safety-related fault or concern. While these faults may be repaired by shops, they are generally handled by a local dealer. Items that have created recalls in the past include potential fuel system leakage problems, exhaust leakage, or electrical malfunctions that could cause a possible fire or cause the engine to stall. Unlike technical service bulletins, whose cost is only covered when the vehicle is within the warranty period, a recall or campaign is always done at no cost to the vehicle owner.

THREADED FASTENERS

Most of the threaded fasteners used on vehicles are cap screws. They are called **cap screws** when they are threaded into a casting. Automotive service technicians usually refer to these fasteners as *bolts*, regardless of how they are used. In this chapter, they are called bolts. Sometimes, studs are used for threaded fasteners. A stud is a short rod with threads on both ends. Often, a stud will have coarse threads on one end and fine threads on the other end. The end of the stud with coarse threads is screwed into the casting. A nut is used on the opposite end to hold the parts together.

The fastener threads *must* match the threads in the casting or nut. The threads may be measured either in fractions of an inch (called fractional) or in metric units. The size is measured across the outside of the threads, called the **crest,** or major diameter, of the thread. See Figure 1-8.

Fractional threads are either coarse or fine. The coarse threads are called **Unified National Coarse (UNC),** and the fine threads are called **Unified National Fine (UNF).** Standard combinations of sizes and number of threads per inch (called **pitch**) are used. Pitch can be measured with a thread pitch gauge, as shown in Figure 1-9. Bolts are identified by their diameter and length as measured from below the head, and not by the size of the head or the size of the wrench used to remove or install the bolt.

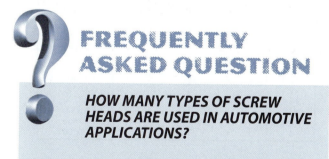

FREQUENTLY ASKED QUESTION

HOW MANY TYPES OF SCREW HEADS ARE USED IN AUTOMOTIVE APPLICATIONS?

Many types of screw heads are used, including Torx, hex (also called Allen), and many others used in custom vans and motorhomes. See Figure 1-10.

Fractional thread sizes are specified by the diameter in fractions of an inch and the number of threads per inch. Typical UNC thread sizes are 5/16–18 and 1/2–13. Similar UNF thread sizes are 5/16–24 and 1/2–20. See Figure 1-11.

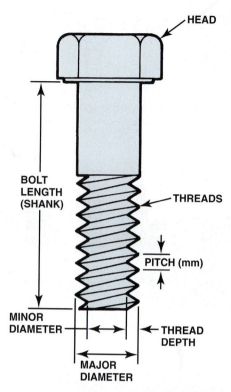

FIGURE 1-8 The dimensions of a typical bolt, showing where sizes are measured.

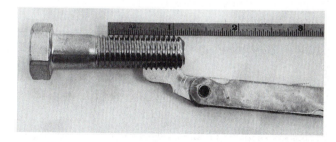

FIGURE 1-9 Thread pitch gauge used to measure the pitch of the thread. This bolt has 13 threads to the inch.

Metric Bolts

The size of a **metric bolt** is specified by the letter *M* followed by the diameter in millimeters (mm) across the outside (crest) of the threads. Typical metric sizes are M8 and M12. Fine metric threads are specified by the thread diameter followed by *X* and the distance between the threads measured in millimeters (e.g., M8 X 1.5). See Figure 1-12.

Grades of Bolts

Bolts are made from many different types of steel, and for this reason some are stronger than others. The strength or

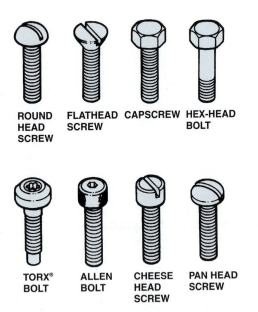

ROUND HEAD SCREW | **FLATHEAD SCREW** | **CAPSCREW** | **HEX-HEAD BOLT**

TORX® BOLT | **ALLEN BOLT** | **CHEESE HEAD SCREW** | **PAN HEAD SCREW**

FIGURE 1-10 Bolts and screws have many different heads; the type of head determines which tool must be used.

classification of a bolt is called the **grade.** The bolt heads are marked to indicate their grade strength.

The actual grade of bolts is two more than the number of lines on the bolt head. Metric bolts have a decimal number to indicate the grade. More lines or a higher grade number indicate a stronger bolt. Higher-grade bolts usually have threads that are rolled rather than cut, which also makes them stronger. See Figure 1-13. In some cases, nuts and machine screws have similar grade markings.

CAUTION: *Never* use hardware store (nongraded) bolts, studs, or nuts on any vehicle steering, suspension, or brake component. Always use the exact size and grade of hardware that is specified and used by the vehicle manufacturer.

Tensile Strength

Graded fasteners have a higher tensile strength than nongraded fasteners. **Tensile strength** is the maximum stress used under tension (lengthwise force) without causing failure of the fastener. Tensile strength is specified in pounds per square inch (psi). See the accompanying chart showing the grade and specified tensile strength.

The strength and type of steel used in a bolt is supposed to be indicated by a raised mark on the head of the bolt. The

Size	Threads per inch		Outside Diameter Inches
	NC UNC	NF UNF	
0	. .	80	0.0600
1	64	. .	0.0730
1	. .	72	0.0730
2	56	. .	0.0860
2	. .	64	0.0860
3	48	. .	0.0990
3	. .	56	0.0990
4	40	. .	0.1120
4	. .	48	0.1120
5	40	. .	0.1250
5	. .	44	0.1250
6	32	. .	0.1380
6	. .	40	0.1380
8	32	. .	0.1640
8	. .	36	0.1640
10	24	. .	0.1900
10	. .	32	0.1900
12	24	. .	0.2160
12	. .	28	0.2160
1/4	20	. .	0.2500
1/4	. .	28	0.2500
5/16	18	. .	0.3125
5/16	. .	24	0.3125
3/8	16	. .	0.3750
3/8	. .	24	0.3750
7/16	14	. .	0.4375
7/16	. .	20	0.4375
1/2	13	. .	0.5000
1/2	. .	20	0.5000
9/16	12	. .	0.5625
9/16	. .	18	0.5625
5/8	11	. .	0.6250
5/8	. .	18	0.6250
3/4	10	. .	0.7500
3/4	. .	16	0.7500
7/8	9	. .	0.8750
7/8	. .	14	0.8750
1	8	. .	1.0000
1	. .	12	1.0000
1 1/8	7	. .	1.1250
1 1/8	. .	12	1.1250
1 1/4	7	. .	1.2500
1 1/4	. .	12	1.2500
1 3/8	6	. .	1.3750
1 3/8	. .	12	1.3750
1 1/2	6	. .	1.5000
1 1/2	. .	12	1.5000
1 3/4	5	. .	1.7500
2	4 1/2	. .	2.0000
2 1/4	4 1/2	. .	2.2500
2 1/2	4	. .	2.5000
2 3/4	4	. .	2.7500
3	4	. .	3.0000
3 1/4	4	. .	3.2500
3 1/2	4	. .	3.5000
3 3/4	4	. .	3.7500
4	4	. .	4.0000

FIGURE 1-11 The American National System is one method of sizing fasteners.

type of mark depends on the standard to which the bolt was manufactured. Most often, bolts used in machinery are made to SAE Standard J429.

Metric bolt tensile strength property class is shown on the head of the bolt as a number, such as 4.6, 8.8, 9.8, and

SAE Bolt Designations

SAE Grade No.	Size Range	Tensile Strength, psi	Material	Head Marking
1	1/4 through 1-1/2	60,000	Low- or medium-carbon steel	
2	1/4 through 3/4	74,000		
	7/8 through 1-1/2	60,000		
5	1/4 through 1	120,000	Medium-carbon steel, quenched and tempered	
	1-1/8 through 1-1/2	105,000		
5.2	1/4 through 1	120,000	Low-carbon martensite steel,* quenched and tempered	
7	1/4 through 1-1/2	133,000	Medium-carbon alloy steel, quenched and tempered	
8	1/4 through 1-1/2	150,000	Medium-carbon alloy steel, quenched and tempered	
8.2	1/4 through 1	150,000	Low-carbon martensite steel,* quenched and tempered	

* Martensite steel is steel that has been cooled rapidly, thereby increasing its hardness. It is named after a German metallurgist, Adolf Martens.

10.9; the higher the number, the stronger the bolt. See Figure 1-14.

Nuts

Most nuts used on cap screws have the same hex size as the cap screw head. Some inexpensive nuts use a hex size larger than the cap screw head. Metric nuts are often marked with dimples to show their strength. More dimples indicates stronger nuts. Some nuts and cap screws use interference-fit threads to keep them from accidentally loosening. This means that the shape of the nut is slightly distorted or that a section of the threads is deformed. Nuts can also be kept from loosening with a nylon washer fastened in the nut or with a nylon patch or strip on the threads. See Figure 1-15.

NOTE: Most "locking nuts" are grouped together and are commonly referred to as **prevailing torque nuts**. This means that the nut will hold its tightness or torque and not loosen with movement or vibration. Most prevailing torque nuts should be replaced whenever removed to ensure that the nut will not loosen during service. Always follow the manufacturer's recommendations. Anaerobic sealers, such as Loctite, are used on the threads where the nut or cap screw must be both locked and sealed.

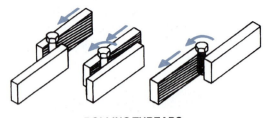

ROLLING THREADS

FIGURE 1-13 Stronger threads are created by cold-rolling a heat-treated bolt blank instead of cutting the threads using a die.

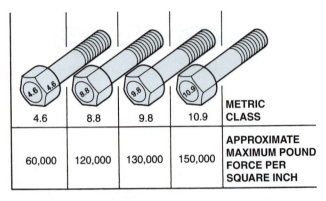

				METRIC CLASS
4.6	8.8	9.8	10.9	
60,000	120,000	130,000	150,000	APPROXIMATE MAXIMUM POUND FORCE PER SQUARE INCH

FIGURE 1-14 Metric bolt (cap screw) grade markings and approximate tensile strength.

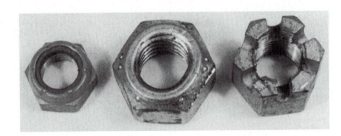

FIGURE 1-15 Types of lock nuts. On the left, a nylon ring; in the center, a distorted shape; and on the right, a castle for use with a cotter key.

Washers

Washers are often used under cap screw heads and under nuts. See Figure 1-16. Plain flat washers are used to provide an even clamping load around the fastener. Lock washers are added to prevent accidental loosening. In some accessories, the washers are locked onto the nut to provide easy assembly.

HAND TOOLS

Wrenches

Wrenches are the hand tool most used by service technicians. Most wrenches are constructed of forged alloy steel, usually chrome-vanadium steel. See Figure 1-17.

METRIC HEXAGON HEAD CAP SCREWS
ALL MEASUREMENTS IN MILLIMETERS

M = NOMINAL THREAD DIAMETER
P = PITCH
D = HEAD SIZE ACROSS FLATS

M	P	D	M	P	D	M	P	D
1.6	0.35	3.2	10	1.00	17	20	1.50	30
1.7	0.35	3.5	10	1.25	17	20	2.50	30
2	0.40	4	10	1.50	17	22	1.50	32
2.3	0.40	4.5	12	1.25	19	22	2.50	32
2.5	0.45	5	12	1.50	19	24	2.00	36
3	0.50	5.5	12	1.75	19	24	3.00	36
3.5	0.60	6	14	1.50	22	27	3.00	41
4	0.70	7	14	2.00	22	30	3.50	46
5	0.80	8	16	1.50	24	33	3.50	50
6	1.00	10	16	2.00	24	36	4.00	55
7	1.00	11	18	1.50	27	39	4.00	60
8	1.00	13	18	2.50	27	42	4.50	65
8	1.25	13				45	4.50	70

FIGURE 1-12 The metric system specifies fasteners by diameter, length, and pitch.

After the wrench is formed, the wrench is hardened and then tempered to reduce brittleness, and then it is chrome plated. There are several types of wrenches.

HEX NUT   JAM NUT   NYLON LOCK NUT   CASTLE NUT   ACORN NUT

FLAT WASHER   LOCK WASHER   STAR WASHER   STAR WASHER

FIGURE 1-16   Various types of nuts (top) and washers (bottom) serve different purposes and all are used to secure bolts or cap screws.

Open-End Wrench

An **open-end wrench** is usually used to loosen or tighten bolts or nuts that do not require a lot of torque. An open-end wrench can be easily placed on a bolt or nut with an angle of 15 degrees, which allows the wrench to be flipped over and used again to continue to rotate the fastener. The major disadvantage of an open-end wrench is the lack of torque that can be applied due to the fact that the open jaws of the wrench only contact two flat surfaces of the fastener. An open-end wrench has two different sizes, one at each end. See Figure 1-18.

Close-End Wrench

A **close-end wrench,** also called a box-end wrench, is placed over the top of the fastener and grips the points of the fastener. A box-end wrench is angled 15 degrees to allow it to clear nearby objects. See Figure 1-19.

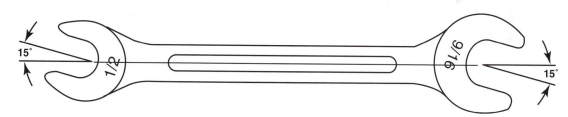

FIGURE 1-17   A forged wrench after it has been forged but before the flashing, extra material around the wrench, has been removed.

FIGURE 1-18   A typical open-end wrench. The size is different on each end, and notice that the head is angled 15 degrees at each end.

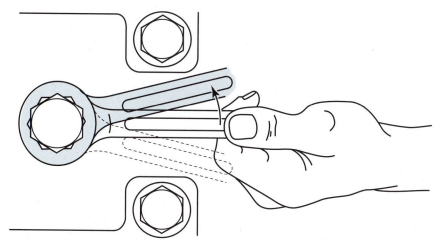

FIGURE 1-19   A typical close-end wrench is able to grip the bolt or nut at points completely around the fastener. Each end is a different size.

Therefore, a box-end wrench should be used to loosen or tighten fasteners. A box-end wrench has two different sizes, one at each end. See Figure 1-20.

Most service technicians purchase **combination wrenches,** which have the open end at one end and the same-size box end on the other end. See Figure 1-21.

A combination wrench allows the technician to loosen or tighten a fastener using the box end of the wrench, turn it around, and use the open end to increase the speed of rotating the fastener.

Adjustable Wrench

An **adjustable wrench** is often used when the exact-size wrench is not available or when a large nut, such as a wheel spindle nut, needs to be rotated but not tightened. An adjustable wrench should not be used to loosen or tighten fasteners because the torque applied to the wrench can cause the moveable jaws to loosen their grip on the fastener, causing it to become rounded. See Figure 1-22.

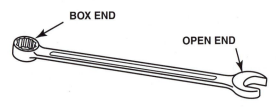

FIGURE 1-20   The end of a box-end wrench is angled 15 degrees to allow clearance for nearby objects or other fasteners.

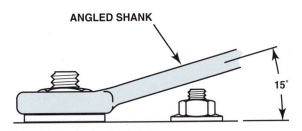

FIGURE 1-21   A combination wrench has an open end at one end and a box end at the other end.

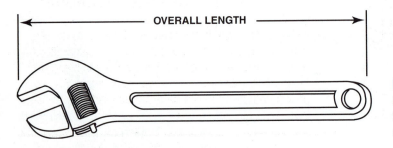

OVERALL LENGTH

Line Wrenches

Line wrenches are also called **flare-nut wrenches,** *fitting wrenches*, or *tube-nut wrenches* and are designed to grip almost all the way around a nut used to retain a fuel or refrigerant line, and yet be able to be installed over the line. See Figure 1-23.

Safe Use of Wrenches. Wrenches should be inspected before use to be sure they are not cracked, bent, or damaged. All wrenches should be cleaned after use before being returned to the tool box. Always use the correct size of wrench for the fastener being loosened or tightened to help prevent the rounding of the flats of the fastener. When attempting to loosen a fastener, pull a wrench—do not push a wrench. If a wrench is pushed, your knuckles can be hurt when forced into another object if the fastener breaks loose.

Ratchets, Sockets, and Extensions

A **socket** fits over the fastener and grips the points and/or flats of the bolt or nut. The socket is rotated (driven) using either a long bar called a **breaker bar** (*flex handle*) or a *ratchet*. See Figures 1-24 and 1-25.

A ratchet turns the socket in only one direction and allows the rotating of the ratchet handle back and forth in a narrow space. Socket **extensions** and **universal joints** are also used with sockets to allow access to fasteners in restricted locations.

Sockets are available in various **drive sizes,** including 1/4-inch, 3/8-inch, and 1/2-inch sizes for most automotive uses. See Figure 1-26 and 1-27.

Many heavy-duty truck and/or industrial applications use 3/4-inch and 1-inch sizes. The drive size is the distance of each side of the square drive. Sockets and ratchets of the same size are designed to work together.

Torque Wrenches

Torque wrenches are socket-turning handles that are designed to apply a known amount of force to the fastener. There are two basic types of torque wrenches:

1. **Clicker type.** This type of torque wrench is first set to the specified torque and then it "clicks" when the set

FIGURE 1-22   An adjustable wrench. Adjustable wrenches are sized by the overall length of the wrench and not by how far the jaws open. Common sizes of adjustable wrenches include 8, 10, and 12 inch.

torque value has been reached. When force is removed from the torque wrench handle, another click is heard. The setting on a clicker-type torque wrench should be set back to zero after use and checked for proper calibration regularly. See Figure 1-28.

2. **Beam-type.** These torque wrenches are used to measure torque, but instead of presenting the value, the actual torque is displayed on the dial of the wrench as the fastener is being tightened. Beam-type torque wrenches are available in 1/4-inch, 3/8-inch, and 1/2-inch drives and both English and Metric units. See Figure 1-29.

FIGURE 1-23   The end of a typical line wrench, which shows that it is capable of grasping most of the head of the fitting.

FIGURE 1-24   A typical ratchet used to rotate a socket. A ratchet makes a ratcheting noise when it is being rotated in the opposite direction from loosening or tightening. A knob or lever on the ratchet allows the user to switch directions.

FIGURE 1-25   A typical flex handle used to rotate a socket, also called a breaker bar because it usually has a longer handle than a ratchet and therefore can be used to apply more torque to a fastener than a ratchet.

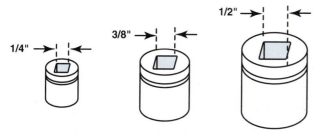

FIGURE 1-26   The most commonly used socket drive sizes include 1/4-inch, 3/8-inch and 1/2-inch drive.

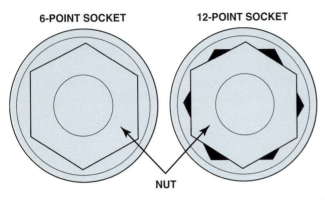

FIGURE 1-27   A 6-point socket fits the head of the bolt or nut on all sides. A 12-point socket can round off the head of a bolt or nut if a lot of force is applied.

TECH TIP

DOUBLE-CHECK THE SPECIFICATIONS

Mis-reading torque specifications is easy to do but can have serious damaging results. Specifications for fasteners are commonly expressed lb-ft. Many smaller fasteners are tightened to specifications expressed in lb-in.

1 lb-ft = 12 lb-in

Therefore, if a fastener were to be accidentally tightened to 24 lb-ft instead of 24 lb-in, the actual torque applied to the fastener will be 288 lb-in instead of the specified 24 lb-in.

This extra torque will likely break the fastener, but it could also warp or distort the part being tightened. Always double-check the torque specifications.

TECH TIP

CHECK TORQUE WRENCH CALIBRATION REGULARLY

Torque wrenches should be checked regularly. For example, Honda has a torque wrench calibration setup at each of its training centers. It is expected that a torque wrench be checked for accuracy before every use. Most experts recommend that torque wrenches be checked and adjusted as needed at least every year and more often if possible. See Figure 1-30.

FIGURE 1-28   Using a torque wrench to tighten connecting-rod nuts on an engine.

FIGURE 1-29   A beam-type torque wrench that displays the torque reading on the face of the dial. The beam display is read as the beam deflects, which is in proportion to the amount of torque applied to the fastener.

Safe Use of Sockets and Ratchets. Always use the proper-size socket that correctly fits the bolt or nut. All sockets and ratchets should be cleaned after use before being placed back into the toolbox. Sockets are available in short- and deep-well designs. See Figure 1-31.

Also select the appropriate drive size. For example, for small work, such as on the dash, select a 1/4-inch drive. For most general service work, use a 3/8-inch drive, and for suspension and steering and other large fasteners, select a 1/2-inch drive. When loosening a fastener, always pull the ratchet toward you rather than pushing it outward.

Screwdrivers

Many smaller fasteners are removed and installed by using a screwdriver. Screwdrivers are available in many sizes and tip shapes. The most commonly used screwdriver is called a flat tip or straight blade.

Flat-tip screwdrivers are sized by the width of the blade, and this width should match the width of the slot in the screw. See Figure 1-32.

FIGURE 1-30 Torque wrench calibration checker.

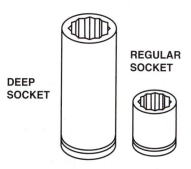

FIGURE 1-31 Deep sockets allow access to a nut that has a stud, as well as other locations needing great depth, such as spark plugs.

CAUTION: Do not use a screwdriver as a pry tool or as a chisel. Always use the proper tool for each application.

Another type of commonly used screwdriver is called a Phillips screwdriver, named for Henry F. Phillips, who invented the crosshead screw in 1934. Due to the shape of the crosshead

TECH TIP

USE SOCKET ADAPTERS WITH CAUTION

Socket adapters are available and can be used for different drive-size sockets on a ratchet. Combinations include:

    1/4-inch drive—3/8-inch sockets
    3/8-inch drive—1/4-inch sockets
    3/8-inch drive—1/2-inch sockets
    1/2-inch drive—3/8-inch sockets

Using a larger drive ratchet or breaker bar on a smaller-size socket can cause the application of too much force to the socket, which could then crack or shatter. Using a smaller-size drive tool on a larger socket will usually not cause any harm, but will greatly reduce the amount of torque that can be applied to the bolt or nut.

TECH TIP

AVOID USING "CHEATER BARS"

When a fastener is difficult to remove, some technicians will insert the handle of a ratchet or a breaker bar into a length of steel pipe. The extra length of the pipe, or **cheater bar,** allows the technician to exert more torque than can be applied using the drive handle alone. However, the extra torque can easily overload the socket and ratchet, causing them to break or shatter, which could cause personal injury.

screw and screwdriver, a Phillips screw can be driven with more torque than can be achieved with a slotted screw.

A Phillips head screwdriver is specified by the length of the handle and the size of the point at the tip. A #1 tip has a sharp point, a #2 tip is the most commonly used, and a #3 tip is blunt and is only used for larger sizes of Phillips head fasteners. For example, a #2 × 3-inch Phillips screwdriver would typically measure 6 inches from the tip of the blade to the end of the handle (3-inch-long handle and 3-inch-long blade) with a #2 tip.

Both straight-blade and Phillips screwdrivers are available with a short blade and handle for access to fasteners with limited room. See Figure 1-33.

Offset Screwdrivers

Offset screwdrivers are used in places where a conventional screwdriver cannot fit. An offset screwdriver is bent at the ends and is used similar to a wrench. Most offset screwdrivers have a straight blade at one end and a Phillips end at the opposite end. See Figure 1-34.

Impact Screwdriver

An impact screwdriver is used to break loose or tighten a screw. A hammer is used to strike the end after the

screwdriver holder is placed in the head of the screw and rotated in the desired direction. The force from the hammer blow does two things. It applies a force downward, holding the tip of the screwdriver in the slot, and then applies a twisting force to loosen (or tighten) the screw. See Figure 1-35.

Safe Use of Screwdrivers. Always use the proper type and size screwdriver that matches the fastener. Try to avoid pressing down on a screwdriver because if it slips, the screwdriver tip could go into your hand, causing serious personal injury. All screwdrivers should be cleaned after use. Do not use a screwdriver as a pry bar; always use the correct tool for the job.

Hammers

Hammers and mallets are used to force objects together or apart. The shape of the back part of the hammer head (called

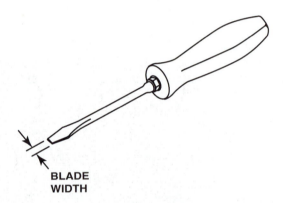

FIGURE 1-32 A flat-tip (straight blade) screwdriver. The width of the blade should match the width of the slot in the fastener being loosened or tightened.

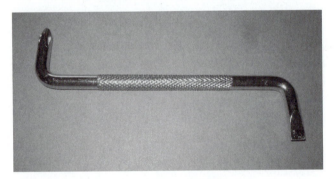

FIGURE 1-34 An offset screwdriver is used to install or remove fasteners that do not have enough space above to use a conventional screwdriver.

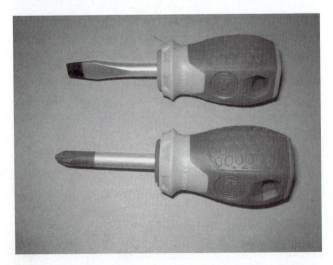

FIGURE 1-33 Two stubby screwdrivers that are used to access screws that have limited space above. A straight blade is on top and a #2 Phillips screwdriver is on the bottom.

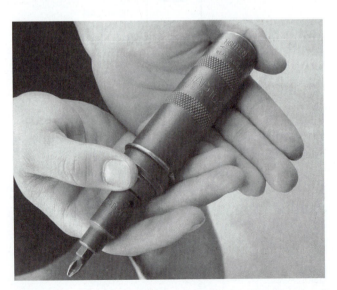

FIGURE 1-35 An impact screwdriver used to remove slotted or Phillips head fasteners that cannot be broken loose using a standard screwdriver.

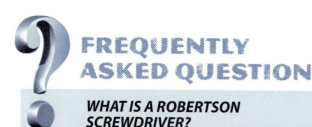

WHAT IS A ROBERTSON SCREWDRIVER?

A Canadian named P. L. Robertson invented the Robertson screw and screwdriver in 1908, which uses a square-shaped tip with a slight taper. The Robertson screwdriver uses color-coded handles because different-size screws require different tip sizes. The colors and sizes include:

Orange (#00)—Number 1 and 2 screws
Yellow (#0)—Number 3 and 4 screws
Green (#1)—Number 5, 6, and 7 screws
Red (#2)—Number 8, 9, and 10 screws
Black (#3)—Number 12 and larger screws

The Robertson screws are rarely found in the United States but are common in Canada.

FIGURE 1-36 A typical ball-peen hammer.

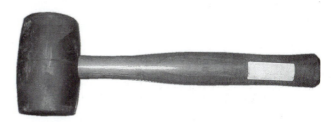

FIGURE 1-37 A rubber mallet used to deliver a force to an object without harming the surface.

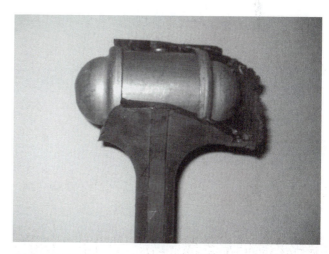

FIGURE 1-38 A dead-blow hammer that was left outside in freezing weather. The plastic covering was damaged, which destroyed this hammer. The lead shot is encased in the metal housing and then covered.

the *peen*) usually determines the name. For example, a ball-peen hammer has a rounded end, like a ball, and the hammer head is used to straighten oil pans and valve covers, whereas the ball peen is used for shaping metal. See Figure 1-36.

NOTE: A claw hammer has a claw used to remove nails and is not used for automotive service.

A hammer is usually sized by the weight of the head of the hammer and the length of the handle. For example, a commonly used ball-peen hammer has an 8-ounce head with an 11-inch handle.

Mallets

Mallets are a type of hammer with a large striking surface, which allows the technician to exert force over a larger area than a hammer, so as not to harm the part or component. Mallets are made from a variety of materials including rubber, plastic, and wood. See Figure 1-37.

A shot-filled plastic hammer is called a *dead-blow hammer*. The small lead balls (shot) inside the plastic head prevent the hammer from bouncing off of the object when struck. See Figure 1-38.

Safe Use of Hammers and Mallets. All mallets and hammers should be cleaned after use and not exposed to extreme

temperatures. Never use a hammer or mallet that is damaged in any way, and always use caution to avoid doing damage to the components and the surrounding area. Always follow the hammer manufacturer's recommended procedures and practices.

Slip-Joint Pliers

Pliers are capable of holding, twisting, bending, and cutting objects and are extremely useful tools. The common household type of pliers is called the *slip-joint pliers*. Two different positions are possible at the junction of the handles to achieve a wide range of sizes of objects that can be gripped. See Figure 1-39.

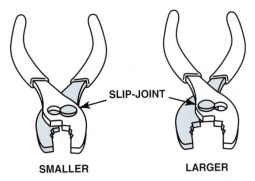

FIGURE 1-39 Typical slip-joint pliers, which are also common house-hold pliers. The slip joint allows the jaws to be opened to two different settings.

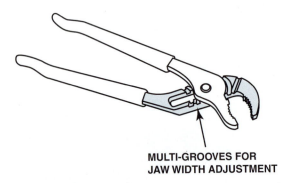

FIGURE 1-40 Multigroove adjustable pliers are known by many names, including the trade name "Channel Locks."

Multigroove Adjustable Pliers

For gripping larger objects, a set of *multigroove adjustable pliers* is a commonly used tool of choice by many service technicians. Because they were originally designed to remove the various-size nuts holding rope seals used in water pumps, the name *water pump pliers* is also used. See Figure 1-40.

Linesman's Pliers

Linesman's pliers are specifically designed for cutting, bending, and twisting wire. While commonly used by construction workers and electricians, linesman's pliers are a very useful tool for the service technician who deals with wiring. The center parts of the jaws are designed to grasp round objects such as pipe or tubing without slipping. See Figure 1-41.

Diagonal Pliers

Diagonal pliers are designed to cut only. The cutting jaws are set at an angle to make it easier to cut wires. Diagonal pliers

are also called *side cuts* or *dikes*. These pliers are constructed of hardened steel and they are used mostly for cutting wire. See Figure 1-42.

Needle-Nose Pliers

Needle-nose pliers are designed to grip small objects or objects in tight locations. Needle-nose pliers have long pointed jaws, which allow the tips to reach into narrow openings or groups of small objects. See Figure 1-43.

Most needle-nose pliers have a wire cutter located at the base of the jaws near the pivot. There are several variations of needle nose pliers, including right-angle jaws or slightly angled jaws to allow access to certain cramped areas.

Locking Pliers

Locking pliers are adjustable pliers that can be locked to hold objects from moving. Most locking pliers also have wire cutters built into the jaws near the pivot point. Locking pliers come in a variety of styles and sizes and are commonly referred to by the trade name VISE-GRIP®. The size is the length of the pliers, not how far the jaws open. See Figure 1-44.

Safe Use of Pliers. Pliers should not be used to remove any bolt or other fastener. Pliers should only be used when specified for use by the vehicle manufacturer.

Snap-Ring Pliers

Snap-ring pliers are used to remove and install snap rings. Many snap-ring pliers are designed to be able to remove and install expanding snap rings, both inward and outward types. Snap-ring pliers can be equipped with serrated tipped jaws for grasping the opening in the snap ring, while others are equipped with points, which are inserted into the holes in the snap ring. See Figure 1-45.

Files

Files are used to smooth metal and are constructed of hardened steel with diagonal rows of teeth. Files are available with a single row of teeth, called a single-cut file, as well as two rows of teeth cut at an opposite angle, called a double-cut file. Files are available in a variety of shapes and sizes, such as small flat files, half-round files, and triangular files. See Figure 1-46.

Safe Use of Files. Always use a file with a handle. Because files only cut when moved forward, a handle must be attached to prevent possible personal injury. After making a forward strike, lift the file and return it to the starting position; avoid dragging the file backward.

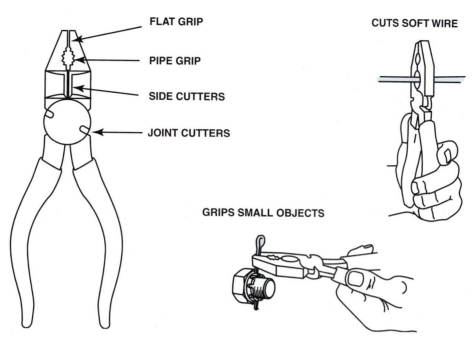

FLAT GRIP

PIPE GRIP

SIDE CUTTERS

JOINT CUTTERS

CUTS SOFT WIRE

GRIPS SMALL OBJECTS

FIGURE 1-41 Linesman's pliers are very useful because they can help perform many automotive service jobs.

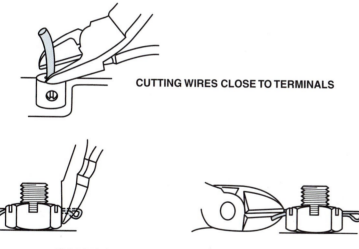

CUTTING WIRES CLOSE TO TERMINALS

PULLING OUT AND SPREADING COTTER PIN

FIGURE 1-42 Diagonal-cut pliers are another common tool with many names.

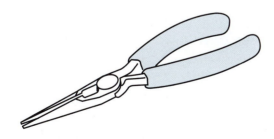

FIGURE 1-43 Needle-nose pliers are used where there is limited access to a wire or pin that needs to be installed or removed.

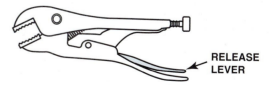

RELEASE LEVER

FIGURE 1-44 Locking pliers are best known by their trade name VISE-GRIPS®.

TECH TIP

BRAND NAME VERSUS PROPER TERM

Technicians often use slang or brand names of tools rather than the proper term. This results in some confusion for new technicians. Some examples are given in the following table.

Brand Name	Proper Term	Slang Name
Crescent wrench	Adjustable wrench	Monkey wrench
Vise-Grips	Locking pliers	
Channel Locks	Water pump pliers or multigroove adjustable pliers	Pump pliers
	Diagonal cutting pliers	Dikes or side cuts

Snips

Service technicians are often asked to fabricate sheet-metal brackets or heat shields, and thus need to use one or more types of cutters available. The simplest is called tin snips. Tin snips are designed to make straight cuts in a variety of materials, such as sheet steel, aluminum, or even fabric. A variation of the tin snips is called aviation tin snips. There are three designs of aviation snips, including one designed to cut straight (called a straight-cut aviation snip), one designed to cut left (called an offset-left aviation snip), and one designed to cut right (called an offset-right aviation snip). See Figure 1-47.

Utility Knife

A utility knife uses a replaceable blade and is used to cut a variety of materials such as carpet, plastic, wood, and paper products such as cardboard. See Figure 1-48.

Safe Use of Cutters. Whenever using cutters, always wear eye protection or a face shield to guard against the possibility

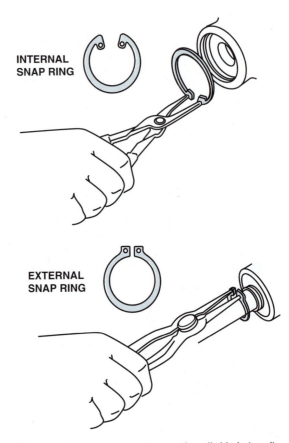

INTERNAL SNAP RING

EXTERNAL SNAP RING

FIGURE 1-45 Snap-ring pliers are also called lock-ring pliers, and most are designed to remove internal and external snap rings (lock rings).

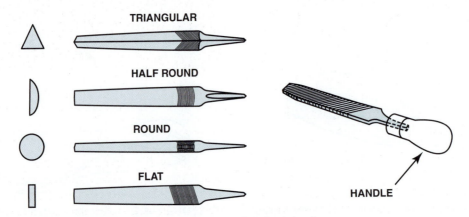

TRIANGULAR

HALF ROUND

ROUND

FLAT

HANDLE

FIGURE 1-46 Files come in many different shapes and sizes. Never use a file without a handle.

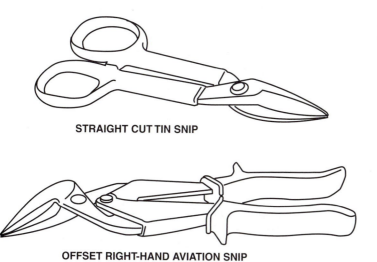

STRAIGHT CUT TIN SNIP

OFFSET RIGHT-HAND AVIATION SNIP

FIGURE 1-47   Tin snips are used to cut thin sheets of metal or carpet.

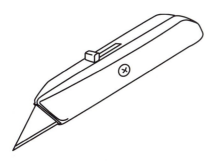

FIGURE 1-48   A utility knife uses replaceable blades and is used to cut carpet and other materials.

of metal pieces being ejected during the cut. Always follow recommended procedures.

Punches

A punch is a small-diameter steel rod that has a smaller-diameter ground at one end. A punch is used to drive a pin out that is used to retain two components. Punches come in a variety of sizes; the size is measured across the diameter of the machined end. Sizes include 1/16", 1/80", 3/16", and 1/40". See Figure 1-49.

Chisels

A chisel has a straight, sharp cutting end that is used for cutting off rivets or to separate two pieces of an assembly. The most common design of chisel used for automotive service work is called a cold chisel.

Safe Use of Punches and Chisels. Always wear eye protection when using a punch or a chisel because the hardened steel is brittle and parts of the punch could fly off and cause serious personal injury. See the warning stamped on the side of the automotive punch in Figure 1-50.

PIN

FIGURE 1-49   A punch used to drive pins from assembled components. This type of punch is also called a pin punch.

WEAR SAFETY GOGGLES

FIGURE 1-50   Warning stamped in the side of a punch noting that goggles should be worn when using this tool. Always follow safety warnings.

Punches and chisels can also have the top rounded off, which is called "mushroomed." This material must be ground off to help avoid the possibility that the overhanging material will be loosened and become airborne during use. See Figure 1-51.

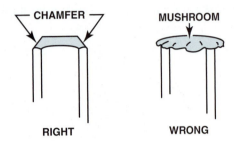

FIGURE 1-51   Use a grinder or a file to remove the mushroom material on the end of a punch or chisel.

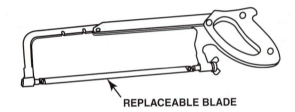

FIGURE 1-52   A typical hacksaw that is used to cut metal. If cutting sheet metal or thin objects, a blade with more teeth should be used.

Hacksaws

A hacksaw is used to cut metals, such as steel, aluminum, brass, or copper. The cutting blade of a hacksaw is replaceable and the sharpness and number of teeth can be varied to meet the needs of the job. Use 14 or 18 teeth per inch (TPI) for cutting plaster or soft metals, such as aluminum and copper. Use 24 or 32 teeth per inch for steel or pipe. Hacksaw blades should be installed with the teeth pointing away from the handle. This means that a hacksaw only cuts while the blade is pushed in the forward direction. See Figure 1-52.

Safe Use of Hacksaws.   Check that the hacksaw is equipped with the correct blade for the job and that the teeth are pointed away from the handle. When using a hacksaw, move the hacksaw slowly away from you, then lift slightly and return for another cut.

BASIC HAND TOOL LIST

Hand tools are used to turn fasteners (bolts, nuts, and screws). The following is a list of hand tools every automotive technician should possess. Specialty tools are not included.

    Safety glasses
    Tool chest
    1/4-inch drive socket set (1/4 in. to 9/16 in. standard
        and deep sockets; 6 mm to 15 mm standard and deep
        sockets)
    1/4-inch drive ratchet

1/4-inch drive 2-inch extension
1/4-inch drive 6-inch extension
1/4-inch drive handle
3/8-inch drive socket set (3/8 in. to 7/8 in. standard
    and deep sockets; 10 mm to 19 mm standard and
    deep sockets)
3/8-inch drive Torx set (T40, T45, T50, and T55)
3/8-inch drive 13/16-inch plug socket
3/8-inch drive 5/8-inch plug socket
3/8-inch drive ratchet
3/8-inch drive 1 1/2-inch extension
3/8-inch drive 3-inch extension
3/8-inch drive 6-inch extension
3/8-inch drive 18-inch extension
3/8-inch drive universal
1/2-inch drive socket set (1/2 in. to 1 in. standard and
    deep sockets)
1/2-inch drive ratchet
1/2-inch drive breaker bar
1/2-inch drive 5-inch extension
1/2-inch drive 10-inch extension
3/8-inch to 1/4-inch adapter
1/2-inch to 3/8-inch adapter
3/8-inch to 1/2-inch adapter
Crowfoot set (fractional inch)
Crowfoot set (metric)
3/8- through 1-inch combination wrench set
10-millimeter through 19-millimeter combination
    wrench set
1/16-inch through 1/4-inch hex wrench set
2-millimeter through 12-millimeter hex wrench set
3/8-inch hex socket
13-millimeter to 14-millimeter flare-nut wrench
15-millimeter to 17-millimeter flare-nut wrench
5/16-inch to 3/8-inch flare-nut wrench
7/16-inch to 1/2-inch flare-nut wrench
1/2-inch to 9/16-inch flare-nut wrench
Diagonal pliers
Needle pliers
Adjustable-jaw pliers
Locking pliers
Snap-ring pliers
Stripping or crimping pliers
Ball-peen hammer
Rubber hammer
Dead-blow hammer
Five-piece standard screwdriver set
Four-piece Phillips screwdriver set
#15 Torx screwdriver
#20 Torx screwdriver
Center punch
Pin punches (assorted sizes)
Chisel
Utility knife

TECH TIP

THE WINTERGREEN OIL TRICK

Synthetic wintergreen oil, available at drugstores everywhere, makes an excellent penetrating oil. So the next time you can't get that rusted bolt loose, use penetrating oil or head for the drugstore. See Figure 1-53.

FIGURE 1-54   A typical beginning technician tool set that includes the basic tools to get started.

FIGURE 1-53   Synthetic wintergreen oil can be used as a penetrating oil to loosen rusted bolts or nuts.

Valve core tool
Filter wrench (large filters)
Filter wrench (smaller filters)
Test light
Feeler gauge
Scraper
Magnet

TOOL SETS AND ACCESSORIES

A beginning service technician may wish to start with a small set of tools before spending a lot of money on an expensive, extensive toolbox. See Figures 1-54 and 1-55.

ELECTRICAL HAND TOOLS

Test Light

A test light is used to test for electricity. A typical automotive test light consists of a clear plastic screwdriver-like handle that contains a light bulb. A wire is attached to one terminal of the

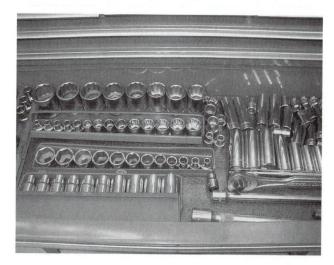

FIGURE 1-55   A typical large tool box, showing just one of many drawers.

bulb, which the technician connects to a clean metal part of the vehicle. The other end of the bulb is attached to a point that can be used to test for electricity at a connector or wire. When there is power at the point and a good connection at the other end, the light bulb illuminates. See Figure 1-56.

Soldering Guns

- **Electric soldering gun.** This type of soldering gun is usually powered by 110- volt AC and often has two power settings expressed in watts. A typical electric soldering gun will produce from 85 to 300 watts of heat at the tip, which is more than adequate for soldering. See Figure 1-57.
- **Electric soldering pencil.** This type of soldering iron is less expensive and creates less heat than an electric

TECH TIP

HIDE THOSE FROM THE BOSS

An apprentice technician started working for a dealership and put his top toolbox on a workbench. Another technician observed that, along with a complete set of good-quality tools, the box contained several adjustable wrenches. The more experienced technician said, "Hide those from the boss." If any adjustable wrench is used on a bolt or nut, the movable jaw often moves or loosens and starts to round the head of the fastener. If the head of the bolt or nut becomes rounded, it becomes that much more difficult to remove.

TECH TIP

NEED TO BORROW A TOOL MORE THAN TWICE? BUY IT!

Most service technicians agree that it is okay for a beginning technician to borrow a tool occasionally. However, if a tool has to be borrowed more than twice, then be sure to purchase it as soon as possible. Also, whenever a tool is borrowed, be sure that you clean the tool and let the technician you borrowed the tool from know that you are returning the tool. These actions will help in any future dealings with other technicians.

TECH TIP

THE VALVE-GRINDING-COMPOUND TRICK

Apply a small amount of valve-grinding compound to a Phillips or Torx screw or bolt head. The gritty valve-grinding compound "grips" the screwdriver or tool bit and prevents the tool from slipping up and out of the screw head. Valve-grinding compound is available in a tube from most automotive parts stores.

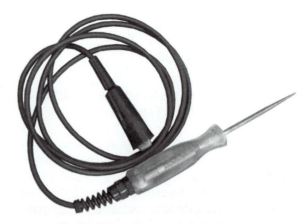

FIGURE 1-56   A typical 12-volt test light.

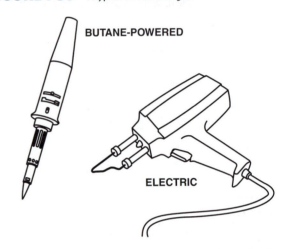

FIGURE 1-57   An electric soldering gun used to make electrical repairs. Soldering guns are used by the wattage rating. The higher the wattage, the greater the amount of created. Most solder guns used for automotive electrical work usually fall within the 60- to 160-watt range.

soldering gun. A typical electric soldering pencil (iron) creates 30 to 60 watts of heat and is suitable for soldering smaller wires and connections.

- **Butane-powered soldering iron.** A butane-powered soldering iron is portable and very useful for automotive service work because an electrical cord is not needed. Most butane-powered soldering irons produce about 60 watts of heat, which is enough for most automotive soldering.

In addition to a soldering iron, most service technicians who do electrical-related work should have the following:

- Wire cutters
- Wire strippers
- Wire crimpers
- Heat gun for heat-shrink tubing

Digital Meter.   A digital meter is a necessary tool for any electrical diagnosis and troubleshooting. A digital multimeter,

TECH TIP

IT JUST TAKES A SECOND

Whenever removing any automotive component, it is wise to screw the bolts back into the holes a couple of threads by hand. This ensures that the right bolt will be used in its original location when the component or part is put back on the vehicle. Often, the same diameter of fastener is used on a component, but the length of the bolt may vary. Spending just a couple of seconds to put the bolts and nuts back where they belong when the part is removed can save a lot of time when the part is being reinstalled. Besides making certain that the right fastener is being installed in the right place, this method helps prevent bolts and nuts from getting lost or kicked away. How much time have you wasted looking for that lost bolt or nut?

abbreviated DMM, is usually capable of measuring the following units of electricity:

- DC volts
- AC volts
- Ohms
- Amperes

SAFETY TIPS FOR USING HAND TOOLS

The following safety tips should be kept in mind whenever you are working with hand tools:

- Always *pull* a wrench toward you for best control and safety. Never push a wrench.
- Keep wrenches and all hand tools clean to help prevent rust and to allow for a better, firmer grip.
- Always use a 6-point socket or a box-end wrench to break loose a tight bolt or nut.
- Use a box-end wrench for torque and an open-end wrench for speed.
- Never use a pipe extension or other type of "cheater bar" on a wrench or ratchet handle. If more force is required, use a larger tool or use penetrating oil and/or heat on the frozen fastener. (If heat is used on a bolt or nut to remove it, always replace it with a new part.)
- Always use the proper tool for the job. If a specialized tool is required, use the proper tool and do not try to use another tool improperly.

- Never expose any tool to excessive heat. High temperatures can reduce the strength ("draw the temper") of metal tools.
- Never use a hammer on any wrench or socket handle unless you are using a special "staking face" wrench designed to be used with a hammer.
- Replace any tools that are damaged or worn.

HAND TOOL MAINTENANCE

Most hand tools are constructed of rust-resistant metals, but they can still rust or corrode if not properly maintained. For best results and long tool life, the following steps should be taken:

- Clean each tool before placing it back into the toolbox.
- Keep tools separated. Moisture on metal tools will cause rust more readily if the tools are in contact with another metal tool.
- Line the drawers of the toolbox with a material that will prevent the tools from moving as the drawers are opened and closed. This helps to quickly locate the proper tool and size.
- Release the tension on all "clicker-type" torque wrenches.
- Keep the toolbox secure.

AIR- AND ELECTRIC-OPERATED TOOLS

Impact Wrench

An impact wrench, either air or electrically powered, is a tool that is used to remove and install fasteners. The air-operated 1/2-inch drive impact wrench is the most commonly used unit. See Figure 1-58.

FREQUENTLY ASKED QUESTION

WHAT IS AN "SST?"

Vehicle manufacturers often specify a **special service tool (SST)** to properly disassemble and assemble components, such as transmissions and other components. These tools are also called *special tools* and are available from the vehicle manufacturer or the manufacturer's tool supplier, such as Kent-Moore and Miller tools. Many service technicians do not have access to special service tools so they use generic versions that are available from aftermarket sources.

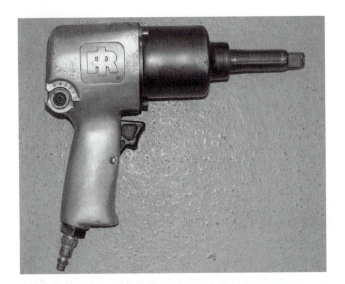

FIGURE 1-58 A typical 1/2-inch drive air-impact wrench.

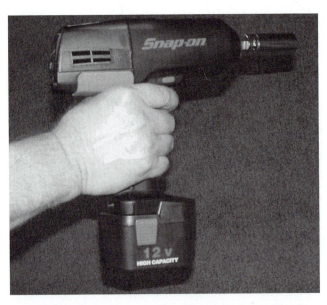

FIGURE 1-60 A typical battery-powered 3/8-inch drive impact wrench.

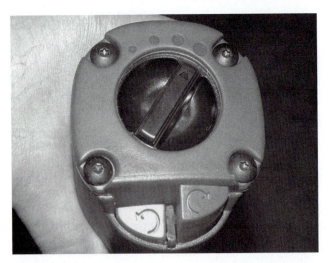

FIGURE 1-59 This air-impact wrench features a variable torque setting using a rotary knob; the direction of rotation can be changed by pressing the buttons at the bottom.

The direction of rotation is controlled by a switch. See Figure 1-59.

Electrically powered impact wrenches commonly include:

- Battery-powered units. See Figure 1-60.
- 110-volt AC-powered units. This type of impact wrench is very useful, especially if compressed air is not readily available.

CAUTION: Always use impact sockets with impact wrenches, and wear eye protection in case the socket or fastener shatters. Input sockets have thicker walls and are constructed with premium alloy steel. They are hardened with a black oxide finish to help prevent corrosion and distinguish them from regular sockets. See Figure 1-61.

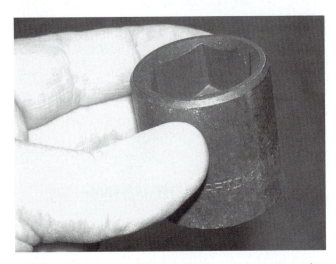

FIGURE 1-61 A black impact socket. Always use impact-type sockets whenever using an impact wrench to avoid the possibility of shattering the socket, which can cause personal injury.

Air Ratchet

An air ratchet is used to remove and install fasteners that would normally be removed or installed using a ratchet and a socket. An air ratchet is much faster, yet has an air hose attached, which reduces accessibility to certain places. See Figure 1-62.

Die Grinder

A die grinder is a commonly used air-powered tool that can also be used to sand or remove gaskets and rust. See Figure 1-63.

FIGURE 1-62   An air ratchet is a very useful tool that allows fast removal and installation of fasteners, especially in areas that are difficult to reach or do not have room enough to move a hand ratchet wrench.

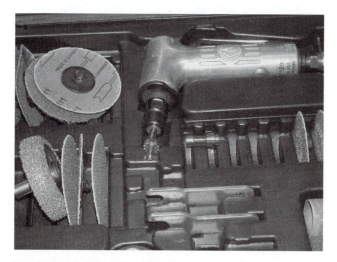

FIGURE 1-63   This typical die grinder surface preparation kit includes the air-operated die grinder as well as a variety of sanding discs for smoothing surfaces or removing rust.

Bench- or Pedestal-Mounted Grinder

These high-powered grinders can be equipped with a wire brush wheel and/or a stone wheel.

- A wire brush wheel is used to clean the threads of bolts as well as to remove gaskets from sheet-metal engine parts.
- A stone wheel is used to grind metal or to remove the mushroom from the top of punches or chisels. See Figure 1-64.

CAUTION: Always wear a face shield when using a wire wheel or a grinder.

FIGURE 1-64   A typical pedestal grinder with a wire wheel on the left side and a stone wheel on the right side. Even though this machine is equipped with guards, safety glasses or a face shield should always be worn whenever working using a grinder or wire wheel.

TECH TIP

WEARING GLOVES SAVES YOUR HANDS

Many technicians wear gloves not only to help keep their hands clean but also to help protect their skin from the effects of dirty engine oil and other possibly hazardous materials. Several types of gloves and their characteristics include:

- *Latex surgical gloves.* These gloves are relatively inexpensive, but tend to stretch, swell, and weaken when exposed to gas, oil, or solvents.
- *Vinyl gloves.* These gloves are also inexpensive and are not affected by gas, oil, or solvents.
- *Polyurethane gloves.* These gloves are more expensive, yet very strong. Even though these gloves are also not affected by gas, oil, or solvents, they do tend to be slippery.
- *Nitrile gloves.* These gloves are exactly like latex gloves, but are not affected by gas, oil, or solvents, yet they tend to be expensive.
- *Mechanic's gloves.* These gloves are usually made of synthetic leather and spandex and provide protection from heat, as well as protection from dirt and grime.

See Figure 1-65.

SAFETY TIPS FOR TECHNICIANS

Personal protective equipment (PPE) is important to help prevent injury during service work on vehicles. Safety is not just a buzzword on a poster in the work area. Safe work habits can reduce accidents and injuries, ease the workload, and keep employees free from pain. Personal protective equipment and suggested safety tips include the following:

- *Safety glasses that meet ANSI Standard Z87.1 should be worn at all times while servicing any vehicle.* See Figure 1-66.
- Watch your toes—always keep your toes protected with steel-toed safety shoes. See Figure 1-67. If safety shoes are not available, then leather-topped shoes offer more protection than canvas or cloth.
- Wear gloves to protect your hands from rough or sharp surfaces. Thin rubber gloves are recommended when working around automotive liquids such as engine oil, antifreeze, transmission fluid, or any other liquids that may be hazardous.
- Service technicians working under a vehicle should wear a **bump cap** to protect the head against under-vehicle objects and the pads of the lift. See Figure 1-68.
- Remove jewelry that may get caught on something or act as a conductor to an exposed electrical circuit. See Figure 1-69.
- Take care of your hands. Keep your hands clean by washing with soap and hot water that is at least 110°F (43°C).
- Avoid loose or dangling clothing.
- Ear protection should be worn if the sound around you requires that you raise your voice (sound level higher than 90 dB). (A typical lawnmower produces noise at a level of about 110 dB. This means that everyone who uses a lawnmower or other lawn or garden equipment should wear ear protection.)
- When lifting any object, get a secure grip with solid footing. Keep the load close to your body to minimize the strain. Lift with your legs and arms, not your back.

FIGURE 1-65 Protective gloves such as these vinyl gloves are available in several sizes. Select the size that allows the gloves to fit snugly. Vinyl gloves last a long time and often can be worn all day to help protect your hands from dirt and possible hazardous materials.

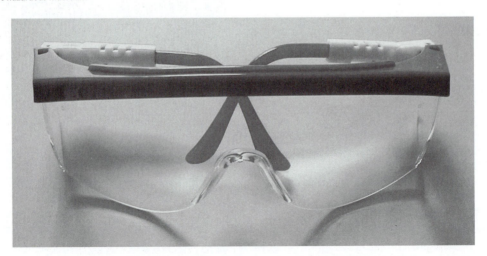

FIGURE 1-66 Safety glasses should be worn at all times when working on or around any vehicle or servicing any component.

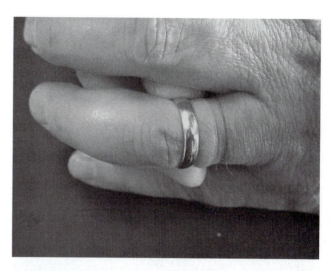

FIGURE 1-69   Remove all jewelry before performing service work on any vehicle.

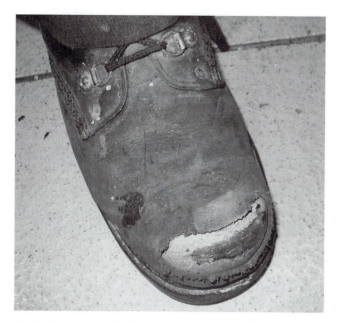

FIGURE 1-67   Steel-toed shoes are a worthwhile investment to help prevent foot injury due to falling objects. Even these well-worn shoes can protect the feet of this service technician.

FIGURE 1-68   One version of a bump cap is this padded plastic insert that is worn inside a regular cloth cap.

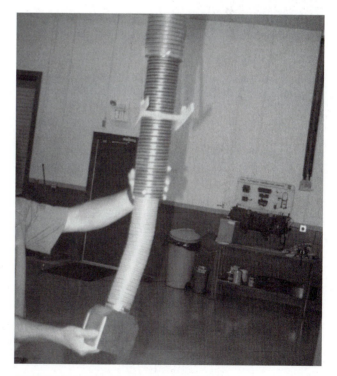

FIGURE 1-70   Always connect an exhaust hose to the tailpipe of the engine of a vehicle to be run inside a building.

- Do not twist your body when carrying a load. Instead, pivot your feet to help prevent strain on the spine.
- Ask for help when moving or lifting heavy objects.
- Push a heavy object rather than pull it. (This is opposite to the way you should work with tools—never push a wrench! If you do and a bolt or nut loosens, your entire weight is used to propel your hand[s] forward. This usually results in cuts, bruises, or other painful injury.)
- Always connect an exhaust hose to the tailpipe of any running vehicle to help prevent the build-up of carbon monoxide inside a closed garage space. See Figure 1-70.

- When standing, keep objects, parts, and tools with which you are working between chest height and waist height. If seated, work at tasks that are at elbow height.
- Always be sure the hood is securely held open. See Figure 1-71.

(a)

HOOD STRUT CLAMP

(b)

FIGURE 1-71 (a) A crude but effective method is to use locking pliers on the chrome-plated shaft of a hood strut. Locking pliers should only be used on defective struts because the jaws of the pliers can damage the strut shaft. (b) A commercially available hood clamp. This tool uses a bright orange tag to help remind the technician to remove the clamp before attempting to close the hood. The hood could be bent if force is used to close the hood with the clamp in place.

SAFETY TIP

SHOP CLOTH DISPOSAL

Always dispose of oily shop cloths in an enclosed container to prevent a fire. See Figure 1-72. Whenever oily cloths are thrown together on the floor or workbench, a chemical reaction can occur that can ignite the cloth even without an open flame. This process of ignition without an open flame is called **spontaneous combustion.**

SAFETY IN LIFTING (HOISTING) A VEHICLE

Many chassis and underbody service procedures require that the vehicle be hoisted or lifted off the ground. The simplest methods involve the use of drive-on ramps or a floor jack and safety (jack) stands, whereas in-ground or surface-mounted lifts provide greater access.

Setting the pads is a critical part of this procedure. All automobile and light-truck service manuals include recommended locations to be used when hoisting (lifting) a vehicle. Newer vehicles have a triangle decal on the driver's door indicating the recommended lift points. The recommended standards for the lift points and lifting procedures are found in SAE Standard JRP-2184. See Figure 1-73.

These recommendations typically include the following points:

1. The vehicle should be centered on the lift or hoist so as not to overload one side or put too much force either forward or rearward. See Figure 1-74.
2. The pads of the lift should be spread as far apart as possible to provide a stable platform.
3. Each pad should be placed under a portion of the vehicle that is strong and capable of supporting the weight of the vehicle.
   a. Pinch welds at the bottom edge of the body are generally considered to be strong.

   CAUTION: Even though **pinch weld seams** are the recommended location for hoisting many vehicles with unitized bodies (unit-body vehicles), care should be taken to not place the pad(s) too far forward or rearward. Incorrect placement of the vehicle on the lift could cause the vehicle to be imbalanced, and the vehicle could fall. This is exactly what happened to the vehicle in Figure 1-75.

   b. Boxed areas of the body are the best places to position the pads on a vehicle without a frame. Be careful to note whether the arms of the lift might come into contact with other parts of the vehicle before the pad touches the intended location. Commonly damaged areas include the following:

1. Rocker panel moldings
2. Exhaust system (including catalytic converter)
3. Tires or body panels (see Figures 1-76 and 1-77)

4. The vehicle should be raised about a foot (30 centimeters [cm]) off the floor, then stopped and shaken to check for stability. If the vehicle seems to be stable when checked at a short distance from the floor, continue raising the vehicle and continue to view the vehicle until it has reached the desired height. The hoist should be lowered onto the mechanical locks, and then raised off of the locks before lowering.

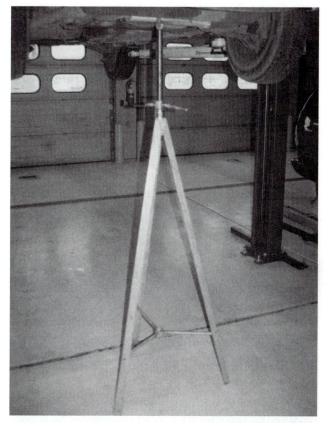

(a)

FIGURE 1-72   All oily shop cloths should be stored in a metal container equipped with a lid to help prevent spontaneous combustion.

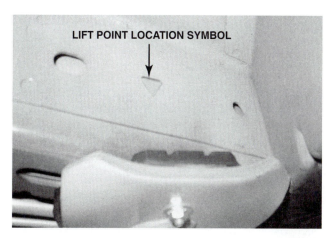

LIFT POINT LOCATION SYMBOL

FIGURE 1-73   Most newer vehicles have a triangle symbol indicating the recommended hoisting lift points.

(b)

FIGURE 1-74   (a) Tall safety stands can be used to provide additional support for a vehicle while on a hoist. (b) A block of wood should be used to avoid the possibility of doing damage to components supported by the stand.

CAUTION: Do not look away from the vehicle while it is being raised (or lowered) on a hoist. Often one side or one end of the hoist can stop or fail, resulting in the vehicle being slanted enough to slip or fall, creating physical damage not only to the vehicle and/or hoist but also to the technician or others who may be nearby.

FIGURE 1-75 This vehicle fell from the hoist because the pads were not set correctly. No one was hurt, but the vehicle was a total loss.

(a)

(b)

FIGURE 1-76 (a) An assortment of hoist pad adapters that are often necessary to safely hoist many pickup trucks, vans, and sport utility vehicles. (b) A view from underneath a Chevrolet pickup truck showing how the pad extensions are used to attach the hoist lifting pad to contact the frame.

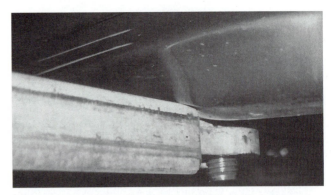

(a)

(b)

FIGURE 1-77 (a) In this photo the pad arm is just contacting the rocker panel of the vehicle. (b) This photo shows what can occur if the technician places the pad too far inward underneath the vehicle. The arm of the hoist has dented in the rocker panel.

NOTE: Most hoists can be safely placed at any desired height. For ease while working, the area in which you are working should be at chest level. When working on brakes or suspension components, it is not necessary to work on them down near the floor or over your head. Raise the hoist so that the components are at chest level.

5. Before lowering the hoist, the safety latch(es) must be released and the direction of the controls reversed. The downward speed is often adjusted to be as slow as possible for additional safety.

JACKS AND SAFETY STANDS

Floor jacks properly rated for the weight of the vehicle being raised are a common vehicle-lifting tool. Floor jacks are portable and relatively inexpensive and must be used with

(a)

(b)

FIGURE 1-78 (a) A typical 3-ton (6,000-pound) capacity hydraulic floor jack. (b) Whenever a vehicle is raised off of the ground, a safety stand should be placed under the frame, axle, or body to support the weight of the vehicle.

safety (jack) stands. The floor jack is used to raise the vehicle off the ground and safety stands should be placed under the frame on the body of the vehicle. The weight of the vehicle should never be kept on the hydraulic floor jack because a failure of the jack could cause the vehicle to fall. See Figure 1-78. The jack is then slowly released to allow the vehicle weight to be supported on the safety stands. If the front or rear of the vehicle is being raised, the opposite end of the vehicle must be blocked.

CAUTION: Safety stands should be rated higher than the weight they support.

DRIVE-ON RAMPS

Ramps are an inexpensive way to raise the front or rear of a vehicle. See Figure 1-79. Ramps are easy to store, but they can be dangerous because they can "kick out" when driving the vehicle onto the ramps.

CAUTION: Professional repair shops do not use ramps because they are dangerous to use. Use only with extreme care.

TECH TIP

POUND WITH SOMETHING SOFTER

If you must pound on something, be sure to use a tool that is softer than what you are about to pound on to avoid damage. Examples are given in the following table.

The Material Being Pounded	What to Pound With
Steel or cast iron or punch	Brass or aluminum hammer
Aluminum	Plastic or rawhide mallet or plastic-covered dead-blow hammer
Plastic	Rawhide mallet or plastic dead-blow hammer

ELECTRICAL CORD SAFETY

Use correctly grounded three-prong sockets and extension cords to operate power tools. Some tools use only two-prong plugs. Make sure these are double insulated and repair or replace any electrical cords that are cut or damaged to prevent the possibility of an electrical shock. When not in use, keep electrical cords off the floor to prevent tripping over them. Tape the cords down if they are placed in high-foot-traffic areas.

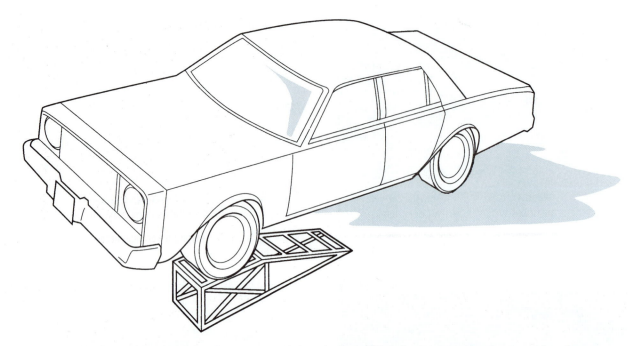

FIGURE 1-79   Drive-on type ramps. The wheels on the ground level *must* be chocked (blocked) to prevent accidental movement down the ramp.

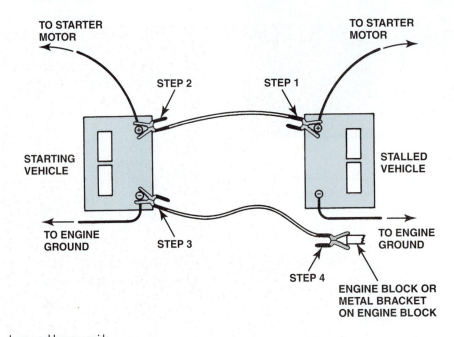

FIGURE 1-80   Jumper cable usage guide.

JUMP STARTING AND BATTERY SAFETY

To jump start another vehicle with a dead battery, connect good-quality copper jumper cables as indicated in Figure 1-80 or a jump box. The last connection made should always be on the engine block or an engine bracket as far from the battery as possible. It is normal for a spark to be created when the jumper cables finally complete the jumping circuit, and this spark could cause an explosion of the gases around the battery. Many newer vehicles have special ground connections built away from the battery just for the purpose of jump starting. Check the owner's manual or service information for the exact location.

Batteries contain acid and should be handled with care to avoid tipping them to greater than a 45-degree angle. Always

SAFETY TIP

AIR HOSE SAFETY

Improper use of an air nozzle can cause blindness or deafness. Compressed air must be reduced to less than 30 psi (206 kPa). See Figure 1-81. If an air nozzle is used to dry and clean parts, make sure the air stream is directed away from anyone else in the immediate area. Coil and store air hoses when they are not in use.

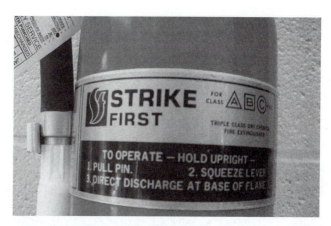

FIGURE 1-82 A typical fire extinguisher designed to be used on type A, B, or C fires.

The class rating is clearly marked on the side of every fire extinguisher. Many extinguishers can be used for multiple types of fires. See Figure 1-82.

When using a fire extinguisher, remember the word "PASS":

P = Pull the safety pin.
A = Aim the nozzle of the extinguisher at the base of the fire.
S = Squeeze the lever to actuate the extinguisher.
S = Sweep the nozzle from side to side.

See Figure 1-83.

Types of Fire Extinguishers

Types of fire extinguishers include the following:

- **Water.** A water fire extinguisher, usually in a pressurized container, is fit for use on Class A fires and works by reducing the temperature to the point where a fire cannot be sustained.
- **Carbon dioxide (CO_2).** A carbon dioxide fire extinguisher is fit for use on almost any type of fire, especially Class B or Class C materials. A CO_2 fire extinguisher works by removing the oxygen from the fire, and the cold CO_2 also helps reduce the temperature of the fire.
- **Dry chemical (yellow).** A dry chemical fire extinguisher is fit for use on Class A, B, or C fires and works by coating the flammable materials, which eliminates the oxygen from the fire. A dry chemical fire extinguisher tends to be very corrosive and will cause damage to electronic devices.

FIRE BLANKETS

Fire blankets are required to be available in the shop areas. If a person is on fire, a fire blanket should be removed from its

FIGURE 1-81 The air pressure going to the nozzle should be reduced to 30 psi or less.

remove jewelry when working around a battery to avoid the possibility of electrical shock or burns, which can occur when the metal comes in contact with a 12-volt circuit and ground, such as the body of the vehicle.

FIRE EXTINGUISHERS

There are four **classes of fire extinguishers.** Each class should be used on specific fires only:

- **Class A** is designed for use on general combustibles, such as cloth, paper, and wood.
- **Class B** is designed for use on flammable liquids and greases, including gasoline, oil, thinners, and solvents.
- **Class C** is used only on electrical fires.
- **Class D** is effective only on combustible metals such as powdered aluminum, sodium, or magnesium.

FIGURE 1-83   A CO$_2$ fire extinguisher being used on a fire set in an open steel drum during a demonstration at a fire department training center.

FIGURE 1-84   A treated wool blanket is kept in this easy-to-open wall-mounted holder and should be placed in a centralized location in the shop.

FIGURE 1-85   A first aid box should be centrally located in the shop and kept stocked with the recommended supplies.

storage bag and thrown over and around the victim to smother the fire. See Figure 1-84, which shows a typical fire blanket.

FIRST AID AND EYE WASH STATIONS

All shop areas must be equipped with a first aid kit and an **eye wash station** centrally located and kept stocked with emergency supplies.

First Aid Kit

A first aid kit should include:

- Bandages (variety)
- Gauze pads
- Roll gauze
- Iodine swab sticks
- Antibiotic ointment
- Hydrocortisone cream
- Burn gel packets
- Eye wash solution
- Scissors
- Tweezers
- Gloves
- First aid guide

See Figure 1-85. Every shop should have a person trained in first aid. If there is an accident, call for help immediately.

Eye Wash Station

An eye wash station should be centrally located and used whenever any liquid or chemical gets into the eyes. If such an emergency does occur, keep the eyes in a constant stream of water and call for professional assistance. See Figure 1-86.

TECH TIP

MARK OFF THE SERVICE AREA

Some shops rope off the service bay area to help keep traffic and distractions to a minimum, which could prevent personal injury. See Figure 1-87.

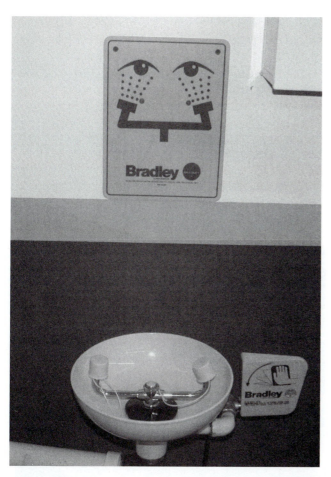

FIGURE 1-86   A typical eye wash station. Often a thorough flushing of the eyes with water is the best treatment in the event of eye contamination.

HYBRID ELECTRIC VEHICLE SAFETY ISSUES

Hybrid electric vehicles (HEVs) use a high-voltage battery pack and an electric motor(s) to help propel the vehicle. See Figure 1-88 for an example of a typical warning label on a hybrid electric vehicle. The gasoline or diesel engine also is equipped with a generator or a combination starter and an integrated starter generator (ISG) or integrated starter alternator (ISA). To safely work around a hybrid electric vehicle, the

SAFETY TIP

INFECTION CONTROL PRECAUTIONS

Working on a vehicle can result in personal injury, including the possibility of being cut or hurt enough to cause bleeding. Some infections such as hepatitis B virus, HIV (which can cause acquired immunodeficiency syndrome, or AIDS), hepatitis C virus, and others are transmitted in the blood. These infections are commonly called blood-borne pathogens. Report any injury that involves blood to your supervisor and take the necessary precautions to avoid coming in contact with blood from another person.

FIGURE 1-87   This area has been blocked off to help keep visitors from the dangerous work area.

FIGURE 1-88   A warning label on a Honda hybrid warns that a person can be killed due to the high-voltage circuits under the cover.

high-voltage (HV) battery and circuits should be depowered following these steps:

Step 1   Turn off the ignition key (if equipped) and remove the key from the ignition switch. (This will shut off all high-voltage circuits if the relay(s) working correctly.)

Step 2   Disconnect the high-voltage circuits.

CAUTION: Some vehicle manufacturers specify that rubber-insulated linesman's gloves be used whenever working around the high-voltage circuits to prevent the danger of electrical shock.

Toyota Prius

In the Toyota Prius, the cutoff switch is located in the trunk. To gain access, remove the three clips holding the upper left portion of the trunk side cover. To disconnect the high-voltage system, pull the orange-handled plug while wearing insulated-rubber linesman's gloves. See Figure 1-89.

Ford Escape/Mercury Mariner

Ford and Mercury specify that the following steps should be included when working with the high-voltage (HV) systems of a hybrid vehicle:

- Four orange cones are to be placed at the four corners of the vehicle to create a buffer zone.

- High-voltage insulated gloves are to be worn with an outer leather glove to protect the inner rubber glove from possible damage.
- The service technician should also wear a face shield, and a fiberglass hook should be in the area to be used to move a technician in the event of electrocution.

The high-voltage shut-off switch is located in the rear of the vehicle under the right side carpet. See Figure 1-90. Rotate the handle to the "service shipping" position, lift it out to disable the high-voltage circuit, and wait 5 minutes before removing high-voltage cables.

FIGURE 1-90   The high-voltage shut-off switch on a Ford Escape hybrid. The switch is located under the carpet at the rear of the vehicle.

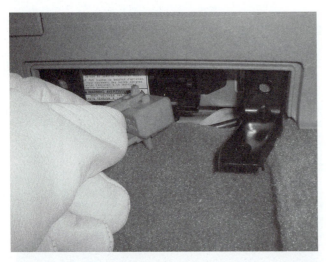

FIGURE 1-89   The high-voltage disconnect switch is in the trunk area on a Toyota Prius. High-voltage linesman's gloves should be worn when removing this plug. *(Courtesy of Tony Martin)*

FIGURE 1-91   The shut-off switch on a GM parallel hybrid truck is green because this system uses 42 volts instead of the higher, and possibly fatal, voltages used in other hybrid vehicles.

Honda Civic

To totally disable the high-voltage system on a Honda Civic, remove the main fuse (labeled number 1) from the driver's side underhood fuse panel. This should be all that is necessary to shut off the high-voltage circuit. If this is not possible, then remove the rear seat cushion and seat back. Remove the metal switch cover labeled "up" and remove the red locking cover. Move the "battery module switch" down to disable the high-voltage system.

Chevrolet Silverado/GMC Sierra Pickup Truck

In these hybrid models, the high-voltage shut-off switch is located under the rear passenger seat. Remove the cover marked "energy storage box" and turn the green service disconnect switch to the horizontal position to turn off the high-voltage circuits. See Figure 1-91.

CAUTION: Do not touch any orange wiring or component without following the vehicle manufacturer's procedures and wearing the specified personal protective equipment (PPE).

HOISTING THE VEHICLE Step-by-Step

STEP 1 The first step in hoisting a vehicle is to properly align the vehicle in the center of the stall.

TIRE PAD

STEP 2 Most vehicles will be correctly positioned when the left front tire is centered on the tire pad.

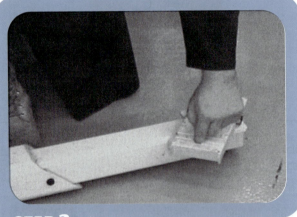

STEP 3 Most pads at the end of the hoist arms can be rotated to allow for many different types of vehicle construction.

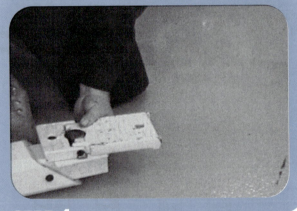

STEP 4 The arms of the lifts can be retracted or extended to accommodate vehicles of many different lengths.

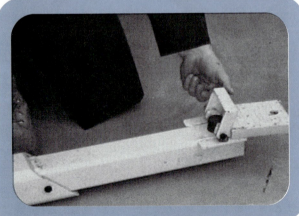

STEP 5 Most lifts are equipped with short pad extensions that are often necessary to use to allow the pad to contact the frame of a vehicle without causing the arm of the lift to hit and damage parts of the body.

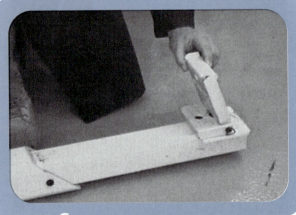

STEP 6 Tall pad extensions can also be used to gain access to the frame of a vehicle. This position is needed to safe hoist many pickup trucks, vans, and sport utility vehicles.

HOISTING THE VEHICLE continued

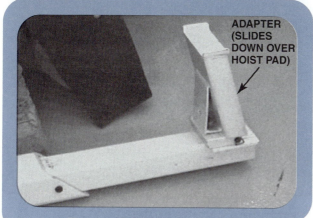

ADAPTER
(SLIDES
DOWN OVER
HOIST PAD)

STEP 7
An additional extension may be necessary to hoist a truck or van equipped with running boards to give the necessary clearance.

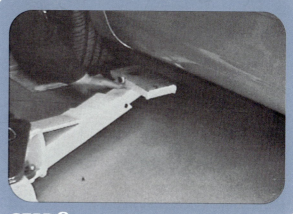

STEP 8
Position the front hoist pads under the recommended locations as specified in the owner's manual and/or service information for the vehicle being serviced.

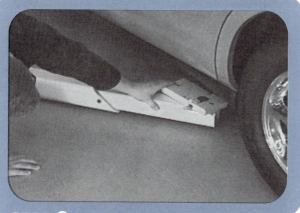

STEP 9
Position the rear pads under the vehicle under the recommended locations.

STEP 10
This photo shows an asymmetrical lift where the front arms are shorter than the rear arms. This design is best used for passenger cars and allows the driver to exit the vehicle more easily because the door can be opened wide without it hitting the verticle support column.

STEP 11
After being sure all pads are correctly positioned, use the electromechanical controls to raise the vehicle.

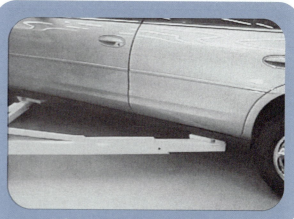

STEP 12
Raise the vehicle about 1 foot (30 cm) and stop to double-check that all pads contact the body or frame in the correct positions.

HOISTING THE VEHICLE continued

STEP 13 With the vehicle raised about a foot off the ground, push down on the vehicle to check to see if it is stable on the pads. If the vehicle rocks, lower the vehicle and reset the pads. If the vehicle is stable, the vehicle can be raised to any desired working level. Be sure the safety is engaged before working on or under the vehicle.

STEP 14 This photo shows the pads set flat and contacting the pinch welds of the body. This method spreads the load over the entire length of the pad and is less likely to dent or damage the pinch weld area.

PINCH WELD

STEP 15 Where additional clearance is necessary for the arms to clear the rest of the body, the pads can be raised and placed under the pinch weld area as shown.

PUSH BUTTON TO RAISE VEHICLE

SAFETY RELEASE

LEVER TO LOWER VEHICLE

STEP 16 When the service work is completed, the hoist should be raised slightly and the safety released before using the hydraulic lever to lower the vehicle.

STEP 17 After lowering the vehicle, be sure all arms of the lift are moved out of the way before driving the vehicle out of the work stall.

STEP 18 Carefully back the vehicle out of the stall. Notice that all of the lift arms have been neatly moved out of the way to provide clearance so that the tires will not contact the arms when the vehicle is driven out of the stall.

SUMMARY

1. Bolts, studs, and nuts are commonly used as fasteners in the chassis. The sizes for fractional and metric threads are different and are not interchangeable. The grade is the rating of the strength of a fastener.
2. Whenever a vehicle is raised above the ground, it must be supported at a substantial section of the body or frame.
3. Wrenches are available in open end, box end, and combination open and box end.
4. An adjustable wrench should only be used when the proper-size wrench is not available.
5. Line wrenches are also called flare-nut wrenches, fitting wrenches, or tube-nut wrenches and are used to remove fuel or refrigerant lines.
6. Sockets are rotated by a ratchet or breaker bar, also called a flex handle.
7. Torque wrenches measure the amount of torque applied to a fastener.
8. Screwdriver types include straight blade (flat tip) and Phillips.
9. Hammers and mallets come in a variety of sizes and weights.
10. Pliers are a useful tool and are available in many different types, including slip-joint, multigroove, linesman's, diagonal, needle-nose, and locking pliers.
11. Other common hand tools include snap-ring pliers, files, cutters, punches, chisels, and hacksaws.

REVIEW QUESTIONS

1. List three precautions that must be taken whenever hoisting (lifting) a vehicle.
2. Describe how to determine the grade of a fastener, including how the markings differ between fractional and metric bolts.
3. List four items that are personal protective equipment (PPE).
4. List the types of fire extinguishers and their usage.
5. Why are wrenches offset 15 degrees?
6. What are the other names for a line wrench?
7. What are the standard automotive drive sizes for sockets?
8. Which type of screwdriver requires the use of a hammer or mallet?
9. What is inside a dead-blow hammer?
10. What type of cutter is available in left and right cutters?

CHAPTER QUIZ

1. The correct location for the pads when hoisting or jacking the vehicle can often be found in the _____.
   a. Service manual
   b. Shop manual
   c. Owner's manual
   d. All of the above
2. For the best working position, the work should be _____.
   a. At neck or head level
   b. At knee or ankle level
   c. Overhead by about 1 foot
   d. At chest or elbow level
3. A high-strength bolt is identified by _____.
   a. A UNC symbol
   b. Lines on the head
   c. Strength letter codes
   d. The coarse threads
4. A fastener that uses threads on both ends is called a _____.
   a. Cap screw
   b. Stud
   c. Machine screw
   d. Crest fastener

5. When working with hand tools, always _____.
   a. Push the wrench—don't pull toward you
   b. Pull a wrench—don't push a wrench

6. The proper term for Channel Locks is _____.
   a. Vise Grips
   b. Crescent wrench
   c. Locking pliers
   d. Multigroove adjustable pliers

7. The proper term for Vise Grips is _____.
   a. Locking pliers
   b. Slip-joint pliers
   c. Side cuts
   d. Multigroove adjustable pliers

8. Two technicians are discussing torque wrenches. Technician A says that a torque wrench is capable of tightening a fastener with more torque than a conventional breaker bar or ratchet. Technician B says that a torque wrench should be calibrated regularly for the most accurate results. Which technician is correct?
   a. Technician A only
   b. Technician B only
   c. Both Technicians A and B
   d. Neither Technician A nor B

9. Which type of screwdriver should be used if there is very limited space above the head of the fastener?
   a. Offset screwdriver
   b. Stubby screwdriver
   c. Impact screwdriver
   d. Robertson screwdriver

10. Which type of hammer is plastic coated, has a metal casing inside, and is filled with small lead balls?
    a. Dead-blow hammer
    b. Soft-blow hammer
    c. Sledgehammer
    d. Plastic hammer

CHAPTER 2

ENVIRONMENTAL AND HAZARDOUS MATERIALS

OBJECTIVES

After studying Chapter 2, the reader should be able to:

1. Prepare for the ASE assumed knowledge content required by all service technicians to adhere to environmentally appropriate actions and behavior.

2. Define the Occupational Safety and Health Act (OSHA).

3. Explain the term Material Safety Data Sheet (MSDS).

4. Identify hazardous waste materials in accordance with state and federal regulations and follow proper safety precautions while handling hazardous waste materials.

5. Define the steps required to safely handle and store automotive chemicals and waste.

KEY TERMS

Safety and the handling of hazardous waste material are extremely important in the automotive shop. The improper handling of hazardous material affects us all, not just those in the shop. Shop personnel must be familiar with their rights and responsibilities regarding hazardous waste disposal. Right-to-know laws explain these rights. Shop personnel must also be familiar with hazardous materials in the automotive shop, and the proper way to dispose of these materials according to state and federal regulations.

OCCUPATIONAL SAFETY AND HEALTH ACT

The U.S. Congress passed the Occupational Safety and Health Act in 1970. This legislation was designed to assist and encourage the citizens of the United States in their efforts to assure safe and healthful working conditions by providing research, information, education, and training in the field of occupational safety and health, as well as to assure safe and healthful working conditions for working men and women by authorizing enforcement of the standards developed under the act. Since approximately 25% of workers are exposed to health and safety hazards on the job, the standards are necessary to monitor, control, and educate workers regarding health and safety in the workplace.

HAZARDOUS WASTE

CAUTION: When handling hazardous waste material, one must always wear the proper protective clothing and equipment detailed in the right-to-know laws. This includes respirator equipment. All recommended procedures must be followed accurately. Personal injury may result from improper clothing, equipment, and procedures when handling hazardous materials.

Hazardous waste materials are chemicals, or components, that the shop no longer needs that pose a danger to the environment and people if they are disposed of in ordinary garbage cans or sewers. However, one should note that no material is considered hazardous waste until the shop has finished using it and is ready to dispose of it. The **Environmental Protection Agency (EPA)** publishes a list of hazardous materials that is included in the **Code of Federal Regulations (CFR).** The EPA considers waste hazardous if it is included on the EPA list of hazardous materials, or if it has one or more of the following characteristics.

Reactive

Any material that reacts violently with water or other chemicals is considered hazardous.

Corrosive

If a material burns the skin, or dissolves metals and other materials, a technician should consider it hazardous. A pH scale is used, with the number 7 indicating neutral. Pure water has a pH of 7. Lower numbers indicate an acidic solution and higher numbers indicate a caustic solution. If a material releases cyanide gas, hydrogen sulfide gas, or similar gases when exposed to low-pH acid solutions, it is considered hazardous.

Toxic

Materials are hazardous if they leak one or more of eight different heavy metals in concentrations greater than 100 times the primary drinking water standard.

Ignitable

A liquid is hazardous if it has a flash point below 140°F (60°C), and a solid is hazardous if it ignites spontaneously.

Radioactive

Any substance that emits measurable levels of radiation is radioactive. When individuals bring containers of a highly radioactive substance into the shop environment, qualified personnel with the appropriate equipment must test them.

WARNING: Hazardous waste disposal laws include serious penalties for anyone responsible for breaking these laws.

RESOURCE CONSERVATION AND RECOVERY ACT (RCRA)

Federal and state laws control the disposal of hazardous waste materials. Every shop employee must be familiar with these laws. Hazardous waste disposal laws include the **Resource Conservation and Recovery Act (RCRA).** This law states that hazardous material users are responsible for hazardous materials from the time they become a waste until the proper waste disposal is completed. Many shops hire an independent hazardous waste hauler to dispose of hazardous waste material. The shop owner, or manager, should have a written contract with the hazardous waste hauler. Rather than have hazardous waste material hauled to an approved hazardous waste disposal site, a shop may choose to recycle the material in the shop. Therefore, the user must store hazardous waste material properly and safely, and be responsible for the transportation of this material until it arrives at an approved

hazardous waste disposal site, where it can be processed according to the law. The RCRA controls these types of automotive waste:

- Paint and body repair products waste
- Solvents for parts and equipment cleaning
- Batteries and battery acid
- Mild acids used for metal cleaning and preparation
- Waste oil, and engine coolants or antifreeze
- Air-conditioning refrigerants and oils
- Engine oil filters

The **right-to-know laws** state that employees have a right to know when the materials they use at work are hazardous. The right-to-know laws started with the Hazard Communication Standard published by the **Occupational Safety and Health Administration (OSHA)** in 1983. Originally, this document was intended for chemical companies and manufacturers that required employees to handle hazardous materials in their work situation. Meanwhile, the federal courts have decided to apply these laws to all companies, including automotive service shops. Under the right-to-know laws, the employer has responsibilities regarding the handling of hazardous materials by their employees. All employees must be trained about the types of hazardous materials they will encounter in the workplace. The employees must be informed about their rights under legislation regarding the handling of hazardous materials.

CLEAN AIR ACT

Air-conditioning (A/C) systems and refrigerant are regulated by the **Clean Air Act (CAA),** Title VI, Section 609. Technician certification and service equipment is also regulated. Any technician working on automotive A/C systems must be certified. A/C refrigerants must not be released or vented into the atmosphere, and used refrigerants must be recovered.

MATERIAL SAFETY DATA SHEETS (MSDSs)

All hazardous materials must be properly labeled, and information about each hazardous material must be posted on **Material Safety Data Sheets (MSDSs)** available from the manufacturer. See Figure 2-1. In Canada, MSDSs are called **Workplace Hazardous Materials Information Systems (WHMIS).**

The employer has a responsibility to place MSDSs where they are easily accessible by all employees. The MSDSs provide the following information about the hazardous material: chemical name, physical characteristics, protective handling

FIGURE 2-1   Material Safety Data Sheets (MSDSs) should be readily available for use by anyone in the area who may come into contact with hazardous materials.

equipment, explosion/fire hazards, incompatible materials, health hazards, medical conditions aggravated by exposure, emergency and first-aid procedures, safe handling, and spill/leak procedures.

The employer also has a responsibility to make sure that all hazardous materials are properly labeled. The label information must include health, fire, and reactivity hazards posed by the material, as well as the protective equipment necessary to handle the material. The manufacturer must supply all warning and precautionary information about hazardous materials. This information must be read and understood by the employee before handling the material.

THE DANGERS OF EXPOSURE TO ASBESTOS

Friction materials such as brake and clutch linings often contain asbestos. While asbestos has been eliminated from most original-equipment friction materials, the automotive service technician cannot know whether or not the vehicle being serviced is or is not equipped with friction materials containing asbestos. It is important that all friction materials be handled as if they do contain asbestos.

Asbestos exposure can cause scar tissue to form in the lungs. This condition is called **asbestosis.** It gradually causes increasing shortness of breath, and the scarring to the lungs is permanent.

Even low exposures to asbestos can cause mesothelioma, a type of fatal cancer of the lining of the chest or abdominal cavity. Asbestos exposure can also increase the risk of lung cancer as well as cancer of the voice box, stomach, and large intestine. It usually takes 15 to 30 years or more for cancer or asbestos lung scarring to show up after exposure. (Scientists call this the latency period.)

Government agencies recommend that asbestos exposure should be eliminated or controlled to the lowest level possible. These agencies have developed recommendations and standards that the automotive service technician and equipment manufacturer should follow. These U.S. federal agencies include the National Institute for Occupational Safety and Health (NIOSH), Occupational Safety and Health Administration (OSHA), and Environmental Protection Agency (EPA).

ASBESTOS OSHA STANDARDS

The Occupational Safety and Health Administration (OSHA) has established three levels of asbestos exposure. Any vehicle service establishment that does either brake or clutch work must limit employee exposure to asbestos to less than 0.2 fibers per cubic centimeter (cc) as determined by an air sample.

If the level of exposure to employees is greater than specified, corrective measures must be performed and a large fine may be imposed.

NOTE: Research has found that worn asbestos fibers such as those from automotive brakes or clutches may not be as hazardous as first believed. Worn asbestos fibers do not have sharp, flared ends that can latch onto tissue, but rather are worn down to a dust form that resembles talc. Grinding or sawing operations on unworn brake shoes or clutch discs *will* contain harmful asbestos fibers. To limit health damage, always use proper handling procedures while working around any component that may contain asbestos.

ASBESTOS EPA REGULATIONS

The federal Environmental Protection Agency (EPA) has established procedures for the removal and disposal of asbestos. The EPA procedures require that products containing asbestos be "wetted" to prevent the asbestos fibers from becoming airborne. According to the EPA, asbestos-containing materials can be disposed of as regular waste. Only when asbestos becomes airborne is it considered to be hazardous.

ASBESTOS HANDLING GUIDELINES

The air in the shop area can be tested by a testing laboratory, but this can be expensive. Tests have determined that asbestos levels can easily be kept below the recommended levels by using a solvent or a special vacuum.

NOTE: Even though asbestos is being removed from brake and clutch lining materials, the service technician cannot tell whether or not the old brake pads, shoes, or clutch disc contain asbestos. Therefore, to be safe, the technician should assume that all brake pads, shoes, or clutch discs contain asbestos.

HEPA Vacuum

A special **high-efficiency particulate air (HEPA) vacuum** system has been proven to be effective in keeping asbestos exposure levels below 0.1 fibers per cubic centimeter.

Solvent Spray

Many technicians use an aerosol can of brake cleaning solvent to wet the brake dust and prevent it from becoming airborne. Commercial brake cleaners are available that use a concentrated cleaner that is mixed with water. See Figure 2-2.

The waste liquid is filtered, and, when dry, the filter can be disposed of as solid waste.

FIGURE 2-2 All brakes should be moistened with water or solvent to help prevent brake dust from becoming airborne.

CAUTION: Never use compressed air to blow brake dust. The fine, talc-like brake dust can create a health hazard even if asbestos is not present or is present in dust rather than fiber form.

Disposal of Brake Dust and Brake Shoes

The hazard of asbestos occurs when asbestos fibers are airborne. Once the asbestos has been wetted down, it is then considered to be solid waste, rather than hazardous waste. Old brake shoes and pads should be enclosed, preferably in a plastic bag, to help prevent any of the brake material from becoming airborne. *Always follow current federal and local laws concerning disposal of all waste.*

USED BRAKE FLUID

Most brake fluid is made from polyglycol, is water soluble, and can be considered hazardous if it has absorbed metals from the brake system.

- Collect brake fluid in containers clearly marked to indicate that they are dedicated for that purpose.
- If your waste brake fluid is hazardous, manage it appropriately and use only an authorized waste receiver for its disposal.
- If your waste brake fluid is nonhazardous (such as old, but unused), determine from your local solid waste collection provider what should be done for its proper disposal.
- Do not mix brake fluid with used engine oil.
- Do not pour brake fluid down drains or onto the ground.
- Recycle brake fluid through a registered recycler.

USED OIL

Used oil is any petroleum-based or synthetic oil that has been used. During normal use, impurities such as dirt, metal scrapings, water, or chemicals can get mixed in with the oil. Eventually, this used oil must be replaced with virgin or re-refined oil. The EPA's used oil management standards include a three-pronged approach to determine if a substance meets the definition of used oil. To meet the EPA's definition of used oil, a substance must meet each of the following three criteria:

- Origin. The first criterion for identifying used oil is based on the oil's origin. Used oil must have been refined from crude oil or made from synthetic materials. Animal and vegetable oils are excluded from the EPA's definition of used oil.
- Use. The second criterion is based on whether and how the oil is used. Oils used as lubricants, hydraulic fluids, heat-transfer fluids, and for other similar purposes are considered used oil. Unused oil, such as bottom clean-out waste from virgin fuel oil storage tanks or virgin fuel oil recovered from a spill, does not meet the EPA's definition of used oil because these oils have never been "used." The EPA's definition also excludes products used as cleaning agents, as well as certain petroleum-derived products such as antifreeze and kerosene.
- Contaminants. The third criterion is based on whether or not the oil is contaminated with either physical or chemical impurities. In other words, to meet the EPA's definition, used oil must become contaminated as a result of being used. This aspect of the EPA's definition includes residues and contaminants generated from handling, storing, and processing used oil.

NOTE: The release of only 1 gallon of used oil (a typical oil change) can make a million gallons of fresh water undrinkable.

If used oil is dumped down the drain and enters a sewage treatment plant, concentrations as small as 50 to 100 PPM (parts per million) in the waste water can foul sewage treatment processes. Never mix a listed hazardous waste, gasoline, waste water, halogenated solvent, antifreeze, or an unknown waste material with used oil. Adding any of these substances will cause the used oil to become contaminated, which classifies it as hazardous waste.

DISPOSAL OF USED OIL

Once oil has been used, it can be collected, recycled, and used over and over again. An estimated 380 million gallons of used oil are recycled each year. Recycled used oil can sometimes be used again for the same job or can take on a completely different task. For example, used engine oil can be re-refined and sold at the store as engine oil or processed for furnace fuel oil. After collecting used oil in an appropriate container (e.g., a 55-gallon steel drum), the material must be disposed of in one of two ways:

- Shipped offsite for recycling
- Burned in an onsite or offsite EPA-approved heater for energy recovery

USED OIL STORAGE

Used oil must be stored in compliance with an existing **underground storage tank (UST)** or an **aboveground storage tank (AGST)** standard, or kept in separate containers. See Figure 2-3. Containers are portable receptacles, such as a 55-gallon steel drum.

Keep Used Oil Storage Drums in Good Condition

This means that they should be covered, secured from vandals, properly labeled, and maintained in compliance with local fire codes. Frequent inspections for leaks, corrosion, and spillage are an essential part of container maintenance.

Never Store Used Oil in Anything Other Than Tanks and Storage Containers

Used oil may also be stored in units that are permitted to store regulated hazardous waste.

Used Oil Filter Disposal Regulations

Used oil filters contain used engine oil that may be hazardous. Before an oil filter is placed into the trash or sent to be recycled, it must be drained using one of the following hot-draining methods approved by the EPA:

- Puncturing the filter anti-drainback valve or filter dome end and hot draining for at least 12 hours
- Hot draining and crushing
- Dismantling and hot draining

FIGURE 2-3   A typical aboveground oil storage tank.

- Any other hot draining method that will remove all the used oil from the filter

After the oil has been drained from the oil filter, the filter housing can be disposed of in any of the following ways:

- Sent for recycling
- Pickup by a service contract company
- Disposed of in regular trash

SOLVENTS

The major sources of chemical danger are liquid and aerosol brake cleaning fluids that contain chlorinated hydrocarbon **solvents.** Several other chemicals that do not deplete the ozone, such as heptane, hexane, and xylene, are now being used in nonchlorinated brake cleaning solvents. Some manufacturers are also producing solvents they describe as environmentally responsible, which are biodegradable and noncarcinogenic.

Sources of Chemical Poisoning

The health hazards presented by brake cleaning solvents occur from three different forms of exposure: ingestion, inhalation, and physical contact. It should be obvious that swallowing brake cleaning solvent is harmful, and such occurrences are not common. Still, brake cleaning solvents should always be handled and stored properly, and kept out of the reach of children. The dangers of inhalation are perhaps the most serious problem, as even very low levels of solvent vapors are hazardous.

Allowing brake cleaning solvents to come in contact with the skin presents a danger because these solvents strip natural oils from the skin and cause irritation of the tissues, plus they can be absorbed through the skin directly into the bloodstream. The transfer begins immediately upon contact, and continues until the liquid is wiped or washed away.

There is no specific standard for physical contact with chlorinated hydrocarbon solvents or the chemicals replacing them. All contact should be avoided whenever possible. The law requires an employer to provide appropriate protective equipment and ensure proper work practices by an employee handling these chemicals.

Effects of Chemical Poisoning

The effects of exposure to chlorinated hydrocarbon and other types of solvents can take many forms. Short-term exposure at low levels can cause headache, nausea, drowsiness, dizziness, lack of coordination, or unconsciousness. It may also cause irritation of the eyes, nose, and throat, and flushing of the face and neck. Short-term exposure to higher concentrations can cause liver damage with symptoms such as yellow jaundice or dark urine. Liver damage may not become evident until several weeks after the exposure.

Health Care Rights

The OSHA regulations concerning on-the-job safety place certain responsibilities on the employer, and give employees specific rights. Any person who feels there might be unsafe conditions where he or she works, whether asbestos exposure, chemical poisoning, or any other problem, should discuss the issue with fellow workers, union representatives (where applicable), and his or her supervisor or employer. If no action is taken and there is reason to believe the employer is not complying with OSHA standards, a complaint can be filed with OSHA and it will be investigated.

The law forbids employers from taking action against employees who file a complaint concerning a health or safety hazard. However, if workers fear reprisal as the result of a complaint, they may request that OSHA withhold their names from the employer.

SAFETY TIP

HAND SAFETY

Service technicians should wash their hands with soap and water after handling engine oil or differential or transmission fluids, or wear protective rubber gloves. Another safety hint is that the service technician should not wear watches, rings, or other jewelry that could come in contact with electrical or moving parts of a vehicle. See Figure 2-4.

SOLVENT HAZARDOUS AND REGULATORY STATUS

Most solvents are classified as hazardous wastes. Other characteristics of solvents include the following:

- Solvents with flash points below 140°F are considered flammable and, like gasoline, are federally regulated by the Department of Transportation (DOT).
- Solvents and oils with flash points above 140°F are considered combustible and, like engine oil, are also regulated by the DOT. See Figure 2-5.

It is the responsibility of the repair shop to determine if its spent solvent is hazardous waste. Waste solvents that are considered hazardous waste have a flash point below 140°F (60°C). Hot water or aqueous parts cleaners may be used to avoid disposing of spent solvent as hazardous waste. Solvent-type parts cleaners with filters are available to greatly extend solvent life and reduce spent-solvent disposal costs. Solvent reclaimers are available that clean and restore the solvent so that it lasts indefinitely.

USED SOLVENTS

Used or spent solvents are liquid materials that have been generated as waste and may contain xylene, methanol, ethyl ether, and methyl isobutyl ketone (MIBK). These materials must be stored in OSHA-approved safety containers with the lids or caps closed tightly. These storage receptacles must show no signs of leaks or significant damage due to dents or rust. In addition, the containers must be stored in a protected

FIGURE 2-4 Washing hands and removing jewelry are two important safety habits all service technicians should practice.

FIGURE 2-5 Typical fireproof flammable storage cabinet.

FIGURE 2-6 All solvents and other hazardous waste should be disposed of properly.

FIGURE 2-7 Used antifreeze coolant should be kept separate and stored in a leakproof container until it can be recycled or disposed of according to federal, state, and local laws. Note that the storage barrel is placed inside another container to catch any coolant that may spill out of the inside barrel.

area equipped with secondary containment or a spill protector, such as a spill pallet. Additional requirements include the following:

- Containers should be clearly labeled "Hazardous Waste" and the date the material was first placed into the storage receptacle should be noted.
- Labeling is not required for solvents being used in a parts washer.
- Used solvents will not be counted toward a facility's monthly output of hazardous waste if the vendor under contract removes the material.
- Used solvents may be disposed of by recycling with a local vendor, such as *SafetyKleen*, to have the used solvent removed according to specific terms in the vendor agreement. See Figure 2-6.
- Use aqueous-based (nonsolvent) cleaning systems to help avoid the problems associated with chemical solvents.

COOLANT DISPOSAL

Coolant is a mixture of antifreeze and water. New antifreeze is not considered to be hazardous even though it can cause death if ingested. Used antifreeze may be hazardous due to dissolved metals from the engine and other components of the cooling system. These metals can include iron, steel, aluminum, copper, brass, and lead (from older radiators and heater cores).

1. Coolant should be recycled either onsite or offsite.
2. Used coolant should be stored in a sealed and labeled container. See Figure 2-7.
3. Used coolant can often be disposed of into municipal sewers with a permit. Check with local authorities and obtain a permit before discharging used coolant into sanitary sewers.

LEAD-ACID BATTERY WASTE

About 70 million spent lead-acid batteries are generated each year in the United States alone. Lead is classified as a toxic metal and the acid used in lead-acid batteries is highly corrosive. The vast majority (95% to 98%) of these batteries are recycled through lead reclamation operations and secondary lead smelters for use in the manufacture of new batteries.

BATTERY HAZARDOUS AND REGULATORY STATUS

Used lead-acid batteries must be reclaimed or recycled in order to be exempt from hazardous waste regulations. Leaking batteries must be stored and transported as hazardous waste. Some states have more strict regulations, which require special handling procedures and transportation. According to the

Battery Council International (BCI), battery laws usually include the following rules:

- Lead-acid battery disposal is prohibited in landfills or incinerators. Batteries are required to be delivered to a battery retailer, wholesaler, recycling center, or lead smelter.
- All retailers of automotive batteries are required to post a sign that displays the universal recycling symbol and indicates the retailer's specific requirements for accepting used batteries.

CAUTION: Battery electrolyte contains sulfuric acid, which is a very corrosive substance capable of causing serious personal injury, such as skin burns and eye damage. In addition, the battery plates contain lead, which is highly poisonous. For this reason, disposing of batteries improperly can cause environmental contamination and lead to severe health problems.

BATTERY HANDLING AND STORAGE

Batteries, whether new or used, should be kept indoors if possible. The storage location should be an area specifically designated for battery storage and must be well ventilated (to the outside). If outdoor storage is the only alternative, a sheltered and secured area with acid-resistant secondary containment is strongly recommended. It is also advisable that acid-resistant secondary containment be used for indoor storage. In addition, batteries should be placed on acid-resistant pallets and never stacked!

FUEL SAFETY AND STORAGE

Gasoline is a very explosive liquid. The expanding vapors that come from gasoline are extremely dangerous. These vapors are present even in cold temperatures. Vapors formed in gasoline tanks on many vehicles are controlled, but vapors from gasoline storage may escape from the can, resulting in a hazardous situation. Therefore, place gasoline storage containers in a well-ventilated space. Although diesel fuel is not as volatile as gasoline, the same basic rules apply to diesel fuel and gasoline storage. These rules include the following:

- Approved gasoline storage cans have a flash-arresting screen at the outlet. These screens prevent external ignition sources from igniting the gasoline within the can when someone pours the gasoline or diesel fuel.
- Technicians must always use red approved gasoline containers to allow for proper hazardous substance identification. See Figure 2-8.
- Do not fill gasoline containers completely full. Always leave the level of gasoline at least 1 inch from the top of the container. This action allows expansion of the gasoline at higher

FIGURE 2-8 This red gasoline container holds about 30 gallons of gasoline and is used to fill vehicles used for training.

temperatures. If gasoline containers are completely full, the gasoline will expand when the temperature increases. This expansion forces gasoline from the can and creates a dangerous spill. If gasoline or diesel fuel containers must be stored, place them in a designated storage locker or facility.

- Never leave gasoline containers open, except while filling or pouring gasoline from the container.
- Never use gasoline as a cleaning agent.
- Always connect a ground strap to containers when filling or transferring fuel or other flammable products from one container to another to prevent static electricity that could result in explosion and fire. These ground wires prevent the build-up of a static electric charge, which could result in a spark and disastrous explosion.

AIRBAG HANDLING

Airbag modules are pyrotechnic devices that can be ignited if exposed to an electrical charge or if the body of the vehicle is subjected to a shock. Airbag safety should include the following precautions:

1. Disarm the airbag(s) if you will be working in the area where a discharged bag could make contact with any part

of your body. Consult service information for the exact procedure to follow for the vehicle being serviced. The usual procedure is to deploy the airbag using a 12-volt power supply, such as a jump start box, using long wires to connect to the module to ensure a safe deployment.

2. Do not expose an airbag to extreme heat or fire.
3. Always carry an airbag pointing away from your body.
4. Place an airbag module facing upward.
5. Always follow the manufacturer's recommended procedure for airbag disposal or recycling, including the proper packaging to use during shipment.
6. Always wash your hands or body well if exposed to a deployed airbag. The chemicals involved can cause skin irritation and possible rash development.
7. Wear protective gloves if handling a deployed airbag.

USED TIRE DISPOSAL

Used tires are an environmental concern for several reasons, including the following:

1. In a landfill, they tend to "float" up through the other trash and rise to the surface.
2. The inside of tires traps and holds rainwater, which is a breeding ground for mosquitoes. Mosquito-borne diseases include encephalitis and dengue fever.
3. Used tires present a fire hazard and, when burned, create a large amount of black smoke that contaminates the air.

Used tires should be disposed of in one of the following ways:

1. Used tires can be reused until the end of their useful life.
2. Tires can be retreaded.
3. Tires can be recycled or shredded for use in asphalt.
4. Derimmed tires can be sent to a landfill (most landfill operators will shred the tires because it is illegal in many states to landfill whole tires).
5. Tires can be burned in cement kilns or other power plants where the smoke can be controlled.
6. A registered scrap tire handler should be used to transport tires for disposal or recycling.

AIR-CONDITIONING REFRIGERANT OIL DISPOSAL

Air-conditioning refrigerant oil contains dissolved refrigerant and is therefore considered to be hazardous waste. This oil must be kept separate from other waste oil or the entire amount of oil must be treated as hazardous. Used refrigerant oil must be sent to a licensed hazardous waste disposal company for recycling or disposal. See Figure 2-9.

FIGURE 2-9 Air-conditioning refrigerant oil must be kept separate from other oils because it contains traces of refrigerant and must be treated as hazardous waste.

TECH TIP

REMOVE COMPONENTS THAT CONTAIN MERCURY

Some vehicles have a placard near the driver's side door that lists the components that contain **mercury**, a heavy metal. See Figure 2-10.

These components should be removed from the vehicle before the rest of the body is sent to be recycled to help prevent the release of mercury into the environment.

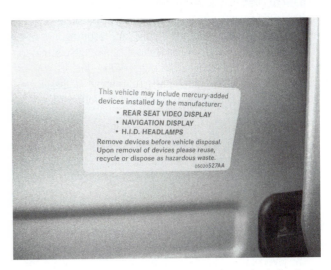

FIGURE 2-10 Placard near driver's door listing the devices in the vehicle that contain mecury.

TECH TIP

WHAT EVERY TECHNICIAN SHOULD KNOW

The Hazardous Material Identification Guide (HMIG) is the standard labeling for all materials. The service technician should be aware of the meaning of the label. See Figure 2-11.

Waste Chart

All automotive service facilities create some waste and while most of it is handled properly, it is important that all hazardous and nonhazardous waste be accounted for and properly disposed. See the chart for a list of typical wastes generated at automotive shops, plus a checklist for keeping track of how these wastes are handled.

Hazardous Materials Identification Guide (HMIG)

TYPE HAZARD		DEGREE	
○	HEALTH		4 - Extreme
○	FLAMMABILITY		3 - Serious
○	REACTIVITY		2 - Moderate
○	PROTECTIVE EQUIPMENT		1 - Slight
			0 - Minimal

HAZARD RATING AND PROTECTIVE EQUIPMENT

Health	Flammable	Reactive
Type of Possible Injury	Susceptibility of materials to burn	Susceptibility of materials to release energy
4 — Highly Toxic. May be fatal on short term exposure. Special protective equipment required.	4 — Extremely flammable gas or liquid. Flash Point below 73°F.	4 — Extreme. Explosive at room temperature.
3 — Toxic. Avoid inhalation or skin contact.	3 — Flammable. Flash Point 73°F to 100°F.	3 — Serious. May explode if shocked, heated under confinement or mixed w/ water.
2 — Moderately Toxic. May be harmful if inhaled or absorbed.	2 — Combustible. Requires moderate heating to ignite. Flash Point 100°F to 200°F.	2 — Moderate. Unstable, may react with water.
1 — Slightly Toxic. May cause slight irritation.	1 — Slightly Combustible. Requires strong heating to ignite.	1 — Slight. May react if heated or mixed with water.
0 — Minimal. All chemicals have a slight degree of toxicity.	0 — Minimal. Will not burn under normal conditions.	0 — Minimal. Normally stable, does not react with water.

Protective Equipment

A	Safety Glasses	E	Safety Glasses + Gloves + Dust Respirator	I	Safety Glasses + Gloves + Combination Dust & Vapor Respirator
B	Safety Glasses + Gloves	F	Safety Glasses + Gloves + Apron + Dust Respirator	J	Chemical Goggles + Gloves + Apron + Combination Dust & Vapor Respirator
C	Safety Glasses + Gloves + Apron	G	Safety Glasses + Gloves + Vapor Respirator	K	Apron + Gloves + Full Protection Suit + Boots
D	Faceshield + Gloves + Apron	H	Chemical Goggles + Gloves + Apron + Vapor Respirator	X	Ask your supervisor for guidance.

FIGURE 2-11 The Environmental Protection Agency (EPA) Hazardous Materials Identification Guide is a standardized listing of the hazards and the protective equipment needed.

Typical Wastes Generated at Auto Repair Shops and Typical Category (Hazardous or Nonhazardous) by Disposal Method

Waste Stream	Typical Category if Not Mixed with Other Hazardous Waste	If Disposed in Landfill and Not Mixed with a Hazardous Waste	If Recycled
Used oil	Used oil	Hazardous waste	Used oil
Used oil filters	Nonhazardous solid waste, if completely drained	Nonhazardous solid waste, if completely drained	Used oil, if not drained
Used transmission fluid	Used oil	Hazardous waste	Used oil
Used brake fluid	Used oil	Hazardous waste	Used oil
Used antifreeze	Depends on characterization	Depends on characterization	Depends on characterization
Used solvents	Hazardous waste	Hazardous waste	Hazardous waste
Used citric solvents	Nonhazardous solid waste	Nonhazardous solid waste	Hazardous waste
Lead-acid automotive batteries	Not a solid waste if returned to supplier	Hazardous waste	Hazardous waste
Shop rags used for oil	Used oil	Depends on used oil characterization	Used oil
Shop rags used for solvent or gasoline spills	Hazardous waste	Hazardous waste	Hazardous waste
Oil spill absorbent material	Used oil	Depends on used oil characterization	Used oil
Spill material for solvent and gasoline	Hazardous waste	Hazardous waste	Hazardous waste
Catalytic converter	Not a solid waste if returned to supplier	Nonhazardous solid waste	Nonhazardous solid waste
Spilled or unused fuels	Hazardous waste	Hazardous waste	Hazardous waste
Spilled or unusable paints and thinners	Hazardous waste	Hazardous waste	Hazardous waste
Used tires	Nonhazardous solid waste	Nonhazardous solid waste	Nonhazardous solid waste

Consolidated Screening Checklist for Automotive Repair Facilities

1. Waste Management		
Waste Management	Has the facility determined which wastes are hazardous wastes?	yes/no
	Does the facility generate more than 100 kg (220 lbs.) of hazardous waste per month?	yes/no
	If yes, does facility have a U.S. EPA hazardous waste generator I.D. number?	yes/no
Used Oil	Are used oil containers and piping leak free, segregated, and labeled "used oil"?	yes/no
	Are hazardous waste fluids mixed with used oil?	yes/no
	Is used oil collected and sent offsite for recycling, or burned in an onsite heater?	recycle/onsite heater/burned offsite/other
	Does the facility accept household used oil?	yes/no
	If yes, is it tested for hazardous waste (solvent/gasoline) contamination?	yes/no
Used Oil Filters	Are used oil filters completely drained before disposal?	yes/no
	How are used oil filters disposed of?	scrap metal/service/trash/other
Used Antifreeze	Is used antifreeze properly contained, segregated, and labeled?	yes/no
	Does the facility generate any antifreeze that is a hazardous waste (>5 ppm lead)?	yes/no/do not know
	If yes, is it recycled onsite in a closed-loop system?	yes/no
	If no, is it counted toward facility generator status?	yes/no
	If used antifreeze is not recycled onsite, how is it disposed of?	recycled offsite/mixed with other fluids/landfill/other
Used Solvents	Are used solvents stored in proper containers and properly labeled?	yes/no/N/A
	How are used solvents disposed of?	service/mixed with other fluids/other
	Does the facility have hazardous waste manifests for shipping papers on file?	yes/no/N/A
Batteries	Does the facility return used batteries to new battery suppliers?	yes/no/N/A
	If not, how are used automotive batteries disposed of?	recycle/hazardous waste landfill/other
	Are used batteries contained and covered prior to disposal?	yes/no
Rags	How are used rags and towels disposed of?	laundry service/burned for heat/trash
	How are used rags stored while onsite?	separate container/shop trash can/floor
Tires	How are used tires disposed of?	resale/retreading/landfill/customer/N/A/other

Consolidated Screening Checklist for Automotive Repair Facilities

Absorbents	Does the facility use sawdust or other absorbents for spills or leaks?	yes/no
	Does the facility determine whether used absorbents are considered hazardous before disposal?	yes/no
	How are absorbents used for oil spills disposed of?	N/A/burned for energy/disposed of as hazardous waste/characterized as nonhazardous and landfilled
2. Wastewater Management		
Floor Drains and Wastewater Management	How does the facility clean shop floor and surrounding area?	uses dry cleanup/uses water
	Are fluids (oil, antifreeze, solvent) allowed to enter floor drains for disposal?	yes/no/no floor drains onsite
	How are fluids disposed of?	municipal sanitary sewer/storm sewer/street/other
	If floor drains discharge to municipal sanitary sewer, to storm sewer system, or the street, has the facility notified Publicly Owned Treatment Works (POTW) about potential contamination in wash water?	yes/no
	If drains discharge directly to surface waters or to an underground injection well, does the facility have an National Pollutant Discharge Elimination System (NPDES) (surface) or UIC (underground) permit?	yes/no/N/A
Stormwater	Does the facility store parts, fluids, and/or other materials outside?	yes/no
	Are materials protected from rain/snow in sealed containers or under tarp or roof?	yes/no/N/A

3. Air Pollution Control

Parts Cleaners	If the facility uses parts-cleaning sinks with halogenated solvents, has the facility submitted a notification report to the EPA?	yes/no/N/A
	Are sinks kept closed and sealed except when actually used for cleaning parts?	yes/no
	Does the facility follow required work and operational practices?	yes/no
Motor Vehicle Air Conditioning (CFCs)	Are Mobile Vehicle Air Conditioning MVAC technicians trained and certified by an accredited program?	yes/no/N/A
	If yes, are certificates on file?	yes/no
	Is CFC recovery and/or recycling equipment EPA approved?	yes/no/N/A
	Is equipment recovery/recycling or recovery only? (circle one)	recover/recycling/ recovery only/N/A
	If recovery only, is refrigerant reclaimed by an EPA-approved reclaimer?	yes/no
Catalytic Converters (CCs)	Does the facility replace CCs that are the correct type based on vehicle requirements?	yes/no/N/A
	Does the facility replace CCs on vehicles covered under original manufacturer's warranty?	yes/no
	If yes, was original CC missing, or is replacement due to state/local inspection program requirement?	yes/no
	Does facility properly mark and keep replaced CCs onsite for at least 15 days?	yes/no
	Does facility completely fill out customer paperwork and maintain onsite for at least 6 months?	yes/no
Fuels	Is Stage I vapor recovery equipment operated properly during unloading of gasoline?	yes/no/N/A
	Is Stage II vapor recovery equipment installed and working at pumps?	yes/no/N/A
	Do fuel delivery records indicate compliance with appropriate fuel requirements?	yes/no/records not available
	Are pumps clearly labeled with the product they contain?	yes/no
	Do gasoline pump nozzles comply with the 10-gallon-per-minute flow rate?	yes/no/don't know
	Is dyed, high-sulfur diesel/kerosene available for sale to motor vehicles?	yes/no

Paints and Thinners	Are paints and thinners properly contained and marked when not in use?	yes/no/N/A
	Does the facility use low-VOC Volatile Organic Compounds paints?	yes/no/N/A
	Does the facility determine whether paints are considered hazardous before disposal?	yes/no
	How are used paints, thinners, and solvents disposed of?	reuse/recycle/mix w/other fluids/ landfill
	Does the facility mix paint amounts according to need?	yes/no
	Does the facility use newer, "high transfer efficiency" spray applications?	yes /no
	If hazardous paints are used, are spray paint booth air filters disposed of properly as hazardous waste?	yes/no
	If filters are not hazardous, how are they disposed of?	recycled/landfill
4. UST/SPCC/Emergency Spill Procedures		
Underground Storage Tanks	Has the state UST program been notified of any USTs located onsite?	yes/no/N/A
	Does the facility conduct leak detection for tank and piping of all onsite UST systems?	yes/no/N/A
	Do USTs at the facility meet requirements for spill, overfill, and corrosion protection?	yes/no/N/A
	Are records and documentation readily available (as applicable) for installation, leak detection, corrosion protection, spill/overfill protection, corrective action, financial responsibility, and closure?	yes/no/N/A
Spill and Emergency Response	Does the facility have a gasoline, fuel oil, or lubricating oil storage capacity total greater than 1,320 gallons (or greater than 660 gallons in any one tank) in aboveground tanks or total underground tank storage capacity greater than 42,000 gallons?	yes/no
	If yes, could spilled gasoline fuel oil or lubricating oil conceivably reach navigable waters?	yes/no
	If yes, does the facility have an SPCC (Spill Prevention Control and Countermeasure plan) signed by a professional engineer?	yes/no
	Are phone numbers of the national, station, and local emergency contact available onsite for immediate reporting of oil or chemical spills?	yes/no

SUMMARY

1. Hazardous materials include common automotive chemicals, liquids, and lubricants, especially those whose ingredients contain *chlor* or *fluor* in their name.
2. Right-to-know laws require that all workers have access to Material Safety Data Sheets (MSDSs).
3. Asbestos fibers should be avoided and removed according to current laws and regulations.
4. Used engine oil contains metals worn from parts and should be handled and disposed of properly.
5. Solvents represent a serious health risk and should be avoided as much as possible.
6. Coolant should be recycled.
7. Batteries are considered to be hazardous waste and should be discarded in a recycling facility.

REVIEW QUESTIONS

1. List five common automotive chemicals or products that may be considered hazardous materials.
2. List five precautions to which every technician should adhere when working with automotive products and chemicals.

CHAPTER QUIZ

1. Hazardous materials include all of the following, *except* _____.
   a. Engine oil
   b. Asbestos
   c. Water
   d. Brake cleaner

2. To determine if a product or substance being used is hazardous, consult _____.
   a. A dictionary
   b. An MSDS
   c. SAE standards
   d. EPA guidelines

3. Exposure to asbestos dust can cause which of the following conditions?
   a. Asbestosis
   b. Mesothelioma
   c. Lung cancer
   d. All of the above are possible

4. Wetted asbestos dust is considered to be _____.
   a. Solid waste
   b. Hazardous waste
   c. Toxic
   d. Poisonous

5. An oil filter should be hot drained for how long before disposing of the filter?
   a. 30 to 60 minutes
   b. 4 hours
   c. 8 hours
   d. 12 hours

6. Used engine oil should be disposed of by all of the following methods, except _____.
   a. Disposed of in regular trash
   b. Shipped offsite for recycling
   c. Burned onsite in a waste-oil-approved heater
   d. Burned offsite in a waste-oil-approved heater

7. All of the following are the proper ways to dispose of a drained oil filter, *except* _____.
   a. Sent for recycling
   b. Picked up by a service contract company
   c. Disposed of in regular trash
   d. Considered to be hazardous waste and disposed of accordingly

8. Which is *not* considered to be a hazardous solvent?
   a. Nonchlorinated hydrocarbon solvent
   b. Tetrachloroethylene
   c. MIBK
   d. Chlorinated hydrocarbon solvent

9. Gasoline should be stored in approved containers that include which color(s)?

   a. A red container with yellow lettering

   b. A red container

   c. A yellow container

   d. A yellow container with red lettering

10. What automotive devices may contain mercury?

   a. Rear seat video displays

   b. Navigation displays

   c. HID headlights

   d. All of the above

CHAPTER 3

WHEELS AND TIRES

OBJECTIVES

After studying Chapter 3, the reader should be able to:

1. Prepare for Suspension and Steering (A4) ASE certification test content area "E" (Wheel and Tire Diagnosis and Repair).

2. Discuss tire sizes and ratings.

3. Describe tire purchasing considerations and maintenance.

4. Explain the construction and sizing of steel and alloy wheels and attaching hardware.

5. Demonstrate the correct lug nut tightening procedure and torque.

KEY TERMS

Aspect Ratio (p. 66)
Back Spacing (p. 84)
Bead (p. 63)
Belt (p. 64)
Body Ply (p. 64)
Bolt Circle (p. 84)
Carcass Ply (p. 64)
Center Section (p. 84)
Conicity (p. 73)
DOT Tire Code (p. 76)
E-metric Tire (p. 79)
Green Tire (p. 65)

High-flotation tires (p. 68)
Hydroplaning (p. 62)
Inner Liner (p. 64)
JWL (p. 87)
LLR (p. 79)
Load Index (p. 69)
Lug Nuts (p. 88)
Major Splice (p. 64)
Offset (p. 84)
Ply Steer (p. 73)
Rim Width (p. 74)
Run-flat Tires (p. 77)

Schrader Valve (p. 87)
Sidewall (p. 63)
Speed Ratings (p. 69)
Spider (p. 84)
TPC (p. 78)
TPMS (p. 79)
Tread (p. 62)
TREAD Act (p. 79)
Unsprung Weight (p. 88)
UTQGS (p. 75)
Wear Bars (p. 62)

The friction (traction) between the tire and the road determines the handling characteristics of any vehicle. Think about this statement for a second. The compounding, construction, and condition of tires are some of the most important aspects of the steering, suspension, alignment, and braking systems of any vehicle. A vehicle that handles poorly or that pulls, darts, jumps, or steers "funny" may be suffering from defective or worn tires. Understanding the construction of a tire is important for the technician to be able to identify tire failure or vehicle handling problems.

Tires are mounted on wheels that are bolted to the vehicle to provide the following:

1. Shock absorber action when driving over rough surfaces
2. Friction (traction) between the wheels and the road

All tires are assembled by hand from many different component parts consisting of various rubber compounds, steel, and various types of fabric material. Tires are also available in many different designs and sizes.

PARTS OF A TIRE

Tread

Tread refers to the part of the tire that contacts the ground. *Tread rubber* is chemically different from other rubber parts of a tire, and is compounded for a combination of traction and tire wear. *Tread depth* is usually 11/32 in. deep on new tires (this could vary, depending on manufacturer, from 9/32 to 15/32 in.). Figure 3-1 shows a tread depth gauge.

NOTE: A tread depth is always expressed in 1/32s of an inch, even if the fraction can be reduced to 1/16s or 1/8s.

Wear indicators are also called **wear bars.** When tread depth is down to the legal limit of 2/32", bald strips appear across the tread. See Figure 3-2.

Tie bars are molded into the tread of most all-season-rated tires. These rubber reinforcement bars are placed between tread blocks on the outer tread rows to prevent unusual wear and to reduce tread noise. As the tire wears normally, the tie bars will gradually appear. This should not be mistaken for an indication of excess outer edge wear. A tire tread with what appears to be a solid band across the entire width of the tread is what the service technician should consider the wear bar indicator.

Grooves are large, deep recesses molded in the tread and separating the tread blocks. These grooves are called *circumferential grooves* or *kerfs.* Grooves running sideways across the tread of a tire are called *lateral grooves.* See Figure 3-3.

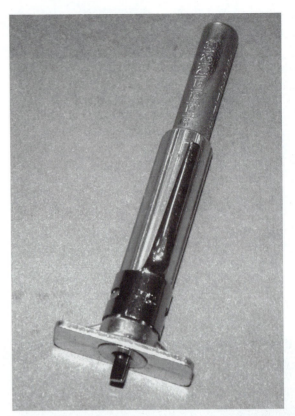

(a)

(b)

FIGURE 3-1 (a) A typical tire tread depth gauge. The center movable plunger is pushed down into the groove of the tire. (b) The tread depth is read at the top edge of the sleeve. In this example, the tread depth is 6/32 in.

Grooves in both directions are necessary for wet traction. The trapped water can actually cause the tires to ride up on a layer of water and lose contact with the ground, as shown in Figure 3-4. This is called **hydroplaning.** With worn tires,

FIGURE 3-2   Wear indicators (wear bars) are strips of bald tread that show when the tread depth is down to 2/32 in, the legal limit in many states.

TIRE TREAD

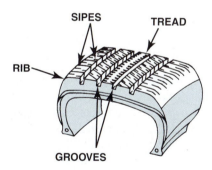

FIGURE 3-3   The tire tread runs around the circumference of the tire, and its pattern helps maintain traction. The ribs provide grip, while the grooves direct any water on the road away from the surface. The sipes help the tire grip the road.

hydroplaning can occur at speeds as low as 30 mph on wet roads. Stopping and cornering is impossible when hydroplaning occurs. *Sipes* are small slits in the tread area to increase wet and dry traction.

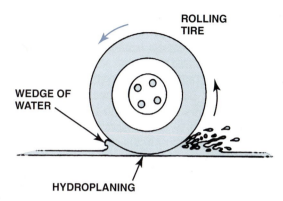

FIGURE 3-4   Hydroplaning can occur at speeds as low as 30 mph (48 km/h). If the water is deep enough and the tire tread cannot evacuate water through its grooves fast enough, the tire can be lifted off the road surface by a layer of water. Hydroplaning occurs at lower speeds as the tire becomes worn.

Sidewall

The **sidewall** is that part of the tire between the tread and the wheel. The sidewall contains all the size and construction details of the tire.

Some tires turn brown on the sidewalls after a short time. This is due to ozone (atmosphere) damage that actually causes the rubber to oxidize. Premium-quality tires contain an anti-oxidizing chemical additive blended with the sidewall rubber to prevent this discoloration.

White Sidewall/Lettered. When pneumatic tires were first constructed in the early 1900s, only natural rubber was used. The entire tire was white. When it was discovered that carbon black greatly increased the toughness of a tire, it was used. The public did not like the change from white tires to black, so tire manufacturers put the carbon black (lamp black) only in the rubber that was to be used for the tread portion of the tire. This tire lasted a lot longer because the black rubber tread that touched the ground was stronger and tougher; it sold well because the sidewalls were white.

White sidewall or white lettered tires actually contain a strip of white rubber under the black sidewall. This is ground off at the factory to reveal the white rubber. Only whitewalls or white letter lines contain this expensive white rubber. Various widths of whitewalls are made possible simply by changing the width of the grinding wheel.

Bead

The **bead** is the foundation of the tire and is located where the tire grips the inside of the wheel rim.

1. The bead is constructed of many turns of copper- or bronze-coated steel wire.

2. The main body plies (layers of material) are wrapped around the bead.

CAUTION: If the bead of a tire is cut or damaged, the tire must be replaced!

---

3. Most radial-ply tires and all truck tires wrap the bead with additional material to add strength.

Body Ply

A tire gets its strength from the layers of material wrapped around both beads under the tread and sidewall rubber. This creates the main framework, or "carcass," of the tire; these **body plies** are often called **carcass plies.** A 4-ply tire has four separate layers of material. If the body plies overlap at an angle (bias), the tire is called a *bias-ply* tire. If only one or two body plies are used and they do not cross at an angle, but lie directly from bead to bead, then the tire is called *radial ply.* See Figure 3-5.

1. Rayon is a body ply material used in many tires because it provides a very smooth ride. A major disadvantage of rayon is that it rots if exposed to moisture.
2. Nylon is a strong body ply material. Though it is still used in some tires, it tends to "flat-spot" after sitting overnight.
3. Aramid is the generic name for aromatic polyamide fibers developed in 1972. Aramid is several times stronger than steel (pound for pound), and is used in high-performance-tire construction. Kevlar is the DuPont brand name for aramid and a registered trademark of E.I. Dupont de Nemours and Co.
4. Polyester is the most commonly used tire material because it provides the smooth ride characteristics of rayon with the rot resistance and strength of nylon.

Belt

A tire **belt** is two or more layers of material applied over the body plies and under the tread area only, to stabilize the tread and increase tread life and handling.

1. Belt material can consist of the following:
    a. Steel mesh
    b. Nylon
    c. Rayon
    d. Fiberglass
    e. Aramid
2. **All radial tires are belted.**

NOTE: Most tires rated for high speed use a nylon "overlay" or "cap belt" between the 2-ply belt and the tread of the tire. This overlay helps stabilize the belt package and helps hold the tire together at high speeds, when centrifugal force acts to tear a tire apart.

Inner Liner

The **inner liner** is the soft rubber lining (usually a butyl rubber compound) on the inside of the tire that protects the body plies and helps provide for self-sealing of small punctures.

Major Splice

When the tire is assembled by a craftsperson on a tire-building machine, the body plies, belts, and tread rubber are spliced together. The fabric is overlapped approximately five threads. The point where the majority of these overlaps occur is called the **major splice,** which represents the stiffest part of the tire. This major splice is visible on most tires on the inside, as shown in Figure 3-6.

NOTE: On most new vehicles and/or new tires, the tire manufacturer paints a dot on the sidewall near the bead, indicating the largest diameter of the tire. The largest diameter of the tire usually is near the major splice. The wheel manufacturer either marks the wheel or drills the valve core hole at the smallest diameter of the wheel. Therefore, the dot should be aligned with the valve core or marked for best balance and minimum radial runout.

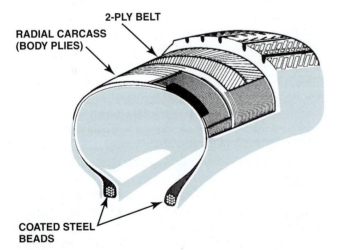

2-PLY BELT

RADIAL CARCASS (BODY PLIES)

COATED STEEL BEADS

FIGURE 3-5   Typical construction of a radial tire. Some tires have only one body ply, and some tires use more than two belt plies.

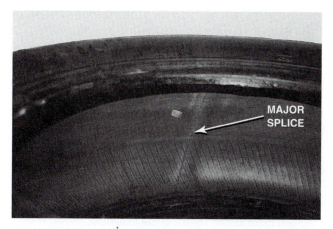

FIGURE 3-6   The major splice of a tire can often be seen and felt on the inside of the tire. The person who assembles (builds) the tire usually places a sticker near the major splice as a means of identification for quality control.

TIRE MOLDING

After the tire has been assembled by the tire builder, it is called a **green tire.** See Figure 3-7. At this stage in construction, the rubber can be returned and reused because it has not been changed chemically. The completed green tire is then placed in a mold where its shape, tread design, and all sidewall markings are formed. See Figure 3-8.

While in the mold, a steam bladder fills the inside of the tire and forces the tire against the outside of the mold. After approximately 30 minutes at 300°F (150°C), the heat changes the chemistry of the rubber. The tire is no longer called a green tire but a *cured tire,* and after inspection and cleaning, it is ready for shipment.

METRIC DESIGNATION

European and Japanese tires use metric designations. For example, 185SR × 14 denotes the following:

185	the tire is 185 millimeters (mm) wide (cross-sectional width)
S	the speed rating
R	radial design
14	fits a 14-in.-diameter wheel

FREQUENTLY ASKED QUESTION

WHY DO I GET SHOCKED BY STATIC ELECTRICITY WHEN I DRIVE A CERTAIN VEHICLE?

Static electricity builds up in insulators due to friction of the tires with the road. Newer tires use silica and contain less carbon black in the rubber, which makes the tires electrically conductive. Because the tires cannot conduct the static electricity to the ground, static electricity builds up inside the vehicle and is discharged through the body of the driver and/or passenger whenever the metal door handle is touched.

NOTE: Toll booth operators report being shocked by many drivers as money is being passed between the driver and the toll booth operator.

Newer tire sidewall designs that use silica usually incorporate carbon sections that are used to discharge the static electricity to ground. To help reduce the static charge build-up, spray the upholstery with an antistatic spray available at discount and grocery stores.

FIGURE 3-7   Tire construction is performed by assembling the many parts of a tire together on a tire-building machine.

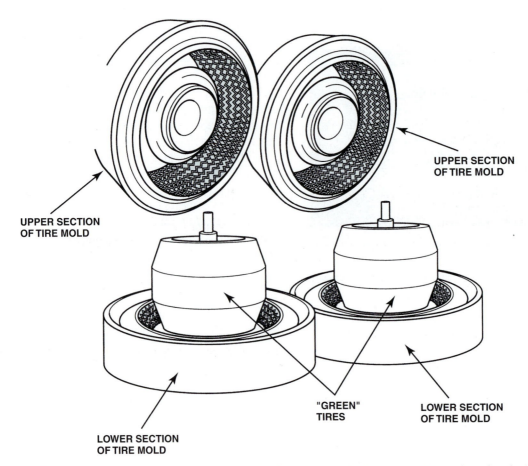

UPPER SECTION OF TIRE MOLD

UPPER SECTION OF TIRE MOLD

"GREEN" TIRES

LOWER SECTION OF TIRE MOLD

LOWER SECTION OF TIRE MOLD

FIGURE 3-8 After the entire tire has been assembled into a completed "green" tire, it is placed into a tire-molding machine where the tire is molded into shape and the rubber is changed chemically by the heat. This nonreversible chemical reaction is called vulcanization.

The European size indicates the exact physical size (width) of the tire and the speed ratings. Because of the lack of speed limits in many countries, this information is important. Because of tire design changes needed for H- and V-rated tires, their cost is usually much higher. European sizes also include the tire's aspect ratio, for example, 185/70SR × 14. If the aspect ratio of a European-sized tire is not indicated, it is generally 83% for most radials.

American Metric Tire Size Designations

After 1980, American tires were also designated using the metric system. For example, P205/75R × 14 denotes the following:

P   passenger vehicle

205   205-mm cross-sectional width

75   75% aspect ratio. The height of the tire (from the wheel to the tread) is 75% as great as its cross-sectional width (the width measured across its widest part). This percentage ratio of height to width is called the **aspect ratio.** (A 60 series tire is 60% as high as it is wide.)

R   radial

14   14-in.-diameter wheel

If a tire is constructed as a bias-ply tire only, then its size designation uses the letter D to indicate *diagonal:* P205/75D × 14.

NOTE: Many "temporary use only" spare tires are constructed with diagonal (bias) plies; the size designation is *T* for *temporary*.

If a tire is constructed as a bias ply with a belt of additional material under the tread area, its size designation uses the letter B to indicate belted: P205/75B × 14. Some tires use letters at the end of the tire size (suffixes) to indicate special applications, including the following:

LT   light truck

ML   mining and logging

MH   mobile home

ST   special trailer

TR   truck

SERVICE DESCRIPTION

Tires built after 1990 use a "service description" method of sidewall information in accordance with ISO 4000 (International Standards Organization) that includes size,

FREQUENTLY ASKED QUESTION

HOW MUCH BIGGER CAN I GO?

Many owners think they can improve their vehicle by upgrading the tire size over the size that comes from the factory to make their vehicle look sportier and ride and handle better. When changing tire size, there are many factors to consider:

1. The tire should be the same outside diameter as the original to maintain the proper suspension, steering, and ride height specifications.
2. Tire size affects vehicle speed sensor values, ABS brake wheel sensor values that can change automatic transmission operation, and ABS operation.
3. The tire should not be so wide as to contact the inner wheel well or suspension components.
4. Generally, a tire that is 10 mm wider is acceptable. For example, an original equipment tire size 205/75 × 15 (outside diameter = 27.1 in.) can be changed to 215/75 × 15 (outside diameter = 27.6 in.). This much change is less than $1/2$ in. in width and increases the outside diameter by $1/2$ in.

NOTE: Outside diameter is calculated by adding the wheel diameter to the cross-sectional height of the tire, multiplied by 2. See Figure 3-9.

5. Whenever changing tires, make sure that the load capacity is the same or greater than that of the original tires.
6. If wider tires are desired, a lower aspect ratio is required to maintain the same, or close to the same, overall outside diameter of the tire.

Old	New
P205/75 × 15	P215/70 × 15
205 × 0.75 = 154 mm	215 × 0.70 = 151 mm

Notice that the overall sidewall height is generally maintained.

If even larger tires are needed, then 225/60 × 15s may be OK—let's check the math:

$$225 \times 0.60 = 135 \text{ mm}$$

Notice that this is much too short a sidewall height when compared with the original tire (see no. 6).

7. Use the "plus 1" or "plus 2" concept. When specifying wider tires, the sidewall height must be reduced to maintain the same, or close to the same, original equipment specifications. The "plus 1" concept involves replacing the wheels with wheels 1 inch larger in diameter to compensate for the lower aspect of wider tires.

Original	Plus 1
205/75 × 15	225/60 × 16

The overall difference in outside diameter is only 0.5 in., even though the tire width has increased from 205 mm to 225 mm and the wheel diameter has increased by 1 inch. If money is no object and all-out performance is the goal, a "plus 2" concept can also be used (use a P245/50 × 17 tire and change to 17-in.-diameter wheels).

Here the overall diameter is within 1/20″ of the original tire/wheel combination, yet the tire width is 1.6 inches (40 mm) wider than the original tire. Refer to the section entitled "Wheels" later in this chapter for proper wheel back spacing and offset when purchasing replacement wheels.

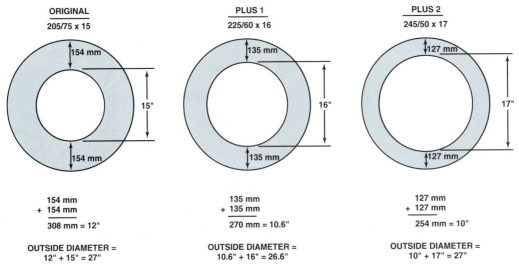

FIGURE 3-9 Notice that the overall outside diameter of the tire remains almost the same and at the same time the aspect ratio is decreased and the rim diameter is increased.

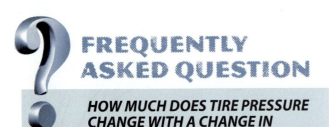

FREQUENTLY ASKED QUESTION

HOW MUCH DOES TIRE PRESSURE CHANGE WITH A CHANGE IN TEMPERATURE?

As the temperature of a tire increases, the pressure inside the tire also increases. The general amount of pressure gain (when temperatures increase) or loss (when temperatures decrease) is as follows:

10°F increase causes 1 psi increase
10°F decrease causes 1 psi decrease

For example, if a tire is correctly inflated to 35 psi when cold and then driven on a highway, the tire pressure may increase 5 psi or more.

CAUTION: DO NOT LET AIR OUT OF A HOT TIRE! If air is released from a hot tire to bring the pressure down to specifications, the tire will be *underinflated* when the tire has cooled. The tire pressure specification is for a cold tire.

Always check the tire pressures on a vehicle that has been driven fewer than 2 miles (3.2 km).

Air pressure in the tires also affects fuel economy. If all four tires are underinflated (low on air pressure), fuel economy is reduced about **0.1 mile per gallon (mpg) for each 1 psi low.** For example, if all four tires were inflated to 25 psi instead of 35 psi, not only is tire life affected but fuel economy is reduced by about 1 mile per gallon ($10 \times 0.1 = 1$ mpg).

load, and speed rating together in one easy-to-read format. See Figure 3-10.

P-Metric Designation	Service Description
P205/75HR × 15	**205/75R × 15 92H**
P passenger vehicle	205 cross-sectional width in mm
205 cross-sectional width in mm	75 aspect ratio
75 aspect ratio	R radial construction
H speed rating (130 mph/210 km/h)	15 rim diameter in inches
R radial construction	92 load index
15 rim diameter in inches	H speed rating (130 mph/210 km/h)

HIGH-FLOTATION TIRE SIZES

High-flotation tires for light trucks are designed to give improved off-road performance on sand, mud, and soft soil and still provide acceptable hard-road surface performance. These tires are usually larger than conventional tires and usually require a wider-than-normal wheel width. High-flotation tires have a size designation such as 33 × 12.50R × 15LT:

33	approximate overall tire diameter in inches
12.50	approximate cross-sectional width in inches
R	radial-type construction
15	rim diameter in inches
LT	light-truck designation

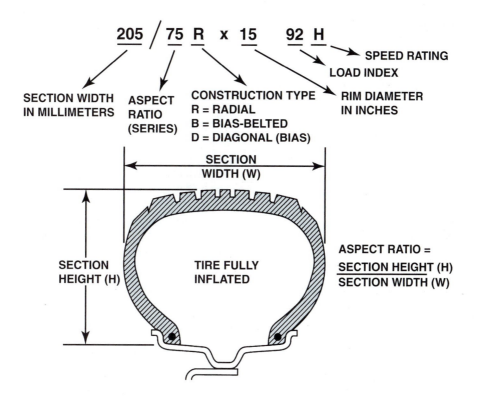

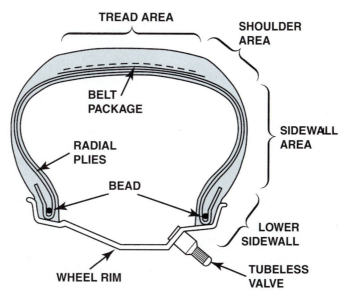

FIGURE 3-10   Cross-sectional view of a typical tire showing the terminology.

LOAD INDEX AND EQUIVALENT LOADS

The **load index,** as shown in Figure 3-11, is an abbreviated method to indicate the load-carrying capabilities of a tire. The weights listed in the chart represent the weight that *each tire* can safely support. Multiply this amount by 4 to get the maximum that the vehicle should weigh fully loaded with cargo and passengers.

SPEED RATINGS

Tires are rated according to the maximum *sustained* speed. A vehicle should never be driven faster than the **speed rating** of the tires.

Load Index	Load (kg)	Load (lb)
75	387	853
76	400	882
77	412	908
78	425	937
79	437	963
80	450	992
81	462	1,019
82	475	1,047
83	487	1,074
84	500	1,102
85	515	1,135
86	530	1,168
87	545	1,201
88	560	1,235
89	580	1,279
90	600	1,323
91	615	1,356
92	630	1,389
93	650	1,433
94	670	1,477
95	690	1,521
96	710	1,565
97	730	1,609
98	750	1,653
99	775	1,709
100	800	1,764
101	825	1,819
102	850	1,874
103	875	1,929
104	900	1,934
105	925	2,039
106	950	2,094
107	975	2,149
108	1,000	2,205
109	1,030	2,271
110	1,060	2,337
111	1,090	2,403
112	1,120	2,469
113	1,150	2,535
114	1,180	2,601
115	1,215	2,679

FIGURE 3-11 Typical sidewall markings for load index and speed rating following the tire size.

CAUTION: A high speed rating does not guarantee that the tires will not fail, even at speeds much lower than the rating. Tire condition, inflation, and vehicle loading also affect tire performance.

As the speed rating of a tire increases, fewer compromises exist for driver comfort and low noise level. The higher speed rating does not mean a better tire. To survive, a high-speed tire must be built with stiff tread compounds, reinforced body (carcass) construction, and fabric angles that favor high speed and high performance over other considerations. For example, a V-rated tire often has less tread depth than a similar tire with an H-speed rating, and therefore will often not give as long of a service life. Since the speed ratings were first developed in Europe, the letters correspond to metric speed in kilometers per hour, with a conversion to miles per hour as noted.

 **FREQUENTLY ASKED QUESTION**

 WHAT EFFECT DOES TIRE SIZE HAVE ON OVERALL GEAR RATIO?

Customers often ask what effect changing tire size has on fuel economy and speedometer readings. If larger (or smaller) tires are installed on a vehicle, many other factors also will change. These include the following:

1. *Speedometer reading.* **If larger-diameter tires are used, the speedometer will read slower** than you are actually traveling. This can result in speeding tickets!

2. *Odometer reading.* Even though larger tires are said to give better fuel economy, just the opposite can be calculated! Since a larger-diameter tire travels farther than a smaller-diameter tire, the larger tire will cause the odometer to read a shorter distance than the vehicle actually travels. For example, if the odometer reads 100 miles traveled on tires that are 10% oversized in circumference, the actual distance traveled is 110 miles.

3. *Fuel economy.* If fuel economy is calculated on miles traveled, the result will be *lower* fuel economy than for the same vehicle with the original tires.

Calculation: $\text{mph} = \dfrac{\text{rpm} \times \text{diameter} \times 3.14}{\text{gear ratio}}$

$\text{rpm} = \dfrac{\text{mph} \times \text{gear ratio}}{\text{diameter} \times 3.14}$

$\text{gear ratio} = \dfrac{\text{rpm} \times \text{diameter} \times 3.14}{\text{mph}}$

FREQUENTLY ASKED QUESTION

IF I HAVE AN OLDER VEHICLE, WHAT SIZE TIRES SHOULD I USE?

Newer radial tires can be used on older-model vehicles if the size of the tires is selected that best matches the original tires. See the following cross-reference chart.

Cross-Reference Chart
(This chart does not imply complete interchangeability.

Pre-1964	1965 to 1972	80 Series Metric	Alpha Numeric 78 Series	P-Metric 75 Series Radial	P-Metric 70 Series Radial
590-13	600-13	165-13	A78-13	P165/75R13	P175/70R13
640-13	650-13	175-13	B78-13	P175/75R13	P185/70R13
725-13	700-13	185-13	D78-13	P185/75R13	P205/70R13
590-14	645-14	155-14	B78-14	P175/75R14	P185/70R14
650-14	695-14	175-14	C78-14	P185/75R14	P195/70R14
700-14	735-14	185-14	E78-14	P195/75R14	P205/70R14
750-14	775-14	195-14	F78-14	P205/75R14	P215/70R14
800-14	825-14	205-14	G78-14	P215/75R14	P225/70R14
850-14	855-14	215-14	H78-14	P225/75R14	P235/70R14
590-15	600-15	165-15	A78-15	P165/75R15	P175/70R15
650-15	685-15	175-15	C78-15	P175/75R15	P185/70R15
640-15	735-15	185-15	E78-15	P195/75R15	P205/70R15
670-15	775-15	195-15	F78-15	P205/75R15	P215/70R15
710-15	815-15	205-15	G78-15	P215/75R15	P225/70R15
760-15	855-15	215-15	H78-15	P225/75R15	P235/70R15
800-15	885-15	230-15	J78-15	P225/75R15	P235/70R15
820-15	900-15	235-15	L78-15	P235/75R15	P255/70R15

NOTE: Vehicles designed for older bias-ply tires may drive differently when equipped with radial tires.

Letter	Maximum Rated Speed
L	120 km/h (75 mph)
M	130 km/h (81 mph)
N	140 km/h (87 mph)
P	150 km/h (93 mph)
Q	160 km/h (99 mph)
R	170 km/h (106 mph)
S	180 km/h (112 mph)
T	190 km/h (118 mph)
U	200 km/h (124 mph)
H	210 km/h (130 mph)
V	240 km/h (149 mph)
W	270 km/h (168 mph)
Y	300 km/h (186 mph)
Z	open-ended*

*The exact speed rating for a particular Z-rated tire is determined by the tire manufacturer and may vary according to size. For example, not all Brand X Z-rated tires are rated at 170 mph, even though one size may be capable of these speeds.

TIRE PRESSURE AND TRACTION

All tires should be inflated to the specifications given by the vehicle manufacturer. Most vehicles have recommended tire inflation figures written in the owner's manual or on a placard or sticker on the door post or glove compartment. See Figure 3-13.

The pressure number molded into the sidewall of a tire should be considered the maximum pressure when the tire is cold. (Pressures higher than that stated on the sidewall may be measured on a hot tire.)

FREQUENTLY ASKED QUESTION

WHAT DOES THE LITTLE "e" MEAN ON THE SIDEWALL?

Most countries have government agencies that regulate standards for motor vehicles sold and/or driven within their jurisdiction. In the United States, the U.S. Department of Transportation and National Highway Traffic Safety Administration are responsible for developing many of the nationwide standards for vehicles. Tires that are certified by their manufacturers to meet U.S. standards are branded with "DOT" (Department of Transportation) preceding the Tire Identification Code on their sidewall.

In Europe, because so much personal and commercial travel extends beyond the borders of any one country, the Economic Commission for Europe (E.C.E.) helps develop uniform motor vehicle standards for its member countries to regulate and standardize passenger and commercial vehicle components.

While sound is a byproduct of modern society, it's one thing that most Europeans would enjoy less of. Excessive noise is considered a form of environmental pollution readily apparent to humans. People who express being disturbed by noise during the day and/or night cite truck, motorcycle, and automobile traffic as the most universal sources.

Besides physical specifications, the E.C.E. standards now require tire "pass-by" noise to meet specific limits. These standards were phased-in starting in 2004. The tires must pass noise emission testing, and the standards will continue to expand in scope until 2009, when the standards will be applied to all tires sold in Europe.

The E.C.E. symbol on a tire's sidewall identifies that the manufacturer certifies that the tire meets all regulations, including the load index and speed symbol that appear in its service description. In order to be E.C.E. branded, tires must receive laboratory approval, pass confirmation testing, and have their manufacturing plant pass quality control inspections.

The letter "e" and number code combination (positioned in a circle or rectangle) identify the country originally granting approval, followed by two digits indicating the Regulation Series under which the tire was approved. Tires that have also been tested and meet the "pass-by" noise limits can have a second E.C.E. branding followed by an "-s" (for *sound*). See Figure 3-12.

The following list indicates selected E.C.E. codes and the countries they represent:

Code	Country	Code	Country
E1	Germany	E14	Switzerland
E2	France	E15	Norway
E3	Italy	E16	Finland
E4	Netherlands	E17	Denmark
E5	Sweden	E18	Romania
E6	Belgium	E19	Poland
E7	Hungary	E20	Portugal
E8	Czech Republic	E21	Russian Federation
E9	Spain	E22	Greece
E10	Yugoslavia	E23	Ireland
E11	United Kingdom	E24	Croatia
E12	Austria	E25	Slovenia
E13	Luxembourg	E26	Slovakia

FIGURE 3-12   The E.C.E. symbol on a sidewall of a tire. Notice the small -s at the end, indicating that the tire meets the "pass-by" noise limits.

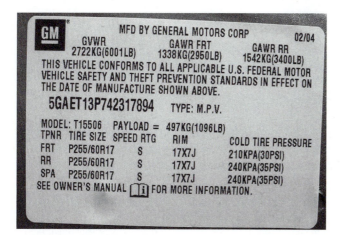

FIGURE 3-13   A typical door placard used on a General Motors vehicle indicating the recommended tire inflation. Note that the information also includes the tire size and speed rating of the tire as well as the recommended wheel size.

TIRE CONICITY AND PLY STEER

Tire **conicity** can occur during the construction of any radial or belted tire when the parts of the tire are badly positioned, causing the tire to be smaller in diameter on one side. When this tire is installed on a vehicle, it can cause the vehicle to pull to one side of the road due to the cone shape of the tire. See Figure 3-14.

Since the cause of conicity is due to the construction of the tire itself, there is nothing the service technician can do

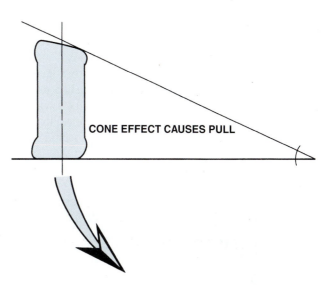

FIGURE 3-14   Conicity is a fault in the tire that can cause the vehicle to pull to one side due to the cone effect (shape) of the tire.

to correct the condition. The exact cause of the conicity is generally due to the slight movement of the belt and tread in the mold during inflation. If a vehicle pulls to one side of the road, the service technician should switch tires left to right (left-side tires to the right side and the right-side tires to the left side of the vehicle). If this swap of tires corrects the pulling condition, then tire conicity was the possible cause.

NOTE: *Radial pull* or *radial tire pull* are other terms often used to describe tire conicity.

Ply steer is another term that describes a slight pulling force on a vehicle due to tire construction. Ply steer is due to the angle of the cords in the belt layers, as seen in Figure 3-15, and not in the ply layer of the carcass (body), as the name implies. Ply steer will cause a slight drift regardless of its direction of rotation. Switching tires left to right will *not* correct a ply steer condition.

NOTE: Whenever a wheel and tire assembly is switched from one side of a vehicle to the other, the tire revolves in the opposite direction.

Ply steer is built into the tire during construction. There is nothing a service technician can do to correct ply steer, except to compensate for it with alignment angles. (See Chapter 16 for details on alignment diagnosis and correction.)

VEHICLE HANDLING AND TIRE SLIP ANGLE

The tire surface contact area or tire patch size is about one-half the area of one page of this book. All accelerating, braking, and cornering forces of a vehicle are transferred to the pavement at just four spots. The combined area of these four spots is about equal to the size of this opened book.

Think about this whenever braking or cornering. As a vehicle is turned, the wheels are moved while the tires remain in contact with the road. These actions "twist" the carcass of the tire and create a slip angle between the direction the wheel is pointing and the direction the tread is pointing. See Figure 3-16.

The contact patch is deformed and snaps back into place as the twisted tire carcass returns to its original shape. This movement causes a slight delay in the turning of the vehicle and causes tire wear as the tread rubber moves in relation to the pavement during cornering.

RIM WIDTH AND TIRE SIZE

As a general rule, for a given **rim width** it is best not to change tire width more than 10 mm (either wider or narrower). For a given tire width, it is best not to vary rim width more than 1/2 in. in either direction. For example, if the original tire size is 195/70 × 14, then either a 185/70 × 14 (−10 mm) or a 205/70 × 14 (+10 mm) *could* be used on the original rim (wheel) without undue harm *if* the replacement tire has proper clearance with the body and suspension components.

Installing a tire on too narrow a wheel will cause the tire to wear excessively in the center of the tread. Installing a tire on too wide a wheel will cause excessive tire wear on both edges.

ANGLED BELT FABRIC

FIGURE 3-15 Notice the angle of the belt material in this worn tire. The angle of the belt fabric can cause a "ply steer" or slight pulling force toward one side of the vehicle.

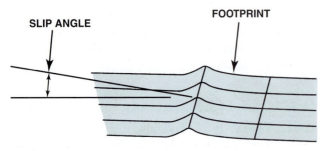

SLIP ANGLE

FOOTPRINT

FIGURE 3-16 Slip angle is the angle between the direction the tire tread is heading and the direction it is pointed.

FREQUENTLY ASKED QUESTION

IS THERE A RULE-OF-THUMB FOR RIM SIZE?

According to the Tire and Rim Association, Inc., the answer is no. Each tire size has a designated rim width on which it is designed to be mounted so as to provide the best performance and wear. The width of the specified rim also varies with rim diameter. A 235/45 × 17 tire may require a 7.5-inch rim but a 235/45 × 19 tire may require an 8.0-inch rim. A rule-of-thumb that has been used is to multiply the width of the rim by 33.55 to determine the approximate tire size for the rim. For example, consider the following.

Rim width 5.0 in. × 33.55 = 167.85 (165 mm) tire
Rim width 5.5 in. × 33.55 = 184.50 (185 mm) tire
Rim width 6.0 in. × 33.55 = 201.30 (195 mm) tire
Rim width 6.5 in. × 33.55 = 218.00 (215 mm) tire
Rim width 7.0 in. × 33.55 = 234.90 (235 mm) tire
Rim width 7.5 in. × 33.55 = 252.00 (245 mm) tire
Rim width 8.0 in. × 33.55 = 268.00 (265 mm) tire
Rim width 8.5 in. × 33.55 = 285.00 (285 mm) tire
Rim width 9.0 in. × 33.55 = 302.00 (305 mm) tire
Rim width 10.0 in. × 33.55 = 335.60 (335 mm) tire

Always check with the tire manufacturer as to the specified tire rim width that should be used.

See a tire store representative for recommended tire sizes that can be safely installed on your rims.

UNIFORM TIRE QUALITY GRADING SYSTEM

The U.S. Department of Transportation (DOT) and the National Highway Traffic Safety Administration (NHTSA) developed a system of tire grading, **the Uniform Tire Quality Grading System (UTQGS),** to help customers better judge the relative performance of tires. The three areas of tire performance are tread wear, traction, and temperature resistance, as shown in Figure 3-17.

NOTE: All tires sold in the United States must have UTQGS ratings molded into the sidewall.

Tread Wear

The tread wear grade is a comparison rating based on the wear rate of a standardized tire, tested under carefully controlled conditions, which is assigned a value of 100. A tire rated 200 should have a useful life twice as long as the standard tire's.

NOTE: The standard tire has a rating for tread wear of 100. This value has generally been accepted to mean a useful life of 20,000 miles of normal driving. Therefore, a tire rated at 200 could be expected to last 40,000 miles.

FIGURE 3-17 Typical "Uniform Tire Quality Grading System" (UTQGS) ratings imprinted on the tire sidewall.

Tread Wear Rating Number	Approximate Number of mi/km
100	20,000/32,000
150	30,000/48,000
200	40,000/64,000
250	50,000/80,000
300	60,000/96,000
400	80,000/129,000
500	100,000/161,000

The tread wear life of any tire is affected by driving habits (fast stops, starts, and cornering will decrease tread life), tire rotation (or lack of tire rotation), inflation, wheel alignment, road surfaces, and climate conditions.

Traction

Traction performance is rated by the letters AA, A, B, and C, with AA being the highest.

NOTE: The traction rating is for wet braking distance only! It does not include cornering traction or dry braking performance.

The traction rating is only one of many other factors that affect wet braking traction, including air inflation, tread depth, vehicle speed, and brake performance.

Temperature Resistance

Temperature resistance is rated by the letters A, B, and C, with A being the highest rating. Tires generate heat while rotating and flexing during normal driving conditions. A certain amount of heat build-up is desirable because tires produce their highest coefficient of traction at normal operating temperatures. For example, race car drivers frequently swerve their cars left and right during the pace laps, causing increased friction between the tire and the road surface, which warms their tires to operating temperature. However, if temperatures rise too much, a tire can start to come apart—the oils and rubber in the tire start to become a liquid! Grade C is the minimum level that all tires must be able to pass under the current Federal Motor Vehicle Safety Standard No. 109.

ALL-SEASON TIRE DESIGNATION

Most all-season tires are rated and labeled as *M & S*, *MS*, or *M + S*, and therefore must adhere to general design features as specified by the Rubber Manufacturers Association (RMA).

Tires labeled M & S are constructed with an aggressive tread design as well as tread compounds and internal construction that are designed for mud and snow. One design feature is that the tire has at least 25% void area. This means that the tread blocks have enough open space around them to allow the blocks to grab and clean themselves of snow and mud. Block angles, dimensional requirements, and minimum cross-sectional width are also a requirement for the M & S designation.

The tread rubber used to make all-season tires is also more flexible at low temperatures. This rubber compound is low-bounce (called high-hysteresis) and is more likely to remain in contact with the road surface. The rubber compound is also called *hydrophilic*, meaning that the rubber has an affinity for water (rather than being *hydrophobic* rubber, which repels water).

NOTE: Most vehicle manufacturers recommend that the same *type* of tire be used on all four wheels even though the size of the tire may vary between front and rear on some high-performance vehicles. Therefore, if all-season replacement tires are purchased, a complete set of four should be used to be assured of proper handling and uniform traction characteristics. While *tire* manufacturers have been recommending this for years—since the late 1980s—most *vehicle* manufacturers are also recommending that all four tires be of the same construction and tread type to help ensure proper vehicle handling.

DOT TIRE CODE

All tires sold in the United States must be approved by the U.S. Federal Department of Transportation (DOT). The **DOT tire code** requirements include resistance to tire damage that could be caused by curbs, chuckholes, and other common occurrences for a tire used on public roads.

NOTE: Most race tires are *not* DOT-approved and must never be used on public streets or highways.

Each tire that is DOT-approved has a DOT number molded into the sidewall of the tire. This number is usually imprinted on only one side of the tire and is usually on the side *opposite the whitewall.* The DOT code includes letters and numbers, such as **MJP2CBDX264.**

The first two letters identify the manufacturer and location. For this example, the first two letters (MJ) mean that the tire was made by the Goodyear Tire and Rubber Company in Topeka, Kansas. The last three numbers are the build date code. The last of these three numbers is the year (1994), and the 26 means that it was built during the 26th week of 1994. Starting with tires manufactured after January 1, 2000, the tire build date includes four digits rather than three digits. A new code such as "3406" means the 34th week of 2006 ("3406"). See Figure 3-18.

FIGURE 3-18   Typical DOT date code. This tire was built the sixth week of 2005.

REAL WORLD FIX

TIRE DATE CODE INFORMATION SAVED ME MONEY!

This author was looking at a three-year-old vehicle when I noticed that the right rear tire had a build date code newer than the vehicle. I asked the owner, "How badly was this vehicle hit?" The owner stumbled and stuttered a little, then said, "How did you know that an accident occurred?" I told the owner that the right rear tire, while the exact same tire as the others, had a date code indicating that it was only one year old, whereas the original tires were the same age as the vehicle. The last three numbers of the DOT code on the sidewall indicate the week of manufacture (the first two numbers of the three-digit date code) followed by the last number of the year.

The owner immediately admitted that the vehicle slid on ice and hit a curb, damaging the right rear tire and wheel. Both the tire and wheel were replaced and the alignment checked. The owner then dropped the price of the vehicle $500! Knowing the date code helps assure that fresh tires are purchased and can also help the technician determine if the tires have been replaced. For example, if new tires are found on a vehicle with 20,000 miles, then the technician should check to see if the vehicle may have been involved in an accident or may have more miles than indicated on the odometer.

SPARE TIRES

Most vehicles today come equipped with space-saver spare tires that are smaller than the wheels and tires that are on the vehicle. The reason for the small size is to reduce the size and weight of the entire vehicle and to increase fuel economy by having the entire vehicle weigh less by not carrying a heavy spare tire and wheel around. The style and type of these spare tires have changed a great deal over the last several years, and different makes and types of vehicles use various types of spare tires.

CAUTION: Before using a spare tire, always read the warning label (if so equipped) and understand all use restrictions. For example, some spare tires are not designed to exceed 50 mph (80 km/h) or be driven more than 500 miles (800 km).

Many small, space-saving spare tires use a higher-than-normal air inflation pressure, usually 60 psi (414 kPa). Even though the tire often differs in construction, size, diameter, and width from the vehicle's original tires, it is amazing that the vehicle usually handles the same during normal driving. Obviously, these tires are not constructed with the same durability as a full-size tire and should be removed from service as soon as possible.

NOTE: When was the last time you checked the tire pressure in your spare tire? The spare tire pressure should be checked regularly.

RUN-FLAT TIRES

Run-flat tires (abbreviated RFT) are designed to operate without any air for a limited distance (usually 50 miles at 55 mph). This feature allows vehicle manufacturers to build vehicles without the extra room and weight of a spare tire and jack assembly.

A typical run-flat tire (also called *extended mobility tire* [EMT] or *zero pressure* [ZP] *tire*) requires the use of an air pressure sensor/transmitter and a dash-mounted receiver to warn the driver that a tire has lost pressure. Because of the reinforced sidewalls, the vehicle handles almost the same with or without air pressure. See Figures 3-19 and 3-20.

CAUTION: Tire engineers warn that rapid cornering should be avoided if a run-flat tire has zero air pressure. The handling during quick maneuvers is often unpredictable and could be dangerous.

PAX Run-Flat Tires

Michelin developed a run-flat tire that has three unique components:

- A special wheel that has two bead seats that are of different diameters. The outside bead seat is 10 mm smaller in diameter than the inside bead seat. This means that a conventional tire cannot be installed on a PAX-style wheel.

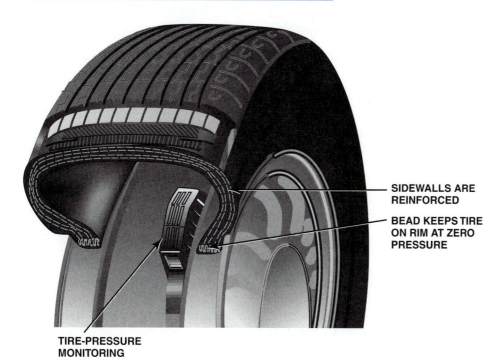

SIDEWALLS ARE REINFORCED

BEAD KEEPS TIRE ON RIM AT ZERO PRESSURE

TIRE-PRESSURE MONITORING SYSTEM

FIGURE 3-19 Cutaway of a run-flat tire showing the reinforced sidewalls and the required pressure sensor.

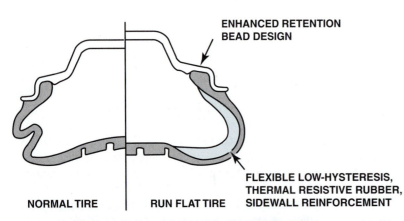

ENHANCED RETENTION
BEAD DESIGN

FLEXIBLE LOW-HYSTERESIS,
THERMAL RESISTIVE RUBBER,
SIDEWALL REINFORCEMENT

NORMAL TIRE   RUN FLAT TIRE

FIGURE 3-20   A conventional tire on the left and a run-flat tire on the right, showing what happens when there is no air in the tire.

FIGURE 3-21   The PAX run-flat tire system is composed of three unique components—a special asymmetrical wheel, a urethane support ring, and special tire.

- A urethane support ring that is designed to support the weight of the vehicle in the event of a flat tire.
- A special tire that is designed to operate without air. See Figure 3-21.

The PAX tire design has a unique sizing, such as:

P245/680R 460A 102V

P	=	passenger
245	=	the cross-section width in millimeters (mm)
680	=	the tire diameter in mm (26.77 inches)
R	=	radial ply construction
460	=	the wheel, diameter in mm (18.1 inches)
A	=	asymmetric wheel, meaning that one bead is smaller than the other bead by 10 mm (0.040 inch)
102	=	the load index
V	=	the speed rating

TECH TIP

PAX REPLACEMENT TIP

In most cases, the fastest and easiest approach to follow if a PAX tire requires replacement is to purchase a replacement tire/wheel assembly. While more expensive than replacing just the tire, this approach is often used to help the vehicle owner get back on the road faster without any concerns as to whether the replacement tire was properly installed.

Servicing a PAX Wheel/Tire Assembly

If a flat tire occurs or when a PAX tire becomes worn and requires replacement, special care should be taken to properly remove the tire from the wheel. Because the urethane support ring prevents the tire bead from entering the dropped center section of the wheel, the outside bead should be broken from the wheel, and then the support ring removed before the tire can be removed from the wheel.

GENERAL MOTORS TPC RATING

All General Motors original equipment (OE) tires have a rating that identifies the size as well as the tread design, wear, traction, and heat resistance factors. All of these factors are combined in a set of numbers and letters that is imprinted in the tire mold. This is referred to as the **Tire Performance Criteria (TPC)** rating of the tire. If a customer wants to have the same tire performance in a replacement tire, then replace the tire with any brand of tire that has the same TPC identification. See Figure 3-22.

FIGURE 3-22 The Tire Performance Criteria (TPC) specification number is imprinted on the sidewall of all tires used on General Motors vehicles from the factory.

TIRE-PRESSURE MONITORING SYSTEM (TPMS)

The **Transportation Recall Enhancement, Accountability and Documentation (TREAD) Act** requires that all vehicles be equipped with a tire-pressure monitoring system that will warn the driver in the event of an underinflated tire.

The National Highway Traffic Safety Administration (NHTSA) requires the installation of **tire-pressure monitoring systems (TPMS)** in passenger vehicles and light trucks manufactured after November 1, 2003.

The NHTSA ruling is part one of a two-part final ruling. Part one establishes a new Federal Motor Vehicle Safety Standard that requires TPMSs to be installed in passenger vehicles and light trucks to warn the driver when a tire is below specified pressure levels. The requirement to equip vehicles with a tire-pressure monitoring system was phased-in starting in 2004 and requires that 100% of the affected vehicles be equipped in 2007.

Indirect

To help compensate for speed variation during cornering, an indirect tire pressure monitoring system checks the rotating speeds of diagonally opposed wheels. The system adds the speeds of the right front and left rear and then subtracts that value from the sum of the left front and right rear tires. If the total is less than or equal to a threshold value, no warning is given. However, if the total is greater than a predetermined value, the TPMS warning light is illuminated. The warning lamp will stay on until air is added to the tire and the ignition is cycled off and on.

NOTE: This system cannot detect if all of the tires are under inflated, only if one tire is under inflated.

FREQUENTLY ASKED QUESTION

WHAT IS A LOW-ROLLING-RESISTANCE TIRE?

Low-rolling-resistance (LLR) tires reduce rolling resistance, which is the power-robbing friction between the tire and crown. The **E-metric tire,** designated for use on electric or hybrid vehicles, operates at higher inflation pressures, reduced load percentages, and lower rolling resistance. These tires were first used on the GM EV-1 electric vehicle.

To soften the ride of tires pumped with additional air, a new tire profile was developed. Narrower rim width and rounder sidewalls make the tire more shock absorbent.

To make the tires roll more freely, low-rolling-resistant tread compounds are molded into smaller tread elements that flex easily and with less friction when they touch the road. LRR tires are available from most major tire manufacturers, including Michelin the Energy MXV4 Plus and Goodyear VIVA 2. According to tire engineers, the basic tradeoff of low rolling resistance is poor wet traction performance. To improve wet road performance and traction requires the use of more silica in the tread, which increases the cost of the tire. Neither a technician nor a vehicle owner can determine the relative rolling resistance unless the tires are compared using a coast-down test from highway speed to zero or a laboratory testing machine.

The ABS-based indirect-measurement system does not meet a NHTSA requirement stating that the system must be able to sense all four tires being incorrectly inflated. The ABS system can only compare the air pressure in all four tires, and therefore can only determine a difference in tire pressures. If the pressure in all four tires is incorrect, but the difference is still within the programmed range, the ABS-based system cannot determine that inflation pressure is incorrect.

Diagnosis. Whenever there is a tire monitoring concern, perform the following:

1. Check tire pressure.
2. Check the tire inflation monitoring function by following the service information chart for Diagnostic System Check Tire Inflation Monitoring. This checks the ability of the EBCM and the body control module (BCM) to communicate with a Scan tool and with other electronic control modules in the vehicle.
3. Check for any stored DTCs. The EBCM will request the IPC to turn on the "low tire pressure" lamp if a DTC related to tire inflation is stored.

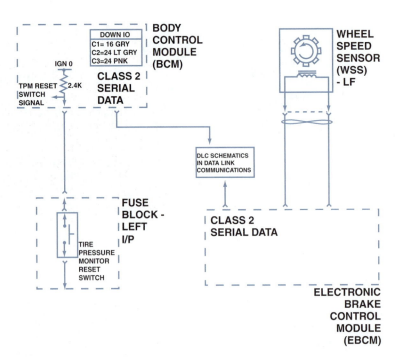

FIGURE 3-23 The indirect tire-pressure monitoring system has a reset switch that should be depressed after rotating or replacing tires.

Reset the Switch. Vehicles with the tire inflation monitoring function are equipped with a TPM reset switch. Typically, the switch is housed in the underhood junction block. Always refer to service information for its exact location. The switch provides the body control module (BCM) with a signal requesting that the EBCM begin to auto-learn the tire pressures at each of the four wheels again. A TPM reset is necessary when tires are rotated or one or more tires are replaced. The BCM sends data messages to the EBCM through a Class 2 data circuit.

The reset switch connects to the BCM with a signal circuit and with a ground connection through the vehicle chassis to the BCM ground circuit. Pressing the switch button causes the switch contacts to close momentarily. See Figure 3-23.

As a part of routine maintenance, the reset switch should be depressed after the tire pressures have been changed or when the tires are rotated. If the reset switch is not depressed, the TPMS function may falsely detect a tire inflation fault and illuminate the "low tire" lamp.

Direct TPMS

There are two types of direct tire-pressure monitoring systems.

- **Wheel-mounted transmitter type**—This type of transmitter uses a strap to hold the unit to the center of the wheel. See Figure 3-24.
- **Tire-valve-mounted transmitter type**—Systems using this type of tire-pressure monitoring usually have a receiver located near the wheel well of each wheel. The sensor inside the wheel then broadcasts.

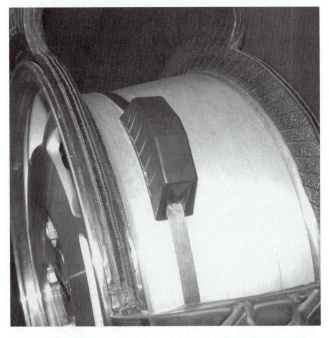

FIGURE 3-24 A wheel-mounted tire-pressure monitoring transmitter.

There is a wireless RF sensor/transmitter unit built into the valve stem of each wheel. It is inserted from the inside of the wheel and retained by a nut torqued to 35 lb-in. and sealed with a grommet. The pressure sensors each weigh about 1 ounce (28 grams) and will most likely be noticed during wheel balancing. A 3-volt lithium battery with 10-year design life powers the sensors, but the sensors do not operate continuously. The

sensors do not operate when the vehicle travels below 20 mph (32 km/h) and they transmit a pressure signal only once each hour when the vehicle is parked, which helps retain battery power. The signal from the sensors is received by either a receiver near each wheel or by the keyless entry system radio receiver. The receiver then sends tire-pressure information to the body control module (BCM) for display on the driver information center (DIC). A warning is sounded automatically if the pressure falls below 24 psi (165 kPa) or rises above 39 psi (269 kPa).

TPMS SENSORS

Depending on the type and manufacturer, tire-pressure monitoring sensors can be any of several different designs, including:

- **Continuous-wave-type sensor**—designed to signal a tester when exposed to 5 to 7 seconds of continuous 125 KHz wave signal.
- **Magnetically-triggered-type sensor**—designed to trigger a tester if exposed to a powerful magnetic force.
- **Pulse-width-modulated-type sensor**—designed to be triggered when exposed to modulated wave 125 KHz signal.

The sensor also can vary according to the frequency at which it transmits tire-pressure information to the receiver in the vehicle. The two most commonly used frequencies are:

- 315 MHz
- 433.92 MHz (commonly listed as 434 MHz)

Programming the TPM Receiver

Whenever the tires are rotated or a new sensor has been installed, the TPM receiver must be reprogrammed to recognize the new sensor locations. Failure to do so will result in the pressure readings being incorrectly displayed on the driver information center. A scan tool will handle this reprogramming task, but if no new sensors were installed, there is also a way to reprogram the receiver without the scan tool. The wireless TPM receiver is housed in the keyless entry system's RF receiver. Using the key fob to place the receiver in "program" mode, the sensor locations can be programmed with a special magnet. See Figure 3-26.

TECH TIP

CHECK THE TPMS SENSORS BEFORE AND AFTER SERVICE

It is wise to check that all of the tire-pressure monitoring system sensors are working before beginning service work. For example, if the tires need to be rotated, the sensors will have to be reprogrammed for their new location. If a tire-pressure monitoring sensor is defective, the procedure cannot be performed. Use an aftermarket or original equipment tire-pressure monitoring sensor tester, as shown in Figure 3-25.

Then the tire-pressure sensors should be checked again after the service to make sure that they are working correctly before returning the vehicle to the customer.

FREQUENTLY ASKED QUESTION

DOESN'T THE TREAD ACT SPECIFY THE TYPE OF SENSOR?

No. The TREAD Act establishes only the tire-pressure standards and does not specify how the vehicle manufacturer must achieve this standard. As a result, different manufacturers have developed various methods to meet the standard. For additional information on TPMS testers, see *www.tipstool.com* or *www.otctools.com*.

FIGURE 3-25 A typical tire-pressure monitoring system tester. The unit should be held near the tire and opposite the valve stem if equipped with a wheel-mounted sensor, and near the valve stem if equipped with a valve-stem-type sensor.

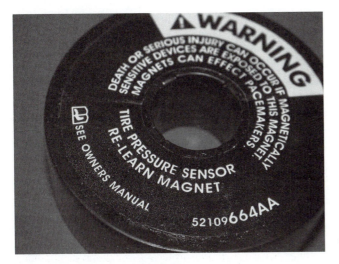

FIGURE 3-26   A magnet is placed around the valve stem to reprogram stem-mounted tire-pressure sensors.

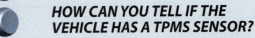

HOW CAN YOU TELL IF THE VEHICLE HAS A TPMS SENSOR?

If the tire/wheel assembly has a tire-pressure monitoring system (TPMS) valve-type sensor, it can usually be identified by the threaded portion of the valve stem. See Figure 3-27.

If the valve stem is black rubber, then it does not have a stem-mounted tire-pressure sensor. However, the wheel may be equipped with a wheel-mounted sensor, so care should still be taken to avoid damaging the sensor during service.

The magnet fits over the valve stem in a way that will force the sensor to turn itself on while stationary, allowing the receiver to "see" it and learn its location while in programming mode. The special magnet tool and a scan tool are both needed when a new sensor has been installed, but the following procedure will allow the service dealer to reprogram the TPM after tire rotation on a General Motors vehicle without using a scan tool.

1. With KOEO (key on, engine off), the "lock" and "unlock" buttons on the key fob should be simultaneously pressed and held. The horn will chirp within 10 seconds, indicating the receiver is in programming mode. The programming procedure must now be completed within five minutes, with no more than one minute between programming.

   NOTE: If the horn does not chirp at the start of this procedure, the TPM option has not been enabled. A scan tool is needed to enable the system.

2. At the left front wheel, the special magnet tool must be held over the valve stem to force the sensor to transmit its code. The horn will chirp once, indicating the TPM system has recognized the sensor. The next sensor must be programmed within one minute.

3. The remaining sensors should be programmed in the following order: RF, RR, LR. The horn will chirp once when each sensor has been detected. It will chirp twice to indicate completion of the programming process.

   NOTE: The technician should not replace either the OEM cap or the valve stem with standard parts. Conventional valve stem parts will inhibit the sensor's ability to transmit its signal.

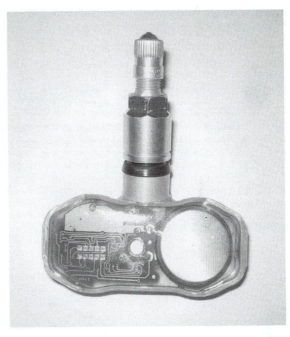

FIGURE 3-27   A clear plastic valve-stem tire-pressure monitoring sensor, showing the round battery on the right and the electronic sensor and transistor circuits on the left.

TIRE SELECTION CONSIDERATIONS

Selecting the proper tire is very important for the proper handling and safety of any vehicle. Do not select a tire by styling or looks alone. For best value and highest satisfaction, follow these guidelines:

Purchasing Suggestions

1. Purchase the same type of tire that came on your vehicle when new.

2. Purchase the same size as the original tire. The width of the tire should be within 10 mm of the width of the original tire. For example, a stock 195/75 × 14 tire's acceptable replacement *could be* 185/75 × 14 or 205/75 × 14.

3. Purchase tires with the same speed rating as the original.

4. Purchase four of the same type of tire. Most vehicle manufacturers recommend against installing snow tires or all-season tires on just the drive wheels.

5. Purchase the same *brand* of tire for both front and/or both rear wheels.

6. Purchase fresh tires. Tires that are older may have been stored in a hot warehouse, where oxygen can attack rubber and cause deterioration.

Reason Why

1. Chassis and tire engineers spend hundreds of hours testing and evaluating the best tire to use for each vehicle.

2. The size of the tire is critical to the handling of any vehicle. Tire width, size, and aspect ratio affect the following:
   a. Braking effectiveness
   b. Headlight aiming
   c. Vehicle height
   d. Acceleration potential
   e. Speedometer calibration

3. When any vehicle is manufactured, it is optimized for its designed use. High-performance tires are generally stiffer and have a speed rating as well. If you purchase non-high-performance tires, the carcass is not as stiff and the suspension is not designed to work with softer tires. Therefore, the cornering and handling, especially fast evasive maneuvers, could be dangerous. The vehicle may be capable of far more speed than the tires are designed to handle.

4. Every vehicle is designed to function best with four tires of the same size, construction, and tread design, unless the vehicle is specifically designed for different sizes of tires at the front and rear. Different tire styles and tread compounds have different slip angles. It is these different slip angles that can cause a vehicle to handle "funny" or cause the vehicle to get out of control in the event of a sudden maneuver.

5. The sizes of tires are nominal and vary according to exact size (and shape) of the mold as well as tire design and construction. The same size of tire from two different manufacturers can often differ in diameter and width. While the differences should be slight, many vehicles are extremely sensitive to these small differences, and poor vehicle handling, torque steer, and pulling could result if different brands of tires are used.

6. Look at the tire build date code (the last three numbers of the DOT code). Try to purchase four tires with the same or similar date codes.

CAUTION: If changing tire sizes or styles beyond the recommendations as stated here, consult a knowledgeable tire store representative for help in matching wheel and tire combinations to your vehicle.

NOTE: Some tires may be five or more years old when purchased. Always check the date code!

WHEELS

The concept of a wheel has not changed in the last 5,000 years, but the style and materials used have changed a lot. Early automotive wheels were constructed from wood with a steel band as the tire.

Today's wheels are constructed of steel or aluminum alloy. The center section of the wheel that attaches to the hub is called the **center section** or **spider** because early wheels used wooden spokes that resembled a spider's web. The rubber tire attaches to the rim of the wheel. The rim has two *bead flanges* where the bead of the tire is held against the wheel when the tire is inflated. The shape of this flange is very important and is designated by Tire and Rim Association letters. For example, a wheel designated $14 \times 6JJ$ means that the diameter of the wheel is 14 in. and the wheel is 6 in. wide measured from inside to inside of the flanges. The letters JJ indicate the *exact* shape of the flange area. See Figure 3-28. This flange area shape and the angle that the rim drops down from the flange are important because of the following:

- They permit a good seal between the rim and the tire.
- They help retain the tire on the rim in the event of loss of air. This is the reason why modern wheels are called "safety rim wheels." See Figure 3-29.
- Run-flat tires (tires that are designed to operate without air for a limited distance without damage) often require a specific wheel rim shape.

Wheel Offset

Offset is a very important variable in wheel design. If the center section (spider) is centered on the outer rim, the offset is zero. Wheel offset is often referred to as ET, which stands for *Einpress Tieffe* in German. See Figure 3-30.

Positive Offset

The wheel has a positive offset if the center section is outward from the wheel centerline. Front-wheel-drive vehicles commonly use positive-offset wheels to improve the loading on the front wheels and to help provide for a favorable scrub radius.

Negative Offset

The wheel has a negative offset if the center section is inboard (or "dished") from the wheel centerline. See Figure 3-31. Avoid using replacement wheels that differ from the original offset.

Back Spacing

Back spacing, also called *rear spacing* or *backside setting,* is the distance between the back rim edge and the wheel center section mounting pad. **This is not the same as offset.** Back spacing can be measured directly with a ruler, as shown in Figure 3-32.

Determining Bolt Circle

On four-lug axles and wheels, the **bolt circle** measurement is simply taken from center to center on opposite studs or holes, as shown in Figure 3-33.

On five-lug axles and wheels, it is a little harder to determine bolt circle. One method is to measure from the far edge of one bolt hole to the center of the hole two over from the first, as shown in Figure 3-34. Another method for a five-lug

FIGURE 3-28 The size of the wheel is usually cast or stamped into the wheel. This wheel is 5 1/2 in. wide. The letters JJ refer to the contours of the seat area of the wheel.

WHEEL RIM CONTOUR

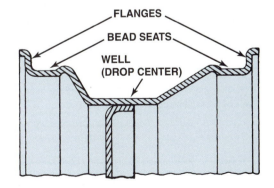

FIGURE 3-29 The wheel rim well provides a space for the tire to fit during mounting; the bead seat provides a tire-to-wheel sealing surface; the flange holds the beads in place.

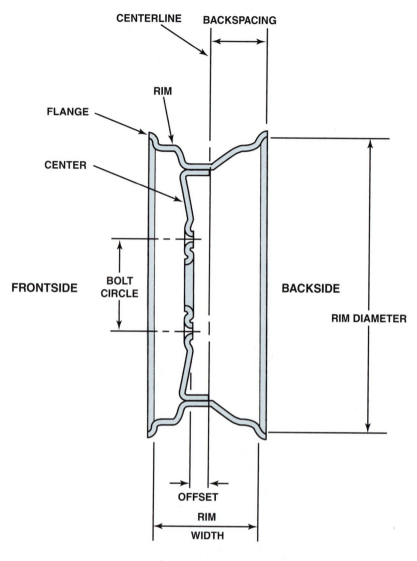

CENTERLINE   BACKSPACING

RIM

FLANGE

CENTER

FRONTSIDE

BOLT
CIRCLE

BACKSIDE

RIM DIAMETER

OFFSET

RIM
WIDTH

FIGURE 3-30 A cross section of a wheel showing part designations.

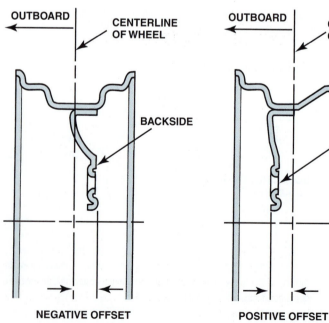

OUTBOARD   CENTERLINE
OF WHEEL

OUTBOARD   CENTERLINE
OF WHEEL

BACKSIDE

BACKSIDE

NEGATIVE OFFSET   POSITIVE OFFSET

FIGURE 3-31 Offset is the distance between the centerline of the wheel and the wheel mounting surface.

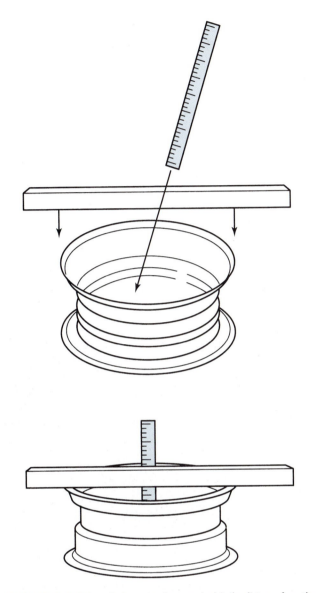

FIGURE 3-32 Back spacing (rear spacing) is the distance from the mounting pad to the edge of the rim. Most custom wheels use this measurement method to indicate the location of the mounting pad in relation to the rim.

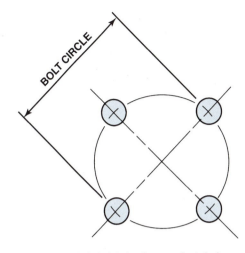

FIGURE 3-33 Bolt circle is the diameter of a circle that can be drawn through the center of each lug hole or stud. The bolt circle is sometimes referred to as PCD for *pitch circle diameter*.

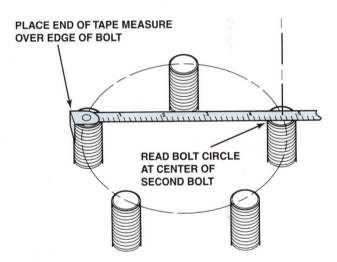

PLACE END OF TAPE MEASURE OVER EDGE OF BOLT

READ BOLT CIRCLE AT CENTER OF SECOND BOLT

FIGURE 3-34 The easiest method to determine the approximate bolt circle of a five-lug wheel.

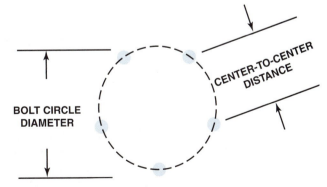

CENTER-TO-CENTER DISTANCE

BOLT CIRCLE DIAMETER

FIGURE 3-35 Measure center-to-center distance and compare the distance to the figures in the chart in the text to determine the diameter for a five-lug bolt circle.

wheel is to measure from center to center between two adjacent studs and convert this measurement into bolt circle diameter, as in the following chart. See Figure 3-35.

Center-to-Center Distance	Bolt Circle Diameter
2.645 in.	4 $\frac{1}{2}$-in. bolt circle
2.792 in.	4 $\frac{3}{4}$-in. bolt circle
2.939 in.	5-in. bolt circle
3.233 in.	5 $\frac{1}{2}$-in. bolt circle

Steel Wheels

Steel is the traditional wheel material. A steel wheel is very strong due to its designed shape and the fact that it is *work hardened* during manufacturing. In fact, most of the strength of a steel wheel is due to its work hardening. Painting and baking cycles also increase the strength of a steel wheel. Steel wheels are formed from welded hoops that are flared and joined to stamped spiders.

Aluminum Wheels

Forged and cast aluminum wheels are commonly used on cars and trucks. *Forged* means that the aluminum is hammered or forged under pressure into shape. A forged aluminum wheel is much stronger than a *cast* aluminum wheel.

A cast aluminum wheel is constructed by pouring liquid (molten) aluminum into a mold. After the aluminum has cooled, the cast aluminum wheel is removed from the mold and machined. Aluminum wheels are usually thicker than steel wheels and require special wheel weights when balancing. Coated or covered wheel weights should be used when balancing aluminum wheels to prevent galvanic corrosion damage to the wheel. Most aluminum wheels use an alloy of aluminum. Aluminum can be combined (alloyed) with copper, manganese, silicon, or other elements to achieve the physical strength and characteristics for the exact product.

Some racing wheels are made from a lighter-weight metal called magnesium. These wheels are called *mag* wheels (an abbreviation for *magnesium*). True magnesium wheels are not practical for production wheels because their cost and corrosion are excessive compared with steel or aluminum alloy wheels. The term *mag wheel*, however, is still heard when referring to alloy (aluminum) wheels.

NOTE: If purchasing replacement aftermarket wheels, check that they are certified by the SFI. SFI is the Specialty Equipment Manufacturers Association (SEMA) Foundation, Incorporated. SEMA and SFI are nongovernment agencies that were formed by the manufacturers themselves to establish standards for safety.

TIRE VALVES

All tires use a tire valve, called a **Schrader valve,** to hold air in the tire. The Schrader valve was invented in New York in 1844 by August Schrader for the Goodyear Brothers: Charles, Henry, and Nelson. Today, Schrader valves are used not only as valves in tires but on fuel-injection systems, air-conditioning systems, and air shock (ride control) systems. Most tire experts agree that the valve stem (which includes the Schrader

FREQUENTLY ASKED QUESTION

WHAT DOES THIS MARK ON A WHEEL MEAN?

The symbol **JWL,** for the Japan Wheel Light Metal Standard Mark, means that the wheel meets the technical standards for passenger-car light-alloy disk wheels. See the mark in Figure 3-36.

The manufacturer is responsible for conducting the inspections set forth in the technical standard, and the JWL mark is displayed on those products that pass the inspection.

FIGURE 3-36   A typical JWL symbol for the Japan Wheel Light Metal Standard Mark.

valve) should be replaced whenever tires are replaced—tires can last four or more years, and in that time the valve stem can become brittle and crack. A defective or leaking valve stem is a major cause of air loss. Low tire pressure can cause the tire to become overheated. Replacement valve stems are therefore a wise investment whenever purchasing new tires. Aluminum (alloy) wheels often require special metal valve stems that use a rubber washer and are actually bolted to the wheel. See Figure 3-37.

UNSPRUNG WEIGHT

The lighter the wheel and tire assembly, the faster it can react to bumps and dips in the road surface and thus the better the ride. The chassis and the body of any vehicle are

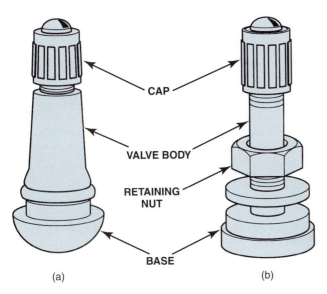

(a)   (b)

FIGURE 3-37   (a) A rubber snap-in style tire valve assembly. (b) A metal clamp-type tire valve assembly used on most high-pressure (over 60 psi) tire applications such as is found on many trucks, RVs, and trailers. The internal Schrader valve threads into the valve itself and can be replaced individually, but most experts recommend replacing the entire valve assembly every time the tires are replaced to help prevent air loss.

supported by some sort of spring suspension system. It is the purpose of the suspension system to isolate the body of the vehicle from the road surface. Also, for best handling, all four tires must remain in contact with the road. After all, a tire cannot grip the road if it leaves the ground after hitting a bump. The wheel and tire are **unsprung weight** because they are not supported by the vehicle's springs. If heavy wheels or tires are used, every time the vehicle hits a bump, the wheel is forced upward. The heavy mass of the wheel and tire would transmit this force through the spring of the vehicle and eventually to the driver and passengers. Obviously, a much lighter wheel and tire assembly reacts faster to bumps and dips in the road surface. The end result is a smoother-riding vehicle with greater control.

An aluminum wheel is *generally* lighter than the same-size stamped steel wheel. This is not always the case, however, so before purchasing aluminum wheels, check their weight!

NOTE: Putting oversized tires on an off-road-type vehicle is extremely dangerous. The increased unsprung weight can cause the entire vehicle to leave the ground after hitting a bump in the road. The increased body height necessary to clear the larger tires seriously affects drive shaft angles and wheel alignment angles, making the vehicle very difficult to control.

LUG NUTS

Lug nuts are used to hold a wheel to the brake disc, brake drum, or wheel bearing assembly. Most manufacturers use a stud in the brake or bearing assembly with a lug nut to hold the wheel. Some models of VW, Audi, and Mazda use a lug *bolt* that is threaded into a hole in the brake drum or bearing assembly.

NOTE: Some aftermarket manufacturers offer a stud conversion kit to replace the lug bolt with a conventional stud and lug nut.

Typical lug nuts are tapered so that the wheel stud will center the wheel onto the vehicle. Another advantage of the taper of the lug nut and wheel is to provide a suitable surface to prevent the nuts from loosening. The taper, usually 60 degrees, forms a wedge that helps ensure that the lug nut will not loosen. Steel wheels are deformed slightly when the lug nut is torqued down against the wheel mounting flange; be certain that the taper is *toward* the vehicle.

Many alloy wheels use a *shank-nut*-type lug nut that has straight sides without a taper. This style of nut must be used with wheels designed for this nut type. If replacement wheels are used on any vehicle, check with the wheel manufacturer as to the proper type and style of lug nut. Figure 3-38 shows several of the many styles of lug nuts that are available.

WHEEL NUTS

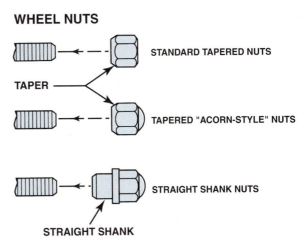

FIGURE 3-38   Various styles of lug nuts.

Size

Lug nuts are sized to the thread size of the stud onto which they screw. The diameter and the number of threads per inch are commonly stated. Since some vehicles use left-hand threads, RH and LH are commonly stated, indicating "right-hand" and "left-hand" threads. A typical size is 7/16-20RH, where the 7/16 indicates the diameter of the wheel stud and 20 indicates that there are 20 threads per inch. Another common fractional size is 1/2 × 20.

Metric sizes such as M12 × 1.5 use a different sizing method.

M	metric
12	12-mm diameter of stud
1.5	1.5-mm distance from one thread peak to another

Other commonly used metric lug sizes include M12 × 1.25 and M14 × 1.5. Obviously, metric wheel studs require metric lug nuts.

TIRE INSPECTION   Step-by-Step

STEP 1   Check the tire information placard, usually located on the driver's door or door jamb, for the specified tire size and tire pressures.

STEP 2   Visually check the tires for abnormal wear or damage.

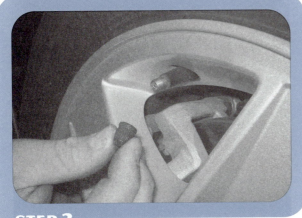

STEP 3   Remove the tire valve cap and visually check the condition of the valve stem.

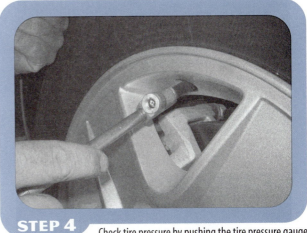

STEP 4   Check tire pressure by pushing the tire pressure gauge straight onto the end of the tire valve.

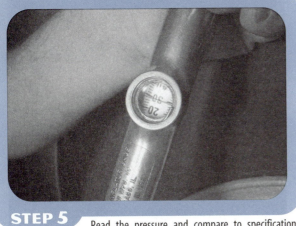

STEP 5   Read the pressure and compare to specifications. Correct as necessary.

STEP 6   A typical tire tread depth gauge.

TIRE INSPECTION   continued

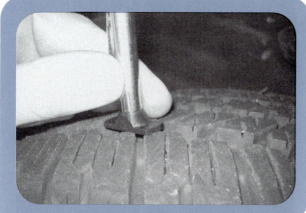

STEP 7   The blade of the tire tread depth gauge is pushed down into the groove of the tire at the lowest part.

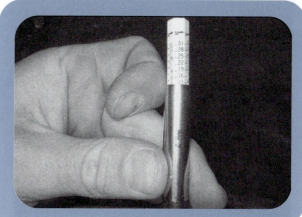

STEP 8   Remove the gauge from the tire and read the tread depth at the metal housing. Tread depth is usually measured in 1/32's of an inch.

STEP 9   If the top of Lincoln's head is visible, then the tread depth is lower than 2/32 in., the legal limit in many states.

SUMMARY

1. New tires have between 9/32 in. and 15/32 in. tread depth. Wear bars (indicators) show up as a bald strip across the tread of the tire when the tread depth gets down to 2/32 in.

2. All tires are assembled by hand from many different materials and chemical compounds. After a green tire is assembled, it is placed into a mold under heat and pressure for about 30 minutes. Tread design and the tire shape are determined by the mold design.

3. A 205/75R × 14 92S tire is 205 mm wide at its widest section and is 75% as high as it is wide. The R stands for radial-type construction. The tire is designed for a 14-in.-diameter rim. The number 92 is the load index of the tire (the higher the number, the more weight the tire can safely support). The S is the speed rating of the tire (S = 112 mph maximum sustained).

4. The Uniform Tire Quality Grading System is a rating for tread wear (100, 150, etc.), traction (A, B, C), and temperature resistance (A, B, C).

5. For best overall handling and satisfaction, always select the same size and type of tire that came on the vehicle when new.

6. Replacement wheels should have the same offset as the factory wheels to prevent abnormal tire wear and/or handling problems.

7. All wheels must be secured with the proper size and style of lug nuts. If a wheel stud is broken, it should be replaced immediately to avoid possible wheel damage or loss of vehicle control.

REVIEW QUESTIONS

1. List the various parts of a tire and explain how a tire is constructed.

2. Explain the effect that aspect ratio has on ride and handling.

3. List the factors that should be considered when purchasing tires.

4. Explain the three major areas of the Uniform Tire Quality Grading System.

5. Explain how to determine proper tire pressure.

CHAPTER QUIZ

1. The part of the tire that is under just the tread of a radial tire is called the _____.
   a. Bead
   b. Body (carcass) ply
   c. Belt
   d. Inner liner

2. The aspect ratio of a tire means _____.
   a. Its width to diameter of a wheel ratio
   b. The ratio of height to width
   c. The ratio of width to height
   d. The ratio of rolling resistance

3. A tire is labeled 215/60R × 15 92T; the T indicates _____.
   a. Its speed rating
   b. Its tread wear rating
   c. Its load rating
   d. Its temperature resistance rating

4. The 92 in the tire designation in question 3 refers to the tire's _____.
   a. Speed rating
   b. Tread wear rating
   c. Load rating
   d. Temperature resistance rating

5. Radial tires can cause a vehicle to pull to one side while driving. This is called "radial tire pull" and is often due to _____.
   a. The angle of the body (carcass) plies
   b. Tire conicity
   c. Tread design
   d. Bead design

6. Tire inflation is very important to the safe and economical operation of any vehicle. Technician A says that the pressure should never exceed the maximum pressure imprinted on the sidewall of the tire. Technician B says to inflate the tires to the pressures recommended on the tire information decal or placard on the driver's door. Which technician is correct?
   a. Technician A only
   b. Technician B only
   c. Both Technicians A and B
   d. Neither Technician A nor B

7. When purchasing replacement tires, do not change tire width from the stock size by more than _____.
   a. 10 mm
   b. 15 mm
   c. 20 mm
   d. 25 mm

8. What do the letters JJ mean in a wheel designation size labeled 14 × 7JJ?
   a. The offset of the rim
   b. The bolt circle code
   c. The back spacing of the rim
   d. The shape of the flange area

9. Technician A says that a PAX run-flat tire uses a special wheel. Technician B says that a standard tire can be used to replace a PAX run-flat tire. Which technician is correct?
   a. Technician A only
   b. Technician B only
   c. Both Technicians A and B
   d. Neither Technician A nor B

10. Technician A says that a tire-pressure monitor system that uses a valve-stem-type transmitter is the direct-reading type of TPMS. Technician B says that a tire-pressure monitoring system that uses a sensor inside and strapped to the wheel is an indirect-reading type of TPMS. Which technician is correct?
    a. Technician A only
    b. Technician B only
    c. Both Technicians A and B
    d. Neither Technician A nor B

WHEEL AND TIRE SERVICE

OBJECTIVES

After studying Chapter 4, the reader should be able to:

1. Prepare for Suspension and Steering (A4) ASE certification test content area "E" (Wheel and Tire Diagnosis and Repair).
2. Discuss proper tire mounting procedures.
3. Describe recommended tire rotation methods.
4. Discuss how to properly balance a tire.
5. Describe tire repair procedures.
6. Explain wheel and tire safety precautions.

KEY TERMS

Proper tire service is extremely important for the safe operation of any vehicle. Premature wear can often be avoided by checking and performing routine service, such as frequent rotation and monthly inflation checks.

TIRE INFLATION

Tires should always be inflated to the pressure indicated on the driver's door or pillar sticker. Tires should be checked when cold, before the vehicle has been driven, because driving on tires increases the temperature and therefore the pressure of the tires. Proper tire inflation is important for the following reasons:

- **Inflation pressure carries the load of the vehicle.** If the pressure is low, the load capacity of the tire is decreased. See Figure 4-1.
- **Inflation pressure varies with temperature.** Tires lose 1 psi for every 10-degree drop in temperature. This means that as the sensors change and the temperature

changes, so does the inflation pressure inside the tires. For example, if tires were inflated to 35 psi on the first day of summer (June 21) when the temperature was 90°F (32°C), then the following pressures would occur, assuming no air loss at all:

Summer (June 21) 90°F—35 psi
Fall (September 21) 80°F—34 psi
Winter (December 21) 30°F—29 psi

Therefore, it is very important to check and correct inflation pressures regularly.

- **Tire inflation affects fuel economy.** A drop in inflation pressure from 30 psi to 23 psi can result in a drop of fuel economy from 20 miles per gallon to 18 miles per gallon. See Figure 4-2.
- **Tire inflation affects tire life.** Even a slight drop in air pressure can have a major effect on the life of a tire. If, for example, the inflation pressure dropped 10 psi, the life of the tire would be reduced by 40%. See Figure 4-3.
- **The TREAD Act specifies that the driver be notified if the inflation of a tire drops by 25%.** However, 25%

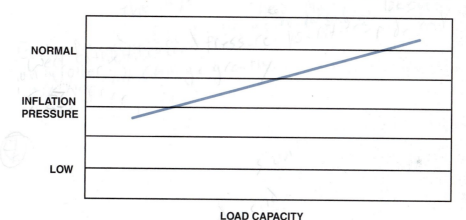

FIGURE 4-1   This chart shows the relationship between tire inflation pressure and load capacity of the tire.

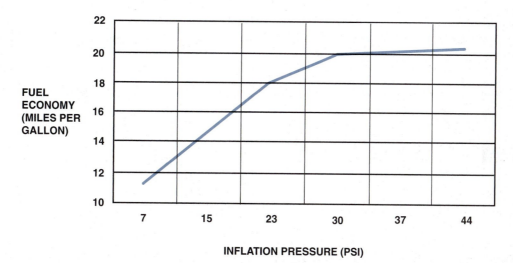

FIGURE 4-2   This chart shows that a drop in inflation pressure has a major effect on fuel economy.

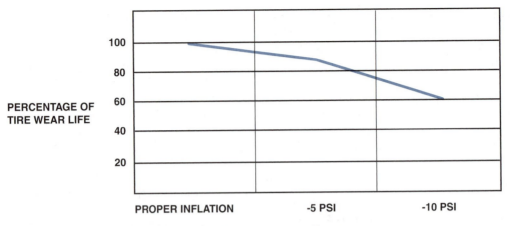

PERCENTAGE OF
TIRE WEAR LIFE

FIGURE 4-3   Notice that if a tire is underinflated by 10 psi, the life expectancy is reduced by 40%.

❓ FREQUENTLY ASKED QUESTION

WHAT IS A "TEMPORARY MOBILITY KIT"?

A temporary mobility kit is a system to inflate a flat tire supplied by the vehicle manufacturer instead of a spare tire. A temporary mobility kit can include:

- A compressor powered by the cigarette lighter with stop leak. See Figure 4-4.
- An aerosol spray can that provides inflation and sealer. See Figure 4-5.

Either type can be found in many vehicles because such devices save weight, increase trunk space, and cost less than a conventional spare tire and jack. However, these kits are designed to be a temporary repair only because the cause of the low tire was never determined. If the tire appears to be fixed, many vehicle owners may think that the tire has been repaired. However, the tire should be carefully inspected inside and out for damage and properly repaired.

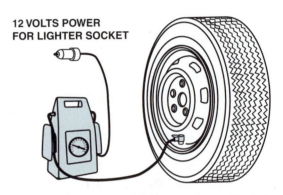

12 VOLTS POWER FOR LIGHTER SOCKET

FIGURE 4-4   A temporary inflation pump that uses 12 volts from the cigarette lighter to inflate the tire.

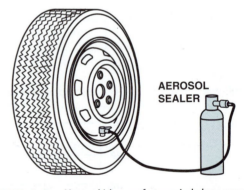

AEROSOL SEALER

FIGURE 4-5   Many vehicle manufacturers include an aerosol can of sealer on vehicles that are not equipped with a conventional spare tire.

represents a loss of air pressure of about 8 psi. A drop of 8 psi means an approximate 2-mpg decrease in fuel economy as well as about a 25% reduction in tread wear.

TIRE MOUNTING RECOMMENDATIONS

1. When removing a wheel from a vehicle for service, mark the location of the wheel and lug stud to ensure that the wheel can be replaced in exactly the same location.

This ensures that tire balance will be maintained if the tire/wheel assembly was balanced on the vehicle.
2. Make certain that the wheel has a good, clean metal-to-metal contact with the brake drum or rotor. Grease, oil, or dirt between these two surfaces could cause the wheel lug nuts to loosen while driving.
3. Always check the rim size. For example, simply by looking it is hard to distinguish a 16-in. wheel from a 16.5-in. wheel used on some trucks. See Figure 4-6. The rim size

is marked on the sidewall of the tire, and the rim's diameter and width are stamped somewhere on the wheel.

4. Install the tire-pressure monitoring system (as shown in Figure 4-7).
5. Many tires have been marked with a paint dot or sticker, as shown in Figure 4-8. This mark represents the largest diameter (high point) and/or stiffest portion

TECH TIP

SPIN THE TIRES

When performing a vehicle inspection and the vehicle has been hoisted on a frame-type lift, check the tires by rotating them by hand. The tires on the nondrive wheels should spin freely.

- On front-wheel-drive vehicles, rear wheels should rotate easily.
- On rear-wheel-drive vehicles, front wheels should rotate easily.
- On all-wheel-drive vehicles, all four wheels may require effort to rotate.

What to Look For:

- When rotating the wheels, look at the tires from the front or rear and check that the tread of the tires does not change or look as if the tread is moving inward or outward. If the tread is moving, this indicates an internal fault with the tire and it should be replaced. This type of fault can cause a vibration even though the tire/wheel assembly has been correctly balanced.
- Look from the side of the vehicle as the wheel/tire assembly is being rotated. Look carefully at the tread of the tire and see if the tire is round. If the tire is out of round, the tread will appear to move up and down as the tire is being rotated.

of the tire. This variation is due to the overlapping of carcass and belt fabric layers, as well as tread and sidewall rubber splices. The tire should be mounted to the rim with this mark lined up with the valve stem. The valve stem hole is typically drilled at the smallest diameter (low point) of the wheel. Mount the tires on the rim with the valve stem matched to (lined up next to) the mark on the tire. This is called **match mounting.**

6. Never use more than 40 psi (275 kPa) to seat a tire bead.
7. Rim flanges must be free of rust, dirt, scale, or loose or flaked rubber build-up prior to mounting the tire. See Figure 4-9.
8. When mounting new tires, do *not* use silicone lubricant on the tire bead. Use special lubricant such as rendered (odorless) animal fat or rubber lubricant to help prevent tire rotation on the rim. This rubber lube is a water-based soap product that is slippery when wet (coefficient of friction when less than 0.3) and acts almost as an adhesive when dry (coefficient of friction when dry of over 0.5 for natural products and over 1.0 for synthetic products). See Figure 4-10. If the wrong lubricant is used, the rubber in the bead area of the tire can be softened or weakened. Also, most other lubricants do not increase in friction when they dry like rubber lubricant does. The result can be the rotation of the tire on the rim (wheel), especially during rapid acceleration or braking.

NOTE: Many experts recommend that when a new tire is installed the vehicle should be driven at less than 50 mph (80 km/h) for the first 50 miles (80 km) to allow the tires to adhere to the rim. During this break-in period, the rubber lube used to mount the tire is drying and the tire is becoming fully seated on the rim. By avoiding high speeds, rapid acceleration, and fast braking, the driver is helping to prevent the tire from rotating on the rim.

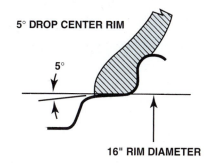
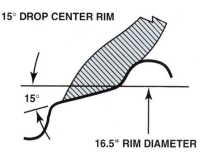

FIGURE 4-6 Note the difference in the shape of the rim contour of the 16-inch and 16 1/2-inch diameter wheels. While it is possible to mount a 16-inch tire on a 16 1/2-inch rim; it cannot be inflated enough to seat against the rim flange. If an attempt is made to seat the tire bead by overinflating (over 40 psi), the tire bead can break, resulting in an explosive force that could cause serious injury or death.

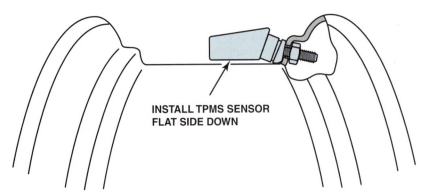

INSTALL TPMS SENSOR
FLAT SIDE DOWN

FIGURE 4-7 When installing a tire-pressure monitoring system sensor, be sure that the flat part of the sensor is parallel to the center section of the rim.

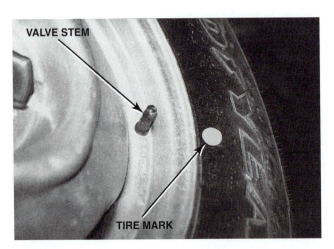

VALVE STEM

TIRE MARK

FIGURE 4-8 This tire on a new vehicle has been match mounted at the factory. The yellow sticker is placed at the largest diameter of the tire. The valve core hole in the wheel is usually drilled at the smallest diameter of the wheel. The best way to make sure the assembly is as round as possible and to reduce the number of wheel weights needed to balance the tire is to align the sticker with the valve core.

WHEEL MOUNTING TORQUE

For **wheel mounting torque,** make certain that the wheel studs are clean and dry, and torqued to the manufacturer's specifications.

CAUTION: Most manufacturers warn that the wheel studs should not be oiled or lubricated with grease; this can cause the wheel lug nuts to loosen while driving. Always follow the vehicle manufacturers' recommended service procedures.

Always tighten lug nuts gradually in the proper sequence— star pattern (tighten one nut, skip one, and tighten the next nut). This helps prevent warping the brake drums or rotors, or bending a wheel. See Figure 4-11.

(a)

(b)

FIGURE 4-9 (a) Cleaning the bead area of an aluminum (alloy) wheel using a handheld wire brush. The technician is using the tire changer itself to rotate the wheel as the brush is used to remove any remnants of the old tire. (b) Using an electric or air-powered wire brush speeds the process, but care should be exercised not to remove any of the aluminum itself. (Remember, steel is harder than aluminum and a steel wire brush could cause recesses to be worn into the aluminum wheel, which would prevent the tire from proper seating in the bead area.)

FIGURE 4-10 Rendered (odorless) animal fat is recommended by some manufacturers of tire changing equipment for use as a rubber lubricant.

TECH TIP

FINE-TUNE HANDLING WITH TIRE-PRESSURE CHANGES

The handling of a vehicle can be changed by changing tire pressures between the front and rear tires.

Understeer—A term used to describe how a vehicle handles when cornering where additional steering input is needed to maintain the corner, or resisting turning into a corner. This is normal handling for most vehicles.

Oversteer—A term used to describe handling where correction while cornering is often necessary because the rear tires lose traction before the front tires.

Tire Pressure	To Decrease Understeer	To Decrease Oversteer
Front tire inflation pressure	Increase	Decrease
Rear tire inflation pressure	Decrease	Increase

CAUTION: Do not exceed the maximum inflation pressure as imprinted on the tire sidewall.

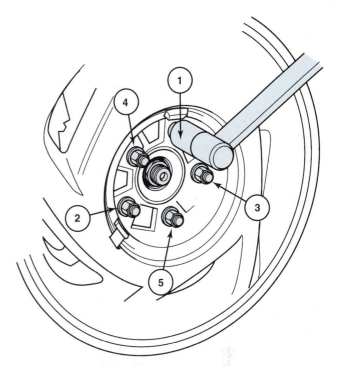

FIGURE 4-11 Always tighten wheel lug nuts (or studs) in a star pattern to ensure even pressure on the axle flange, brake rotors or drums, and the wheel itself. *(Courtesy of DaimlerChrysler Corporation)*

If the exact torque value is not available, use the following chart as a guide for the usual value based on the size (diameter) of the lug studs.

Stud Diameter	Torque (lb-ft)
3/8 in.	35–45
7/16 in.	55–65
1/2 in.	75–85
9/16 in.	95–115
5/8 in. (usually only trucks)	125–150
12 mm	70–80
14 mm	85–95

Many factory-installed and aftermarket wheels use antitheft wheel lug nuts, as shown in Figure 4-12, usually on only one wheel stud. When removing or installing a locked lug nut, be sure the key is held square to the lug nut to prevent damaging either the nut or the key.

Whenever you install a brand new set of aluminum wheels, re-torque the wheels after the first 25 miles. The soft aluminum often compresses slightly, loosening the torque on the wheels.

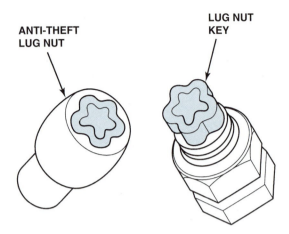

ANTI-THEFT LUG NUT

LUG NUT KEY

FIGURE 4-12 Most manufacturers recommend using hand tools rather than an air impact wrench to remove and install lock-type lug nuts to prevent damage. If either the key or the nut is damaged, the nut may be very difficult to remove!

AIR IMPACT WRENCH

TORQUE LIMITING ADAPTER

FIGURE 4-13 A torque-limiting adapter for use with an air impact wrench still requires care to prevent overtightening. The air pressure to the air impact should be limited to 125 psi (860 kPa) in most cases, and the proper adapter must be selected for the vehicle being serviced. The torque adapter absorbs any torque beyond its designed rating. Most adapters are color coded for easy identification as to the size of lug nut and torque value.

NOTE: The use of torque-absorbing adapters (torque-limiting shank sockets) on lug nuts with an air impact wrench properly set has proved to give satisfactory results. See Figure 4-13 for a photo of a torque-absorbing adapter.

REAL WORLD FIX

I THOUGHT THE LUG NUTS WERE TIGHT!

Proper wheel nut torque is critical, as one technician discovered when a customer returned complaining of a lot of noise from the right rear wheel. See Figure 4-14 for a photo of what the technician discovered. The lug (wheel) nuts had loosened and ruined the wheel.

CAUTION: Most vehicle manufacturers also specify that the wheel studs/nuts should *not* be lubricated with oil or grease. The use of a lubricant on the threads could cause the lug nuts to loosen.

FIGURE 4-14 This wheel was damaged because the lug nuts were not properly torqued.

TIRE ROTATION

To ensure long life and even tire wear, **tire rotation** is essential. It is important to rotate each tire to another location. Some rear-wheel-drive vehicles, for example, may show premature tire wear on the front tires. The wear usually starts on the outer tread row. This wear usually appears as a front-to-back (high and low) wear pattern on individual tread blocks. These *blocks of tread* rubber are deformed during cornering, stopping, and turning. This type of tread block wear can cause tire noise and/or tire roughness. While some shoulder wear on front tires is normal, it can be reduced by proper inflation, alignment, and tire rotation. For best results, tires should be rotated every 6,000 miles or every six months. See Figure 4-15 for suggested methods of rotation, such as the **modified X.**

NOTE: Radial tires can cause a radial pull due to their construction. If wheel alignment is correct, attempt to correct a pull by rotating the tires front to rear or, if necessary, side to side.

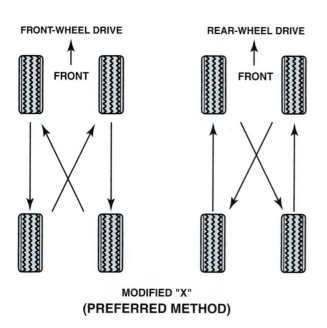

FRONT-WHEEL DRIVE

REAR-WHEEL DRIVE

FRONT

FRONT

MODIFIED "X"
(PREFERRED METHOD)

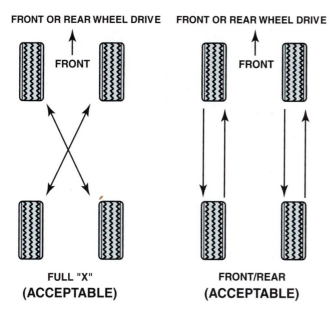

FRONT OR REAR WHEEL DRIVE

FRONT OR REAR WHEEL DRIVE

FRONT

FRONT

FULL "X"
(ACCEPTABLE)

FRONT/REAR
(ACCEPTABLE)

FIGURE 4-15   The method most often recommended is the modified X method. Using this method, each tire eventually is used at each of the four wheel locations. An easy way to remember the sequence, whether front wheel drive or rear wheel drive, is to say to yourself, "Drive wheels straight, cross the nondrive wheels."

TECH TIP

TIRE ROTATION

Tire rotation should be done at every *other* oil change. Most manufacturers recommend changing the engine oil every 3,000 miles (4,800 km) or every three months; tire rotation is recommended every 6,000 miles (9,600 km), or every six months.

Some tire manufacturers do not recommend rotating the tires on front-wheel-drive vehicles because the front tires often wear three times as fast as the rear. They recommend replacing just front tires, because the rear tires often last over 90,000 miles (145,000 km).

General Motors also warns that the wheels on many vehicles such as the Pontiac Trans Am and the newer Grand Prix cannot be rotated front to rear because the wheels and tires are different sizes. Always check service information as to the specified tire rotation procedure to follow on the vehicle being serviced.

TIRE INSPECTION

All tires should be carefully inspected for faults in the tire itself or for signs that something may be wrong with the steering or suspension systems of the vehicle. See Figures 4-16 through 4-18 for examples of common problems.

FIGURE 4-16   Tire showing excessive shoulder wear resulting from underinflation and/or high-speed cornering.

FIGURE 4-17   Tire showing excessive wear in the center, indicating overinflation or heavy acceleration on a drive wheel.

WEAR ON OUTSIDE SHOULDER

FIGURE 4-18   Wear on the outside shoulder only is an indication of an alignment problem.

TECH TIP

ALL-WHEEL-DRIVE TIRE CONCERNS

It is very important that all-wheel-drive vehicles be equipped with tires that are all the same outside diameter. If, for example, the vehicle has 20,000 miles and the tires are half worn, all of the tires should be replaced in the event of a problem requiring replacement of only one tire.

Most vehicle manufacturers specify that all tires must be within 2/32 inch of tread depth without causing a constant strain on the drive train.

RADIAL RUNOUT

Even though a tire has no visible faults, it can be the cause of vibration. If vibration is felt above 45 mph, regardless of the engine load, the cause is usually an out-of-balance or a defective out-of-round tire. Both of these problems cause a **tramp** or *up-and-down*-type vibration. If the vibration is seen in the hood of the vehicle or felt in the steering wheel, then the problem is usually the *front* tires. If the vibration is felt throughout the entire vehicle or in the seat of your pants, then the rear tires (or drive shaft, in rear-wheel-drive vehicles) are the problem. This can be checked by using a runout gauge and checking for **radial runout**. See Figures 4-19 and 4-20. To check

FIGURE 4-19   A tire runout gauge being used to measure the radial runout of a tire.

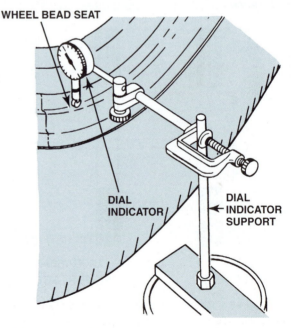

WHEEL BEAD SEAT

DIAL INDICATOR

DIAL INDICATOR SUPPORT

FIGURE 4-20   To check wheel radial runout, the dial indicator plunger tip rides on a horizontal surface of the wheel, such as the bead seat.

I THOUGHT RADIAL TIRES COULDN'T BE ROTATED!

When radial tires were first introduced by American tire manufacturers in the 1970s, rotating tires side-to-side was *not* recommended because of concerns about belt or tread separation. Since the late 1980s, most tire manufacturers throughout the world, including the United States, have used tire-building equipment specifically designed for radial-ply tires. These newer radial tires are constructed so that the tires can now be rotated from one side of the vehicle to the other without fear of causing a separation by the resulting reversal of the direction of rotation.

radial runout (checking for out of round) and lateral runout (checking for side-to-side movement), follow these steps:

1. Raise the vehicle so that the tires are off the ground approximately 2 in. (5 cm).
2. Place the runout gauge against the tread of the tire in the center of the tread and, while rotating the tire, observe the gauge reading.
3. Note that maximum radial runout should be less than 0.060 in. (1.5 mm). Little, if any, tramp will be noticed with less than 0.030 in. (0.8 mm) runout. If the reading is over 0.125 in. (3.2 mm), replacement of the tire is required.
4. Check all four tires.

Correcting Radial Runout

Excessive radial runout may be corrected by one of several methods:

1. Try relocating the wheel on the mounting studs. Mark one stud and remount the wheel two studs away from its original position. Excessive wheel hole and/or stud tolerance may be the cause. If the radial runout is now satisfactory, re-mark the stud and wheel to prevent a future occurrence of the problem.
2. Remount the tire on the wheel 180degrees from its original location. This can solve a runout problem, especially if the tire was not match mounted to the wheel originally.
3. If runout is still excessive, remove the tire from the wheel and check the runout of the *wheel.* If the wheel is within 0.035 in. (0.9 mm), yet the runout of the tire/wheel assembly is excessive, the problem has to be a defective tire and it should be replaced.

Sometimes a problem within the tire itself can cause a vibration, and yet not show up as being out of round when tested for radial runout. A condition called **radial force variation** can cause a vibration even if correctly balanced. A **tire problem detector (TPD)** can be used to find a defective tire by revolving the tire with normal vehicle weight on the roller and measuring the movement of the spindle with a dial indicator, as shown in Figure 4-21.

NOTE: Some tire balancers are equipped with a roller that is pressed against the tread of the tire to measure radial force variations. Follow the instructions as shown on the balancer display to correct for excessive radial force variations.

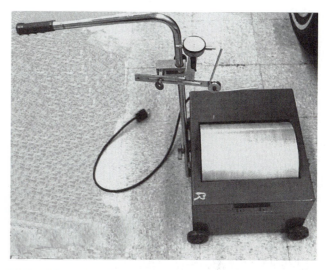

FIGURE 4-21 Tire problem detector. A similar device equipped with grinding wheels can be used to "true" or "match grind" a tire.

IS THE AGE OF A TIRE IMPORTANT?

Yes. The National Highway Traffic Safety Administration (NHTSA) recommends that any tire six years old or older should be replaced regardless of tread depth. This means that tires that look almost like new but are six years old or older should be replaced because the NHTSA determined that age, not tread depth, was a major factor in tire failures.

LATERAL RUNOUT

Another possible problem that tires can cause is a type of vibration called **shimmy.** This *rapid back-and-forth motion* can be transmitted through the steering linkage to the steering wheel. Excessive runout is usually noticeable by the driver of the vehicle as a side-to-side vibration, especially at low speeds between 5 and 45 mph (8 and 72 km/h). Shimmy can be caused by an internal defect of the tire or a bent wheel. This can be checked using a runout gauge on the side of the tire or wheel to check for **lateral runout.**

Place the runout gauge against the side of the tire and rotate the wheel. Observe the readings. The maximum allowable reading is 0.045 in. (1.1 mm). If close to or above 0.045 in. (1.1 mm), check on the edge of the wheel to see if the cause of the lateral runout is due to a bent wheel, as shown in Figure 4-22.

Most manufacturers specify a maximum lateral runout of 0.035 in. (0.9 mm) for alloy wheels and 0.045 in. (1.1 mm) for steel wheels.

Correcting Lateral Runout

Excessive lateral runout may be corrected by one of several methods:

1. Re-torque the wheel in the proper star pattern to the specified torque. Unequal or uneven wheel torque can cause excessive lateral runout.
2. Remove the wheel and inspect the wheel mounting flange for corrosion or any other reason that could prevent the wheel from seating flat against the brake rotor or drum surface.
3. Check the condition of the wheel or axle bearings. Looseness in the bearings can cause the wheel to wobble.

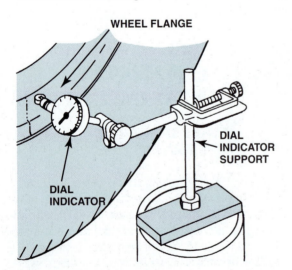

FIGURE 4-22   To check lateral runout, the dial indicator plunger tip rides on a vertical surface of the wheel, such as the wheel flange.

REAL WORLD FIX

THE GREASED WHEEL CAUSES A VIBRATION

Shortly after an oil change and a chassis lubrication, a customer complained of a vibration at highway speed. The tires were checked for excessive radial runout to be certain the cause of the vibration was not due to a defective out-of-round tire. After removing the wheel assembly from the vehicle, excessive grease was found on the inside of the rim. Obviously, the technician who greased the lower ball joints had dropped grease on the rim. After cleaning the wheel, it was checked for proper balance on a dynamic computer balancer and found to be properly balanced. A test drive confirmed that the problem was solved.

TIRE BALANCING

Proper tire balance is important for tire life, ride comfort, and safety. Tire balancing is needed because of the lack of uniform weight and stiffness (due to splices) and a combination of wheel runout and tire runout. Balancing a tire can compensate for most of these conditions. However, if a tire or wheel is excessively out of round or bent, then replacement of the wheel or tire is required.

Static Balance

The term **static balance** means that the weight mass is evenly distributed around the axis of rotation. See Figure 4-23.

1. For example, if a wheel is spun and stops at different places with each spin, then the tire is statically balanced.
2. **If the static balance is not correct, wheel tramp-type (vertical shake) vibration and uneven tire wear can result.**
3. Static balance can be tested with the tire stationary or while being spun to determine the heavy spot (sometimes called *kinetic balance*).

Dynamic Balance

The term **dynamic balance** means that the centerline of weight mass is in the same plane as the centerline of the wheel. See Figure 4-24.

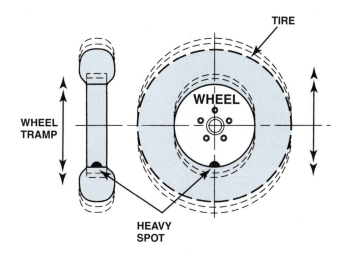

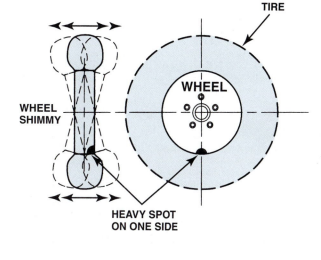

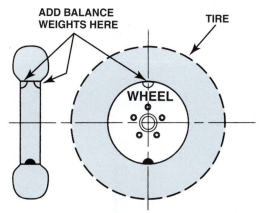

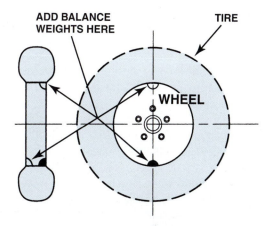

FIGURE 4-23 Weights are placed opposite the heavy spot of the tire/wheel assembly to balance the tire statically and prevent wheel tramp-type (up-and-down) vibration.

FIGURE 4-24 Weights are added to correct not only imbalance up and down but also any "wobble" caused by the tire/wheel assembly being out of balance dynamically.

1. Dynamic balance must be checked while the tire and the wheel are rotated, to determine side-to-side as well as up-and-down out of balance.
2. **Incorrect dynamic balance causes shimmy.** Shimmy-type vibration causes the steering wheel to shake from side to side.

Prebalance Checks

Before attempting to balance any tire, the following should be checked and corrected to ensure good tire balance:

1. Check the wheel bearing adjustment for looseness or wear.
2. Check the radial runout.
3. Check the lateral runout.
4. Remove stones from the tread.
5. Remove grease or dirt build-up on the inside of the wheel.

6. Check for dragging or misadjusted brakes.
7. Check for loose or backward lug nuts.
8. Check for proper tire pressures.
9. Remove all of the old weights.
10. Check for bent or damaged wheel covers.

Wheel Weights

Wheel weights are available in a variety of styles and types, including the following:

1. Clip-on lead weights for standard steel rims.
2. Clip-on weights for Cadillac steel rims. These weights use a longer clip that allows the use of full wheel covers without their hitting the weights near the rim edge.
3. Clip-on weights for alloy (aluminum) wheels.
   a. Uncoated—generally *not* recommended by wheel or vehicle manufacturers because corrosion often

REAL WORLD FIX

THE VIBRATING FORD VAN

A technician was asked to solve a vibration problem on a rear-wheel-drive Ford van. During a test drive, the vibration was felt everywhere—the dash, the steering wheel, the front seat, the shoulder belts; everything was vibrating! The technician balanced all four tires on a computer balancer. Even though wheel weights were put on all four wheels and tires, the vibration was even worse than before. The technician rebalanced all four wheels time after time, but the vibration was still present. The shop supervisor then took over the job of solving the mystery of the vibrating van. The supervisor balanced one wheel/tire assembly and then tested it again after installing the weights. The balance was way off! The supervisor broke the tire down and found about 1 quart (1 liter) of liquid in the tire! Liquid was found in all four tires. No wonder the tires couldn't be balanced! Every time the tire stopped, the liquid would settle in another location.

The customer later admitted to using a tire stop-leak liquid in all four tires. Besides stop leak, another common source of liquid in tires is water that accumulates in the storage tank of air compressors, which often gets pumped into tires when air is being added. All air compressor storage tanks should be drained of water regularly to prevent this from happening. See Figure 4-25.

occurs where the lead weight contacts the alloy wheel surface.

b. Coated—lead weights that are painted or coated in a plastic material are usually the *recom-mended* type of weight to use on alloy wheels. See Figure 4-26.

Weights are usually coated with a nylon or polyester-type material that often matches the color of the aluminum wheels.

4. Stick-on weights come with an adhesive backing that is most often used on alloy wheels. See Figure 4-27.

TECH TIP

Stop leak should never be used in a tire that is equipped with the TPMS sensor because the sensor can be damaged.

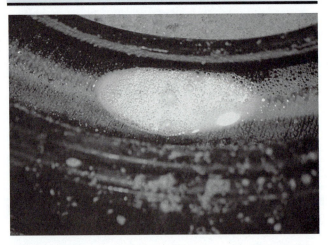

FIGURE 4-25 Liquid tire stop leak was found in all four tires. This liquid caused the tires to be out of balance.

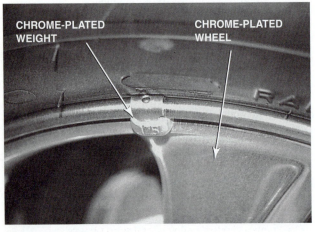

(a)

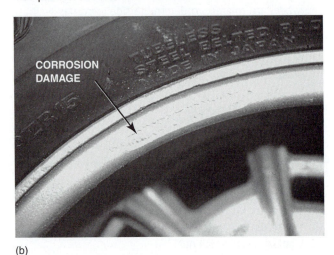

(b)

FIGURE 4-26 (a) A chrome-plated wheel weight used on a new vehicle equipped with chrome-plated aluminum (alloy) wheels. (b) Note the corrosion on this alloy wheel caused by the use of standard lead wheel weights. Using a coated wheel weight would have prevented this damage to an expensive wheel.

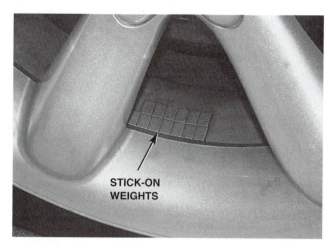

FIGURE 4-27 Stick-on weights are used from the factory to balance the alloy wheels of this Prowler.

Most wheel weights come in 1/4-ounce (0.25 oz) increments (oz × 28 = grams).

0.25 oz = 7 gm	1.75 oz = 49 gm
0.50 oz = 14 gm	2.00 oz = 56 gm
0.75 oz = 21 gm	2.25 oz = 63 gm
1.00 oz = 28 gm	2.50 oz = 70 gm
1.25 oz = 35 gm	2.75 oz = 77 gm
1.50 oz = 42 gm	3.00 oz = 84 gm

Bubble Balancer

This type of static balancer is commonly used and is accurate, if calibrated and used correctly. A bubble balancer is portable and can be easily stored away when not in use. It is also easy to use and is relatively inexpensive. See Figure 4-28.

Computer Balancer

The most popular type of tire balancer is the computer dynamic balancer. Most computer balancers are designed to balance wheels and tires off the vehicle. Computer dynamic balancers spin the tire at a relatively slow speed (approximately 20 mph). Sensors attached to the spindle of the balancer determine the amount and location of weights necessary to balance the tire dynamically. All computer balancers must be programmed with the actual rim size and tire location for the electronic circuits to calibrate the required weight locations. Some computer balancers can perform loaded radial force and lateral force variation testing on the tire/wheel assembly and display corrective actions. See Figure 4-29.

Most computer balancers will be accurate to within 1/4 oz (0.25 oz), while some are accurate to within 1/8 oz (0.125 oz). (Most drivers can feel an out-of-balance of 1 oz or more, but few can feel a vibration caused by just 1/4 oz.) For sensitive drivers or vehicles used for high speeds, such as racing, most computer balancers can be programmed to balance within

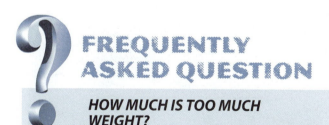

FREQUENTLY ASKED QUESTION

HOW MUCH IS TOO MUCH WEIGHT?

Whenever balancing a tire, it is wise to use as little amount of weight as possible. For most standard-size passenger vehicle tires, most experts recommend that no more than 5.5 oz of weight be added to correct an imbalance condition. If more than 5.5 oz is needed, remove the tire from the wheel (rim) and carefully inspect for damage to the tire or the wheel. If the tire still requires more than 5.5 oz and the wheel is not bent or damaged, replace the tire.

FREQUENTLY ASKED QUESTION

ARE THE BRAKE DRUMS AND ROTORS BALANCED?

Whenever an off-the-vehicle computer balancer is used, a question often asked by beginning technicians is, "What about the balance of the brake drums and rotors?" Brake drums and rotors are balanced at the factory, usually to within 0.5 oz-in. Imbalance measured in oz-in. means that any imbalance force is measured in ounces, then multiplied by the distance from the center measured in inches. This means that at a distance of 1 inch from the center of the drum or rotor, it is within 0.5 ounce of being perfectly balanced. Being within 0.5 ounce-inch also means that at 5 inches from the center, the imbalance is only 0.1 ounce.

What this means to the technician is that most drums and rotors are balanced well enough not to be a problem when using off-the-vehicle balancers. However, the smart technician should look for evidence that weights have been removed from brake drums to permit aluminum wheels to fit, or other cases where the factory balance of the drums and rotors has been changed.

1/8 oz (0.125 oz). Refer to the manufacturer's instructions for the exact capabilities and procedures for your computer balancer.

Most vehicle manufacturers specify that no more than 5.5 oz (150 gm) be used to balance any tire, with no more than 3.5 oz (100 gm) used per side of each wheel.

REPLACEMENT WHEELS

Whenever a replacement wheel is required, the same offset should be maintained. If wider or larger-diameter wheels are to be used, consult a knowledgeable wheel or tire salesperson to determine the correct wheel for your application.

CAUTION: Never remove the weights that are welded to the surface of the brake drum facing the wheel. See Figure 4-30. If replacement wheels do not fit without removing these weights, either replace the brake drum (one without a weight) or select another brand or style of wheel. Removing the weights from a brake drum can cause severe vibration at highway speeds.

(a)

(b)

(c)

FIGURE 4-28 (a) Typical portable bubble wheel balancer. (b) When properly balanced, the bubble should be in the center of the crosshairs. The triangle mark is placed on the gauge to be used to line up the valve stem of the tire. This allows the technician to reinstall the tire/wheel assembly back onto the balancer after pounding on the weights in the same location. (c) Most bubble balancers use oil to allow the gauge to float freely. Be careful when moving this type of balance because the oil can easily spill out if tilted.

FIGURE 4-29 A tire balancer that can also detect radial and lateral force variation and instruct the operator where to rotate the tire to achieve the best ride, or indicate a bent wheel.

FIGURE 4-30 Most brake drums do not have this much attached weight.

REAL WORLD FIX

IT HAPPENED TO ME—IT COULD HAPPEN TO YOU

During routine service, I rotated the tires on a Pontiac Trans Am. Everything went well and I even used a torque wrench to properly torque all of the lug nuts. Then, when I went to drive the car out of the service stall, I heard a horrible grinding sound. When I hoisted the car to investigate, I discovered that the front wheels were hitting the outer tie rod ends. See Figure 4-31. The 16-inch wheels had a different back spacing front and rear, and therefore these wheels could not be rotated. Always check replacement or aftermarket wheels for proper fit before driving the vehicle.

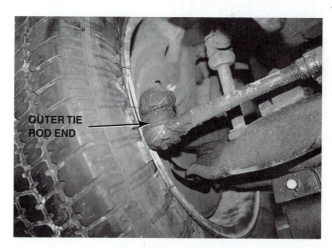

FIGURE 4-31 Notice that the rim touches the tie rod end.

NITROGEN INFLATION

Some shops recommend and inflate tires using nitrogen instead of using compressed air. Compressed air contains about 78% nitrogen, 21% oxygen, and 1% other gases. If air already contains mostly nitrogen, why use pure nitrogen? There are several reasons, including:

- The nitrogen molecule is slightly larger than the oxygen molecule so the tire will lose pressure faster if air is used instead of nitrogen.

- Compressed nitrogen contains less moisture than compressed air. When the tire heats up, moisture in the tire vaporizes and expands, causing the pressure inside the tire to increase. Even small changes in tire pressure can noticeably affect the handling of the vehicle.
- Race teams use nitrogen because they already come to the track with a cylinder of nitrogen to power the air tools.
- Race teams also have more control over how much the pressure will increase when the tires heat up, because nitrogen has less tendency to change pressure with temperature change.
- Some oxygen in the tires could, over a long period of time, cause the oxidation of the inner liner of the tire and the corrosion of the wheel. See Figure 4-32.

TIRE REPAIR

Tread punctures, nail holes, or cuts up to 1/4 in. (2.6 mm) can be repaired. Repairs should be done from the inside of the tire using plugs or patches. The tire should be removed from the rim to make the repair. With the tire off the wheel, inspect the wheel and the tire for hidden damage. The proper steps to follow for a tire repair are as follows:

1. Mark the location of the tire on the wheel.

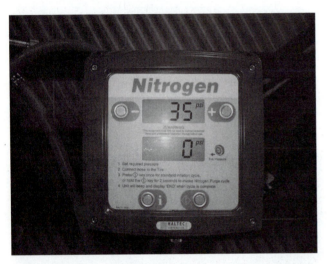

FIGURE 4-32 Nitrogen inflation machines are capable of removing nitrogen from the air.

FREQUENTLY ASKED QUESTION

WHAT ARE HUBCENTRIC WHEELS?

Most wheels are designed to fit over and be supported by the axle hub. Some wheels use an enlarged center hub section and rely on the wheel studs for support and to keep the wheel centered on the axle. Some aftermarket wheels may be designed to fit several different vehicles. As a result, the wheel manufacturers use plastic hubcentric adapter rings. See Figure 4-33.

2. Dismount the tire; inspect and clean the punctured area with a prebuff cleaner. DO NOT USE GASOLINE!
3. Buff the cleaned area with sandpaper or a tire-buffing tool until the rubber surface has a smooth, velvet finish. See Figure 4-34.
4. Ream the puncture with a fine reamer from the inside. Cut and remove any loose wire material from the steel belts.
5. Fill the puncture with contour filling material, and cut or buff the material flush with the inner liner of the tire.
6. Apply chemical vulcanizing cement and allow to dry.

NOTE: Most vulcanizing (rubber) cement is highly flammable. Use out of the area of an open flame. Do not smoke when making a tire repair.

(a)   (b)

FIGURE 4-33   (a) A hubcentric plastic ring partially removed from an aftermarket wheel. (b) A hubcentric plastic ring left on the hub when removing a wheel.

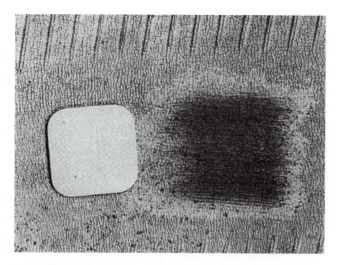

FIGURE 4-34   The area of the repair should be buffed slightly larger than the patch to be applied.

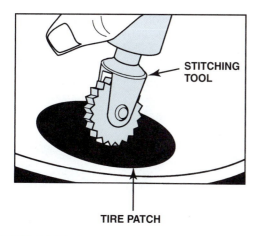

STITCHING TOOL

TIRE PATCH

FIGURE 4-35   A stitching tool being used to force any trapped air out from under the patch.

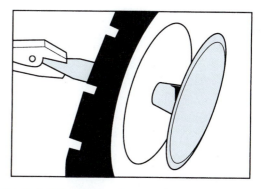

FIGURE 4-36   A rubber plug being pulled through a hole in the tire. The stem is then cut off flush with the surface of the tire tread.

7. Apply the patch and use a stitching tool from the center toward the outside of the patch to work any air out from between the patch and the tire. See Figure 4-35. Another excellent tire repair procedure uses a rubber plug. Pull the stem through the hole in the tire, as shown in Figure 4-36.
8. Remount the tire on the rim, aligning the marks made in step 1. Inflate to the recommended pressure and check for air leaks.

There are many tire repair products on the market. Always follow the installation and repair procedures exactly per the manufacturer's instructions.

CAUTION: Most experts agree that tire repairs should be done from the inside. Many technicians have been injured and a few killed when the tire they were repairing exploded as a steel reamer tool was inserted into the tire. The reamer can easily create a spark as it is pushed through the steel wires of a steel-belted tire. This spark can ignite a combustible mixture of gases inside the tire caused by using stop leak or inflator cans. Since there is no way a technician can know if a tire has been inflated with a product that uses a combustible gas, always treat a tire as if it could explode.

TECH TIP

DISPOSE OF OLD TIRES PROPERLY

Old tires cannot be thrown out in the trash. They must be disposed of properly. Tires cannot be buried because they tend to come to the surface. They also trap and hold water, which can be a breeding ground for mosquitoes. Used tires should be sent to a local or regional recycling center where the tires will be ground up and used in asphalt paving or other industrial uses. Because there is often a charge to dispose of old tires, it is best to warn the customer of the disposal fee.

TECH TIP

OPEN-END WRENCHES MAKE IT EASIER

Tire repair is made easier if two open-end wrenches are used to hold the beads of the tire apart. See step 4 in the tire repair photo sequence.

TIRE MOUNTING Step-by-Step

STEP 1 A typical tire-changing machine showing the revolving table and movable arm used to remove a tire from the wheel.

STEP 2 The foot-pedal controls allow the service technician to break the tire bead, damp the wheel (rim) to the machine, rotate the tire/wheel assembly, and still have both hands free to help with the changing of the tire.

STEP 3 Using a tire valve removal tool, unscrew the valve core using extreme caution because the valve is under pressure and can be forced outward and cause personal injury.

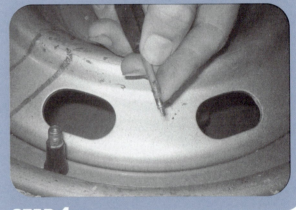

STEP 4 The valve core removed from the tire valve. Allow all of the air in the tire to escape.

STEP 5 A bead breaker is being used to separate the tire from the bead seat of the wheel. Repeat as needed to break the bead on both sides of the wheel.

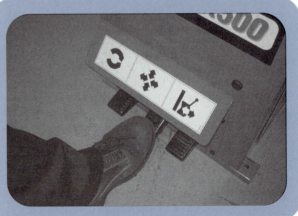

STEP 6 After breaking the beads from both sides of the tire, install the wheel/tire assembly flat onto the machine and, using the foot-pedal control, lock the wheel to the changer.

TIRE MOUNTING continued

STEP 7 To remove the tire from the wheel, position the arm of the changer against the rim of the wheel and lock in position.

STEP 8 The tire tool (flat bar) is placed between the bead of the tire and the wheel.

STEP 9 The foot pedal that causes the table to rotate is depressed and the tire is removed from the wheel.

STEP 10 Reposition the tire tool to remove the lower bead of the tire from the wheel.

STEP 11 As the table of the tire changer is rotated, the tire is released from the wheel and can be lifted off the wheel.

STEP 12 Before installing a tire, inspect and clean the bead seat.

TIRE MOUNTING continued

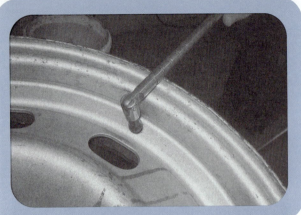

STEP 13 Before installing a new tire, most experts recommend replacing the tire valve, being installed here, using a tool that pulls the valve through the hole in the wheel.

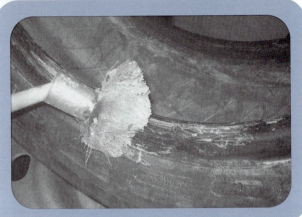

STEP 14 Apply tire soap or rubber lubricant to both beads of the tire.

STEP 15 Rotate the tire on the wheel and position the arm so that the tire will be guided onto the rim as the wheel is rotated.

STEP 16 Repeat for the upper bead.

STEP 17 Inflate the tire, being careful to not exceed 40 psi.

STEP 18 Install the tire valve core and inflate the tire to specifications.

TIRE REPAIR Step-by-Step

STEP 1 The source of the leak was detected by spraying soapy water on the inflated tire. Needle-nose pliers are being used to remove the object that caused the flat tire.

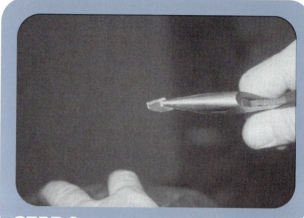

STEP 2 A part of a razor blade was found to be the cause of the flat tire.

STEP 3 A teamer is being used to clean the puncture hole.

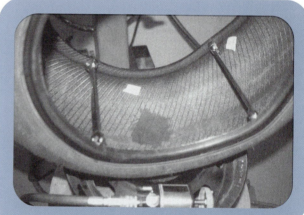

STEP 4 A method used by some technicians is to hold the beads apart with two open-end wrenches. In this case, two line wrenches were used, and this provided more than enough room to gain access to the inside of the tire.

STEP 5 The surrounding area is being buffed using an air-powered die grinder equipped with a special buffing tool specifically designed for this process.

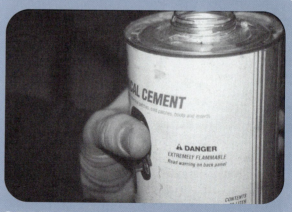

STEP 6 Rubber cement is applied to the buffed area.

TIRE REPAIR continued

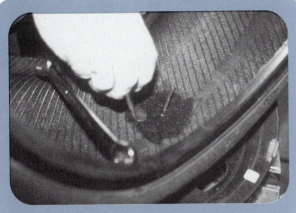

STEP 7 The brush included with the rubber cement makes the job easy. Be sure to cover the entire area around the puncture.

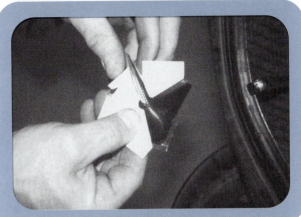

STEP 8 Peel off the paper from the adhesive on the patch. Insert the tip of the patch through the puncture from the inside of the tire.

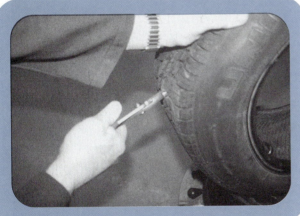

STEP 9 Use a pair of pliers to pull the plug of the patch through the puncture.

STEP 10 This view of the patch is from the inside of the tire.

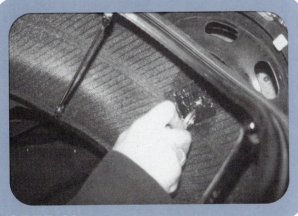

STEP 11 To be assured of an air-tight patch, the adhesive of the patch should be "stitched" to the inside of the tire using a serrated roller called a stitching tool.

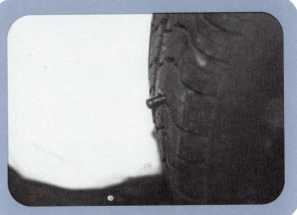

STEP 12 A view of the plug from the outside of the tire after metal covering used to pierce the puncture is removed from the patch plug. The plug can be trimmed to the level of the tread using side cutters or a knife.

SUMMARY

1. For safety and proper vehicle handling, all four tires of the vehicle should be of the same size, construction, and type, except where specified by the manufacturer, such as on some high-performance sports cars.

2. Wheels should always be tightened with a torque wrench to the proper torque in a star pattern.

3. Tires should be rotated every 5,000 to 7,000 miles (8,000 to 11,000 km), or at every other oil change.

4. Wheels should be cleaned around the rim area whenever tires are changed and carefully inspected for cracks or other defects such as excessive lateral or radial runout.

5. Properly balanced tires prolong tire life. Wheel tramp or an up-and-down type of vibration results if the tires are statically out of balance or if the tire is out of round.

6. Dynamic balance is necessary to prevent side-to-side vibration, commonly called shimmy.

7. Only coated or stick-on-type wheel weights should be used on alloy wheels to prevent corrosion damage.

REVIEW QUESTIONS

1. List the precautions and recommendations regarding tire selection and maintenance.

2. Determine the proper wheel mounting torque for your vehicle from the guidelines provided.

3. Determine the proper bolt circle, wheel diameter, and wheel width for your vehicle.

4. Describe the difference between static and dynamic balance.

CHAPTER QUIZ

1. A tire is worn excessively on both edges. The most likely cause of this type of tire wear is _____.
   a. Overinflation
   b. Underinflation
   c. Excessive radial runout
   d. Excessive lateral runout

2. When seating a bead of a tire, never exceed _____ psi.
   a. 30
   b. 40
   c. 50
   d. 60

3. For best tire life, most vehicle and tire manufacturers recommend tire rotation every _____.
   a. 3,000 miles
   b. 6,000 miles
   c. 9,000 miles
   d. 12,000 miles

4. What lubricant should be used when mounting a tire?
   a. Silicone spray
   b. Grease
   c. Water-based soap
   d. SAE 10W-30 engine oil

5. The most common torque specification range for lug nuts is _____.
   a. 125–150 lb-ft
   b. 100–120 lb-ft
   c. 80–100 lb-ft
   d. 60–80 lb-ft

6. Which statement is *false?*
   a. Excessive radial runout can cause a tramp-type vibration.
   b. Excessive lateral runout can cause a tramp-type vibration.
   c. A tire out of balance dynamically can cause a shimmy-type vibration.
   d. A tire out of balance statically can cause a tramp-type vibration.

7. The recommended type of wheel weight to use on aluminum (alloy) wheels is _____.
   a. Lead with plated spring steel clips
   b. Coated (painted) lead weights
   c. Lead weights with longer-than-normal clips
   d. Aluminum weights

8. Most vehicle and tire manufacturers recommend that no more than _____ ounces of balance weight be added to a wheel/tire assembly.
   a. 2.5
   b. 3.5
   c. 4.5
   d. 5.5

9. A vehicle vibrates at highway speed. Technician A says that water in the tire(s) could be the cause. Technician B says that an out-of-round tire could be the cause. Which technician is correct?
   a. Technician A only
   b. Technician B only
   c. Both Technicians A and B
   d. Neither Technician A nor B

10. Proper tire inflation pressure information is found _____.
   a. On the driver's door or post
   b. In the owner's manual
   c. On the sidewall of the tire
   d. Both a and b

CHAPTER 5

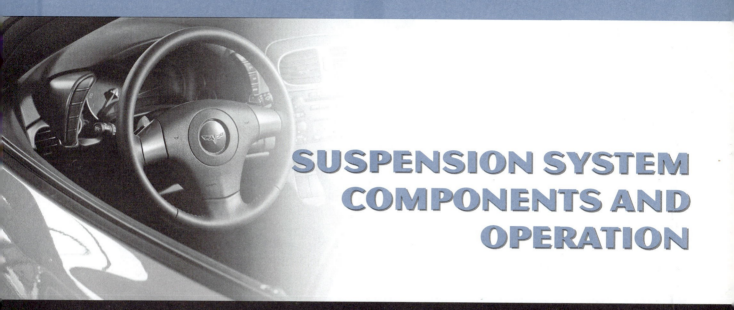

SUSPENSION SYSTEM COMPONENTS AND OPERATION

OBJECTIVES

After studying Chapter 5, the reader should be able to:

1. Prepare for the Suspension and Steering (A4) ASE certification test content area "B" (Suspension System Diagnosis and Repair).
2. List various types of suspensions and their component parts.
3. Explain how coil, leaf, and torsion bar springs work.
4. Describe how suspension components function to allow wheel movement up and down and provide for turning.
5. Describe how shock absorbers control spring forces.

KEY TERMS

Air Spring (p. 144)
Anti-Dive (p. 131)
Anti-Squat (p. 131)
Ball Joints (p. 134)
Bulkhead (p. 121)
Bump Stop (p. 146)
Center Bolt (p. 127)
Coil Springs (p. 123)
Composite Leaf Spring (p. 130)
Control Arms (p. 134)
Cradle (p. 120)
Full Frame (p. 120)
GVW (p. 121)
Hooke's Law (p. 123)
Independent Suspension (p. 122)

Insulators (p. 127)
Kingpin (p. 132)
Ladder Frame (p. 120)
Lateral Links (p. 130)
Leaf Springs (p. 127)
Load-Carrying Ball Joint (p. 134)
Mono Leaf (p. 128)
Non-Load-Carrying Ball Joint (p. 134)
Perimeter Frame (p. 120)
Platforms (p. 121)
Rebound Clips (p. 128)
Shackles (p. 127)
Shock Absorbers (p. 137)
Space Frame (p. 121)
Spring Pocket (p. 127)

Spring Rate (p. 123)
Springs (p. 122)
Sprung Weight (p. 122)
Stabilizer Bars (p. 137)
Steering Knuckles (p. 132)
Stress Riser (p. 127)
Strut Rod (p. 135)
Struts (p. 145)
Stub-Type Frame (p. 120)
Torsion Bar (p. 130)
Unit-Body (p. 120)
Unsprung Weight (p. 122)
Wheel Rate (p. 126)

Street-driven cars and trucks use a suspension system to keep the tires on the road and to provide acceptable riding comfort. A vehicle with a solid suspension, or no suspension, would bounce off the ground when the tires hit a bump. If the tires are off the ground, even for a fraction of a second, loss of control is possible. The purpose of the suspension is to provide the vehicle with the following:

1. A smooth ride
2. Accurate steering
3. Responsive handling
4. Support for the weight of the vehicle
5. Maintenance of acceptable tire wear

FRAME CONSTRUCTION

Frame construction usually consists of channel-shaped steel beams welded and/or fastened together. The frame of a vehicle supports all the "running gear" of the vehicle, including the engine, transmission, rear axle assembly (if rear-wheel drive), and all suspension components.

This frame construction, referred to as **full frame,** is so complete that most vehicles can usually be driven without the body. Most trucks and larger rear-wheel-drive cars use a full frame.

Ladder Frame

A **ladder frame** is a common name for a type of perimeter frame where the transverse (lateral) connecting members are straight across. See Figures 5-1 and 5-2. When viewed with the body removed, the frame resembles a ladder. Most pickup trucks are constructed with a ladder-type frame.

Perimeter Frame

A **perimeter frame** consists of welded or riveted frame members around the entire perimeter of the body. This means that

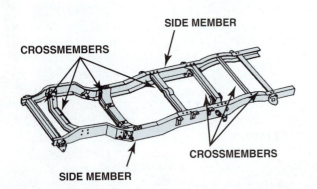

FIGURE 5-1   A typical truck frame is an excellent example of a ladder-type frame. The two side members are connected by a crossmember.

LADDER FRAME

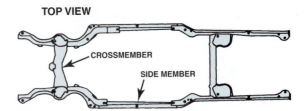

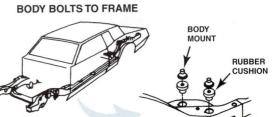

FIGURE 5-2   Rubber cushions used in body or frame construction isolate noise and vibration from traveling to the passenger compartment.

the frame members provide support underneath the sides as well as for the suspension and suspension components.

Stub-Type Frames

A **stub-type frame** is a partial frame often used on unit-body vehicles to support the power train and suspension components. It is also called a **cradle** on many front-wheel-drive vehicles. See Figure 5-3.

Unit-Body Construction

Unit-body construction (sometimes called *unibody*) is a design that combines the body with the structure of the frame. The body supports the engine and drive line components, as well as the suspension and steering components. The body is composed of many individual stamped-steel panels welded together.

The strength of this type of construction lies in the *shape* of the assembly. The typical vehicle uses 300 separate and different stamped steel panels that are spot-welded to form a vehicle's body. See Figure 5-4.

NOTE: A typical vehicle contains about 10,000 individual parts.

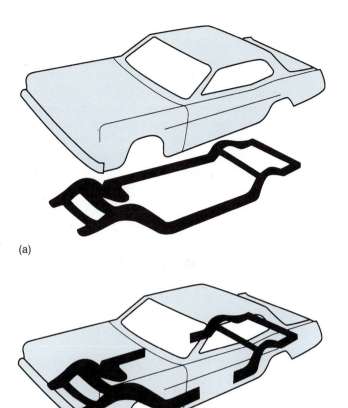

(a)

(b)

FIGURE 5-3   (a) Separate body and frame construction; (b) unitized construction: the small frame members are for support of the engine and suspension components. Many vehicles attach the suspension components directly to the reinforced sections of the body and do not require the rear frame section.

UNIT-BODY CONSTRUCTION

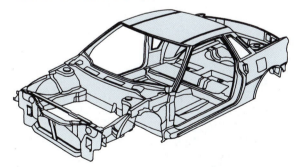

FIGURE 5-4   Welded metal sections create a platform that combines the body with the frame using unit-body construction.

Space Frame Construction

Space frame construction consists of formed sheet steel used to construct a framework for the entire vehicle. The vehicle is drivable without the body, which uses plastic or steel panels to cover the steel framework.

FREQUENTLY ASKED QUESTION

WHAT DOES GVW MEAN?

GVW, gross vehicle weight, is the weight of the vehicle plus the weight of all passengers the vehicle is designed to carry (× 150 lb [68 kg] each), plus the maximum allowable payload or luggage load. *Curb weight* is the weight of a vehicle when *wet*, meaning with a full tank of fuel and all fluids filled, but without passengers or cargo (luggage). *Model weight* is the weight of a vehicle wet and with passengers.

The GVW is found stamped on a plate fastened to the doorjamb of most vehicles. A high GVW rating does not mean that the vehicle itself weighs a lot more than other vehicles. For example, a light truck with a GVW of 6,000 lbs (2,700 kg) will not ride like an old 6,000-lb luxury car. In fact, a high GVW rating usually requires stiff springs to support the payload; these stiff springs result in a harsh ride. Often technicians are asked to correct a harsh-riding truck that has a high GVW rating. The technician can only check that everything in the suspension is satisfactory and then try to convince the owner that a harsher-than-normal ride is the result of a higher GVW rating.

PLATFORMS

The **platform** of any vehicle is its basic size and shape. Various vehicles of different makes can share the same platform, and therefore many of the same drive train (engine, transmission, and final drive components) and suspension and steering components.

A platform of a unit-body vehicle includes all major sheet-metal components that form the load-bearing structure of the vehicle, including the front suspension and engine-supporting sections. The area separating the engine compartment from the passenger compartment is called the **bulkhead.** The height and location of this bulkhead panel to a large degree determines the shape of the rest of the vehicle.

Other components of vehicle platform design that affect handling and ride are the track and wheelbase of the vehicle. *The track of a vehicle is the distance between the wheels, as viewed from the front or rear.* A wide-track vehicle is a vehicle with a wide wheel stance; this increases the stability of the vehicle, especially when cornering. *The wheelbase of a vehicle is the distance between the center of the front wheel and the*

TECH TIP

HOLLANDER INTERCHANGE MANUAL

Most salvage businesses that deal with wrecked vehicles use a reference book called the *Hollander Interchange Manual*. In this yearly publication, every vehicle part is given a number. If a part from another vehicle has the same Hollander number, then the parts are interchangeable.

center of the rear wheel, as viewed from the side. A vehicle with a long wheelbase tends to ride smoother than a vehicle with a short one.

Examples of common platforms include the following:

1. Chevrolet Impala and Pontiac Grand Prix
2. Toyota Camry and Lexus ES 350
3. Buick Lucerne and Cadillac DTC

UNSPRUNG WEIGHT

A suspension system has to be designed to allow the wheels to move up and down quickly over bumps and dips without affecting the entire weight of the car or truck. In fact, the lighter the total weight of the components that move up and down, the better the handling and ride. This weight is called **unsprung weight.** The idea of very light weight resulted in magnesium wheels for racing cars, which are very light yet strong. Aftermarket wheels that resemble racing car wheels are often referred to as *mag* wheels. For best handling and ride, the unsprung weight should be kept as low as possible.

Sprung weight is the term used to identify the weight of the car or truck that does *not* move up and down and is supported or *sprung* by the suspension.

TYPES OF SUSPENSIONS

Early suspension systems on old horse wagons, buggies, and older vehicles used a solid axle for front and rear wheels. See Figure 5-5. If one wheel hit a bump, the other wheel was affected, as shown in Figure 5-6.

Most vehicles today use a separate control-arm-type of suspension for each front wheel, which allows for movement of one front wheel without affecting the other front wheel. This type of front suspension is called **independent suspension.** See Figure 5-7.

Many rear suspensions also use independent-type suspension systems. Regardless of the design type of suspension, all suspensions use springs in one form or another.

Springs

A suspension **spring** serves two purposes. First, it acts as a buffer between the suspension and frame to absorb vertical wheel and suspension movement without passing it on to the frame.

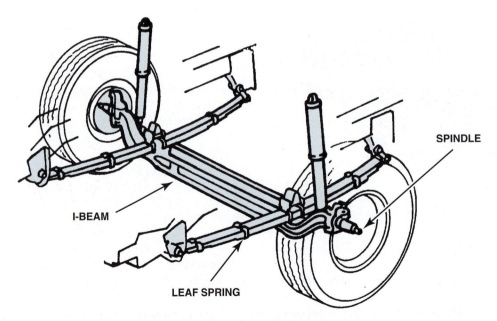

SPINDLE

I-BEAM

LEAF SPRING

FIGURE 5-5   Solid I-beam axle with leaf springs.   *(Courtesy of Hunter Engineering Company)*

Second, each spring transfers part of the vehicle weight to the suspension component it rests on, which transfers it to the wheels.

The basic method by which springs absorb road shocks varies according to the type of spring. Simply stated, leaf springs flatten, coil springs and air springs compress, and torsion bars twist. What all springs have in common is that they somehow give way to absorb the vertical force of the moving wheel during jounce, then release that force during rebound as they return to their original shape and position.

Spring Materials. Most springs are made of a tempered steel alloy known as spring steel, usually chrome silicon or chrome-vanadium alloy. Tempering is a process of heating and cooling metal under controlled conditions, which increases the resilience of the metal. Resilience is the ability of the metal to return to, or spring back to, its original shape after being twisted or compressed.

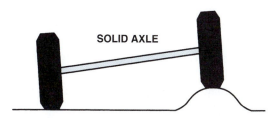

FIGURE 5-6 When one wheel hits a bump or drops into a hole, both left and right wheels are moved. Because both wheels are affected, the ride is often harsh and feels stiff.

HOOKE'S LAW

Regardless of type, all suspensions use springs that share a common characteristic described by **Hooke's Law.** Robert Hooke (1635–1703), an English physicist, discovered the force characteristics of springs: *The deflection (movement or deformation) of a spring is directly proportional to the applied force.*

What this means is that when a coil spring (for example) is depressed 1 in., it pushes back with a certain force (in pounds), such as 400 pounds. If the spring is depressed another inch, the force exerted by the spring is increased by another 400 pounds. The **spring rate** or force constant for this spring is therefore "400 lb per inch," usually symbolized by the letter K. Since the force constant is the force per unit of displacement (movement), it is a measure of the stiffness of the spring. The higher the spring rate (K), the stiffer the spring. See Figure 5-8.

COIL SPRINGS

Coil springs are made of special round spring steel wrapped in a helix shape. The strength and handling characteristics of a coil spring depend on the following:

1. Coil diameter
2. Number of coils

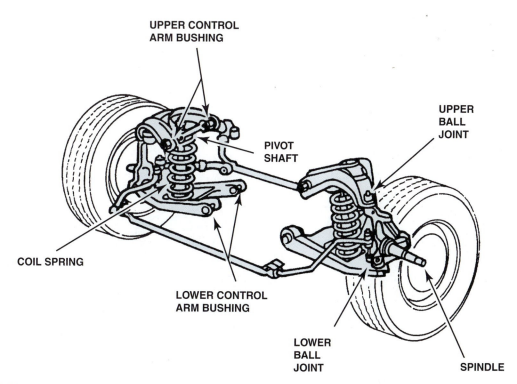

FIGURE 5-7 A typical independent front suspension used on a rear-wheel-drive vehicle. Each wheel can hit a bump or hole in the road *independently* without affecting the opposite wheel. *(Courtesy of Hunter Engineering Company)*

3. Height of spring
4. Diameter of the steel coil that forms the spring (see Figure 5-9)

The spring rate (K) for coil springs is expressed by the formula:

$$K = \frac{Gd4}{8ND3}$$

where

G = 11,250,000 (constant for steel)
d = diameter of wire
N = number of coils
D = diameter of the coil

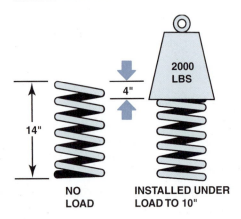

FIGURE 5-8 This spring was depressed 4 inches due to a weight of 2,000 lb. This means that this spring has a spring rate (K) of 500 lb per inch (2000 ÷ 4 in. = 500 lb./in.) *(Courtesy of Moog)*

Coil springs are used in front and/or rear suspensions. The larger the diameter of the steel, the "stiffer" the spring.
The shorter the height of the spring, the stiffer the spring.
The fewer the coils, the stiffer the spring.

Springs are designed to provide desired ride and handling and come in a variety of spring ends, as shown in Figure 5-10.

CAUTION: The use of spacers between the coils of a coil spring is *not* recommended because the force exerted by the spacers on the springs can cause spring breakage. When a spacer is installed between the coils, the number of coils is reduced and the spring becomes stiffer. The force exerted on the coil spring at the contact points of the spacer can cause the spring to break.

Spring Rate

Spring rate, also called *deflection rate*, is a value that reflects how much weight it takes to compress a spring a certain amount. Generally, spring rate is specified in pounds per inch, which is the weight in pounds it takes to compress the spring 1 inch. In other words, if a 100-pound weight causes a spring to compress 1 inch, the spring has a spring rate of 100 pounds.

A constant-rate spring continues to compress at the same rate throughout its complete range of deflection. For example, if a constant-rate spring compresses 1 inch under a 100-pound load, it will compress 2 inches under a 200-pound load, and so on. See Figure 5-11. Many automotive suspension springs,

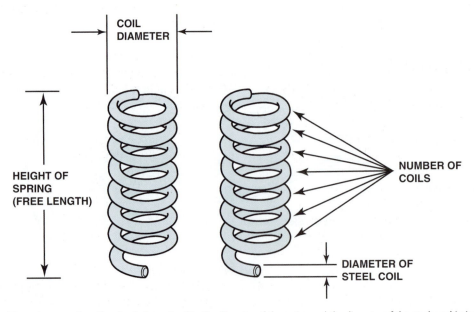

FIGURE 5-9 The spring rate of a coil spring is determined by the diameter of the spring and the diameter of the steel used in its construction plus the number of coils and the free length (height). *(Courtesy of Moog)*

COIL SPRING ENDS

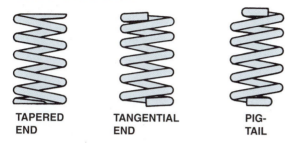

TAPERED END   TANGENTIAL END   PIG-TAIL

FIGURE 5-10   Coil spring ends are shaped to fit the needs of a variety of suspension designs.

CONSTANT-RATE SPRING

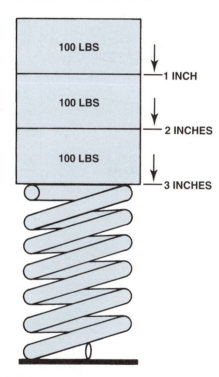

100 LBS — 1 INCH
100 LBS — 2 INCHES
100 LBS — 3 INCHES

FIGURE 5-11   A constant-rate spring compresses at the same rate regardless of the amount of weight that is applied.

VARIABLE-RATE SPRINGS

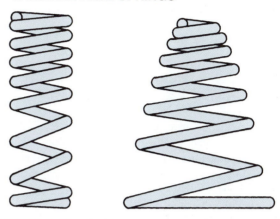

FIGURE 5-12   Variable-rate springs come in a variety of shapes and compress more slowly as weight is applied.

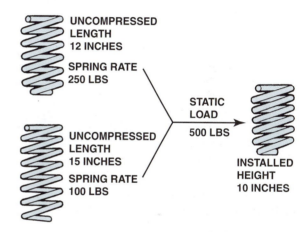

UNCOMPRESSED LENGTH 12 INCHES
SPRING RATE 250 LBS

UNCOMPRESSED LENGTH 15 INCHES
SPRING RATE 100 LBS

STATIC LOAD 500 LBS

INSTALLED HEIGHT 10 INCHES

FIGURE 5-13   Two springs, each with a different spring rate and length, can provide the same ride height even though the higher-rate spring will give a stiffer ride.

compresses the spring. Therefore, the uncompressed length and the spring rate must be such that the spring has room to compress and keep the vehicle at the correct ride height *after* the static load is applied. See Figure 5-13.

Typical Front-Wheel-Drive Sedan Springs

	Force @ Height	*Spring Rate*
LF	1,343 lbs. @ 7.6 in.	256 lb/in.
RF	1,300 lbs. @ 7.6 in.	254 lb/in.
LR	638 lbs. @ 9.38 in.	200 lb/in.
RR	610 lbs. @ 9.38 in.	195 lb/in.

Notice that each of the four coil springs used on this vehicle is unique. The higher spring rate on the left is used to help support the weight of the driver. Because each spring is designed for each location on the vehicle, they should be marked if they are removed from a vehicle during service.

both coil and leaf, compress at a variable rate. That is, they become stiffer and exert more force the further they compress. For example, a variable-rate spring may compress 1 inch under a 100-pound load, but only compress an additional 1/2 inch under a 200-pound load. Variable-rate springs offer a soft, comfortable ride under normal circumstances but will not bottom out as quickly when adverse road conditions compress them further. See Figure 5-12.

Before a spring is installed on a vehicle or any load is placed on it, it is at its uncompressed length, or free length. Once installed, the weight of the corner of the vehicle resting on the spring is called its *static load*. The static load constantly

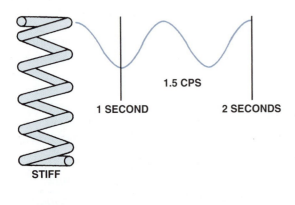

FREQUENTLY ASKED QUESTION

DOES THE SPRING RATE CHANGE AS THE VEHICLE GETS OLDER?

No, the spring rate of a spring does not change, but the spring load can change due to fatigue. The spring rate is the amount of force it takes to compress the spring 1 inch. The spring load is the amount of weight that a spring can support at any given compressed height. When a spring fatigues, the spring's load capacity decreases and the vehicle will sag.

Spring Frequency

Spring frequency is a value that reflects the speed at which a spring oscillates, or bounces, after it is released from compression or extension. Frequency is typically measured in cycles per second (CPS) or hertz (Hz). See Figure 5-14. There is a direct correlation between spring rate and spring frequency: the higher the spring rate, the higher the spring frequency. This means that stiffer springs bounce at a higher frequency, while softer springs bounce more slowly.

SPRING FREQUENCY

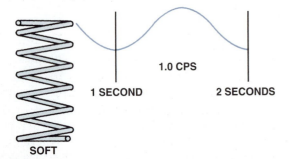

FIGURE 5-14   Stiffer springs bounce at a higher frequency than softer springs.

Wheel Rate

Depending on the suspension design, springs are installed a certain distance away from the wheel, which determines the ratio of wheel travel to spring travel, or **wheel rate.** See Figure 5-15. For example, if a coil spring is mounted on the

WHEEL RATE

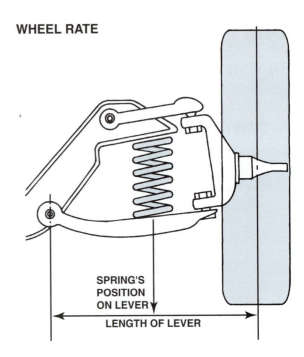

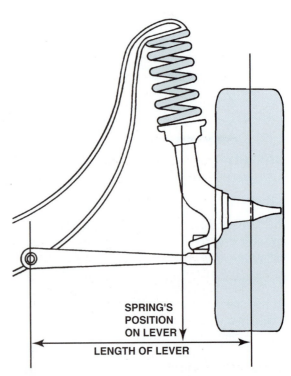

FIGURE 5-15   The wheel and arm acts as a lever to compress the spring. The spring used on the top picture must be stiffer than the spring used on the strut-type suspension shown on the bottom because the length of the lever arm is shorter.

midpoint of a control arm, or halfway between the center of the wheel and the arm pivot points, it compresses approximately 1 inch when the wheel travels vertically 2 inches. On a strut-type suspension, the coil spring has a more direct ratio because it is closer to the wheel, so when the wheel of a strut travels vertically 2 inches, the spring also compresses 2 inches. This means that a coil spring used on a strut-type suspension is less than half the spring rate of a coil spring used on suspensions that use control arms.

Coil Spring Mounting

Coil springs are usually installed in a **spring pocket** or spring seat. Hard rubber or plastic cushions or **insulators** are usually mounted between the coil spring and the spring seat. See Figure 5-16. The purpose of these insulators is to isolate and dampen road noise and vibration from the vehicle body. The type of end on the coil spring also varies and determines the style of the spring mount.

Spring Coatings

All springs are painted or coated with epoxy to help prevent breakage. A scratch, nick, or pit caused by corrosion can cause a **stress riser** that can lead to spring failure. The service technician should be careful not to remove any of the protective coating. Whenever a service operation requires the spring to be compressed, always use a tool that will not scratch or nick the surface of the spring.

LEAF SPRINGS

Leaf springs are constructed of one or more strips of long, narrow spring steel. These metal strips, called leaves, are assembled with plastic or synthetic rubber insulators between

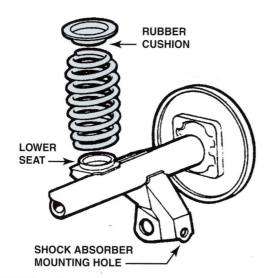

RUBBER CUSHION

LOWER SEAT

SHOCK ABSORBER MOUNTING HOLE

FIGURE 5-16   The spring cushion helps isolate noise and vibration from being transferred to the passenger compartment.   *(Courtesy of Moog)*

TECH TIP

DON'T CUT THOSE COIL SPRINGS!

Chassis service technicians are often asked to lower a vehicle. One method is to remove the coil springs and cut off half or more coils from the spring. While this *will* lower the vehicle, this method is generally *not* recommended for the following reasons:

1. A coil spring could be damaged during the cutting-off procedure, especially if a torch is used to do the cutting.
2. The spring will get stiffer when shortened, often resulting in a very harsh ride.
3. The amount the vehicle is lowered is *less* than the amount cut off from the spring. This is because as the spring is shortened, it becomes stiffer. The stiffer spring will compress less than the original.

Instead of cutting springs to lower a vehicle, several preferable methods are available if the vehicle *must* be lowered:

1. There are replacement springs designed specifically to lower that model vehicle. A change in shock absorbers may be necessary because the shorter springs change the operating height of the stock (original) shock absorbers. Consult spring manufacturers for exact installation instructions and recommendations. See Figure 5-17.
2. There are replacement spindles designed to *raise* the location of the wheel spindle, thereby lowering the body in relation to the ground. Except for ground clearance problems, this is the method recommended by many chassis service technicians. Replacement spindles keep the same springs, shock absorbers, and ride, while lowering the vehicle without serious problems.

the leaves, allowing for freedom of movement during spring operation. See Figure 5-18.

The ends of the spring are rolled or looped to form eyes. Rubber bushings are installed in the eyes of the spring and act as noise and vibration insulators. See Figure 5-19.

The leaves are held together by a **center bolt**, also called a *centering pin*. See Figure 5-20.

One end of a leaf spring is mounted to a hanger with a bolt and rubber bushings directly attached to the frame. The other end of the leaf spring is attached to the frame with movable mounting hangers called **shackles**. See Figure 5-21.

FIGURE 5-17   The replacement coil spring (left) designed to lower a vehicle is next to the original taller spring (right).

FIGURE 5-18   A typical leaf spring used on the rear of a pickup truck showing the plastic insulator between the leaves, which allows the spring to move without creating wear or noise.

LEAF SPRING

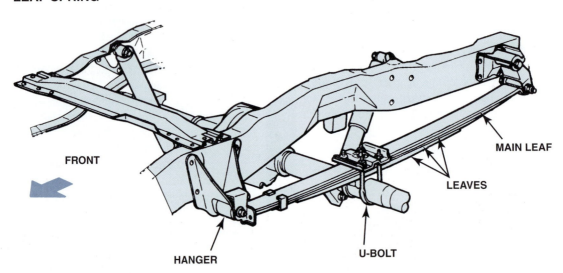

FIGURE 5-19   A typical leaf spring installation. The longest leaf, called the *main leaf*, attaches to the frame through a shackle and a hanger.

The shackles are necessary because as the spring hits a bump, the slightly curved spring (semi-elliptical) becomes longer and straighter, and the shackles allow for this rearward movement. **Rebound clips,** or spring alignment clips, help prevent the leaves from separating whenever the leaf spring is rebounding from hitting a bump or rise in the roadway. See Figure 5-22.

Single leaf steel springs, called **mono leaf,** are used on some vehicles. A single or mono leaf spring is usually tapered to produce a variable spring rate. Leaf springs are used for rear suspensions on cars and many light trucks. A variable rate can be accomplished with a leaf spring suspension by providing contacts on the mount that effectively shorten the spring once

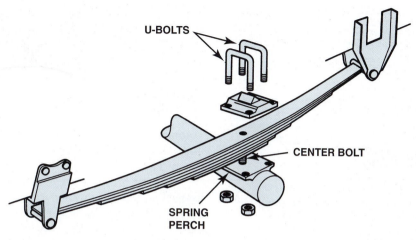

FIGURE 5-20   All multileaf springs use a center bolt to not only hold the leaves together but also help retain the leaf spring in the center of the spring perch.   *(Courtesy of Moog)*

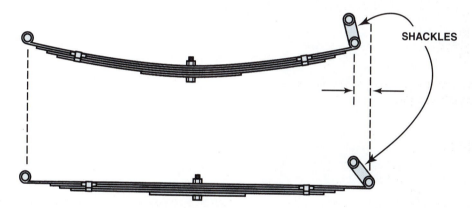

FIGURE 5-21   When a leaf spring is compressed, the spring flattens and becomes longer. The shackles allow for this lengthening.

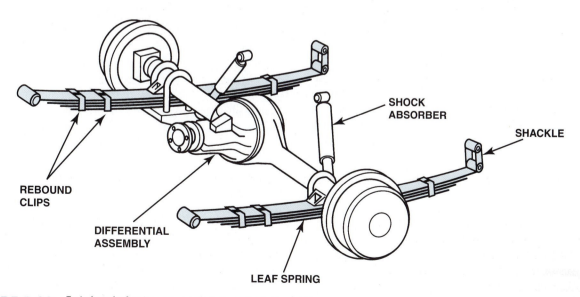

FIGURE 5-22   Typical rear leaf-spring suspension of a rear-wheel-drive vehicle.

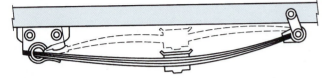

FIGURE 5-23 As the vehicle is loaded, the leaf spring contacts a section of the frame. This shortens the effective length of the spring, which makes it stiffer.

FIGURE 5-24 Many pickup trucks, vans, and sport utility vehicles (SUVs) use auxiliary leaf springs that contact the other leaves when the load is increased.

it is compressed to a certain point. This provides a smoother ride when the load is light and still provides a stiffer spring when the load is heavy. See Figure 5-23.

To provide additional load-carrying capacity, especially on trucks and vans, auxiliary or *helper* leaves are commonly used. This extra leaf becomes effective only when the vehicle is heavily loaded. See Figure 5-24.

Leaf springs are used on the front suspension of many four-wheel-drive trucks, especially medium and heavy trucks.

Composite Leaf Springs

Since the early 1980s, fiberglass-reinforced epoxy plastic **composite leaf springs** have been used on production vehicles. They save weight: An 8-pound spring can replace a conventional 40-pound steel leaf spring. The secret to making a strong plastic leaf spring is the glass fibers running continuously from one end of the spring to the other, and the use of 70% fiberglass with 30% epoxy composite. The single-leaf composite spring helps isolate road noise and vibrations. It is more efficient

than a multileaf spring because it eliminates the interleaf friction of the steel leaves and requires less space. See Figure 5-25.

Leaf spring rate increases when the thickness increases, and decreases as the length increases.

TORSION BARS

A **torsion bar** is a spring that is a long, *round*, hardened steel bar similar to a coil spring except that it is a *straight* bar. See Figure 5-26.

One end is attached to the lower control arm of a front suspension and the other end to the frame. When the wheels hit a bump, the bar twists and then untwists. General Motors pickup trucks use torsion-bar front suspension longitudinally. See Figure 5-27.

Many manufacturers of pickup trucks currently use torsion-bar-type suspensions, especially on their four-wheel-drive models. Torsion bars allow room for the front drive axle and constant velocity joint and still provide for strong suspension.

As with all automotive springs, spring action is controlled by the shock absorbers. Unlike other types of springs, torsion bars may be adjustable for correct ride height. See Figure 5-28.

Most torsion bars are labeled *left* or *right*, usually stamped into the end of the bars. The purpose of this designation is to make sure that the correct bar is installed on the original side of the vehicle. Torsion bars are manufactured without any built-in direction or preload. However, after being in a vehicle, the bar takes a set; reversing the side the torsion bar is used on causes the bar to be twisted in the opposite direction. Even though the bars are usually interchangeable, proper ride height can be accomplished even if the bars were installed on the side opposite from the original. But because the bar is being "worked" in the opposite direction, it can weaken and break. If a torsion bar breaks, the entire suspension collapses; this can cause severe vehicle damage, as well as a serious accident.

SUSPENSION PRINCIPLES

Suspensions use various links, arms, and joints to allow the wheels to move freely up and down; front suspensions also have to allow the front wheels to turn. All suspensions must provide for the following supports:

1. **Transverse (or side-to-side) wheel support.** As the wheels of the vehicle move up and down, the suspension must accommodate this movement and still keep the wheel from moving away from the vehicle or inward toward the center of the vehicle. See Figure 5-29. The control arm pivots on the vehicle frame. The wheels attach to a spindle that attaches to the ball joint at the end of the control arm. Transverse links are also called **lateral links.**
2. **Longitudinal (front-to-back) wheel support.** As the wheels of the vehicle move up and down, the suspension must allow for this movement and still keep the wheels

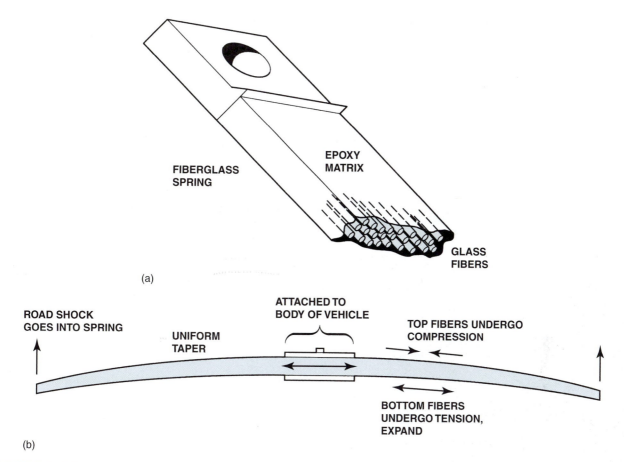

(a)

(b)

FIGURE 5-25   (a) A fiberglass spring is composed of long fibers locked together in an epoxy (resin) matrix. (b) When the spring compresses, the bottom of the spring expands and the top compresses.

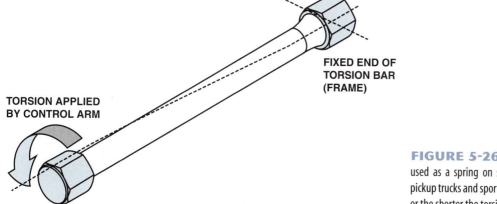

FIGURE 5-26   A torsion bar resists twisting and is used as a spring on some cars and many four-wheel-drive pickup trucks and sport utility vehicles. The larger the diameter, or the shorter the torsion bar, the stiffer the bar.

from moving backward whenever a bump is hit. Note in Figure 5-29 how the separation of the pivot points, where the control arm meets the frame, provides support to prevent front-to-back wheel movement.

At least two suspension links or arms are required in order to provide for freedom of movement up or down, and to *prevent* any in-out or forward-back movement. Some suspension designs use an additional member to control forward-back movement. See Figure 5-30.

The design of the suspension and the location of the suspension mounting points on the frame or body are critical to proper vehicle handling. Two very important design factors are called **anti-squat** and **anti-dive**.

FIGURE 5-27 Longitudinal torsion bars attach at the lower control arm at the front and at the frame at the rear of the bar. *(Courtesy of Dana Corporation)*

TORSION BAR

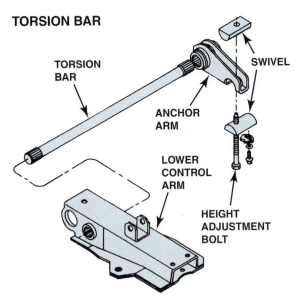

FIGURE 5-28 One end of the torsion bar attaches to the lower control arm and the other to an anchor arm that is adjustable.

1. **Anti-squat.** Anti-squat refers to the reaction of the body of a vehicle during acceleration. It is normal in most designs for the vehicle to squat down at the rear while accelerating. Most drivers feel comfortable feeling this reaction, even on front-wheel-drive vehicles. Anti-squat refers to the degree to which this normal force is neutralized. If 100% anti-squat were designed into the suspension system, the vehicle would remain level while accelerating.

2. **Anti-dive.** Anti-dive refers to the force that causes the front of the vehicle to drop down while braking. Some front-nose dive feels normal to most drivers. If 100% anti-dive were designed into a vehicle, it would remain perfectly level while braking.

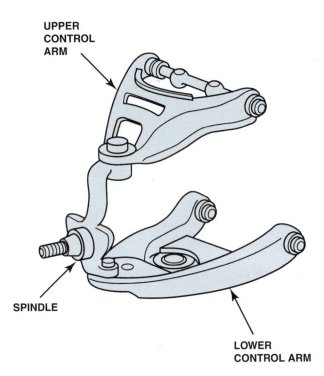

FIGURE 5-29 The spindle supports the wheels and attaches to the control arm with ball-and-socket joints called ball joints. The control arm attaches to the frame of the vehicle through rubber bushings to help isolate noise and vibration between the road and the body. *(Courtesy of Moog)*

The service technician cannot, and should not, attempt to change anti-squat or anti-dive characteristics built into the design of the vehicle. However, if the customer notices more squat or dive than normal, then the technician should carefully inspect all suspension components, especially those mounting points to the frame or body.

STEERING KNUCKLES

A **steering knuckle** is hard to classify either as part of the suspension or as part of the wheel. A knuckle serves two purposes:

- To join the suspension to the wheel
- To provide pivot points between the suspension and wheel

Knuckles are used with independent suspensions and at the wheels that steer the vehicle. See Figure 5-31.

The only knuckle that uses a **kingpin** is a steering knuckle on an I-beam or twin I-beam front suspension. See Figure 5-32. A kingpin steering knuckle keeps the wheel rigid in relation to the I-beam during up-and-down wheel movement, but rotates around the steering axis to turn the wheels

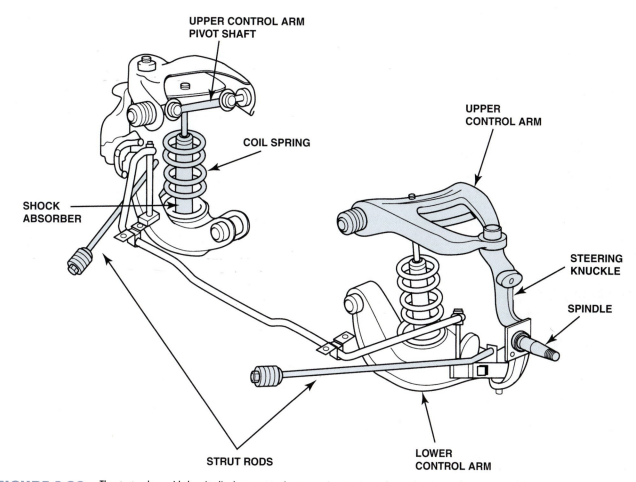

UPPER CONTROL ARM
PIVOT SHAFT

UPPER
CONTROL ARM

COIL SPRING

SHOCK
ABSORBER

STEERING
KNUCKLE

SPINDLE

STRUT RODS

LOWER
CONTROL ARM

FIGURE 5-30   The strut rods provide longitudinal support to the suspension to prevent forward or rearward movement of the control arms.

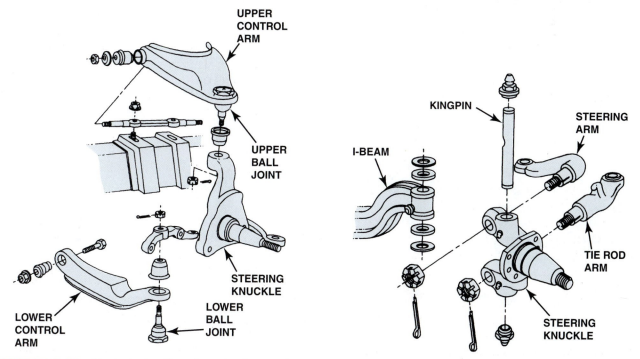

UPPER
CONTROL
ARM

UPPER
BALL
JOINT

STEERING
KNUCKLE

LOWER
BALL
JOINT

LOWER
CONTROL
ARM

KINGPIN

STEERING
ARM

I-BEAM

TIE ROD
ARM

STEERING
KNUCKLE

FIGURE 5-31   The steering knuckle used on a short/long-arm front suspension.

FIGURE 5-32   A kingpin is a steel shaft or pin that joins the steering knuckle to the suspension and allows the steering knuckle to pivot.

left and right. The steering axis is the vertical center of the kingpin.

CONTROL ARMS

A **control arm** is a suspension link that connects a knuckle or wheel flange to the frame. One end of a control arm attaches to the knuckle or wheel flange, generally with either a ball joint or bushing. The opposite end of the arm, which attaches to a frame member, usually pivots on a bushing. See Figure 5-33. The end attached to the frame must pivot to allow the axle or knuckle to travel vertically.

BALL JOINTS

Ball joints are actually ball-and-socket joints, similar to the joints in a person's shoulder. Ball joints allow the front wheels to move up and down, as well as side to side (for steering).

A vehicle can be equipped with coil springs, mounted either above the upper control arm *or* on the lower control arm. See Figure 5-34.

If the coil spring is attached to the top of the upper control arm, then the upper ball joint is carrying the weight of the vehicle and is called the **load-carrying ball joint.** The lower ball joint is called the **non-load-carrying,** or *follower*, **ball joint**. See Figure 5-35.

If the coil spring is attached to the lower control arm, then the lower ball joint is the load-carrying ball joint and the upper joint is the follower ball joint. See Figure 5-36.

If a torsion-bar-type spring is used, the lower ball joint is a load-carrying joint because the torsion bar is attached to the lower control arm on most vehicles that use torsion bars.

Ball Joint Design

There are two basic designs of ball joints: compression loaded and tension loaded. If the control arm rests on the steering knuckle, the ball joint is *compressed* into the control arm by the weight of the vehicle. If the knuckle rests on the control arm, the weight of the vehicle tends to pull the ball joint back into the control arm by *tension*. The type used is determined by the chassis design engineer, and the service technician cannot change the type of ball joint used for a particular application. See Figure 5-37.

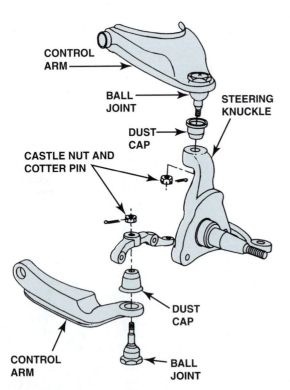

FIGURE 5-33 Control arms are used to connect the steering knuckle to the frame or body of the vehicle and provide the structural support for the suspension system.

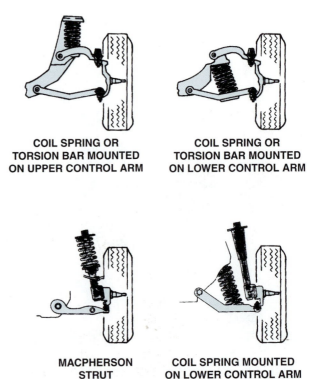

FIGURE 5-34 Ball joints provide the freedom of movement necessary for steering and suspension movements. *(Courtesy of Dana Corporation)*

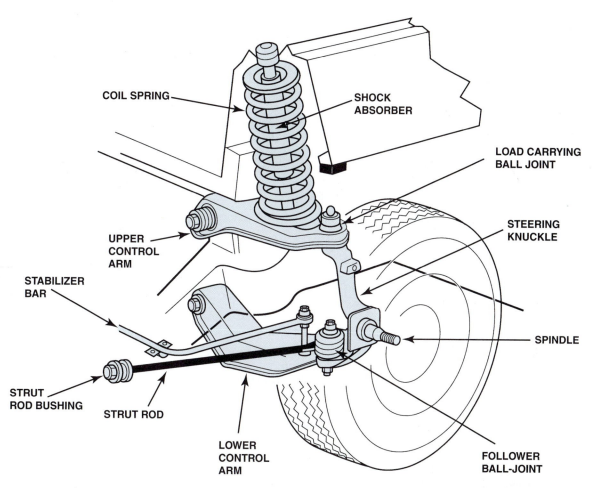

FIGURE 5-35   The upper ball joint is load carrying in this type of suspension because the weight of the vehicle is applied through the spring, upper control arm, and ball joint to the wheel. The lower control arm is a lateral link, and the lower ball joint is called is called a follower ball joint.

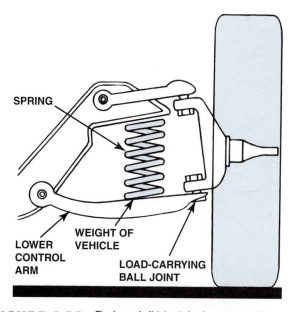

FIGURE 5-36   The lower ball joint is load carrying in this type of suspension because the weight of the vehicle is applied through the spring, lower control arm, and ball joint to the wheel.

A specific amount of stud-turning resistance is built into each ball joint to stabilize steering. A ball joint that does not support the weight of the vehicle and acts as a suspension pivot is often called a follower ball joint or a friction ball joint. The load-carrying (weight-carrying) ball joint is subjected to the greatest amount of wear and is the most frequently replaced.

STRUT RODS

Some vehicles are equipped with round steel rods that are attached between the lower control arm at one end and the frame of the vehicle with rubber bushings, called strut rod bushings, at the other end. The purpose of these **strut rods** is to provide forward/backward support to the control arms. Strut rods are used on vehicles equipped with MacPherson struts and many short/long-arm-type suspensions. The bushings are very important in maintaining proper wheel alignment while providing the necessary up-and-down movement of the control arms during suspension travel. Strut rods

LOAD-CARRYING BALL JOINTS

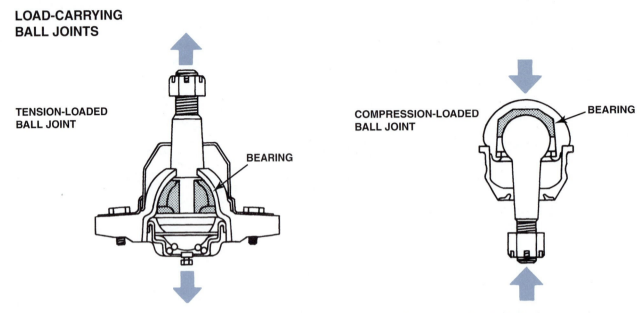

TENSION-LOADED
BALL JOINT

BEARING

COMPRESSION-LOADED
BALL JOINT

BEARING

FIGURE 5-37   All ball joints, whether tension or compression loaded, have a bearing surface between the ball stud and socket.

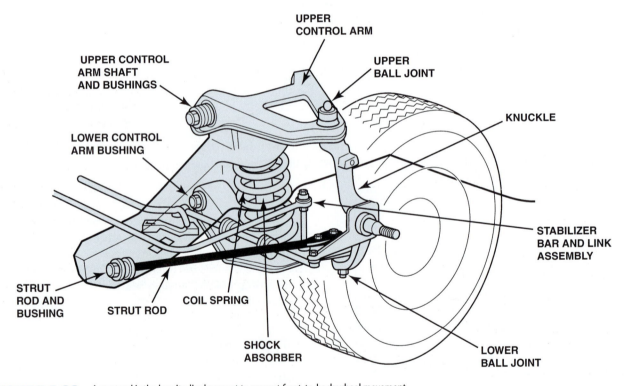

UPPER
CONTROL ARM

UPPER CONTROL
ARM SHAFT
AND BUSHINGS

UPPER
BALL JOINT

KNUCKLE

LOWER CONTROL
ARM BUSHING

STABILIZER
BAR AND LINK
ASSEMBLY

STRUT
ROD AND
BUSHING

STRUT ROD

COIL SPRING

SHOCK
ABSORBER

LOWER
BALL JOINT

FIGURE 5-38   A strut rod is the longitudinal support to prevent front-to-back wheel movement.

prevent lower control arm movement back and forth during braking. See Figure 5-38.

Strut rods are also called tension or compression rods or simply TC rods. Tension rods attach in *front* of the wheels to the body or frame where the rod is being pulled in tension.

Compression rods attach to the body or frame *behind* the wheels where the rod is being pushed or compressed. Some vehicle manufacturers call the strut rod a drag rod because it is attached in front of the wheels, and therefore acts on the lower control arm as if to drag the wheels behind their attachment points.

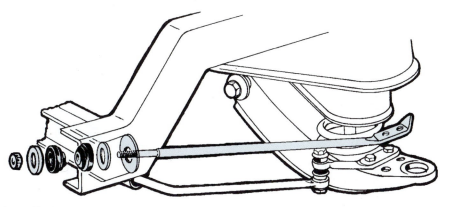

FIGURE 5-39   Strut rod bushings insulate the steel bar from the vehicle frame or body.   *(Courtesy of Moog)*

The bushings are replaceable by removing a nut on the frame end of the strut rod. See Figure 5-39. If a strut rod has a nut on *both* sides of the bushings, then the strut rod is used to adjust *caster.* See Chapters 15 and 16 for information on caster and other alignment angles.

STABILIZER BARS

Most cars and trucks are equipped with a **stabilizer bar** on the front suspension, which is a round, hardened steel bar (usually SAE 4560 or 4340 steel) attached to both lower control arms with bolts and rubber bushing washers called stabilizer bar bushings. See Figure 5-40.

A stabilizer bar is also called an anti-sway bar (sway bar) or anti-roll bar (roll bar). A stabilizer bar operates by *twisting* the bar if one side of the vehicle moves up or down in relation to the other side, such as during cornering, hitting bumps, or driving over uneven road surfaces. See Figure 5-41.

The purpose of the stabilizer bar is to prevent excessive body roll while cornering and to add to stability while driving over rough road surfaces. The stabilizer bar is also used as a longitudinal (front/back) support to the lower control arm on many vehicles equipped with MacPherson struts. The effective force of a stabilizer bar is increased with the diameter of the bar. Therefore, optional suspensions often include larger-diameter stabilizer bars and bushings.

Stabilizer links connect the ends of the stabilizer bar to the lower control arm. See Figures 5-42 and 5-43. Careful inspection of the stabilizer bar links is important. Links are commonly found to be defective (cracked rubber washers or broken spacer bolts) because of the great amount of force

that is transmitted through the links and the bushings. Defective links and/or bushings can cause unsafe vehicle handling and noise.

SHOCK ABSORBERS

Shock absorbers are used on all conventional suspension systems to dampen and control the motion of the vehicle's springs. Without shock absorbers (dampers), the vehicle would continue to bounce after hitting bumps. See Figure 5-44.

The major purpose of any shock or strut is to control ride and handling. Standard shock absorbers *do not* support the weight of a vehicle. *The springs support the weight of the vehicle; the shock absorbers control the actions and reactions of the springs.* Shock absorbers are also called dampers.

Most shock absorbers are *direct acting* because they are connected directly between the vehicle frame or body and the axles. See Figures 5-45 and 5-46.

As a wheel rolls over a bump, the wheel moves toward the body and compresses the spring(s) of the vehicle. As the spring compresses, it stores energy. The spring then releases this stored energy, causing the body of the vehicle to rise (rebound). See Figure 5-47.

After the energy in the spring is used up, the body starts downward, causing the spring to compress. Without shock absorbers, the energy released from the spring would be very rapid and violent. The shock absorber helps dampen the rapid up-and-down movement of the vehicle springs by converting energy of movement into heat by forcing hydraulic fluid through small holes inside the shock absorber.

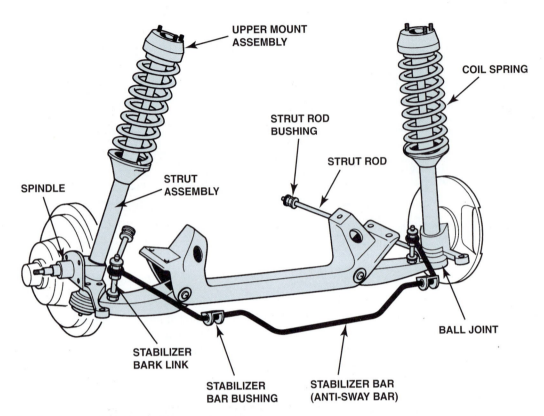

FIGURE 5-40   Typical stabilizer bar installation.

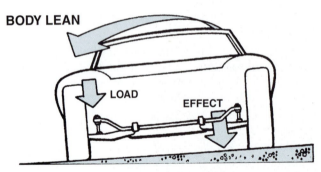

FIGURE 5-41   As the body of the vehicle leans, the stabilizer bar is twisted. The force exerted by the stabilizer bar counteracts the body lean. *(Courtesy of Moog)*

Shock Absorber Operation

The hydraulic shock absorber operates on the principle of fluid being forced through a small opening (orifice). See Figures 5-48 and 5-49. Besides small openings, pressure relief valves are built into most shock absorbers to control vehicle ride under all operating conditions. The greater the pressure drop of the fluid inside the shock and the greater the amount of fluid moved through the orifice, the greater the amount of dampening; therefore, larger shock absorbers can usually provide better dampening than smaller units.

Gas-Charged Shocks

Most shock absorbers on new vehicles are gas charged. Pressurizing the oil inside the shock absorber helps smooth the ride over rough roads. This pressure helps prevent air pockets from forming in the shock absorber oil as it passes through the small passages in the shock. After the oil is forced through small passages, the pressure drops and the oil expands. As the oil expands, bubbles are created. The oil becomes foamy. This air-filled oil does not effectively provide dampening. The result of all of this aeration (air being mixed with the oil) is lack of dampening and a harsh ride.

The use of higher-pressure radial tires and lighter vehicle weight has created the need for more effective shock absorbers. To meet this need, shock absorber design engineers use a pressurized gas that does not react chemically with the oil in the shock. If a substance does not react with any other

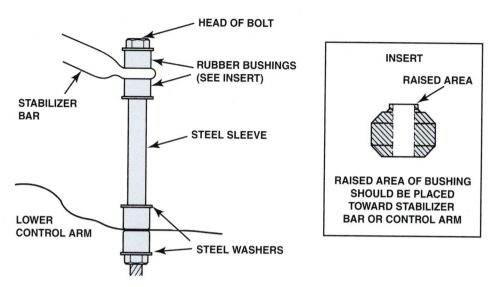

FIGURE 5-42   Stabilizer bar links are sold as a kit consisting of the long bolt with steel sleeve and rubber bushings. Steel washers are used on both sides of the rubber bushings as shown.

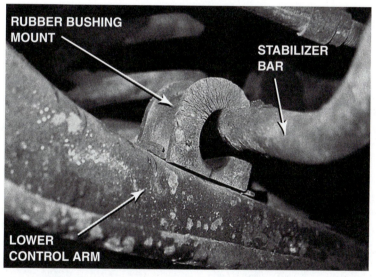

FIGURE 5-43   Notice how the stabilizer bar pulls down on the mounting bushing when the vehicle is hoisted off the ground, allowing the front suspension to drop down. These bushings are a common source of noise, especially when cold. Lubricating the bushings with paste silicone grease often cures the noise.

substances, it is called *inert*. The gas most often used is nitrogen, which is about 78% of our atmosphere. Typical gas-charged shocks are pressurized with 130 to 150 psi (900 to 1,030 kPa) to aid in both handling and ride control. Some shocks use higher pressures, but the higher the pressure, the greater the possibility of leaks and the harsher the ride.

Some gas-charged shock absorbers use a single tube that contains two pistons that separate the high-pressure gas from the working fluid. Single-tube shocks are also called monotube or DeCarbon after the French inventor of the principle and manufacturer of suspension components. See Figure 5-50.

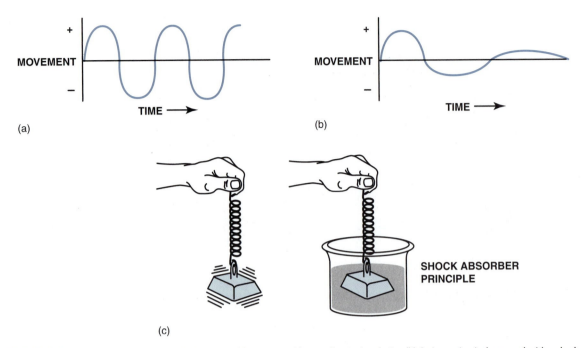

(a)

(b)

(c)

FIGURE 5-44   (a) Movement of the vehicle is supported by springs without a damponing device. (b) Spring action is dampened with a shock absorber. (c) The function of any shock absorber is to dampen the movement or action of a spring, similar to using a liquid to control the movement of a weight on a spring.

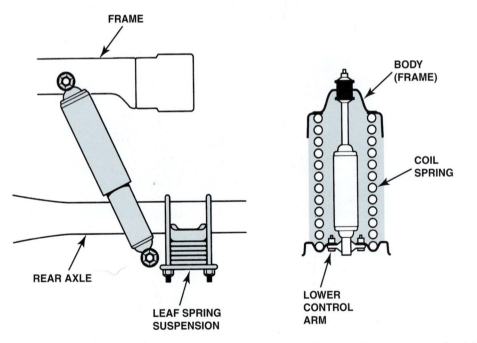

FIGURE 5-45   Shock absorbers work best when mounted as close to the spring as possible. Shock absorbers that are mounted straight up and down offer the most dampening.

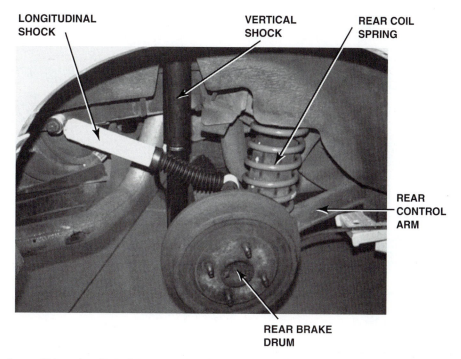

LONGITUDINAL SHOCK

VERTICAL SHOCK

REAR COIL SPRING

REAR CONTROL ARM

REAR BRAKE DRUM

FIGURE 5-46   Some vehicles such as this Ford Mustang use four shock absorbers on the rear suspension. The vertical shock absorbers control vertical body movement and react with the rear coil springs. The longitudinal shocks help control the rear axle during acceleration and deceleration.

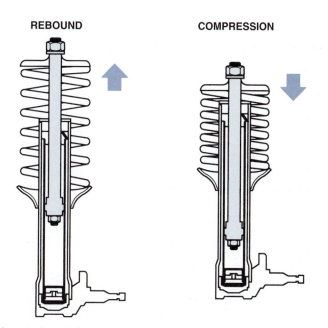

REBOUND

COMPRESSION

FIGURE 5-47   When a vehicle hits a bump in the road, the suspension moves upward. This is called compression. Rebound is when the spring (coil, torsion bar, or leaf) returns to its original position.

142   CHAPTER 5

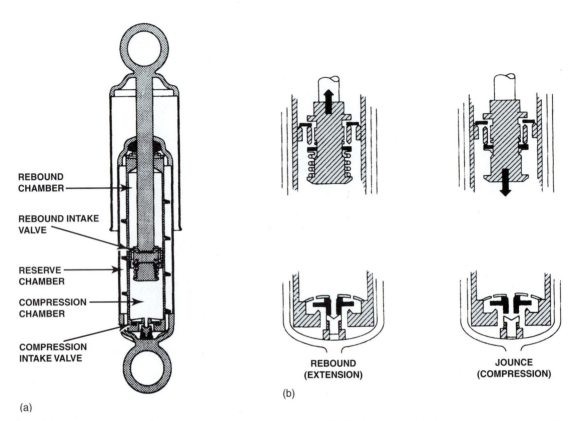

FIGURE 5-48   (a) A cutaway drawing of a typical double-tube shock absorber. (b) Notice the position of the intake and compression valve during rebound (extension) and compression.

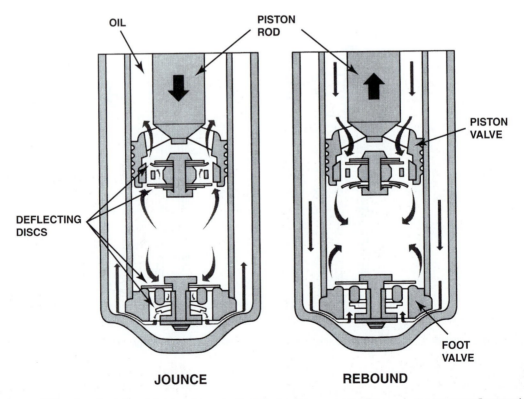

FIGURE 5-49   Oil flow through a deflected disc-type piston valve. The deflecting disc can react rapidly to suspension movement. For example, if a large bump is hit at high speed, the disc can deflect completely and allow the suspension to reach its maximum jounce distance while maintaining a controlled rate of movement.

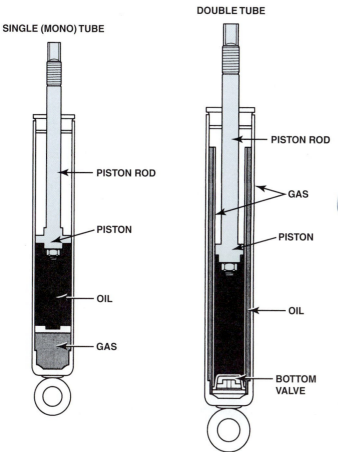

SINGLE (MONO) TUBE

- PISTON ROD
- PISTON
- OIL
- GAS

DOUBLE TUBE

- PISTON ROD
- GAS
- PISTON
- OIL
- BOTTOM VALVE

FIGURE 5-50 Gas-charged shock absorbers are manufactured with a double-tube design similar to conventional shock absorbers and with a single or monotube design.

? FREQUENTLY ASKED QUESTION

WHAT ARE REMOTE RESERVOIR SHOCKS?

Remote reservoir shock absorbers are units designed for heavy-duty use that use a separate container for the working fluid. See Figure 5-51.

The purpose of the remote fluid reservoir is to keep the temperature of the fluid stable, which helps the shock absorber provide consistent dampening under all conditions.

FIGURE 5-51 The shock absorber is on the right and the fluid reservoir for the shock is on the left.

Air Shocks/Struts

Air-inflatable shock absorbers or struts are used in the rear of vehicles to provide proper vehicle ride height while carrying heavy loads. Many air shock/strut units are original equipment. They are often combined with a built-in air compressor and ride height sensor(s) to provide automatic ride height control.

Air-inflatable shocks are standard shock absorbers with an air chamber with a rubber bag built into the dust cover (top) of the shock. See Figure 5-52.

Air pressure is used to inflate the bag, which raises the installed height of the shock. As the shock increases in height, the rear of the vehicle is raised. Typical maximum air pressure in air shocks ranges from 90 to 150 psi (620 to 1,030 kPa). As the air pressure increases in the air-inflatable reservoir of the shock, the stiffness of the suspension increases. This additional stiffness is due to the shock taking weight from the spring, and therefore the air in the air shock becomes an air spring. Now, with two springs to support the vehicle, the spring rate increases and a harsher ride often results. *It is important that the load capacity of the vehicle not be exceeded or serious damage can occur to the vehicle's springs, axles, bearings, and shock support mounts.*

AIR SHOCK ABSORBER

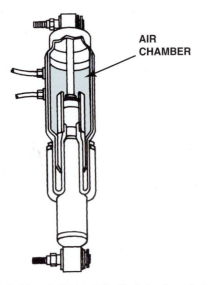

AIR CHAMBER

FIGURE 5-52 A rubber tube forms an inflatable air chamber at the top of an air shock. The higher the air pressure in the chamber, the stiffer the shock.

Air Springs

Some electronically controlled suspension systems use air springs. A basic **air spring** consists of a rubber air chamber, generally closed at the bottom by a piston fitted into a control arm, or by a strut shock absorber. See Figure 5-53.

Electronically controlled suspension systems that use air springs as the only springs are available on some Hummer, and many Ford, Mercury and Lincoln vehicles.

Some air springs are in effect auxiliary springs inside a coil-spring strut. In these designs, the coil spring supports the weight of the vehicle, while the air spring raises or lowers the body to adjust ride height according to load. See Figure 5-54.

Coil-Over Shocks

A coil-over shock absorber uses the force of an external coil spring to boost the performance of the basic shock absorber. See

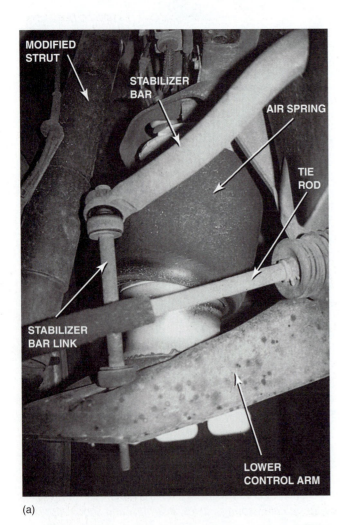

MODIFIED STRUT

STABILIZER BAR

AIR SPRING

TIE ROD

STABILIZER BAR LINK

LOWER CONTROL ARM

(a)

AIR SPRING

REAR AXLE HOUSING

(b)

FIGURE 5-53 (a) The front suspension of a Lincoln with an air-spring suspension. (b) The rear suspension of the same Lincoln.

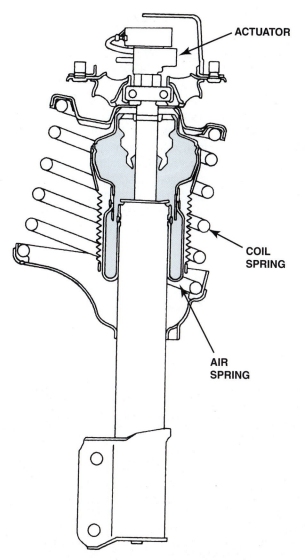

FIGURE 5-54   Some air springs are auxiliary units to the coil spring and are used to control ride height while the coil spring is the weight-bearing unit.

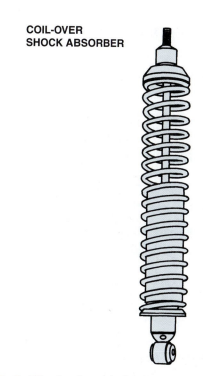

FIGURE 5-55   A coil-over shock is a standard hydraulic shock absorber with a coil spring wrapped around it to increase stiffness and/or take some of the carrying weight off of the springs.

MacPherson Struts

The MacPherson strut, which is named after Earle S. MacPherson, who developed the suspension design in the late 1940s and patented it in 1953, is the most commonly used type. A MacPherson strut includes the suspension spring—a coil spring that surrounds the strut casing—so that it transfers the weight of the body to the wheel. See Figure 5-56.

A MacPherson strut typically incorporates an upper and a lower spring seat, a shock absorber mount and dust cap, a dust cover for the piston rod, and a bump stop. The upper mount secures the upper spring seat to the strut tower. A rubber bushing at the top of the strut absorbs vibrations. A bearing on a front-wheel strut allows it to rotate on the vertical steering axis without rubbing against the strut tower when the steering knuckle turns. The lower spring seat is attached to the strut casing.

Modified Struts

Unlike a MacPherson unit, a modified strut does not include a spring as part of the assembly and is used in the front on some vehicles and on the rear of others. See Figure 5-57. Most modified strut rear suspensions use coil springs mounted on the lower control arm.

Figure 5-55. The spring usually extends from the upper shock mount to a seat on the lower portion of the cylinder. The spring rate added to the hydraulic resistance makes the shock stiffer.

STRUTS

A **strut** is a sturdy shock absorber that is also a structural component of the suspension. A strut is a suspension link as well as a shock absorber. The casing of a strut must be strong and rigid to function as a suspension link. The shock absorber assembles inside the casing of a strut, and may be either a removable cartridge or an integral part of the strut.

BUMP STOPS

All suspension systems have a limit of travel. If the vehicle hits a large bump in the road, the wheels are forced upward toward the vehicle with tremendous force. This force is absorbed by the springs of the suspension system. If the bump is large enough, the suspension is compressed to its mechanical limit. Instead of allowing the metal components of the suspension to hit the frame or body of the vehicle, a rubber or foam bumper is used to absorb and isolate the suspension from the frame or body. See Figure 5-58.

These bumpers are called **bump stops,** suspension bumpers, strike-out bumpers, or jounce bumpers. *Jounce* means jolt, or to cause to bounce or move up and down. Bumpers are made from rubber or microcellular urethane. Urethane is a high-strength material with good resistance to wear and tear as well as good chemical resistance to most fluids. Forming urethane foam with small, regular air cells makes the material ideal for jounce bumpers.

Damaged suspension-limiting bump stops can be caused by the following:

1. Sagging springs that result in lower-than-normal ride (trim) height
2. Worn or defective shock absorbers

Most suspensions also use a rubber or foam stop to limit the downward travel of the suspension during rebound. The rebound stop also prevents metal-to-metal contact of the suspension on the frame when the vehicle is on a body-contact-type hoist and the wheels are allowed to hang or droop down. Some stops are built into the shock absorber or strut.

MACPHERSON STRUT

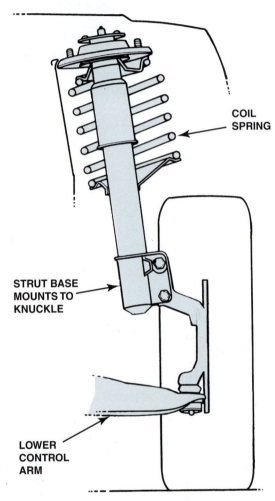

COIL SPRING

STRUT BASE MOUNTS TO KNUCKLE

LOWER CONTROL ARM

FIGURE 5-56   A strut is a structural part of the suspension and includes the spring and shock absorber in one assembly.

MODIFIED STRUT

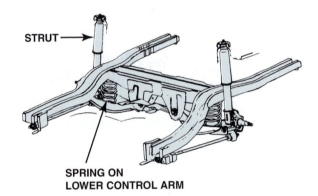

STRUT

SPRING ON LOWER CONTROL ARM

FIGURE 5-57   A modified strut used on the rear suspension; it is part of the structural part of the assembly.

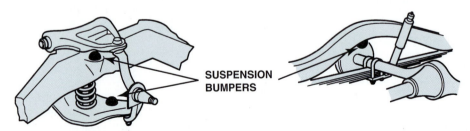

SUSPENSION BUMPERS

FIGURE 5-58   Suspension bumpers are used on all suspension systems to prevent metal-to-metal contact between the suspension and the frame or body of the vehicle when the suspension "bottoms out" over large bumps or dips in the road.   *(Courtesy of Moog)*

SUMMARY

1. The lighter the wheel/tire combination, the lower the unsprung weight and the better the ride and handling of the vehicle.
2. All springs—including the coil, leaf, and torsion bar types—share Hooke's Law, which states that the force exerted by the spring is directly proportional to the amount the spring is deflected.
3. All springs are similar to torsion bars. As the torsion bar becomes longer or smaller in diameter, it becomes easier to twist. If a coil spring is cut, the remaining spring is shorter, yet stiffer.
4. Ball joints attach to control arms and allow the front wheels to move up and down, as well as turn.
5. Suspension designs include a straight or solid-axle, two-control-arm-type called an SLA or a MacPherson strut.
6. All shock absorbers dampen the motion of the suspension to control ride and handling.

REVIEW QUESTIONS

1. List the types of suspensions and name their component parts.
2. Explain Hooke's Law.
3. Describe the purpose and function of a stabilizer bar.
4. Explain the difference between a load-carrying and a friction ball joint.

CHAPTER QUIZ

1. The spring rate of a spring is measured in units of _____.
   a. lb per inch
   b. ft-lb
   c. psi
   d. in.-lb

2. Two technicians are discussing torsion bars. Technician A says that many torsion bars are adjustable to allow for ride height adjustment. Technician B says that torsion bars are usually marked left and right and should not be switched side to side. Which technician is correct?
   a. Technician A only
   b. Technician B only
   c. Both Technicians A and B
   d. Neither Technician A nor B

3. A vehicle makes a loud noise while traveling over bumpy sections of road. Technician A says that worn or deteriorated control arm bushings could be the cause. Technician B says that worn or deteriorated strut rod bushings could be the cause. Which technician is correct?
   a. Technician A only
   b. Technician B only
   c. Both Technicians A and B
   d. Neither Technician A nor B

4. Two technicians are discussing MacPherson struts. Technician A says that in most applications the entire strut assembly rotates when the front wheels are turned. Technician B says a typical MacPherson strut suspension system uses only one control arm and one ball joint per side. Which technician is correct?
   a. Technician A only
   b. Technician B only
   c. Both Technicians A and B
   d. Neither Technician A nor B

5. Technician A says that regular replacement shock absorbers will raise the rear of a vehicle that is sagging down. Technician B says that replacement springs will be required to restore the proper ride height. Which technician is correct?

   a. Technician A only

   b. Technician B only

   c. Both Technicians A and B

   d. Neither Technician A nor B

6. A vehicle used for 24-hour-a-day security was found to have damaged suspension-limiting rubber jounce bumpers. Technician A says sagging springs could be the cause. Technician B says defective or worn shock absorbers could be the cause. Which technician is correct?

   a. Technician A only

   b. Technician B only

   c. Both Technicians A and B

   d. Neither Technician A nor B

7. The part of many rear suspension systems that controls side-to-side movement is called the _____.

   a. Rear control arm

   b. Track rod or panhard rod

   c. Stabilizer bar

   d. Trailing arm

8. Two technicians are discussing air shocks. Technician A says that air is forced through small holes to dampen the ride. Technician B says that air shocks are conventional hydraulic shock absorbers with an airbag to control vehicle ride height. Which technician is correct?

   a. Technician A only

   b. Technician B only

   c. Both Technicians A and B

   d. Neither Technician A nor B

9. The owner of a pickup truck wants to cut the coil springs to lower the vehicle. Technician A says that the ride will be harsher than normal if the springs are cut. Technician B says that the springs could be damaged, especially if a cutting torch is used to cut the springs. Which technician is correct?

   a. Technician A only

   b. Technician B only

   c. Both Technicians A and B

   d. Neither Technician A nor B

10. A MacPherson strut is a structural part of the vehicle.

   a. True

   b. False

CHAPTER **6**

FRONT SUSPENSION AND SERVICE

OBJECTIVES

After studying Chapter 6, the reader should be able to:

1. Prepare for the Suspension and Steering (A4) ASE certification test content area "B" (Suspension System Diagnosis and Repair).
2. Explain how to perform a road test, a dry park test, a visual inspection, and a bounce test.
3. Discuss the procedures for testing load-carrying and follower-type ball joints.
4. Describe ball joint replacement procedures.
5. List the steps required to replace control arm and stabilizer bar bushings.
6. Explain routine service procedures of the suspension system.

KEY TERMS

A-arm (p. 151)
Cow Catcher (p. 170)
Cuppy Tire Wear (p. 167)
Dry Park Test (p. 156)
Durometer (p. 175)
Indicator Ball Joints (p. 158)
Kingpin (p. 150)

Pinch Bolt (p. 161)
Radius Rod (p. 150)
SLA (p. 151)
Steering Knuckle (p. 150)
Strut Suspension (p. 153)
Twin I-beam (p. 150)

FRONT SUSPENSION TYPES

Solid Axles

Early cars and trucks used a solid (or *straight*) front axle to support the front wheels. See Figure 6-1.

A solid-axle front suspension is very strong and is still being used in the manufacture of medium and heavy trucks. The main disadvantage of solid-axle design is its lack of ride quality. When one wheel hits a bump or dip in the road, the forces are transferred through the axle to the opposite wheel. Solid axles are currently used in the rear of most vehicles.

Kingpins

At the end of many solid I-beam or tube axles are **kingpins** that allow the front wheels to rotate for steering. Kingpins are hardened steel pins that attach the steering knuckle to the front axle, allowing the front wheels to move for steering. Kingpins usually have grease fittings to lubricate the kingpin bushings. Failure to keep these bushings lubricated with chassis grease can cause wear and freeplay or can cause the pins to become galled (seized or frozen), resulting in hard steering and/or loud noise while turning. See Figure 6-2.

Twin I-Beams

A **twin I-beam** front suspension was used for over 30 years on Ford pickup trucks and vans, beginning in the mid-1960s. Strong steel twin beams that cross provide independent front suspension operation with the strength of a solid front axle.

Early versions of the twin I-beam systems used kingpins, while later models used ball joints to support the **steering knuckle** and spindle. Coil springs are usually used on twin I-beam suspensions, even though the original design and patent used leaf springs. See Figure 6-3.

To control longitudinal (front-to-back) support, a **radius rod** is attached to each beam and is anchored to the frame of the truck using rubber bushings. These bushings allow the front axle to move up and down while still insulating road noise and vibration from the frame and body.

TECH TIP

RADIUS ROD BUSHING NOISE

When the radius rod bushing on a Ford truck or van deteriorates, the most common complaint from the driver is noise. See Figure 6-4 on page 152. Besides causing tire wear, worn or defective radius rod bushing deterioration can cause the following:

1. A clicking sound when braking (it sounds as if the brake caliper may be loose).
2. A clunking noise when hitting bumps.

When the bushing deteriorates, the axles can move forward and backward with less control. Noise is the first sign that something is wrong. Without proper axle support, handling and cornering can also be affected.

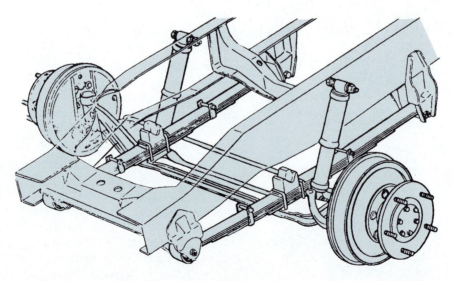

FIGURE 6-1   A solid-axle suspension with leaf springs. *(Courtesy of Dana Corporation)*

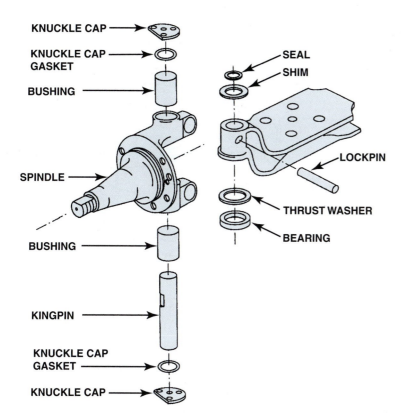

KNUCKLE CAP
KNUCKLE CAP GASKET
BUSHING
SEAL
SHIM
SPINDLE
LOCKPIN
BUSHING
THRUST WASHER
BEARING
KINGPIN
KNUCKLE CAP GASKET
KNUCKLE CAP

FIGURE 6-2 Typical kingpin used with a solid axle. *(Courtesy of Dana Corporation)*

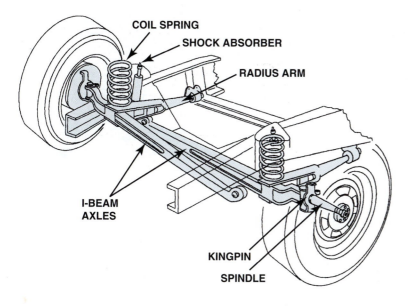

COIL SPRING
SHOCK ABSORBER
RADIUS ARM
I-BEAM AXLES
KINGPIN
SPINDLE

FIGURE 6-3 Twin I-beam front suspension. *(Courtesy of Dana Corporation)*

SHORT/LONG-ARM SUSPENSIONS

The short/long-arm suspension uses a short upper control arm and a longer lower control arm and usually is referred to as the *SLA-type suspension*.

The two main links in a **short/long-arm (SLA)** suspension are the upper control arm and the lower control arm. The upper control arm is shorter than the lower one. See Figure 6-5. This type of suspension system goes by a variety of names, including unequal-arm suspension, double-wishbone suspension, or **A-arm** suspension. Unequal arm refers to the fact that the two arms are of different lengths, while double-wishbone

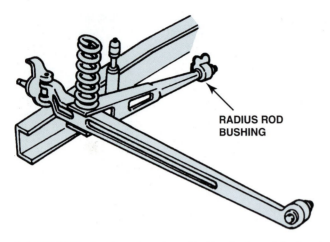

FIGURE 6-4 The rubber radius rod bushing absorbs road shocks and helps isolate road noise. *(Courtesy of Moog)*

SHORT/LONG-ARM (SLA) SUSPENSION

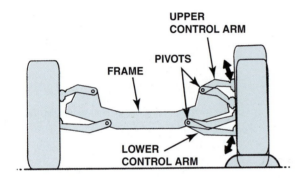

FIGURE 6-5 The upper control arm is shorter than the lower control arm on a short/long-arm (SLA) suspension.

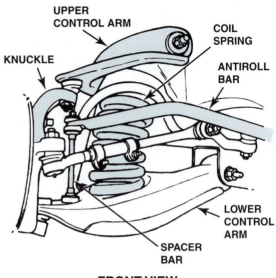

FRONT VIEW

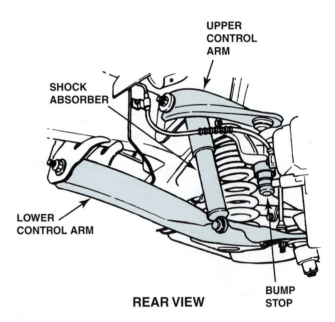

REAR VIEW

FIGURE 6-6 A typical SLA front suspension using coil springs.

and A-arm derive from the shape of the arms, which are frequently triangular with one mounting point at the knuckle and two at the frame. When an SLA suspension uses a straight, two-point lower control arm, there is almost always a strut rod that braces the lower arm against the frame. The strut rod can attach to the frame at a point either forward or to the rear of the control arm.

A strut rod, also called a *reaction rod,* provides support to the axle during braking and acceleration forces.

Using a strut rod provides triangulation between the wheel and the frame. *Triangulation* means that the front suspension has a three-point brace that resists forces from every direction, while still allowing the wheels to pivot on the steering axis.

Locating the coil spring on the lower control arm is the most common SLA-type suspension configuration. See Figure 6-6.

The upper control arm is A-shaped, with two mounting points at the frame side member and one at the steering

knuckle. The inboard ends of the arm attach to a pivot bar that is rigidly bolted to the frame, and the outboard end connects to the steering knuckle with a ball joint. Bushings between the inner arm mounts and the pivot bar allow the arm to swing vertically. The lower control arm is also A-shaped with two inboard pivot mounts and a ball joint connection at the knuckle. Bolts attach the inboard ends of the lower arm to brackets that extend from the bottom of the frame crossmember. Bushings on the inboard mounts allow the arm to pivot vertically.

The coil springs seat between the lower control arm and a bracket below the frame side member. The shock absorber attaches to the lower control arm and the frame side member.

SLA SUSPENSION - COIL SPRING ON UPPER ARM

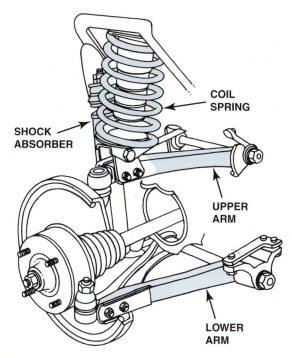

FIGURE 6-7 An SLA-type suspension with the coil spring placed on top of the upper control arm.

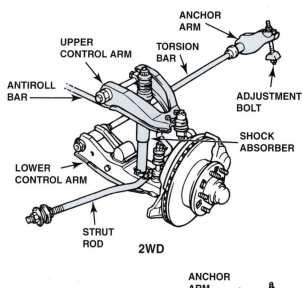

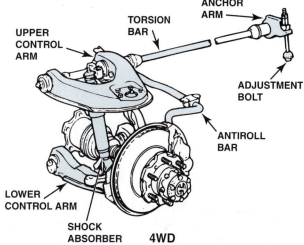

FIGURE 6-8 A torsion bar SLA suspension can use either the lower or the upper control arm.

In a typical coil spring on the upper control arm design, a portion of the unit-body wheel well is reinforced to withstand spring force and act as the upper spring seats. See Figure 6-7. Short/long-arm suspensions use longitudinal torsion bars, especially in trucks.

The forward end of the torsion bar has external splines and shares the splined socket of the torque arm with the control arm through a bolt. Because the torque arm is rigidly bolted to the control arm, motion transfers to the torsion bar whenever the control arm pivots. The torsion bar extends rearward from the control arm and connects to an anchor arm that attaches to a frame crossmember. The torsion bar splines to the anchor arm and the anchor arm is secured to the frame by a bolt and adjusting nut. The adjusting nut varies the spring force of the torsion bar to establish the ride height of the vehicle. See Figure 6-8.

STRUT SUSPENSION

Strut suspension can be of several types. A MacPherson strut includes the suspension spring that transfers the weight of the body to the wheel. A MacPherson strut is the main, load-carrying suspension spring. See Figure 6-9.

A MacPherson strut typically incorporates an upper and a lower spring seat, a shock absorber mount and dust cap, a dust cover for the piston rod, and a bump stop. The upper mount secures the upper spring seat to the strut tower. A rubber bushing at the top of the strut absorbs vibrations. In most applications, a bearing on a front-wheel strut allows it to rotate on the vertical steering axis without rubbing against the strut tower when the steering knuckle turns. The lower spring seat is attached to the strut casing. The piston rod dust cover is similar to the dust cover on a conventional shock absorber, and a bump stop at the top of the piston rod keeps the strut from bottoming out during suspension jounce.

A modified strut does not include a spring as part of the assembly. See Figure 6-10. A modified strut is used on the rear of some GM vehicles. Except for the lack of a spring and spring seats, the construction and function of a modified strut are basically the same as those of a MacPherson strut. When used on the front suspension, a modified strut also rotates on the steering axis when the wheels turn.

MACPHERSON STRUT SUSPENSION

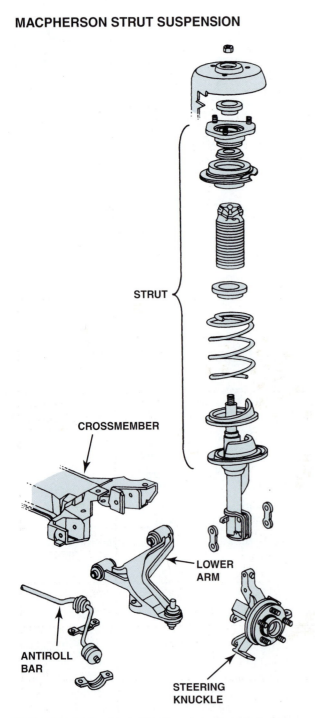

FIGURE 6-9 A typical MacPherson strut showing all of the components of the assembly.

A multilink front suspension uses two control arms as well as a structural strut assembly. This type of suspension is also called a strut/SLA or long spindle, short/long-arm suspension. See Figure 6-11 on page 156.

MODIFIED STRUT SUSPENSION

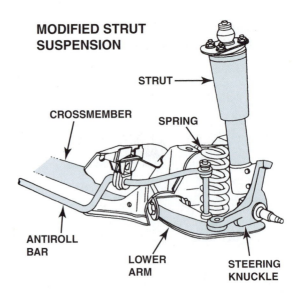

FIGURE 6-10 The modified strut front suspension is similar to a MacPherson strut suspension except that the coil spring is seated on the lower control arm and is not part of the strut assembly.

SERVICING THE SUSPENSION SYSTEM

Suspension systems are designed and manufactured to provide years of trouble-free service with a minimum amount of maintenance. In fact, the suspension system is often "invisible" or "transparent" to the driver because the vehicle rides and handles as expected. It is when the driver notices that the vehicle is not riding or handling as it did, or should, that a technician is asked to repair or align the vehicle and fix the problem.

The smart technician should always road test any vehicle before and after servicing (see Tech Tip for details). *The purpose of any diagnosis is to eliminate known good components.* (See the suspension diagnostic chart for a list of components that can cause the problem or customer complaint.)

ROAD TEST DIAGNOSIS

If possible, perform a road test of the vehicle with the owner of the vehicle. It is also helpful to have the owner drive the vehicle. While driving, try to determine when and where the noise or problem occurs, such as the following:

1. In cold or warm weather
2. With cold or warm engine/vehicle
3. While turning, left only, right only

Suspension Problem Diagnosis Chart

Item or System to Check	Concern/Problem					
	Noise	Instability/Wander	Pull to One Side	Excessive Steering Play	Hard Steering	Shimmy
Tires/Wheels	Road/tire noise	Low/uneven air pressure	Low/uneven air pressure, mismatched tire sizes	Low/uneven air pressure	Low/uneven air pressure	Wheel out of balance/ uneven tire wear/overworn tires
Shock Absorbers (Struts)	Loose/worn mounts/ bushings	Loose/worn mounts/bushings, worn/damaged struts/shock absorbers	Loose/worn mounts/bushings		Loose/worn mounts/bushings on strut assemblies	Worn/damaged struts/shock absorbers
Strut Rods (If Equipped)	Loose/worn mounts/ bushings	Loose/worn mounts/bushings	Loose/worn mounts/bushings			Loose/worn mounts/bushings
Springs	Brakes damaged	Brakes damaged	Brakes damaged, especially rear			
Control Arms	Steering knuckle contacting control arm stop, worn/ damaged mounts/ bushings	Worn/damaged mounts/bushings	Worn/damaged mounts/bushings		Worn/damaged mounts/bushings	Worn/damaged mounts/bushings
Steering System	Component wear/damage	Component wear/damage	Component wear/damage	Component wear/ damage	Component wear/damage	Component wear/damage
Wheel Alignment		Front and rear, especially caster	Front, camber and caster	Front alignment	Front, especially caster	Front, especially caster
Wheel Bearings	Front-wheel bearings	Loose/worn (front and rear)	Loose/worn (front and rear)	Loose/worn (front and rear)		Loose/worn (front and rear)
Brake System			Stuck caliper/slide			
Other					Ball joint lubrication	Loose/worn friction ball joints

Caution: More than one factor may be the cause of a problem. Be sure to inspect all suspension components, and repair all parts that are worn or damaged. Failure to do so may allow the problem to reoccur and cause premature failure of other suspension components.

STRUT/SLA SUSPENSION

MAZDA

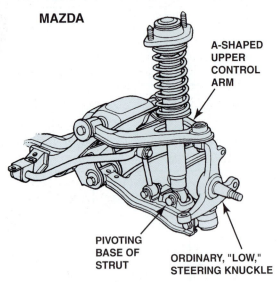

A-SHAPED UPPER CONTROL ARM

PIVOTING BASE OF STRUT

ORDINARY, "LOW," STEERING KNUCKLE

HONDA

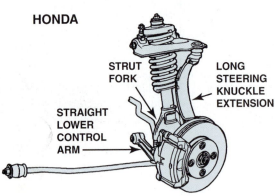

STRUT FORK

LONG STEERING KNUCKLE EXTENSION

STRAIGHT LOWER CONTROL ARM

NISSAN

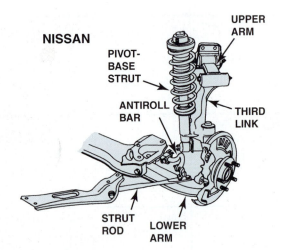

UPPER ARM

PIVOT-BASE STRUT

ANTIROLL BAR

THIRD LINK

STRUT ROD   LOWER ARM

FIGURE 6-11 Multilink front suspension design varies depending on the vehicle manufacturer.

A proper road test for any suspension system problem should include the following:

1. **Drive beside parked vehicles.** Any noise generated by the vehicle suspension or tires is reflected off solid objects, such as a row of parked vehicles along a street. For best results, drive with the windows down and drive close to the parked vehicles or a retaining wall on the left side. Repeat the drive for the right side. Defective wheel bearings or power steering pumps usually make noise and can be heard during this test.

2. **Drive into driveways.** Suspension problems often occur when turning at the same time the suspension hits a bump. This action is best repeated by driving slowly into a driveway with a curb. The curb causes the suspension to compress while the wheels are turned (see the Real World Fix titled "The Rock-Hard Problem" for an example). Defective stabilizer bar bushings, control arm bushings, and ball joints will usually make noise during this test procedure.

3. **Drive in Reverse while turning.** This technique is usually used to find possible defective outer CV joints used on the drive axle shaft of front-wheel-drive vehicles. This technique also forces the suspension system to work in reverse of normal. Any excessive clearances in the suspension system are reversed and often make noise or cause a vibration during the test. Besides defective CV joints, this test can often detect worn control arm bushings, ball joints, stabilizer bar bushings, or links. This test can also detect defective or worn steering system components such as an idler arm, tie rod end, or center link.

4. **Drive over a bumpy road.** Worn or defective suspension (and steering) components can cause the vehicle to bounce or dart side to side while traveling over bumps and dips in the road. Worn or defective ball joints, control arm bushings, stabilizer bar bushings, stabilizer bar links, or worn shock absorbers can be the cause.

Once the problem has been confirmed, then a further inspection can be performed in the service bay.

DRY PARK TEST (SUSPENSION)

A **dry park test** can also be used to help locate worn or defective suspension components. The dry park test is performed by having an assistant move the steering wheel side to side while feeling and observing for any freeplay in the steering or suspension. For best results, the vehicle should be on a level floor or on a drive-on-type hoist with the front wheels pointing straight ahead. In this suspension analysis using the dry park test, the technician should observe the following for any noticeable play or unusual noise:

1. **Front wheel bearings.** Loose or defective wheel bearings are often overlooked as a possible cause of poor handling or darting vehicle performance. (See Chapter 12 for wheel bearing inspection and service procedures.)

2. **Control arm bushing wear or movement.** Check for any abnormal movement in upper control arm bushings or lower control arm bushings.

3. **Ball joint movement.** Check for any noticeable play or noise from both load-carrying and follower-type ball joints on both sides of the vehicle.

NOTE: The dry park test (and many other chassis system tests) relies on the experience of the technician to be able to judge normal wear from abnormal wear. It is extremely important that all beginning technicians work closely with an experienced technician to gain this knowledge.

TECH TIP

ROAD TEST— BEFORE AND AFTER

Many times technicians will start to work on a vehicle based on the description of the problem by the driver or owner. A typical conversation was overheard where the vehicle owner complained that the vehicle handled "funny," especially when turning. The owner wanted a wheel alignment, and the technician and shop owner wanted the business. The vehicle was aligned, but the problem was still present. The real problem was a defective tire. The service technician should have road-tested the vehicle *before* any service work was done to confirm the problem and try to determine its cause. Every technician should test drive the vehicle *after* any service work is performed to confirm that the service work was performed correctly and that the customer complaint has been resolved. This is especially true for any service work involving the steering, suspension, or braking systems.

VISUAL INSPECTION

All suspension components should be carefully inspected for signs of wear or damage. A thorough visual inspection should include checking all of the following:

1. Shock absorbers (see Figure 6-12)
2. Springs (see Figure 6-13)
3. Stabilizer bar links
4. Stabilizer bar bushings
5. Upper and lower shock absorber mounting points
6. Bump stops
7. Body-to-chassis mounts
8. Engine and transmission (transaxle) mounts
9. Suspension arm bushings (see Figure 6-14)

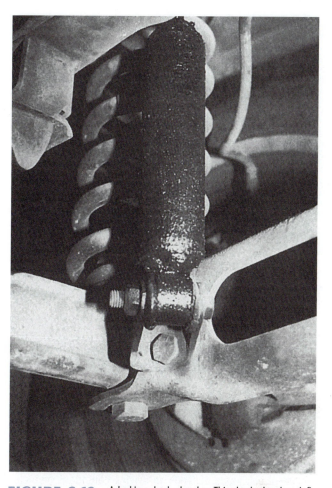

FIGURE 6-12 A leaking shock absorber. This shock absorber definitely needs to be replaced.

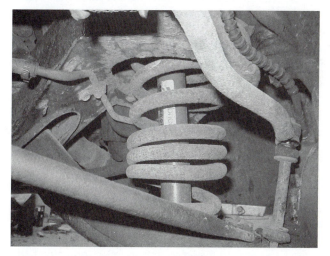

FIGURE 6-13 This front coil spring looks as if it has been heated with a torch in an attempt to lower the ride height of the vehicle. Both front springs will require replacement.

Alignment equipment and procedures can often determine if a suspension component is bent or has been moved out of position. A careful *visual* inspection can often reveal suspected damaged components by observing scrape marks or

FIGURE 6-14 It is easy to see that this worn control arm bushing needed to be replaced. The new bushing is shown next to the original.

rusty sections that could indicate contact with the road or another object.

While an assistant bounces the vehicle up and down, check to see if there is any freeplay in any of the suspension components.

BALL JOINTS

Diagnosis and Inspection

The life of ball joints depends on driving conditions, vehicle weight, and lubrication. Even with proper care and lubrication, the load-carrying (weight-carrying) ball joints wear more than the follower ball joints. Ball joints should be replaced in pairs, both lower or both upper, to ensure the best handling.

Defective or worn ball joints can cause looseness in the suspension and the following common driver complaints:

1. Loud popping or squeaking whenever driving over curbs, such as into a driveway
2. Shimmy-type vibration felt in the steering wheel
3. Vehicle wander or a tendency not to track straight
4. Excessive freeplay in the steering wheel

A ball joint inspection should also be performed when an alignment is performed or as part of any other comprehensive vehicle inspection.

Many load-carrying ball joints have wear indicators with a raised area around the grease fitting, called **indicator ball joints**. See Figures 6-15 and 6-16.

Always check wear-indicator-type ball joints with the wheels of the vehicle on the ground. If the raised area around the grease fitting is flush or recessed with the surrounding area, the ball joint is worn more than 0.050 in. and must be replaced.

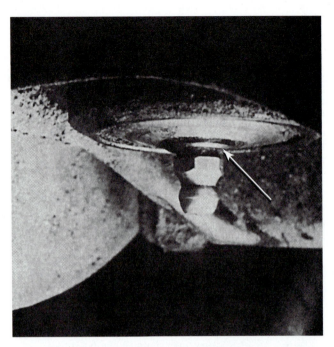

FIGURE 6-15 Grease fitting projecting down from the surrounding area of a ball joint. The ball joint should be replaced when the area around the grease fitting is flush or recessed.

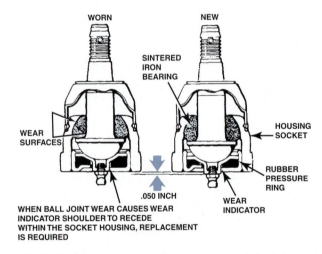

FIGURE 6-16 Indicator ball joints should be checked with the weight of the vehicle on the ground. *(Courtesy of Moog)*

NOTE: Most ball joints must be replaced if the joint has more than 0.050 in. axial (up-and-down) movement. To help visualize this distance, consider that the thickness of an American nickel coin is about 0.060 in. It is helpful to know that maximum wear should be less than the thickness of a nickel. There are dial indicators (gauges) available that screw into the grease-fitting hole of the ball joint that can accurately measure the wear. See Figure 6-17.

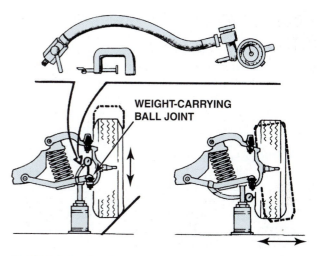

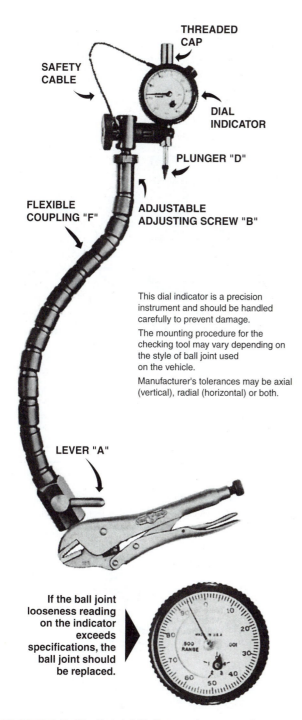

THREADED CAP

SAFETY CABLE

DIAL INDICATOR

PLUNGER "D"

FLEXIBLE COUPLING "F"

ADJUSTABLE ADJUSTING SCREW "B"

This dial indicator is a precision instrument and should be handled carefully to prevent damage.

The mounting procedure for the checking tool may vary depending on the style of ball joint used on the vehicle.

Manufacturer's tolerances may be axial (vertical), radial (horizontal) or both.

LEVER "A"

If the ball joint looseness reading on the indicator exceeds specifications, the ball joint should be replaced.

FIGURE 6-17   Typical dial indicator used to measure the suspension component movement. The locking pliers attach the gauge to a stationary part of the vehicle and the flexible coupling allows the dial indicator to be positioned at any angle. *(Courtesy of Moog)*

To perform a proper non-indicator-type ball joint inspection, the force of the vehicle's springs *must* be *unloaded* from the ball joint. If this force is not relieved, the force of the spring pushes the ball and socket joint tightly together and any wear due to movement will not be detected.

WEIGHT-CARRYING BALL JOINT

FIGURE 6-18   If the spring is attached to the lower control arm as in this SLA suspension, the jack should be placed under the lower control arm as shown. A dial indicator should be used to measure the amount of freeplay in the ball joints. Be sure that the looseness being measured is not due to normal wheel bearing endplay. *(Courtesy of Dana Corporation)*

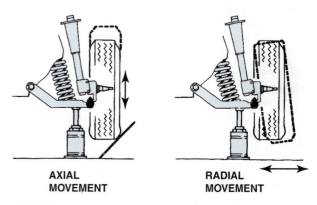

AXIAL MOVEMENT

RADIAL MOVEMENT

FIGURE 6-19   The jack should be placed under the lower control arm of this modified MacPherson-type suspension. *(Courtesy of Dana Corporation)*

NOTE: The location of the load-carrying ball joint is closest to the seat of the spring or torsion bar.

If the coil spring or torsion bar is attached to the *lower* control arm, the *lower* ball joint is the load-carrying ball joint. See Figure 6-18. This includes vehicles equipped with modified MacPherson-strut-type suspension. See Figure 6-19.

1. Place the jack under the lower control arm as close to the ball joint as possible and raise the wheels approximately 1 to 2 in. (2.5 to 5 cm) off the ground to unload the lower ball joint.
2. Using a pry bar under the tire, lift the wheel up. If there is excessive vertical movement in the ball joint itself, it must

be replaced. Most manufacturers specify a maximum vertical play of approximately 0.050 in. (1.3 mm), or the thickness of a nickel. Always check the manufacturer's specifications for exact maximum allowable movement. Vertical movement of a ball joint is often called axial play because the looseness is in the same axis as the ball joint stud. To check for *lateral* play, grip the tire at the top and bottom and move your hands in opposite directions.

NOTE: Be sure that the cause of any freeplay or looseness is not due to the wheel bearing. Closely observe the exact source of the freeplay movement.

If the coil spring is attached to the *upper* control arm, the *upper* ball joint is the load-carrying ball joint. See Figure 6-20.

1. Place a block of wood (2 × 4 in.) between the upper control arm and the frame, or use a special tool designed for this purpose. See Figure 6-21.
2. Place the jack under the vehicle's *frame* and raise the wheel approximately 1 in. to 2 in. off the ground. (The wood block or special tool keeps the weight of the vehicle off the upper ball joint.)
3. Using a pry bar under the tire, lift the wheel. If there is excessive vertical movement in the ball joint itself, it must be replaced. Always check the manufacturer's specifications for exact maximum allowable movement.

Follower ball joints (friction ball joints) should also be inspected while testing load-carrying ball joints. Grasp the tire at the top and the bottom and attempt to shake the wheel assembly while looking directly at the follower ball joint. Generally, there should be no lateral or axial movement at all in the follower ball joint. However, some manufacturers specify a maximum of 0.250 in. (1/4 in. or 0.6 cm) measured at the top of the tire. Always check the manufacturer's specifications before condemning a ball joint because of excessive play.

MacPherson-strut-equipped vehicles do not have a load-carrying ball joint. The weight of the vehicle is carried through the upper strut mount and bearing assembly. See Figure 6-22.

After checking axial play in a ball joint, grasp the tire from the side at the top and bottom and alternately push and pull. *Any* lateral movement at the ball joint should generally be considered a good reason to replace the ball joints. See Figure 6-23.

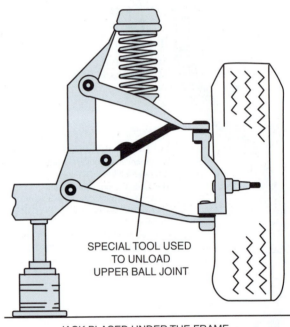

JACK PLACED UNDER THE FRAME

FIGURE 6-21   A special tool or a block of wood should be inserted between the frame and the upper control arm before lifting the vehicle off the ground. This tool stops the force of the spring against the upper ball joint so that a true test can be performed on the condition of the ball joint.

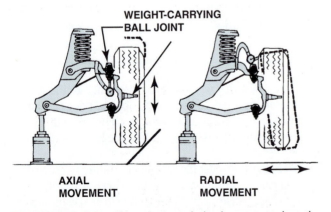

FIGURE 6-20   If the spring is attached to the upper control arm, the jack should be placed under the frame to check for ball joint wear. *(Courtesy of Dana Corporation)*

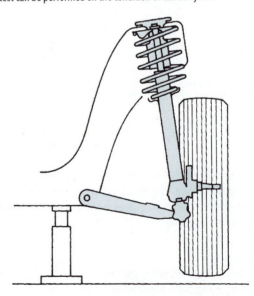

FIGURE 6-22   The jacking point is under the frame for checking the play of a lower ball joint used with a MacPherson strut.

FIGURE 6-23 This worn and rusty ball joint was found by moving the wheel and looking for movement in the joint.

FREQUENTLY ASKED QUESTION

WHAT IS THE DIFFERENCE BETWEEN A LOW-FRICTION BALL JOINT AND A STEEL-ON-STEEL BALL JOINT?

Before the late 1980s, most ball joints were constructed with a steel ball that rubbed on a steel socket. This design created friction and provided for a tight high-friction joint until wear caused looseness in the joint.

Newer designs use a polished steel ball that is installed in a hard plastic polymer, resulting in a low-friction joint assembly. Because of the difference in friction characteristics, the vehicle may handle differently than originally designed if incorrect-style ball joints are installed. Most component manufacturers state that low-friction ball joints in a vehicle originally equipped with steel-on-steel high-friction ball joints are usually acceptable, but high-friction replacement ball joints should be avoided on a vehicle originally equipped with low-friction ball joints.

Ball Joint Removal

Take care to avoid damaging grease seals when separating ball joints from their mounts. *The preferred method to separate tapered parts is to use a puller-type tool that applies pressure to the tapered joint as the bolt is tightened on the puller.* See Figure 6-24.

Sometimes the shock of a hammer can be used to separate the ball joint from the steering knuckle. For best results, another hammer should be used as a backup while striking the joint to be separated on the side with a heavy hammer.

CAUTION: The use of tapered "pickle forks" should be avoided, unless the part is to be replaced, because they often damage the grease seal of the part being separated.

Some ball joint studs have a slot or groove where a **pinch bolt** is used to hold the ball joint to the steering knuckle. See Figure 6-25. Use penetrating oil in the steering knuckle groove and rotate the knuckle several times. Do not use a hammer on

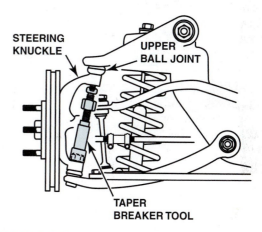

FIGURE 6-24 Taper breaker tool being used to separate the upper ball joint from the steering knuckle. This is especially important for vehicles equipped with aluminum alloy control arms.

FIGURE 6-25 A pinch bolt attaches the steering knuckle to the ball joint. Remove the pinch bolt by turning the nut, not the bolt. *(Courtesy of Moog)*

the pinch bolt because this can cause damage to the bolt and the ball joint. Do not widen the slot in the steering knuckle. Once separated, check the shape of the steering knuckle. See Figure 6-26. If the pinch bolt has been deformed by overtightening, the steering knuckle should be replaced.

When removing ball joints that are riveted in place, always cut off or drill rivet heads before separating the ball joint from the spindle. This provides a more solid base to assist in removing rivets. *The preferred method to remove rivets from ball joints is to center punch and drill out the center of the rivet before using a drill or an air-powered chisel to remove the rivet heads.* Be careful not to drill or chisel into the control arms. See Figures 6-27 through 6-30.

Press-in-type ball joints are removed and installed using a special C-clamp-type tool. See Figure 6-31 on page 164.

NOTE: Many replacement press-in-type ball joints are slightly larger in diameter—about 0.050 in. (1.3 mm)—than the original ball joint to provide the same press fit. If the ball joints have been replaced before, then the control arm must be replaced.

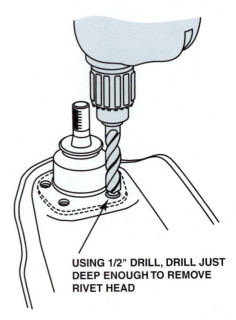

USING 1/2" DRILL, DRILL JUST DEEP ENOUGH TO REMOVE RIVET HEAD

FIGURE 6-28 The head of the rivet can be removed by using a larger-diameter drill bit as shown.

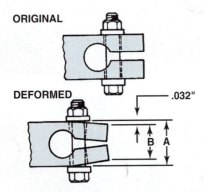

FIGURE 6-26 If the pinch bolt is overtightened, the steering knuckle can be deformed. A deformed knuckle can cause the pinch bolt to break and the ball joint could become separated from the steering knuckle. *(Courtesy of Moog)*

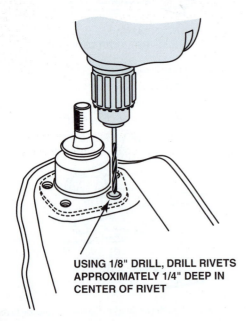

USING 1/8" DRILL, DRILL RIVETS APPROXIMATELY 1/4" DEEP IN CENTER OF RIVET

FIGURE 6-27 By drilling into the rivet, the holding force is released.

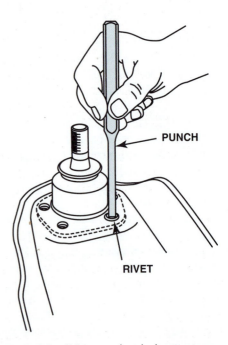

PUNCH

RIVET

FIGURE 6-29 Using a punch and a hammer to remove the rivet after drilling down through the center and removing the head of the rivet.

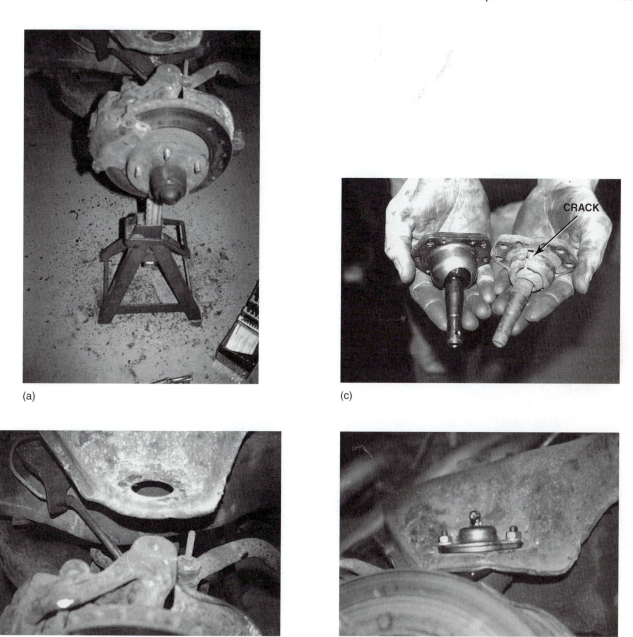

(a)

(b)

(c)

CRACK

(d)

FIGURE 6-30 (a) A safety stand is used to support the weight of the vehicle by placing it under the lower control arm while replacing the upper ball joint. (b) The old ball joint has been removed. (c) The new replacement ball joint is on the left and the old ball joint is on the right. Note the crack right down the middle of the old ball joint—it is a miracle that the vehicle made it into the shop. (d) The replacement ball joint is bolted in place using the hardened steel bolts and nuts supplied with the replacement ball joint.

Avoid using heat to remove suspension or steering components. Many chassis parts use rubber and plastic that can be damaged if heated with a torch. *If heat is used to remove a part, it must be replaced.* For best results, try soaking with a penetrating oil and use the proper tools and procedures as specified by the manufacturer.

Many vehicles are equipped with nonreplaceable ball joints, and the entire control arm must be replaced if the ball joint is worn or defective.

CAUTION: Always follow manufacturers' recommended installation instructions whenever replacing any suspension or other chassis component part. Tie rod ends and ball joints use a taper to provide the attachment to other components. Whenever a nut is used to tighten a tapered part, it is important not to back off (loosen) the nut after tightening. As the nut is being tightened, the taper is being pulled into the taper of the adjoining part. The specified torque on the nut ensures that the two pieces of the taper are properly joined. If the cotter key does not line up with the hole in the tapered stud when the nut has been properly torqued, tighten it more to line up a hole—never loosen the nut.

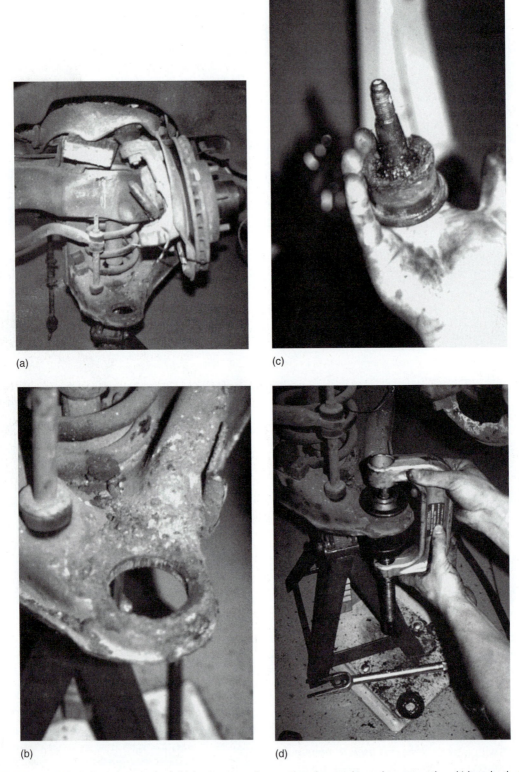

(a)

(b)

(c)

(d)

FIGURE 6-31   (a) A block of wood was used to hold the upper control arm, and a safety stand is used to support the vehicle under the lower control arm during the replacement of the lower ball joint. (b) A photo of the lower control arm after the old press-in-type ball joint was removed. (c) The old press-in ball joint was replaced because the wear indicator was recessed (instead of extended) in the housing, indicating that the joint was worn beyond serviceable limits. (d) A large C-clamp press is being used with adapters and sleeves to install the replacement ball joint.

REAL WORLD FIX

THE RATTLE STORY

A customer complained that a rattle was heard every time the vehicle hit a bump. The noise sounded as if it came from the rear. All parts of the exhaust system and suspension system were checked. Everything seemed OK until the vehicle was raised with a frame-type hoist instead of a drive-on type. Then, whenever the right rear wheel was lifted, the noise occurred. The problem was a worn (elongated) shock absorber mounting hole. A washer with the proper-size hole was welded over the worn lower frame mount and the shock absorber was bolted back into place.

KINGPIN DIAGNOSIS AND SERVICE

Kingpins are usually used on trucks, sport utility vehicles, and other heavy-duty vehicles. See Figure 6-32.

King pins are designed to rotate inside kingpin bushings with a clearance between them of approximately 0.001 to 0.003 in. (0.025 to 0.075 mm). As wear occurs, this clearance distance increases and the kingpin becomes loose. Looseness in the kingpin causes looseness in the wheels and steering. *Kingpins can also gall or seize due to lack of lubrication, resulting in very hard steering.*

After supporting the vehicle safely off the ground, inspect for looseness by positioning a dial gauge (indicator) on the extreme inside bottom of the edge of the wheel and rock the tire. If the dial indicator registers more than 1/4 inch (6 mm), replace the kingpin and/or kingpin bushings.

To remove a typical kingpin, follow these basic steps:

Step 1   Remove the tire, brake drum, and backing plate or caliper.
Step 2   Remove the lockpin. The lockpin is usually tapered with a threaded end for the nut. Drive the lockpin out with a drift (punch).
Step 3   Remove the grease caps and drive the kingpin from the steering knuckle and axle with a hammer and a brass punch or a hydraulic press, if necessary. See Figure 6-33.

To replace the kingpin bushings and/or kingpin, refer to the manufacturer's procedure and specifications. See Figure 6-34.

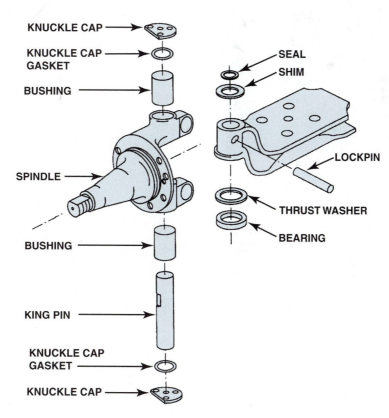

FIGURE 6-32   Typical kingpin assembly. *(Courtesy of Dana Corporation)*

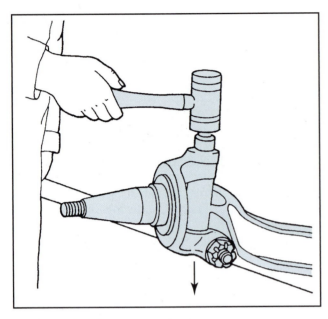

FIGURE 6-33   Driving a kingpin out with a hammer. *(Courtesy of Dana Corporation)*

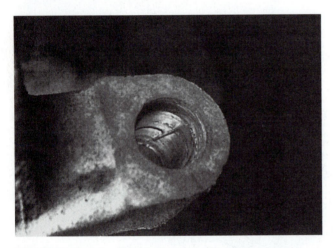

FIGURE 6-34   This galled kingpin bushing must be replaced.

Some bronze bushings must be sized by reaming or honing to provide from 0.001 to 0.003 in. (0.025 to 0.075 mm) clearance between the kingpin and the bushing.

SHOCK ABSORBERS AND STRUTS

Diagnosis

Shock absorber life depends on how and where the vehicle is driven. Original equipment (OE) shock absorbers are carefully matched to the vehicle springs and bushings to provide the best ride comfort and control. As the control arm bushings and

TECH TIP

THE SHOCK STUD TRICK

Front shock absorbers used on many rear-wheel-drive vehicles equipped with an SLA-type front suspension are often difficult to remove because the attaching nut is rusted to the upper shock stub. A common trick is to use a deep-well 9/16-in. socket and a long extension and simply bend the shock stud until it breaks off. At first you would think that this method causes harm, and it does ruin the shock absorber—but the shock absorber is not going to be reused and will be discarded anyway.

The usual procedure followed by many technicians is to simply take a minute or two to break off the upper shock stud, then hoist the vehicle to allow access to the lower two shock bolts, and then the shock can easily be removed. To install the replacement shock absorber, attach the lower bolts, lower the vehicle, and attach the upper rubber bushings and retaining nut.

ball joints age, the energy built up in the springs of the vehicle is controlled less by the friction of these joints and bushings, requiring more control from the shock absorbers. Shock absorber action is also reduced as the seals inside wear. Replacement shock absorbers may be required when any or all of the following symptoms appear:

1. **Ride harshness.** As the effectiveness of the shock absorber decreases, the rapid forces of the springs are not as dampened or controlled. Worn shocks can cause ride harshness and yet not cause the vehicle to bounce after hitting a bump.
2. **Frequent bottoming out on rough roads.** Shock absorbers provide a controlled movement of the axle whenever the vehicle hits a bump or dip in the road. As fluid is lost or wear occurs, the shock absorber becomes weaker and cannot resist the forces acting on the axle. The worn shock absorber can allow the spring to compress enough so that the axle contacts the jounce bumper (bump stop) on the body or frame of the vehicle.

NOTE: Frequent bottoming out is also a symptom of reduced ride height due to sagging springs. Before replacing the shock absorbers, always check for proper ride height as specified in the vehicle service manual or any alignment specification booklet available from suppliers or companies of alignment or chassis parts and equipment.

3. **Extended vehicle movement after driving on dips or a rise in the road.** The most common shock absorber test is the bounce test. Push down on the body of the vehicle and let go; the vehicle should return to its normal ride height and stop. Worn shock absorbers can cause poor driver control due to excessive up-and-down suspension movements. If the vehicle continues to bounce two or three times, then the shocks or struts are worn and must be replaced.

4. **Cuppy-type tire wear.** Defective shock absorbers can cause **cuppy tire wear.** This type of tire wear is caused by the tire's bouncing up and down as it rotates.

5. **Leaking hydraulic oil.** When a shock or strut leaks oil externally, this indicates a defective seal. The shock absorber or strut cannot function correctly when low on oil inside.

6. **Springs and shock absorbers should be replaced in pairs.** Both front or both rear shocks should be replaced together to provide the best handling and control.

NOTE: Shock absorbers do not affect ride height except where special air shocks or coil overload carrying shocks are used. If a vehicle is sagging on one side or in the front or the rear, the springs should be checked and replaced if necessary.

Shock absorbers are filled with fluid and sealed during production. They are not refillable; if worn, damaged, or leaking, they must be replaced. A slight amount of fluid may bleed by the rod seal in cold weather and deposit a light film on the upper area of the shock absorber. This condition will not hurt the operation of the shock and should be considered normal. If noisy when driving, always check the tightness and condition of all shock absorber mounts.

Replacement shock absorbers and/or struts should match the original equipment unit in physical size.

Front Shock Replacement

Front shock absorbers provide ride control and are usually attached to the lower control arm by bolts and nuts. The upper portion of the shock usually extends through the spring housing and is attached to the frame of the vehicle with rubber grommets to help insulate noise, vibration, and harshness.

Most front shock absorbers can be replaced either with the vehicle still on the ground or while on a hoist. The front suspension of most vehicles allows the removal of the shocks without the need to support the downward travel of the lower control arm. The downward travel limit is stopped by a rubber stop or by the physical limit of the suspension arms.

Special sockets and other tools are available to remove the nut from the shocks that use a single mounting stem. The removal of the lower mounting of most front shock absorbers

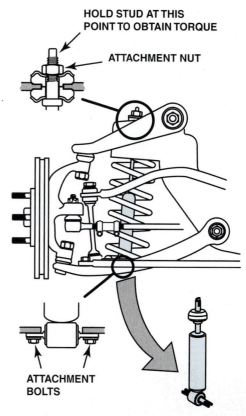

HOLD STUD AT THIS POINT TO OBTAIN TORQUE

ATTACHMENT NUT

ATTACHMENT BOLTS

FIGURE 6-35 Most shock absorbers used on the front suspension can be removed from underneath the vehicle after removing the attaching bolts or nuts.

usually involves the removal of two bolts. After removal of the attaching hardware, the shock absorber is simply pulled through the front control arm. See Figure 6-35.

Reverse the removal procedure to install replacement shock absorbers. Always consult the manufacturer's recommended procedures and fastener tightening torque.

MACPHERSON STRUT REPLACEMENT

On most vehicles equipped with MacPherson strut suspensions, strut replacement involves the following steps.

CAUTION: Always follow the manufacturer's recommended methods and procedures whenever replacing a MacPherson strut assembly or component.

---

1. Hoist the vehicle, remove the wheels, and mark the attaching bolts/nuts.
2. Remove the upper strut mounting bolts except for one to hold the strut until ready to remove the strut assembly. See Figure 6-36.

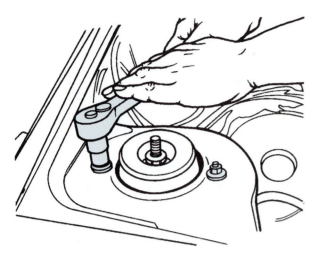

FIGURE 6-36 Removing the upper strut mounting bolts. Some experts recommend leaving one of the upper strut mount nuts loosely attached to prevent the strut from falling when the lower attaching bolts are removed. *(Courtesy of Dana Corporation)*

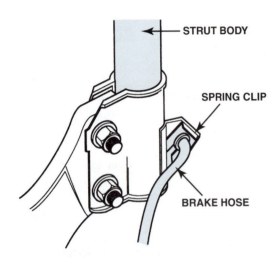

STRUT BODY

SPRING CLIP

BRAKE HOSE

FIGURE 6-37 A brake hydraulic hose is often attached to the strut housing. Sometimes all that is required to separate the line from the strut is to remove a spring clip.

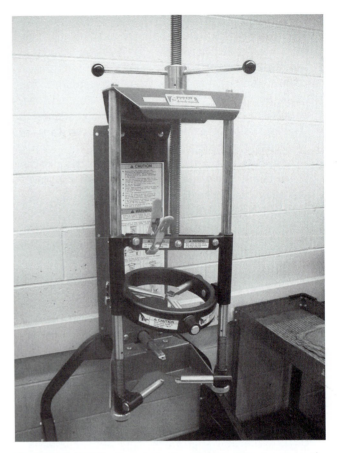

FIGURE 6-38 Use a strut spring compressor fixture to compress the spring on a MacPherson strut before removing the strut retaining nut.

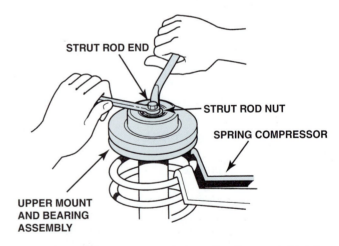

STRUT ROD END

STRUT ROD NUT

SPRING COMPRESSOR

UPPER MOUNT AND BEARING ASSEMBLY

FIGURE 6-39 Removing the strut rod nut. The strut shaft is being helped with one wrench while the nut is being removed with the other wrench. Notice that the spring is compressed before the nut is removed.

3. Remove the brake caliper or brake hose from the strut housing. See Figure 6-37.
4. After removing all lower attaching bolts, remove the final upper strut bolt and remove the strut assembly from the vehicle. Place the strut assembly into a strut spring compressor fixture or use manual spring compressors as shown in Figure 6-38.
5. Compress the coil spring enough to relieve the tension on the strut rod nut. Remove the strut rod nut as shown in Figure 6-39.
6. After removing the strut rod nut, remove the upper strut bearing assembly and the spring. See Figure 6-40.

NOTE: The bearing assembly should be carefully inspected and replaced if necessary. Some automotive experts recommend replacing the bearing assembly whenever the strut is replaced.

Replacement

To replace a strut rod bushing, the nut on the end of the strut rod has to be removed. See Figure 6-46. As the nut is being removed, the lower control arm is likely to move forward or backward, depending on the location of the strut rod frame mount. After removing the strut rod nut, remove the one or two fasteners that retain the strut rod to the lower control arm. The strut rod can now be removed from the vehicle and the replacement rubber bushings can be installed. Install the strut rod in the reverse order of installation. Most bushings use a serrated spacer to maintain the proper force on the rubber bushings; this prevents the technician from compressing the rubber bushing when the strut rod nut is tightened. See Figure 6-47.

CAUTION: Some suspension bushings are directional and must be installed according to the vehicle manufacturer's instructions. For example, on some vehicles, the bushings have a slit or void which must face the front of the vehicle. Always check service information when installing new bushings.

FRONT COIL SPRINGS

Diagnosis

Coil springs should be replaced in pairs if the vehicle ride height is lower than specifications. Sagging springs can cause the tires to slide laterally (side to side) across the pavement, causing excessive tire wear. See Figure 6-48. Sagging springs can also cause the vehicle to bottom out against the suspension bumpers when traveling over normal bumps and dips in the road.

If a vehicle is overloaded, the springs of the vehicle can *take a set* and not recover to the proper ride height. This commonly occurs with all types of vehicles whenever a heavy load is carried, even on a short trip.

It is normal for the rear of a vehicle to sag when a heavy load is carried, but it can permanently damage the spring by exceeding the yield point of the steel spring material.

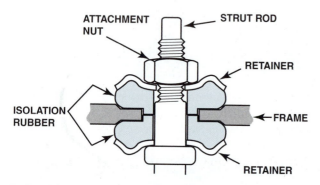

FIGURE 6-46 Typical strut rod bushing with rubber on both sides of the frame to help isolate noise, vibration, and harshness from being transferred to the passengers.

FIGURE 6-47 Parts of a strut rod bushing. Note that the serrated spacers are used between the two rubber bushings to maintain a fixed distance between the bushings. This bushing helps prevent the nut from being tightened too much, thereby compressing the bushings too much.

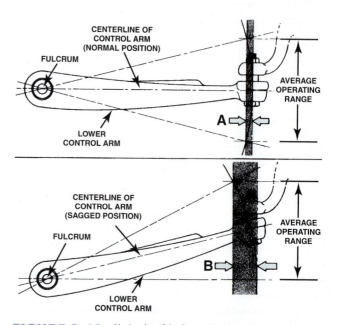

FIGURE 6-48 Notice that if the front coil springs are sagging, the resulting angle of the lower control arm causes the wheels to move from side to side as the suspension moves up and down. Note the difference between the distance at "A" with good springs and the distance at "B" with sagging springs. *(Courtesy of Moog)*

Replacement

The only solution recommended by the vehicle manufacturer is to replace the damaged springs in pairs (both front and both rear, or all four). Several aftermarket alternatives include the following:

- **Helper or auxiliary left springs.** These helper springs are usually designed to increase the load-carrying capacity of leaf springs or to restore the original ride height to sagging springs.
- **Spring inserts for coil springs.** Hard rubber or metal spacers are *not recommended* because they create concentrated pressure points on the coils that can cause the spring to break. Hard rubber stabilizers that bridge the gap between two coils without raising the ride height stiffen the ride by locking two coils together. With two coils connected, the spring rate increases and the spring becomes stiffer.
- **Air shocks or airbag devices.** Air shocks or airbags are generally used to restore or increase the load-carrying capacity to the rear of the vehicle. While these devices do allow the ride height to be maintained, the extra load is still being supported by the tires and rear axle bearings. Caution should be used not to overload the basic chassis or power train of the vehicle.

There are two designs for vehicles that use coil springs. The most commonly used design places the coil spring between the vehicle frame and the lower control arm.

Both front-suspension designs require that the front shock absorbers be removed in order to replace the coil springs. This first step in the coil spring removal procedure can be performed on the ground or on any type of hoist. After removing the shock absorber, use a coil spring compressor and install it through the center of the coil spring. See Figure 6-49. Hook the arms of the coil spring compressor over the rungs of the coil spring and rotate the adjusting nut on the spring compressor with a wrench to shorten the spring. Coil spring clips can also be used to retain the coil spring.

CAUTION: When compressed, all springs contain a great deal of stored energy. If a compressed spring were to become disconnected from its spring compressor or clips, it could be projected outward with enough force to cause injury or death.

After the coil spring is retained, the control arm can be separated from the steering knuckle and the coil spring can be removed as shown in Figures 6-50 and 6-51.

Replacement springs should be compressed and installed using the reverse procedure.

FIGURE 6-49 Spring compressing tool in place to hold the spring as the ball joint is separated. Note that the stabilizer bar links have been removed to allow the lower control arm to move downward enough to remove the coil spring.

FIGURE 6-50 The steering knuckle has been disconnected from the ball joints. The lower control arm and coil spring are being held up by a floor jack.

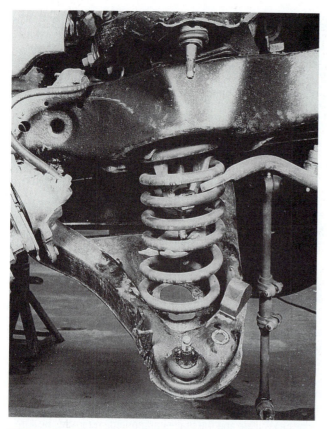

FIGURE 6-51 The spring is being held with a spring compressor as the lower control arm is being pushed down to release the spring.

NOTE: Many automotive experts recommend that new coil insulators be installed every time the coil springs are replaced.

Make sure that the spring is positioned correctly in the control arm and that the spring insulators are installed correctly. See Figure 6-52. Most control arms use two holes for the purpose of coil spring seating. The end of the spring should cover one hole completely and partially cover the second hole. See Figure 6-53.

STEERING KNUCKLES

Diagnosis

Most steering knuckles are constructed of cast or forged cast iron. The steering knuckle usually incorporates the wheel spindle and steering arm. The steering knuckle/steering arm can become bent if the vehicle is in an accident or hits a curb sideways. Often this type of damage is not apparent until vehicle handling or excessive tire wear is noticed. Unless a thorough inspection is performed during a wheel alignment, a bent steering knuckle is often overlooked.

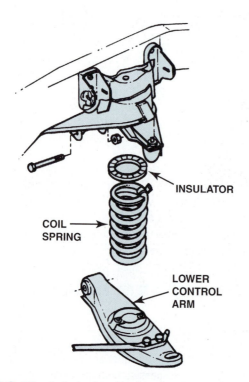
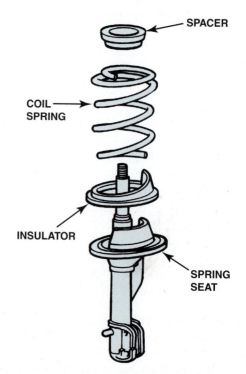

FIGURE 6-52 Spring insulators install between the spring seat and the coil spring to reduce noise.

SHOULD BE OPEN OR PARTIALLY COVERED

SHOULD BE COMPLETELY COVERED

FIGURE 6-53 The holes in the lower arm are not only used to allow water to drain from the spring seat, but also are used as a gauge to show the service technician that the coil spring is correctly seated.

REAL WORLD FIX

THE ROCK-HARD PROBLEM

The owner of a six-month-old full-size pickup truck complained that occasionally when the truck was driven up into a driveway, a loud grinding sound was heard. Several service technicians worked on the truck, trying to find the cause for the noise. After the left front shock absorber was replaced, the noise did not occur for two weeks, and then started again. Finally, the service manager told the technician to replace anything and everything in the front suspension in an attempt to solve the customer's intermittent problem. Five minutes later, a technician handed the service manager a small, deformed rock. This technician had taken a few minutes to *carefully* inspect the entire front suspension. Around the bottom coil spring seat, the technician found the rock. Apparently, when the truck made a turn over a bump, the rock was forced between the coils of the coil spring, making a very loud grinding noise. But the rock did not always get between the coils. Therefore, the problem occurred only once in a while. The technician handed the rock to the very happy customer.

Replacement

If the steering knuckle is bent or damaged, it must be replaced. It should *not* be bent back into shape or repaired. To replace the steering knuckle, both ball joints must be disconnected from the knuckle and the brake components removed. Be sure to support the control arm and spring properly during the procedure. See a factory service manual for the exact procedure and fastener torque for the vehicle you are servicing.

TORSION BARS

Adjustment

Most torsion bar suspensions are designed with an adjustable bolt to permit the tension on the torsion bar to be increased or decreased to change the ride height. Unequal side-to-side ride height can be corrected by adjusting (turning) the torsion bar tension bolt. See Figure 6-54.

Torsion bar adjustment should be made if the difference in ride height from one side to another exceeds 1/8 in. (0.125 in. or 3.2 mm). If the ride height difference side to side is greater than 1/8 in., the vehicle will tend to wander or be unstable, with constant steering wheel movements required to maintain straight-ahead direction.

CONTROL ARM BUSHINGS

Diagnosis

Defective control arm bushings are a common source of vehicle handling and suspension noise problems. Most suspension

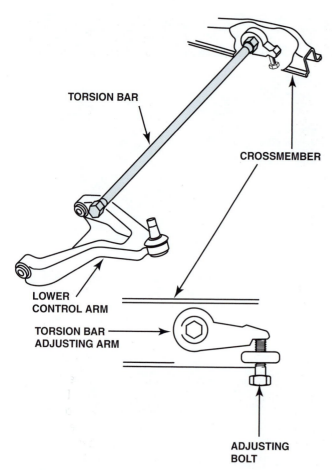

FIGURE 6-54 By rotating the adjusting bolt, the vehicle can be raised or lowered.

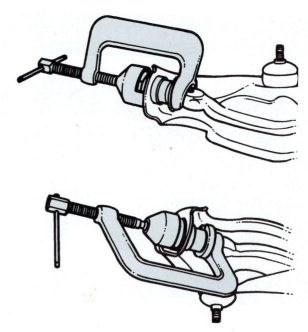

FIGURE 6-55   An adapter and a press or large clamp are used to remove the old bushing from the control arm and to install a new bushing.

NOTE: Some replacement control arm bushings have a higher durometer, or hardness, rating than the original. Urethane bushings are often used in sporty or race-type vehicles and deflect less than standard replacement bushings. These harder bushings also transfer more road noise, vibration, and harshness to the body.

control arm bushings are constructed of three parts: an inner metal sleeve, the rubber bushing itself, and an outer steel sleeve. (Some vehicles use a two-piece bushing that does not use an outer sleeve.)

Replacement

To remove an old bushing from a control arm, the control arm must first be separated from the suspension and/or frame of the vehicle. Several methods can be used to remove the bushing from the control arm, but all methods apply force to the *outer* sleeve. While an air chisel is frequently used to force the steel sleeve out of the suspension member, a puller tool is most often recommended by General Motors. See Figure 6-55. The puller can be used to remove the old bushing and install the replacement bushing without harming the control arm or the new bushing. All bushings should be tightened with the vehicle on the ground and the wheels in a straight-ahead position; this prevents the rubber bushing from exerting a pulling force on the suspension.

The upper control arm bushings can be replaced in most vehicles that use a short/long-arm-type suspension by following just four easy steps:

Step 1   Raise the vehicle and support the lower control arm with a safety stand or floor jack.

Step 2   Disconnect the upper control arm from the frame by removing the frame-attaching nuts or bolts.

Step 3   Using the upper ball joint as a pivot, rotate the upper control arm outward into the wheel well area. With the control arm accessible, it is much easier to remove and replace the upper control arm pivot shaft and rubber bushings.

Step 4   After replacing the bushings, simply rotate the upper control arm back into location and reattach the upper control arm pivot shaft to the vehicle frame.

NOTE: An alignment should always be performed after making any suspension-related repairs.

STRUT REPLACEMENT Step-by-Step

STEP 1 The tools needed to replace a front strut assembly include several sockets and a ball-peen hammer, plus a strut compressor.

STEP 2 After safely hoisting the vehicle to elbow height and removing the wheel covers, remove the front tire/wheel assembly.

STEP 3 Remove the two strut retaining nuts.

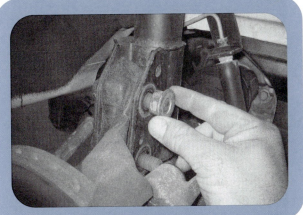

STEP 4 Before using a hammer to drive the retaining bolts from the steering knuckle, thread the nut into the bolt backwards to prevent causing damage to the threads.

STEP 5 Remove the retaining bolts and separate the strut from the steering knuckle.

STEP 6 Lower the vehicle and remove the upper strut retaining fasteners.

STRUT REPLACEMENT continued

STEP 7 Hold the strut while removing the last upper retaining nut and then remove the strut assembly.

STEP 8 After the strut has been removed from the vehicle, install the assembly into a strut compressor.

STEP 9 Position the jaws of the compressor under the bearing assembly as per the vehicle manufacturer's instructions.

STEP 10 Turn the compressor wheel until all tension of the spring has been relieved from the upper bearing assembly.

STEP 11 Remove the strut retaining nut.

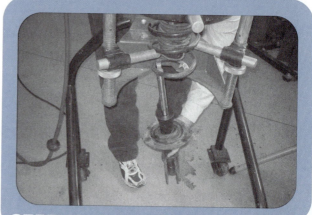

STEP 12 Remove the strut assembly.

(continued)

STRUT REPLACEMENT continued

STEP 13 Before installing the replacement strut, check the upper bearing by exerting a downward force on the bearing while rotating and check for roughness. Replace if necessary.

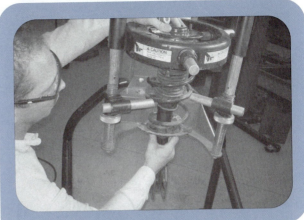

STEP 14 Install the strut from underneath the spring compressor fixture.

STEP 15 Install the strut retaining nut.

STEP 16 Before loosening the tension, check that the coil spring is correctly located at both the top and the bottom, then release the tension on the spring.

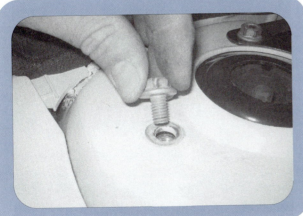

STEP 17 Remove the strut assembly from the compressor and back into the vehicle and install the upper fasteners. Do not torque to specifications until the lower fasteners have been installed.

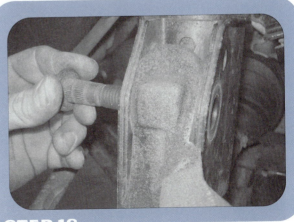

STEP 18 Attach the lower strut to the steering knuckle using the original hardened bolts and nuts.

STRUT REPLACEMENT continued

STEP 19 Using a torque wrench, torque all fasteners to factory specifications.

STEP 20 Install the tire/wheel assembly, lower the vehicle, and torque the lug nuts to factory specifications. Align the vehicle before returning it to the customer.

SUMMARY

1. A thorough road test of a suspension problem should include driving beside parked vehicles and into driveways in an attempt to determine when and where the noise occurs.

2. A dry park test should be performed to help isolate defective or worn suspension components.

3. Ball joints must be unloaded before testing. The ball joints used on vehicles with a MacPherson strut suspension are *not* load carrying. Wear-indicator ball joints are observed with the wheels on the ground.

4. Always use a taper-braker puller or two hammers to loosen tapered parts to remove them. Never use heat unless you are replacing the part; heat from a torch can damage rubber and plastic parts.

5. When installing a tapered part, always tighten the attaching nut to specifications. Never loosen the nut to install a cotter key. If the cotter key will not line up with a hole in the tapered part, tighten the nut more until the cotter key hole lines up with the nut and stud.

6. Defective shock absorbers can cause ride harshness as well as frequent bottoming out on rough roads.

7. Always follow manufacturers' recommended procedures whenever replacing springs or MacPherson struts. Never remove the strut end nut until the coil spring is compressed and the spring force is removed from the upper bearing assembly.

REVIEW QUESTIONS

1. Describe how to perform a proper road test for the diagnosis of suspension-related problems.

2. List four symptoms of worn or defective shock absorbers.

3. Explain the procedure for replacing front shock absorbers on an SLA-type suspension vehicle.

4. Describe the testing procedure for ball joints.

5. Describe the correct general procedure to remove and replace tapered suspension components.

CHAPTER QUIZ

1. Unusual noise during a test drive can be caused by _____.

   a. Defective wheel bearings or stabilizer bar links

   b. Defective or worn control arm bushings or ball joints

   c. Worn or defective CV joints

   d. All of the above

2. Two technicians are discussing non-indicator-type ball joint inspection. Technician A says that the vehicle should be on the ground with the ball joints *loaded,* then checked for freeplay. Technician B says that the ball joints should be *unloaded* before checking for freeplay. Which technician is correct?

   a. Technician A only

   b. Technician B only

   c. Both Technicians A and B

   d. Neither Technician A nor B

3. Most manufacturers specify a maximum axial play for ball joints of about _____.

   a. 0.003 in. (0.076 mm)

   b. 0.010 in. (0.25 mm)

   c. 0.030 in. (0.76 mm)

   d. 0.050 in. (1.27 mm)

4. The preferred method to separate tapered chassis parts is to use _____.

   a. A pickle fork tool

   b. A torch to heat the joint until it separates

   c. A puller tool or two hammers to shock and deform the taper

   d. A drill to drill out the tapered part

5. A light film of oil is observed on the upper area of a shock absorber. Technician A says that this condition should be considered normal. Technician B says that a rod seal may bleed fluid during cold weather, causing the oil film. Which technician is correct?

   a. Technician A only

   b. Technician B only

   c. Both Technicians A and B

   d. Neither Technician A nor B

6. Before the strut insert can be removed from a typical MacPherson strut assembly, which operation is necessary to prevent possible personal injury?

   a. The brake caliper and/or brake hose should be removed from the strut housing

   b. The coil spring should be compressed

   c. The upper strut mounting bolts should be removed

   d. The lower attaching bolts should be removed

7. What should the technician do when replacing stabilizer bar links?

   a. The stabilizer bar should be removed from the vehicle before replacing the links.

   b. The links can be replaced individually, yet the manufacturer often recommends that the links at both ends be replaced together.

   c. The stabilizer bar must be compressed using a special tool before removing or installing stabilizer bar links.

   d. Both b and c are correct.

8. A noise and a pull toward one side during braking is a common symptom of a worn or defective _____.

   a. Shock absorber

   b. Strut rod bushing

   c. Stabilizer bar link

   d. Track rod bushing

9. To help prevent vehicle wandering on a vehicle with torsion bars, the ride height (trim height) should be within _____ side to side.

   a. 0.003 in. (0.076 mm)

   b. 0.050 in. (1.27 mm)

   c. 0.100 in. (2.5 mm)

   d. 0.125 in. (3.2 mm)

10. Two technicians are discussing suspension bushings. Technician A says that replacing control arm bushings usually requires special tools. Technician B says using high-performance urethane bushings may cause excessive noise to be transferred to the passenger compartment. Which technician is correct?

    a. Technician A only

    b. Technician B only

    c. Both Technicians A and B

    d. Neither Technician A nor B

REAR SUSPENSION AND SERVICE

OBJECTIVES

After studying Chapter 7, the reader should be able to:

1. Prepare for the Suspension and Steering (A4) ASE certification test content area "B" (Suspension System Diagnosis and Repair).
2. Describe the various types and styles of rear suspension.
3. Explain the difference among the different types of rear axles.
4. List the steps necessary to replace rear shock absorbers.
5. Explain how to replace rear leaf and coil springs.

KEY TERMS

Axle Windup (p. 183)
Chapman Strut (p. 186)
Hotchkiss Drive (p. 184)
IRS (p. 186)
Live Axle (p. 184)
Panhard Rod (p. 185)
Semi-Independent Suspension (p. 187)

Semi-Trailing Arm (p. 186)
Solid Axle (p. 183)
Torque Arm (p. 184)
Track Rod (p. 185)
Trailing Arm (p. 184)
Watts Linkage (p. 186)

All suspensions have two basic jobs: keeping the tires on the ground and providing a smooth ride.

SOLID REAR AXLES

A **solid axle** can be used at the rear of either a rear-wheel-drive or front-wheel-drive vehicle. See Figure 7-1. On a rear-wheel-drive vehicle, a solid rear axle consists of the differential gears and axle shafts inside a solid housing. On a front-wheel-drive vehicle, a solid axle is usually a simple U-shaped or tubular beam that may contain a torsion bar, rod, or tube to allow some twisting action.

Certain characteristics apply to any solid rear axle, while other characteristics vary by the type of suspension used to attach the axle to the frame.

Solid axles have some handling characteristics that are inferior to those of an independent suspension. Disadvantages of a solid axle include the following:

- Increased proportion of unsprung weight
- Side-to-side road shock transference
- Poorer tire adhesion

Increasing the proportion of unsprung weight decreases ride quality. Transferring road shock from side-to-side causes wheel tramp and shimmy, and poor tire adhesion accelerates tire wear. See Figure 7-2.

The sprung weight of the frame and body must be heavy to oppose the unsprung weight of a solid axle, especially on a driven axle. Unsprung weight, wheel tramp, and shimmy all

reduce tire adhesion. The effects of these problems are more noticeable in rear-wheel-drive vehicles due to the weight of the rear axle and differential assembly. On a typical front-wheel-drive vehicle, the simple axle beam is not heavy enough to decrease ride quality or cause extreme tire wear. In fact, the rear tires of a front-wheel-drive model always wear more slowly than the front tires because the rear axle is so much lighter than the power train.

SOLID AXLES

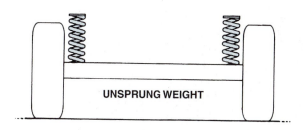

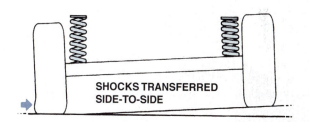

FIGURE 7-2   A solid axle supports the springs, so the axle and suspension components are unsprung weight. When one wheel rides over a bump, the shock transfers through the solid axle to the opposite side, leading to unstable handling.

FREQUENTLY ASKED QUESTION

WHAT IS AXLE WINDUP?

Axle windup is a product of the law of physics, which states that every action produces an equal and opposite reaction. As the axle shafts rotate in one direction to drive the wheels, the axle housing attempts to rotate in the opposite direction. The force of this reaction tends to lift the front end of the vehicle during acceleration. See Figure 7-3. Axle windup is a particular problem with a solid, driven rear axle because the axle housing concentrates the reacting force. Under extreme acceleration, the reacting force can actually tilt the drive shaft upward and lift the front wheels off the ground. Leaf springs, control arms, pinion snubbers, and torque arms all are means of controlling axle windup.

SOLID REAR AXLES

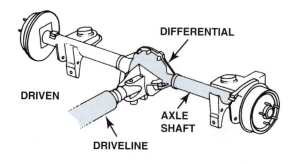

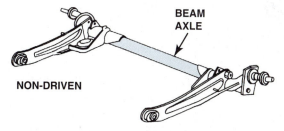

FIGURE 7-1   Solid axles are used on rear-wheel-drive vehicles as well as front-wheel-drive vehicles.

AXLE WINDUP

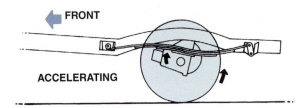

FIGURE 7-3 When the axle housing reacts against the force of axle shaft rotation, the front of the differential tilts upward, creating axle windup.

If engine torque is applied to the rear axle to drive the vehicle, the axle is referred to as a **live axle.**

LEAF SPRING REAR SUSPENSIONS

A leaf spring suspension is a simple system because it does not require control arms to brace and position the axle. The leaf springs link the axle to the frame and effectively serve two purposes:

- Absorbing road shock
- Locating the axle under the vehicle

Most rear-wheel-drive trucks use a solid rear axle with leaf springs in an arrangement called a **Hotchkiss drive.** See Figure 7-4. Leaf springs on a driven axle control axle windup by transferring force from the axle housing to the frame. The front portion of the leaf spring, from the axle housing to the frame mount, acts like a trailing control arm. However, if the front section of the leaf spring is too flexible, it may not control axle windup as well. To compensate, some manufacturers make the front section of the spring shorter, and therefore less flexible, than the rear section.

Leaf springs are used on the rear of many light- and medium-duty trucks and vans. See Figure 7-5. The wheel spindles bolt to the flanges, the centers of the leaf springs rest on the seats, and U-bolts secure the springs to the axle. A shackle attaches the rear of each spring to the unit-body frame, while the front of each spring pivots through a bolt and bushing connected to a hanger that bolts to the body.

TRAILING ARM REAR SUSPENSIONS

A **trailing arm** extends from a frame crossmember located ahead of the rear axle back to the axle housing or a wheel knuckle. Trailing arms run parallel to the centerline of the chassis. See Figure 7-6. A trailing arm mounts to the frame

LEAF SPRING SUSPENSION - DRIVEN AXLE

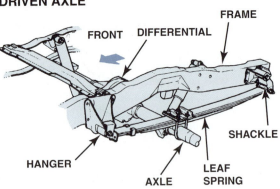

FIGURE 7-4 A typical rear-wheel-drive pickup truck rear suspension equipped with leaf springs. This type of arrangement is called a Hotchkiss drive and the drive train forces are controlled by the rear suspension components.

LEAF SPRING SUSPENSION - BEAM AXLE

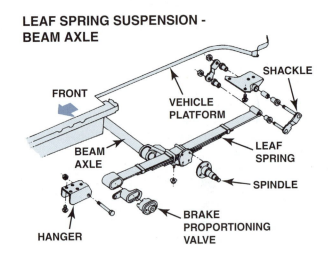

FIGURE 7-5 An exploded view of a beam axle with multi-leaf springs.

with bushings, which allows the arm to pivot as the wheel rides over bumps. Some rear suspensions use two sets of trailing arms, one set positioned higher in the chassis than the other. Although the arms in this type of arrangement are commonly referred to as the *upper control arms* and *lower control arms*, they are usually called trailing arms. The word *trailing* applies to any link where the supported member trails the arm. Trailing arms may be used to brace either a driven or nondriven solid rear axle against front-to-rear forces, but they do not provide much resistance to side-to-side, or lateral, forces. The axle itself is one means of locating the wheels side-to-side, and solid rear suspensions frequently use another rod to provide additional support. Trailing arms transfer axle windup force to the frame and control front-to-rear axle movement. On a few models, especially those with a high-performance suspension, a **torque arm** provides additional resistance to axle windup. See Figure 7-7. The torque arm extends parallel to

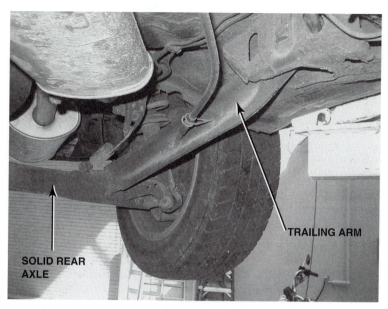

FIGURE 7-6   A trailing arm rear suspension with a solid axle used on a front-wheel-drive vehicle.

TRAILING ARM SUSPENSION - DRIVEN AXLE

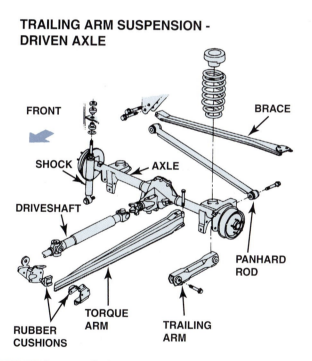

FIGURE 7-7   The Camaro and Firebird rear suspension systems use a torque arm to control axle windup.

TRAILING ARM SUSPENSION - BEAM AXLE

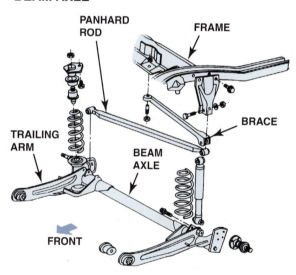

FIGURE 7-8   A typical beam axle rear suspension, which uses trailing arms and coil springs along with a track rod, also called a Panhard rod, to control side-to-side axle movement.

the drive shaft between the rear axle and the transmission. One end of the torque arm is rigidly bolted to the differential housing, while the other end attaches to the transmission through a cushioned bracket to allow some flex.

A trailing arm rear suspension on a nondriven solid axle virtually always includes a **track rod,** also called a **Panhard rod.** A track rod is a rod attached to the body or frame on one end and the rear axle on the other. The purpose of the track

rod is to keep the rear axle centered under the vehicle. The suspension may use either coil springs or struts.

The rear axle is a U-shaped steel beam that is open on the bottom. See Figure 7-8. Flat metal axle end plates, to which the wheel spindles bolt, are attached to each end of the beam. A torsion tube or rod fits inside the beam and is welded to the axle end plates.

The trailing arms, which are welded to the outboard ends of the axle, extend forward and attach to the frame with pivot bushing mounts. A bracket on top of the beam axle locates the ring-type lower strut mount, and the upper strut mount attaches to a reinforced area of the wheel well.

SEMI-TRAILING ARM REAR SUSPENSIONS

A **semi-trailing arm** is similar to a trailing arm in that it extends back from a frame member to the axle. However, a trailing arm is parallel to the vehicle centerline whereas a semi-trailing arm pivots at an angle to the vehicle centerline. Semi-trailing arms have an advantage over trailing arms because they control both side-to-side and front-to-rear motion. Typically, a semi-trailing arm suspension uses coil springs, air springs, or pivot-base struts.

A semi-trailing arm suspension may be used with either a solid axle or an independent suspension.

The Ford suspension uses two pairs, upper and lower, of semi-trailing arms and a center pivot arrangement to locate the driven rear axle. This axle centering pivot bracket and linkage is called a **Watts linkage.** See Figure 7-9.

INDEPENDENT REAR SUSPENSIONS

The use of **independent rear suspension**, called **IRS,** has grown dramatically over the past several decades to the point where such systems are now fairly common, especially on front-wheel-drive vehicles and some rear-wheel-drive vehicles. Although rarely used on trucks, a number of rear-wheel-drive vehicles do feature an independent rear suspension.

The reduction in unsprung weight is particularly noticeable for driven axles, which are constructed to transfer the weight of the differential and axles to the frame. See Figure 7-10. A vehicle with an independent rear suspension rides and holds better than a similar vehicle equipped with a solid rear axle. An SLA-type of independent suspension may be used at the rear of a rear-wheel-drive vehicle. See Figure 7-11.

The differential carrier bolts to the rear subframe, which bears the weight of the axle. Equal-length axle shafts with constant-velocity (CV) joints at either end connect the differential to the rear wheels, and allow the wheels to move independently of each other.

The main benefit of an SLA suspension is that it reduces tire scrub and improves traction. The positioning of the control arms determines the suspension roll center location. In general, the lower the roll center, the less body roll.

Unit-body front-wheel-drive vehicles frequently use strut suspensions at the rear axle. Typically, the strut mounts to the knuckle and replaces the upper control arm. The first designer to put MacPherson-type struts in a rear suspension was an Englishman, Colin Chapman. For this reason, a rear strut suspension is often referred to as a **Chapman strut** suspension by European manufacturers and engineers.

The MacPherson strut system is the most popular independent rear suspension for late-model front-wheel-drive vehicles. See Figure 7-12. Modified strut rear suspensions are found on a variety of front-wheel-drive models from a number of different manufacturers. See Figure 7-13.

INDEPENDENT SUSPENSION

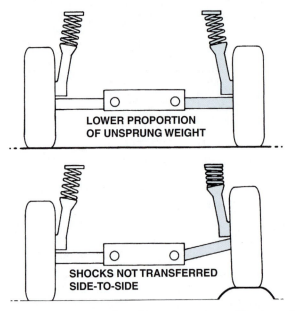

FIGURE 7-10   An independent rear suspension provides a better ride because less weight is unsprung and the suspension is able to react quickly to bumps in the road without affecting the opposite side.

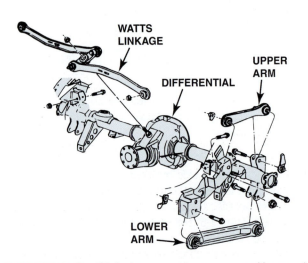

FIGURE 7-9   This Ford rear suspension uses upper and lower semi-trailing arms to mount the rear axle and a Watts linkage to control side-to-side movement.

SHORT-LONG-ARM (SLA) SUSPENSION

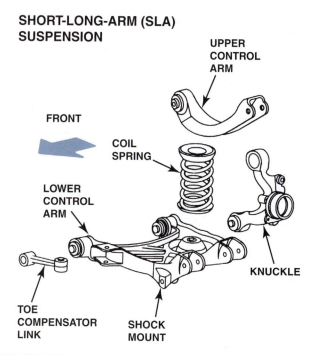

FIGURE 7-11   A typical short/long-arm independent rear suspension.

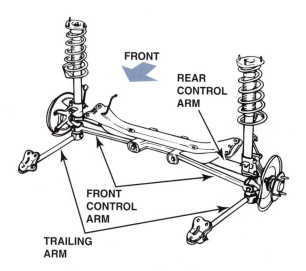

FIGURE 7-12   This independent rear suspension uses a MacPherson strut, two parallel lower transverse control arms, and a trailing arm.

General Motors produced two different rear modified strut systems with transverse leaf springs. See Figure 7-14. A transverse leaf spring is also used on the Chevrolet Corvette and the Cadillac XLR.

SEMI-INDEPENDENT REAR SUSPENSIONS

A **semi-independent suspension** is used only at a non-driven rear axle. The semi-independent design is based on a

MODIFIED STRUT SUSPENSION - COIL SPRING

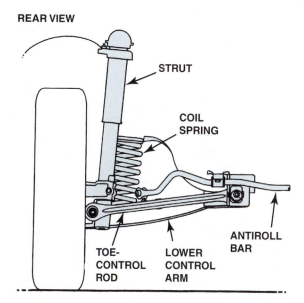

FIGURE 7-13   The toe-control rod provides an extra brace to keep the rear wheels straight ahead during braking and acceleration on this modified-strut-type independent rear suspension.

crossbeam that is similar to the beam axle of a solid, non-driven rear suspension. However, on a semi-independent design the crossbeam is placed ahead, rather than at the centerline, of the wheels. See Figure 7-15. Trailing arms extend rearward from the crossbeam to the wheels. The name *semi-independent* indicates that although an axle does not directly link the wheels, the wheels are not completely independent of each other because they are indirectly connected through the crossbeam.

Some semi-independent rear suspensions use struts. See Figure 7-16.

REAR SUSPENSION SERVICE

Rear suspension service starts with a thorough test drive, to observe any unusual noises or vibrations that may be caused by a fault with a rear suspension component.

After a test drive, safely hoist the vehicle and perform a thorough visual inspection. Use an appropriate prybar and move all of the bushings and joints, checking for deterioration or freeplay. See Figure 7-17 on page 189.

Inspect the shock absorber or struts for leakage or damage. Inspect the bump stops for damage. See Figure 7-18 on page 189. If the bump stops are damaged, this may indicate that the springs are fatigued and the vehicle is at lower-than-normal

MODIFIED STRUT SUSPENSION TRANSVERSE LEAF SPRING

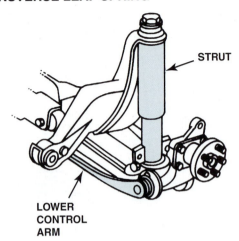

STRUT

LOWER
CONTROL
ARM

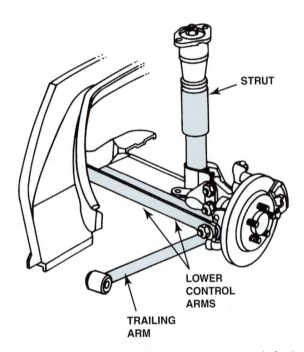

STRUT

LOWER
CONTROL
ARMS

TRAILING
ARM

FIGURE 7-14 The upper drawing shows a transverse-leaf-spring-type independent rear suspension that uses an "H"-shaped lower control arm. The lower drawing shows a transverse leaf spring suspension that uses two parallel lower links and a trailing arm.

ride height, or that the shocks or studs are unable to control the springs. See Figure 7-19.

REAR SHOCK REPLACEMENT

Before removing the rear shock absorbers, the rear axle must be supported to prevent stretching of the rear brake flexible

SEMI-INDEPENDENT SUSPENSIONS

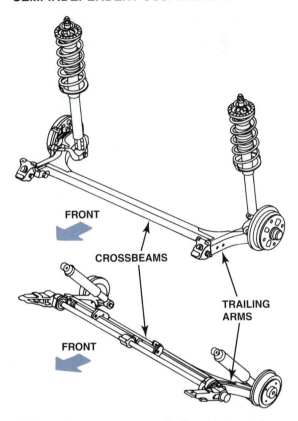

FRONT

CROSSBEAMS

TRAILING
ARMS

FRONT

FIGURE 7-15 The crossbeam is placed toward the front of the vehicle rather than the centerline of the rear wheels on a semi-independent-type rear suspension.

SEMI-INDEPENDENT SUSPENSION-STRUT

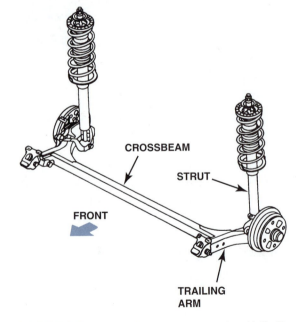

CROSSBEAM

STRUT

FRONT

TRAILING
ARM

FIGURE 7-16 A semi-independent rear suspension with MacPherson struts.

FIGURE 7-17 Check all rubber bushings for excessive cracking.

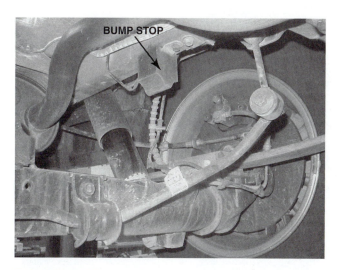

FIGURE 7-18 Carefully inspect the bump stops for damage during a thorough visual inspection.

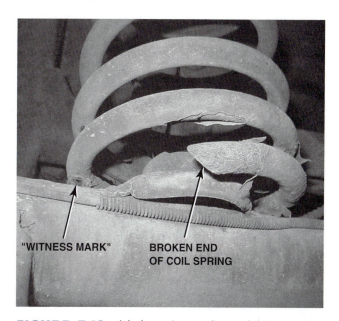

"WITNESS MARK" BROKEN END OF COIL SPRING

FIGURE 7-19 A broken spring was discovered during a routine under-vehicle visual inspection. Notice the witness marks that show that the spring coils have been hitting each other.

SHOCK ABSORBER

TALL SAFETY STAND

FIGURE 7-20 Whenever replacing shock absorbers (especially rear shock absorbers), be sure to support the rear axle. The rear axle assembly could drop and cause damage to the vehicle and possible personal injury if the axle is not supported and the shock absorber attaching bolt (or nut) is removed.

hose. See Figure 7-20. Shocks are attached to the frame or body of the vehicle at the top and to a bracket on the rear axle housing at the bottom. Often, the top of the rear shock absorber is fastened *inside* the vehicle. Consult the vehicle manufacturer's service information for exact procedures and fastener torque values.

NOTE: Shock absorbers and/or struts should always be replaced as a pair.

Air Shock Installation

Air-adjustable shock absorbers are a popular replacement for conventional rear shock absorbers. Air shocks can be used to level the vehicle while towing a trailer or when heavily loaded. When the trailer or load is removed, air can be released from the air shocks to return the vehicle height to normal.

Most replacement air shocks are directional and are labeled *left* and *right*. This ensures that the plastic air hose line exits the shock absorber toward the center or rear of the vehicle and is kept away from the wheels.

The plastic air shock line attaches to the shock absorber with an O-ring or brass ferrule and nut. An air leak can result if this O-ring or ferrule is not installed according to the manufacturer's recommendations. Route the plastic air line along the body, keeping it away from the exhaust and any other body parts where the line could be damaged. Attach the line to both shocks to a junction at a convenient location for adding or releasing air.

Rear Coil Springs

Replacement. Coil springs in the rear are easily replaced on both front-wheel-drive and rear-wheel-drive vehicles. The procedure includes the following steps:

1. Raise the vehicle safely on a hoist.
2. Remove both rear wheels.
3. Support the rear axle assembly with tall safety stands.
4. Remove the lower shock absorber mounting bolts/nuts and disconnect the shock absorber from the rear axle assembly.
5. Slowly lower the rear axle assembly by either lowering the height of the adjustable safety stands or raising the height of the vehicle on the hoist.
6. Lower the rear axle just enough to remove the coil springs. See Figure 7-21.

CAUTION: The shock absorber is usually the only component that limits the downward movement of the rear axle to allow removal of the rear coil springs. Some vehicles may be equipped with rear suspension height sensors for the adjustable suspension system or an adjustable rear proportioning valve for the rear brakes. Some vehicles also require that the rear stabilizer bar or track rod be disconnected or removed before lowering the rear axle assembly. Always consult service information for the exact procedure and torque specifications for the vehicle being serviced.

Rear Leaf Springs

Replacement. Rear leaf springs often need replacement due to one of the following common causes:

1. **Individual leaves of a leaf spring often crack, then break.** When a leaf spring breaks, the load-carrying

FIGURE 7-21   Coil spring being removed from a rear suspension.

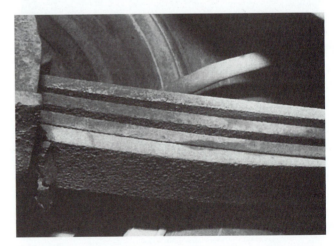

FIGURE 7-22   The leaves of this leaf spring are probably broken because the rear of the vehicle is sagging and the leaves are separated.

capacity of the vehicle decreases and it often sags on the side with the broken spring. Metal fatigue, corrosion, and overloading are three of the most common causes of leaf spring breakage. See Figure 7-22.

NOTE: When one rear spring on one side sags, the opposite front end of the vehicle tends to *rise.* For example, if the right rear spring breaks or sags down, the left front of the vehicle tends to rise higher than the right front. This unequal vehicle height can make the vehicle difficult to handle, especially around corners or curves.

2. **If the center bolt breaks,** the individual leaves can move and the rear axle is no longer held in the correct location. When one side of the rear axle is behind the other side, the vehicle will *dog track.* Dog tracking refers to the sideways angle of the vehicle while traveling straight. It is commonly caused by the rear axle steering the vehicle toward one side, while the driver controls the direction of the vehicle with the front wheels.

NOTE: Leaf springs should be replaced in pairs.

To replace leaf springs in the rear of a rear-wheel-drive vehicle, follow these steps:

1. Raise the vehicle safely on a hoist.
2. Support the rear axle with safety stands.
3. Remove the rear shackle bolts and forward mounting bolt or mounting bracket.
4. Remove the U-bolts.
5. Being careful of any nearby brake line, remove the spring.
6. Install the new spring, being careful to position the center bolt correctly into the hole on the axle pedestal.

TROUBLESHOOTING REAR ELECTRONIC LEVELING SYSTEMS

The first step with any troubleshooting procedure is to check for normal operation. Some leveling systems require that the

ignition key be on (run), while other systems operate all the time. Begin troubleshooting by placing approximately 300 lb (135 kg) on the rear of the vehicle. If the compressor does not operate, check to see if the sensor is connected to a rear suspension member and that the electrical connections are not corroded.

Also check the condition of the compressor ground wire. It must be tight and free of rust and corrosion where it attaches to the vehicle body. If the compressor still does not run, check to see if 12 volts are available at the power lead to the compressor. If necessary, use a fused jumper wire directly from the positive (+) of the battery to the power lead of the compressor. If the compressor does not operate, it must be replaced.

If the ride height compressor runs excessively, check the air compressor, the air lines, and the air shocks (or struts) with soapy water for air leaks. Most air shocks or air struts are not repairable and must be replaced. Most electronic leveling systems provide some adjustments of the rear ride height by adjusting the linkage between the height sensor and the rear suspension. See Figure 7-23.

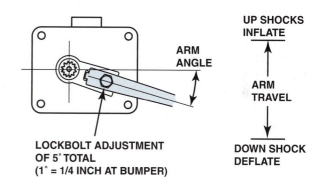

FIGURE 7-23 Most electronic level-control sensors can be adjusted, such as this General Motors unit.

SUMMARY

1. Solid rear axles are commonly used on rear-wheel-drive and front-wheel-drive vehicles.

2. A Hotchkiss rear suspension uses the leaf springs to absorb axle windup.

3. Trailing arms run parallel to the centerline of the vehicle and are used to locate a solid rear axle.

4. A track rod (Panhard rod) or Watts linkage is used to keep the rear axle centered under the vehicle.

5. Independent rear suspension (IRS) usually uses coil springs but can use a transversely mounted leaf spring.

6. The rear suspension should be supported whenever replacing the rear shock absorbers.

REVIEW QUESTIONS

1. What are the disadvantages of a solid rear axle?

2. What is the purpose of a torque arm?

3. What must be done to ensure safety when replacing the rear shock absorbers?

CHAPTER QUIZ

1. A vehicle equipped with a coil spring front suspension and a leaf spring rear suspension "dog tracks" while driving on a straight, level road. Technician A says that a broken center bolt could be the cause. Technician B says defective rear shock absorbers could be the cause. Which technician is correct?
   a. Technician A only
   b. Technician B only
   c. Both Technicians A and B
   d. Neither Technician A nor B

2. When axle windup is controlled by the rear-leaf spring during acceleration, this system is called _____.
   a. Trailing arm
   b. Semi-trailing arm
   c. Torque arm
   d. Hotchkiss drive

3. A loud "bang" is heard and felt every time the accelerator is depressed or released on a rear-wheel-drive vehicle. Technician A says that a leaf spring could be the cause. Technician B says a broken torque arm could be the cause. Which technician is correct?
   a. Technician A only
   b. Technician B only
   c. Both Technicians A and B
   d. Neither Technician A nor B

4. Technician A says that all leaf springs are mounted lengthwise on the rear of many vehicles. Technician B says that some vehicles use a transversely mounted leaf spring on the rear. Which technician is correct?
   a. Technician A only
   b. Technician B only
   c. Both Technicians A and B
   d. Neither Technician A nor B

5. A strut-type suspension is used _____.
   a. In the front only
   b. In the rear only
   c. In both the front and rear
   d. In rare vehicles no longer in production

6. Two technicians are discussing rear shock absorbers. Technician A says that if one shock is leaking, then both rear shock absorbers should be replaced. Technician B says that the rear axle should be supported before removing rear shock absorbers. Which technician is correct?
   a. Technician A only
   b. Technician B only
   c. Both Technicians A and B
   d. Neither Technician A nor B

7. Technician A says that installing new gas shock absorbers will raise the rear of the vehicle. Technician B says that the shock absorbers usually limit the downward travel of the rear suspension. Which technician is correct?
   a. Technician A only
   b. Technician B only
   c. Both Technicians A and B
   d. Neither Technician A nor B

8. The left front of the vehicle is higher than the right front and the right rear is lower than the left rear. What is the most likely cause of this problem?
   a. A weak right-rear shock absorber
   b. A broken track rod
   c. A broken left-front shock absorber
   d. A sagging right-rear spring

9. One rear leaf spring is broken. Technician A says that both rear leaf springs should be replaced. Technician B says that only the broken spring needs to be replaced. Which technician is correct?
   a. Technician A only
   b. Technician B only
   c. Both Technicians A and B
   d. Neither Technician A nor B

10. Two technicians are discussing electronic leveling systems. Technician A says that a weight should be placed in the vehicle as part of the diagnostic procedure. Technician B says many ride height sensors are adjustable. Which technician is correct?
    a. Technician A only
    b. Technician B only
    c. Both Technicians A and B
    d. Neither Technician A nor B

CHAPTER 8

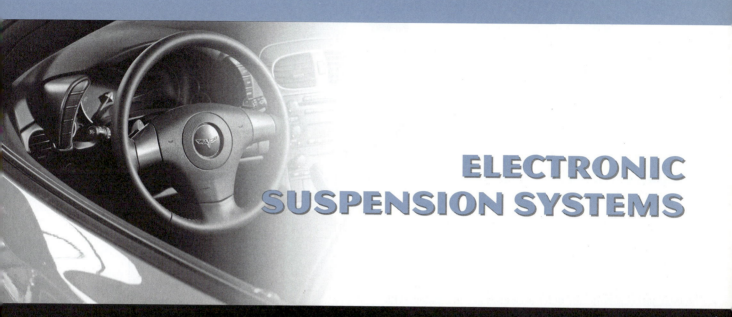

ELECTRONIC SUSPENSION SYSTEMS

OBJECTIVES

After studying Chapter 8, the reader should be able to:

1. Prepare for the Suspension and Steering (A4) ASE certification test content area "B" (Suspension System Diagnosis and Repair).
2. Describe how suspension height sensors function.
3. Explain the use of the various sensors used for electronic suspension control.
4. Discuss the steering wheel position sensor.
5. Explain how solenoids and actuators are used to control the suspension.

KEY TERMS

Actuator (p. 194)
Air Suspension (p. 195)
Armature (p. 201)
AS (p. 202)
Automatic Level Control (ALC) (p. 202)
CCVRTMR (p. 210)
Computer Command Ride (CCR) (p. 199)
Desiccant (p. 210)
Driver Select Switch (p. 199)
EBCM (p. 196)
ECU (p. 194)
Electromagnet (p. 199)
ESC (p. 205)
ESP (p. 206)
Handwheel Position Sensor (p. 196)

Height Sensor (p. 194)
Input (p. 194)
Lateral Accelerometer Sensor (p. 197)
LED (p. 194)
Loose (p. 206)
Magneto-Rheological (MR) (p. 210)
Mode Select Switch (p. 202)
Motor (p. 201)
MRRTD (p. 210)
Output (p. 194)
Perform Ride Mode (p. 204)
Photocell (p. 194)
Phototransistor (p. 194)
Plowing (p. 206)
Pulse Width (p. 201)

Pulse-Width Modulation (p. 201)
Real-Time Dampening (RTD) (p. 196)
RPO (p. 205)
RSS (p. 196)
Selectable Ride (SR) (p. 199)
Solenoid (p. 200)
Solenoid Controlled Damper (p. 207)
Stabilitrack (p. 207)
Steering Wheel Position Sensor (p. 196)
Tight (p. 206)
Touring Ride Mode (p. 204)
Vehicle Stability Enhancement System (VSES) (p. 197)
VS Sensor (p. 197)
Yaw Rate Sensor (p. 198)

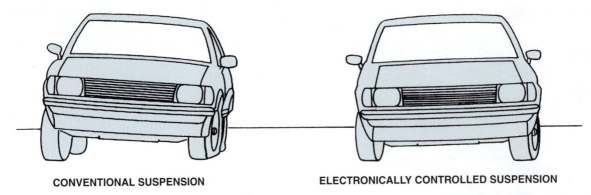

CONVENTIONAL SUSPENSION   ELECTRONICALLY CONTROLLED SUSPENSION

FIGURE 8-1   An electronically controlled suspension system can help reduce body roll and other reactions better than most conventional suspension systems.

Since the mid-1980s, many vehicle manufacturers have been introducing models with electronic suspension controls that provide a variable shock stiffness or spring rate. The main advantage of electronic controls is that the suspension can react to different conditions. The system provides a firm suspension feel for fast cornering and quick acceleration and braking, with a soft ride for cruising. See Figure 8-1.

ELECTRONIC CONTROLS AND SENSORS

Sensors and switches provide **input** to the electronic control module (ECM), or system computer. The ECM, which may also be referred to as the **electronic control unit (ECU)**, is a small computer that receives input in the form of electrical signals from the sensors and switches and provides **output** electrical signals to the system actuators. See Figure 8-2. The electrical signal causes an **actuator** to perform some type of mechanical action.

Height Sensors

Sensors, which are the input devices that transmit signals to the ECM, monitor operating conditions and component functions. A **height sensor** senses the vertical relationship between the suspension component and the body. Its signal indicates to the ECM how high the frame or body is, or how compressed the suspension is. A number of sensor designs are used to determine ride height, including a **photocell** type of sensor. See Figure 8-3.

Four height sensors, one at each wheel, deliver an input signal to the ECM. All four sensors are similar and use a control link, lever, slotted disc, and four photo interrupters to transmit a signal. Each photo interrupter consists of a **light-emitting diode (LED)** and a **phototransistor,** which reacts to the LED.

Inside the sensor, the LEDs and phototransistors are positioned opposite each other on each side of the slotted disc. See

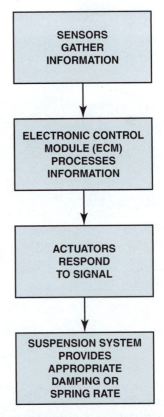

FIGURE 8-2   Input devices monitor conditions and provide information to the electronic control module, which processes the information and operates the actuators to control the movement of the suspension.

Figure 8-4. When the system is activated, the ECM applies voltage to the LEDs, which causes them to illuminate. Light from an LED shining on the phototransistor causes the transistor to generate a voltage signal. Signals generated by the phototransistors are delivered to the ECM as an input that reflects ride height.

As suspension movement rotates the disc, the slots, or windows, on the disc either allow light from the LEDs to shine on the phototransistors or prevent it. The windows are

HEIGHT SENSOR

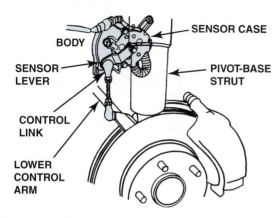

FIGURE 8-3 A typical electronic suspension height sensor, which bolts to the body and connects to the lower control arm through a control link and lever.

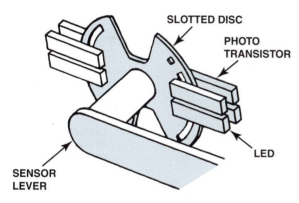

FIGURE 8-4 When suspension action moves the lever, it rotates the slotted disc and varies how much of the photo transistor is exposed to the LEDs, which vary the input signal.

positioned in such a manner that, in combination with the four LEDs and transistors, the sensor is capable of generating 16 different levels of voltage. This variable voltage, which is transmitted to the ECM as an input signal, directly corresponds to 1 of 16 possible positions of the suspension. This input signal tells the ECM the position of the suspension in relation to the body. Whether the input voltage signal is increasing or decreasing allows the ECM to determine if the suspension is compressing or extending.

The ECM can also determine the relative position of the body to the suspension, or the attitude of the vehicle, from the four height sensors. Comparing front-wheel input signals to those of the rear wheels determines the amount of pitch caused by forces of acceleration or deceleration. A side-to-side comparison allows the ECM to determine the amount of body roll generated by cornering force.

General Motors Electronic Suspension Sensors

There are five different sensors found on electronic suspension systems, and GM vehicles can have between one and four of these sensors, depending on the system.

Depending on the vehicle, the *suspension position sensor* may be called by a different name. It can be called:

- An automatic level control sensor
- An electronic suspension position sensor
- A position sensor
- An air suspension sensor

The sensor provides the control module with information regarding the relative position and movement of suspension components. The common mounting location is between the vehicle body and the suspension control arm. See Figure 8-5.

The operation of the sensor is either an air suspension sensor two-wire type or a potentiometer three-wire type. The **air suspension** sensor is also known as a *linear Hall Effect* sensor. The air suspension sensor operation consists of a moveable iron core linked to the components. As the core moves, it varies the inductance of the internal sensor coil relative to suspension position.

The suspension control module energizes and de-energizes the coil approximately 20 times a second, thereby measuring sensor inductance as it relates to suspension position. The potentiometer three-wire sensor requires reference and ground voltage. Similar to the throttle position (TP) sensor, it produces a variable analog voltage signal. See Figure 8-6.

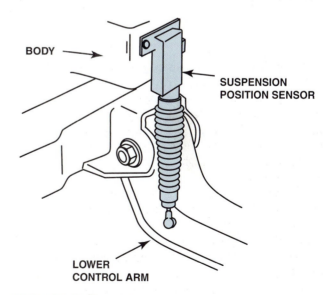

FIGURE 8-5 Typical suspension position sensor.

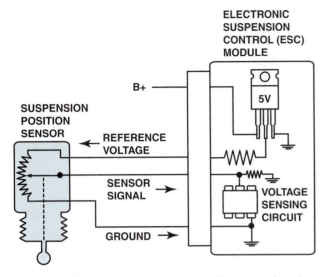

FIGURE 8-6   A three-wire suspension position sensor schematic.

FIGURE 8-7   A suspension height sensor.

As the suspension moves up or down, an arm moves on the suspension position sensor through a ball-and-cup link. See Figure 8-7.

Suspension position sensor voltage changes relative to this movement. The sensor receives a 5-volt reference signal from the control module. The position sensor returns a voltage signal between 0 and 5 volts depending on suspension arm position.

NOTE: Some systems may require sensor learning or "reprogramming" after replacement. For instance, the sensor used on the Tahoe or Suburban needs to be programmed if replaced. Always check service information for the details and procedures to follow when replacing a sensor on the suspension.

Steering Wheel Position Sensor

Depending on the vehicle, the **steering wheel position sensor** may also be called a **handwheel position sensor.** The function of this sensor is to provide the control module with signals relating to steering wheel position, the speed and direction of handwheel position.

The sensor is found on most **real-time dampening (RTD)** and **road-sensing suspension (RSS)** applications. The sensor is typically located at the base of the steering column. Always refer to service information for vehicle-specific information. See Figure 8-8 and 8-9.

The handwheel sensor produces two digital signals, which are used by the **electronic brake control module (EBCM).** These signals are produced as the steering wheel is rotated. The sensor can also produce more than two signals. As an example, the Cadillac Escalade handwheel sensor produces one analog and three digital signals.

The sensor uses a 5-volt signal reference. Analog signal voltage values increase or decrease, between 0 and 5 volts, as the steering wheel is moved left and right of center. The digital signal is also a standard power-to-ground circuit as shown in the schematic.

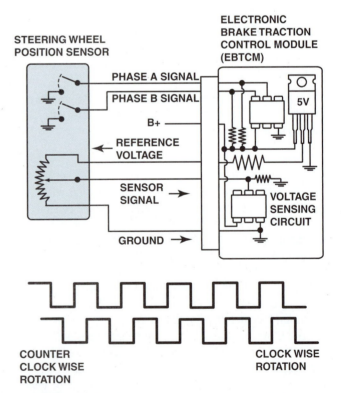

FIGURE 8-8   The steering wheel position (handwheel position) sensor wiring schematic and how the signal varies with the direction that the steering wheel is turned.

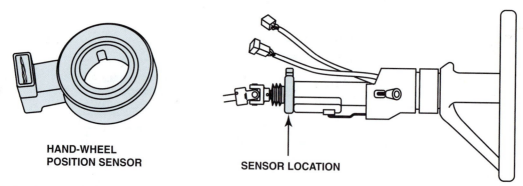

HAND-WHEEL POSITION SENSOR

SENSOR LOCATION

FIGURE 8-9   The handwheel position sensor is located at the base of the steering column.

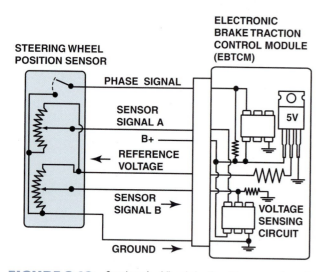

FIGURE 8-10   Steering wheel (handwheel) position sensor schematic.

There are three possible digital signals:

- Phase A
- Phase B
- Index pulse

These signals provide the suspension control module with steering wheel speed and direction information. Digital signals are either high or low, 5 volts or 0 volts. See Figure 8-10.

The Tech 2 provides DTC faults for this sensor. If there is an intermittent concern with a steering wheel position sensor, select Tech 2 snapshot and slowly turn the steering wheel lock to lock. After the snapshot is complete, plot the analog sensor voltage to see if the signal dropped out. Any dropout is an indication of an intermittent problem.

Vehicle Speed Sensor

The **vehicle speed (VS) sensor** is used by the EBCM to help control the suspension system. The vehicle speed sensor is a magnetic sensor and generates an analog signal whose frequency increases as the speed increases. The ride is made firmer at high speeds and during braking and acceleration and less firm at cruise speeds. See Figure 8-11.

Pressure Sensor

A pressure transducer (sensor) is typically mounted on the compressor assembly. This sensor is typically found on suspension systems that use a compressor assembly. The main function of the pressure sensor is to provide feedback to the suspension control module about the operation of the compressor. The sensor assures both that a minimum air pressure is maintained in the system and that a maximum value is not exceeded. A pressure transducer (sensor) is typically mounted on the compressor assembly. This sensor is typically found on systems such as air suspension, real-time damping, and road-sensing suspension that use a compressor assembly. See Figure 8-12.

The operation of the pressure sensor requires a 5-volt reference, a ground, and a signal wire to provide feedback to the control module. The voltage output on the signal wire will vary from 0 to 5 volts based upon pressure in the system. A high voltage indicates high pressure and low voltage indicates a low pressure.

Lateral Accelerometer Sensor

The function of the **lateral accelerometer sensor** is to provide the suspension control module with feedback regarding vehicle cornering forces. This type of sensor is also called a G-sensor, with the letter "G" representing the force of gravity. For example, when a vehicle enters a turn, the sensor provides information as to how hard the vehicle is cornering. This information is processed by the suspension control module to provide appropriate damping on the inboard and outboard dampers during cornering events. The lateral accelerometer sensor is found on the more complex suspensions systems, such as RTD and RSS systems that incorporate the **vehicle stability enhancement system (VSES).**

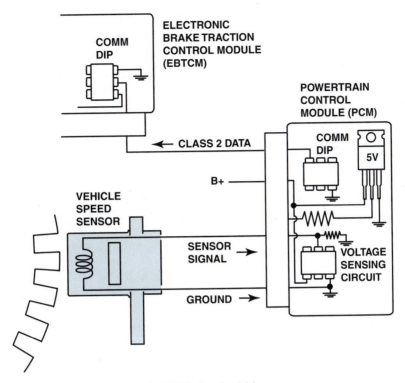

FIGURE 8-11   The VS sensor information is transmitted to the EBCM by Class 2 serial data.

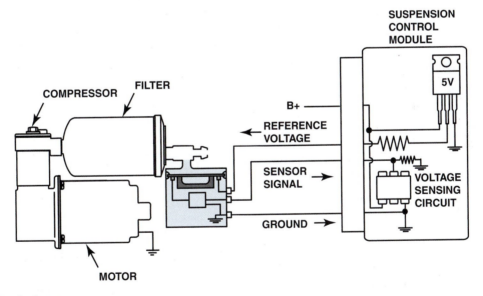

FIGURE 8-12   An air pressure sensor.

This sensor can be either a stand-alone unit or combined with the yaw rate sensor. Typically, the sensor is mounted in the passenger compartment under a front seat, center console, or package shelf.

The sensor produces a voltage signal of 0 to 5 volts as the vehicle maneuvers left or right through a curve. The signal is an input to the EBCM. If zero lateral acceleration, the sensor input is 2.5 volts. Check service information for specific codes that can be set.

If driving the vehicle and the voltage values increase or decrease during cornering events, this indicates proper operation. See Figure 8-13.

Yaw Rate Sensor

The **yaw rate sensor** provides information to the suspension control module and the EBCM. This information is used to determine how far the vehicle has deviated from the driver's

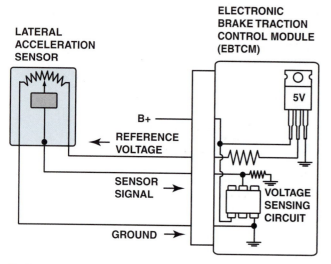

FIGURE 8-13 A schematic showing the lateral acceleration sensor and the EBCM.

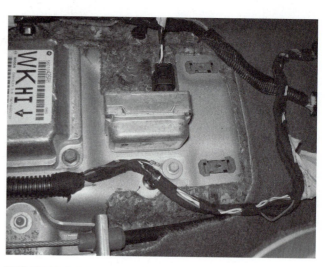

FIGURE 8-14 The lateral accelerometer sensor (G-sensor) is usually located under the center console.

TECH TIP

QUICK AND EASY "G" SENSOR TEST

Most factory scan tools will display the value of sensors, including the lateral accelerometer sensor (G-sensor). However, the G-sensor value will read zero unless the vehicle is cornering. A quick and easy test of the sensor is to simply unbolt the sensor and rotate it 90 degrees with the key on engine off. See Figure 8-14. Now the sensor is measuring the force of gravity and should display 1.0 G on the scan tool. If the sensor does not read close to 1.0 G or reads zero all of the time, the sensor or the wiring is defective.

intended direction. The yaw sensor is used on vehicles equipped with Electronic Stability Control (ESC).

This sensor can be either a stand-alone unit or combined with the lateral accelerometer sensor. Typically, the sensor is mounted in the passenger compartment under the front seat, center console, or on the rear package shelf.

The sensor produces a voltage signal of 0 to 5 volts as the vehicle yaw rate changes. The voltage signal is an input to the EBCM. The yaw rate input to the EBCM indicates the number of degrees that the vehicle deviates from its intended direction.

For example, with a 0-degree yaw rate, the sensor output is 2.5 volts. During an emergency maneuver, the signal will vary above or below 2.5 volts. This sensor does set DTC codes. These codes can be found in service information. See Figure 8-15.

Driver Selector Switch

The **driver select switch** is a two- or three-mode switch, usually located in the center console, and is an input to the suspension control module.

The switch that is used to select either touring (soft) or performance (firm) ride is found on the **Selectable Ride (SR)** and the **Computer Command Ride (CCR)** systems. The mode select switch status is generally displayed on a scan tool. The three-position switch is used on the Corvette RTD system, and allows the driver to select three modes of operation:

- Tour
- Sport
- Performance

ELECTRONIC SUSPENSION SYSTEM ACTUATORS

Each actuator in an electronically controlled suspension system receives output signals from the ECM and responds to these signals, or commands, by performing a mechanical action. Actuators are usually inductive devices that operate using an electromagnetic field. A simple **electromagnet** consists of a soft iron core with a coil of wire, usually copper, wrapped around it. See Figure 8-16.

Electrical current traveling through the coiled wire creates a magnetic field around the core. All magnets are polarized; that is, they have a north, or positive, and a south, or negative, pole. When the opposite poles of two magnets are placed near each other—positive-to-negative—the magnets attract each other. Place the same poles together, positive-to-positive or negative-to-negative, and the magnets repel each other. See

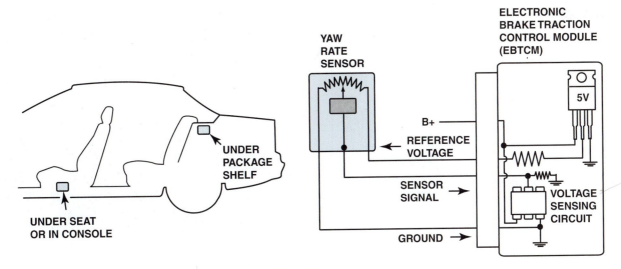

FIGURE 8-15   Yaw rate sensor showing the typical location and schematic.

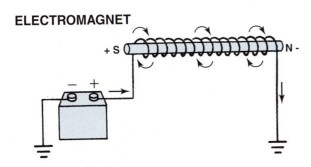

FIGURE 8-16   A magnetic field is created whenever an electrical current flows through a coil of wire wrapped around an iron core.

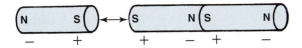

FIGURE 8-17   When magnets are near each other, like poles repel and opposite poles attract.

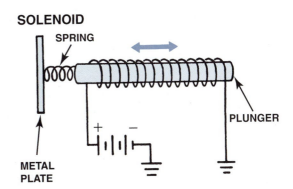

FIGURE 8-18   When electrical current magnetizes the plunger in a solenoid, the magnetic field moves the plunger against spring force. With no current, the spring pushes the plunger back to its original position.

Figure 8-17. Magnets also attract and are attracted to certain types of metals, especially iron and steel.

When an electromagnet has more than one coil, the stronger primary coil can induce voltage into the weaker secondary coil. This inductive transfer occurs even though there is no physical connection between the two coils.

Solenoids

In a **solenoid,** the core of the electromagnet also acts as a plunger to open and close a passage or to move a linkage. Solenoids are cylindrically shaped with a metal plate at one end and open at the other end to allow the plunger to move in and out. The electromagnetic coils are placed along the sides of the cylinder. A preload spring forces the plunger toward one end of the device when the solenoid is de-energized, or there is no current in the coil.

When the solenoid is energized, current passes through the coil and magnetizes the core. The magnetized core is attracted to the metal plate and the strength of the magnetic field overcomes spring force to pull the plunger inward. See Figure 8-18. When the electrical current switches off, the solenoid de-energizes and spring force returns the plunger to its rest position.

An airflow control valve is an example of a solenoid used in an electronically controlled suspension. See Figure 8-19. As the solenoid plunger extends and retracts, it opens and closes air passages between the system air-pressure tank and the air springs. The position of the plunger determines whether the springs receive more pressure or whether pressure bleeds out of them. Increasing the pressure in the air springs lifts the body higher, and decreasing the pressure by bleeding air from the springs lowers the body.

SOLENOID OFF

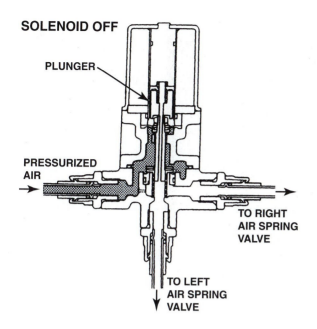

PLUNGER

PRESSURIZED AIR →

TO RIGHT AIR SPRING VALVE

TO LEFT AIR SPRING VALVE

SOLENOID ON

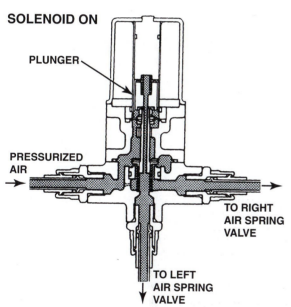

PLUNGER

PRESSURIZED AIR →

TO RIGHT AIR SPRING VALVE

TO LEFT AIR SPRING VALVE

FIGURE 8-19   This air supply solenoid blocks pressurized air from the air spring valves when off. The plunger pulls upward to allow airflow to the air spring valves when the solenoid is energized.

Solenoids are digital devices that are either on or off. However, the ECM can vary the amount a solenoid opens by pulsing the output signal to the coil. If the signal is rapidly switched on and off, spring and magnetic forces do not have enough time to react and effectively move the plunger between the signal changes. The amount of time the current is on compared to the amount of time it is off is called **pulse width**, and the control of a solenoid using this pulsing-on-and-off method is called **pulse-width modulation.**

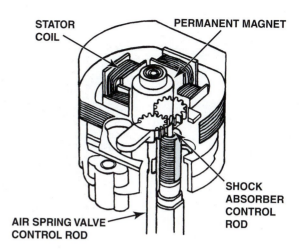

STATOR COIL

PERMANENT MAGNET

SHOCK ABSORBER CONTROL ROD

AIR SPRING VALVE CONTROL ROD

FIGURE 8-20   An actuator motor uses a permanent magnet and four stator coils to drive the air spring control rod.

Actuator Motors

If a current-carrying conductor is placed in a magnetic field, it tends to move from the stronger field area to the weaker field area. A **motor** uses this principle to convert electrical energy into mechanical movement. Electrical current is directed through the field coils on the motor frame to create a magnetic field within the frame. By applying an electrical current to the **armature,** which is inside the motor frame, the armature rotates from a strong field area to a weaker field area. Armature movement can in turn move another part, such as a gear, pulley, or shaft, attached to it.

Located at the top mount of the air spring variable shock assembly of each wheel, the suspension control actuator moves a control rod that regulates air pressure to the spring, which determines ride height. The actuator is an electromagnetic device consisting of four stator coils and a permanent magnet core. See Figure 8-20.

The ECM applies current to two stator coils at a time to create opposing magnetic fields around the core, which causes the core to rotate into a new position. Which coils are energized determines how far and in which direction the core rotates. See Figure 8-21. By switching current from one pair of coils to the other, the ECM moves the core into a new position, and a third position is available by reversing the polarity of the coils.

A gear at the base of the permanent magnet connects to a rod that operates the air valve to the air spring. The gear also drives another gear, which operates the control rod of the variable shock absorber. Therefore, the three positions of the suspension control actuator motor provide three shock absorber stiffness settings in addition to a variable air spring.

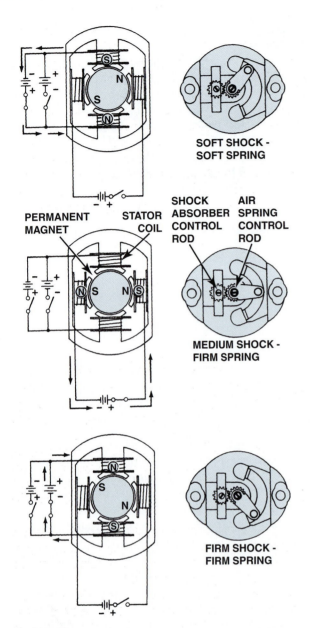

FIGURE 8-21   The stator coils of the actuator are energized in three ways to provide soft, medium, or firm ride from the air springs and shock absorbers.

TYPES OF ELECTRONIC SUSPENSION

The types of electronic suspension systems used on General Motors vehicles, as examples, include:

1. Selectable Ride
2. Automatic Level Control
3. Air Suspension
4. Computer Command Ride
5. Real-Time Dampening/Road-Sensing Suspension

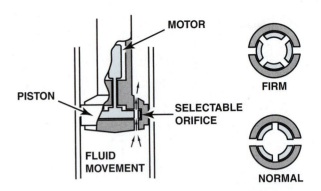

FIGURE 8-22   Selectable Ride as used on Chevrolet and GMC C/K trucks.

6. Vehicle Stability Enhancement System
7. Magneto-Rheological Suspension (F55)

Selectable Ride (SR)

The Selectable Ride (SR) system is the most basic of the electronic systems offered by General Motors. Selectable Ride (SR) allows the driver to choose between two distinct damping levels:

- Firm
- Normal

SR is found on Chevrolet and GMC full-size (C/K) trucks. See Figure 8-22.

A switch is used to control four electronically controlled gas-charged dampers. The **mode select switch** activates the bi-state (two settings) dampers at all four corners of the vehicle, allowing the driver to select vehicle ride characteristics. The system is either energizing or de-energizing the bi-state dampers to provide a firm or normal ride.

Automatic Level Control

The **Automatic Level Control (ALC)** system automatically adjusts the rear height of the vehicle in response to changes in vehicle loading and unloading. Automatic Level Control is found on many General Motors vehicles. ALC controls rear leveling by monitoring the rear suspension position sensor and energizing the compressor to raise the vehicle or energizing the exhaust valve to lower the vehicle. ALC has several variations across the different platforms. See Figure 8-23.

Air Suspension (AS)

Air Suspension (AS) is a system very similar to the ALC system. The purpose of the AS system includes:

1. Keep the vehicle visually level
2. Provide optimal headlight aiming
3. Maintain optimal ride height

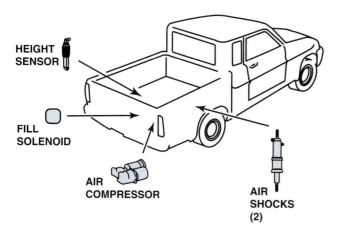

FIGURE 8-23   ALC maintains the same ride height either loaded or unloaded.

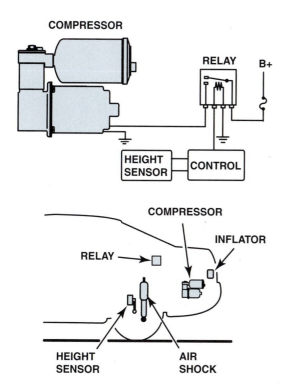

FIGURE 8-24   A typical schematic showing the air suspension compressor assembly and sensor.

The AS system includes the following components:

- An air suspension compressor assembly
- Rear air springs
- Air suspension sensors

The AS system is designed to maintain rear trim height within 4 mm in all loading conditions, and the leveling function will deactivate if the vehicle is overloaded.

The AS system also includes an accessory air inflator found in the rear cargo area. See Figure 8-24.

Variable-Rate Air Springs

In an air spring system with ordinary shock absorbers, the ECM uses the air springs to control trim height and is used on many Ford, Mercury, and Lincoln vehicles.

The three height sensors transmit a signal to the ECM that reflects trim height at each axle. See Figure 8-25. The ignition and brake light switches tell the ECM whether the ignition switch is on or off, and if the brake pedal is depressed. The dome light switch indicates whether any doors are open. The on/off switch disables the air spring system to avoid unexpected movement while towing or servicing the vehicle.

CAUTION: Failure to turn off the system will cause the air springs to be vented when the vehicle is hoisted. This will cause the vehicle to drop almost to the ground when the vehicle is lowered. This can cause damage to the air springs and/or to the vehicle.

The ECM receives information from the height sensors indicating that the trim height is too high or too low, and it energizes the actuators to add or bleed air from the air springs. The system actuators can still operate for up to an hour after the ignition is switched off.

Any time the ignition is switched to the "run" position, the ECM raises the vehicle, if necessary, within the first 45 seconds. If trim height is too high and the vehicle must be lowered, the ECM delays doing so for 45 seconds after the ignition is switched on.

An air compressor with a regenerative dryer provides the air change required to inflate the air springs on the air suspension system, and a vent solenoid is used to relieve air pressure and deflate the springs. See Figure 8-26.

By energizing the compressor relay, the ECM directs current to turn on the compressor motor when trim height needs to be raised. The ECM command to lower the vehicle is an electrical signal that opens the vent solenoid to bleed air pressure out of the system. See Figure 8-27.

General Motors Computer Command Ride

The General Motors Computer Command Ride (CCR) system controls ride firmness by automatically controlling an actuator in each of the four struts to increase ride firmness as speed increases.

The three damping modes are:

- Comfort
- Normal
- Sport

VARIABLE-RATE AIR SPRINGS

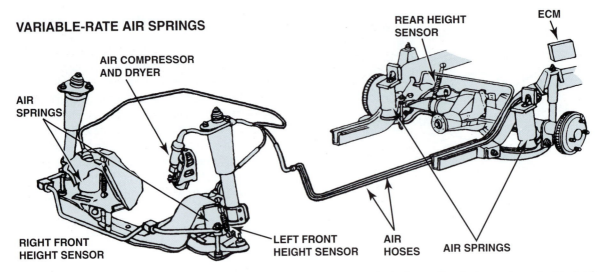

FIGURE 8-25   The typical variable-rate air spring system uses three height sensors, two in the front and one in the rear, to monitor trim height and to provide input signals to the ECM.

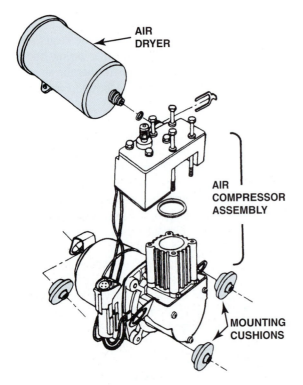

FIGURE 8-26   The air spring compressor assembly is usually mounted on rubber cushions to help isolate it from the body of the vehicle. All of the air entering or leaving the air springs flows through the regenerative air dryer.

Damping mode selection is controlled by the CCR control module according to vehicle speed conditions, driver select switch position, and any error conditions that may exist.

In the **perform ride mode,** the system will place the damping level in the firm mode regardless of vehicle speed.

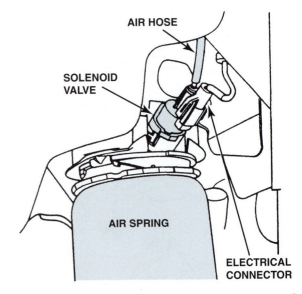

FIGURE 8-27   A solenoid valve at the top of each spring regulates airflow into and out of the air spring.

In the **touring ride mode,** the damping level depends on vehicle speed. See Figure 8-28.

Real-Time Dampening and Road-Sensing Suspension

Real-time dampening (RTD) independently controls a solenoid in each of the four shock absorbers in order to control the vehicle ride characteristics and is capable of making changes within milliseconds (0.001 second).

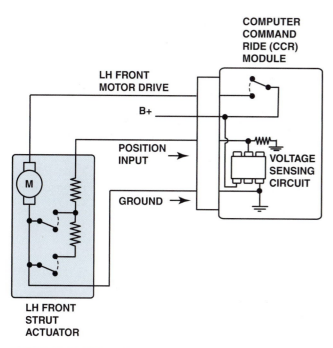

FIGURE 8-28 Schematic showing Computer Command Ride (CCR) system.

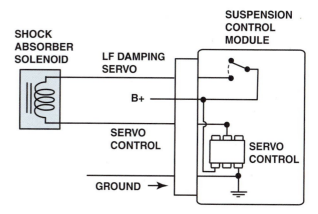

FIGURE 8-29 Schematic showing the shock control used in the RSS system.

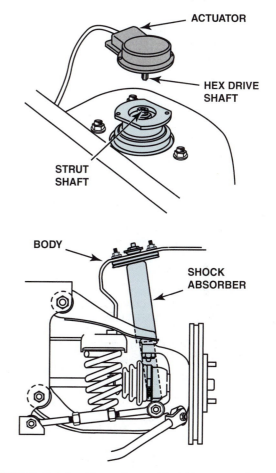

FIGURE 8-30 Bi-state dampers (shocks) use a solenoid to control fluid flow in the unit to control compression and rebound actions.

TECH TIP

CHECK THE RPO CODE

Whenever working on the suspension system check the **RPO (regular production option)** code for the type of suspension used. For example, the F55 RPO may be called by a different name depending on the make and model of vehicle. Also, service procedures will be different on the same vehicle depending on whether it is equipped with an F45 or an F55 system.

Road-sensing suspension (RSS), along with ALC, controls damping forces in the front struts and rear shock absorbers in response to various road and driving conditions.

RTD and RSS incorporate the following components:

- An electronic suspension control module,
- Front and rear suspension position sensors,
- Bi-state dampers
- A ride select switch, and
- An air compressor is used on some models.

See Figures 8-29 and 8-30.

ELECTRONIC STABILITY CONTROL

Electronic Stability Control (ESC) uses the steering wheel position sensor and the G-force and/or yaw sensor to determine if a vehicle is not under control. The ESC system, also called the **Electronic Stability Program (ESP)**, then applies individual wheel brakes to bring the vehicle under control. The following occurs if the vehicle is oversteering or understeering.

Oversteering

In the oversteering condition, the rear of the vehicle breaks loose, resulting in the vehicle spinning out of control. This condition is also called **loose.** If the condition is detected during a left turn, the ESC system would apply the right front brake to bring the vehicle back under control.

Understeering

In understeering condition, the front of the vehicle continues straight ahead when turning, a condition that is also called **plowing** or **tight.** If this condition is detected during a right turn, the ESC system would apply the right rear wheel brake to bring the vehicle back under control. See Figure 8-31.

NOTE: When the brakes are applied during these corrections, a thumping sound and vibration may be sensed.

Stability control systems are offered under the following names:

- Acura: Vehicle Stability Assist (VSA)
- Audi: Electronic Stabilization Program (ESP)
- BMW: Dynamic Stability Control (DSC), including Dynamic Traction Control
- Chrysler: Electronic Stability Program (ESP)
- Dodge: Electronic Stability Program (ESP)
- DaimlerChrysler: Electronic Stability Program (ESP)
- Ferrari: Controllo Stabilita (CST)
- Ford: Advance Trac and Interactive Vehicle Dynamics (IVD)
- GM: StabiliTrak (except Corvette—Active Handling)
- Hyundai: Electronic Stability Program (ESP)
- Honda: Electronic Stability Control (ESC) and Vehicle Stability Assist (VSA) and Electronic Stability Program (ESP)
- Infiniti: Vehicle Dynamic Control (VDC)
- Jaguar: Dynamic Stability Control (DSC)
- Jeep: Electronic Stability Program (ESP)
- Kia: Electronic Stability Program (ESP)
- Land Rover: Dynamic Stability Control (DSC)
- Lexus: Vehicle Dynamics Integrated Management (VDIM) with Vehicle Stability Control (VSC) and Traction Control (TRAC) systems
- Lincoln: AdvanceTrak
- Maserati: Maserati Stability Program (MSP)
- Mazda: Dynamic Stability Control
- Mercedes: Electronic Stability Program (ESP)
- Mercury: AdvanceTrak
- MINI Cooper: Dynamic Stability Control
- Mitsubishi: Active Skid and Traction Control MULTIMODE
- Nissan: Vehicle Dynamic Control (VDC)
- Porsche: Porsche Stability Management (PSM)

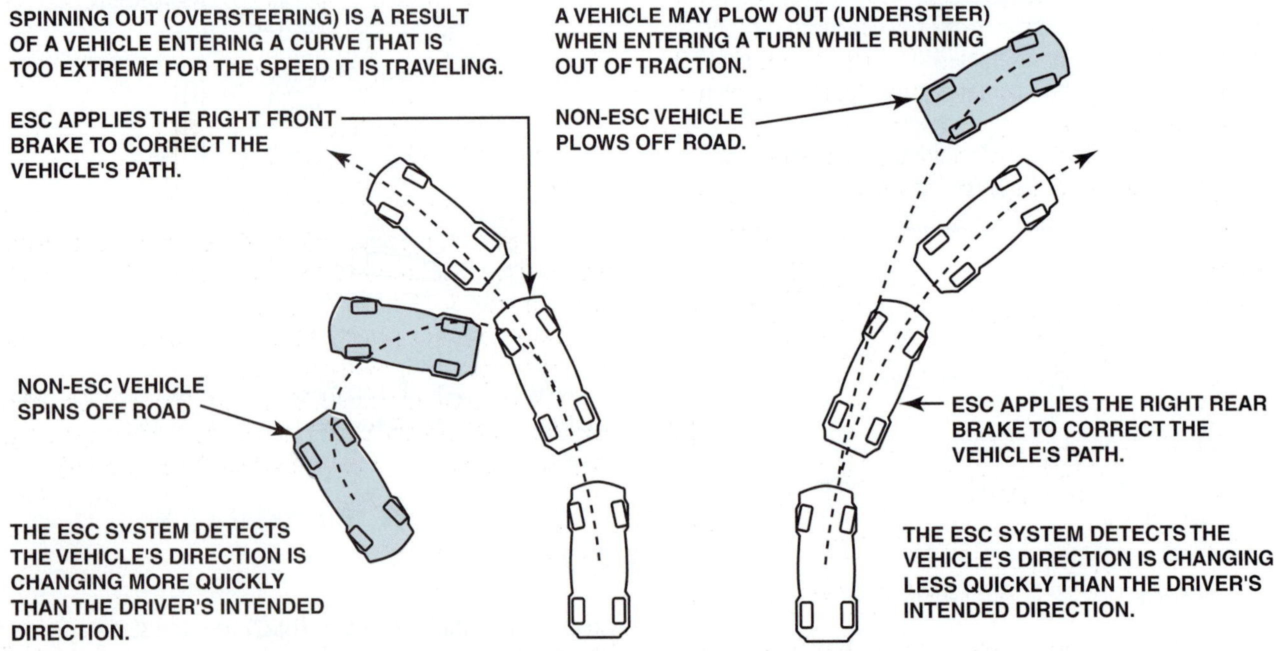

SPINNING OUT (OVERSTEERING) IS A RESULT OF A VEHICLE ENTERING A CURVE THAT IS TOO EXTREME FOR THE SPEED IT IS TRAVELING.

ESC APPLIES THE RIGHT FRONT BRAKE TO CORRECT THE VEHICLE'S PATH.

NON-ESC VEHICLE SPINS OFF ROAD

THE ESC SYSTEM DETECTS THE VEHICLE'S DIRECTION IS CHANGING MORE QUICKLY THAN THE DRIVER'S INTENDED DIRECTION.

A VEHICLE MAY PLOW OUT (UNDERSTEER) WHEN ENTERING A TURN WHILE RUNNING OUT OF TRACTION.

NON-ESC VEHICLE PLOWS OFF ROAD.

ESC APPLIES THE RIGHT REAR BRAKE TO CORRECT THE VEHICLE'S PATH.

THE ESC SYSTEM DETECTS THE VEHICLE'S DIRECTION IS CHANGING LESS QUICKLY THAN THE DRIVER'S INTENDED DIRECTION.

FIGURE 8-31 The Electronic Stability Control (ESC) system applies individual wheel brakes to keep the vehicle under control of the driver.

- Rover: Dynamic Stability Control (DSC)
- Saab: Electronic Stability Program (ESP)
- Saturn: StabiliTrak
- Subaru: Vehicle Dynamics Control Systems (VDCS)
- Suzuki: Electronic Stability Program (ESP)
- Toyota: Vehicle Dynamics Integrated Management (VDIM) with Vehicle Stability Control (VSC)
- Volvo: Dynamic Stability and Traction Control (DSTC)
- VW: Electronic Stability Program (ESP)

The purpose of the vehicle stability enhancement system along with the antilock brake system (ABS) is to provide vehicle stability enhancement during oversteer, or understeer conditions.

Bi-State and Tri-State Dampers

The bi-state damper is also known as a **solenoid controlled damper.** Bi-state dampers are found on the RTD, RSS, and SR systems. Each of the suspension dampers used in these systems have an integral solenoid. The solenoid valve provides various amounts of damping by directing hydraulic damping fluid in the suspension shock absorber or strut. See Figure 8-32.

The General Motors version of ESC is called the vehicle stability enhancement system (VSES) and includes an additional level of vehicle control to the EBCM. VSES is also known as **Stabilitrak.**

The purpose of the vehicle stability enhancement system along with the antilock brake system (ABS) is to provide vehicle stability enhancement during oversteer or understeer conditions.

The pulse-width modulation (PWM) voltage signal from the suspension control module controls the amount of current flow through each of the damper solenoids. With a low PWM signal de-energized, more hydraulic damping fluid is allowed to bypass the main suspension damper passage, resulting in a softer damping mode.

As the PWM signal increases, or is energized, the damping mode becomes more firm. See Figure 8-33.

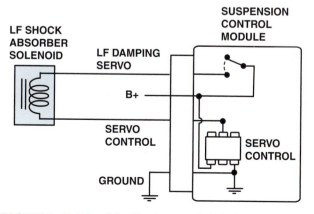

FIGURE 8-32 Solenoid valve controlled shock absorber circuit showing the left front (LF) shock as an example.

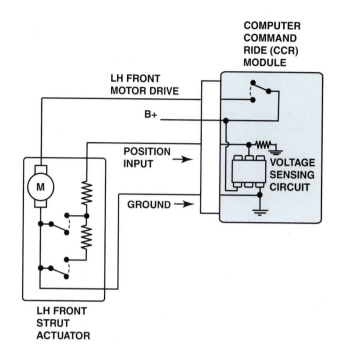

FIGURE 8-33 A typical CCR module schematic.

NOTE: If the suspension module does not control the shock absorber solenoid, a full soft damping mode results. In some system malfunctions, the module may command one or all of the damper solenoids to a full soft damping.

As the PWM signal increases, or is energized, the damping mode becomes more firm. The main difference between a tri-state damper and a bi-state damper is that the tri-state damper uses an electrical actuator, whereas the bi-state damper is solenoid controlled.

The three damping modes include:

- Comfort
- Normal
- Sport

A tri-state damper has an integral electrical strut actuator that rotates a selector valve to change the flow of hydraulic damping fluid. See Figure 8-34.

The CCR module controls the operation of the strut actuators to provide the three damping modes.

The strut position input provides feedback to the CCR module. The strut position input is compared to the commanded actuator position to monitor system operation. See Figure 8-35.

AUTOMATIC LEVEL CONTROL (ALC)

Vehicles that have an air inflator system as part of the ALC system also have an air inflator switch. The air inflator

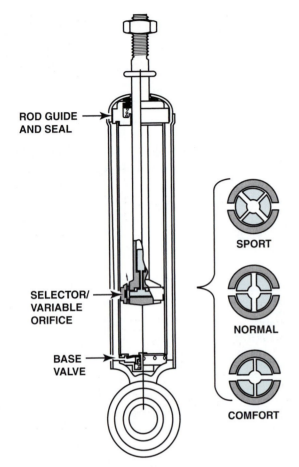

ROD GUIDE
AND SEAL

SELECTOR/
VARIABLE
ORIFICE

BASE
VALVE

SPORT

NORMAL

COMFORT

FIGURE 8-34   The three dampening modes of a CCR shock absorber.

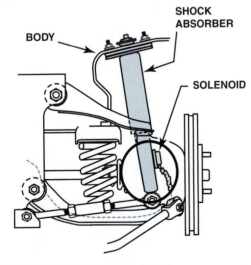

BODY

SHOCK
ABSORBER

SOLENOID

FIGURE 8-35   Integral shock solenoid.

switch is an input to the ALC and AS system. The inflator switch is used to control the air inflator system operation and provides a signal to the ALC or AS module to initiate compressor activation.

FREQUENTLY ASKED QUESTION

WHAT ARE SELF-LEVELING SHOCKS?

A German company, ZF Sachs, supplies a self-leveling shock absorber to several vehicle manufacturers, such as DaimlerChrysler for use on the rear of minivans, plus BMW, Saab, and Volvo. The self-leveling shocks are entirely self-contained and do not require the use of height sensors or an external air pump. See Figure 8-36.

The shock looks like a conventional shock absorber but contains the following components:

- Two reservoirs in the outer tube
- An oil reservoir (low-pressure reservoir)
- A high-pressure chamber

Inside the piston rod is the pump chamber containing an inlet and an outlet valve. When a load is placed in the rear of the vehicle, it compresses the suspension and the shock absorber. When the vehicle starts to move, the internal pump is activated by the movement of the body. Extension of the piston rod causes oil to be drawn through the inlet valve into the pump. When the shock compresses, the oil is forced through the outlet valve into the high-pressure chamber. The pressure in the oil reserve decreases as the pressure in the high-pressure chamber increases. The increasing pressure is applied to the piston rod, which raises the height of the vehicle.

When the vehicle's normal height is reached, no oil is drawn into the chamber. Because the shock is mechanical, the vehicle needs to be moving before the pump starts to work. It requires about 2 miles of driving for the shock to reach the normal ride height. The vehicle also needs to be driven about 2 miles after a load has been removed from the vehicle for it to return to normal ride height.

With the ignition on, the driver can turn the system to ON. The switch will command the compressor to run for up to 10 minutes, allowing time to inflate a tire or other items requiring air.

NOTE: There are no DTCs associated with compressor assembly.

Inflator or Compressor Relay

The suspension control module energizes the relay to activate the compressor motor. This adjusts the rear trim height as needed. The suspension control module controls the compressor relay for normal operation or for the accessory air inflator.

To avoid compressor overheating, the timer within the suspension control module limits the compressor run time to 10 minutes. See Figure 8-37.

On RTD or RSS systems with a compressor, the Tech 2 may display DTCs associated with compressor relay operation. On some vehicle applications, the Tech 2 will display data relating to relay operation and can be used to command the relay to verify proper operation.

Compressor

The compressor is a positive-displacement air pump and can generate up to 150 lbs. of pressure per square inch (psi). The compressor is found on the ALC, AS, RTD, and RSS systems. A 12-volt permanent magnet motor drives the compressor. The compressor supplies compressed air to the rear air shock absorbers or struts to raise the vehicle. See Figure 8-38.

FIGURE 8-36   A typical ZF Sachs self-leveling shock, as used on the rear of a DaimlerChrysler minivan.

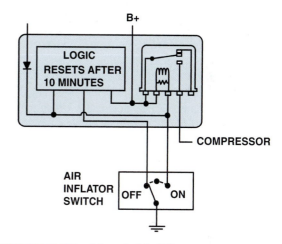

FIGURE 8-37   Schematic of the ALC system.

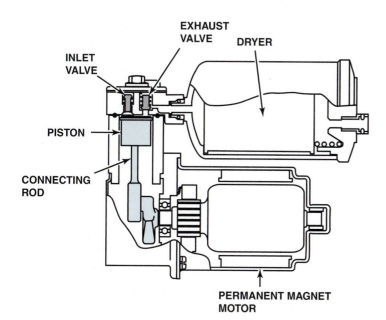

FIGURE 8-38   Air compressor assembly can be located at various locations depending on the vehicle.

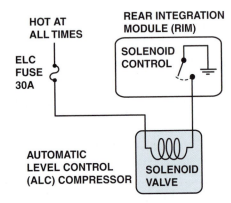

FIGURE 8-39 The exhaust solenoid is controlled by the rear integration module (RIM).

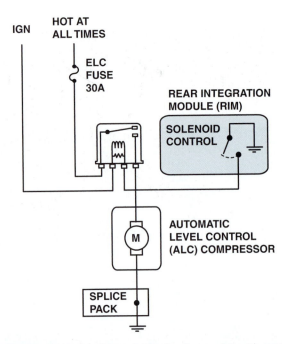

FIGURE 8-40 Schematic showing the rear integration module (RIM) and how it controls the ALC compressor.

Air Dryer. Within the compressor is an air dryer. The air dryer is responsible for removing moisture from the compressor system. Improper air dryer operation can cause a premature failure in the system if an air line restriction occurs due to excessive moisture build-up. A dryer on the output side of the compressor contains silica gel **desiccant**, which removes moisture from the discharge air before it travels through the nylon air hoses to the air chamber of the rear shocks.

Exhaust Solenoid. The exhaust solenoid, which is located on the compressor, relieves pressure in the system. The ground-side switched exhaust solenoid has three main functions:

1. It releases compressed air from the shock absorbers or air springs to lower the vehicle body.
2. It relieves compressor head pressure. By exhausting air, it protects compressor start-up from high head pressure, which can possibly cause fuse failure.
3. The solenoid acts as a pressure relief valve, which limits overall system pressure.

The special functions on the Tech 2 can be used to command the solenoid and to verify its operation. See Figures 8-39 and 8-40.

MAGNETO-RHEOLOGICAL (MR) SUSPENSION

MR fluid shocks use a working fluid inside the shock that can change viscosity rapidly depending on electric current sent to an electromagnetic coil in each device. The fluid is called **magneto-rheological (MR)** and is used in monotube-type shock absorbers. This type of shock and suspension system is

FIGURE 8-41 Vehicles that use magneto-rheological shock absorbers have a sensor located near each wheel, as shown on this C6 Corvette.

called the **magneto-rheological real-time damping (MRRTD)** or **chassis continuously variable real-time dampening magneto-rheological suspension (CCVRTMR).**

Under normal operating conditions, the fluid flows easily through orifices in the shock and provides little dampening. When a large or high-frequency bump is detected, a small electrical current is sent from the chassis controller to an electromagnetic coil in each shock and the iron particles in the fluid respond within 3 milliseconds (ms), aligning themselves in fiber-like strands. See Figures 8-41 and 8-42.

FIGURE 8-42   The controller for the magneto-rheological suspension system on a C6 Corvette is located behind the right front wheel.

FREQUENTLY ASKED QUESTION

CAN COMPUTER CONTROLLED SHOCK ABSORBERS AND STRUTS BE REPLACED WITH CONVENTIONAL UNITS?

Maybe. If the vehicle was manufactured with or without electronic or variable shock absorbers, it may be possible to replace the originals with the standard replacement units. The electrical connector must be disconnected, and this may cause the control system to store a diagnostic trouble code (DTC) and/or turn on a suspension fault warning light on the dash. Some service technicians have used a resistor equal in resistance value of the solenoid or motor across the terminals of the wiring connector to keep the controller from setting a DTC. All repairs to a suspension system should be done to restore the vehicle to like-new condition, so care should be exercised if replacing electronic shocks with nonelectronic versions.

This causes the MR fluid to become thick like peanut butter and increases the firmness of the shock. This type of shock absorber is used to control squat during acceleration and brake dive as well as to reduce body roll during cornering by the chassis controller. See Figure 8-43.

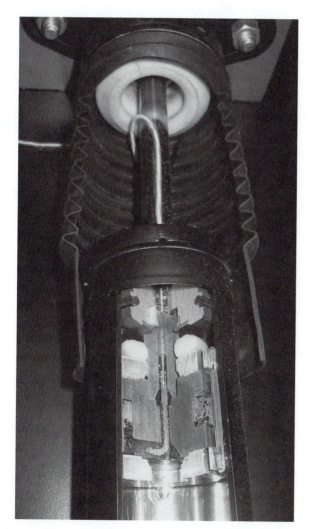

FIGURE 8-43   A cutaway of a magneto-rheological shock absorber as displayed at the Corvette Museum in Bowling Green, Kentucky.

SUMMARY

1. General Motors uses seven types of electronic suspension under many different names.
2. Suspension height sensors and steering wheel (handwheel) position sensors are used in many systems.
3. A vehicle speed sensor signal is used to control the suspension at various speeds.
4. Many electronic suspension systems use a lateral accelerometer sensor, which signals the suspension computer when the vehicle is rapidly accelerating, braking, or cornering.
5. Solenoids and motors are used to control the suspension movement by moving valves in the shock absorbers or air springs.
6. An air pump and air shocks are used to raise the rear of the vehicle to compensate for a heavy load.

REVIEW QUESTIONS

1. What type of sensor is usually used on electronically controlled suspensions to sense the height of the vehicle?
2. Why is the vehicle speed sensor used as input for many electronic suspension systems?
3. What is a lateral accelerometer sensor and why is it used?
4. Why does the output side of the suspension air compressor contain a desiccant?

CHAPTER QUIZ

1. What type of sensor is used as a height sensor on vehicles equipped with an electronically controlled suspension?
   a. Hall-effect
   b. Photo cell
   c. Potentiometer
   d. All of the above

2. Which sensors do most vehicles use if equipped with electronic suspension?
   a. Height sensors
   b. Steering wheel position sensors
   c. Lateral accelerometer sensors
   d. All of the above

3. A lateral acceleration sensor is used to provide the suspension control module with feedback regarding _____ force.
   a. Cornering
   b. Acceleration
   c. Braking
   d. All of the above

4. A steering wheel position sensor is being discussed. Technician A says that the sensor is used to determine the direction the steering wheel is turned. Technician B says that the sensor detects how fast the steering wheel is turned. Which technician is correct?
   a. Technician A only
   b. Technician B only
   c. Both Technicians A and B
   d. Neither Technician A nor B

5. Technician A says that an electronic control module used in the suspension system is the same as that used for engine control. Technician B says that most electronically controlled suspension systems use a separate electronic control module. Which technician is correct?
   a. Technician A only
   b. Technician B only
   c. Both Technicians A and B
   d. Neither Technician A nor B

6. What type of actuator is used on electronically controlled suspensions?

   a. Solenoid

   b. Relay

   c. Electric motor

   d. All of the above

7. Why is the typical rear load-leveling system connected to the ignition circuit?

   a. To keep the system active for a given time after the ignition is switched off

   b. To prevent the system from working unless the ignition key is on

   c. To keep the compressor from running for an extended period of time

   d. All of the above

8. If a vehicle is detected to be oversteering while rounding a left curve, which wheel brake would the ESC system apply to help regain control?

   a. RF

   b. LF

   c. RR

   d. LR

9. The *firm* setting is usually selected by the electronic suspension control module whenever which of the following occurs?

   a. High speed

   b. Rapid braking

   c. Rapid acceleration

   d. All of the above

10. Which of the following is the *least likely* sensor to cause an electronic suspension fault?

    a. Yaw sensor

    b. Throttle position (TP) sensor

    c. Steering wheel position sensor

    d. Vehicle speed sensor

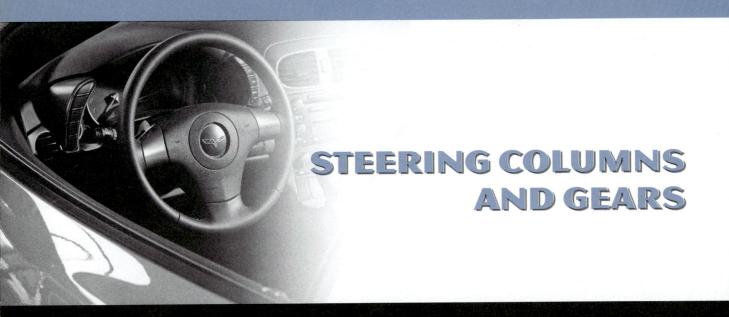

CHAPTER 9

STEERING COLUMNS AND GEARS

OBJECTIVES

After studying Chapter 9, the reader should be able to:

1. Prepare for the Suspension and Steering (A4) ASE certification test content area "A" (Steering System Diagnosis and Repair).

2. Discuss steering columns and intermediate shafts.

3. Explain how a recirculating ball-nut and worm gear steering gear system works.

4. Describe how a rack-and-pinion steering gear works.

KEY TERMS

When the driver turns the steering wheel in a circle, or in a rotary motion, the steering linkage moves side to side, or in a lateral motion, to steer the wheels.

STEERING WHEELS

The steering wheel, which consists of a rigid rim and a number of spokes connecting the rim to a center hub, attaches to the top of the steering shaft at its center. Most steering wheel hubs have internal splines that fit over external splines on the steering shaft. A bolt or nut at the center of the hub secures the wheel to the shaft. The steering wheel may also contain controls for the cruise control and audio controls, as well as the driver's airbag.

Horn Operation

The horn circuit is in a series circuit in which electricity has one path that it can follow when the circuit is complete. A normally open switch in an electrical circuit is inside the horn button. When the driver pushes the horn button, the contacts on the switch close, allowing electrical current through the circuit to operate the horn. See Figure 9-1. A relay circuit is a more common method of wiring the horn. In a relay, closing a switch in a low-current series circuit triggers the high-current circuit that powers the horn.

Airbags

An airbag is a device made of nylon cloth that is covered with neoprene. The airbag is folded and stored in the front center of the steering wheel. In a front-end collision, the airbag inflates in a fraction of a second to provide a cushion between the driver and the steering wheel and dashboard. See Figure 9-2. The part of the steering wheel where the airbag is stored is called the **inflator module.** The module also contains an igniter, a canister of flammable gas, and a number of sodium azide pellets. The sodium azide pellets burn quickly, and rapidly release nitrogen gas while they burn. The nitrogen gas fills the airbag. As it inflates, the airbag tears open the module cover and spreads out across the steering wheel, windshield, and dashboard. The entire process, from sensor reaction to full airbag deployment, takes 30 to 65 milliseconds. Within a second of inflating, the bag deflates partially as the nitrogen gas escapes through exhaust vents in the side of the airbag. Once deployed, an airbag cannot be reused.

The module fits in front of the nut that secures the steering wheel to the steering shaft. Bolts at the back of the steering wheel fasten the airbag module to the steering wheel. Electrical current is provided to the airbag through the spiral cable, which is also known as a coil. The spiral cable connects to the airbag module with two wire leads. The spiral cable is a tightly coiled metal strip that allows steering wheel rotation while maintaining electrical continuity. See Figure 9-3.

CAUTION: Whenever working on the steering column, consult service information for the recommended airbag disabling procedure.

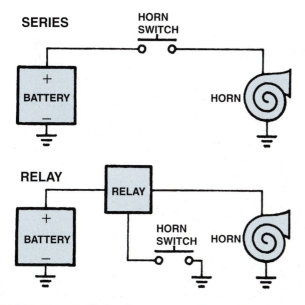

FIGURE 9-1   The horn button is a normally open (NO) switch. When the button is depressed, the switch closes, which allows electrical current to flow from the battery to sound the horn. Most horn circuits use a relay to conduct the horn current.

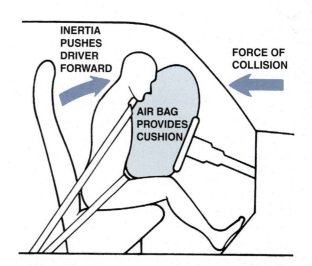

FIGURE 9-2   The airbag inflates at the same time the driver moves toward the steering wheel during a front-end collision and supplements the protection of the safety belt.

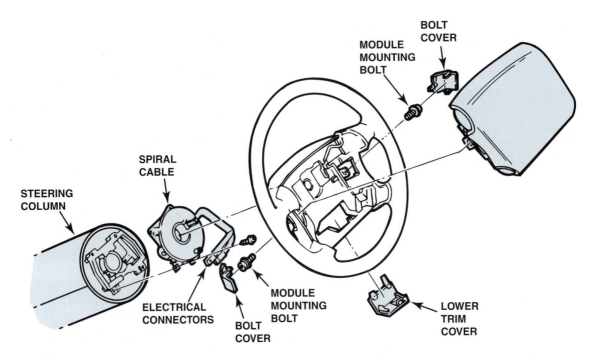

FIGURE 9-3   The airbag module attaches to the steering wheel and is removed as an assembly to service the steering wheel and column.

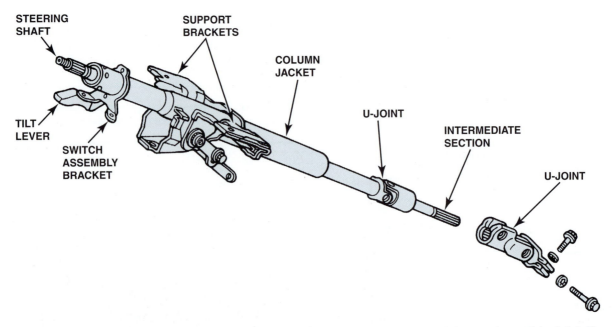

FIGURE 9-4   The steering shaft links the steering wheel to the steering gear while the column jacket, which surrounds part of the shaft, holds support brackets and switches. This steering shaft has a small intermediate section between the main section and the steering gear.

STEERING COLUMNS

The steering shaft transmits rotary motion from the steering wheel to the steering gear, while the column jacket that encases it attaches to the vehicle body and offers a stationary mounting point for a number of switches and mechanisms. See Figure 9-4.

Steering Shaft

The **steering shaft** extends from the steering wheel to the steering gear. A bolt or nut secures the shaft to the steering wheel, and a flexible coupling joins it to the steering gear input shaft. The coupling can be a simple rubber or fabric insert, a universal joint (U-joint), or a pot joint. In addition to allowing a directional change of the shaft, a pot joint permits a limited amount of plunging motion. See Figure 9-5.

Universal Joint

A **universal joint,** or U-joint, consists of two yokes with a steel crosspiece joining them together. See Figure 9-6. Universal joints allow changes in the angle between two rotating shafts. In a steering shaft, U-joints allow rotary motion transfer between the steering wheel and the steering gear even though the steering shaft meets the steering gear input shaft at an angle. On some models the steering shaft itself is assembled in sections that are connected by U-joints. This permits the

steering shaft to bend around obstacles between the steering wheel and the steering gear.

Flexible Coupling

A **flexible coupling** is a simple device made of rubber, or rubber reinforced with fabric, that is placed between two shafts to allow for a change in angle between them. See Figure 9-7. The rubber in a steering shaft flexible coupling absorbs vibrations and helps keep the steering wheel from shaking. A fail-safe connection between the steering shaft and the steering gear input shaft keeps the two shafts linked should the rubber coupling wear out or break. This allows the

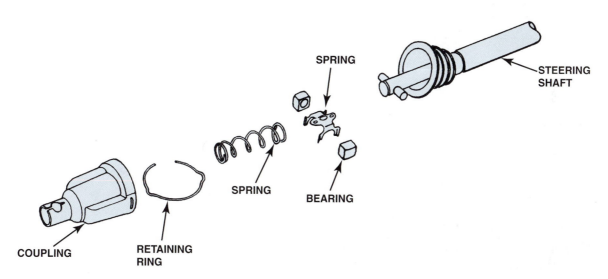

FIGURE 9-5   A pot joint is a flexible coupling used to join two shafts that allow plunging motion.

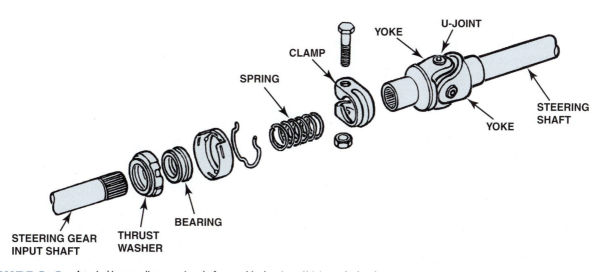

FIGURE 9-6   A typical intermediate steering shaft assembly showing a U-joint and related components.

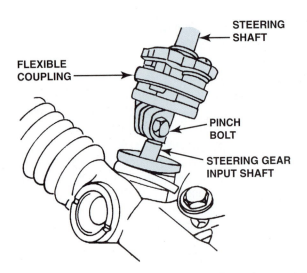

FIGURE 9-7   A flexible coupling is used to isolate road noise and vibration from the steering shaft.

driver to maintain steering control, although the steering feels loose when this happens.

Column Cover

To keep the wiring from the jacket-mounted switches out of sight, the part of the steering column that extends into the passenger compartment is shrouded by the column cover. See Figure 9-8. The column cover is usually at least two separate pieces, top and bottom. A knee bolster that mounts under the steering column is a safety feature designed to keep the driver from sliding forward during a collision. Knee bolsters are part of the passive restraint system required to meet U.S. federal safety standards on certain vehicles.

Collapsible Column

Federal law requires that all vehicles sold in the United States have steering columns and shafts that collapse, **collapsible columns,** during a head-on collision to absorb some of the energy of the crash and lessen the danger of injury to the driver. See Figure 9-9. One early method used a section of the steering column constructed out of mesh, which would collapse easily during a crash. Another method is to use a two-piece column. One section of the column has a smaller diameter so that it fits inside the other and rides on a roller bearing. During a collision, the smaller section slides down into the larger one to collapse like a telescope.

Tilt Mechanisms

Many steering columns have tilt mechanisms, which allow the driver to adjust the angle of the steering wheel relative to the

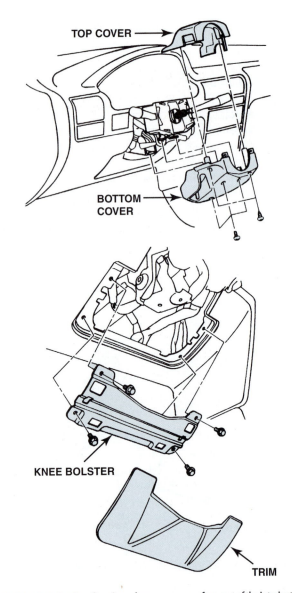

FIGURE 9-8   Steering column covers are often part of the interior trim.

TECH TIP

DO NOT POUND ON THE STEERING COLUMN

Always use a steering wheel puller and/or the special tools recommended by the vehicle manufacturer when servicing the steering column. If a hammer is used on the steering shaft in an attempt to remove a steering wheel, the shaft could collapse, requiring the replacement of the entire steering column assembly.

COLLAPSIBLE STEERING COLUMNS

MESH

BEARING

BREAKAWAY SUPPORT BRACKETS

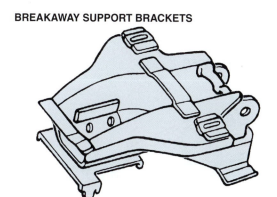

FIGURE 9-9 Collapsible steering columns include a mesh design that crushes easily, a bearing design that allows one section of the column to slide into the other, and a breakaway device that separates the steering column from the body of the vehicle in the event of a front-end collision.

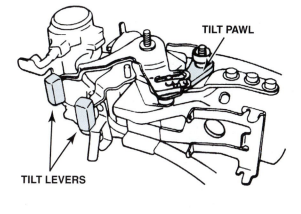

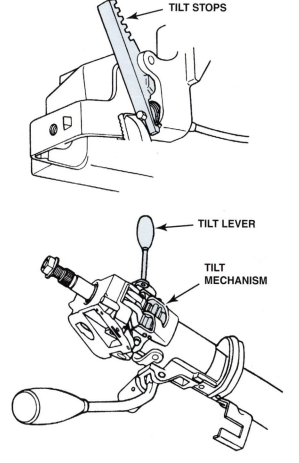

FIGURE 9-10 Tilt mechanisms vary by design and vehicle manufacturer, although most use a ratchet to position the top portion of the steering column.

steering column. In a typical **tilt steering column,** the steering shaft has a short section at the top joined to the rest of the steering shaft either by a U-joint or gears. Most tilt mechanisms are some sort of ratchet device that enables the driver to lift the steering wheel and the top section of the shaft and place them in the desired position. See Figure 9-10. Usually, spring tension locks the steering wheel in place on the ratchet, and a release lever compresses the spring to allow tilt adjustment.

Telescoping Steering Columns

Some steering columns are designed to **telescope,** which means that the top of the steering shaft and jacket can be pulled out toward the driver or pushed in toward the dashboard, and then locked into the new position.

Steering Column Construction

The steering shaft is at the center of the steering column. See Figures 9-11 and 9-12. The top end of the steering shaft splines to the center of the steering wheel, and a large nut fastens the steering wheel to the shaft. The lock housing, which contains

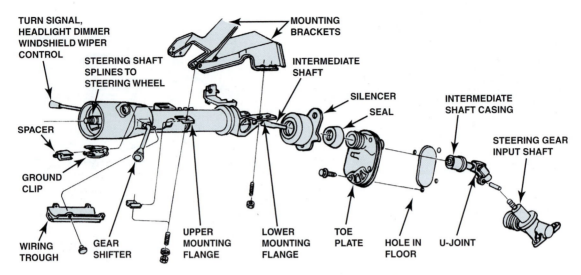

FIGURE 9-11   Typical steering column showing all of the components from the steering wheel to the steering gear.

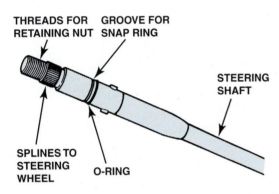

FIGURE 9-12   The steering shaft splines onto the steering wheel.

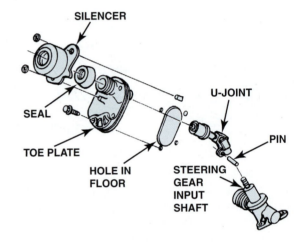

FIGURE 9-13   The toe plate seals the hole from the steering shaft and helps seal out noise and moisture.

the ignition lock cylinder, encases the top part of the steering shaft. The steering column jacket covers the shaft under the ignition lock housing, and the gear selector lever housing fits over a portion of the column jacket.

A U-joint connects the lower end of the steering shaft to a small intermediate shaft, often called a **stub shaft.** Because this steering column includes a gear selector lever, the lower end of the column also incorporates an attachment point that connects the shift tube to the gear shift rod. The intermediate shaft extends through a hole in the floor where it is coupled to the steering gear input shaft by a U-joint.

A toe plate bolts to the floor of the passenger compartment to cover the shaft opening and to protect the interior from noise, drafts, and dirt. See Figure 9-13. The toe plate has a tube for the intermediate shaft, and a seal and silencer fit on top of the tube.

Two sections at the upper end of the steering column house the column-mounted controls. See Figure 9-14. The lock housing, seated on top of the column jacket, is the topmost piece and contains the turn signal lever, hazard light control, and ignition lock. The gear selector lever and its

housing are just below the lock housing, and the housing encases the top of the steering column jacket.

The lock housing contains the ignition lock cylinder, several electrical switches, and a steering shaft bearing. Some of the switches have driver-operated controls on the outside of the lock housing.

A multifunction switch operates the turn signals, the windshield wiper and washer switch, and the dimmer switch.

Most steering shafts ride on at least two bearings, one near the top and one near the bottom of the shaft, to allow the shaft to rotate freely without affecting other parts of the steering column. See Figure 9-15. A snap ring at the center of the bearing housing rests in a groove on the steering shaft to secure the bearing, and an O-ring on the steering shaft keeps lubricant in the bearing.

Underneath the bearing and housing is a **lock plate** and coil spring that lock the steering shaft into position when the driver removes the ignition key. See Figure 9-16. The ignition

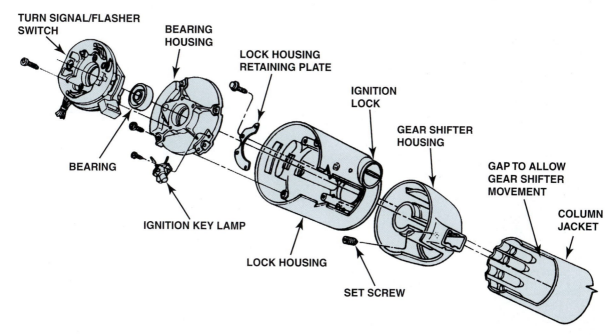

FIGURE 9-14   The upper section of the steering column includes the lock housing and switches.

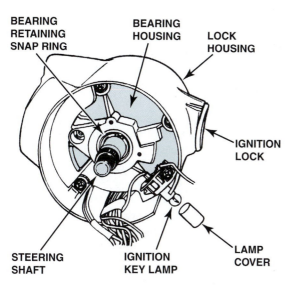

FIGURE 9-15   The upper section of the steering column contains the steering shaft bearing.

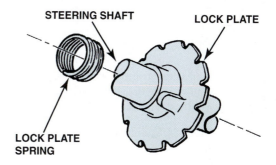

FIGURE 9-16   The lock plate engages an ignition lock pawl to keep the steering wheel in one position when the ignition is off.

lock cylinder, which is under the lock plate, moves a bellcrank that in turn operates a spring and lever assembly linked to the ignition switch actuating rod.

CONVENTIONAL STEERING GEARS

All steering gears have an input gear, which transmits rotary movement from the steering wheel into the steering gear, and an output gear, which causes the steering linkage to move laterally. The rotation of the steering wheel is transferred to the front wheels through a steering gear and linkage. The intermediate shaft is splined to a **worm gear** inside a conventional steering gear. Around the worm gear is a nut with gear teeth that meshes with the teeth on a section of a gear called a **sector gear.** The sector gear is part of a **pitman shaft,** also known as a **sector shaft,** as shown in Figure 9-17.

Ball, roller, or needle bearings support the sector shaft and the worm gear shaft, depending on the make and model of the gear assembly.

As the steering wheel is turned, the movement is transmitted through the steering gear to an arm attached to the bottom end of the pitman shaft. This arm is called the **pitman arm.** Whenever the steering wheel is turned, the pitman arm moves.

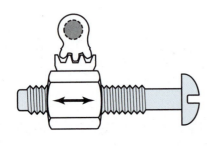

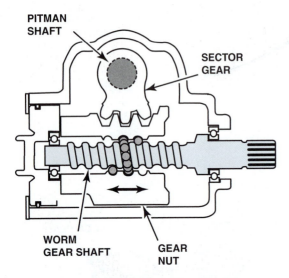

FIGURE 9-17 As the steering wheel is turned, the nut moves up or down on the threads, shown using a bolt to represent the worm gear and the nut representing the gear nut that meshes with the teeth of the sector gear.

Steering Gear Ratio

When the steering wheel is turned, the front wheels turn on their steering axis. If the steering wheel is rotated 20 degrees and results in the front wheels rotating 1 degree, then the steering gear ratio is 20:1 (read as "20 to 1"). See Figure 9-18. The front wheels usually are able to rotate through 60 to 80 degrees of rotation. The steering wheel, therefore, has to rotate 20 times the number of degrees that the wheels move.

20 × 60 degrees = 1,200 degrees, or about three full revolutions (360 degrees = 1 full turn) of the steering wheel

20 × 80 degrees = 1,600 degrees, or over four revolutions of the steering wheel

A vehicle that turns three complete revolutions from full left to full right is said to have three turns "lock to lock."

A high ratio, such as 22 to 1 (22:1), means that the steering wheel must be rotated 22 degrees to move the front wheels 1 degree. This high ratio means that the steering wheel is easier to turn than a steering wheel with a lower ratio such as

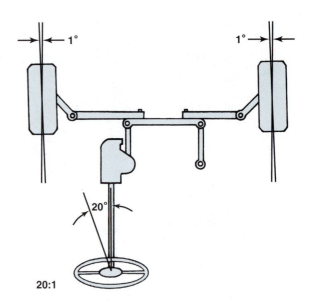

FIGURE 9-18 Steering gear ratio is the ratio between the number of degrees the steering wheel is rotated to the number of degrees the front wheel turns.

14:1. The 14:1 ratio is considered to be "faster" than the 22:1 ratio. This fast ratio allows the front wheels to be turned with less movement of the steering wheel, yet more force may be required to turn the wheel. This is considered by some to be more "sporty."

Most steering gears and some rack-and-pinion steering gears feature a **variable ratio.** This feature causes the steering ratio to decrease as the steering wheel is turned from the on-center position. The high on-center ratio (such as 16:1) provides good steering feel at highway speeds while the reduced off-center ratio (13:1) provides fewer steering wheel turns during turning and parking. The ratio is accomplished by changing the length of the gear teeth on the sector gear. See Figure 9-19 for an example of the teeth of a constant-ratio sector gear.

See Figure 9-20 for an example of the teeth on a variable-ratio sector gear.

The sector gear meshes with the ball nut inside the steering gear, as shown in Figure 9-21.

WORM AND ROLLER STEERING GEAR

The steering gear input shaft splines to a U-joint at the base of the steering column or steering shaft to provide the rotary motion to the steering gear. The input shaft may be called the "worm shaft," because the worm gear and the input shaft are one assembly. This type of steering gear is usually used in heavy-truck applications. See Figure 9-22. An oil seal prevents

FIGURE 9-19   Constant-ratio steering gear sector shaft. Notice that all three gear teeth are the same size.

FIGURE 9-20   Variable-ratio steering gear sector shaft. Notice the larger center gear tooth.

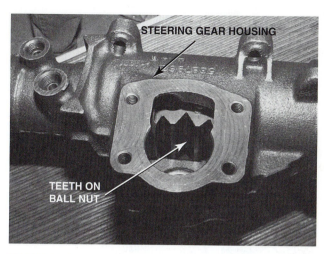

FIGURE 9-21   The sector gear meshes with the gear teeth on the ball nut.

WORM AND ROLLER STEERING GEAR

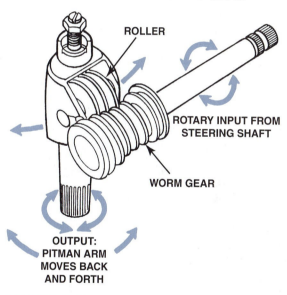

FIGURE 9-22   A typical worm and roller steering gear design used mostly in heavy-truck applications.

lubricant from leaking where the shaft enters the housing. The worm gear is hourglass-shaped to keep it in mesh with the roller as the roller and shroud turn, but the depth of the worm gear thread remains the same along the entire length of the worm gear.

Two thrust bearings reduce friction between the worm gear and the steering gear housing. The upper bearing rides between the tapered top of the worm gear and the inside of the housing, and the lower bearing rides between the tapered bottom of the worm gear and the end plate.

In addition to reducing friction, the tight fit of the thrust bearings between the worm gear and housing keeps the worm gear from moving up and down inside the housing. In other words, the thrust bearings help control axial play, which is up-and-down movement in line with the axis of a shaft. Axial play measured at the end of a shaft is commonly called **endplay.**

The end plate holds the bearings, worm gear, and shaft in place in the steering gear housing. Four bolts secure the end plate to the housing, and a gasket between them provides a seal to prevent lubricant leakage. See Figure 9-23.

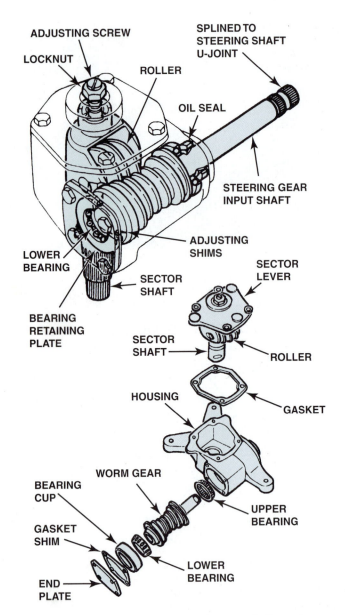

FIGURE 9-23 An exploded view of a worm and roller steering gear used on a medium-duty truck.

RECIRCULATING BALL STEERING GEAR

A recirculating ball steering gear is the most commonly used conventional steering gear. See Figure 9-24.

The end of the steering gear input shaft, or worm shaft, splines to the steering shaft U-joint and provides rotary input to the steering gear. An oil seal prevents fluid leakage where the input shaft enters the steering gear housing. At the top and the bottom of the worm gear are the upper and lower thrust bearings. The upper bearing cup seats in the housing, and the

lower bearing cup seats in the adjuster plug. The thrust bearings reduce friction between the worm gear and the steering gear housing and control worm endplay.

The adjuster plug at the lower end of the worm gear holds the worm gear, shaft, and bearings inside the steering gear housing.

The ball nut, which has internal grooves that match the worm gear thread, fits over the worm gear. Steel balls roll through the tunnels formed by the ball nut grooves and the worm gear thread. Crescent-shaped ball-return guides link the ends of the ball-nut tunnels together, so the balls continuously circulate through the ball nut and worm gear, into the ball-return guides, and back again. A clamp secured by screws holds the return guides in place on one side of the ball nut. Gear teeth mesh with the teeth of the sector gear machined into the outside of the ball nut on the side opposite the ball-return guides.

The sector gear is an integral part of the sector shaft, which runs through the center of the sector gear, and forms the axis of the gear. One end of the sector shaft extends out of the steering gear housing and splines to the pitman arm. An oil seal prevents lubricant leakage where the sector shaft goes through the opening in the housing. To reduce friction, the sector shaft rides on two bushings. One bushing fits inside the housing and the other is part of the housing side cover. See Figure 9-25 on page 226.

STEERING GEAR ADJUSTMENTS

For the steering gear to operate efficiently, the internal parts must be positioned correctly in relation to the housing and each other. As parts wear, clearances inside the housing and between parts increase, causing looseness and excessive play. The acceptable clearance between any two mechanical parts is called their tolerance. Insufficient tolerance causes binding between parts, increasing steering effort. Excessive tolerance causes delayed reaction to steering input and too much steering wheel freeplay.

Worm bearing preload, also referred to as worm endplay, is a measurement of how much force is required to turn the steering gear input shaft against the force, or **preload,** that the thrust bearings apply to the worm gear and shaft. Worm endplay, which is the distance the worm gear can move end-to-end between the thrust bearings, is directly related to preload. The higher the force the bearings push against the worm gear, the less endplay there is, and the more force it takes to turn the input shaft and worm gear. Worm bearing preload is adjusted by one of two methods: turning an adjustment nut or screw or installing selectively sized shims. Either adjustment method increases or decreases the worm endplay.

Worm endplay is a linear measurement, made in fractions of inches or millimeters, of how far the worm gear and shaft can slide axially. See Figure 9-26 on page 226. Worm bearing preload is a measurement of how much force it takes to overcome bearing pressure in order to turn the input shaft. Preload is a

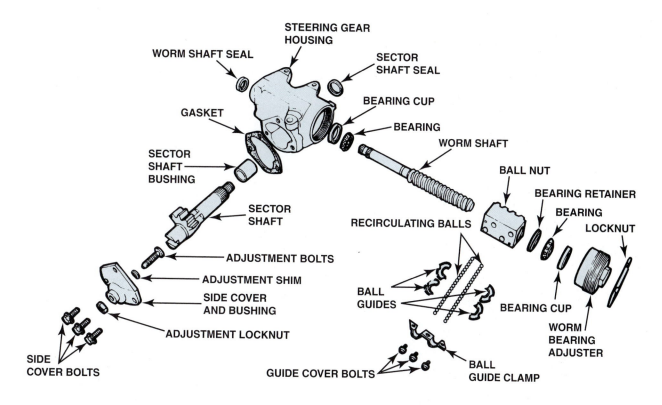

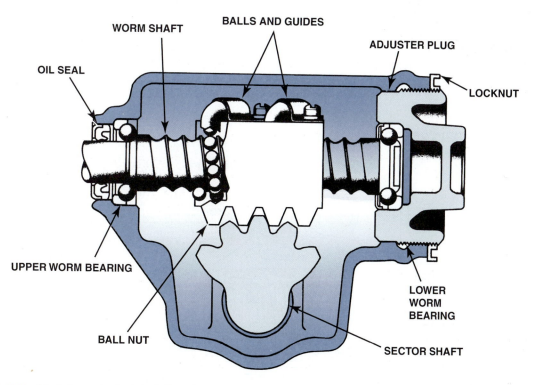

FIGURE 9-24   A typical manual recirculating ball steering gear.

torque, or turning force, measurement made in inch-pounds or Newton-meters. Because endplay and preload are related, one measurement affects the other. When measuring and adjusting the worm bearing preload, a technician measures preload and adjusts endplay. The endplay is correct when the preload measurement is correct. See Figures 9-27 and 9-28.

Gear mesh preload is a measurement of how closely the teeth of the ball-nut gear and sector gear, or the worm gear and roller, fit together. Gear mesh preload is related to another measurement, called sector lash or **gear lash.**

Gear mesh preload is a measurement of how much turning force must be applied to the input shaft to overcome the resistance of the sector gear and move it. Gear mesh preload

is usually measured in a 90-degree turn across the center of the input shaft movement. General Motors calls this adjustment the **overcenter adjustment.** Gear mesh preload (overcenter adjustment) determines how sensitive the steering gear is to small steering wheel movements during straight-ahead driving. Insufficient preload contributes to steering wander.

If there is too much gear lash, the steering becomes unresponsive because the steering gear does not transmit small steering wheel movements to the linkage. Insufficient lash makes the gears bind, offering too much resistance to steering wheel movement. See Figure 9-29.

Sector shaft endplay is a measurement of how much room the sector shaft has to slide axially. See Figure 9-30 on page 228. If provision is made to measure sector shaft endplay, the measurement is taken in fractions of inches or millimeters. Some steering gears provide an external adjusting method, but it is more common for sector shaft endplay to be adjusted by internal shims, if it is adjustable.

RACK-AND-PINION STEERING GEAR

The term "rack and pinion" is simply a description of the basic design of this type of steering gear. The **rack-and-pinion** steering gear is widely used because it is light in weight and takes less space than a conventional steering gear. The input gear of a rack-and-pinion steering gear is a pinion gear that receives rotary input from the steering shaft. The rack is a rod with gear teeth machined into one side. The pinion gear teeth mesh with the teeth on the rack so that when the pinion gear turns, it pushes the rack from side to side. See Figure 9-31 on page 228. The rack connects directly to the tie rod in the steering linkage to move the linkage back and forth in a straight line.

The steering gear input shaft is splined to the steering shaft U-joint. See Figure 9-32 on page 228. At the end of the

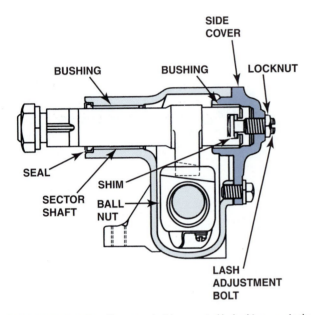

FIGURE 9-25   The sector shaft is supported by bushings, one in the housing and one in the side cover.

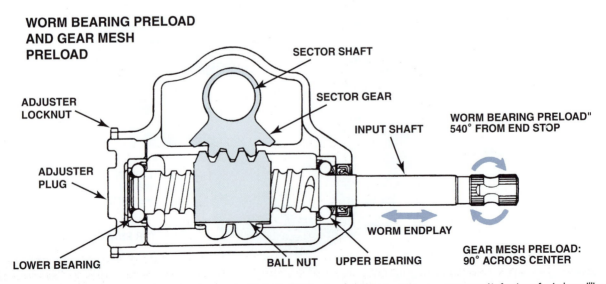

FIGURE 9-26   Worm bearing preload is a turning force measured in in.-lb or N-M, and worm endplay is axial movement measured in fractions of an inch or millimeters.

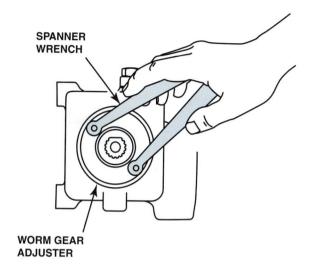

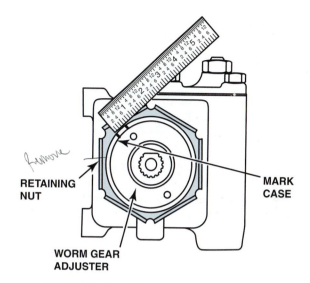

FIGURE 9-27   The first step to adjust worm gear freeplay is to bottom the worm gear nut, using a spanner wrench designed to fit into the two holes in the nut labeled 2.

FIGURE 9-28   After the worm gear nut has been tightened, measure 1/2 inch (13 mm) and mark the case. Using the spanner wrench, rotate the worm gear nut counterclockwise 1/2 inch, align the marks, and then tighten the retaining the nut. This procedure gives the proper worm gear endplay.

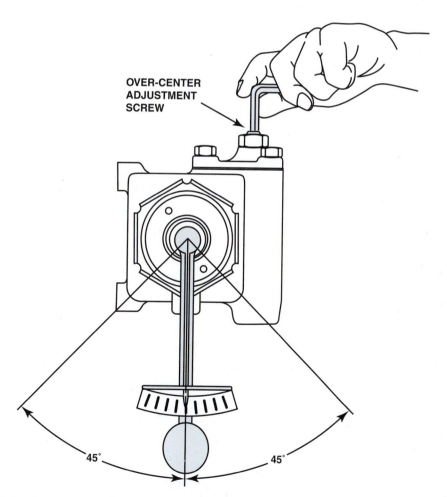

FIGURE 9-29   Performing an overcenter adjustment requires the use of a beam-type inch-lb torque wrench. After the worm bearing preload procedure has been completed, use the torque wrench to measure the rotating torque, which should be 6 to 15 lb-in. If the rotating torque is within the specified range, adjust the overcenter adjustment screw until you achieve 6 to 10 lb-in. more rotating torque and then tighten the retaining nut.

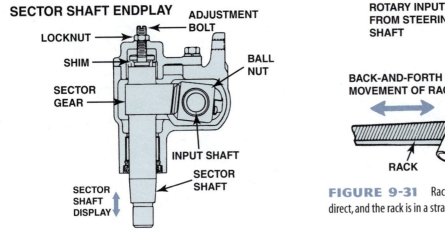

SECTOR SHAFT ENDPLAY

LOCKNUT
SHIM
SECTOR GEAR
ADJUSTMENT BOLT
BALL NUT
INPUT SHAFT
SECTOR SHAFT
SECTOR SHAFT DISPLAY

FIGURE 9-30   Sector shaft endplay is the measurement of how far the sector shaft can move axially and is measured in fractions of an inch or millimeters.

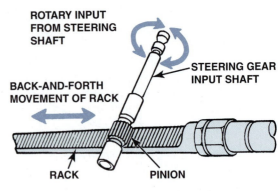

ROTARY INPUT FROM STEERING SHAFT
STEERING GEAR INPUT SHAFT
BACK-AND-FORTH MOVEMENT OF RACK
RACK
PINION

FIGURE 9-31   Rack-and-pinion steering gear operation is simple, direct, and the rack is in a straight line to the front wheels.

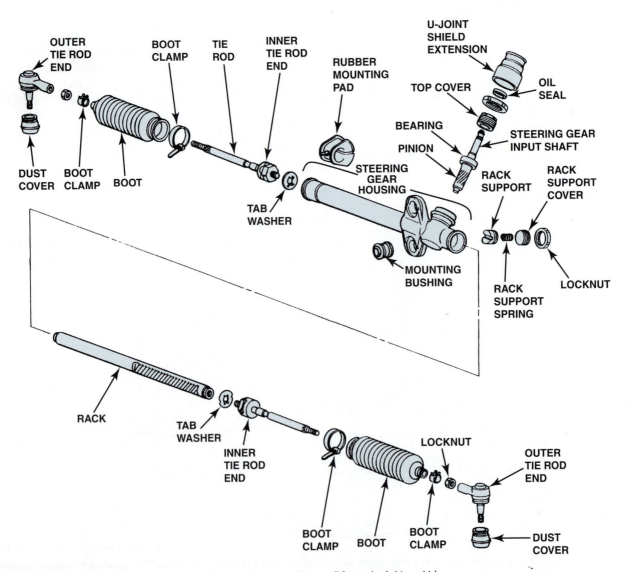

FIGURE 9-32   A typical manual rack-and-pinion steering gear used in a small front-wheel-drive vehicle.

steering gear input shaft, which extends into the rack housing, is the pinion gear. Two ball bearings reduce friction between the shaft and the steering gear housing. The upper bearing is a press-fit on the input shaft, and the lower bearing installs inside the housing at the bottom of the pinion gear. A cover, which fits around the shaft and threads into the housing, seats on top of the upper ball bearing to preload it and close the top of the steering gear housing. An oil seal between the top cover and the input shaft keeps lubricant from leaking out of the housing. A lock nut holds the top cover in position.

The teeth of the pinion gear mesh with the teeth of the rack. The teeth are at one end of the rack and the pinion is offset at one side of the housing.

The rack is encased in the long, tubular steering gear housing with a mounting flange on the pinion end. Rubber bushings fit into the mounting flange bolt holes to absorb vibration and isolate the assembly from the frame.

A spring-loaded **rack support** and related hardware install through a hole at the back of the steering gear housing to position the rack. See Figure 9-33. The face of the rack support curves to match the back of the rack, which rests on it and slides back and forth across it. A spring behind the rack support cushions the rack from vibration and shocks. While the rack support provides a sliding surface to reduce friction at the pinion end of the rack, the rack rides in a bushing pressed into the steering gear housing at the opposite end to reduce friction.

To adjust the rack-and-pinion gear preload, follow these steps (see Figure 9-34):

1. Loosen the adjuster plug lock nut.

2. Turn the adjuster plug clockwise until the adjuster plug bottoms in the gear assembly.

3. Turn the adjuster plug back 50 degrees to 70 degrees (approximately one flat).

Most rack-and-pinion units use a small metal tube running along the outside of the housing to connect the two boots and transfer air from one to the other. See Figure 9-35. If there were no means for air displacement between the boots, they might collapse as they expanded or explode as they compressed.

Internal threads on each end of the rack allow attachment of the externally threaded tie rods.

A rubber boot at each side of the steering gear housing covers the end of the rack and the inner tie rod end to prevent dirt, water, and other contaminants from entering the assembly. Band clamps fasten the ends of the boots to the housing and tie rods. The tie rods move back and forth with the rack and connect it to the wheels through the steering linkage.

The housing generally bolts to either a flange on the firewall or to the subframe or engine cradle. See Figure 9-36. The mounting points have rubber cushions to isolate the steering gear from shock and vibration. If the driver can feel vibration and road shocks through the steering wheel, the condition is called **kickback.** Some kickback is inevitable with a rack-and-pinion steering gear.

RACK-AND-PINION ADJUSTMENTS

Some rack-and-pinion steering gears can be adjusted. **Pinion torque** is a measurement of how much turning force is

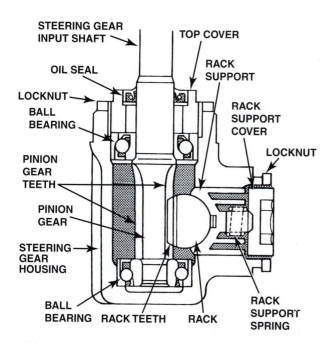

FIGURE 9-33   The spring-loaded rack support positions the rack to keep it from rubbing against the housing and establishes the pinion torque.

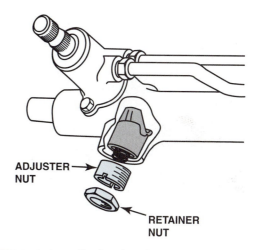

FIGURE 9-34   To adjust the rack-and-pinion gear preload, loosen the retaining nut and tighten the adjuster nut until it bottoms. Then loosen 60 degrees (one "flat" of the six-sided retainer). Tighten retaining nut.

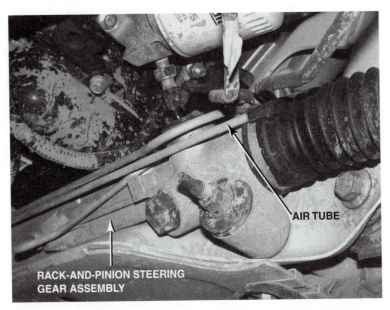

AIR TUBE

**RACK-AND-PINION STEERING
GEAR ASSEMBLY**

FIGURE 9-35   A small air tube is used to transfer air between the boots as they extend and compress during turns.

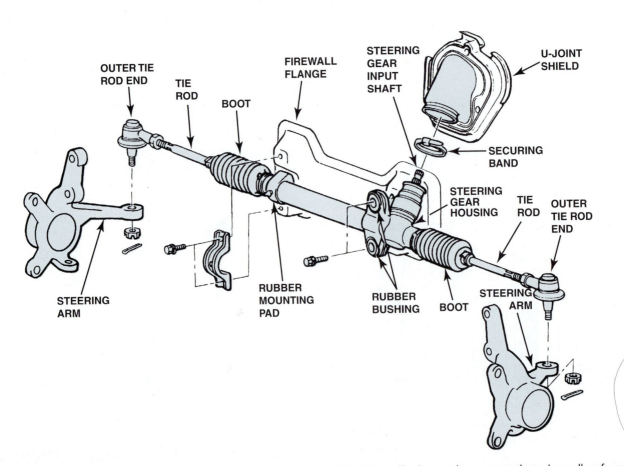

OUTER TIE
ROD END

TIE
ROD

BOOT

FIREWALL
FLANGE

STEERING
GEAR
INPUT
SHAFT

U-JOINT
SHIELD

SECURING
BAND

STEERING
GEAR
HOUSING

TIE
ROD

OUTER
TIE ROD
END

STEERING
ARM

RUBBER
MOUNTING
PAD

RUBBER
BUSHING

BOOT

STEERING
ARM

FIGURE 9-36   This manual rack-and-pinion steering gear mounts to the bulkhead (firewall), whereas others mount to the engine cradle or frame of the vehicle.

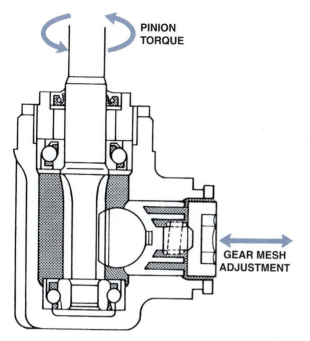

PINION
TORQUE

GEAR MESH
ADJUSTMENT

FIGURE 9-37   Pinion torque is a turning torque force measured in inch-pounds or Newton-meters. Tightening the rack support against the rack increases the pinion torque.

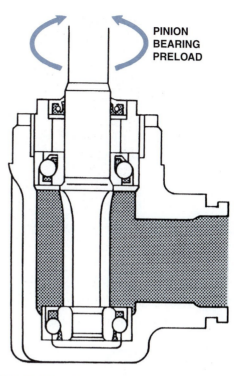

PINION
BEARING
PRELOAD

FIGURE 9-38   Pinion bearing preload is a measurement of the turning force required to overcome the resistance of the pinion shaft bearings.

needed at the input shaft for the pinion to overcome the resistance of the rack and move it. See Figure 9-37. The measurement gives an indication of how closely meshed the pinion teeth and the rack teeth are. Like gear mesh preload in a standard steering gear, pinion torque indicates steering system responsiveness. The adjustment method is to thread the rack support cover farther into the steering gear housing to reduce gear lash, or thread it out to increase gear lash. Manufacturers specify an acceptable range of pinion torque in inch-pounds or Newton-meters. Because the middle teeth on the rack wear before the teeth at either end, pinion torque should be checked across the whole stroke of the rack. Otherwise, reducing gear lash to a very close tolerance in the middle may cause binding as the pinion travels toward the end of the rack.

Pinion bearing preload in a rack-and-pinion steering gear is the same concept as worm bearing preload in a standard steering gear. That is, it is a measurement of how much force is required to turn the steering gear input shaft against the force, or preload, that the bearings apply to the pinion gear and shaft. See Figure 9-38. To provide adjustable pinion bearing preload, there may be a threaded adjustment mechanism or selectively sized shims that install behind a shim cover.

To set pinion bearing preload, the rack may need to be removed or loosened to prevent false readings caused by the resistance of the gears. Therefore, pinion bearing preload, when adjustable, must be set before pinion torque is measured and adjusted.

SUMMARY

1. Most horn circuits use a relay. The horn button or contact on the steering wheel completes the control circuit of the relay, which then completes the power circuit to the horn(s).

2. The driver's side airbag uses a clockspring spiral cable in the steering column electronically connecting the airbag inflator module.

3. The steering column, which connects the steering wheel to the steering gear, includes the steering shaft universal joint and flexible coupling.

4. Conventional steering gears consist of an input gear and output gear, also called the sector gear.

5. Steering gear ratio is the number of degrees the steering wheel is rotated compared to the number of degrees the

front wheels are rotated. Most steering gears provide a ratio of between 14:1 and 22:1.

6. A recirculating-ball-type steering gear is the most commonly used conventional steering gear.

7. A rack-and-pinion steering gear ties the two tie rods together in a straight line.

REVIEW QUESTIONS

1. What components are included in a typical steering column assembly?

2. When the driver turns the steering wheel, how is the motion transferred to the front wheels through a conventional steering gear?

3. Why are recirculating balls used in the recirculating ball steering gear?

4. What steering gear adjustments are possible on a conventional recirculating-ball-type steering gear?

5. What steering gear adjustments are possible on a typical rack-and-pinion steering gear?

CHAPTER QUIZ

1. The circuit to the airbag inflation module is connected from the steering column to the steering wheel through what component?
   a. Slip ring and carbon brushes
   b. Clockspring (coil)
   c. Magnetic field sensor
   d. Hall-effect switch

2. Which part in the steering column allows for changes in the angle between the upper and lower shafts?
   a. Flexible coupling
   b. Column cover
   c. Universal joint
   d. Collapsible section

3. Technician A says that the ignition switch is located where the key is inserted. Technician B says that the ignition switch is controlled by the ignition lock cylinder through a lever and actuating rod. Which technician is correct?
   a. Technician A only
   b. Technician B only
   c. Both Technicians A and B
   d. Neither Technician A nor B

4. The pitman shaft is also called the _____.
   a. Sector
   b. Input
   c. Worm
   d. Spline

5. The driver rotates the steering wheel one-half of one revolution (180 degrees) on a vehicle equipped with a steering gear with a 20:1 gear ratio. How many degrees will the front wheels be rotated?
   a. 9 degrees
   b. 0.1 degree
   c. 90 degrees
   d. 11.1 degrees

6. What causes a variable-ratio steering gear to be able to change the ratio as the steering wheel is turned?
   a. Using two or three different sector gears depending on design
   b. Using a variable-length pitman arm
   c. Changing the number of teeth on the worm gear
   d. Changing the length of the teeth on the sector gear

7. Recirculating steel balls are used in most conventional sleeving gears because they _____.
   a. Provide for a variable ratio
   b. Keep the steering wheel centered
   c. Reduce friction
   d. Help provide feedback to the driver regarding the road surface

8. Which conventional steering gear adjustment should be the first performed?
   a. Worm bearing preload
   b. Tolerance adjustment
   c. Gear mesh preload
   d. Sector shaft endplay

9. The two rack-and-pinion steering gear adjustments include _____.

    a. Worm bearing preload and tolerance adjustment

    b. Pinion bearing preload and rack support

    c. Sector shaft and stub shaft preload

    d. Stub shaft endplay and sector shaft preload

10. A driver of a vehicle equipped with a rack-and-pinion steering gear complains that the steering wheel jerks whenever the vehicle is being driven into a curbed driveway approach at an angle. Technician A says that the rack-and-pinion gears may have too little clearance between the teeth of the gears. Technician B says that a lack of lubrication of the rack-and-pinion is the most likely cause. Which technician is correct?

    a. Technician A only

    b. Technician B only

    c. Both Technicians A and B

    d. Neither Technician A nor B

STEERING LINKAGE AND SERVICE

OBJECTIVES

After studying Chapter 10, the reader should be able to:

1. Prepare for Suspension and Steering (A4) ASE certification test content area "A" (Steering System Diagnosis and Service).
2. Identify steering linkage components.
3. Describe how the movement of the steering wheel causes the front wheels to turn.
4. Describe how to perform a dry park test to determine the condition of steering system components.
5. Perform an under-the-vehicle inspection of the steering system components.
6. List the service procedures for under-the-vehicle steering system service.
7. Explain how to replace steering linkage parts.

KEY TERMS

The proper operation of the steering system is critical to the safe operation of any vehicle. Always follow the service procedures specified by the vehicle manufacturer.

STEERING LINKAGE

The steering linkage relays steering forces from the steering gear to the front wheels. Most conventional steering linkages use the **parallelogram**-type design. A parallelogram is a geometric box shape where opposite sides are parallel and equal distance. A parallelogram-type linkage uses four **tie rods,** two inner and two outer (left and right), a **center link** (between the tie rods), and an idler arm on the passenger side and a **pitman arm** attached to the steering gear output shaft (pitman shaft). See Figure 10-1.

As the steering wheel is rotated, the pitman arm is moved. The pitman arm attaches to a center link. At either end of the center link are inboard (inner) tie rods, adjusting sleeves, and outboard (outer) tie rods connected to the steering arm, which moves the front wheels. The passenger side of all these parts is supported and held horizontal by an idler arm that is bolted to the frame. The center link may be known by several names, including the following:

Center link
Connecting link
Connecting rod
Relay rod
Intermediate rod
Drag link (usually a truck term only)

Other types of steering linkages often used on light trucks and vans include the **cross-steer linkage.** See Figure 10-2 for a comparison of parallelogram and cross-steer-type steering linkage arrangements.

NOTE: Many light trucks, vans, and some luxury cars use a steering dampener attached to the linkage. A **steering dampener** is similar to a shock absorber, and it absorbs and dampens sudden motions in the steering linkage. See Figure 10-3.

Connections between all steering component parts are constructed of small ball-and-socket joints. These joints allow side-to-side movement to provide steering of both front wheels, and allow the joints to move up and down, which is required for normal suspension travel.

It is important that all of these joints be lubricated with chassis grease through a **grease fitting,** also called a **zerk fitting,** at least every six months or per the vehicle manufacturer's specifications.

Some vehicles come equipped with sealed joints and do not require periodic servicing. Some vehicles come from the factory with plugs that need to be removed and replaced with grease fittings and then lubricated.

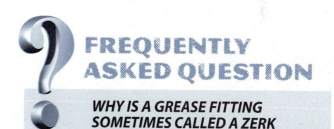

FREQUENTLY ASKED QUESTION

WHY IS A GREASE FITTING SOMETIMES CALLED A ZERK FITTING?

In 1922 the *zerk* fitting was developed by Oscar U. Zerk, an employee of the Alemite Corporation, a manufacturer of pressure lubrication equipment. A zerk or grease fitting is also known as an *Alemite fitting*.

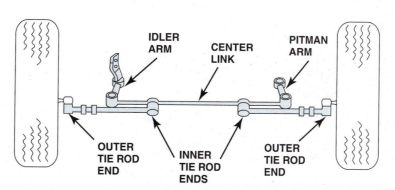

FIGURE 10-1   Steering movement is transferred from the pitman arm that is splined to the sector shaft (pitman shaft), through the center link and tie rods, to the steeting knuckle at each front wheel. The idler arm supports the passenger side of the center link and keeps the steering linkage level with the road. *(Courtesy of Dana Corporation)*

PARALLELOGRAM STEERING LINKAGE

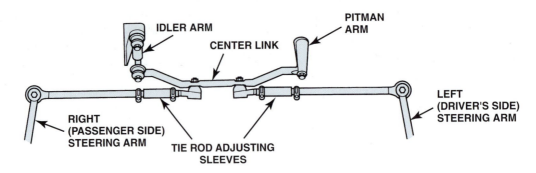

CROSS-STEER LINKAGE

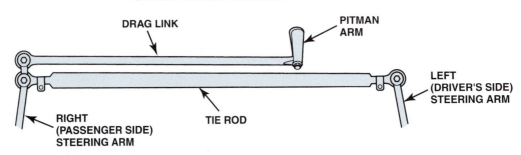

FIGURE 10-2   The most common type of steering is the parallelogram. The cross-steer and Haltenberger linkage designs are used on some trucks and vans.

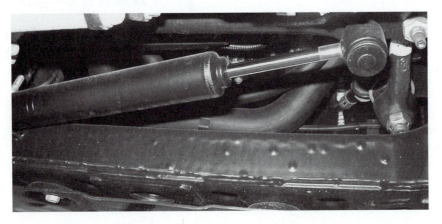

FIGURE 10-3   Typical steering dampener used on a Hummer H2.

Tie Rod Ends

Tie rod ends connect the steering linkage to the steering knuckles and to other steering linkage components. Conventional tie rod ends use a hardened steel ball stud assembled into a hardened steel and thermoplastic bearing. An internal preload spring limits the ball stud endplay and helps compensate for ball-and-socket wear. See Figure 10-4 for two designs of tie rod ends.

For many years, Ford Motor Company used tie rod ends that included a rubber-bonded steel ball stud. Because there is no sliding friction inside the tie rod end, no lubrication was

needed. This type of tie rod end is called **RBS (rubber-bonded socket).** See Figure 10-5.

RACK-AND-PINION INNER TIE ROD ENDS

Inner tie rod end assemblies used on rack-and-pinion steering units require special consideration and often special tools. The inner tie rod end is also called a **ball socket assembly.**

The inner tie rod assemblies are attached to the end of the steering rack by one of several methods. See Figure 10-6.

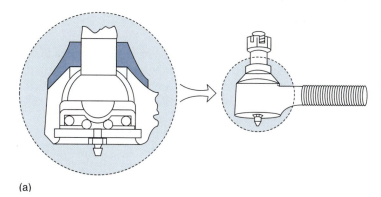

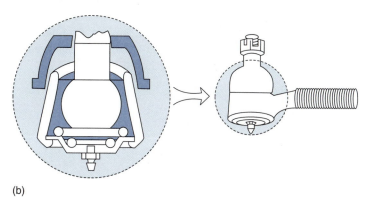

(a)

(b)

FIGURE 10-4   (a) A dual bearing design with a preload spring. The use of two bearing surfaces allows for one surfaces for rotation (for steering) and another surface for pivoting (to allow for suspension up-and-down movement). (b) The nylon wedge bearing type allows for extended lube intervals. Wear is automatically compensated for by the tapered design and spring-loaded bearing. *(Courtesy of Dana Corporation)*

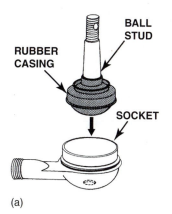

BALL
STUD

RUBBER
CASING

SOCKET

(a)

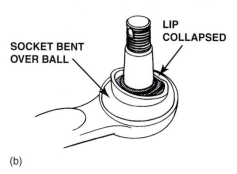

LIP
COLLAPSED

SOCKET BENT
OVER BALL

(b)

FIGURE 10-5   (a) A rubber-bonded socket is constructed of a rubber casing surrounding the ball stud, which is then inserted into the socket of the tie rod end. The hole in the socket allows air to escape as the ball stud is installed and there is not a place for a grease fitting. (b) The socket is crimped over the ball so that part of the socket lip retains the stud.

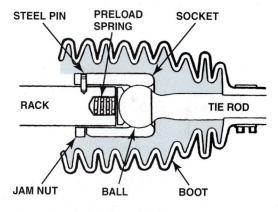

STEEL PIN   PRELOAD   SOCKET
SPRING

RACK   TIE ROD

JAM NUT   BALL   BOOT

FIGURE 10-6   Rack-and-pinion steering systems use a ball-and-socket-type inner tie rod end.

Staked

This method is common on Saginaw-style rack-and-pinion steering units found on General Motors vehicles.

The flange around the outer tie rod must be restaked to the flat on the end of the rack.

Riveted or Pinned

This method is commonly found on Ford vehicles. Some roll pins require a special puller, or the pin can be drilled out.

Many styles use an aluminum rivet. A special, very deep socket or a large open-end wrench can usually be used to shear the aluminum rivet by unscrewing the socket assembly from the end of the rack while the rack-and-pinion unit is still in the vehicle. See Figure 10-7.

Center Take-Off Racks

For the **center take-off racks,** use bolts to secure the inner tie rods to the rack, as shown in Figure 10-8.

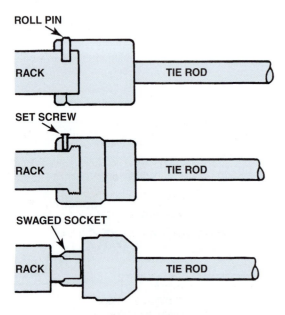

FIGURE 10-7 A variety of methods are used to secure the inner tie rod end socket assembly to the end of the rack.

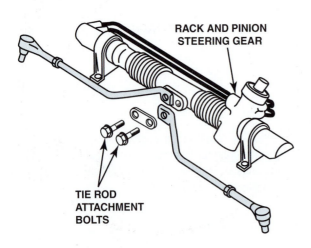

FIGURE 10-8 Exploded view of a center-take-off-style rack-and-pinion steering gear assembly.

Front Steer versus Rear Steer

Front steer, also called *forward steer*, is the term used to describe a vehicle that has the steering gear in front of the front wheel centerline. Having the steering gear located in this position improves handling and directional stability, especially when the vehicle is heavily loaded.

Front-steer vehicles usually produce an understeer effect that makes the vehicle feel very stable while cornering. If the steering gear linkage is located behind the wheels, it is called **rear steer** and the cornering forces are imposed on the steering in the direction of the turn. This is an oversteer effect. It tends to make the steering easier and makes the vehicle feel less stable.

Most front-wheel-drive vehicles are rear steering, with the rack-and-pinion steering unit attached to the bulkhead or subframe behind the engine. See Figure 10-9.

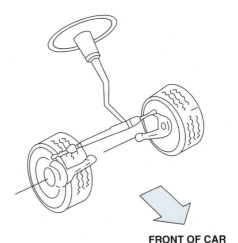

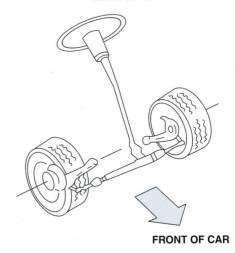

FIGURE 10-9 In a rear-steer vehicle, the steering linkage is behind the centerline of the front wheels, whereas the linkage is in front on a front-steer vehicle. *(Courtesy of Dana Corporation)*

FOUR-WHEEL STEERING

Some vehicles were equipped with a system that steers all four wheels. Two terms are commonly used when discussing four-wheel steering:

1. **Same-phase steering.** Same-phase steering means that the front and rear wheels are steered in the same direction. Same-phase steering improves steering response, especially during rapid-lane-change-type maneuvers.
2. **Opposite-phase steering.** Also called *negative-phase mode*, opposite-phase steering is when the front wheels and rear wheels are steered in the opposite direction. See Figure 10-10. Opposite-phase steering will quickly change the vehicle's direction, but may cause a feeling of oversteering.

Opposite-phase steering is best at low speeds; same-phase steering is best for higher-speed handling and lane-change maneuvers.

Quadrasteer

Quadrasteer™ is a four-wheel steering system that dramatically enhances low-speed maneuverability, high-speed stability, and towing capability. See Figure 10-11.

The system is an electrically powered rear wheel steering system comprised of the following components:

- A steerable, solid rear axle
- A heavy-duty wiring harness and fuse
- A programmable control module

- A power relay in the control module
- A rack-and-pinion-style steering actuator mounted on the rear differential cover
- An electric motor assembly on top of the rear steering actuator
- Three Hall-effect switches in the motor assembly
- A shorting relay in the motor assembly
- A rear wheel position sensor located under a cover on the bottom of the actuator, below the motor assembly
- A steering wheel position sensor located at the base of the steering column
- A mode select switch on the dash

See Figure 10-12 for an overall view of the components of the Quadrasteer system.

The rear wheel steering control module has the following inputs:

- Battery voltage
- Switched battery voltage
- Class 2 serial data
- Steering wheel position sensor analog signal, via class 2 message from the body control module (BCM)
- Steering wheel position sensor phase A
- Steering wheel position sensor phase B
- Steering wheel position sensor marker pulse

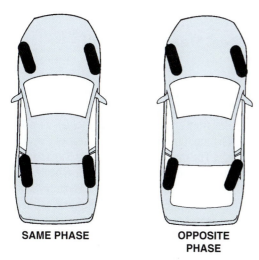

SAME PHASE   **OPPOSITE PHASE**

FIGURE 10-10   Opposite-phase four-wheel steer is usually used only at low vehicle speed to help in parking maneuvers. Sample-phase steering helps at higher speeds and may not be noticeable by the average driver.

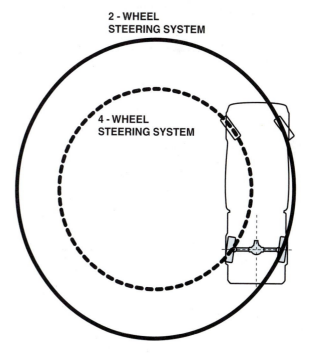

2 - WHEEL STEERING SYSTEM

4 - WHEEL STEERING SYSTEM

FIGURE 10-11   Being equipped with four-wheel steer allows a truck to make shorter turns than would otherwise be possible.

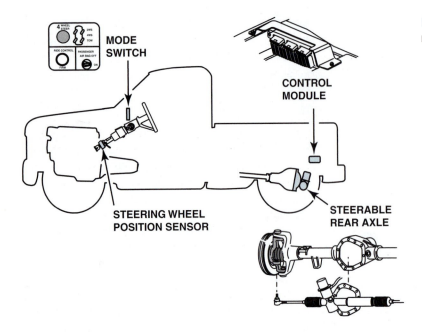

FIGURE 10-12 The Quadrasteer system includes many components that all work together.

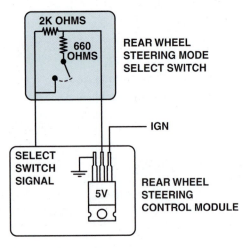

FIGURE 10-13 Rear steer select switch schematic.

- Rear wheel position sensor position 1
- Rear wheel position sensor position 2
- Rear wheel steering motor Hall sensor A
- Rear wheel steering motor Hall sensor B
- Rear wheel steering motor Hall sensor C
- Vehicle speed signal from the instrument panel cluster (IPC)
- Rear wheel steering mode switch signal

See Figure 10-13.

The system operates in three principal modes, as follows:

- **Two-wheel steer mode.** Normal steering operation—the rear wheels are held in a centered position and rear wheel steering is disabled while in this mode.

- **Four-wheel steer mode.** The four-wheel steering mode provides three principal phases of steering: negative phase, neutral phase, and positive phase. Negative phase occurs at low speeds and the rear wheels turn opposite of the front wheels. In the neutral phase, the rear wheels are centered and do not turn. Positive phase occurs at higher speeds and the rear wheels turn in the same direction as the front wheels.

- **Four-wheel steer tow mode.** The four-wheel steer tow mode provides more positive-phase steering than the normal four-wheel steering at high speed. During low-speed driving, the four-wheel steer tow mode provides similar negative-phase steering as it does in the normal four-wheel steering mode.

Rear Wheel Steering Control Module

The rear wheel steering control module controls all functions of the rear wheel steering system. The module has a dedicated power feed line from an underhood fuse holder, via a 125-amp mega fuse. The module is located in the rear of the vehicle on the underbody. The module uses the inputs listed earlier to determine when and how far to turn the rear wheels. The module uses the Hall switches in the motor assembly, a shorting relay, and a motor control relay to monitor and control the direction and speed of the motor. The module also controls the duty cycle of the phase leads to the motor. The motor control relay is part of the rear wheel steering control module and is not serviceable.

The control module allows the vehicle rear wheels to turn a maximum of 12 degrees left or right. When the vehicle is operated in reverse, the maximum rear wheel steering angle is 5 degrees left or right. When the vehicle is sitting still in the test mode, the system will move a maximum of 5 degrees left or right.

Rear Wheel Steering Mode Switch

The mode switch located in the instrument panel allows the driver the option of selecting two-wheel steering, four-wheel steering, or four-wheel steering tow modes of operation. The mode switch has indicators that show which mode the rear wheel steering system is in. When all indicators are lit the rear wheel steering control module has lost its memory settings and the scan tool must be used to recalibrate the rear wheel steering control module. During a mode change, the indicator for the selected mode will flash until the mode change is complete. The rear wheel steering control module will wait for the steering wheel to pass the center position before entering the selected mode. The indicators on the mode switch are LEDs; the switch is also back lit. See Figure 10-14.

Rear Wheel Steering Motor Assembly. The rear wheel steering motor assembly is a three-phase, six-pole, brushless DC motor. The motor assembly is located on the top of the rear steering actuator, and transmits its power through a planetary gearset inside the actuator. There are three Hall switches inside the assembly: Hall A, Hall B, and Hall C. The rear wheel steering control modules uses the Hall switch inputs to monitor the position, speed, and direction of the motor.

Steering Wheel Position Sensor. The **steering wheel position sensor (SWPS)** provides one analog signal and three digital signals. The digital signals—Phase A, Phase B, and marker pulse—are direct inputs to the rear wheel steering control module. The analog signal is input to the body

control module (BCM) and is sent via a class 2 message to the rear wheel steering control module. Battery voltage is supplied to the sensor from the cruise fuse to operate the digital portion of the sensor. A 12-volt reference is provided by the rear wheel steering control module to the Phase A, Phase B, and marker pulse circuits of the SWPS. The module monitors each circuit as it is either remains high or is pulled low by the SWPS. The scan tool displays the Phase A and Phase B data parameters as either high or low when the steering wheel is being rotated. Each change from high to low, or low to high, represents 1 degree of steering wheel rotation. When observing with the scan tool, the parameters for Phase A and Phase B will not always display the same value at the same time. The marker pulse is a digital pulse signal that is displayed as high by the scan tool with the steering wheel angle between +10 degrees and −10 degrees. At greater than 10 degrees steering wheel angle in either direction, the marker pulse data will be displayed as low. The BCM provides the 5-volt reference and low reference for the analog portion of the SWPS. The BCM reads the SWPS analog signal in voltage, which is typically 2.5 volts with the steering wheel on center. The voltage ranges from 0.25 volts at approximately one full turn left to 4.75 volts at approximately one full turn right. The voltage will then remain at that level for the remainder of steering wheel travel. This voltage can be monitored in BCM data display on a scan tool. The sensor may also be utilized by other optional systems. See Figures 10-15 through 10-18.

Rear Wheel Position Sensor. The rear wheel position sensor has two signal circuits: position 1 and position 2. Position 1 is a linear measurement of voltage per degree. The voltage range for position 1 is from 0.25 to 4.75 volts, and the angular measurement range is from −620 degrees to +620 degrees. At 0.25 volts the steering wheel has been rotated −600 degrees past center. At 4.75 volts the steering wheel has

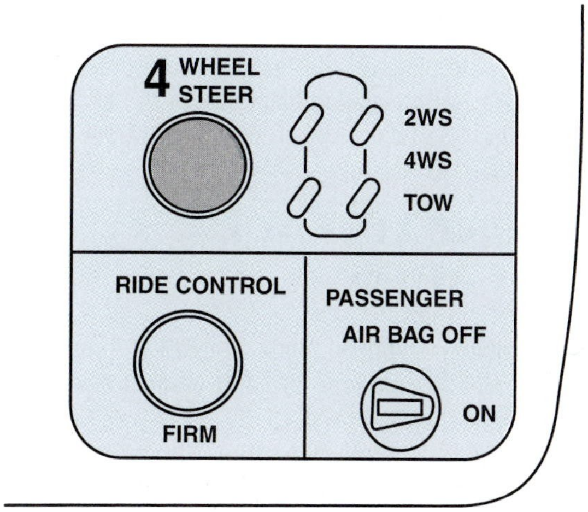

FIGURE 10-14 The dash-mounted select switch showing the three positions for the four-wheel steer system.

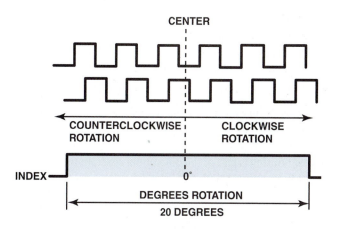

FIGURE 10-15 The output of the handwheel sensor digital signal.

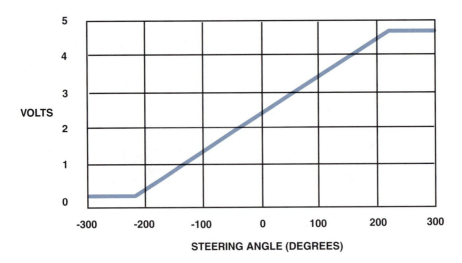

FIGURE 10-16   Handwheel analog signal.

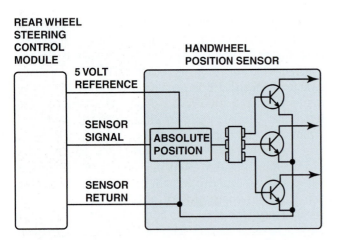

FIGURE 10-17   Handwheel position sensor analog signal to control module.

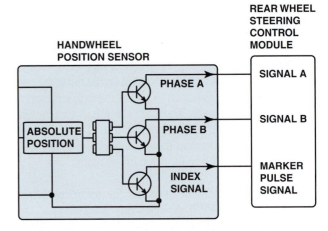

FIGURE 10-18   Handwheel position sensor digital signal to control module.

been rotated +600 degrees past center. The position 2 circuit is a linear measurement of voltage per degree. The voltage for position 2 increases or decreases from 0.25 to 4.75 volts every 180 degrees. When the steering wheel is 0 degrees center, the position 1 and position 2 output signals each measure 2.5 volts.

Steerable Rear Axle. The steerable rear axle has a rack-and-pinion-style actuator mounted to the differential cover, specially designed axle shafts, and movable hub and bearing assemblies mounted by upper and lower ball joints. The actuator housing is part of the differential cover. In the event of a system malfunction, the actuator returns the rear wheels to the center position through internal springs. The actuator has specially designed inner and outer tie rod ends. There are inner tie rod boots to prevent contaminants from entering the actuator. The actuator has the rear wheel steering

motor assembly attached to the upper housing. There are shields and a skid plate on the rear axle to protect the actuator. There are no internal adjustments to the actuator. See Figure 10-19.

STEERING LINKAGE LUBRICATION

Keeping all joints equipped with a grease fitting properly greased is necessary for long life and ease of steering. See Figure 10-20.

During a chassis lubrication, do not forget to put grease on the *steering stop,* if so equipped. **Steering stops** are the projections or built-up areas on the control arms of the front suspension designed to limit the steering movement at full lock. See Figure 10-21 on page 244.

FIGURE 10-19   A Quadrasteer system showing all of the components. The motor used to power the rear steering rack can draw close to 60 amperes during a hard turn and can be monitored using a Tech 2.

FREQUENTLY ASKED QUESTION

WHAT IS "GOOFY MODE"?

Trucks that are equipped with the Quadrasteer system have a three-position switch on the dash:

1. 2WS
2. 4WS
3. Tow

The Quadrasteer module then determines the right amount of rear steer and in which direction based on vehicle speed and steering wheel angle. If trailer towing mode is selected and the truck is *not* towing a trailer, the computer will adjust the steering as if there is a trailer and will slightly delay the rear steering action when changing lanes and other maneuvers. As a result, when the steering wheel is turned the front wheels will of course turn in direct proportion to the input from the steering wheel; however, the rear wheels will be delayed in their action to allow the trailer to track properly. If, however, a trailer is not being towed, this delay feels "goofy" and could result in customer concerns about the proper operation of the Quadrasteer system. Be sure that the control switch is placed in the off or normal modes unless a trailer is in fact being towed.

FIGURE 10-20   Greasing a tie rod end. Some joints do not have a hole for excessive grease to escape, and excessive grease can destroy the seal.

NOTE: Many rack-and-pinion steering units are designed with a rack-travel-limit internal stop and do not use an external stop on the steering knuckle or control arm.

When the steering wheel is turned as far as it can go, the steering should *not* stop inside the steering gear! Forces exerted by the power steering system can do serious damage to the steering gear if absorbed by the steering gear rather than the steering stop.

Most steering stops are designed so that the lower control arm hits a small section of the body or frame when the steering wheel is turned to the full "lock" position. Steering stops should be lubricated to prevent a loud grinding

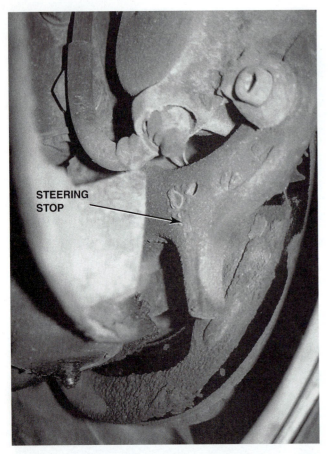

FIGURE 10-21 Part of steering linkage lubrication is applying grease to the steering stops. If these stops are not lubricated, a grinding sound may be heard when the vehicle hits a bump when the wheels are turned all the way one direction or the other. This often occurs when driving into or out of a driveway that has a curb.

noise when turning while the vehicle is going over a bump. This noise is usually noticeable when turning into or out of a driveway.

DRY PARK TEST

Since many steering (and suspension) components do *not* have exact specifications for replacement purposes, it is extremely important that the beginning service technician work closely with an experienced veteran technician. While most technicians can determine when a steering component such as a tie rod end is definitely in need of replacement, marginally worn parts are often hard to spot and can lead to handling problems. One of the most effective, yet easy to perform, steering component inspection methods is called the **dry park test.**

FREQUENTLY ASKED QUESTION

WHY DO ONLY A FEW VEHICLES USE GREASE FITTINGS?

Many years ago, all vehicles were equipped with grease fittings, while today very few vehicles are so equipped. The reasons for this, as given by engineers, include the following:

- It has been determined that the use of the wrong type of grease can cause more harm than good.
- If a grease fitting is used to allow grease to enter the suspension or steering joint, then water can also get inside the joint.
- Grease fittings are often ignored or the greasing of the joint is not performed by the service technician.
- Low-friction joints do not require routine service like the older metal-to-metal joints required.

FIGURE 10-22 Checking for freeplay in the steering.

Excessive play in the steering wheel can be caused by worn or damaged steering components. Looseness in the steering components usually causes freeplay in the steering wheel. Freeplay refers to the amount of movement of the steering wheel required to cause movement of the front wheels. The exact cause of freeplay in the steering should be determined if the freeplay exceeds 2 in. (5 cm) for parallelogram-type steering linkages, or 3/8 in. (1 cm) for rack-and-pinion steering. See Figure 10-22.

This simple test is performed with the vehicle on the ground or on a drive-on ramp-type hoist, moving the steering wheel back and forth *slightly* while an assistant feels for movement at each section of the steering system. The technician can start checking for any looseness in the steering linkage starting either at the outer tie rod ends and working toward the steering column, or from the steering column toward the outer tie rod ends. It is important to check each and every joint and component of the steering system, including the following:

1. The intermediate shaft and flexible coupling.
2. All steering linkage joints, including the inner tie rod end ball socket. See Figure 10-23.
3. Steering gear mounting and rack-and-pinion mounting bushings.

TECH TIP

JOUNCE/REBOUND TEST

All steering linkage should be level and "work" at the same angle as the suspension arms, as shown in Figure 10-24. A simple test to check these items is performed as follows:

1. Park on a hard, level surface with the wheels straight ahead and the steering wheel in the *unlocked* position.
2. Bounce (jounce) the vehicle up and down at the front bumper while watching the steering wheel.

The steering wheel should *not* move during this test. If the steering wheel moves while the vehicle is being bounced, look for a possible bent steering linkage, suspension arm, or steering rack. See Figure 10-25.

COMMON WEAR ITEMS

On a vehicle equipped with a conventional steering gear and parallelogram linkage, as shown in Figure 10-26, typical items that wear first, second, and so on include the following:

Steering Component	Estimated Mileage to Wear Out*
1. Idler arm	40,000–60,000 miles (60,000–100,000 km)
2. Outer tie rod ends (replaced in pairs only)	60,000–100,000 miles (100,000–160,000 km)
3. Inner tie rod ends	80,000–120,000 miles (130,000–190,000 km)

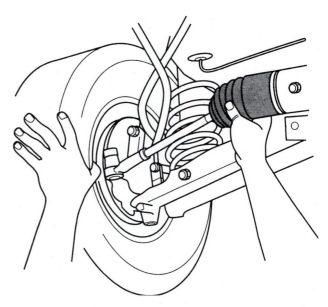

FIGURE 10-23   All joints should be felt during a dry park test. Even inner tie rod ends (ball socket assemblies) can be felt through the rubber bellows on many rack-and-pinion steering units.

4. Center link	90,000–130,000 miles (140,000–180,000 km)
5. Pitman arm	100,000–150,000 miles (160,000–240,000 km)

*Mileage varies greatly due to different road conditions and levels of vehicle maintenance. This chart should be used as a guide only.

Note that there are overlapping mileage intervals for several components. Also note that the mileage interval for an idler arm is such that by the time other components are worn, the idler arm may need to be replaced a second time.

For vehicles that use rack-and-pinion-type steering systems, the list is shorter because there are fewer steering components and the forces exerted on a rack-and-pinion system are in a straight line. The first to wear are usually outer tie rod ends (one or both) followed by the inner tie rod ball-and-socket joints, usually after 60,000 miles (100,000 km) or more. Intermediate shaft U-joints usually become worn and can cause steering looseness after 80,000 miles (130,000 km) or more.

NOTE: Experienced front-end technicians can often guess the mileage of a vehicle simply by careful inspection of the steering linkage. For example, if the idler arm is a replacement part and again needs to be replaced, and the outer tie rods also need replacement, then the vehicle probably has at least 60,000 miles and usually more! When inspecting a used vehicle for possible purchase, perform a careful steering system inspection. This is one area of the vehicle where it is difficult to hide long or hard service.

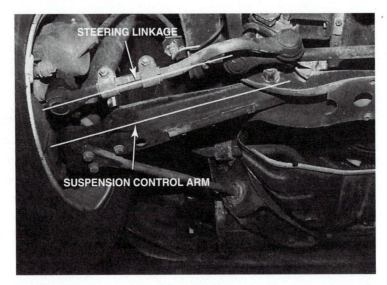

FIGURE 10-24   The steering and suspension arms must remain parallel to prevent the up-and-down motion of the suspension from causing the front wheels to turn inward or outward.

PARALLELISM

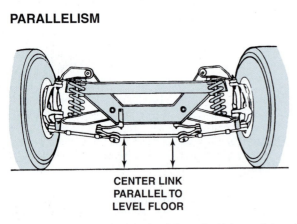

CENTER LINK PARALLEL TO LEVEL FLOOR

FIGURE 10-25   The steering linkage should be parallel to the ground.

TECH TIP

WEAR AND NONWEAR CENTER LINKS

Some center links are equipped with ball-and-socket joints, which can wear. Other center links are manufactured with holes for ball joint studs only. See Figure 10-27. Generally, the center links that do not use joints are unlikely to need replacement unless a joint becomes loose and wears the tapered stud hole. Knowing which style of center link is used will help determine the most likely location to check for excessive steering linkage play.

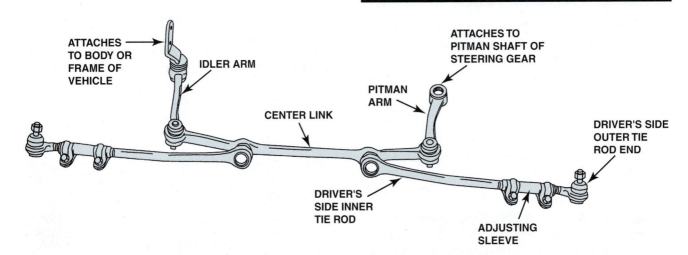

FIGURE 10-26   Typical parallelogram steering linkage. The center link can also be named the relay rod, drag link, or connecting link.

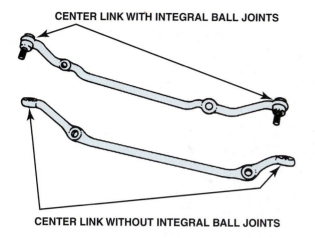

CENTER LINK WITH INTEGRAL BALL JOINTS

CENTER LINK WITHOUT INTEGRAL BALL JOINTS

FIGURE 10-27　Some center links have ball joints while others have tapered socket holes to accept ball joints on the pitman arm, idler arm, and inner tie rod ends.

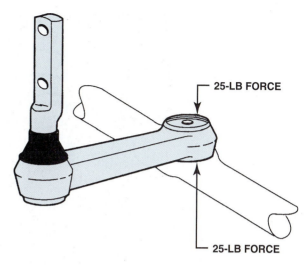

— 25-LB FORCE

— 25-LB FORCE

FIGURE 10-28　To check an idler arm, most vehicle manufacturers specify that 25 pounds of force be applied by hand up and down to the idler arm. The idler arm should be replaced if the total movement (up and down) exceeds $^{1}/_{4}$ in. (6mm). *(Courtesy of Dana Corporation)*

UNDER-VEHICLE INSPECTION

After checking the steering system components as part of a dry park test, hoist the vehicle and perform a thorough part-by-part inspection:

1. Inspect each part for damage due to an accident or bent parts due to the vehicle's hitting an object in the roadway.

   CAUTION: Never straighten a bent steering linkage; always replace with new parts.

2. Idler arm inspection is performed by using *hand* force of 25 lb (110 N-m) up and down on the arm. If the *total* movement exceeds 1/4 in. (6 mm), the idler arm should be replaced. See Figure 10-28.
3. All other steering linkage should be tested *by hand* for any vertical or side-to-side looseness. Tie rod ends use ball-and-socket joints to allow for freedom of movement for suspension travel and to transmit steering forces to the front wheels. It is therefore normal for tie rods to rotate in their sockets when the tie rod sleeve is rocked. **Endplay in any tie rod should be zero.** Many tie rods are spring loaded to help keep the ball-and-socket joint free of play as the joint wears. Eventually, the preloaded spring cannot compensate for the wear, and endplay occurs in the joint. See Figures 10-29 and 10-30.
4. All steering components should be tested with the wheels in the straight-ahead position. If the wheels are turned, some apparent looseness may be noticed due to the angle of the steering linkage.

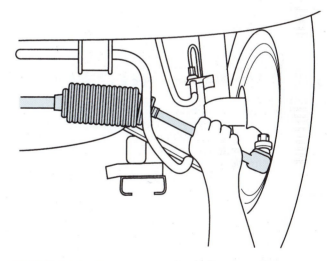

FIGURE 10-29　Steering system component(s) should be replaced if any noticeable looseness is detected when moved by hand.

CAUTION: Do not turn the front wheels of the vehicle while suspended on a lift to check for looseness in the steering linkage. The extra leverage of the wheel and tire assembly can cause a much greater force to be applied to the steering components than can be exerted by hand alone. This extra force may cause some apparent movement in good components that may not need replacement.

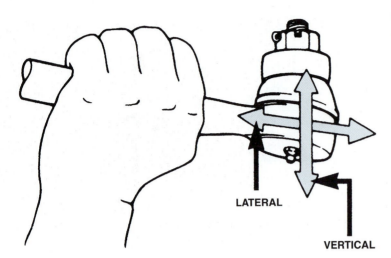

FIGURE 10-30 All joints should be checked by hand for any lateral or vertical play. *(Courtesy of Moog)*

LATERAL

VERTICAL

TECH TIP

THE KILLER Bs

The "three Bs" that can cause steering and suspension problems are bent, broken, or binding components. Always inspect each part under the vehicle for each of the killer B's.

REAL WORLD FIX

BUMP STEER

Bump steer, or *orbital steer*, is used to describe what happens when the steering linkage is not level: The front tires turn inward or outward as the wheels and suspension move up and down. (Automotive chassis engineers call it *roll steer*.) The vehicle's direction is changed *without moving the steering wheel* whenever the tires move up and down over bumps, dips in the pavement, or even over gentle rises!

This author experienced bump steer once and will never forget the horrible feeling of not having control of the vehicle. After replacing an idler arm and aligning the front wheels, everything was OK until about 40 mph (65 km/h); then the vehicle started darting from one lane of the freeway to another. Because there were no "bumps" as such, bump steer was not considered as a cause. Even when holding the steering wheel perfectly still and straight ahead, the vehicle would go left, then right. Did a tie rod break? It certainly felt exactly like that's what happened. I slowed down to below 30 mph and returned to the shop.

After several hours of checking everything, including the alignment, I discovered that the idler arm was not level with the pitman arm. This caused a pull on the steering linkage whenever the suspension moved up and down. As the suspension compressed, the steering linkage pulled inward on the tie rod on that side of the vehicle. As the wheel moved inward (toed in), it created a pull just as if the wheel were turned by the driver.

This is why all steering linkages must be parallel with the lower control. The reason for the bump steer was that the idler arm was bolted to the frame, which was slotted vertically. I didn't pay any attention to the location of the original idler arm and simply bolted the replacement to the frame. After raising the idler arm back up where it belonged (about 1/2 in. [13 mm]), the steering problem was corrected.

Other common causes of bump steer are worn or deteriorated rack mounting bushings, a noncentered steering linkage, or a bent steering linkage. If the steering components are not level, any bump or dip in the road will cause the vehicle to steer one direction or the other. See Figure 10-31.

Always check the steering system carefully whenever a customer complains about any "weird" handling problem.

STEERING LINKAGE REPLACEMENT

Parallelogram Type

When replacing any steering system component, it is best to replace all defective and marginally good components at the same time. Use the following guidelines.

Parts that can be replaced *individually* include the following:

Idler arm
Center link
Pitman arm

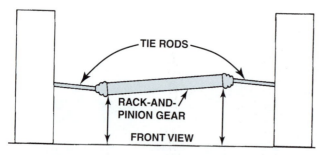

FIGURE 10-31   If a rack-and-pinion or any other steering linkage system is not level, the front tires will be moved inward and/or outward whenever the wheels of the vehicle move up or down.

Intermediate shaft
Intermediate shaft U-joint

Parts that should be replaced in *pairs only* include the following:

Outer tie rod ends
Inner tie rod ends
Idler arm (if there are two on the same vehicle, such as GM's Astro van)

Replacing steering system components involves these steps:

Step 1   Hoist the vehicle safely with the wheels in the straight-ahead position. Remove the front wheels, if necessary, to gain access to the components.

Step 2   Loosen the retainer nut on tapered components, such as tie rod ends. Use a tie rod removal puller (also called a *taper breaker*), as shown in Figure 10-32, or use hammers to slightly deform the taper, as shown in Figure 10-33.

CAUTION: Vehicle manufacturers often warn not to use a tapered pickle-fork tool to separate tapered parts. The wedge tool can tear the grease seal and damage both the part being removed and the adjoining part.

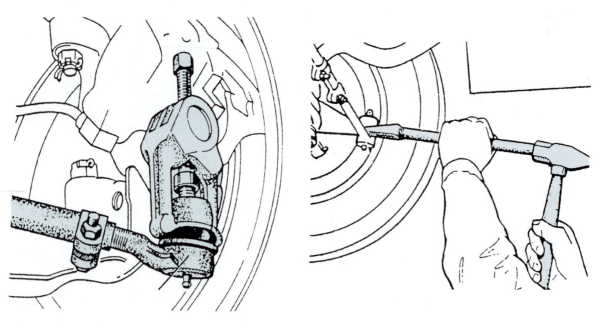

FIGURE 10-32   The preferred method for separating the tie rod end from the steering knuckle is to use a puller such as the one shown. A pickle-fork-type tool should only be used if the tie rod end is going to be replaced. A pickle-fork-type tool can damage or tear the rubber grease boot.

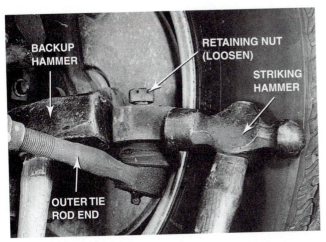

FIGURE 10-33 — Two hammers being used to disconnect a tie rod end from the steering knuckle. One hammer is used as a backing for the second hammer. Notice that the attaching nut has been loosened, but not removed. This prevents the tie rod end from falling when the tapered connection is knocked loose.

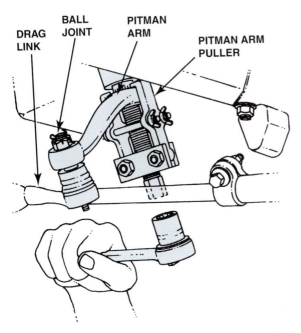

FIGURE 10-34 — A pitman arm puller is used to remove the pitman arm from the pitman shaft.

FIGURE 10-35 — Pitman arm and pitman shaft indexing splines.

FIGURE 10-36 — Align the hole in the tie rod end with the slot in the retaining nut. If the holes do not line up, always tighten the nut further (never loosen) until the hole lines up.

Pitman arms require a larger puller to remove the pitman arm from the splines of the pitman shaft. See Figures 10-34 and 10-35.

Step 3 — Replace the part using the hardware and fasteners supplied with the replacement part. *Do not reuse the precrimped torque prevailing nuts used at the factory as original equipment on many tie rod ends.*

CAUTION: Whenever tightening the nuts of tapered parts such as tie rods, *DO NOT* loosen after reaching the proper assembly torque to align the cotter key hole. If the cotter key does not fit, *tighten* the nut further until the hole lines up for the cotter key. See Figure 10-36. Always use a new cotter key.

When replacing tie rod ends, use the adjusting sleeve to adjust the total length of the tie rod to the same position and length as the original. Measure the original length of the tie rods and assemble the replacement tie rod(s) to the same overall length. See Figure 10-37.

When positioning the tie rod end(s), check that the stud is centered in the socket, as shown in Figure 10-38. This permits maximum steering linkage movement without getting into a bind if the steering linkage is pivoted beyond the angle the tie rod end can move in the socket.

NOTE: To ensure proper wheel alignment, install the adjusting sleeve with an equal number of threads showing at each end of the sleeve. Some manufacturers also specify a *minimum* of three threads showing at each end. If the sleeve itself is corroded or bent, it should be replaced along with either or both of the tie rod ends (inner and outer). See Figure 10-39.

Service of Ball Socket Assemblies

Inner tie rod end assemblies used on rack-and-pinion steering units require special consideration and often special tools. The inner tie rod end, also called a ball socket assembly, should be replaced whenever there is any noticeable freeplay in the ball-and-socket joint. Another test of this joint is performed by disconnecting the outer tie rod end and measuring the effort required to move the tie rod in the socket, as shown in Figure 10-40. This is called the **articulation test.**

NOTE: The articulation test is to be used on metal-to-metal ball socket assemblies. Low-friction joints (polished ball and plastic liner-type joints) may require less effort to move and still be serviceable.

The inner tie rod assemblies are attached to the end of the steering rack by one of several methods.

Removing a ball socket assembly usually requires the use of two wrenches or a special tool. See Figure 10-41.

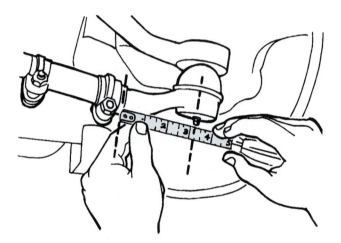

FIGURE 10-37   Replacement tie rods should be of the same overall length as the originals. Measure from the edge of the tie rod sleeve to the center of the grease fitting. When the new tie rod is threaded to this dimension, the toe setting will be close to the original. *(Courtesy of Dana Corporation)*

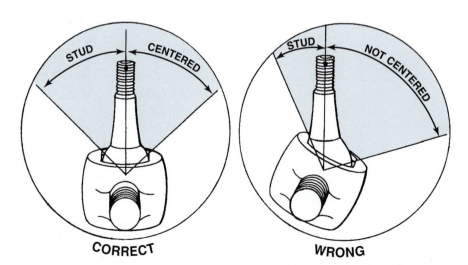

CORRECT   WRONG

FIGURE 10-38   All tie rod ends should be installed so that the stud is in the center of its operating range, as shown. *(Courtesy of Dana Corporation)*

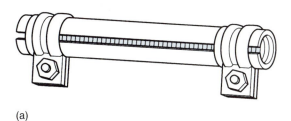

(a)

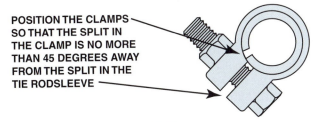

CLAMP ALIGNMENT

POSITION THE CLAMPS
SO THAT THE SPLIT IN
THE CLAMP IS NO MORE
THAN 45 DEGREES AWAY
FROM THE SPLIT IN THE
TIE RODSLEEVE

CORRECT

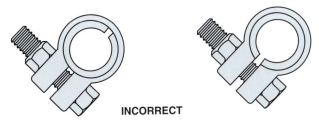

INCORRECT

FIGURE 10-39   (a) Tie rod adjusting sleeve. *(Courtesy of Dana Corporation)* (b) Be sure to position the clamp correctly on the sleeve.

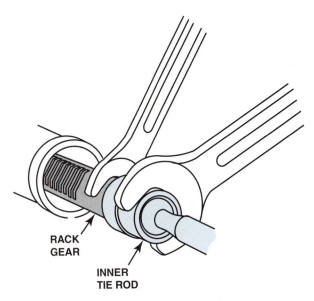

RACK
GEAR

INNER
TIE ROD

FIGURE 10-41   Removing a staked inner tie rod assembly requires two wrenches—one to hold the rack and the other to unscrew the joint from the end of the steering rack.

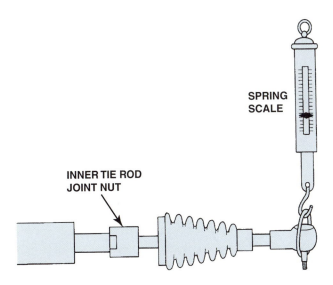

SPRING
SCALE

INNER TIE ROD
JOINT NUT

FIGURE 10-40   An articulation test uses a spring scale to measure the amount of force needed to move the tie rod in the ball socket assembly. Most manufacturers specify a minimum of 1 lb (4.4 N) of force and a maximum of 6 lb (26 N).

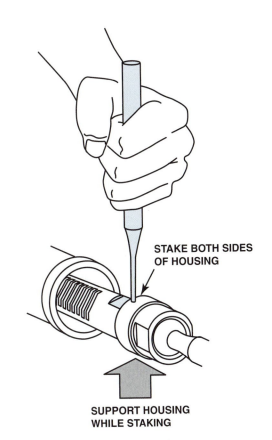

STAKE BOTH SIDES
OF HOUSING

SUPPORT HOUSING
WHILE STAKING

FIGURE 10-42   When the inner tie rod end is reassembled, both sides of the housing must be staked down onto the flat shoulder of the rack.

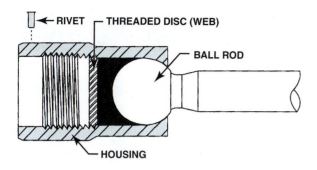

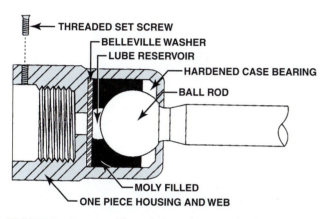

FIGURE 10-43 After replacing an inner tie rod end, the socket assembly should be secured with a rivet or set screw depending on the style of the replacement part. *(Courtesy of Dana Corporation)*

The flange around the outer tie rod must be restaked to the flat shoulder on the end of the rack, as shown in Figure 10-42.

Always follow the instructions that come with the replacement part(s). See Figure 10-43.

NOTE: When replacing a rack-and-pinion assembly, specify a *long rack* rather than a *short rack*. A short rack does not include the bellows (boots) or inner tie rod ends (ball socket assemblies). The labor and cost required to exchange or replace these parts usually make it easier and less expensive to replace the entire steering unit.

DRY PARK TEST   Step-by-Step

STEP 1   Drive the vehicle onto a drive-on-type hoist and have an assistant gently rotate the steering wheel back and forth about 2 inches (50 mm).

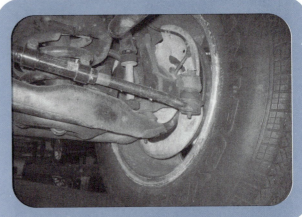

STEP 2   Perform a visual inspection of the steering and suspension system, looking for damage from road debris or other faults.

STEP 3   As the assistant wiggles the steering wheel, grasp the joint at the outer tie rod end on the driver's side to check for any movement.

STEP 4   Next, check for any freeplay at the pitman arm.

DRY PARK TEST continued

STEP 5 Check the joint between the left inner tie rod end and the center link for play.

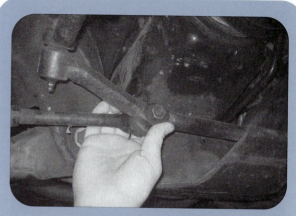

STEP 6 Move to the passenger side and check for any looseness at the joint between the center link and the right-side inner tie rod end.

STEP 7 Check for looseness at the idler arm connector to the center link and the idler arm at the frame mount.

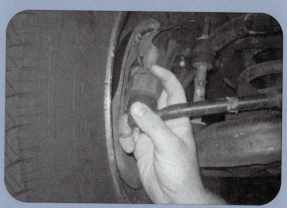

STEP 8 Check for looseness at the passenger-side outer tie rod end. After the inspection, record the results on the work order.

SUMMARY

1. The dry park test is a very important test to detect worn or damaged steering parts. With the vehicle on the ground, have an assistant move the steering wheel back and forth while the technician feels for any looseness in each steering system part.

2. The steering system must be level side-to-side to prevent unwanted bump steer. Bump steer is when the vehicle's direction is changed when traveling over bumps or dips in the road.

3. The idler arm usually is the first steering system component to wear out in a conventional parallelogram-type steering system. Following the idler arm in wear are the tie rods, center link, and then the pitman arm.

4. Steering components should be checked for wear using hand force only.

5. All steering components should be installed and tightened with the front wheels in the straight-ahead position.

6. Always use a tie rod remover/puller or a taper breaker when separating tapered components, such as tie rods.

REVIEW QUESTIONS

1. Describe how to perform a dry park test.

2. List the steering parts that should be replaced in pairs.

3. What test procedure can be used to check that the steering linkage is straight and level?

4. What is the difference between a wear and nonwear center link?

CHAPTER QUIZ

1. A "dry park" test to determine the condition of the steering components and joints should be performed with the vehicle _____.
   a. On level ground on a drive-on lift
   b. On turn plates that allow the front wheels to move
   c. On a frame contact lift with the wheels off the ground
   d. Lifted off the ground about 2 in. (5 cm)

2. Two technicians are discussing bump steer. Technician A says that an unlevel steering linkage can be its cause. Technician B says that if the steering wheel moves when the vehicle is bounced up and down, the steering linkage may be bent. Which technician is correct?
   a. Technician A only
   b. Technician B only
   c. Both Technicians A and B
   d. Neither Technician A nor B

3. A vehicle has an excessive amount of freeplay in the steering wheel and it is difficult to keep it traveling straight on a straight and level road. Which is the *least likely* cause?
   a. Worn tie rod ends
   b. Excessive play in the ball socket assemblies
   c. Worn idler arms
   d. Loose pitman arm retaining nut

4. How are the inner tie rods attached to the rack on a center-take-off-type rack-and-pinion steering gear?
   a. Staked
   b. Bolted
   c. Riveted
   d. Pinned

5. What is the *most likely* cause of bump steer?
   a. Worn outer tie rod ends
   b. A worn center link
   c. Worn or oil-soaked rack bushings
   d. A lack of proper lubrication of all ball-and-socket joints

6. How much endplay is usually acceptable in tie rod ends?
   a. Zero
   b. 0.0010 to 0.030 in.
   c. 0.030 to 0.050 in.
   d. 0.050 to 0.100 in.

7. Technician A says that outer tie rod ends should be replaced in pairs, even if only one is worn. Technician B says that inner tie rod ends should be replaced in pairs, even if only one is worn. Which technician is correct?
   a. Technician A only
   b. Technician B only
   c. Both Technicians A and B
   d. Neither Technician A nor B

8. Which tool is *not* recommended to be used to separate tapered steering components because it can do harm?
   a. Taper breaker
   b. Pickle fork
   c. Tie rod removal puller
   d. Two hammers

9. Technician A says that torque prevailing nuts can be reused unless damaged. Technician B says that a new cotter key should always be used. Which technician is correct?
   a. Technician A only
   b. Technician B only
   c. Both Technicians A and B
   d. Neither Technician A nor B

10. New tie rods are being installed. Technician A says to tighten the retaining nuts to specification and then loosen, if needed, to align the cotter pin hole. Technician B says to tighten further to align the cotter key hole. Which technician is correct?
    a. Technician A only
    b. Technician B only
    c. Both Technician A and B
    d. Neither Technician A nor B

CHAPTER 11

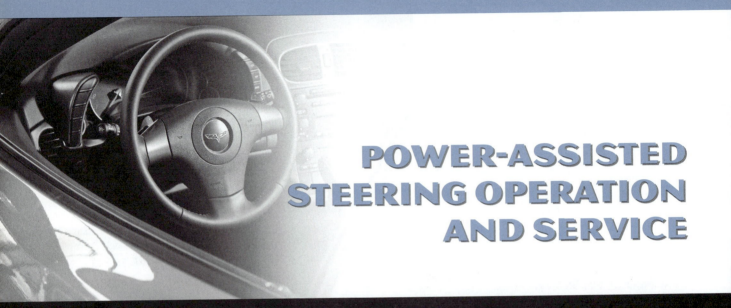

POWER-ASSISTED STEERING OPERATION AND SERVICE

OBJECTIVES

After studying Chapter 11, the reader should be able to:

1. Prepare for Suspension and Steering (A4) ASE certification test content area "A" (Steering Systems Diagnosis and Repairs).

2. Discuss the components and operation of power steering pumps.

3. List the components of a typical power-recirculating-ball-nut steering gear system.

4. Describe the operation of a power rack-and-pinion steering system.

KEY TERMS

BPP (p. 278)
Cold Climate Fluid (p. 281)
EHPS (p. 277)
EPS (p. 274)
EVO (p. 270)
Flow Control Valve (p. 260)
Force (p. 259)
Integral Reservoir (p. 259)
Magnasteer (p. 270)
Pascal's Law (p. 259)
Poppet Valve Steering Gear (p. 267)

Pressure (p. 259)
Pressure-Relief Valve (p. 263)
PSCM (p. 275)
PSP (p. 262)
Remote Reservoir (p. 260)
Rotary Control Valve (p. 263)
Self-Park (p. 277)
SPS (p. 276)
SSS (p. 270)
TFE (p. 270)
VES (p. 270)

Power-assisted steering hydraulically boosts the mechanical steering gear operation so the driver can turn the steering wheel with less effort for the same response. Hydraulic power steering has been available since the 1950s, and many late-model systems are enhanced by electronic controls.

POWER STEERING HYDRAULIC SYSTEMS

Hydraulics is the study of liquids and their use to transmit force and motion. Hydraulic systems transmit force and motion through the use of fluid pressure. **Force** is a push or pull acting on an object and is usually measured in pounds or Newtons. **Pressure** is force applied to a specific area. Pressure is usually measured in force per unit of area, such as pounds per square inch (psi), or kilopascals (kPa). One psi is equal to 6.895 kPa.

The Pascal is a unit of measure named after the French scientist Blaise Pascal (1623–1662), who studied the behavior of fluids in closed systems. One of his discoveries, known as **Pascal's law,** was that pressure on a confined fluid is transmitted equally in all directions and acts with equal force on equal areas.

Hydraulic systems can transmit force and motion through liquids because, for all practical purposes, a liquid cannot be compressed. No matter how much pressure is placed on a liquid, its volume remains the same. This allows a liquid to transmit force much like a mechanical lever. See Figure 11-1.

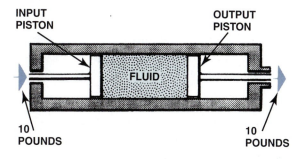

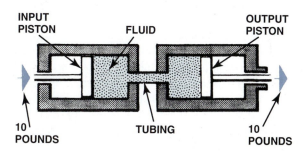

FIGURE 11-1   Hydraulic fluid transmits the same force whether it passes through a single chamber or two chambers connected by a narrow passage.

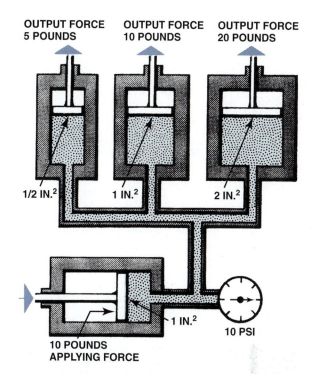

FIGURE 11-2   A fluid applies a force equal to the applied force on a surface that is equal in size to the applying surface. If the surface is half the size, then the fluid exerts half the force: if the surface is twice as large, the fluid exerts twice the force.

The advantage of a liquid over a mechanical lever is that a liquid has volume but does not have a fixed shape. Because it assumes the shape of its container, a liquid can transfer force around obstacles or through pipes and passages of any shape. As explained by Pascal's Law, a liquid can also decrease or increase the force it transmits depending on the area of the output surface to which the force is applied. See Figure 11-2.

POWER STEERING PUMP AND RESERVOIR

The power steering pump draws fluid from the reservoir, pressurizes it, and delivers it to the power steering system. A power steering pump produces a high-pressure stream of fluid, typically in the 1,500-psi (10,500 kPa) range. The fluid reservoir may be either integral to (built into) the pump or remotely mounted and connected to the pump by a hose. The power steering fluid reservoir is usually made of either plastic or stamped metal, and it includes the fluid filler neck, cap, and dipstick. It can be integral to or remote from the pump. An **integral reservoir** is part of the pump, and the pump itself operates submerged in power steering fluid. See Figure 11-3. Although once common, steering pumps with an integral reservoir have given way to those with a remote reservoir on many current-production vehicles. This is because the remote

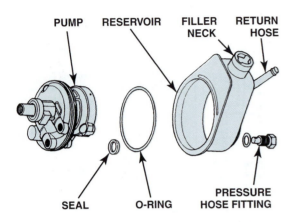

FIGURE 11-3 A typical integral power stering pump when the pump is mounted inside the reservoir.

FIGURE 11-4 Typical remote reservoir.

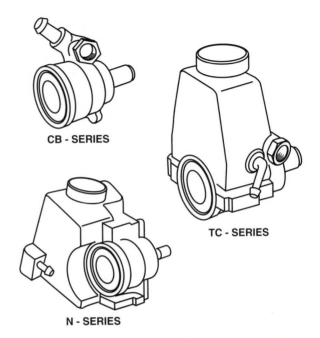

FIGURE 11-5 Typical integral power steering pump assemblies.

reservoir allows for a smaller, more compact pump assembly that is better suited to the cramped engine compartment of a modern vehicle.

A **remote reservoir** is a separate assembly from the pump and provides fluid to it through a suction hose. See Figure 11-4.

A typical power steering system requires only 2 to 3.5 lb (0.9 to 1.6 kg) of effort to turn the steering wheel.

Most power steering systems use an engine-driven hydraulic pump. Power steering hydraulic pumps are usually belt driven from the front crankshaft pulley of the engine, as shown in Figure 11-5.

The power steering pump delivers a constant flow of hydraulic fluid to the power steering gear or rack. A typical power steering pump requires less than 1/2 horsepower, which is less than 1% of engine power while driving straight ahead. Even while parking at low speed, the power steering requires only about 3 horsepower while providing high

hydraulic pressures. Typical pressures generated by a power steering system include the following.

Straight ahead	less than 150 psi (1,400 kPa)
Cornering	about 450 psi (3,100 kPa)
Parking (maximum)	750–1400 psi (5,200–10,000 kPa)

The power steering pump drive pulley is usually fitted to a chrome-plated shaft with a press fit. The shaft is applied to a rotor with vanes that rotate between a thrust plate and a pressure plate. See Figure 11-6.

Some power steering pumps are of the slipper or roller design instead of the vane type. When the engine starts, the drive belt rotates the power steering pump pulley and the rotor assembly inside the power steering pump.

With a vane-type pump, centrifugal force and hydraulic pressure push the vanes of the rotor outward into contact with the pump ring. The shape of the pump ring causes a change in the volume of fluid between the vanes. As the volume increases, the pressure is decreased in the space between the vanes and draws in fluid from the pump reservoir. When the volume between the vanes decreases, the pressure is increased and flows out the pump discharge port. See Figures 11-7, 11-8, and 11-9.

The pressure outlet hose connects to a fitting that threads into the outlet port of the pump body. A modulator valve, commonly called a **flow control valve,** installs in the same bore as the hose fitting. See Figure 11-10 on page 262.

The modulator valve is a spring-loaded pressure-relief device that bleeds off excess pressure to prevent system damage.

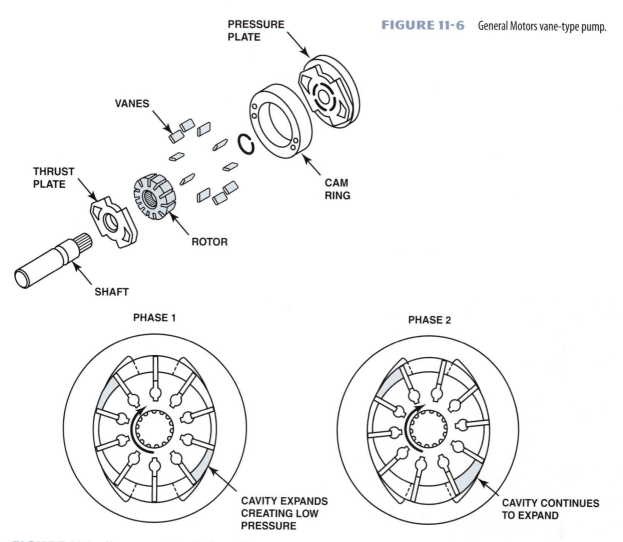

FIGURE 11-6   General Motors vane-type pump.

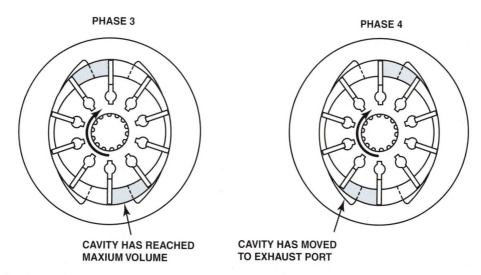

FIGURE 11-7   Vane pump operation. In phase 1, the rotor moves past the opposed suction ports, and the vanes move out to maintain contact with the ring. This creates a low-pressure area, drawing fluid into the cavities formed by the vanes. As the rotor continues to move during phase 2, the vanes follow the contour of the ring. The contour of the ring forms a larger cavity between the vanes. This increases the suction and draws more fluid into the pump.

FIGURE 11-8   Vane pump operation—continued. At phase 3, the vanes are at the end of the intake port of the pump and the cavity has reached its maximum volume. In phase 4, the rotor moves into alignment with the opposed discharge ports.

PHASE 5

PHASE 6

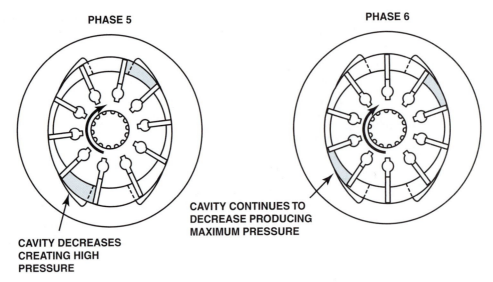

CAVITY CONTINUES TO
DECREASE PRODUCING
MAXIMUM PRESSURE

CAVITY DECREASES
CREATING HIGH
PRESSURE

FIGURE 11-9   Vane pump operation—continued. As the rotor continues to move during phase 5, the volume of the cavity decreases, which increases the discharge pressure. At phase 6, the last phase, the contour of the ring results in the minimum cavity volume, and the discharge of fluid is completed.

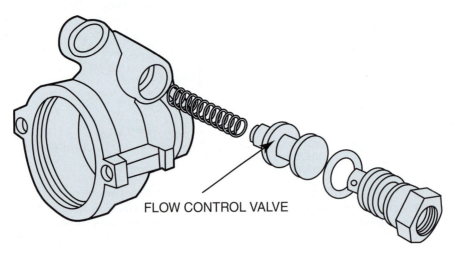

FLOW CONTROL VALVE

FIGURE 11-10   Flow control valve.

When pump output is more than the power steering system requires, the excess pressure overcomes spring force and moves the valve down in its bore. This uncovers an orifice through which the fluid can flow back into the inlet passages. An orifice is a small opening that regulates fluid pressure and flow. It can be a restriction in a fluid line or a hole between two fluid chambers. This particular opening is called a *variable orifice* because the size of the opening varies with the amount of pressure applied to the valve. When fluid pressure is not high, spring force keeps the valve seated so that all of the pressurized fluid flows through the outlet port and into the pressure hose.

Because the engine drives the pump, the power steering pump places a load on the engine whenever the engine is running. Under certain conditions, such as when the steering wheel is turned to or near full stop for more than a few seconds, pressure builds in the system and the pump must work harder to keep up with the demand. As a result, the pump draws more power from the engine. If the engine is running at idle, the extra load can cause it to stall. A pressure switch, known as the **power steering pressure (PSP)** switch, transmits an electronic signal to the powertrain control module (PCM) when the pressure in the system is high enough to increase the load on the engine. In response to the PSP switch signal, the PCM increases the engine idle speed to prevent stalling.

The pressure increases when the steering wheel is turned to its full stop in either direction. To handle the excess pressure, a pressure-relief passage runs from a point near the pressure hose fitting to the spring end of the modulator valve. Inside the passage is a **pressure-relief valve.** The spring end of the modulator valve forms a seat for the pressure-relief check ball. Under normal circumstances, the check ball remains seated.

The parts of the pressure-relief valve are the following:

- Spring
- Valve piston
- Check ball
- Seat

A shim installs on the check ball seat to adjust the pressure at which the check ball unseats to open the pressure-relief valve. Normally, the spring force holds the piston against the check ball to keep it in its seat. When pressure becomes excessive in the pressure-relief passage, the check ball raises off its seat to allow fluid to flow through the relief passage and out through an orifice in the modulator valve. See Figure 11-11. The pressure when this occurs varies from 750 to 1,400 psi (5,200 to 10,000 kPa) depending on the calibration of the pressure-relief valve. When power steering systems are pushed to the limit, most will make a chattering or squealing noise until the pressure is reduced.

POWER STEERING HOSES

Because the power steering pump and the steering gear are not part of the same assembly, the system requires two hoses to connect the power steering pump and gear assembly. The pressure hose is connected to the flow control/relief valve. This hose supplies pressurized fluid to the steering gear. The second hose is called the return hose and it returns the fluid from the steering gear to the pump. Some vehicles will use a cooler in the return path to the pump. The cooler is used to reduce the temperature of the fluid before it enters the pump. See Figure 11-12.

INTEGRAL POWER STEERING

In an integral power steering system, the control valve and the power piston are incorporated into the steering gear construction. The control valve regulates the application of pressurized fluid against the power piston, and the power piston helps move the output member of the steering gear when pressure is applied to one side of it.

Integral Standard Steering Gear

Most standard steering gears with power assist are the recirculating-ball type, and the ball nut functions as the power piston. Hydraulic pressure from the steering gear control valve is applied directly against the ball nut to help move it through the housing. The ball nut in this type of power steering gear is called the *power piston* because hydraulic pressure moves it as if it were a piston traveling in a cylinder. See Figure 11-13.

Rotary Control Valve

A **rotary control valve** is a two-piece assembly that operates by rotating an inner valve within an outer valve. A steering

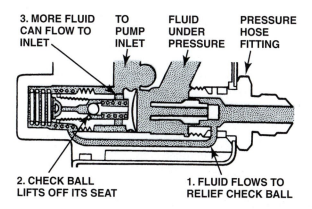

FIGURE 11-11 The pressure-relief check ball unseats, allowing fluid to flow back into the pump inlet if the pressure rises above a certain limit.

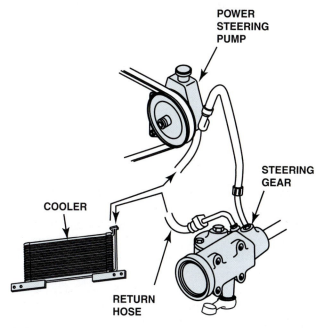

FIGURE 11-12 The power steering fluid cooler, if used, is located in the return hose.

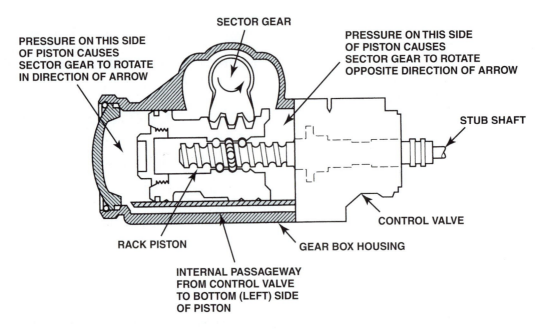

FIGURE 11-13   Forces acting on the rack piston of an integral power steering gear.

gear with a rotary control valve is also a *torsion bar steering gear,* because a small torsion bar is used to control valve movement.

The rotary control valve consists of two cylindrical elements: the inner valve element and outer valve element. The inner valve element is secured to the steering gear input shaft and the torsion bar. In the valve, the inner element and the input shaft are one piece, and the torsion bar attaches to them. See Figure 11-14. The inner element assembly fits inside the outer valve element, and is also secured to the torsion bar by a pin. The outer valve element is also the steering worm gear. The torsion bar acts as a spring between the two elements to allow movement between them when the steering shaft turns. The spring force of the torsion bar tends to pull the elements back to their neutral positions when the steering wheel is released or returned to center. The strength of the torsion bar determines steering feel. A weak torsion bar moves easily and provides soft steering, while a strong bar resists movement and makes steering feel firm.

The facing surfaces of the inner and outer elements have grooves machined into them through which fluid can flow. Passages carry fluid from some of the inner-element grooves to the center of the element, where it travels through the return line to the pump reservoir. The outer element has three sets of fluid passages that connect the outside of the element to a groove at the inside. One set of passages carries fluid into the element from the pressure hose fitting, the second set carries fluid to and from the left-turn side of the power piston, and the third carries it to and from the right-turn side.

When the steering wheel is aimed straight ahead, the valve is in its neutral position. Fluid enters the valve and flows

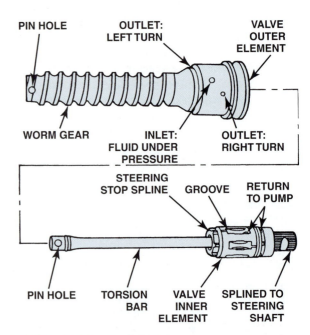

FIGURE 11-14   The rotary valve consists of inner and outer elements. The worm gear is part of the outer element and the torsion bar is part of the inner element. A pin attaches the worm gear to the bottom of the torsion bar to join the two elements together.

equally to both sides of the steering gear piston and to the return line. See Figure 11-15.

When the steering wheel and steering shaft turn to the left, the inner element twists on the torsion bar and repositions the valve ports. In this left-turn position, pressurized fluid flowing into the valve can only exit through the left-turn

STRAIGHT-AHEAD

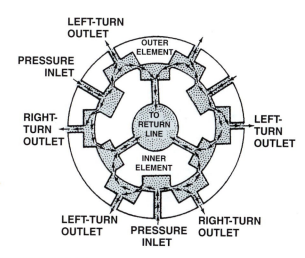

FIGURE 11-15 When the steering wheel is in the straight-ahead position, all of the ports in a rotary valve are open equally to the pressure and return circuits.

LEFT TURN

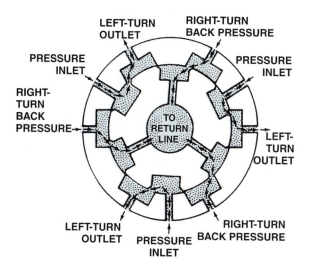

FIGURE 11-16 During a left turn, the inner element turns so that the left-turn circuits are open to pressure and the right-turn circuits are open to the return circuit.

ports. See Figure 11-16. Meanwhile, the right-turn ports align with the return ports to bleed off residual pressure from the opposite side of the power piston. Pressurized fluid flowing through the left-turn ports is directed into the steering gear, where it applies force to the power piston and reduces the effort needed to turn the steering linkage to the left. See Figure 11-17. As the piston moves, it forces fluid out of the right-turn side, and that fluid returns through the control valve to the pump reservoir. Exactly the opposite flow occurs during a right-hand turn: The right-turn ports are opened and the left-turn ports exhaust to the return line. See Figure 11-18. Hydraulic pressure moves the piston up the housing bore during a right-hand turn. See Figure 11-19.

When the steering wheel is released, the spring force of the torsion bar returns the two elements to their natural positions. Fluid pressure equalizes throughout the steering gear and recenters the piston in the middle of the steering gear.

Power Rack-and-Pinion Steering

The rotary control valve on a power rack-and-pinion steering gear is located between the steering gear input shaft and the pinion gear. See Figure 11-20.

Fluid discharged by the valve travels through external steel lines to either side of the power piston. A steel air-transfer tube allows air displacement between the boots as they compress and expand, since the power piston prevents air from passing through the rack housing. The rotary valve in a rack-and-pinion steering unit operates in the same manner as the one previously described for a standard steering gear. During a left-hand turn, the control valve directs fluid flow into the left-turn steel line, which routes it to the right-hand side of the

power piston in order to move the rack to the left. As this happens, fluid on the opposite side of the power piston is forced out through the right-turn steel line and back to the control valve, where it is exhausted to the return circuit. When the steering wheel is turned to the right, fluid flow is reversed so the power piston moves to the right and fluid in the left-turn chamber is exhausted to the return circuit. See Figure 11-21.

Flow Control Valve Operation

When the power steering pump begins operation, the fluid from the output of the pump flows into the control valve. The fluid then flows through the orifice, where a pressure differential is formed. The pressure differential results in a higher pressure on the pump side than on the system side. The fluid from the orifice flows into the power steering system and through a passage on the backside of the control valve. See Figure 11-22.

The fluid on the backside of the control valve is used to assist the spring force acting on the valve. At this point, the combination of the spring force and hydraulic pressure is higher than the output pressure of the pump. This causes the control valve to block the passage to the pump intake. When the output pressure is higher than the spring force, the pressure behind the valve forces the control valve to move. The movement of the valve opens the passage to the intake side of the pump. This allows some of the fluid to flow into the passage. As the pump speed continues to increase, the valve moves more to compensate for the higher pressure and flow. The pressure and flow in the power steering system must remain in the correct range or the steering system components can be damaged. Failure of the control valve to regulate the pressure in the power steering system can result in excessive pressure and temperature. As long

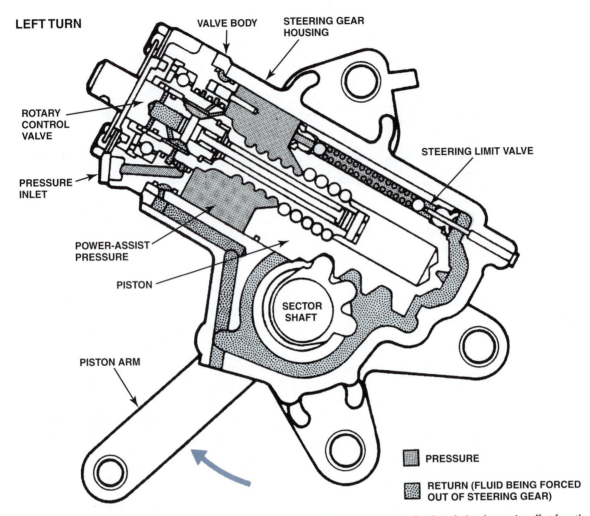

LEFT TURN

VALVE BODY

STEERING GEAR HOUSING

ROTARY CONTROL VALVE

STEERING LIMIT VALVE

PRESSURE INLET

POWER-ASSIST PRESSURE

PISTON

SECTOR SHAFT

PISTON ARM

▓ PRESSURE

▓ RETURN (FLUID BEING FORCED OUT OF STEERING GEAR)

FIGURE 11-17   During a left turn, the high-pressure fluid helps push the piston along the worm gear, thereby reducing the steering effort from the driver.

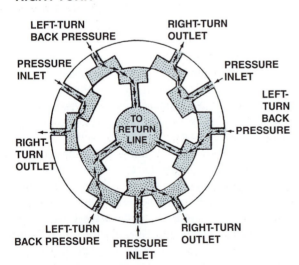

RIGHT TURN

LEFT-TURN BACK PRESSURE

RIGHT-TURN OUTLET

PRESSURE INLET

PRESSURE INLET

TO RETURN LINE

LEFT-TURN BACK PRESSURE

RIGHT-TURN OUTLET

LEFT-TURN BACK PRESSURE

PRESSURE INLET

RIGHT-TURN OUTLET

FIGURE 11-18   During a right turn, the inner element turns so that the right-turn outlets are open to pressure and the left-turn outlets are open to the return circuit.

as fluid can flow through the system, the control valve can regulate the pressure. See Figure 11-23.

However, there are times during normal operation when the flow in the system will stop. Fluid flow can stop during parking maneuvers and when the steering wheel is turned to the extreme right and left positions.

When the fluid flow through the system stops, the pressure equalizes on both sides of the orifice. This creates equal pressure on both sides of the control valve. Because the backside of the valve has a spring, the combination of the hydraulic pressure and spring force positions the control valve to prevent flow into the pump intake passage. As the pump continues to operate, the pressure in the system builds. If the pressure is not relieved, the system can be damaged. To prevent this, the control valve has a check valve inside of it. At a specific pressure, the check valve opens to relieve the pressure on the backside of the control valve. This creates a pressure differential and allows the control valve to move. With the control valve moved, the high pressure is allowed into the pump intake passage. At this point, the check valve and control valve seat. See Figure 11-24.

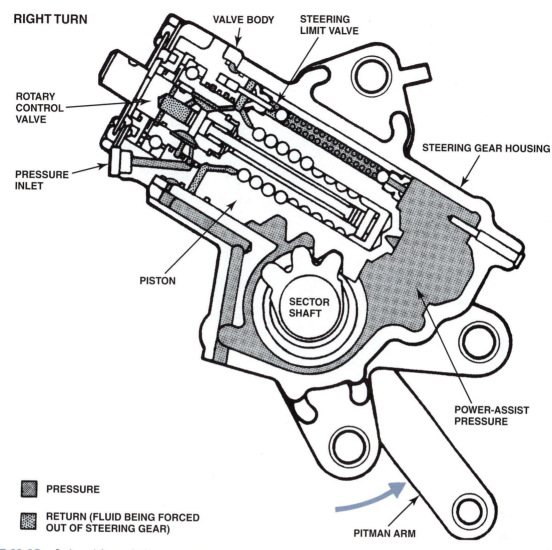

RIGHT TURN

VALVE BODY

STEERING LIMIT VALVE

ROTARY CONTROL VALVE

STEERING GEAR HOUSING

PRESSURE INLET

PISTON

SECTOR SHAFT

POWER-ASSIST PRESSURE

PITMAN ARM

PRESSURE

RETURN (FLUID BEING FORCED OUT OF STEERING GEAR)

FIGURE 11-19   During a right turn, high-pressure fluid pushes the piston up the worm gear, moving the sector shaft and pitman arm to provide assist during a right turn.

FREQUENTLY ASKED QUESTION

WHAT IS A POPPET VALVE STEERING GEAR?

A **poppet valve steering gear** is used on General Motors medium-duty trucks and is manufactured by TRW/ROSS. It is similar in operation to the Saginaw steering gear except that it delays power assist until after the steering wheel has been rotated one-third of a revolution by using a poppet valve.

This prevents oversteering in a medium-duty truck. Turning the steering wheel left causes the poppet valve on the pressure side of the rack piston (the left side) to

be unseated by hydraulic pressure. The poppet valve on the other side (the right side) contacts a bolt inside the housing within a one-third rotation of the steering wheel. This connects the pressure and return lines to both sides of the rack piston.

This prevents power-assisted steering. When the steering is turned right, the poppet valve on the right side of the rack piston is unseated by hydraulic pressure. The poppet valve on the left side contacts a bolt within a one-third rotation of the steering wheel. Both sides of the rack piston are connected to the pressure and return lines, and power-assisted steering is prevented. See Figure 11-25 on page 270.

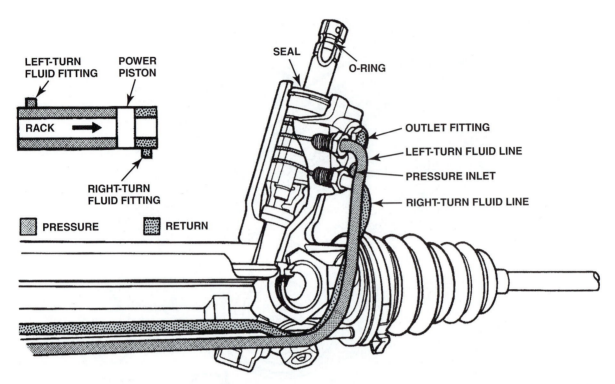

FIGURE 11-20   During a left turn, the control valve directs pressure into the left-turn fluid line and the rack moves left. (See inset.) Fluid pushed out of the right-turn fluid chamber travels back through the right-turn fluid line and control valve to the return circuit.

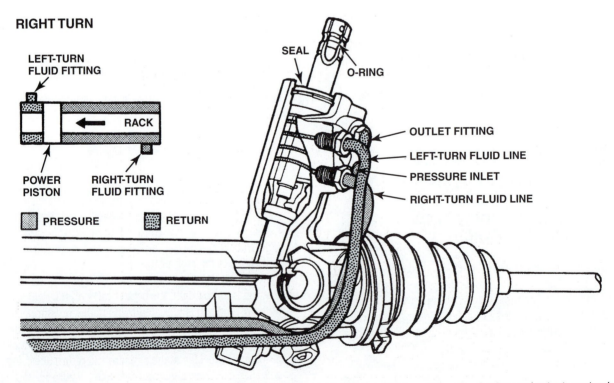

FIGURE 11-21   The control valve routes high-pressure fluid to the left-hand side of the power piston, which pushes the piston and assists in moving the rack toward the right when the steering wheel is turned right.

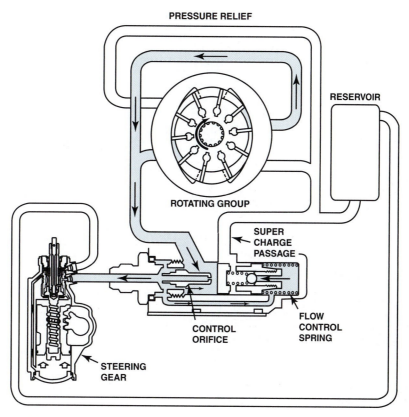

FIGURE 11-22   Low-speed flow control.

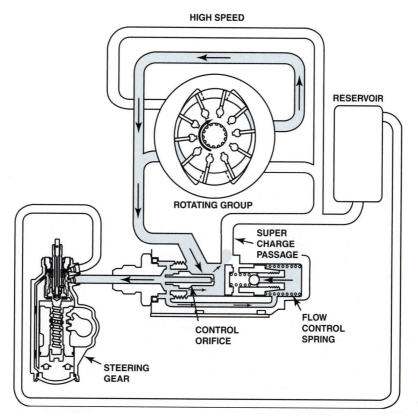

FIGURE 11-23   High-speed flow control operation.

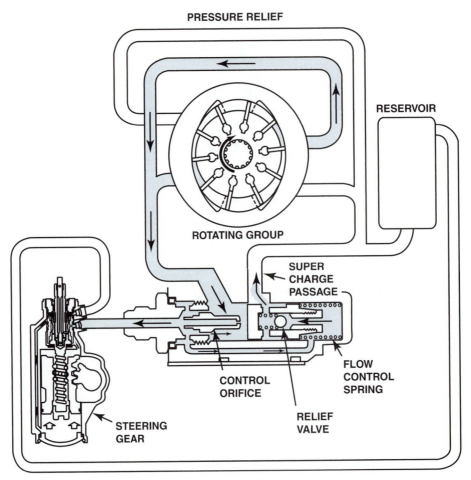

FIGURE 11-24   Pressure-relief mode. In this mode the steering gear has blocked the flow of fluid from the pump and the pressure rises, which unseats the pressure-relief valve. Now fluid flows back to the inlet through the pressure-relief orifice and passage.

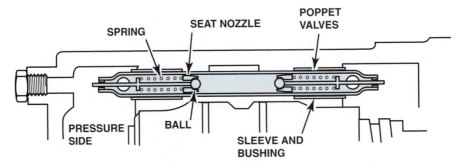

FIGURE 11-25   A TRW/ROSS poppet valve steering gear.

VARIABLE-EFFORT STEERING

Variable-effort steering (VES) systems are designed to provide variable power-assisted steering. The amount of power assist increases at lower vehicle speeds to aid parking maneuvers and decreases at higher speeds for greater road feel.

An examples, General Motors uses four different variable-effort steering systems:

- Electronic Variable Orifice (EVO)
- Two-Flow Electronic (TFE)
- Speed Sensitive Steering (SSS)
- Magnasteer

The Electronic Variable Orifice (EVO) system provides a wide range of power-assisted steering based on the vehicle's operating conditions. See Figure 11-26.

The system uses vehicle speed and steering wheel speed to regulate the current to a solenoid that changes the orifice size of the flow control valve.

The size of the orifice controls the flow rate through the valve and the pressure in the hydraulic system. The desired amount is then directed to the steering gear for the power assist. The second type of power assist is the TFE system, which provides two rates of power assist:

- At low speeds, the TFE solenoid provides maximum power assist.
- At high speeds, the solenoid provides minimum power assist.

Another type of power assist is the Speed Sensitive Steering (SSS) system, which uses hydraulic pressure to resist movement in the steering gear as speed increases. This provides a firmer sense of control and stability in the steering gear at higher speeds.

Electronic Variable Orifice (EVO) System Components

The main components of the EVO system are:

- Vehicle speed sensor
- Power steering control module
- Steering wheel speed sensor
- Power steering gear
- Power steering pump and solenoid actuator

The actuator is a solenoid-operated pintle valve. Electrical current flow through the solenoid controls the position of the pintle in relation to the orifice.

As the vehicle speed increases, the control module provides a higher current flow and the solenoid positions the pintle to change the size of the orifice.

This increased speed results in a reduced amount of hydraulic flow and provides less hydraulic pressure to the steering gear.

The control module uses the signal from the vehicle speed sensor to calculate the required amperage for the solenoid.

The amperage has a direct effect on steering effort and the flow rate to the gear. As the vehicle speed increases, the solenoid extends the pintle and reduces the size of the orifice. Hydraulic pressure is being reduced as the vehicle speed increases and less power assist is available.

The other sensor for the EVO system is the steering wheel speed sensor. This sensor is used to determine if the vehicle operator is performing an evasive steering maneuver.

In this situation, the controller increases the hydraulic pressure to assist the operator. The faster the driver turns the steering wheel, the stronger the signal generated by the sensor. The faster the steering wheel is rotated, the more the solenoid retracts the pintle and enlarges the size of the orifice. This increases hydraulic pressure to the steering gear and provides more power assist for the operator.

Two-Flow Electronic (TFE) System

The main components of the TFE system are:

- Power steering pump and solenoid actuator
- Steering rack-and-pinion gear
- Powertrain control module (PCM)

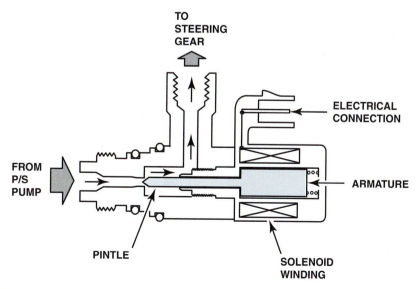

FIGURE 11-26   EVO actuator assembly.

The TFE actuator is a solenoid-operated pintle valve. The pintle valve only has two positions—maximum assist and reduced assist. When the solenoid is provided a ground from the chime module, the pintle extends out from the orifice and provides maximum assist. When the chime module opens the ground path, the pintle moves in to restrict the orifice and thus reduces steering assist.

The PCM provides the chime module with a vehicle speed signal. The logic circuits in the chime module determine when to energize the solenoid. The solenoid is energized whenever the vehicle speed is approximately 20 mph (32 km/h) or lower and the pintle is extended, causing the power steering pressure to increase. This provides maximum assist and the steering effort is low. When the vehicle speed is higher than 20 mph (32 km/h), the pintle is moved in and the steering pressure is low. This provides reduced assist and higher steering effort.

SSS System

The major components of the SSS system are:

- Power steering pump
- SSS actuator
- Steering gear
- Road sensing suspension control module

The actuator is a solenoid-operated valve that controls the flow of fluid into the chambers of the steering gear valve. As more fluid flows into the chamber, pressure is built against the four pistons that are located around the spool shaft. As the pistons are loaded and pushed against the spool shaft, steering effort is increased.

Unlike the EVO and TFE systems, the SSS system uses hydraulic pressure to resist movement in the steering gear. The amount of fluid allowed into the chambers is based on the electrical current flow through the solenoid.

The Road Sensing Suspension (RSS) control module, using the signal from the vehicle speed sensor, calculates the required amperage for the solenoid.

The amperage has a direct effect on steering effort and the hydraulic flow rate into the chambers of the spool shaft. As the vehicle's speed increases, more hydraulic pressure is built against the pistons and the steering effort is increased. The steering effort adjustment begins at a vehicle speed of 20 mph (32 km/h).

Magnasteer

The fourth type of VES steering system used by General Motors is the Magnasteer system. This system uses a variable bi-directional magnetic rotary actuator built into the steering rack. The bi-directional magnetic rotary actuator has no effect on the hydraulic operation of the steering rack.

The main components in the system include:

- Power steering pump
- Magnasteer actuator assembly
- Steering gear
- Electronic brake control module (EBCM)

The Magnasteer system uses a conventional rack-and-pinion steering gear and an engine-driven hydraulic pump to provide power assist. The Magnasteer actuator consists of the following:

- A permanent magnet attached to the rotary input shaft
- A pole-piece assembly attached to the pinion
- An electromagnetic coil mounted in the steering gear housing

Integrated with the pinion shaft is a spool valve that senses the level of torque in the shaft and applies hydraulic pressure to the steering rack whenever assistance is needed. The electromagnet acts in parallel with the input shaft from the steering wheel to open or close the spool valve.

The electromagnet generates variable torque, which can either increase or diminish the amount of steering torque that is needed to open the spool valve. See Figures 11-27 and 11-28.

To vary the amount of steering assist, the EBCM uses the signal from the wheel speed sensor to calculate the required amperage and direction of current flow to the Magnasteer actuator.

The amperage and direction of current flow have a direct effect on steering effort and the flow rate to the rack piston. When the vehicle is stationary, approximately 1.6 amps of current flow through the electromagnetic coil.

As the vehicle speed increases to approximately 45 mph, the current decreases to 0 amps. The EBCM then switches the direction of current flow. Current flow through the electromagnetic coil causes either a magnetic attraction or repelling in the Magnasteer actuator.

At low vehicle speeds below 45 mph, the direction of current flow creates a magnetic field that opposes the permanent magnet. The repelling force of the magnetic field assists the spool valve in moving out of alignment with the valve body, and this increases the power assist.

With vehicle speeds below 45 mph, increased current provides increased steering assist. At vehicle speeds above 45 mph, the direction of current through the electromagnetic coil creates a magnetic field that attracts the permanent magnet.

- The magnet helps keep the spool valve aligned with the valve body, and this reduces the power assist and provides a greater road feel.
- As the vehicle speed increases, the amount of effort required to overcome the attracting force of the magnetic field increases.

With vehicle speeds above 45 mph, increased current flow provides decreased steering assist.

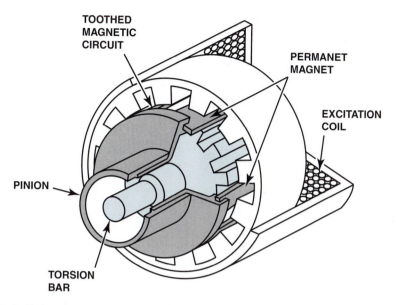

FIGURE 11-27 Integrated with the pinion shaft is a spool valve that senses the level of torque in the shaft and applies hydraulic pressure to the steering rack whenever assistance is needed. The electromagnet acts in parallel with the input shaft from the steering wheel to open or close the spool valve. The electromagnet generates variable torque, which can either increase or diminish the amount of steering torque that is needed to open the spool valve.

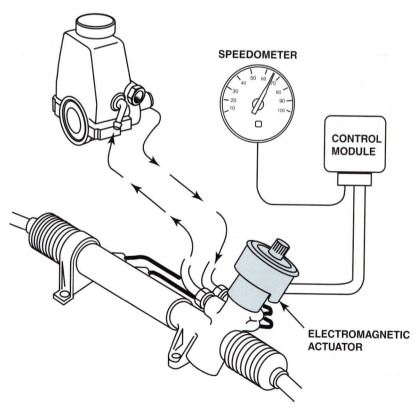

FIGURE 11-28 Magnasteer system.

ELECTRIC POWER STEERING SYSTEM

Most electric power steering units use a DC electric motor. Some operate from 42 volts while others operate from 12 volts. The **electric power steering (EPS)** is also called electric power-assisted steering (EPAS).

The Toyota system on a Prius uses a DC motor, reduction gear, and torque sensor all mounted to the steering column. See Figure 11-29.

The electric power steering (EPS) is controlled by the EPS ECU, which calculates the amount of needed assist based on the input from the steering torque sensor. The steering torque sensor is a noncontact sensor that detects the movement and torque applied to the torsion bar. The torsion bar twists when the drive exerts torque to the steering wheel, and the more torque applied the further the bar will twist. This generates a higher-voltage signal to the EPS ECU. See Figure 11-30.

The steering shaft torque sensor and the steering wheel position sensor are not serviced separately from each other or from the steering column assembly. The steering column assembly does not include the power steering motor and module assembly. The detection ring 1 and detection ring 2 are mounted on the input shaft and detection ring 3 is mounted on the output shaft. The input shaft and the output shaft are connected by a torsion bar. When the steering wheel is turned, the difference in relative motion between detection rings 2 and 3 is sensed by the detection coil and it sends two signals to the EPS ECU. These two signals are called Torque Sensor Signal 1 and Torque Signal 2. The EPS ECU uses these signals to control the amount of assist, and also uses the signals for diagnosis.

NOTE: If the steering wheel, steering column, or steering gear is removed or replaced, the zero point of the torque sensors must be reset.

The Toyota Highlander and Lexus RX 400h use a different electric power steering unit due to the larger size of the vehicles. This unit uses a brushless DC on the steering rack. See Figures 11-31 and 11-32.

The Honda electric power steering uses an electric motor to provide steering assist and replaces the need for a hydraulic pump, hoses, and gear. A torque sensor is used to measure road resistance and the direction that the driver is turning the steering wheel. The torque sensor input and the vehicle speed are used by the EPS controller to supply the EPS motor with the specified current to help assist the steering effort. See Figure 11-33.

The motor turns the pinion shaft using a worm gear. The worm gear is engaged with the worm wheel so that the motor turns the pinion shaft directly when providing steering assist. The steering rack is unique because the tie rods are mounted to the center of the rack rather than at the ends of the rack as in a conventional Honda power steering arrangement. See Figure 11-34.

If a major fault were to occur, the control module would first try to maintain power-assisted steering even if some sensors had failed. If the problem is serious, then the vehicle can be driven and steered manually. The EPS control unit will turn on the EPS dash warning light if a fault has been detected. A fault in the system will not cause the malfunction indicator light to come on because that light is reserved for emission-related faults only. Fault codes can be retrieved by using a scan tool and the codes will be displayed by the flashing of the EPS warning lamp.

The EPS system includes the following components and inputs/outputs:

- Powertrain control module (PCM)
- Body control module (BCM)
- Power steering control module (PSCM)
- Battery voltage
- Steering shaft torque sensor
- Steering wheel position sensor
- Power steering motor
- Driver information center (DIC)
- Serial data circuit to perform the system functions.

FIGURE 11-29 A Toyota Prius EPS assembly. *(Courtesy of Tony Martin)*

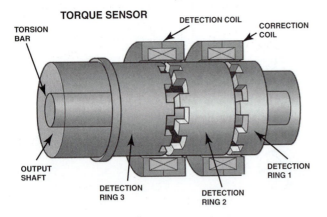

FIGURE 11-30 The torque sensor converts the torque the driver is exerting to the steering wheel into a voltage signal. *(Courtesy of Toyota)*

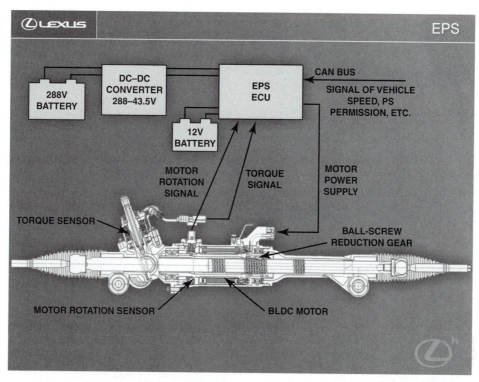

FIGURE 11-31 The electric power steering in Toyota/Lexus SUVs uses a brushless DC (labeled BLDC) motor around the rack of the unit and operates on 42 volts. *(Courtesy of University of Toyota and Toyota Motor Sales, U.S.A. Inc).*

FIGURE 11-32 Photo of the electric power steering gear on a Lexus 400h taken from underneath the vehicle.

The **power steering control module (PSCM)** and the power steering motor are serviced as an assembly and are serviced separately from the steering column assembly. See Figure 11-35.

The steering shaft torque sensor and the steering wheel position sensor are not serviced separately from each other or from the steering column assembly. The steering column assembly does not include the power steering motor and module assembly.

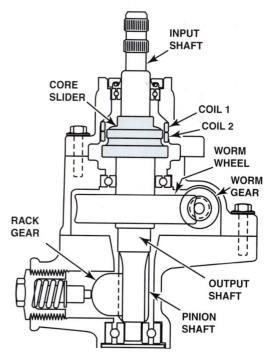

FIGURE 11-33 A cross-sectional view of a Honda electric power steering (EPS) gear showing the torque sensor and other components.

Steering Shaft Torque Sensor

The PSCM uses the steering shaft torque sensor as a main input for determining steering direction and the amount of assist

FIGURE 11-34 Honda electric power steering unit cutaway.

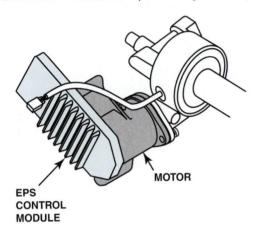

EPS
CONTROL
MODULE

MOTOR

FIGURE 11-35 The Power Steering Control Module (PSCM) is attached to the motor of the electric power steering assembly.

needed. The steering column has an input shaft, from the steering wheel to the torque sensor, and an output shaft, from the torque sensor to the steering shaft coupler. The input and output shafts are separated by a section of torsion bar, where the torque sensor is located. The sensor is a 5-volt dual-analog inverse signal device with a signal voltage range of 0.25 to 4.75 volts. The sensors are used to detect the direction the steering wheel is being rotated.

- When torque is applied to the steering column shaft during a right turn, the sensor signal 1 voltage increases, while the signal 2 voltage decreases.
- When torque is applied to the steering column shaft during a left turn, the sensor signal 1 voltage decreases, while the signal 2 voltage increases.

The PSCM recognizes this change in signal voltage as steering direction and steering column shaft torque.

Steering Wheel Position Sensor

The PSCM uses the **steering position sensor (SPS)** to determine the steering system on-center position. Because the power steering motor provides a slight amount of return-to-center assist, the PSCM will command the power steering motor to the steering system center position and not beyond. The sensor is a 5-volt dual-analog signal device with a signal voltage range of 0 to 5 volts. The sensor's signal 1 and signal 2 voltage values will increase and decrease within 2.5 to 2.8 volts of each other as the steering wheel is turned. See Figure 11-36.

Power Steering Motor

The power steering motor is a 12-volt brushless DC reversible motor with a 65-amp rating. The motor assists steering through a worm gear and reduction gear located in the steering column housing.

Power Steering Control Module (PSCM)

The PSCM uses a combination of steering shaft torque sensor input, vehicle speed, calculated system temperature, and steering tuning to determine the amount of steering assist. When the steering wheel is turned, the PSCM uses signal voltage from the steering shaft torque sensor to detect the amount of torque and steering direction being applied to the steering column shaft and then commands the proper amount of current to the power steering motor. The PSCM receives a vehicle speed message from the PCM by way of the serial data circuit. At low speeds more assist is provided for easy turning during parking maneuvers, and at higher speeds, less assist is provided for improved road feel and directional stability.

NOTE: The PSCM and the power steering motor are not designed to handle 65 amps continuously. If the power steering system is exposed to excessive amounts of static steering conditions, the PSCM will go into a protection mode to avoid thermal damage to the power steering components. In this mode the PSCM will limit the amount of current commanded to the power steering motor, which reduces system temperature and steering assist levels. The PSCM has the ability to detect malfunctions within the power steering system. Any malfunction detected will cause the DIC to display the *power steering* warning message and/or the *service vehicle soon* indicator.

The PSCM must also be set up with the correct steering tunings, which are different in relation to the vehicle's power train configuration, model type, tire and wheel size.

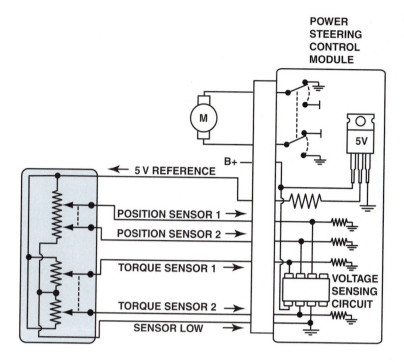

POWER STEERING CONTROL MODULE

5 V REFERENCE
POSITION SENSOR 1
POSITION SENSOR 2
TORQUE SENSOR 1
TORQUE SENSOR 2
SENSOR LOW
B+
5V
VOLTAGE SENSING CIRCUIT

FIGURE 11-36 Schematic showing the electric power steering and the torque/position sensor.

SELF-PARKING SYSTEM

Several vehicle manufacturers offer a **self-parking** feature that uses the electric power steering to steer the vehicle. The driver has control of the brakes. Most systems use the following sensors:

- Wheel speed sensor (WSS)
- Steering-angle sensor
- Ultrasonic sensors, which are used to plot a course into a parking space

Some systems, such as those manufactured by Valeo for Volkswagen, allow the driver to control the accelerator as well as the brakes, making it possible to add power to park uphill. The Toyota/Lexus system stops working if the accelerator is depressed during a self-parking event. The Toyota/Lexus system is camera based and uses the navigation system to display the parking spot with touch-screen controls. The system displays a green video box to indicate that the spot is large enough and a red box to indicate that the spot is too small. The driver positions a yellow flag on the video screen to mark the front corner of the parking spot and then the vehicle backs into the space at idle speed. The driver has to complete the parking event by straightening the vehicle and pulling forward in the spot.

Diagnosis and Testing

Self-parking systems use many sensors to achieve the parking event, and a fault in any one sensor will disable self-parking. Before trying to diagnose a self-parking fault, be sure that the driver is operating the system as designed. For example, the self-parking event is cancelled if the accelerator pedal is depressed on some units. Always follow the factory-recommended diagnostic and testing procedures.

ELECTRO-HYDRAULIC POWER STEERING

Electro-hydraulic power steering is used on the Chevrolet Silverado hybrid truck.

The **electro-hydraulic power steering (EHPS)** module controls the power steering motor, which has the function of providing hydraulic power to the brake booster and the steering gear.

A secondary function includes the ability to improve fuel economy by operating on a demand basis and the ability to provide speed-dependent variable-effort steering.

The EHPS module controls the EHPS powerpack, which is an integrated assembly consisting of the following components:

- Electric motor
- Hydraulic pump
- Fluid reservoir
- Reservoir cap
- Fluid level sensor
- Electronic controller
- Electrical connectors

See Figure 11-37.

FIGURE 11-37 An electro-hydraulic power steering assembly on a Chevrolet hybrid pickup truck.

EHPS Module

The electro-hydraulic power steering (EHPS) module is operated from the 36-volt (nominal) power supply. The EHPS module uses class 2 for serial communications. A 125-amp, 36-volt fuse is used to protect the EHPS module. If this fuse were to blow open, the EHPS system would not operate and communication codes would be set by the modules that communicate with the EHPS module. The powertrain control module (PCM) is the gateway that translates controller area network (CAN) messages into class 2 messages when required for diagnostic purposes. The EHPS module receives the following messages from the CAN bus:

- Vehicle speed
- Service disconnect status
- PRNDL (shift lever) position
- Torque converter clutch (TCC)/Cruise Dump signal (gives zero-adjust brake switch position)

The EHPS module outputs the following messages to the CAN bus:

- Brake pedal rate, position, in-range rationality, and out-of-range diagnosis
- EHPS system status
- Diagnostic messages to driver information center (DIC) via hybrid control module (HCM)
- Diagnostic information requested by service technicians via Tech 2 link (class 2 via PCM)
- Steering wheel sensor diagnostic message (in-range, out-of-range failure)

The EHPS module is not attached to class 2 data and receives several signals through wiring. The signals received and used by the EHPS module include:

- The digital steering wheel speed signals from the steering wheel sensor mounted on the steering column. The steering wheel speed sensor output contains three digital signals that indicate the steering wheel position. The signals are accurate to within 1 degree. The index output references a steering wheel position of 0 degrees plus or minus 10 degrees (steering wheel centered) and is repeated every 360 degrees of steering wheel rotation.
- An analog brake pedal position signal from the brake-pedal-mounted **brake pedal position (BPP)** sensor. The BPP sensor outputs an analog signal, referenced to 5 volts, that increases or decreases with brake pedal depression. The electrical range of the BPP sensor motion is −55 degrees to +25 degrees. The mechanical range of the BPP sensor is −70 degrees to +40 degrees.
- The EHPS module also receives ignition key position signals. These signals are the ignition signal and the accessory signal. The EHPS module receives an input from the ignition 0 circuit indicating when the key is in the ACCY position. This input is used to provide an independent wake-up signal in the event of loss of the ignition input, and to activate the EHPS module when the key remains in the ACCY position.

EHPS system performance may be reduced with power steering fluid temperature change.

The temperature range at which full performance is achieved is approximately zero to +220°F (−20 to +105°C). The EHPS system performance will be affected as follows:

- At less than −40°F (−40°C), the system will be disabled.
- At −40 to −20°F (−40 to −29°C), the hydraulic output power reduction will be less than 50%.
- At approximately −29 to −20°C (−20 to −4°F), the hydraulic output power reduction will be less than 20%.
- At zero to +221°F (−20 to +105°C), the hydraulic output power will be at full performance.
- At greater than 275°F (135°C), the system will be disabled.

EHPS system performance may also be reduced with voltage changes from the specified 34 to 50 volts. The EHPS system performance will be affected as follows:

- At less than 18 volts, the EHPS system will be disabled.
- At between 18 and 33 volts, the EHPS system performance will be reduced.
- At between 34 and 50 volts, the EHPS module will be at full performance.
- At greater than 55 volts, the EHPS module will be disabled.

Whenever a replacement EHPS powerpack is installed, reprogramming is necessary. If the EHPS powerpack is not programmed, a DTC C0564 will be set.

POWER STEERING DIAGNOSIS AND TROUBLESHOOTING

Power steering systems are generally very reliable, yet many problems are caused by not correcting simple service items such as the following:

1. **A loose, worn, or defective power steering pump drive belt.** This can cause jerky steering and belt noise, especially when turning. It is generally recommended that all belts, including the serpentine (or Poly V) belts, be replaced every four years.

    If the vehicle does not use a belt tensioner, then a belt tension gauge is needed to achieve the specified belt tension. Install the belt and operate the engine with all of the accessories turned on to "run-in" the belt for at least five minutes. Adjust the tension of the accessory drive belt to factory specifications or use the following table for an example of the proper tension based on the size of the belt.

Serpentine Belts

Number of Ribs Used	Tension Range (lbs.)
3	45–60
4	60–80
5	75–100
6	90–125
7	105–145

Replace any serpentine belt if more than three cracks appear in any one ribs within a 3-inch span.

NOTE: Do not guess at the proper belt tension. Always use a belt tension gauge or observe the marks on the tensioner. See Figure 11-38.

2. **A bent or misaligned drive pulley** is usually caused by an accident or improper reassembly of the power steering pump after an engine repair procedure. This can cause a severe grinding noise whenever the engine is running and may sound like an engine problem.

3. **Low or contaminated power steering fluid** is usually caused by a slight leak at the high-pressure hose or defective inner rack seals on a power rack-and-pinion power steering system. This can cause a loud whine and a lack of normal power steering assist. See the Tech Tip, "The Visual Test"

4. **Broken or loose power steering pump mounting brackets.** In extreme cases, the pump mounting bolts

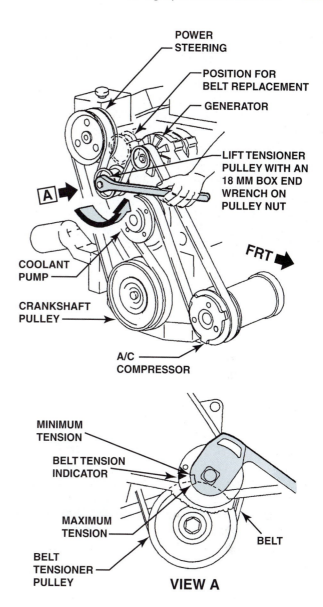

FIGURE 11-38 A typical service manual illustration showing the method to use to properly tension the accessory drive belt.

can be broken. These problems can cause jerky steering. It is important to inspect the pump mounting brackets and hardware carefully when diagnosing a steering-related problem. The brackets tend to crack at the adjustment points and pivot areas. Tighten all the hardware to ensure the belt will remain tight and not slip, which would cause noise or a power-assist problem.

5. **Underinflated tires.**
6. **Engine idle speed below specifications.**
7. **A defective power steering pressure switch.** If this switch fails, the computer will not increase engine idle speed while turning.
8. **Internal steering gear mechanical binding.**

TECH TIP

THE VISUAL TEST

Whenever diagnosing any power steering complaint, check the level *and* condition of the power steering fluid. Often this is best accomplished by putting your finger down into the power steering fluid reservoir and pulling it out to observe the texture and color of the fluid. See Figure 11-39.

A common problem with some power rack-and-pinion units is the wearing of grooves in the housing by the Teflon sealing rings of the spool (control) valve. When this wear occurs, aluminum particles become suspended in the power steering fluid, giving it a grayish color and thickening the fluid.

Normally clear power steering fluid that is found to be grayish in color and steering that is difficult when cold are clear indications as to what has occurred and why the steering is not functioning correctly.

As part of a complete steering system inspection and diagnosis, a steering wheel turning effort test should be performed. The power steering force, as measured by a spring scale during turning, should be less than 5 lb (2.3 kg).

NOTE: Some vehicles use power steering reservoir caps with *left-hand threads.* Always clean the top of the cap and observe all directions and cautions. Many power steering pump reservoirs and caps have been destroyed by technicians attempting to remove a cap in the wrong direction using large pliers.

Power Steering Fluid

The correct power steering fluid is *critical* to the operation and service life of the power steering system! The *exact* power steering fluid to use varies as to vehicle manufacturer. There are even differences within the same company because of various steering component suppliers.

NOTE: Remember, multiple-purpose power steering fluid does not mean *all*-purpose power steering fluid. Always consult the power steering reservoir cap, service manual, or owner's manual for the exact fluid to be used in the vehicle being serviced.

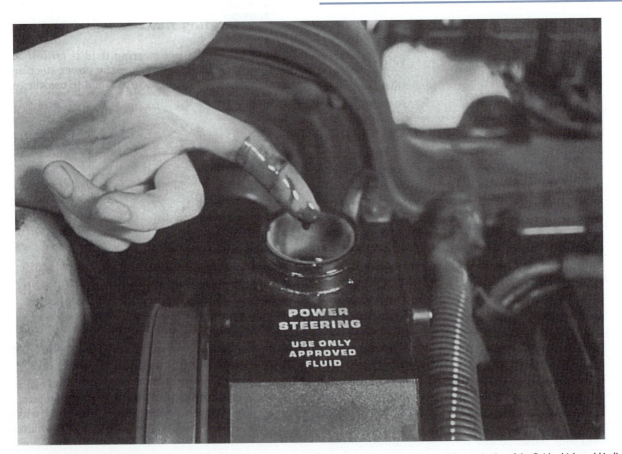

FIGURE 11-39   A check of the power steering fluid should include inspecting not only the level but the condition and color of the fluid, which could indicate a possible problem with other components in the steering system.

FIGURE 11-40 Some power steering fluid is unique to the climate, such as this **cold climate fluid** recommended for use in General Motors vehicles when temperatures are low.

The main reason for using the specified power steering fluid is the compatibility of the fluid with the materials used in seals and hoses of the system. Using the wrong fluid (substituting ATF, for example) can lead to seal or hose deterioration and/or failure and fluid leaks.

NOTE: Always use the power steering fluid recommended by the manufacturer. The correct fluid to use is usually imprinted on or near the power steering reservoir fill cap. See Figure 11-40.

1. Check the power steering fluid level. Bleed the air from the system by turning the steering wheel lock-to-lock with the engine cranking.
2. Check the condition and tension of the drive belt. If in doubt, replace the belt.
3. Inspect the condition of all hoses, checking for any soft hose or places where the hose could touch another component.
4. Check the tightness of all mounting bolts of the pump and gear.

Power Steering Fluid Flushing Procedure

Whenever there is any power steering service performed, such as replacement of a defective pump or steering gear or rack-and-pinion unit, the entire system should be flushed. If all of the old fluid is not flushed from the system, small pieces of a failed bearing or rotor could be circulated through the system. These metal particles can block paths in the control valve and cause failure of the new power steering pump or gear assembly.

NOTE: Besides flushing the old power steering fluid from the system and replacing it with new fluid, many technical experts recommend installing a filter in the low-pressure return line as an added precaution against serious damage from debris in the system. Power steering filters are commonly available through vehicle dealer parts departments, as well as aftermarket sources from local auto supply stores.

Always follow the vehicle manufacturer's recommended flushing procedure. Two people are needed to flush the system. Use the following steps:

Step 1   Raise the front wheels off the ground.
Step 2   Remove the low-pressure return hose from the pump and plug the line fitting on the pump.
Step 3   Place the low-pressure return hose into an empty container.
Step 4   Fill the pump reservoir with fresh fluid and start the engine.
Step 5   As the old and dirty power steering fluid is being pumped into the container, keep the reservoir full of clean fluid while the assistant turns the steering wheel full lock one way to full lock the other way.

CAUTION: Never allow the pump reservoir to run dry of power steering fluid. Severe internal pump damage can result.

Step 6   When the fluid runs clean, stop the engine and reattach the low-pressure return hose to the pump reservoir.
Step 7   Restart the engine and fill the reservoir to the full mark. Turn the steering wheel back and forth, avoiding the stops one or two times to bleed any trapped air in the system.

Bleeding Air out of the System

If the power steering fluid is tan, there may be air bubbles trapped in the fluid. Stop the engine and allow the air to burp out to the surface for several minutes. Lift the vehicle off the ground, then rotate the steering wheel. This method prevents the breakup of large air bubbles into thousands of smaller bubbles that are more difficult to bleed out of the system.

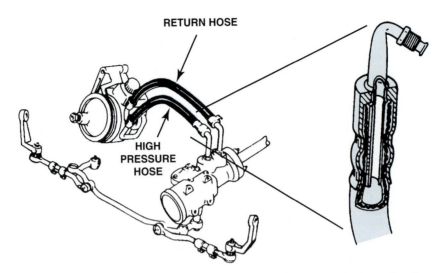

FIGURE 11-41   Inspect both high-pressure and return power steering hoses. Make sure the hoses are routed correctly and not touching sections of the body to prevent power steering noise from being transferred to the passenger compartment. *(Courtesy of Moog)*

NOTE: To help rid the power steering system of unwanted trapped air, it is recommend that the engine be cranked and that the wheels be turned from stop to stop *with the tires off the ground.* Do not crank the engine for longer than 15 seconds to prevent starter damage due to overheating. Allow the starter to cool at least 30 seconds before cranking again.

Sometimes trapped air just cannot be bled out of the system using ordinary methods. This trapped air makes the pump extremely noisy and this noise sometimes convinces the technician that the pump itself is defective. If the power steering system has been opened for repairs and the system has been drained, trapped air may be the cause.

Hose Inspection

Both high-pressure and low-pressure return hoses should be inspected as part of any thorough vehicle inspection. While the low-pressure return hose generally feels softer than the high-pressure return hose, neither should feel *spongy.* A soft, spongy hose should always be replaced. See Figure 11-41.

When replacing any power steering hose, make certain that it is routed the same as the original and does not interfere with any accessory drive belt, pulley, or other movable component such as the intermediate steering shaft.

Pressure Testing

Use of a power steering pressure tester involves the following steps:

1. Disconnect the pressure hose at the pump.

2. Connect the leads of the tester to the pump and the disconnected pressure line. See Figure 11-42.
3. Open the valve on the tester.
4. Start the engine. Allow the power steering system to reach operating temperatures.
5. The pressure gauge should register 80 to 125 psi (550 to 860 kPa). If the pressure is greater than 150 psi (1,400 kPa), check for restrictions in the system, including the operation of the poppet valve located in the inlet of the steering gear.
6. Fully close the valve three times. (Do not leave the valve closed for more than five seconds!) All three readings should be within 50 psi (345 kPa) of each other and the peak pressure should be higher than 1,000 psi (6,900 kPa).
7. If the pressure readings are high enough *and* within 50 psi (345 kPa) of each other, the pump is OK.
8. If the pressure readings are high enough, yet not within 50 psi (345 kPa) of each other, the flow control valve is sticking.
9. If the pressure readings are less than 1,000 psi (6,900 kPa), replace the flow control valve and recheck. If the pressures are still low, replace the rotor and vanes in the power steering pump.
10. If the pump is OK, turn the steering wheel to both stops. If the pressure at both stops is not the same as the maximum pressure, the steering gear (or rack and pinion) is leaking internally and should be repaired or replaced.

Many vehicle manufacturers recommend using a power steering analyzer that measures both pressure and volume, as shown in Figure 11-43.

Knowing the volume flow in the system provides information to the technician in addition to that of the pressure gauge. Many manufacturers' diagnostic procedures specify

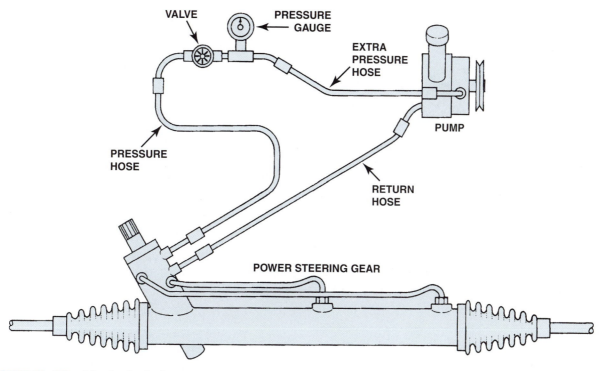

FIGURE 11-42 A drawing showing how to connect a power steering analyzer to the system.

volume measurements and test results that can help pinpoint flow control or steering gear problems. Always follow the vehicle manufacturer's recommended testing procedures. Pressure and volume measurements specified by the manufacturer usually fall within the range noted in the following chart.

Typical Power Steering Pressures and Volume

Steering Action	Pressure, psi (kPa)	Volume* (gal/min) (l/min)
Straight ahead, no steering	Less than 150 psi (1,000 kPa)	2.0 to 3.3 gpm (10 to 15 lpm)
Slow cornering	300–450 psi (2,000–3,000 kPa)	Within 1 gpm (4 lpm) of straight ahead
Full turn at stops	750–1,450 psi** (5,200–10,000 kPa)	Less than 1 gpm (4 lpm)

*Volume is determined by orifice size in the outlet of the pump and is matched to the steering gear.

**Upper-limit pressure is determined by the calibration of the pressure-relief valve.

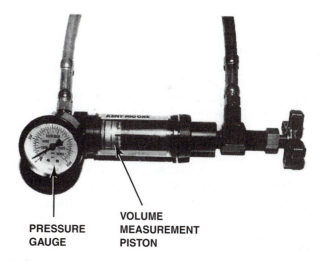

FIGURE 11-43 A power steering analyzer that measures both pressure and volume. The shut-off valve at the right is used to test the maximum pressure of the pump.

Pump Service

Some power steering pump service can usually be performed without removing the pump, including the following:

1. Replacing the high-pressure and return hoses
2. Removing and cleaning the flow control valve assembly (See Figure 11-44.)

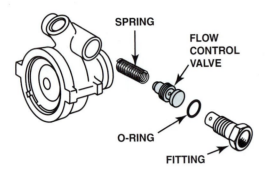

FIGURE 11-44 Typical power steering pump showing the order of assembly. The high-pressure (outlet) hose attaches to the fitting (#16). The flow control valve can be removed from the pump by removing the fitting.

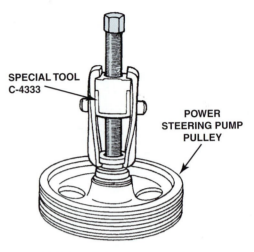

REMOVE DRIVE PULLEY (TYPICAL)

Most power steering pump service requires the removal of the pump from the engine mounting and/or removal of the drive pulley.

NOTE: Most replacement pumps are not equipped with a pulley. The old pulley must be removed and installed on the new pump. The old pulley should be carefully inspected for dents, cracks, or warpage. If the pulley is damaged, it must be replaced.

The pulley must be removed and installed with a pulley removal and installation tool. See Figure 11-45.

CAUTION: Do not hammer the pump shaft or pulley in an attempt to install the pulley. The shock blows will damage the internal components of the pump.

After removing the pump from the vehicle and removing the drive pulley, disassemble the pump according to the manufacturer's recommended procedure. See Figures 11-46 through 11-50 for the disassembly and reassembly of a typical power steering pump.

Clean all parts in power steering fluid. Replace any worn or damaged parts and all seals.

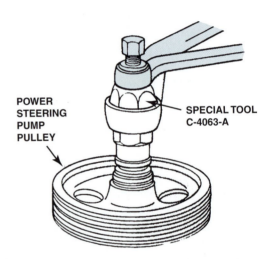

INSTALL DRIVE PULLEY (TYPICAL)

FIGURE 11-45 Typical tools required to remove and install a drive pulley on a power steering pump. Often these tools can be purchased at a relatively low cost from automotive parts stores and will work on many different makes of vehicles. *(Courtesy of DaimlerChrysler Corporation)*

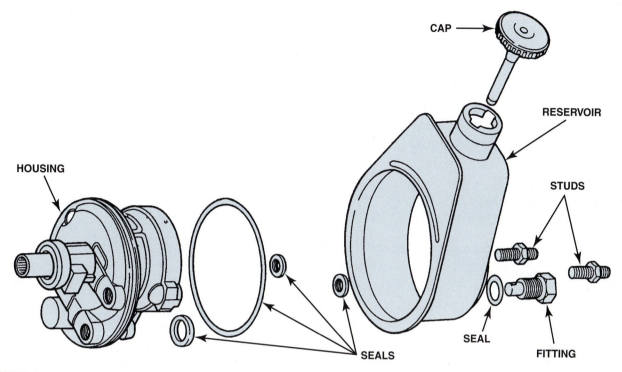

CAP

RESERVOIR

STUDS

HOUSING

SEALS

SEAL

FITTING

FIGURE 11-46   A typical submerged-type power steering pump. The pump is housed inside the fluid reservoir. *(Courtesy of DaimlerChrysler Corporation)*

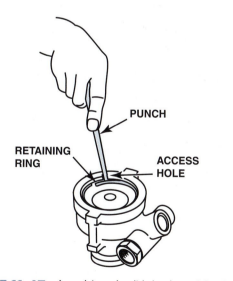

PUNCH

RETAINING
RING

ACCESS
HOLE

FIGURE 11-47   A punch is used to dislodge the retaining ring.

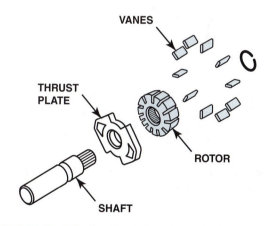

VANES

THRUST
PLATE

ROTOR

SHAFT

FIGURE 11-48   The drive shaft attaches to the drive pulley at one end and is splined to the pump rotor at the other end. The vanes are placed in the slots of the rotor.

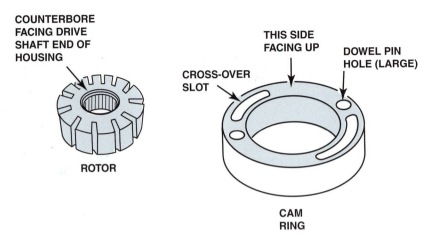

COUNTERBORE FACING DRIVE SHAFT END OF HOUSING

ROTOR

CROSS-OVER SLOT

THIS SIDE FACING UP

DOWEL PIN HOLE (LARGE)

CAM RING

FIGURE 11-49 The pump ring *must* be installed correctly. If it is installed upside down, the internal passages will not line up and the pump will have no output.

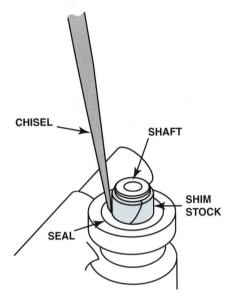

CHISEL

SHAFT

SHIM STOCK

SEAL

FIGURE 11-50 The shaft seal must be chiseled out. A thin metal shim stock should be used to protect the shaft from damage.

TECH TIP

POCKET THE IGNITION KEY TO BE SAFE

When replacing any steering gear such as a rack-and-pinion steering unit, be sure that no one accidentally turns the steering wheel! If the steering wheel is turned without being connected to the steering gear, the airbag wire coil (clock spring) can become off center. This can cause the wiring to break when the steering wheel is rotated after the steering gear has been replaced. To help prevent this from occurring, simply remove the ignition key from the ignition and put it in your pocket while servicing the steering gear.

SUMMARY

1. Always use a belt tension gauge when checking, replacing, or tightening a power steering drive belt. The proper power steering fluid should always be used to prevent possible seal or power steering hose failure.

2. Power steering troubles can usually be diagnosed using a power steering pressure gauge. Lower-than-normal pump pressure could be due to a weak (defective) power steering pump or internal leakage inside the steering gear itself. If the pressure reaches normal when the shut-off valve on the gauge is closed, then the problem is isolated to being a defective gear.

3. Care should be taken when repairing or replacing any steering gear assembly to follow General Motors' recommended procedures exactly; do not substitute parts from one steering gear to another.

REVIEW QUESTIONS

1. List five possible causes for hard steering.

2. Explain the procedure for flushing a power steering system.

3. Briefly describe adjustment and service procedures for a conventional power steering gear.

4. Briefly describe adjustment and service procedures for a power rack-and-pinion steering unit.

CHAPTER QUIZ

1. Two technicians are discussing the proper procedure for bleeding air from a power steering system. Technician A says that the front wheels of the vehicle should be lifted off the ground before bleeding. Technician B says that the steering wheel should be turned left and right with the engine off during the procedure. Which technician is correct?

   a. Technician A only
   b. Technician B only
   c. Both technicians A and B
   d. Neither technician A nor B

2. A power steering pressure test is being performed, and the pressure is higher than specifications with the engine running and the steering wheel stationary in the straight-ahead position. Technician A says that a restricted high-pressure line could be the cause. Technician B says that internal leakage inside the steering gear or rack-and-pinion unit could be the cause. Which technician is correct?

   a. Technician A only
   b. Technician B only
   c. Both Technicians A and B
   d. Neither Technician A nor B

3. A vehicle with power rack-and-pinion steering is hard to steer when cold (temporary loss of power assist when cold). The most likely cause is _____.

   a. Leaking rack seals
   b. A defective or worn power steering pump
   c. Worn grooves in the housing by the spool valve seals
   d. Use of incorrect power steering fluid

4. Integral power steering gears use _____ for lubrication of the unit.

   a. SAE 80W-90 gear lube
   b. Chassis grease (NLGI #2)
   c. Power steering fluid in the system
   d. Molybdenum disulfide

5. Two technicians are discussing replacement of the pitman shaft seal on an integral power steering gear. Technician A says that the pitman arm must be removed before the old seal can be removed. Technician B says that the steering gear unit should be removed from the vehicle before the seal can be removed. Which technician is correct?

   a. Technician A only
   b. Technician B only
   c. Both Technicians A and B
   d. Neither Technician A nor B

6. High-pressure hoses have to be used on the high-pressure side of the power steering system because pressures can reach as high as _____.

    a. 200 psi

    b. 750 psi

    c. 1,500 psi

    d. 2,500 psi

7. Some vehicles are equipped to signal the computer whenever the power steering pressures increase so that the idle speed can be increased to prevent stalling during turns at low speeds. What component signals the computer?

    a. Pressure-relief valve

    b. Power steering pressure switch

    c. Rotary valve

    d. Flow control valve

8. Some high-performance vehicles have firmer steering than other similar vehicles. Technician A says that the power steering pump pulley size is larger on those with stiffer steering, which reduces the speed of the pump. Technician B says that a torsion bar inside of the rotary valve is larger in diameter. Which technician is correct?

    a. Technician A only

    b. Technician B only

    c. Both Technicians A and B

    d. Neither Technician A nor B

9. Electronically controlled variable-assist power steering systems vary the amount of boost by _____.

    a. Varying the pump output orifice size

    b. Speeding up or slowing down the power steering pump

    c. Changing the flow of fluid through the steering gear

    d. Bypassing some of the fluid back into the reservoir

10. Power steering fluid is discovered to be pink in color. Technician A says that air could be trapped in the fluid. Technician B says that engine coolant has leaked into the power steering fluid. Which technician is correct?

    a. Technician A only

    b. Technician B only

    c. Both Technicians A and B

    d. Neither Technician A nor B

WHEEL BEARINGS AND SERVICE

OBJECTIVES

After studying Chapter 12, the reader should be able to:

1. Prepare for Suspension and Steering (A4) ASE certification test content area "C" (Related Suspension and Steering Service).

2. Discuss the various types, designs, and parts of automotive antifriction wheel bearings.

3. Describe the symptoms of defective wheel bearings.

4. Explain wheel bearing inspection procedures and causes of spalling and brinelling.

5. List the installation and adjustment procedures for front wheel bearings.

6. Explain how to inspect, service, and replace rear wheel bearings and seals.

KEY TERMS

Bearings allow the wheels of a vehicle to rotate and still support the weight of the entire vehicle.

ANTIFRICTION BEARINGS

Antifriction bearings use rolling parts inside the bearing to reduce friction. Four styles of rolling contact bearings include ball, roller, needle, and tapered roller bearings, as shown in Figure 12-1. All four styles convert sliding friction into rolling motion. All of the weight of a vehicle or load on the bearing is transferred through the rolling part. In a ball bearing, all of the load is concentrated into small spots where the ball contacts the inner and outer races (rings). See Figure 12-2.

Ball Bearings

While **ball bearings** cannot support the same weight as roller bearings, there is less friction in ball bearings and they generally operate at higher speeds. Ball bearings can control thrust movement of an axle shaft because the balls ride in grooves on the inner and outer races. The groove walls resist lateral movement of the wheel on the spindle. The most frequent use of ball bearings is at the rear wheels of a rear-wheel-drive vehicle with a solid rear axle. See Figure 12-3. These bearings are installed into the axle housing and are often press-fitted to the axle shaft. Many front-wheel-drive vehicles use sealed double-row ball bearings as a complete sealed unit, which are nonserviceable except as an assembly.

FIGURE 12-1   Rolling contact bearings include (left to right) ball, roller needle, and tapered roller.

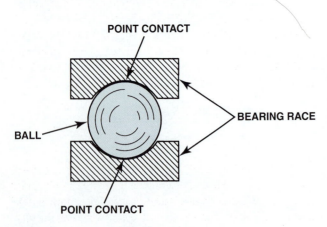

FIGURE 12-2   Ball bearing point contact.

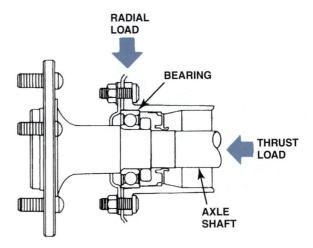

FIGURE 12-3   Radial load is the vehicle weight pressing on the wheels. The thrust load occurs as the chassis components exert a side force during cornering.

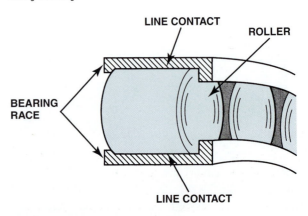

FIGURE 12-4   Roller bearing line contact.

Roller Bearings

A **roller bearing** having a greater (longer) contact area can support heavier loads than a ball bearing. See Figure 12-4.

A needle bearing is a type of roller bearing that uses smaller rollers called needle rollers. The clearance between the diameter of the ball or straight roller is manufactured into the bearing to provide the proper radial clearance and is *not adjustable*.

Tapered Roller Bearings

The most commonly used automotive wheel bearing is the **tapered roller bearing.** Not only is the bearing itself tapered, but the rollers are also tapered. By design, this type of bearing can withstand **radial** (up and down) as well as **axial** (thrust) loads in one direction. See Figure 12-5.

Many nondrive wheel bearings use tapered roller bearings. The taper allows more weight to be handled by the friction-reducing bearings because the weight is directed over the entire length of each roller rather than concentrated on a small spot, as with ball bearings. Because of the taper, these bearings are

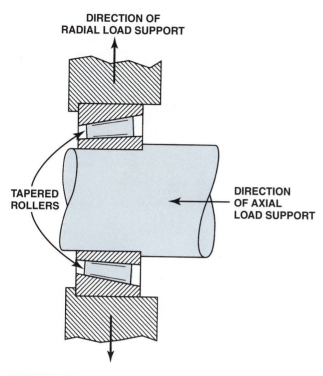

FIGURE 12-5   A tapered roller bearing will support a radial load and an axial load in only one direction.

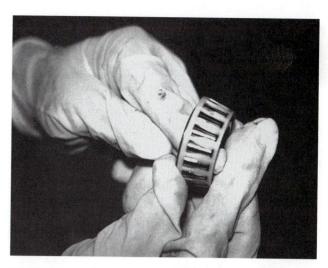

FIGURE 12-6   Many tapered roller bearings use a plastic cage to retain the rollers.

FIGURE 12-7   Non-driven-wheel hub with inner and outer tapered roller bearings. By angling the inner and outer bearings in opposite directions, axial (thrust) loads are supported in both directions.

called tapered roller bearings. The rollers are held in place by a **cage** between the inner race (also called the inner ring or **cone**) and the outer race (also called the outer ring or **cup**). Tapered roller bearings must be loose in the cage to allow for heat expansion. Tapered roller bearings should always be adjusted for a certain amount of freeplay to allow for heat expansion. On nondrive-axle vehicle wheels, the cup is tightly fitted to the wheel hub and the cone is loosely fitted to the wheel spindle. New bearings come packaged with the rollers, cage, and inner race assembled together, with the outer race wrapped with moisture-resistant paper. See Figure 12-6.

Inner and Outer Wheel Bearings

Many rear-wheel-drive vehicles use an inner and an outer wheel bearing on the front wheels. The inner wheel bearing is always the larger bearing because it is designed to carry most of the vehicle weight and transmit the weight to the suspension through to the spindle. See Figure 12-7. Between the inner wheel bearing and the spindle, there is a grease seal that prevents grease from getting onto the braking surface and prevents dirt and moisture from entering the bearing.

Standard Bearing Sizes

Bearings use standard dimensions for inside diameter, width, and outside diameter. The standardization of bearing sizes helps interchangeability. The dimensions that are standardized include bearing bore size (inside diameter), bearing series

(light to heavy usage), and external dimensions. When replacing a wheel bearing, note the original bearing brand name and number. Replacement bearing catalogs usually have crossover charts from one brand to another. The bearing number is usually the same because of interchangeability and standardization within the wheel bearing industry.

Sealed Front-Wheel-Drive Bearings

Most front-wheel-drive (FWD) vehicles use a sealed, nonadjustable front wheel bearing. This type of bearing can include either two preloaded tapered roller bearings or a double-row ball bearing. This type of sealed bearing is also used on the rear of many front wheel drive vehicles.

BALL-BEARING ASSEMBLY

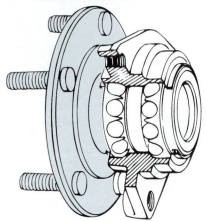

TAPERED ROLLER BEARING ASSEMBLY

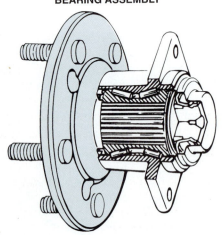

FIGURE 12-8 Sealed bearing and hub assemblies are used on the front and rear wheels of many vehicles.

Double-row ball bearings are often used because of their reduced friction and greater seize resistance. See Figures 12-8 and 12-9.

BEARING GREASES

Vehicle manufacturers specify the type and consistency of grease for each application. The technician should know what these specifications mean. **Grease** is an oil with a thickening agent to allow it to be installed in places where a liquid lubricant would not stay. Greases are named for their thickening agent, such as aluminum, barium, calcium, lithium, or sodium.

Grease Additives

Commonly used additives in grease include the following:

- Antioxidants
- Antiwear agents

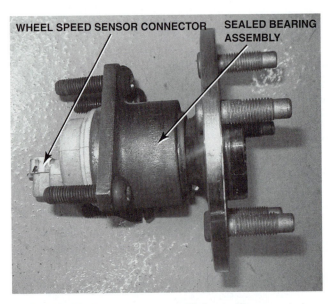

WHEEL SPEED SENSOR CONNECTOR   **SEALED BEARING ASSEMBLY**

FIGURE 12-9 Sealed bearing and hub assemblies are serviced as a complete unit as shown. This assembly includes the wheel speed sensor.

- Rust inhibitors
- Extreme pressure (EP) additives such as sulfurized fatty oil or chlorine

Grease also contains a dye to not only provide product identification but also to give the grease a consistent color. Grease also contains a solid such as graphite or molybdenum disulfide (moly), which acts as an antisieze additive.

NLGI Classification

The **National Lubricating Grease Institute (NLGI)** uses the penetration test as a guide to assign the grease a number. Low numbers are very fluid and higher numbers are more firm or hard. See the following chart.

National Lubricating Grease Institute (NLGI) Numbers

NLGI Number	Relative Consistency
000	Very fluid
00	Fluid
0	Semi-fluid
1	Very soft
2	Soft (typically used for wheel bearings)
3	Semi-firm
4	Firm
5	Very firm
6	Hard

FREQUENTLY ASKED QUESTION

WHAT DO DIFFERENT GREASE COLORS MEAN?

Nothing. According to grease manufacturers, grease is colored for identification, marketing, and color consistency reasons.

- *Identification.* The color is often used to distinguish one type of grease from another within the same company. The blue grease from one company may be totally different from the blue grease produced or marketed by another company.
- *Marketing.* According to grease manufacturers, customers tend to be attracted to a particular color of grease and associate that color with quality.
- *Consistency of color.* All greases are produced in batches, and the color of the finished product often varies in color from one batch to another. By adding color to the grease, the color can be made consistent.

Always use the grease recommended for the service being performed.

Grease is also classified according to quality. Wheel bearing classifications include the following:

- GA—mild duty
- GB—moderate duty
- GC—severe duty, high temperature (frequent stop-and-go service)

GC indicates the highest quality. Chassis greases, such as is used to lubricate steering and suspension components, includes the following:

- LA—mild duty (frequent relubrication)
- LB—high loads (infrequent relubrication)

LB indicates the highest quality. Most multipurpose greases are labeled with both wheel bearing and chassis grease classifications, such as **GC-LB.**

More rolling bearings are destroyed by overlubrication than by underlubrication because the heat generated in the bearings cannot be transferred easily to the air through the excessive grease. Bearings should never be filled beyond one-third to one-half of their grease capacity by volume.

SAFETY TIP

SMOKING CAN KILL YOU

Some greases contain polymers such as Teflon® that turn to a deadly gas when burned. Always wash your hands thoroughly after handling grease that contains these ingredients before smoking. If some of the grease is on the cigarette paper and is burned, these polymers turn into nitrofluoric acid—a deadly toxin.

SEALS

Seals are used in all vehicles to keep lubricant, such as grease, from leaking out and to prevent dirt, dust, or water from getting into the bearing or lubricant. Two general applications of seals are static and dynamic. **Static seals** are used between two surfaces that do not move. **Dynamic seals** are used to seal between two surfaces that move. Wheel bearing seals are dynamic-type seals that must seal between rotating axle hubs and the stationary spindles or axle housing. Most dynamic seals use a synthetic rubber lip seal encased in metal. The lip is often held in contact with the moving part with the aid of a **garter spring**, as shown in Figure 12-10.

The sealing lip should be installed toward the grease or fluid being contained. See Figure 12-11.

FIGURE 12-10 Typical lip seal with a garter spring.

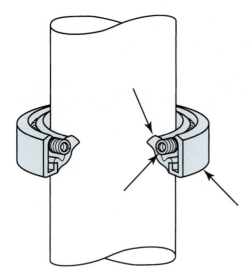

FIGURE 12-11   A garter spring helps hold the sharp lip edge of the seal tight against the shaft. *(Courtesy of Dana Corporation)*

SYMPTOMS AND DIAGNOSIS OF DEFECTIVE BEARINGS

Wheel bearings control the positioning and reduce the rolling resistance of vehicle wheels. Whenever a bearing fails, the wheel may not be kept in position and noise is usually heard. Symptoms of defective wheel bearings include the following:

1. A hum, rumbling, or growling noise that increases with vehicle speed
2. Roughness felt in the steering wheel that changes with the vehicle speed or cornering
3. Looseness or excessive play in the steering wheel, especially while driving over rough road surfaces
4. A loud grinding noise in severe cases of a defective front wheel bearing
5. Pulling during braking

With the vehicle off the ground, rotate the wheel by hand, listening and feeling carefully for bearing roughness. Grasp the wheel at the top and bottom and wiggle it back and forth, checking for bearing looseness.

NOTE: Excessive looseness in the wheel bearings can cause a low brake pedal. If any of the symptoms just mentioned are present, carefully clean and inspect the bearings.

TECH TIP

"BEARING OVERLOAD"

It is not uncommon for vehicles to be overloaded. This is particularly common with pickup trucks and vans. Whenever there is a heavy load, the axle bearings must support the entire weight of the vehicle, including its cargo. If a bump is hit while driving with a heavy load, the balls of a ball bearing or the rollers of a roller bearing can make an indent in the race of the bearing. This dent or imprint is called brinelling, named after Johann A. Brinell, a Swedish engineer who developed a process of testing for surface hardness by pressing a hard ball with a standard force into a sample material to be tested.

Once this imprint is made, the bearing will make noise whenever the roller or ball rolls over the indent. Continued use causes wear to occur on all of the balls or rollers and eventual failure. While this may take months to fail, the *cause* of the bearing failure is often overloading of the vehicle. Avoid shock loads and overloading for safety and for longer vehicle life.

NONDRIVE WHEEL BEARING INSPECTION AND SERVICE

The steps in a nondrive wheel bearing inspection include the following:

1. Hoist the vehicle safely.
2. Remove the wheel.
3. Remove the brake caliper assembly and support it with a coat hanger or other suitable hook to avoid allowing the caliper to hang by the brake hose.
4. Remove the grease cap (dust cap). See Figure 12-12.
5. Remove the old cotter key and discard.

NOTE: The term *cotter*, as in *cotter key* or *cotter pin*, is derived from the old English verb meaning "to close or fasten."

6. Remove the spindle nut (castle nut).
7. Remove the washer and the outer wheel bearing. See Figure 12-13.
8. Remove the bearing hub from the spindle. The inner bearing will remain in the hub and may be removed

FIGURE 12-12 Removing the grease cap with grease cap pliers.

FIGURE 12-13 After wiggling the brake rotor slightly, the washer and outer bearing can be easily lifted out of the wheel hub.

FIGURE 12-14 Some technicians remove the inner wheel bearing and the grease seal at the same time by jerking the rotor off the spindle after reinstalling the spindle nut. While this is a quick-and-easy method, sometimes the bearing is damaged (deformed) from being jerked out of the hub using this procedure.

TECH TIP

BEARING NOISE— TIRE NOISE

A defective wheel bearing is often difficult to diagnose because the noise is similar to a noisy winter tire or a severely cupped tire. Customers often request that tires be replaced as a result of the noise when the real problem is a bad wheel bearing. To help determining if the noise is caused by a wheel bearing or a tire, try these tips:

Tip 1   Drive the vehicle over a variety of road surfaces. If the noise changes with a change in road surface, then the noise is caused by a tire(s). If the noise remains the same, then the cause is a defective wheel bearing.

Tip 2   Try temporarily overinflating the tires. If the noise changes, then the tires are the cause. If the noise is the same, then defective wheel bearings are the cause.

(simply lifted out) after the grease seal is pried out. See Figure 12-14.

9. Most vehicle and bearing manufacturers recommend cleaning the bearing thoroughly in solvent or acetone. If there is no acetone, clean the solvent off the bearings with denatured alcohol to make certain that the thin solvent layer is completely washed off and dry. *All solvent must be removed or allowed to dry from the bearing because the new grease will not stick to a layer of solvent.*

10. Carefully inspect the bearings and the races for the following:
   a. The outer race for lines, scratches, or pits. See Figure 12-15.
   b. The cage should be round. If the round cage has straight sections, this is an indication of an overtightened adjustment or a dropped cage.

   If either of these conditions is observed, then the bearing, including the outer race, must be replaced.

BENT CAGE
CAGE DAMAGE CAUSED BY IMPROPER HANDLING OR TOOL USE

GALLING
METAL SMEARS OR ROLLER ENDS CAUSED BY OVERHEATING, OVERLOADING, OR INADEQUATE LUBRICATION

STEP WEAR
NOTCHED WEAR PATTERN ON ROLLER ENDS CAUSED BY ABRASIVES IN THE LUBRICANT

ETCHING AND CORROSION
EATEN AWAY BEARING SURFACE WITH GRAY OR GRAY-BLACK COLOR CAUSED BY MOISTURE CONTAMINATION OF THE LUBRICANT

PITTING AND BRUISING
PITS, DEPRESSIONS, AND GROOVES IN THE BEARING SURFACES CAUSED BY PARTICULATE CONTAMINATION OF THE LUBRICANT

SPALLING
FLAKING AWAY OF THE BEARING SURFACE METAL CAUSED BY FATIGUE

MISALIGNMENT
SKEWED WEAR PATTERN CAUSED BY BENT SPINDLE OR IMPROPER BEARING INSTALLATION

HEAT DISCOLORATION
FAINT YELLOW TO DARK BLUE DISCOLORATION FROM OVERHEATING CAUSED BY OVERLOADING OR INADEQUATE LUBRICATION

BRINELLING
INDENTATIONS IN THE RACES CAUSED BY IMPACT LOADS OR VIBRATION WHEN THE BEARING IS NOT TURNING

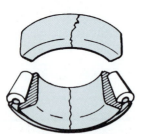

CRACKED RACE
CRACKING OF THE RACE CAUSED BY EXCESSIVE PRESS FIT, IMPROPER INSTALLATION OR DAMAGED BEARING SEATS

SMEARING
SMEARED METAL FROM SLIPPAGE CAUSED BY POOR FIT, POOR LUBRICATION, OVERLOADING, OVERHEATING, OR HANDLING DAMAGE

FRETTAGE
ETCHING OR CORROSION CAUSED BY SMALL RELATIVE MOVEMENTS BETWEEN PARTS WITH NO LUBRICATION

FIGURE 12-15   Wheel bearing inspection chart.

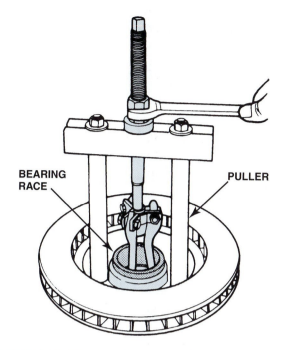

FIGURE 12-16   A wheel bearing race puller.

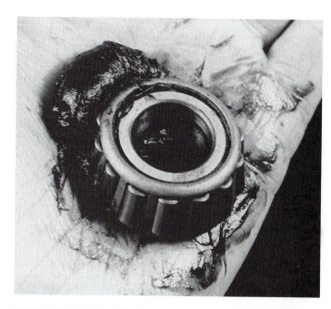

FIGURE 12-18   When packing grease into a cleaned bearing force grease around each roller as shown.

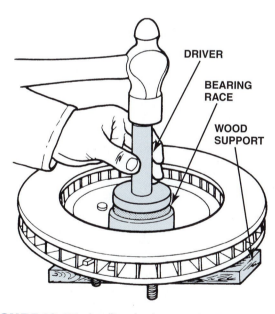

FIGURE 12-17   Installing a bearing race with a driver.

Failure to replace the outer race (which is included when purchasing a bearing) could lead to rapid failure of the new bearing. See Figures 12-16 and 12-17.

11. Pack the cleaned or new bearing thoroughly with clean, new, approved wheel bearing grease using hand packing or a wheel-bearing packer. Always clean out all of the old grease before applying the recommended type of new grease. *Because of compatibility problems,*

it is not recommended that greases be mixed. See Figure 12-18.

NOTE: Some vehicle manufacturers do *not* recommend that "stringy-type" wheel bearing grease be used. Centrifugal force can cause the grease to be thrown outward from the bearing. Because of the stringy texture, the grease may not flow back into the bearing after it has been thrown outward. The final result is a lack of lubrication and eventual bearing failure.

12. Place a thin layer of grease on the outer race.
13. Apply a thin layer of grease to the spindle, being sure to cover the outer bearing seat, inner bearing seat, and shoulder at the grease seal seat.
14. Install a new **grease seal** (also called a grease retainer) flush with the hub using a seal driver.
15. Place approximately 3 tablespoons of grease into the grease cavity of the wheel hub. Excessive grease could cause the inner grease seal to fail, with the possibility of grease getting on the brakes. Place the rotor with the inner bearing and seal in place over the spindle until the grease seal rests on the grease seal shoulder.
16. Install the outer bearing and the bearing washer.
17. Install the spindle nut and, while rotating the tire assembly, tighten to about 12 to 30 lb-ft with a wrench to "seat" the bearing correctly in the race (cup) and on the spindle. See Figure 12-19.
18. While still rotating the tire assembly, loosen the nut approximately one-half turn and then *hand tighten only* (about 5 lb-in.).

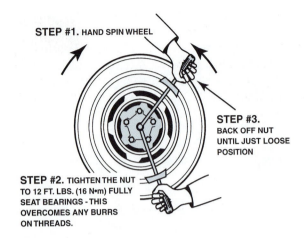

STEP #1. HAND SPIN WHEEL

STEP #3.
BACK OFF NUT
UNTIL JUST LOOSE
POSITION

STEP #2. TIGHTEN THE NUT
TO 12 FT. LBS. (16 N•m) FULLY
SEAT BEARINGS - THIS
OVERCOMES ANY BURRS
ON THREADS.

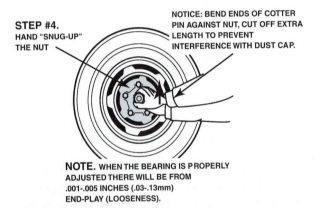

STEP #5. LOOSEN NUT UNTIL EITHER
HOLE IN THE SPINDLE LINES UP WITH
A SLOT IN THE NUT – THEN INSERT
COTTER PIN.

STEP #4.
HAND "SNUG-UP"
THE NUT

NOTICE: BEND ENDS OF COTTER
PIN AGAINST NUT, CUT OFF EXTRA
LENGTH TO PREVENT
INTERFERENCE WITH DUST CAP.

NOTE. WHEN THE BEARING IS PROPERLY
ADJUSTED THERE WILL BE FROM
.001-.005 INCHES (.03-.13mm)
END-PLAY (LOOSENESS).

FIGURE 12-19   The wheel bearing adjustment procedure as specified for rear-wheel-drive General Motors vehicles.

NOTE: If the wheel bearing is properly adjusted, the
wheel will still have about 0.001 to 0.005 in. (0.03 to
0.13 mm) of endplay. This looseness is necessary to allow the tapered roller bearing to expand when hot and
not bind or cause the wheel to lock up.

19. Install a new cotter key. (An old cotter key could break a
part off where it was bent and lodge in the bearing, causing major damage.)

NOTE: Most vehicles use a cotter key that is 1/8 in. in
diameter by 1 1/2 in. long.

20. If the cotter key does not line up with the hole in the spindle, loosen slightly (no more than 1/16 in. of a turn) until the hole lines up. Never tighten more than hand tight.

21. Bend the cotter key ends up and around the nut, not
over the end of the spindle where the end of the cotter
key could rub on the grease cap, causing noise. See
Figure 12-20.

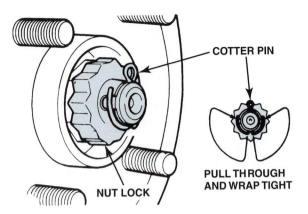

COTTER PIN

PULL THROUGH
AND WRAP TIGHT

NUT LOCK

FIGURE 12-20   A properly secured wheel bearing adjust nut.

TECH TIP

WHEEL BEARING LOOSENESS TEST

Looseness in a front wheel bearing can allow the rotor
to move whenever the front wheel hits a bump, forcing
the caliper piston in, which causes the brake pedal to
kick back and creates the feeling that the brakes are
locking up.

Loose wheel bearings are easily diagnosed by removing the cover of the master cylinder reservoir and
watching the brake fluid as the front wheels are turned
left and right with the steering wheel. If the brake fluid
moves while the front wheels are being turned, caliper
piston(s) are moving in and out, caused by loose wheel
bearing(s). If everything is OK, the brake fluid should
not move.

NOTE: Loose wheel bearings can also cause the brake pedal to sink
due to movement of the rotor, causing the caliper piston to move. This
sinking brake pedal is usually caused by a defective master cylinder.
Before replacing a master cylinder, check the wheel bearings.

22. Install the grease cap (dust cap) with a rubber mallet or
soft-faced hammer to help prevent denting or distorting
the grease cap. Install the wheel cover or hub cap.

CAUTION: Clean grease off the disc brake rotors or
drums after servicing the wheel bearings. Use a brake
cleaner and a shop cloth. Even a slight amount of grease
on the friction surfaces of the brakes can harm the friction lining and/or cause brake noise.

SEALED BEARING REPLACEMENT

Most front-wheel-drive vehicles use a sealed bearing assembly that is bolted to the steering knuckle and supports the drive axle or the rear, as shown in Figure 12-21.

Many front-wheel-drive vehicles use a bearing that must be pressed off the steering knuckle. Special aftermarket tools are also available to remove many of the bearings without removing the knuckle from the vehicle. Check the factory service manual and tool manufacturers for exact procedures for the vehicle being serviced. See Figures 12-22 and 12-23.

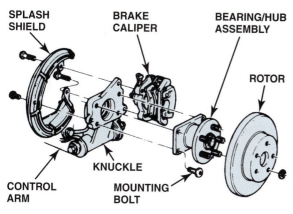

FIGURE 12-21   A rear-wheel sealed bearing hub assembly.

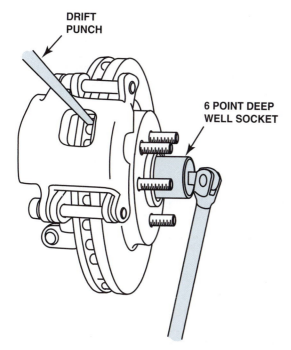

FIGURE 12-22   Removing the drive axle shaft hub nut. This nut is usually very tight and the drift (tapered) punch wedged into the cooling fins of the brake rotor keeps the hub from revolving when the nut is loosened.

Diagnosing a defective front bearing on a front-wheel-drive vehicle is sometimes confusing. A defective wheel bearing is usually noisy while driving straight, and the noise increases with vehicle speed (wheel speed). A drive-axle-shaft U-joint (CV joint) can also be the cause of noise on a front-wheel-drive vehicle, but usually makes *more noise* while turning and accelerating.

REAR DRIVE AXLE CLASSIFICATIONS

There are three rear drive axle classifications:

- Full-floating
- Three-quarter-floating
- Semi-floating

These terms indicate whether the axle shafts or the axle housing supports the wheels. Which category an axle belongs in is determined by how the wheels and wheel bearings mount to the axle or housing.

Full-Floating Axle

On a full-floating axle, the bearings are mounted and retained in the hub of the brake drum or rotor. The hub and bearing mount onto the axle housing, and are held in place by a bearing retainer or adjustment nuts and safety locks. The flanged end of the drive axle is attached to the hub by bolts or nuts. The inner end of the axle splines into the differential side gears. The wheel mounts onto the hub, and lug bolts or nuts retain it. In this design, the axle shafts "float" in the axle housing and drive the wheels without supporting their weight. Because the axle shafts do not retain the wheel, the

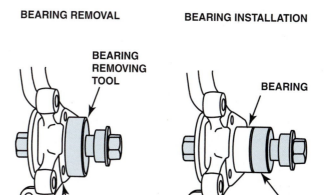

FIGURE 12-23   A special puller makes the job of removing the hub bearing from the knuckle easy without damaging any component.

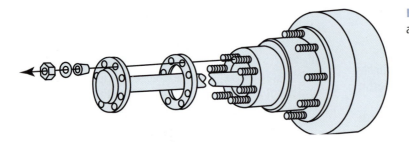

FIGURE 12-24 A typical full-floating rear axle assembly.

axle shafts can usually be removed from the vehicle while it is standing on the wheels. Most three-quarter-ton pickups, all heavy-duty truck tractors, and trailers use full-floating axles. See Figure 12-24.

Three-Quarter-Floating Axle

The bearings in a three-quarter-floating axle are mounted and retained in the brake drum or rotor hub, which mounts onto the axle housing. The outer extension of the hub fits onto the end of the axle, which is usually splined and tapered, and a nut and cotter pin secure the hub to the axle. The axle shaft splines to the side gears inside the differential. The wheels are mounted on the hub and retained by lug bolts or nuts. As in the full-floating axle, the axle housing and bearings in the hub support the weight in a three-quarter-floating axle. Because of the construction of a three-quarter-floating axle, the wheel must be removed before removing the axle shaft from the vehicle.

Semi-Floating Axle

The wheel bearings in a semi-floating axle either press onto the axle shaft or are installed in the outer end of the axle housing. A retainer plate at the outer end of the axle shaft or a C-clip inside the differential at the other end keeps the axle shaft in the housing. The brake drum or rotor fits onto the end of the axle, and lug bolts or nuts fasten the wheel to the drum or rotor and to the axle. These axles are called "semi-floating" because only the inboard ends of the axle shaft "float" in the housing. The outboard end of the shaft retains the wheel and transmits the weight of the wheel to the housing. Most solid-axle rear-wheel-drive cars and light trucks use a semi-floating type of axle. See Figure 12-25.

REAR AXLE BEARING AND SEAL REPLACEMENT

The rear bearings used on rear-wheel-drive vehicles are constructed and serviced differently from other types of wheel

THREE-QUARTER-FLOATING

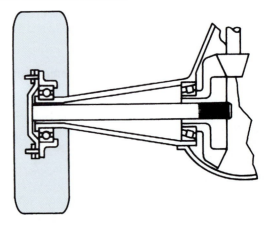

SEMI-FLOATING

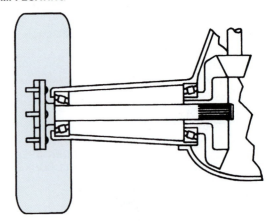

FIGURE 12-25 Rear axle shafts may be full-floating, three-quarter-floating, or semi-floating, depending on whether the shafts or the axle housing support the wheels.

bearings. Rear axle bearings are either sealed or lubricated by the rear-end lubricant. The rear axle must be removed from the vehicle to replace the rear axle bearing. There are two basic types of axle retaining methods, **retainer-plate-type** and the **C-lock.**

Retainer-Plate-Type Axles

The retainer-plate-type rear axle uses four fasteners that retain the axle in the axle housing. To remove the axle shaft and the

rear axle bearing and seal, the retainer bolts or nuts must be removed.

NOTE: If the axle flange has an access hole, then a retainer-plate-type axle is used.

The hole or holes in the wheel flange permit socket-wrench access to the fasteners. After the fasteners have been removed, the axle shaft must be removed from the rear axle housing. With the retainer-plate-type rear axle, the bearing and the retaining ring are press-fit onto the axle and the bearing cup (outer race) is also tightly fitted into the axle housing tube. See Figure 12-26.

See Figure 12-27 for one way to remove the axle shaft.

It is often necessary to remove the axle to perform a visual inspection, especially if trying to diagnose drive line noises. See Figure 12-28.

C-Lock-Type Axles

Vehicles that use C-locks (clips) use a straight roller bearing supporting a semi-floating axle shaft inside the axle housing. The straight rollers do not have an inner race. The rollers ride on the axle itself. If a bearing fails, both the axle and the

FIGURE 12-27   A slide-hammer-type axle puller can also be used.

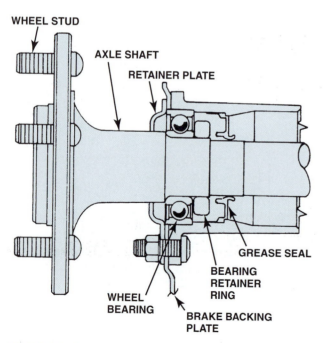

FIGURE 12-26   A retainer-plate-type rear axle bearing. Access to the fasteners is through a hole in the axle flange.

FIGURE 12-28   The ball bearings fell out onto the ground when this axle was pulled out of the axle housing. Diagnosing the cause of the noise and vibration was easy on this vehicle.

TECH TIP

THE BRAKE DRUM SLIDE-HAMMER TRICK

To remove the axle from a vehicle equipped with a retainer-plate-type rear axle, simply use the brake drum as a slide hammer to remove the axle from the axle housing. See Figure 12-29. If the brake drum does not provide enough force, a slide hammer can also be used to remove the axle shaft.

(a)

(b)

FIGURE 12-29 (a) To remove the axle from this vehicle equipped with a retainer-plate rear axle, the brake drum was placed back onto the axle studs backward so that the drum itself can be used as a slide hammer to pull the axle out of the axle housing. (b) A couple of pulls and the rear axle is pulled out of the axle housing.

bearing usually need to be replaced. The outer bearing race holding the rollers is pressed into the rear axle housing. The axle bearing is usually lubricated by the rear-end lubricant and a grease seal is located on the outside of the bearing.

NOTE: Some available replacement bearings are designed to ride on a fresh, unworn section of the old axle. These bearings allow the use of the original axle, saving the cost of a replacement axle.

The C-lock-type rear axle retaining method requires that the differential cover plate be removed.

After removal of the cover, the differential pinion shaft has to be removed before the C-lock that retains the axle can be removed. See Figures 12-30 and 12-31.

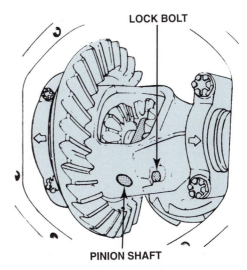

FIGURE 12-30 To remove the C-lock (clip), the lock bolt has to be moved before the pinion shaft.

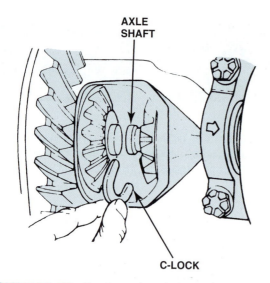

FIGURE 12-31 The axle must be pushed inward slightly to allow the C-lock to be removed. After the C-lock has been removed, the axle can be easily pulled out of the axle housing.

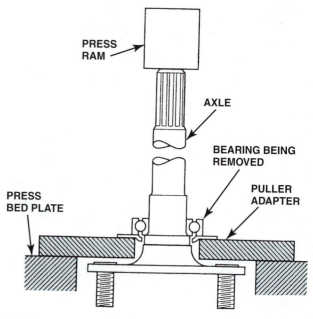

FIGURE 12-32 Using a hydraulic press to press an axle bearing from the axle. When pressing a new bearing back onto the axle, pressure should only be on the inner bearing race to prevent damaging the bearing.

NOTE: When removing the differential cover, rear axle lubricant will flow from between the housing and the cover. Be sure to dispose of the old rear axle lubricant in the environmentally approved way, and refill with the proper type and viscosity (thickness) of rear-end lubricant. Check the vehicle specifications for the recommended grade.

Once the C-lock has been removed, the axle simply is pulled out of the axle tube. Axle bearings with inner races are pressed onto the axle shaft and must be pressed off using a hydraulic press. A bearing retaining collar should be chiseled or drilled into to expand the collar, allowing it to be removed. See Figure 12-32.

Always follow the manufacturer's recommended bearing removal and replacement procedures. Always replace the rear axle seal whenever replacing a rear axle bearing. See Figure 12-33 for an example of seal removal.

Always check the differential vent to make sure it is clear. A clogged vent can cause excessive pressure to build up inside the differential and cause the rear axle seals to leak. If rear-end lubricant gets on the brake linings, the brakes will not have the proper friction and the linings themselves are ruined and must be replaced.

FIGURE 12-33 Removing an axle seal using the axle shaft as the tool.

FIGURE 12-34 This is a normally worn bearing. If it does not have too much play, it can be reused. *(Courtesy of SKF USA Inc.)*

(a)   (b)

FIGURE 12-35 (a) When corrosion etches into the surface of a roller or race, the bearing should be discarded. (b) If light corrosion stains can be removed with an oil-soaked cloth, the bearing can be reused. *(Courtesy of SKF USA Inc.)*

(a)   (b)

FIGURE 12-36 (a) When just the end of a roller is scored, it is because of excessive preload. Discard the bearing. (b) This is a more advanced case of pitting. Under load, it will rapidly lead to spalling. *(Courtesy of SKF USA Inc.)*

BEARING FAILURE ANALYSIS

Whenever a bearing is replaced, the old bearing must be inspected and the cause of the failure eliminated. See Figures 12-34 through 12-40 for examples of normal and abnormal bearing wear.

For example, a wheel bearing may fail for several reasons, including:

Metal Fatigue. Long vehicle usage, even under normal driving conditions, causes metal to fatigue. Cracks often

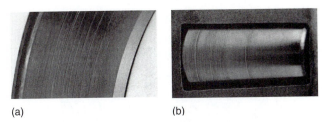

(a)   (b)

FIGURE 12-37 (a) Always check for faint grooves in the race. This bearing should not be reused. (b) Grooves like this are often matched by grooves in the race (above). Discard the bearing. *(Courtesy of SKF USA Inc.)*

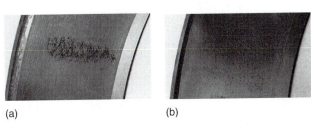

(a)   (b)

FIGURE 12-38 (a) Regular patterns of etching in the race are from corrosion. This bearing should be replaced. (b) Light pitting comes from contaminants being pressed into the race. Discard the bearing. *(Courtesy of SKF USA Inc.)*

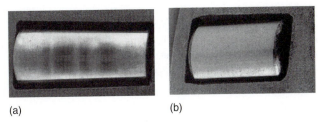

(a)   (b)

FIGURE 12-39 (a) This bearing is worn unevenly. Notice the stripes. It should not be reused. (b) Any damage that cause low spots in the metal renders the bearing useless. *(Courtesy of SKF USA Inc.)*

(a)   (b)

FIGURE 12-40 (a) In this more advanced case of pitting, you can see how the race has been damaged. (b) Discoloration is a result of overheating. Even a lightly burned bearing should be replaced. *(Courtesy of SKF USA Inc.)*

(a)   (b)

FIGURE 12-41 (a) Pitting eventually leads to spalling, a condition where the metal falls away in large chunks. (b) In this spalled roller, the metal has actually begun to flake away from the surface. *(Courtesy of SKF USA Inc.)*

FIGURE 12-42 These dents resulted from the rollers "hammering" against the race, a condition called brinelling. *(Courtesy of SKF USA Inc.)*

TECH TIP

WHAT'S THAT SOUND?

Defective wheel bearings usually make noise. The noise most defective wheel bearings make sounds like noisy off-road or aggressive tread, or mud and snow tires. Wheel bearing noise will remain constant while driving over different types of road surfaces, whereas tire tread noise usually changes with different road surfaces. In fact, many defective bearings have been ignored by the vehicle owners and technicians because it was thought that the source of the noise was the aggressive tread design of the mud and snow tires. Always suspect defective wheel bearings whenever you hear what seems to be extremely or unusually loud tire noise.

appear, and eventually these cracks expand downward into the metal from the surface. The metal between the cracks can break out into small chips, slabs, or scales of metal. This process of breaking up is called spalling. See Figure 12-41.

Shock Loading. Dents can be formed in the race of a bearing, which eventually leads to bearing failure. See the Tech Tip titled "Bearing Overload" and Figure 12-42.

SUMMARY

1. Wheel bearings support the entire weight of a vehicle and are used to reduce rolling friction. Ball and straight roller-type bearings are nonadjustable, whereas tapered roller-type bearings must be adjusted for proper clearance.

2. Most front-wheel-drive vehicles use sealed bearings, either two preloaded tapered roller bearings or double-row ball bearings.

3. Most wheel bearings are available in standardized sizes.

4. A defective bearing can be caused by metal fatigue that leads to **spalling,** shock loads that cause **brinelling,** or damage from electrical arcing due to poor body ground wires or improper electrical welding on the vehicle.

5. Bearing grease is an oil with an added thickener. The higher the NLGI number of the grease, the thicker or harder the grease consistency.

6. Tapered wheel bearings must be adjusted by hand tightening the spindle nut after properly seating the bearings. A new cotter key must always be used.

7. Defective wheel bearings usually make more noise while turning because more weight is applied to the bearing as the vehicle turns.

8. All bearings must be serviced, replaced, and/or adjusted using the vehicle manufacturer's recommended procedures as stated in the service manual.

REVIEW QUESTIONS

1. List three common types of automotive antifriction bearings.

2. Explain the adjustment procedure for a typical tapered roller wheel bearing.

3. List four symptoms of a defective wheel bearing.

4. Describe how the rear axle is removed from a C-lock-type axle.

CHAPTER QUIZ

1. Which type of automotive bearing can withstand radial and thrust loads, yet must be adjusted for proper clearance?
   a. Roller bearing
   b. Tapered roller bearing
   c. Ball bearings
   d. Needle roller bearing

2. Most sealed bearings used on the front wheels of front-wheel-drive vehicles are usually which type?
   a. Roller bearing
   b. Single tapered roller bearing
   c. Double-row ball bearing
   d. Needle roller bearing

3. On a bearing that has been shock loaded, the race (cup) of the bearing can be dented. This type of bearing failure is called _____.
   a. Spalling
   b. Arcing
   c. Brinelling
   d. Fluting

4. The bearing grease most often specified is rated NLGI _____.
   a. #00
   b. #0
   c. #1
   d. #2

5. A nondrive wheel bearing adjustment procedure includes a final spindle nut tightening torque of _____.
   a. Finger tight
   b. 5 lb-in.
   c. 12 to 30 lb-ft.
   d. 12 to 15 lb-ft. plus 1/16 in. turn

6. After a nondrive wheel bearing has been properly adjusted, the wheel should have how much endplay?
   a. Zero
   b. 0.001 to 0.005 in.
   c. 0.10 to 0.30 in.
   d. 1/16 to 3/32 in.

7. The differential cover must be removed before removing the rear axle on which type of axle?
   a. Retainer plate
   b. C-lock
   c. Press-fit
   d. Welded tube

8. What part(s) should be replaced when servicing a wheel bearing on a nondrive wheel?
   a. The bearing cup
   b. The grease seal
   c. The cotter key
   d. Both the grease seal and the cotter key

9. Technician A says that a defective wheel or axle bearing often makes a growling or rumbling noise. Technician B says that a defective wheel or axle bearing often makes a noise similar to a tire with an aggressive mud or snow design. Which technician is correct?
   a. Technician A only
   b. Technician B only
   c. Both Technicians A and B
   d. Neither Technician A nor B

10. Two technicians are discussing differentials. Technician A says all differentials are vented. Technician B says that a clogged vent can cause the rear axle seal to leak. Which technician is correct?
    a. Technician A only
    b. Technician B only
    c. Both Technicians A and B
    d. Neither Technician A nor B

DRIVE AXLE SHAFTS AND CV JOINTS

OBJECTIVES

After studying Chapter 13, the reader should be able to:

1. Prepare for Suspension and Steering (A4) ASE certification test content area "C" (Related Suspension and Steering Service).
2. Name drive shaft and U-joint parts, and describe their function and operation.
3. Describe how CV joints work.
4. Explain how the working angles of the U-joints are determined.
5. List the various types of CV joints and their applications.
6. Explain the operation of a differential.
7. Describe how various four-wheel-drive systems operate.

KEY TERMS

A drive axle shaft transmits engine torque from the transmission or transaxle (if front wheel drive) to the rear axle assembly or drive wheels. See Figures 13-1 and 13-2.

Drive shaft is the term used by the Society of Automotive Engineers (SAE) to describe the shaft between the transmission and the rear axle assembly on a rear-wheel-drive vehicle. General Motors and some other manufacturers use the term **propeller shaft** or *prop shaft* to describe this same part. The SAE term will be used throughout this textbook.

A typical drive shaft is a hollow steel tube. A splined end yoke is welded onto one end that slips over the splines of the output shaft of the transmission. See Figure 13-3. An end yoke is welded onto the other end of the drive shaft. Some drive shafts use a center support bearing.

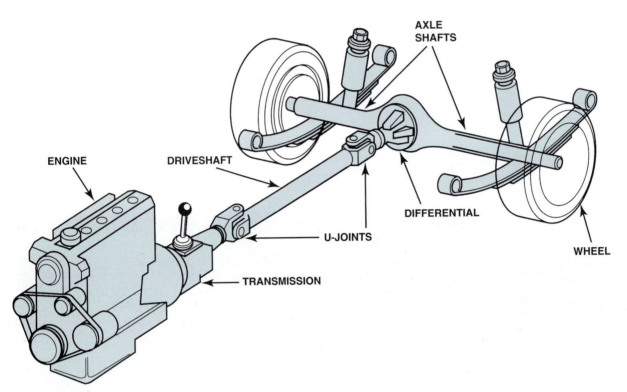

FIGURE 13-1 Typical rear-wheel-drive power train arrangement. The engine is mounted longitudinal (lengthwise).

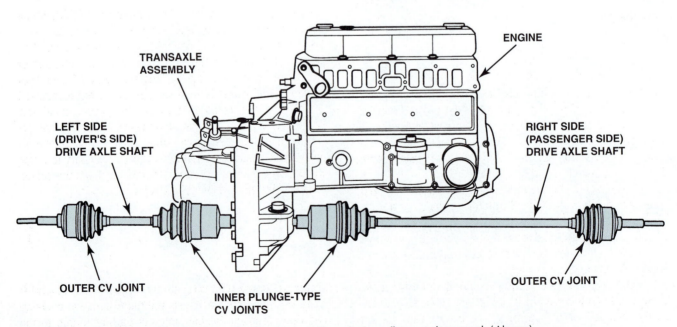

FIGURE 13-2 Typical front-wheel-drive power train arrangement. The engine is usually mounted transversely (sideways).

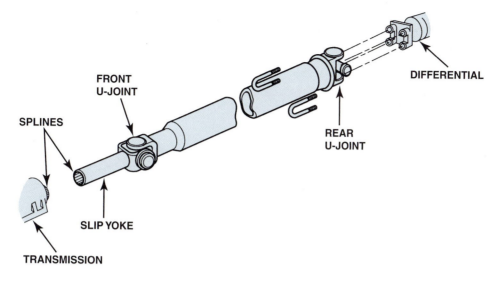

SPLINES

FRONT
U-JOINT

DIFFERENTIAL

REAR
U-JOINT

SLIP YOKE

TRANSMISSION

FIGURE 13-3   Typical drive shaft (also called a *propeller shaft*). The driver shaft transfers engine power from the transmission to the differential.

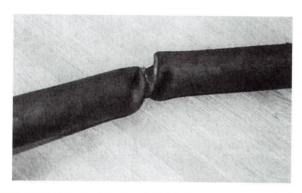

FIGURE 13-4   This drive shaft failed because it had a slight dent caused by a rock. When engine torque was applied, the drive shaft collapsed, twisted, and then broke.

DRIVE SHAFT DESIGN

Most drive shafts are constructed of hollow steel tubing. *The forces are transmitted through the surface of the drive shaft tubing.* The surface is therefore in tension, and cracks can develop on the outside surface of the drive shaft due to metal fatigue. Drive shaft tubing can bend and, if dented, can collapse. See Figure 13-4.

Most rear-wheel-drive cars and light trucks use a one- or two-piece drive shaft. A steel tube drive shaft has a maximum length of about 65 in. (165 cm). Beyond this critical length, a **center support bearing** must be used, as shown in Figure 13-5. A center support bearing is also called a steady bearing or hanger bearing.

Some vehicle manufacturers use aluminum drive shafts; these can be as long as 90 in. (230 cm) with no problem. Many extended-cab pickup trucks and certain vans use aluminum drive shafts to eliminate the need (and expense) of a

center support bearing. Composite-material drive shafts are also used in some vehicles. These carbon-fiber-plastic drive shafts are very strong yet lightweight, and can be made in extended lengths without the need for a center support bearing.

To dampen drive shaft noise, it is common to line the inside of the hollow drive shaft with cardboard. This helps eliminate the tinny sound whenever shifting between drive and reverse in a vehicle equipped with an automatic transmission. See Figure 13-6.

DRIVE SHAFT BALANCE

All drive shafts are balanced. Generally, any drive shaft whose rotational speed is greater than 1,000 RPM must be balanced. Drive shaft balance should be within 0.5% of the drive shaft weight. (This is one of the biggest reasons why aluminum or composite drive shafts can be longer because of their light weight.) (See Chapter 17 for drive shaft balancing procedures.)

Drive shafts are often not available by make, model, and year of the vehicle. There are too many variations at the factory, such as transmission type, differential, or U-joint type. To get a replacement drive shaft, it is usually necessary to know the series of U-joints (type or style of U-joint) and the center-to-center distance between the U-joints.

U-JOINT DESIGN AND OPERATION

Universal joints (U-joints) are used at both ends of a drive shaft. U-joints allow the wheels and the rear axle to move up and down, remain flexible, and still transfer torque to the drive wheels. A simple universal joint can be made from two

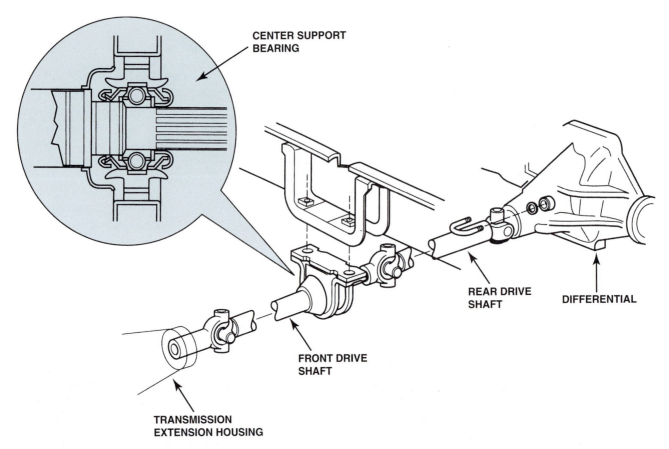

CENTER SUPPORT BEARING

REAR DRIVE SHAFT

DIFFERENTIAL

FRONT DRIVE SHAFT

TRANSMISSION EXTENSION HOUSING

FIGURE 13-5   A center support bearing is used on many vehicles with long drive shafts.

FIGURE 13-6   Some drive shafts use rubber between an inner and outer housing to absorb vibrations and shocks to the drive line.

Y-shaped yokes connected by a crossmember called a cross or **spider.** The four arms of the cross are called **trunnions.** See Figure 13-7 for a line drawing of a simple U-joint with all part names identified. A similar design is the common U-joint used with a socket wrench set.

Most U-joints are called cross-yoke joints or **Cardan joints.** *Cardan* is named for a sixteenth-century Italian mathematician who worked with objects that moved freely in any direction. Torque from the engine is transferred through the U-joint. The engine drives the U-joint at a constant speed, but the output speed of the U-joint changes because of the angle of the joint. The speed changes twice per revolution. *The greater the angle, the greater the change in speed (velocity).* See Figure 13-8.

If only one U-joint were used in a drive line, this change in speed of the driven side (output end) would generate vibrations in the drive line. To help reduce vibration, another U-joint is used at the other end of the drive shaft. If the angles of both joints are nearly equal, the acceleration and deceleration of one joint is offset by the alternate deceleration and acceleration of the second joint. *It is very important that both U-joints operate at about the same angle to prevent excessive drive line vibration.* See Figure 13-9.

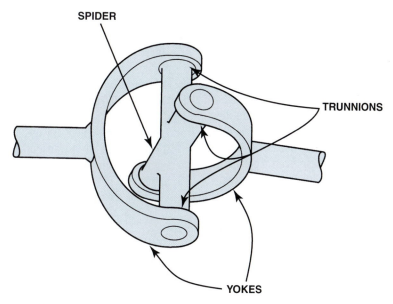

FIGURE 13-7   A simple universal joint (U-joint).

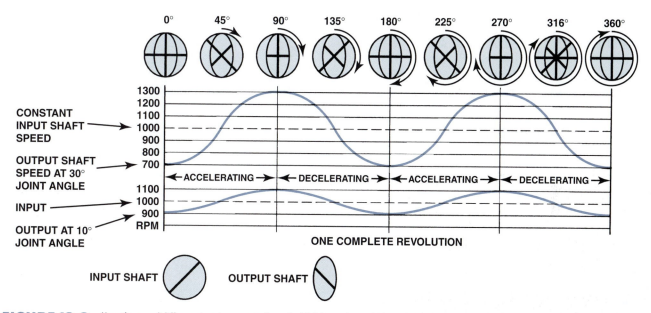

FIGURE 13-8   How the speed difference on the output of a typical U-joint varies with the speed and the angle of the U-joint. At the bottom of the chart, the input speed is a constant 1,000 RPM, while the output speed varies from 900 RPM to 1,100 RPM when the angle difference in the joint is only 10°. At the top part of the chart, the input speed is a constant 1,000 RPM, yet the output speed varies from 700 to 1,200 RPM when the angle difference in the joint is changed to 30°. *(Courtesy of Dana Corporation)*

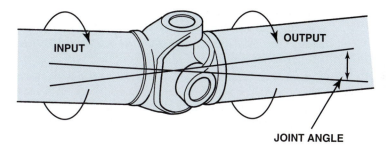

FIGURE 13-9   The joint angle is the difference between the angles of the joint. *(Courtesy of Dana Corporation)*

Acceptable Working Angles

Universal joints used in a typical drive shaft should have a *working angle* of 1/2 to 3 degrees. See Figure 13-10. The working angle is the angle between the driving end and the driven end of the joint. If the drive shaft is perfectly straight (0-degree working angle), then the needle bearings inside the bearing cap are not revolving because there is no force (no difference in angles) to cause the rotation of the needle bearings. If the needle bearings do not rotate, they can exert a constant pressure in one place and damage the bearing journal. If a two-piece drive shaft is used, one U-joint (usually the front) runs at a small working angle of about 1/2 degree, just enough to keep the needle bearings rotating. The other two U-joints (from the center support bearing and rear U-joint at the differential) operate at typical working angles of a single-piece drive shaft.

If the U-joint working angles differ by more than 1/2 degree, a vibration is usually produced that is *torque sensitive.* As the vehicle is first accelerated from a stop, engine torque can create unequal drive shaft angles by causing the differential to rotate on its suspension support arms. This vibration is most noticeable when the vehicle is heavily loaded and being accelerated at lower speeds. The vibration usually diminishes at higher speeds due to decrease in the torque being transmitted. If the drive shaft angles are excessive (over 3 degrees), a vibration is usually produced that increases as the speed of the vehicle (and drive shaft) increases.

CONSTANT VELOCITY JOINTS

Constant velocity joints, commonly called **CV joints,** are designed to rotate without changing speed. Regular U-joints are usually designed to work up to 12 degrees of angularity. If two Cardan-style U-joints are joined together, the angle at which this **double-Cardan joint** can function is about 18 to 20 degrees. See Figure 13-11.

FIGURE 13-10 The angle of this rear U-joint is noticeable.

FREQUENTLY ASKED QUESTION

WHAT IS A 1350-SERIES U-JOINT?

Most universal joints are available in sizes to best match the torque that they transmit. The larger the U-joint, the higher the amount of torque. Most U-joints are sized and rated by series numbers. See the accompanying chart for series numbers and sizes.

Series Number	Cap Diameter (inches)	Overall Length (inches)	Trunnion Diameter (inches)
1000	15/16	2 5/64	1/2
1100	15/16	2 13/64	1/2
1260/1270	1 1/16	2 31/32	19/32
1280	1 1/16	2 31/32	39/64
1310	1 1/16	2 31/32	21/32
1330	1 1/16	3 3/8	21/32
1350	1 3/16	3 3/8	49/64
1410	1 3/16	3 15/16	49/64
1480	1 3/8	3 7/8	57/64

Double-Cardan U-joints were first used on large rear-wheel-drive vehicles to help reduce drive-line-induced vibrations, especially when the rear of the vehicle was fully loaded and drive shaft angles were at their greatest. As long as a U-joint (either single or double Cardan) operates in a straight line, the driven shaft will rotate at the same constant speed (velocity) as the driving shaft. As the angle increases, the driven shaft speed or velocity varies during each revolution. This produces pulsations and a noticeable vibration or surge. The higher the shaft speed and the greater the angle of the joint, the greater the pulsations.

NOTE: Many four-wheel-drive light trucks use standard Cardan-style U-joints in the front drive axles. If the front wheels are turned sharply and then accelerated, the entire truck often shakes due to the pulsations created by the speed variations through the U-joints. This vibration is normal and cannot be corrected. It is characteristic of this type of design and is usually not noticeable in normal driving.

The first constant velocity joint was designed by Alfred H. Rzeppa (pronounced shep'pa) in the mid-1920s. The **Rzeppa joint** transfers torque through six round balls that are held in position midway between the two shafts. This design causes the angle between the shafts to be equally split regardless of the angle. See Figure 13-12. Because the angle is always split equally, torque is transferred equally without the change in speed (velocity) that occurs in Cardan-style U-joints. This style of joint results in a constant velocity between driving and driven shafts. It can also function at angles greater than simple U-joints can, up to 40 degrees.

NOTE: CV joints are also called LOBRÖ joints, the brand name of an original equipment manufacturer.

While commonly used today in all front-wheel-drive vehicles and many four-wheel-drive vehicles, its first use was on the front-wheel-drive 1929 Cord. Built in Auburn, Indiana, the Cord was the first front-wheel-drive car to use a CV-type drive axle joint.

Outer CV Joints

The Rzeppa-type CV joint is most commonly used as an outer joint on most front-wheel-drive vehicles. See Figure 13-13. The outer joint must do the following:

1. Allow up to 40 degrees or more of movement to allow the front wheels to turn

FIGURE 13-11   A double-Cardan U-joint.

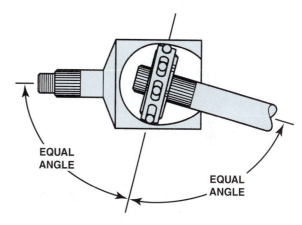

FIGURE 13-12   A constant velocity (CV) joint can operate at high angles without a change in velocity (speed) because the joint design results in equal angles between input and output. *(Courtesy of TRW Inc.)*

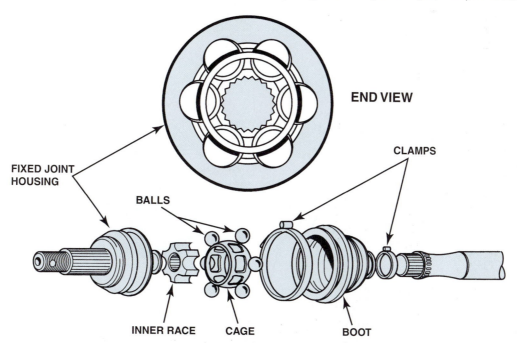

FIGURE 13-13   A Rzeppa fixed joint. This type of CV joint is commonly used at the wheel side of the drive axle shaft. This joint can operate at high angles to compensate for suspension travel and steering angle changes. *(Courtesy of Dana Corporation)*

2. Allow the front wheels to move up and down through normal suspension travel in order to provide a smooth ride over rough surfaces

3. Be able to transmit engine torque to drive the front wheels

Outer CV joints are called **fixed joints.** The outer joints are also attached to the front wheels. They are more likely to suffer from road hazards that often can cut through the protective outer flexible boot. See Figure 13-14. Once this boot has been split open, the special high-quality grease is thrown out and contaminants such as dirt and water can enter. Some joints cannot be replaced individually if worn. See Figure 13-15.

FIGURE 13-14 The protective CV joint boot has been torn away on this vehicle and all of the grease has been thrown outward onto the brake and suspension parts. The driver of this vehicle noticed a "clicking" noise, especially when turning.

NOTE: Research has shown that in as few as eight hours of driving time, a CV joint can be destroyed by dirt, moisture, and a lack of lubrication if the boot is torn. The technician should warn the owner as to the possible cost involved in replacing the CV joint itself whenever a torn CV boot is found.

Inner CV Joints

Inner CV joints attach the output of the transaxle to the drive axle shaft. Inner CV joints are therefore inboard, or toward the center of the vehicle. See Figure 13-16.

Inner CV joints have to be able to perform two very important movements:

1. Allow the drive axle shaft to move up and down as the wheels travel over bumps.
2. Allow the drive axle shaft to change length as required during vehicle suspension travel movements (lengthening and shortening as the vehicle moves up and down; same as the slip yoke on a conventional RWD drive shaft). CV joints are also called **plunge joints.**

Drive Axle Shafts

Unequal-length **drive axle shafts** (also called **half shafts**) result in unequal drive axle shaft angles to the front drive wheels. See Figure 13-17. This unequal angle often results in a pull on the steering wheel during acceleration. This pulling to one side during acceleration due to unequal engine torque being applied to the front drive wheels is called torque steer. To help reduce the effect of torque steer, some vehicles are

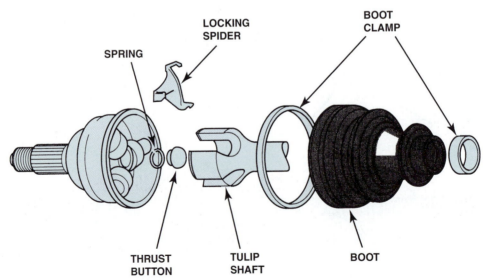

SPRING   LOCKING SPIDER   BOOT CLAMP

THRUST BUTTON   TULIP SHAFT   BOOT

FIGURE 13-15 A tripod fixed joint. This type of joint is found on some Renault and Japanese vehicles. If the joint wears out, it is to be replaced with an entire drive axle shaft assembly. *(Courtesy of Dana Corporation)*

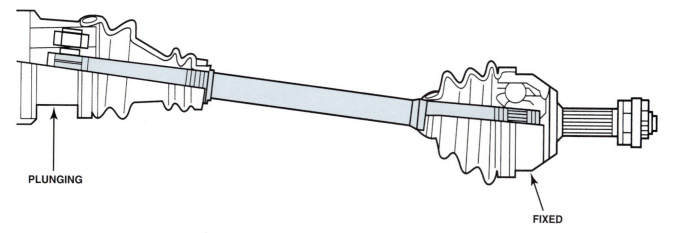

PLUNGING

FIXED

FIGURE 13-16   The fixed outer joint is required to move in all directions because the wheels must turn for steering as well as move up and down during suspension movement. The inner joint has to be able to not only move up and down but also plunge in and out as the suspension moves up and down. *(Courtesy of Dana Corporation)*

UNEQUAL LENGTH DRIVESHAFT

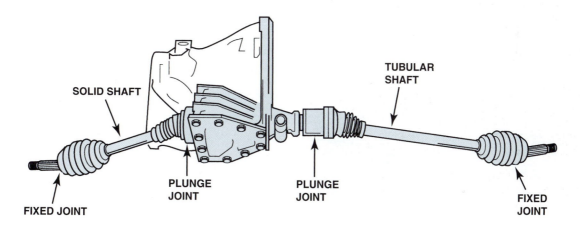

SOLID SHAFT

TUBULAR SHAFT

PLUNGE JOINT

PLUNGE JOINT

FIXED JOINT

FIXED JOINT

EQUAL LENGTH DRIVESHAFT

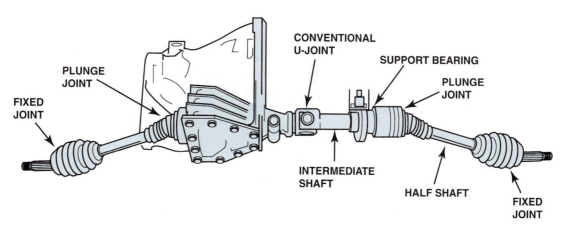

PLUNGE JOINT

CONVENTIONAL U-JOINT

SUPPORT BEARING

PLUNGE JOINT

FIXED JOINT

INTERMEDIATE SHAFT

HALF SHAFT

FIXED JOINT

FIGURE 13-17   Unequal-length drive shafts result in unequal drive axle shaft angles to the front drive wheels. This unequal angle side-to-side often results in a steering of the vehicle during acceleration called torque steer. By using an intermediate shaft, both drive axles are the same angle and the torque steer effect is reduced. *(Courtesy of Dana Corporation)*

FREQUENTLY ASKED QUESTION

WHAT IS THAT WEIGHT FOR ON THE DRIVE AXLE SHAFT?

Some drive axle shafts are equipped with what looks like a balance weight. See Figure 13-18. It is actually a dampener weight used to dampen out certain drive line vibrations. The weight is not used on all vehicles and may or may not appear on the same vehicle depending on engine, transmission, and other options. The service technician should always try to replace a defective or worn drive axle shaft with the exact replacement. When replacing an entire drive axle shaft, the technician should always follow the manufacturer's instructions regarding either transferring or not transferring the weight to the new shaft.

FIGURE 13-18   A typical drive axle shaft with dampener weight.

manufactured with an intermediate shaft that results in equal drive axle shaft angles. Both designs use fixed outer CV joints with plunge-type inner joints.

Typical types of inner CV joints that are designed to move axially, or *plunge,* include the following:

1. Tripod. See Figure 13-19.
2. Cross groove. See Figure 13-20.
3. Double offset. See Figure 13-21.

CV joints are also used in rear-wheel-drive vehicles and in many four-wheel-drive vehicles.

CV Joint Boot Materials

The pliable boot surrounding the CV joint, or **CV joint boot,** must be able to remain flexible under all weather conditions and still be strong enough to avoid being punctured by road debris. There are four basic types of boot materials used over CV joints:

1. *Natural rubber* (black) uses a bridge-type stainless steel clamp to retain.
2. *Silicone rubber* (gray) is a high-temperature-resistant material that is usually only used in places that need heat protection, such as the inner CV joint of a front-wheel-drive vehicle.
3. *Hard thermoplastic* (black) is a hard plastic material requiring heavy-duty clamps and a lot of torque to tighten (about 100 lb-ft!).
4. *Urethane* (usually blue) is a type of boot material usually found in an aftermarket part. See Figure 13-22 for examples of various types of CV joint boots depending on the manufacturer of the CV joints and shafts.

NOTE: Some aftermarket companies offer a split-style replacement CV joint boot. Being split means that the boot can be replaced without having to remove the drive axle shaft. Vehicle manufacturers usually do *not* recommend this type of replacement boot because the joint cannot be disassembled and properly cleaned with the drive axle still in the vehicle. The split boots must also be kept perfectly clean (a hard job to do with all the grease in the joint) in order to properly seal the seam on the split boot.

It is important that boot seals be inspected regularly and replaced if damaged. The inboard (plunging joint) can often pump water into the joint around the seals or through small holes in the boot material itself because the joint moves in and out. Seal retainers are used to provide a leakproof connection between the boot seal and the housing or axle shaft.

CV Joint Grease

CV joints require special greases. Grease is an oil with thickening agents. Greases are named for the thickening agents used.

Most CV joint grease is molybdenum-disulfide-type grease, commonly referred to as *moly* grease. The exact composition of grease can vary depending on the CV joint manufacturer. *The grease supplied with a replacement CV joint or boot kit should be the only grease used.*

The exact mix of chemicals, viscosity (thickness), wear, and corrosion-resistant properties varies from one CV joint application to another. Some technicians mistakenly think that the *color* of the grease determines in which CV joint it is used. The color—such as black, blue, red, or tan—is used to identify the grease during manufacturing and packaging as well as to give the grease a consistent, even color (due to blending of various ingredients in the grease).

TRIPOD TYPE PLUNGE JOINT

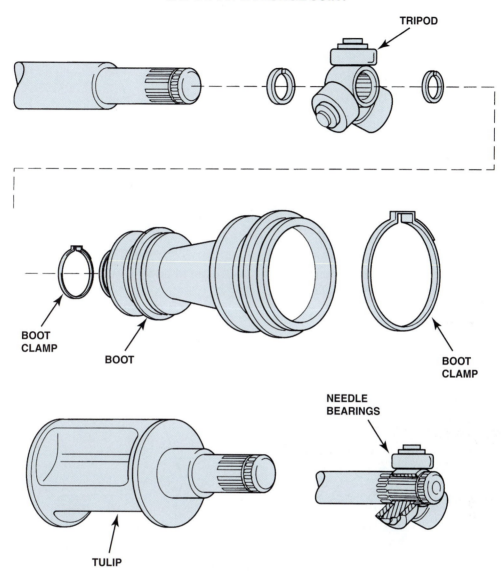

FIGURE 13-19   A tripod joint is also called a tripot, tripode, or tulip design. *(Courtesy of Dana Corporation)*

The exact grease to use depends on many factors, including the following:

1. The type (style) of CV joint. For example, outer (fixed) and inner (plunging) joints have different lubricating needs.
2. The location of the joint on the vehicle. For example, inner CV joints are usually exposed to the greatest amount of heat.
3. The type of boot. The grease has to be compatible with the boot material.

DIFFERENTIALS

A **differential** is used on the drive wheels of vehicles to allow for the transmission of torque to the drive wheels and to permit the drive wheels to rotate at different speeds. A differential is also called a rear end, or abbreviated simply as **diff.** Whenever any vehicle makes a turn, the outside wheel must travel a greater distance than the inside wheel. See Figure 13-23.

The drive shaft applies torque to the pinion gear that meshes below the centerline of a **ring gear.** This type of

CROSS-GROOVE PLUNGE JOINT

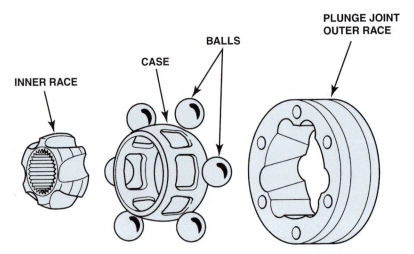

FIGURE 13-20 A cross-groove plunge joint is used on many German front-wheel-drive vehicles and as both inner and outer joints on the rear of vehicles that use an independent-type rear suspension. *(Courtesy of Dana Corporation)*

DOUBLE-OFFSET
BALL-TYPE PLUNGE JOINT

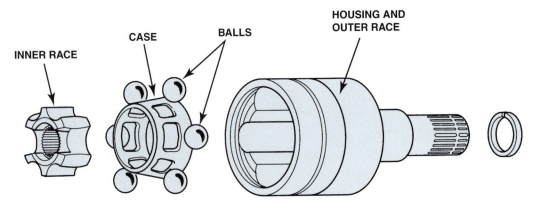

FIGURE 13-21 Double-offset ball-type plunge joint. *(Courtesy of Dana Corporation)*

gearset is called a **hypoid gearset** and requires gear lubrication specifically designed for this type of service. The ring gear is attached to a differential case that also contains small beveled **spider gears** or pinion gears. A pinion shaft passes through the two pinion gears in the case. In mesh with the pinion gears are two **side gears** that are splined to the inner ends of the axles. See Figure 13-24.

Differential Operation

When traveling straight, both rear wheels are turning at the same speed. The ring gear and the case with the pinion shaft rotate the differential pinion gears. The teeth on the differential pinion gears mesh with and apply torque to the axle side gears and axles. See Figure 13-25.

When turning a corner, the outside wheel is turning faster than the inside wheel because the outer wheel has to travel a greater distance.

The outer axle and side gear rotate faster than the inside axle and its side gear. This difference in speed between the side gears causes the differential pinion gears to rotate on the differential pinion shaft. Thrust washers are used to allow the pinion gears and side gears to move without wearing the internal surfaces of the differential case.

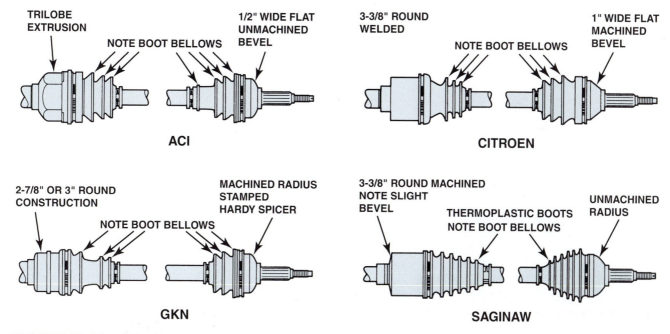

TRILOBE
EXTRUSION

NOTE BOOT BELLOWS

1/2" WIDE FLAT
UNMACHINED
BEVEL

ACI

3-3/8" ROUND
WELDED

NOTE BOOT BELLOWS

1" WIDE FLAT
MACHINED
BEVEL

CITROEN

2-7/8" OR 3" ROUND
CONSTRUCTION

NOTE BOOT BELLOWS

MACHINED RADIUS
STAMPED
HARDY SPICER

GKN

3-3/8" ROUND MACHINED
NOTE SLIGHT
BEVEL

THERMOPLASTIC BOOTS
NOTE BOOT BELLOWS

UNMACHINED
RADIUS

SAGINAW

FIGURE 13-22 Getting the correct boot kit or parts from the parts store is more difficult on many Chrysler front-wheel-drive vehicles because Chrysler has used four different manufacturers for its axle shaft assemblies. *(Courtesy of Dana Corporation)*

NOTE: These thrust washers can easily become worn if the drive wheels are allowed to spin on a slippery surface such as ice or snow. The wheel with the least traction receives the engine torque and spins at *twice* the speed indicated by the speedometer. These thrust washers can also wear if unequal-size tires are used on the drive wheels.

Because a conventional differential allows for the drive wheels to rotate at different speeds, when one wheel has little or no traction, the engine torque is applied to the wheel with the *least* traction and causes one wheel to spin on ice or other slippery surfaces.

Limited Slip Differentials

Limited slip differentials use clutches and other parts to limit the amount of slippage that can occur from one wheel to another. Different vehicle and axle manufacturers use different names for their design of limited slip differentials. Some differentials, such as the Eaton locking differential, will lock, sending torque to both rear wheels without any slippage. Other designs allow a limited amount of torque to be transferred to the wheel with the lower traction, hence the term *limited slip*. See Figure 13-26.

Some transaxles (transmission and differentials in one unit) are equipped with limited slip differentials. Figure 13-27 is a photo of a silicone viscous coupling final drive from a front-wheel-drive vehicle. This type of coupling permits both drive wheels to receive the same amount of engine torque.

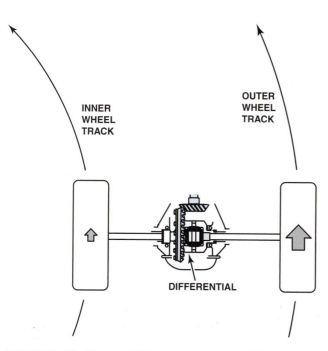

INNER
WHEEL
TRACK

OUTER
WHEEL
TRACK

DIFFERENTIAL

FIGURE 13-23 The difference between the travel distance of the drive wheels is controlled by the differential.

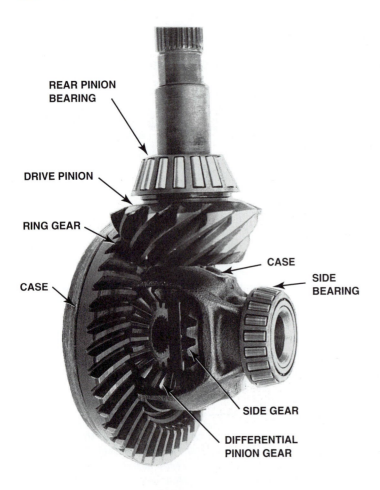

REAR PINION
BEARING

DRIVE PINION

RING GEAR

CASE

CASE

SIDE
BEARING

SIDE GEAR

DIFFERENTIAL
PINION GEAR

FIGURE 13-24 Pinion gears and side gears mounted in the case. The ring gear is bolted to the case and meshes with the pinion gear. This entire assembly is placed in the differential housing.

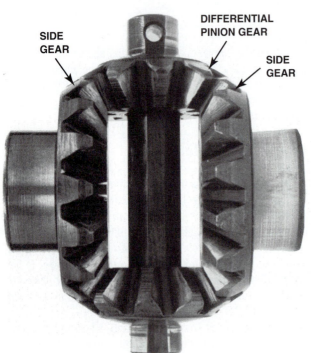

SIDE
GEAR

DIFFERENTIAL
PINION GEAR

SIDE
GEAR

FIGURE 13-25 Differential pinion gears assembled with two side gears.

If there is very little difference in speeds between the two drive wheels, the silicone fluid is thinner and allows for small changes in speed to allow for road bumps, dips, and turns. If there is a big difference in speed, the viscous silicone fluid increases in viscosity and tends to act as a solid, thereby holding both drive wheels together at the same speed.

Differential Lubricant

Because all differentials use hypoid gearsets, a special lubricant is necessary because the gears both roll and slide between their meshed teeth. Gear lubes are specified by the **American Petroleum Institute (API)** as follows:

GL-1 Straight mineral oil
GL-2 Worm-type gear lubricant
GL-3 Mild-type EP lubricant (will *not* protect hypoid gears)
GL-4 Mild-type EP lubricant suitable for manual transmissions/transaxles
GL-5 EP-type; OK for hypoid gears (meets military Mil-L2150B type requirements)
GL-6 EP-type; used where additional protection against gear scoring is needed, such as in racing or heavy-duty applications

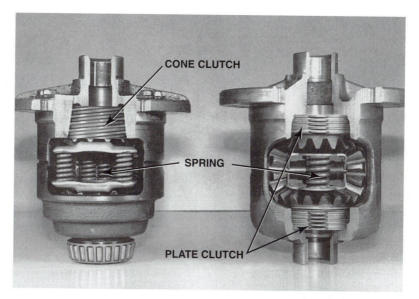

FIGURE 13-26   Cutaway sections of limited-slip-type differential cases showing a cone-type clutch (left) and a plate-type clutch (right).

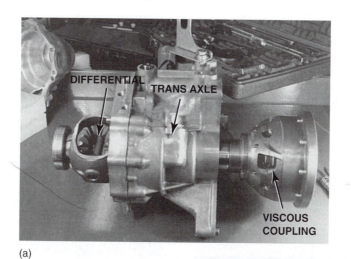

(a)

(b)

(c)

FIGURE 13-27   (a) A manual transaxle assembly showing the final drive unit (differential) and viscous coupling that acts as a limited slip differential on this front-wheel-drive vehicle. (b) The inside of the viscous coupling consists of thin metal discs. (c) Viscous silicone fluid is used between the metal discs.

Extreme pressure (EP) additives are sulfurized esters and organic sulfur-phosphorous compounds. They are useful as lubricants between steel and steel. They are not effective between steel and soft metal. In some cases, they accelerate corrosive wear of the soft metal. Lubricants containing EP additives should *not* be used with babbitt, aluminum, copper, or bronze bearing materials. Most differentials require the following:

1. SAE 80W-90 GL-5
2. SAE 75W-90 GL-5
3. SAE 80W GL-5

NOTE: Always check the *exact* specification before adding or replacing rear axle lubricant. For example, manual transmissions or transaxles may require any one of four possible lubricants, including the following:

SAE 80W-90 GL-5
STF (synchromesh transmission fluid) similar to ATF, but with friction characteristics designed for manual transmissions
ATF (automatic transmission fluid)
Engine oil (usually SAE 5W-30)

Limited slip differentials (often abbreviated LSD) usually use an additive that modifies the friction characteristics of the rear axle lubricant to prevent chattering while cornering. See Figure 13-28.

FOUR-WHEEL-DRIVE SYSTEMS

Two-wheel-drive vehicles use engine torque to turn either the front or the rear wheels. A differential is required to allow the

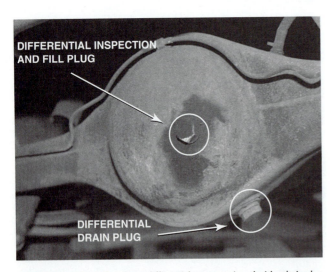

FIGURE 13-28 Some differentials come equipped with a drain plug as well as an inspection and fill plug, making it easier to change the differential lubricant.

drive wheels to travel different distances and speeds while cornering or driving over bumps or dips in the road. A four-wheel-drive vehicle therefore requires two differentials: one for the front wheels and one for the rear wheels.

NOTE: The term 4×4 means a four-wheeled vehicle that has engine torque applied to all four wheels (four-wheel drive). A 4×2 means a four-wheeled vehicle that has engine torque applied to only two wheels (two-wheel drive).

Four-wheel-drive vehicles require more than just two differentials. The front and the rear wheels of a four-wheel-drive vehicle also travel different distances and speeds whenever cornering or running over dips or rises in the road. There are three different methods used to allow for front-to-rear drive line speed variation.

Method 1: Locking Hubs

Engine torque from the transmission is applied directly to the rear differential through the *transfer case*. See Figure 13-29. The transfer case permits the driver to select a low-speed, high-torque gear ratio inside the transfer case while in four-wheel drive. These positions and their meanings include the following:

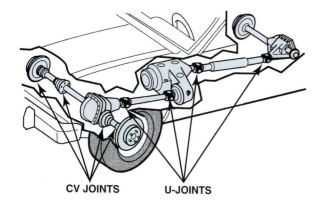

CV JOINTS   U-JOINTS

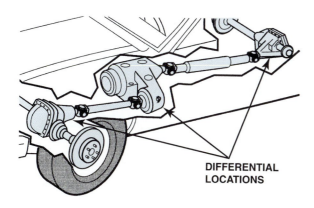

DIFFERENTIAL
LOCATIONS

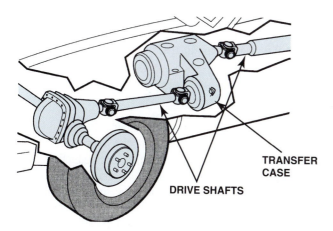

TRANSFER
CASE
DRIVE SHAFTS

FIGURE 13-29 Many light trucks and sport utility vehicles use a transfer case to provide engine power to all four wheels and to allow a gear reduction for maximum power to get through mud or snow. *(Courtesy of Dana Corporation)*

- 4 H   Four-wheel drive with no gear reduction in the transfer case.
- 4 L   Four-wheel drive with gear reduction. Use of this position is usually restricted to low speeds on slippery surfaces.
- 2H   Two-wheel drive (rear wheels only) in high range, meaning no gear reduction in the transfer case.

CAUTION: Check the owner's manual or service manual for the recommended procedure to follow when changing from one position to another in the transfer case. Some vehicles require that the vehicle be stopped before selecting between two- and four-wheel drive, and between high and low range.

The transfer case also applies torque to the front differential. Torque is then applied to the front wheels through the drive axles to the locking hubs. In normal 4H driving on hard surfaces, the front hubs *must* be in the unlocked position. On loose road surfaces that can absorb and allow for tire slippage due to the different tire speeds front to back, the front hubs are locked. Some four-wheel-drive vehicles, such as the GM S-10 pickup truck, use a clutch or disconnect device that disengages the front drive axle shaft from the front wheels. This clutch is built into the front differential housing.

CAUTION: Failure to unlock the front wheel hubs while driving on a hard road surface can cause serious drive line vibrations and damage to drive shafts, U-joints, and bearings, as well as to the transfer case, transmission, and even the engine.

Method 2: Auto-Locking Hubs

This method uses a clutch arrangement built into the hub assembly. Whenever driving on smooth, hard road surfaces, the hubs *freewheel* and allow the front wheels to rotate at different speeds from the rear wheels. When the speed difference between the wheels and the front drive axle is great, the hubs will automatically lock and allow engine torque to be applied to the front wheels. Figure 13-30 shows an auto-locking hub with the cover removed.

FIGURE 13-30   Automatic-locking hub with the cover removed.

Method 3: Full-Time Four-Wheel Drive

This method uses a center differential to allow front and rear wheels to travel at different speeds under all operating conditions. While this method is the easiest to operate both on and off the road, the center differential can cause the vehicle to get stuck in mud or snow even though it is a "four-wheel-drive vehicle." All open-style differentials allow for speed differences. Torque is applied to the side of the differential with the *least* traction. This is why many vehicles are spinning just one wheel when stuck on ice or snow.

If a center differential is used, and one rear wheel starts to spin, all of the engine torque is applied to the spinning wheel and not to the front wheels, where it is most needed. The most common solution to this problem is to lock the center differential to prevent this from happening. A **viscous**

REAL WORLD FIX

THE JERKY VOLVO STORY

The owner of a Volvo XC70 complained that at about 40 mph, the vehicle would jerk if accelerating, but not jerk at the same speed when decelerating. A visual inspection showed one new tire on the right front that was replaced due to curb damage on the old tire. The vehicle had 29,000 miles and the tread looked to be serviceable on the other three tires. However, this vehicle is equipped with an all-wheel-drive system and equal size tires are very important. The service technician installed the wheels and tires from another similar vehicle as a test and the jerking was not felt. After replacing the other three tires, the problem was solved. According to many experts, the tread depth should be within 1/16 inch for all tires used on vehicles equipped with all-wheel drive.

coupling is commonly used on many four-wheel-drive vehicles to provide an automatic lockup of the center differential. A viscous coupling is a type of fluid clutch. When the speed difference between the front and rear wheels is high enough, the silicone fluid inside the coupling stiffens to reduce the speed difference between the front and rear drive shafts. This center differential lock, combined with a limited-slip-type rear differential, greatly helps the vehicle maintain traction under all road and weather conditions.

ALL-WHEEL DRIVE

Some cars and light trucks are equipped with an all-wheel-drive system that uses a transfer case with a center differential and only one speed (high). Low-range gear reduction is not used. A viscous coupling is usually incorporated into the center differential to provide superior all-weather traction. Combined with a limited slip differential in the rear, and sometimes also in the front, an all-wheel-drive system can provide ideal road traction under all driving conditions without any action by the driver.

SUMMARY

1. The drive shaft of a rear-wheel-drive vehicle transmits engine torque from the transmission to the differential.

2. Drive shaft length is usually limited to about 65 inches due to balancing considerations unless a two-piece or a composite material shaft is used.

3. Universal joints (U-joints) allow the drive shaft to transmit engine torque while the suspension and the rear axle assembly are moving up and down during normal driving conditions.

4. Acceptable working angles for a Cardan-type U-joint fall within 1/2 to 3 degrees. Some angle is necessary to cause the roller bearings to rotate; a working angle of greater than 3 degrees can lead to drive line vibrations.

5. Constant velocity (CV) joints are used on all front-wheel-drive vehicles and many four-wheel-drive vehicles to provide a smooth transmission of torque to the drive wheels regardless of angularity of the wheel or joint.

6. Outer or fixed CV joints commonly use a Rzeppa design, while inner CV joints are the plunging or tripod type.

7. In a typical differential in a rear-wheel-drive vehicle, the drive shaft applies engine torque to the pinion gear that meshes with and turns a ring gear attached to the differential case. The axles are splined to side gears that rotate with the differential case and mesh with the pinion gears. When a corner is turned, the inside wheel slows down, causing the pinion gear to rotate on the pinion shaft.

8. Limited slip differentials limit the amount of slippage that can occur between the two drive wheels of the drive axle. Special hypoid gear lubricant is required in all differentials, and limited slip units usually require a special friction additive.

9. Four-wheel-drive vehicles use two differentials, one for the front wheels and one for the rear wheels. Locking hubs with or without a center differential and transfer case are used to transmit engine torque to all four wheels.

REVIEW QUESTIONS

1. Explain why Cardan-type U-joints on a drive shaft must be within 1/2-degree working angles.

2. Describe how the differential allows the outside drive wheel to travel faster than the inside drive wheel while the vehicle is turning a corner.

3. Explain why many four-wheel-drive vehicles should not be driven on a smooth, hard surface with the front hubs locked.

4. What makes a constant velocity joint able to transmit engine torque through an angle at a constant velocity?

5. What type of grease must be used in CV joints?

CHAPTER QUIZ

1. The name most often used to describe the universal joints on a conventional rear-wheel-drive vehicle drive shaft is _____.
   a. Trunnion
   b. Cardan
   c. CV
   d. Spider

2. A rear-wheel-drive vehicle shudders or vibrates when first accelerating from a stop. The vibration is less noticeable at higher speeds. The most likely cause is _____.
   a. Drive shaft unbalance
   b. Excessive U-joint working angles
   c. Unequal U-joint working angles
   d. Brinelling of the U-joint

3. All drive shafts are balanced.
   a. True
   b. False

4. The maximum difference between the front and rear working angle of a drive shaft is _____.
   a. 1/4 degree
   b. 1/2 degree
   c. 1 degree
   d. 3 degrees

5. An all-wheel-drive vehicle has how many differentials?
   a. One
   b. Two
   c. Three
   d. Four

6. The owner of a full-size four-wheel-drive pickup truck complains that whenever the vehicle is in four-wheel drive and turning sharply while accelerating rapidly, a severe vibration is created. Technician A says that the drive shaft may be out of balance. Technician B says that this is normal if conventional Cardan U-joints are used to drive the front wheels. Which technician is correct?
   a. Technician A only
   b. Technician B only
   c. Both Technicians A and B
   d. Neither Technician A nor B

7. The outer CV joints used on front-wheel-drive vehicles are _____.
   a. Fixed type
   b. Plunge type

8. The proper grease to use with a CV joint is _____.
   a. Black chassis grease
   b. Dark blue EP grease
   c. Red moly grease
   d. The grease that is supplied with the boot kit

9. The pinion gears in a differential spin on the pinion shaft whenever the vehicle is driven _____.
   a. On a straight road
   b. Around a curve or corner

10. Which component is *not* used on a vehicle equipped with all-wheel drive?
    a. Front differential
    b. Rear differential
    c. Center differential
    d. Locking hubs

DRIVE AXLE SHAFT AND CV JOINT SERVICE

OBJECTIVES

After studying Chapter 14, the reader should be able to:

1. Prepare for Suspension and Steering (A4) ASE certification test content area "C" (Related Suspension and Steering Service).
2. Explain how to perform a U-joint inspection.
3. List the steps necessary to replace a U-joint.

4. Explain how to perform a measurement of the working angles of a U-joint.
5. Describe the service procedures for replacing CV joints and boots.
6. Describe the routine maintenance service procedures required for drive axle shafts and universal CV joints.
7. Describe differential service and adjustment procedures.

KEY TERMS

Inclinometer (p. 332)
Pin Bushings (p. 332)
Pinch Bolt (p. 334)
Spline Bind (p. 338)

Synthetic Retainers (p. 331)
Torque Prevailing Nut (p. 336)
U-joints (p. 328)

The drive shaft of a typical rear-wheel-drive (RWD) vehicle rotates about three times faster than the wheels. This is due to the gear reduction that occurs in the differential. The differential not only provides gear reduction but also allows for a difference in the speed of the rear wheels that is necessary whenever turning a corner.

The drive shaft rotates at the same speed as the engine if the transmission ratio is 1 to 1 (1:1). The engine speed, in revolutions per minute (RPM), is transmitted through the transmission at the same speed. In lower gears, the engine speed is many times faster than the output of the transmission. Most transmissions today, both manual and automatic, have an overdrive gear. This means that at highway speeds, the drive shaft is rotating faster than the engine (the engine speed is decreased or overdriven to help reduce engine speed and improve fuel economy).

The drive shaft must travel up and down as the vehicle moves over bumps and dips in the road while rotating and transmitting engine power to the drive wheels. The drive shaft and universal joints should be carefully inspected whenever any of the following problems or symptoms occur:

1. Vibration or harshness at highway speed
2. A clicking sound whenever the vehicle is moving either forward or in reverse

NOTE: A click-click-click sound while moving in reverse is usually the first indication of a defective U-joint. This clicking occurs in reverse because the needle bearings are being forced to rotate in a direction opposite the usual.

REAL WORLD FIX

THE SQUEAKING PICKUP TRUCK

The owner of a pickup truck complained that a squeaking noise occurred while driving in reverse. The "eeeee-eeeee-eeee" sound increased in frequency as the truck increased in speed, yet the noise did not occur when driving forward.

Because there was no apparent looseness in the U-joints, the service technician at first thought that the problem was inside either the transmission or the rear end. When the drive shaft was removed to further investigate the problem, it became obvious where the noise was coming from. The U-joint needle bearing had worn the cross-shaft bearing surface of the U-joint. See Figure 14-1. The noise occurred only in reverse because the wear had occurred in the forward direction, and therefore only when the torque was applied in the opposite direction did the needle bearing become bound up and start to make noise. A replacement U-joint solved the squeaking noise in reverse.

FIGURE 14-1   Notice how the needle bearings have worn grooves into the bearing surface of the U-joint.

3. A clunking sound whenever changing gears, such as moving from Drive to Reverse

DRIVE SHAFT AND U-JOINT INSPECTION

The drive shaft should be inspected for the following:

1. Any dents or creases caused by incorrect hoisting of the vehicle or by road debris.

   CAUTION: A dented or creased drive shaft can collapse, especially when the vehicle is under load. This collapse of the drive shaft can cause severe damage to the vehicle and may cause an accident.

2. Undercoating, grease, or dirt build-up on the drive shaft can cause a vibration.
3. Undercoating should be removed using a suitable solvent and a rag. Always dispose of used rags properly.

The **U-joints** should be inspected every time the vehicle chassis is lubricated, or four times a year. Original equipment (OE) U-joints are permanently lubricated and have no provision for greasing. If there is a grease fitting, the U-joint should be lubricated by applying grease with a grease gun. See Figures 14-2 and 14-3.

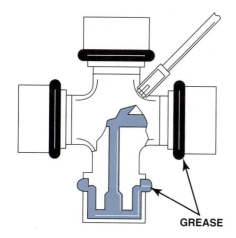

GREASE

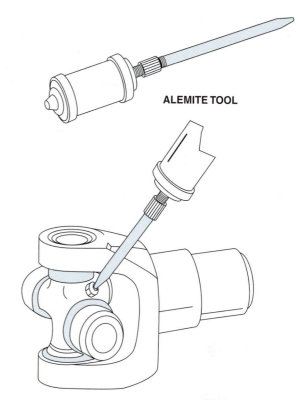

ALEMITE TOOL

FIGURE 14-3   Many U-joints require a special grease gun tool to reach the grease fittings.

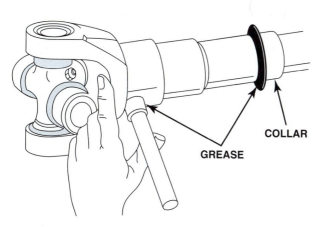

COLLAR

GREASE

FIGURE 14-2   All U-joints and spline collars equipped with a grease fitting should be greased four times a year as part of a regular lubrication service.

In addition to periodic lubrication, the drive shaft should be grabbed and moved to see if there is any movement of the U-joints. If *any* movement is noticed when the drive shaft is moved, the U-joint is worn and must be replaced.

NOTE: U-joints are not serviceable items and cannot be repaired. If worn or defective, they must be replaced.

U-joints can be defective and still not show noticeable free movement. *A proper U-joint inspection can be performed only by removing the drive shaft from the vehicle.*

Before removing the drive shaft, always mark the position of all mating parts to ensure proper reassembly. White correction fluid, also known as "White Out" or "Liquid Paper," is an easy and fast-drying marking material. See Figure 14-4.

To remove the drive shaft from a rear-wheel-drive vehicle, remove the four fasteners at the rear U-joint at the differential. See Figure 14-5.

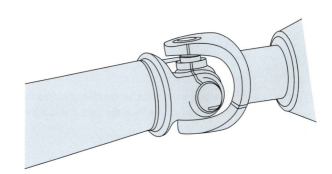

FIGURE 14-4   Always mark the original location of U-joints before disassembly.

Push the drive shaft forward toward the transmission and then down and toward the rear of the vehicle. The drive shaft should slip out of the transmission spline and can be removed from underneath the vehicle.

NOTE: With the drive shaft removed, transmission lubricant can leak out of the rear extension housing. To prevent a mess, use an old spline the same size as the one being removed or place a plastic bag over the extension housing to hold any escaping lubricant. A rubber band can be used to hold the bag onto the extension housing.

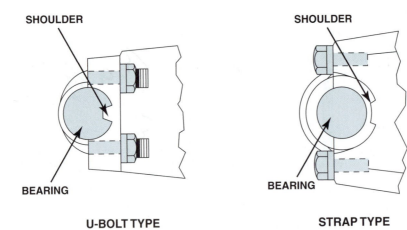

FIGURE 14-5 Two types of retaining methods that are commonly used at the rear U-joint at the differential.

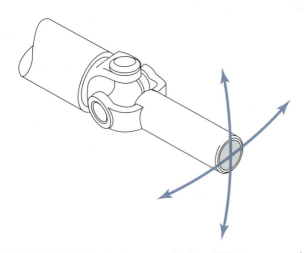

FIGURE 14-6 The best way to check any U-joint is to remove the drive shaft from the vehicle and move each joint in all directions. A good U-joint should be free to move without binding.

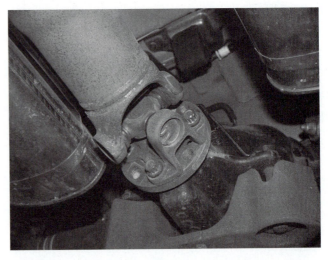

FIGURE 14-7 Typical U-joint that uses an outside snap ring. This style of joint bolts directly to the companion flange that is attached to the pinion gear in the differential.

To inspect U-joints, move each joint through its full travel, making sure it can move (articulate) freely and equally in all directions. See Figure 14-6.

U-JOINT REPLACEMENT

All movement in a U-joint should occur between the trunnions and the needle bearings in the end caps. The end caps are press-fit to the yokes, which are welded to the drive shaft. Three types of retainers are used to keep the bearing caps on the U-joints: the outside snap ring (see Figure 14-7), the inside retaining ring (see Figure 14-8), and injected synthetic (usually nylon).

After removing the retainer, use a press or a vise to separate the U-joint from the yoke. See Figure 14-9.

TECH TIP

USE TAPE TO BE SAFE

When removing a drive shaft, use tape to prevent the rear U-joint caps from falling off. If the caps fall off the U-joint, all of the needle bearings will fall out and scatter over the floor. See Figure 14-10.

FIGURE 14-8   Removing an inside retaining ring (snap ring).

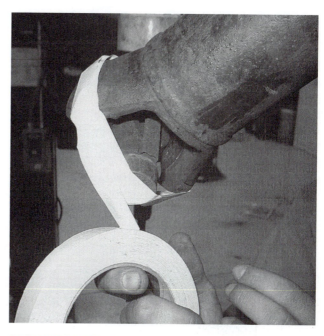

FIGURE 14-10   Taping the U-joint to prevent the caps from coming off.

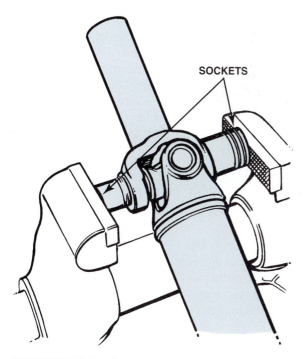

FIGURE 14-9   Use a vise and two sockets to replace a U-joint. One socket fits over the bearing cup and one fits on the bearing to press fit the cups from the crosspiece.

U-joints that use **synthetic retainers** must be separated using a press and a special tool to press onto both sides of the joint in order to shear the plastic retainer, as shown in Figure 14-11.

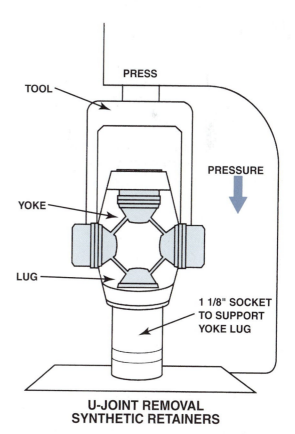

**U-JOINT REMOVAL
SYNTHETIC RETAINERS**

FIGURE 14-11   A special tool being used to press apart a U-joint that is retained by injected plastic. Heat from a propane torch may be necessary to soften the plastic to avoid exerting too much force on the U-joint.

Replacement U-joints use spring clips instead of injected plastic. Remove the old U-joint from the yoke, as shown in Figure 14-12, and replace with a new U-joint. Replacement U-joints should be *forged* (never cast) and use up to 32 needle bearings (also called **pin bushings**) instead of just 24 needle bearings, as used in lower-quality U-joints. Replacement U-joints usually have a grease fitting so that the new replacement U-joint can be properly lubricated. See Figure 14-13.

After removing any dirt or burrs from the yoke, press in a new U-joint. Rotate the new joint after installation to make sure it moves freely, without binding or stiffness. If a U-joint is stiff, it can cause a vibration.

FIGURE 14-12 Removing the worn cross from the yoke.

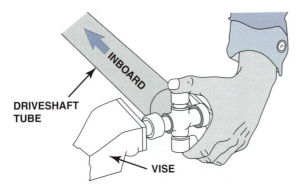

FIGURE 14-13 When installing a new U-joint, position the grease fitting on the inboard side (toward the drive shaft tube) and in alignment with the grease fitting of the U-joint at the other end.

NOTE: If a U-joint is slightly stiff after being installed, strike the U-joint using a brass punch and a light hammer. This often frees a stiff joint and is often called "relieving the joint." The shock aligns the needle bearings in the end caps.

U-Joint Working Angles

Unequal or incorrect U-joint working angles can cause severe vibrations. Drive shaft and U-joint angles may change from the original factory setting due to one or more of the following:

1. Defective or collapsed engine or transmission mounts
2. Defective or sagging springs, especially the rear springs due to overloading or other causes
3. Accident damage or other changes to the chassis of the vehicle
4. Vehicle modification that raises or lowers the ride height

Replace any engine or transmission mount that is cracked or collapsed. When a mount collapses, the engine drops from its original location. Now the drive shaft angles are changed and a vibration may be felt.

Rear springs often sag after many years of service or after being overloaded. This is especially true of pickup trucks. Many people carry as much as the cargo bed can hold, often exceeding the factory-recommended carry capacity or gross vehicle weight (GVW) of the vehicle.

To measure U-joint and drive shaft angles, the vehicle must be hoisted using an axle contact or drive-on-type lift so as to maintain the same drive shaft angles as the vehicle has while being driven.

The working angles of the two U-joints on a drive shaft should be within 1/2 degree of each other in order to cancel out speed changes. See Figure 14-14.

To measure the working angle of a U-joint, follow these steps:

Step 1   Place an **inclinometer** (a tool used to measure angles) on the rear U-joint bearing cap. Level the bubble and read the angle. See Figure 14-15; the pictured reading is 19.5 degrees.

Step 2   Rotate the drive shaft 90 degrees and read the angle of the rear yoke. For example, this reading is 17 degrees.

Step 3   Subtract the smaller reading from the larger reading to obtain the working angle of the joint. In this example, it is 2.5 degrees (19.5 degrees − 17 degrees = 2.5 degrees).

Repeat the same procedure for the front U-joint. The front and rear working angles should be within 0.5 degrees. If the two working angles are not within 0.5 degrees, shims can be added to bring the two angles closer together. The angle of the rear joint is changed by installing a tapered shim between the leaf spring and the axle, as shown in Figure 14-16.

CAUTION: Use caution whenever using wedges between the differential and the rear leaf spring to restore the correct U-joint working angle. Even though wedges are made to raise the front of the differential, the tilt often prevents rear-end lubricant from reaching the pinion bearing, resulting in pinion bearing noise and eventual failure.

The angle of the front joint is changed by adding or removing shims from the mount under the transmission. See Figure 14-17.

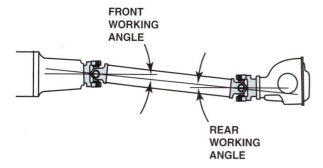

FIGURE 14-14 The working angle of most U-joints should be at least 1/2 degree (to permit the needle bearing to rotate in the U-joints) and should not exceed 3 degrees or a vibration can occur in the drive shaft, especially at higher speeds. The difference between the front and rear working angles should be within 1/2 degree of each other.

CV JOINT DIAGNOSIS

When a CV joint wears or fails, the most common symptom is noise while driving. An outer fixed CV joint will most likely be heard when turning sharply and accelerating at the same time. This noise is usually a clicking sound. While inner joint failure is less common, a defective inner CV joint often creates a loud

FIGURE 14-15   Inclinometer reads 19 1/2 degrees at this rear U-joint.

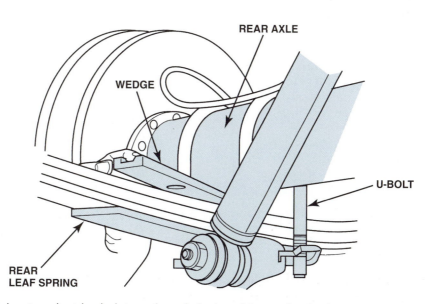

FIGURE 14-16   Placing a tapered metal wedge between the rear leaf spring and the rear axle pedestal to correct rear U-joint working angles.

FIGURE 14-17 A transmission oil pan gasket leak allowed automatic transmission fluid (ATF) to saturate the rear transmission mount rubber, causing it to collapse. After replacing the defective mount, proper drive shaft angles were restored and the drive line vibration was corrected.

TECH TIP

QUICK AND EASY BACKLASH TEST

Whenever a drive line clunk is being diagnosed, one possible cause is excessive backlash (clearance) between the ring gear teeth and differential pinion teeth in the differential. Another common cause of excessive differential backlash is too much clearance between differential carrier pinion teeth and side gear teeth. A quick test to check backlash involves three easy steps:

Step 1 Hoist the vehicle on a frame contact lift, allowing the drive wheels to be rotated.

Step 2 Have an assistant hold one drive wheel and the drive shaft to keep them from turning.

Step 3 Move the other drive wheel, observing how far the tire can rotate. This is the amount of backlash in the differential; it should be less than 1 in. (25 mm) of movement measured *at the tire*.

If the tire can move more than 1 in. (25 mm), then the differential should be inspected for wear and parts should be replaced as necessary. If the tire moves *less* than 1 in. (25 mm), then the backlash between the ring gear and pinion is probably *not* the cause of the noise.

clunk while accelerating from rest. To help verify a defective joint, drive the vehicle in reverse while turning and accelerating. This almost always will reveal a defective outer joint.

REPLACEMENT SHAFT ASSEMBLIES

Front-wheel-drive vehicles were widely used in Europe and Japan long before they became popular in North America. The standard repair procedure used in these countries is the replacement of the entire drive assembly if there is a CV joint failure. Replacement boot kits are rarely seen in Europe because it is felt that even a slight amount of dirt or water inside a CV joint is unacceptable. Vehicle owners simply wait until the joint wear causes severe noise, and then the entire assembly is replaced.

The entire drive axle shaft assembly can easily be replaced and the defective unit can be sent to a company for remanufacturing. Even though cost to the customer is higher, the parts and repair shop does not have to inventory every type, size, and style of boot kit and CV joint. Service procedures and practices therefore vary according to location and the availability of parts. For example, some service technicians use replacement drive axle assemblies from salvage yards with good success.

NOTE: Some drive axle shafts have a weight attached between the inner and outer CV joints. This is a dampener weight. It is not a balance weight, and it need not be transferred to the replacement drive axle shaft (half shaft) unless instructed to do so in the directions that accompany the replacement shaft assembly.

CV JOINT SERVICE

The hub nut must be removed whenever servicing a CV joint or shaft assembly on a front-wheel-drive vehicle. Since these nuts are usually torqued to almost 200 lb-ft (260 N·m), keep the vehicle on the ground until the hub nut is loosened and then follow these steps (see Figure 14-18):

Step 1 Remove the front wheel and hub nut.

NOTE: Most manufacturers warn against using an air impact wrench to remove the hub nut. The impacting force can damage the hub bearing.

Step 2 To allow the knuckle room to move outward enough to remove the drive axle shaft, some or all of the following will have to be disconnected:
a. Lower ball joint or **pinch bolt** (see Figure 14-19).
b. Tie rod end (see Figure 14-20).
c. Stabilizer bar link.
d. Front disc brake caliper.

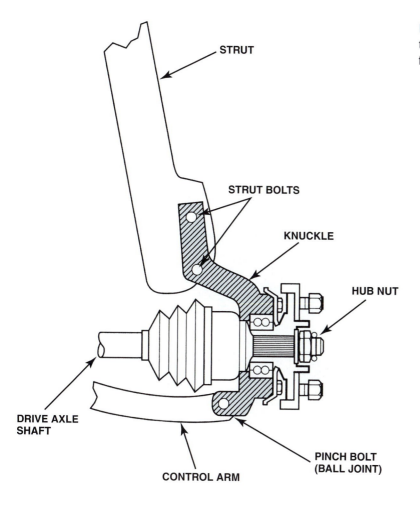

STRUT

STRUT BOLTS

KNUCKLE

HUB NUT

DRIVE AXLE
SHAFT

PINCH BOLT
(BALL JOINT)

CONTROL ARM

FIGURE 14-18   The hub nut must be removed before the hub bearing assembly or drive axle shaft can be removed from the vehicle.

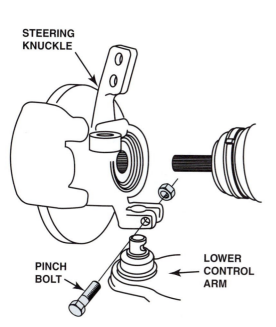

STEERING
KNUCKLE

PINCH
BOLT

LOWER
CONTROL
ARM

FIGURE 14-19   Many knuckles are attached to the ball joint on the lower control arm by a pinch bolt.

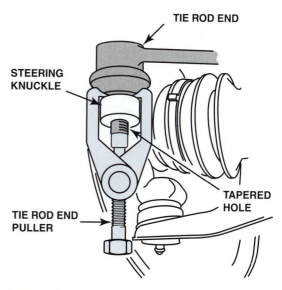

TIE ROD END

STEERING
KNUCKLE

TIE ROD END
PULLER

TAPERED
HOLE

FIGURE 14-20   A tie rod end puller can be used to separate the tapered stud of the tie rod from the tapered hole on the steering knuckle after the retaining nut is removed. Without a puller, a tie rod end can be separated from a knuckle by prying upward on the tie rod end and striking the knuckle with a heavy hammer. The shock "breaks the taper," releasing the tie rod end stud.

Step 3   Remove the splined end of the axle from the hub bearing. Sometimes a special puller may be necessary, but in most cases the shaft can be tapped inward through the hub bearing with a light hammer and a brass punch can be used. To protect the threads of the drive axle shaft, install the hub nut temporarily. See Figures 14-21 and 14-22.

Step 4   Use a prybar or special tool with a slide hammer, as shown in Figure 14-23, and remove the inner joint from the transaxle.

Step 5   Disassemble, clean, and inspect all components. See Figures 14-24 through 14-30.

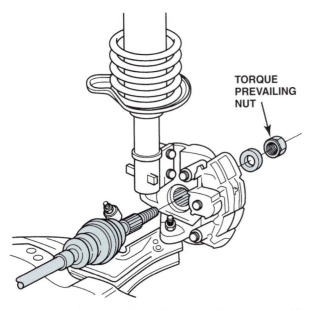

FIGURE 14-21   Many drive axles are retained by **torque prevailing nuts** that must not be reused. Torque prevailing nuts are slightly deformed or contain a plastic insert that holds the nut tight (retains the torque) to the shaft without loosening.

FIGURE 14-22   A special General Motors tool is being used to separate the drive axle shaft from the wheel hub bearing.

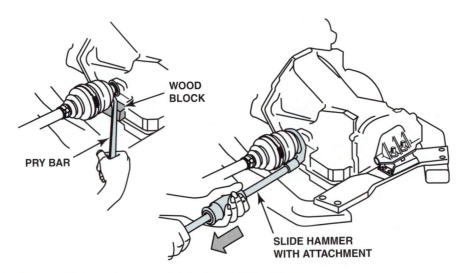

FIGURE 14-23   Most inner CV joints can be separated from the transaxle with a prybar.

FIGURE 14-24   When removing a drive axle shaft assembly, use care to avoid pulling the plunge joint apart.

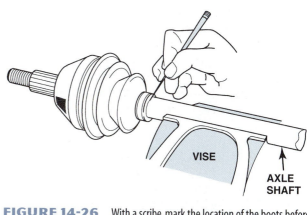

FIGURE 14-26   With a scribe, mark the location of the boots before removal. The replacement boots must be in the same location.

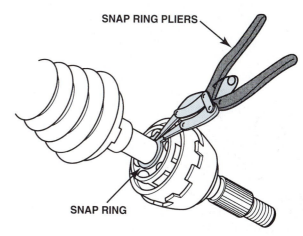

FIGURE 14-27   Most CV joints use a snap ring to retain the joint on the drive axle shaft.

FIGURE 14-25   If other service work requires that just one end of the drive axle shaft be disconnected from the vehicle, be sure that the free end is supported to prevent damage to the protective boots or allowing the joint to separate. The method shown using a shop cloth to tie up one end may not be very pretty, but at least the technician took precautions to support the end of the shaft while removing the transaxle to replace a clutch.

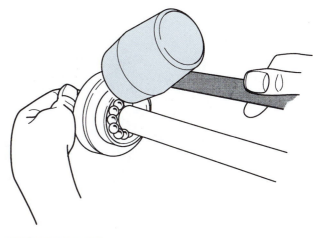

FIGURE 14-28   After releasing the snap ring, most CV joints can be tapped off the shaft using a brass or shot-filled plastic (dead-blow) hammer.

FIGURE 14-29 Typical outer CV joint after removing the boot and the joint from the drive axle shaft. This joint was removed from the vehicle because a torn boot was found. After disassembly and cleaning, this joint was found to be OK and was put back into service. Even though the grease looks terrible, there was enough grease in the joint to provide enough lubrication to prevent any wear from occurring.

FIGURE 14-30 The cage of this Rzeppa-type CV joint is rotated so that one ball at a time can be removed. Some joints require that the technician use a brass punch and a hammer to move the cage.

TECH TIP

SPLINE BIND CURE

Drive line "clunk" often occurs in rear-wheel-drive vehicles when shifting between drive and reverse or when accelerating from a stop. Often the cause of this noise is excessive clearance between the teeth of the ring and pinion in the differential. Another cause is called **spline bind,** where the changing rear pinion angle creates a binding in the spline when the rear springs change in height. For example, when a pickup truck stops, the weight transfers toward the front and unloads the rear springs. The front of the differential noses downward and forward as the rear springs unload. When the driver accelerates forward, the rear of the truck squats downward, causing the drive shaft to be pulled rearward when the front of the differential rotates upward. This upward movement on the spline often causes the spline to bind and make a loud clunk when the bind is finally released.

The method recommended by vehicle manufacturers to eliminate this noise is to follow these steps:

1. Remove the drive shaft.
2. Clean the splines on both the drive shaft yoke and the transmission output shaft.
3. Remove any burrs on the splines with a small metal file (remove all filings).
4. Apply a high-temperature grease to the spline teeth of the yoke. Apply grease to each spline, but do not fill the splines. Synthetic chassis grease is preferred because of its high temperature resistance.
5. Reinstall the drive shaft.

Step 6   Replace the entire joint if there are *any* worn parts. Pack *all* the grease that is supplied into the assembly or joint. See Figure 14-31. Assemble the joint and position the boot in the same location as marked. Before clamping the last seal on the boot, be sure to release trapped air to prevent the boot from expanding when heated and collapsing when cold. This is sometimes called *burping the boot.* Clamp the boot according to the manufacturer's specifications.

Step 7   Reinstall the drive axle shaft in the reverse order of removal, and torque the drive axle nut to factory specifications. See Figure 14-32.

FIGURE 14-31 Be sure to use *all* of the grease supplied with the replacement joint or boot kit. Use only the grease supplied and do not use substitute grease.

FIGURE 14-32 A screwdriver is shown, but a punch would be better, to keep the rotor from rotating while removing or installing the drive axle shaft spindle nut.

REAL WORLD FIX

THE VIBRATING BUICK

The owner of a front-wheel-drive Buick complained that it vibrated during acceleration only. The vehicle would also pull toward one side during acceleration. An inspection discovered a worn (cracked) engine mount. After replacing the mount, the CV joint angles were restored and both the vibration and the pulling to one side during acceleration were solved. See Figure 14-33.

(a)

(b)

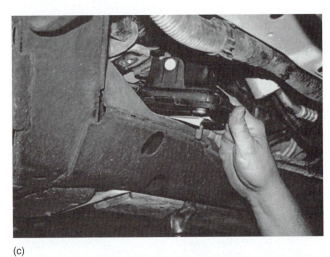

(c)

FIGURE 14-33   (a) Before the engine mount could be replaced, the vehicle was hoisted and a tall safety stand was placed under the engine. The stand was adjustable, thereby allowing the technician to raise the engine slightly to get the old mount out. (b) The old engine mount was torn and shorter than the replacement. (c) The engine had to be raised higher to get the new (noncollapsed) engine mount installed.

DRIVE AXLE SHAFT REPLACEMENT   Step-by-Step

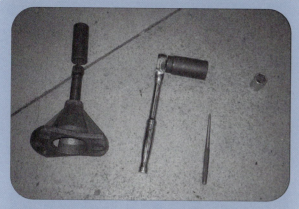

STEP 1   Tools needed to replace a drive axle shaft on a General Motors vehicle include a drift, sockets, plus a prybar bearing/axle shaft special tool.

STEP 2   The drive axle shaft retaining nut can be loosened with the tire on the ground, or use a drift inserted into the rotor cooling fins before removing the nut.

STEP 3   Using a special tool to push the drive axle splines from the bearing assembly.

STEP 4   Remove the disc brake caliper and support it out of the way. Then, remove the disc brake rotor.

STEP 5   To allow for the removal of the drive axle shaft, the strut is removed from the steering knuckle assembly.

STEP 6   A prybar is used to separate the inner drive axle shaft joint from the transaxle.

(continued)

DRIVE AXLE SHAFT REPLACEMENT continued

STEP 7 After the inner joint splines have been released from the transaxle, carefully remove the drive axle shaft assembly from the vehicle.

STEP 8 To install, reverse the disassembly procedure and be sure to install the washer under the retainer-nut, and always use a new prevailing torque nut.

STEP 9 Reinstall the disc brake rotor and caliper and then torque the drive axle shaft retaining nut to factory specifications.

SUMMARY

1. A defective U-joint often makes a *clicking* sound when the vehicle is driven in reverse. Severely defective U-joints can cause drive line vibrations or a *clunk* sound when the transmission is shifted from Reverse to Drive or from Drive to Reverse.

2. Incorrect drive shaft working angles can result from collapsed engine or transmission mounts.

3. Drive line clunk noise can often be corrected by applying high-temperature chassis grease to the splines of the front yoke on the drive shaft.

4. CV joints require careful cleaning, inspection, and lubrication with specific CV joint grease.

REVIEW QUESTIONS

1. List two items that should be checked when inspecting a drive shaft.

2. List the steps necessary to measure drive shaft U-joint working angles.

3. Describe how to replace a Cardan-type U-joint.

4. Explain the proper steps to perform when replacing a CV joint.

CHAPTER QUIZ

1. Two technicians are discussing U-joints. Technician A says that a defective U-joint could cause a loud clunk when the transmission is shifted between Drive and Reverse. Technician B says a worn U-joint can cause a clicking sound only when driving the vehicle in reverse. Which technician is correct?
   a. Technician A only
   b. Technician B only
   c. Both Technicians A and B
   d. Neither Technician A nor B

2. Incorrect or unequal U-joint working angles are most likely to be caused by _____.
   a. A bent drive shaft
   b. A collapsed engine or transmission mount
   c. A dry output shaft spline
   d. Defective or damaged U-joints

3. A defective outer CV joint will usually make a _____.
   a. Rumbling noise
   b. Growling noise
   c. Clicking noise
   d. Clunking noise

4. The last step after installing a replacement CV boot is to _____.
   a. "Burp the boot"
   b. Lubricate the CV joint with chassis grease
   c. Mark the location of the boot on the drive axle shaft
   d. Separate the CV joint before installation

5. Cardan-type U-joints should be removed from a drive shaft yoke using _____.
   a. A special tool
   b. A torch
   c. A press or a vise
   d. A torque wrench

6. Two technicians are discussing CV joints. Technician A says that the entire front suspension has to be disassembled to remove most CV joints. Technician B says that most CV joints are bolted onto the drive axle shaft. Which technician is correct?
   a. Technician A only
   b. Technician B only
   c. Both Technicians A and B
   d. Neither Technician A nor B

7. The splines of the drive shaft yoke should be lubricated to prevent _____.

   a. A vibration

   b. Spline bind

   c. Rust

   d. Transmission fluid leaking from the extension housing

8. It is recommended by many experts that an air impact wrench *not* be used to remove or install the drive axle shaft nut because the impacting force can damage the hub bearing.

   a. True

   b. False

9. Front and rear drive shaft U-joint working angles should be within _____ degrees of each other.

   a. 0.5

   b. 1.0

   c. 3.0

   d. 4.0

10. A defective (collapsed) engine mount on a front-wheel-drive vehicle can cause a vibration.

    a. True

    b. False

CHAPTER 15

WHEEL ALIGNMENT PRINCIPLES

OBJECTIVES

After studying Chapter 15, the reader should be able to:

1. Prepare for Suspension and Steering (A4) ASE certification test content area "D" (Wheel Alignment Diagnosis, Adjustment, and Repair).

2. Discuss which vehicle handling problems can and cannot be corrected by an alignment.

3. Define camber, toe, caster, SAI, included angle, scrub radius, turning radius, setback, and thrust line.

4. Explain how camber, caster, and toe affect the handling and tire wear of the vehicle.

KEY TERMS

BJI (p. 358)
Camber (p. 347)
Camber Roll (p. 350)
Caster (p. 350)
Drift (p. 346)
Four-Wheel Alignment (p. 364)
Included Angle (p. 358)
KPI (p. 358)
Lead (p. 346)
MSI (p. 358)
Pull (p. 346)
Returnability (p. 351)
Road Crown (p. 346)

SAI (p. 358)
Scrub Radius (p. 358)
Setback (p. 362)
Shimmy (p. 346)
Steering Dampener (p. 352)
Steering Offset (p. 359)
Thrust Line (p. 363)
Toe (p. 353)
TOOT (p. 361)
Tracking (p. 364)
Tramp (p. 346)
Wander (p. 346)

A wheel alignment is the adjustment of the suspension and steering to ensure proper vehicle handling with minimum tire wear. When a vehicle is new, the alignment angles are set at the factory. After many miles and/or months of driving, the alignment angles can change slightly. The change in alignment angles may result from one or more of the following conditions:

1. Wear of the steering and the suspension components
2. Bent or damaged steering and suspension parts
3. Sagging springs, which can change the ride height of the vehicle and therefore the alignment angles

By adjusting the suspension and steering components, proper alignment angles can be restored. An alignment includes checking and adjusting, if necessary, both front and rear wheels.

ALIGNMENT-RELATED PROBLEMS

Most alignment diagnosis is symptom-based diagnosis. This means that the problem with the alignment is determined from symptoms such as excessive tire wear or a pull to one side of the road. The definitions of alignment symptom terms used in this book are discussed next.

Pull

A **pull** is generally defined as a definite tug on the steering wheel toward the left or the right while driving straight on a level road. See Figure 15-1. Bent, damaged, or worn suspension and/or steering components can cause this problem, as well as a tire problem.

Lead or Drift

A **lead** or **drift** is a mild pull that does not cause a force on the steering wheel that the driver must counteract. A lead or drift is observed by momentarily removing your hands from the steering wheel while driving on a straight, level road. When the vehicle moves toward one side or the other, this is called a lead or a drift.

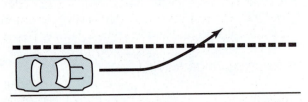

PULL

FIGURE 15-1 A pull is usually defined as a tug on the steering wheel toward one side or the other.

CAUTION: When test-driving a vehicle for a lead or a drift, make sure that the road is free of traffic and that your hands remain close to the steering wheel. Your hands should be held away from the steering wheel for just a second or two—just long enough to check for a lead or drift condition.

Road Crown Effects

Most roads are constructed with a slight angle to permit water to drain from the road surface. On a two-lane road, the center of the road is often higher than the berms, resulting in a **road crown.** See Figure 15-2.

On a four-lane expressway (freeway), the crown is often *between the two sets* of lanes. Because of this slight angle to the road, some vehicles may lead or drift away from the road crown. In other words, it may be perfectly normal for a vehicle to lead toward the right while being driven in the slow lane and toward the left while being driven in the fast (or inside) lane of a typical divided highway.

Wander

A **wander** is a condition where constant steering wheel corrections are necessary to maintain a straight-ahead direction on a straight, level road. See Figure 15-3.

Worn suspension and/or steering components are the most likely cause of this condition. Incorrect or unequal alignment angles such as caster and toe, as well as defective tire(s), can also cause this condition.

Stiff Steering or Slow Return to Center

Hard-to-steer problems are commonly caused by leaks, either low tire pressure (due to the leak of air) and/or lack of proper power steering (due to the leak of power steering fluid). Other causes include excessive positive caster on the front wheels or binding steering linkage.

Tramp or Shimmy Vibration

Tramp is a vertical-type (up-and-down) vibration usually caused by out-of-balance or defective tires or wheels. **Shimmy** is a back-and-forth vibration that can be caused by an out-of-balance tire or defective wheel or by an alignment problem.

NOTE: Wheel alignment will not correct a tramp-type vibration.

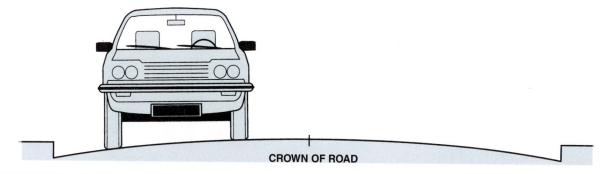

FIGURE 15-2   The crown of the road refers to the angle or slope of the roadway needed to drain water off the pavement.

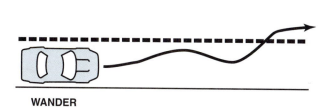

WANDER

FIGURE 15-3   Wander is an unstable condition requiring constant driver corrections.

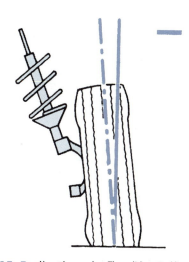

FIGURE 15-5   Negative camber. The solid vertical line represents true vertical, and the dotted line represents the angle of the tire. *(Courtesy of Hunter Engineering Company)*

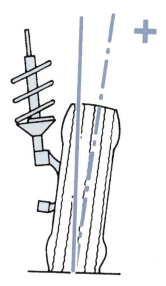

FIGURE 15-4   Positive camber. The solid vertical line represents true vertical, and the dotted line represents the angle of the tire. *(Courtesy of Hunter Engineering Company)*

CAMBER

Camber *is the inward or outward tilt of the wheels from true vertical as viewed from the front or rear of the vehicle.*

1. If the top of the tire is tilted out, then camber is positive (+), as shown in Figure 15-4.

2. If the top of the tire is tilted in, then camber is negative (−), as shown in Figure 15-5.
3. Camber is zero (0 degrees) if the tilt of the wheel is true vertical, as shown in Figure 15-6.
4. Camber is measured in degrees or fractions of degrees.
5. *Camber can cause tire wear if not correct.*
   a. *Excessive positive camber* causes scuffing and wear on the outside edge of the tire, as shown in Figure 15-7.
   b. *Excessive negative camber* causes scuffing and wear on the inside edge of the tire, as shown in Figure 15-8.
6. Camber can cause pull if it is unequal side-to-side. **The vehicle will pull toward the side with the most positive camber.** A difference of more than 1/2 degree from one side to the other will cause the vehicle to pull. See Figures 15-9 through 15-11.
7. Incorrect camber can cause excessive wear on wheel bearings, as shown in Figures 15-12 and 15-13. Many vehicle manufacturers specify positive camber so that the vehicle's weight is applied to the larger inner wheel bearing and spindle. As the vehicle is loaded or when the

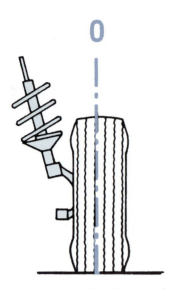

FIGURE 15-6   Zero camber. Note that the angle of the tire is true vertical. *(Courtesy of Hunter Engineering Company)*

springs sag, camber usually decreases. If camber is kept positive, then the running camber is kept near zero degrees for best tire life.

NOTE: Many front-wheel-drive vehicles that use sealed wheel bearings often specify negative camber.

8. Camber is *not* adjustable on many vehicles.
9. If camber is adjustable, the change is made by moving the upper or the lower control arm or strut assembly by means of one of the following methods:
    a. Shims
    b. Eccentric cams
    c. Slots
       See Chapter 16 for camber adjustment methods and procedures.
10. Camber should be equal on both sides; however, if camber cannot be adjusted exactly equal, make certain that

FIGURE 15-7   Excessive positive camber and how the front tires would wear due to the excessive camber. *(Courtesy of Hunter Engineering Company)*

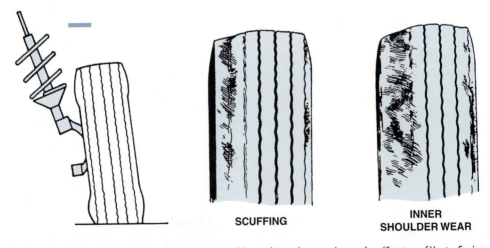

FIGURE 15-8   Excessive negative camber and how the front tires would wear due to the excessive camber. *(Courtesy of Hunter Engineering Company)*

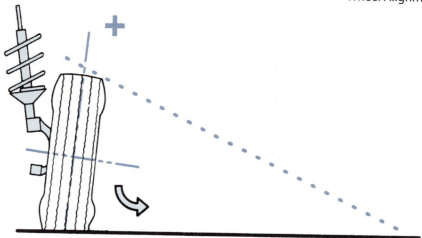

FIGURE 15-9   Positive camber tilts the tire and forms a cone shape that causes the wheel to roll away or pull outward toward the point of the cone. *(Courtesy of Hunter Engineering Company)*

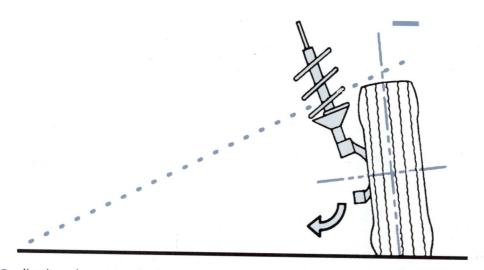

FIGURE 15-10   Negative camber creates a pulling force toward the center of the vehicle. *(Courtesy of Hunter Engineering Company)*

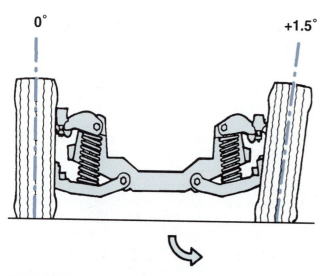

FIGURE 15-11   If camber angles are different from one side to the other, the vehicle will pull toward the side with the most camber. *(Courtesy of Hunter Engineering Company)*

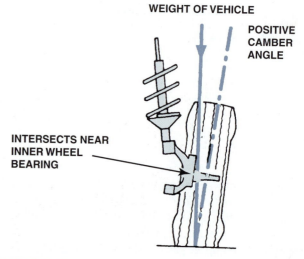

FIGURE 15-12   Positive camber applies the vehicle weight toward the larger inner wheel bearing. This is desirable because the larger inner bearing is designed to carry more vehicle weight than the smaller outer bearing. *(Courtesy of Hunter Engineering Company)*

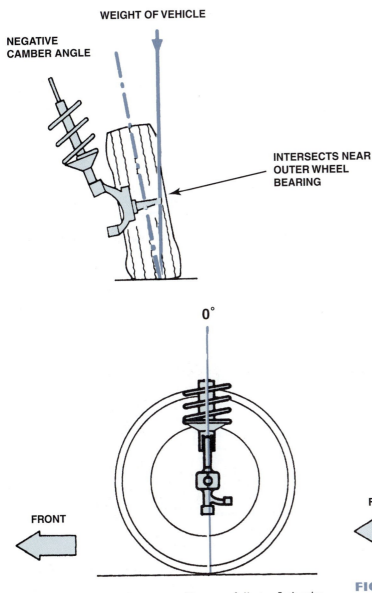

NEGATIVE CAMBER ANGLE

WEIGHT OF VEHICLE

INTERSECTS NEAR OUTER WHEEL BEARING

FIGURE 15-13 Negative camber applies the vehicle weight to the smaller outer wheel bearing. Excessive negative camber, therefore, may contribute to outer wheel bearing failure. *(Courtesy of Hunter Engineering Company)*

0°

FRONT

FIGURE 15-14 Zero caster. *(Courtesy of Hunter Engineering Company)*

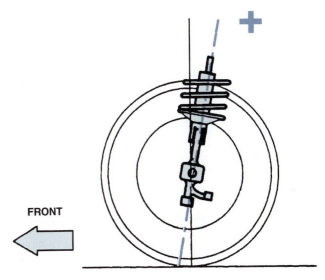

+

FRONT

FIGURE 15-15 Positive (+) caster. *(Courtesy of Hunter Engineering Company)*

there is more camber on the front of the left side to help compensate for the road crown (1/2 degree maximum difference).

CASTER

Caster *is the forward or rearward tilt of the steering axis in reference to a vertical line as viewed from the side of the vehicle.* The steering axis is defined as the line drawn through the upper and lower steering pivot points. On an SLA suspension system, the upper pivot is the upper ball joint and the lower pivot is the lower ball joint. On a MacPherson strut system, the upper pivot is the center of the upper bearing mount and the lower pivot point is the lower ball joint. Zero caster

means that the steering axis is straight up and down, also called 0 degrees or perfectly vertical, as shown in Figure 15-14.

1. Positive (+) caster is present when the upper suspension pivot point is behind the lower pivot point (ball joint) as viewed from the side. See Figure 15-15.
2. Negative (−) caster is present when the upper suspension pivot point is ahead of the lower pivot point (ball joint) as viewed from the side. See Figure 15-16.
3. Caster is measured in degrees or fractions of degrees.
4. Caster is not a tire-wearing angle, but positive caster does cause changes in camber during a turn. See Figure 15-17. This condition is called **camber roll** (see the Tech Tip titled "Caster Angle Tire Wear").

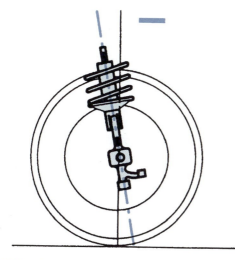

FRONT

FIGURE 15-16 Negative (−) caster is seldom specified on today's vehicles because it tends to make the vehicle unstable at highway speeds. Negative caster was specified on some older vehicles not equipped with power steering to help reduce the steering effort. *(Courtesy of Hunter Engineering Company)*

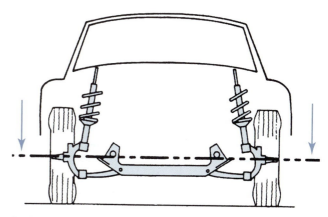

FIGURE 15-18 Vehicle weight tends to lower the spindle, which returns the steering to the straight-ahead position. *(Courtesy of Hunter Engineering Company)*

FIGURE 15-17 As the spindle rotates, it lifts the weight of the vehicle due to the angle of the steering axis. *(Courtesy of Hunter Engineering Company)*

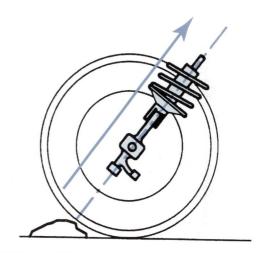

FIGURE 15-19 High caster provides a road shock path to the vehicle. *(Courtesy of Hunter Engineering Company)*

5. Caster is a stability angle.
   a. If caster is excessively positive, the vehicle steering will be very stable (will tend to go straight with little steering wheel correction needed). This degree of caster helps with steering wheel **returnability** after a turn. See Figure 15-18.
   b. If the caster is positive, steering effort will increase with increasing positive caster. Greater road shocks will be felt by the driver when driving over rough road surfaces. See Figure 15-19. Vehicles with as many as 11 degrees positive caster usually use a steering dampener to control possible shimmy at high speeds and to dampen the snap-back of the spindle after a turn. See Figure 15-20.

   c. If caster is negative, or excessively unequal, the vehicle will not be as stable and will tend to wander (constant steering wheel movement will be required to maintain straight-ahead direction). If a vehicle is heavily loaded in the rear, caster increases. See Figure 15-21.
6. Caster can cause pull if unequal; **the vehicle will pull toward the side with the least positive caster**. However, the pulling force of unequal caster is only about one-fourth the pulling force of camber. It would require a difference of caster of one full degree to equal the pulling force of only $1/4$-degree difference of camber.
7. Caster is *not* adjustable on many vehicles.

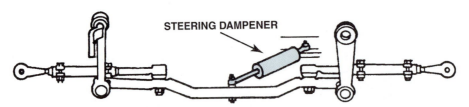

FIGURE 15-20 A **steering dampener** is used on many pickup trucks, sport utility vehicles (SUVs), and many luxury vehicles designed with a high-positive-caster setting. The dampener helps prevent steering wheel kickback when the front tires hit a bump or hole in the road and also helps reduce steering wheel shimmy that may result from the high-caster setting. *(Courtesy of Hunter Engineering Company)*

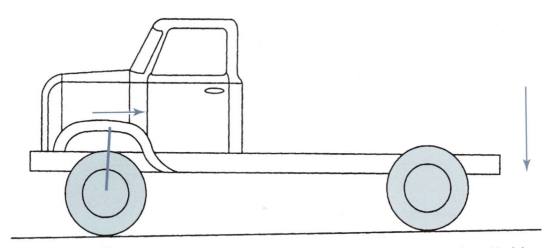

FIGURE 15-21 As the load increases in the rear of a vehicle, the top steering axis pivot point moves rearward, increasing positive (+) caster. *(Courtesy of Hunter Engineering Company)*

8. If caster is adjustable, it is changed by moving either the lower or the upper pivot point forward or backward by means of the following:
   a. Shims
   b. Eccentric cams
   c. Slots
   d. Strut rods
9. Caster should be equal on both sides; however, if caster cannot be adjusted to be exactly equal, make certain that there is more caster on the right side (maximum 1/2-degree difference) to help compensate for the crown of the road.

NOTE: Caster is only measured on the front turning wheels of the vehicle. While some caster is built into the rear suspension of many vehicles, rear caster is not measured as part of a four-wheel alignment.

TECH TIP

CASTER ANGLE TIRE WEAR

The caster angle is generally considered to be a *non-tire-wearing* angle. However, excessive or unequal caster can *indirectly* cause tire wear. When the front wheels are turned on a vehicle with a lot of positive caster, they become angled. This is called *camber roll.* (Caster angle is a measurement of the difference in camber angle from when the wheel is turned inward compared to when the wheel is turned outward.) Most vehicle manufacturers have positive caster designed into the suspension system. This positive caster increases the directional stability.

However, if the vehicle is used exclusively in city driving, positive caster can cause tire wear to the outside shoulders of both front tires. See Figure 15-22.

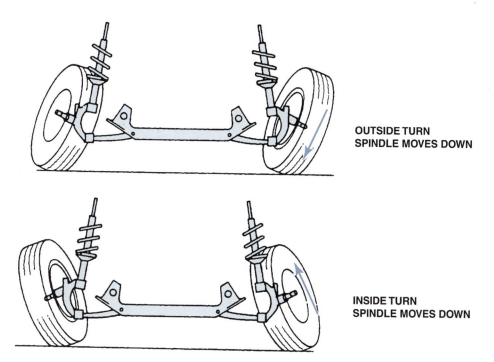

**OUTSIDE TURN
SPINDLE MOVES DOWN**

**INSIDE TURN
SPINDLE MOVES DOWN**

FIGURE 15-22   Note how the front tire becomes tilted as the vehicle turns a corner with positive caster. The higher the caster angle, the more the front tires tilt, causing camber-type tire wear. *(Courtesy of Hunter Engineering Company)*

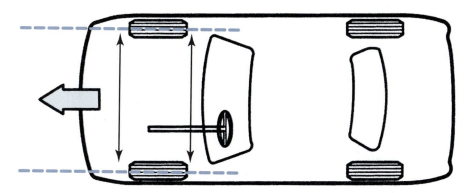

FIGURE 15-23   Zero toe. Note how both tires are parallel to each other as viewed from above the vehicle. *(Courtesy of Hunter Engineering Company)*

TOE

Toe *is the difference in distance between the front and rear of the tires.* As viewed from the top of the vehicle (a bird's eye view), zero toe means that both wheels on the same axle are parallel, as shown in Figure 15-23.

Toe is also described as a comparison of horizontal lines drawn through both wheels on the same axle, as shown in Figure 15-24.

If the front of the tires is closer than the rear of the same tires, then the toe is called *toe-in* or positive (+) toe. See Figure 15-25.

If the front of the tires is farther apart than the rear of the same tires, then the wheels are *toed-out,* or have negative (−) toe. See Figure 15-26.

The purpose of the correct toe setting is to provide maximum stability with a minimum of tire wear when the vehicle is being driven.

1. Toe is measured in fractions of degrees or in fractions of an inch (usually 1/16s), millimeters (mm), or decimals of an inch (such as 0.06 in.).
2. *Incorrect toe is the major cause of excessive tire wear!* See Figure 15-27.

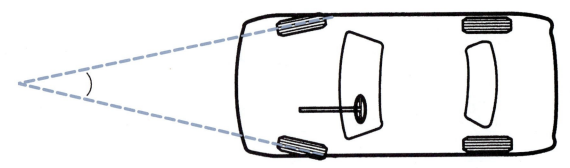

FIGURE 15-24 Total toe is often expressed as an angle. Because both front wheels are tied together through the tie rods and center link, the toe angle is always equally split between the two front wheels when the vehicle moves forward. *(Courtesy of Hunter Engineering Company)*

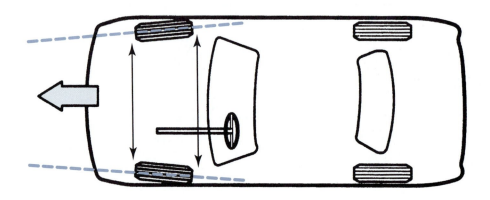

FIGURE 15-25 Toe-in, also called positive (+) toe. *(Courtesy of Hunter Engineering Company)*

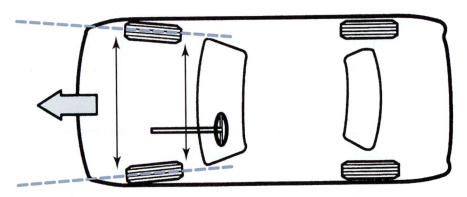

FIGURE 15-26 Toe-out, also called negative (−) toe. *(Courtesy of Hunter Engineering Company)*

NOTE: If the toe is improper by just 1/8 in. (3 mm), the resulting tire wear is equivalent to dragging a tire sideways 28 feet (8.5 m) for every mile traveled (1.6 km).

If not correct, toe causes camber-type wear on one side of the tire. See Figures 15-28 and 15-29. Feather-edge wear is also common, especially if the vehicle is equipped with nonradial tires. See Figure 15-30.

3. *Incorrect front toe does not cause a pull condition.* Incorrect toe on the front wheels is split equally as the vehicle is driven because the forces acting on the tires are exerted through the tie rod and steering linkage to both wheels.

4. *Incorrect (or unequal) rear toe can cause tire wear.* See Figures 15-31 through 15-33. If the toe of the rear wheels is not equal, the steering wheel will not be straight and will pull toward the side with the most toe-in.

5. Front toe adjustment must be made correctly by adjusting the tie rod sleeves. See Figure 15-34.

FIGURE 15-27 This tire is just one month old! It was new and installed on the front of a vehicle that had about $\frac{1}{4}$ inch (6 mm) of toe-out. By the time the customer returned to the tire store for an alignment, the tire was completely bald on the inside. Note the almost new tread on the outside.

6. Many vehicle manufacturers specify a slight amount of toe-in to compensate for the natural tendency of the front wheels to spread apart (become toed-out) due to centrifugal force of the rolling wheels acting on the steering linkage.

NOTE: Some manufacturers of front-wheel-drive vehicles specify a toe-out setting to compensate for the toe-in forces created by the engine drive forces on the front wheels.

7. Normal wear to the tie rod ends and other steering linkage parts usually causes toe-out.

Excessive front toe-out will cause wandering (lack of directional stability), especially during braking. Incorrectly set toe will cause an uncentered steering wheel. If toe is unequal in the *rear*, the vehicle will pull toward the side with the most toe-in.

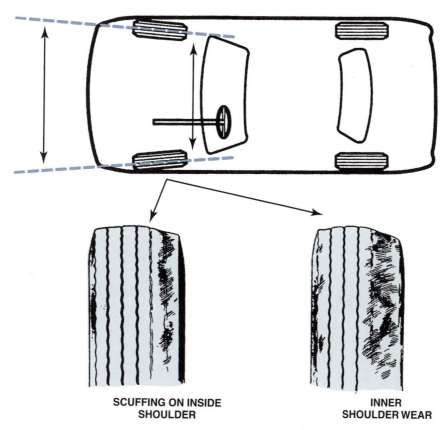

SCUFFING ON INSIDE SHOULDER

INNER SHOULDER WEAR

FIGURE 15-28 Excessive toe-out and the type of wear that can occur to the inside of the left front tire. *(Courtesy of Hunter Engineering Company)*

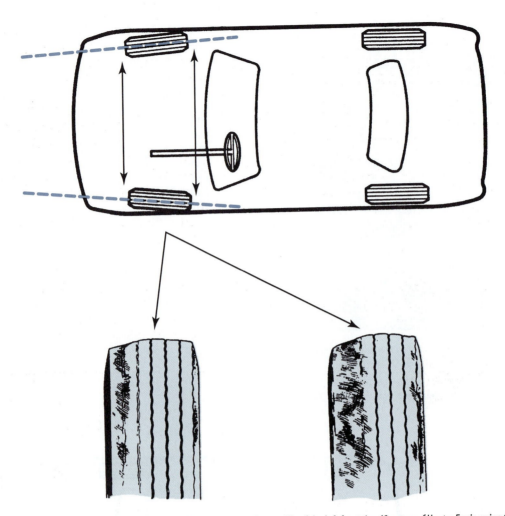

FIGURE 15-29 Excessive toe-in and the type of wear that can occur to the outside of the left front tire. *(Courtesy of Hunter Engineering Company)*

FIGURE 15-30 Feather-edge wear pattern caused by excessive toe-in or toe-out. *(Courtesy of Hunter Engineering Company)*

FREQUENTLY ASKED QUESTION

WHY DOESN'T UNEQUAL FRONT TOE ON THE FRONT WHEELS CAUSE THE VEHICLE TO PULL?

Each wheel could have individual toe, but as the vehicle is being driven, the forces on the tires tend to split the toe, causing the steering wheel to cock at an angle as the front wheels both track the same. If the toe is different on the rear of the vehicle, the rear will be "steered" similar to a rudder on a boat because the rear wheels are not tied together as are the front wheels.

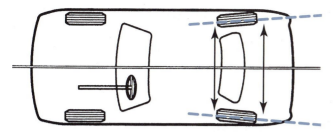

FIGURE 15-31   Rear toe-in (+). The rear toe (unlike the front toe) can be different for each wheel while the vehicle is moving forward because the rear wheels are not tied together as they are in the front. *(Courtesy of Hunter Engineering Company)*

FIGURE 15-32   Incorrect toe can cause the tire to run sideways as it rolls, resulting in a diagonal wipe. *(Courtesy of Hunter Engineering Company)*

FIGURE 15-33   Diagonal wear such as shown here is usually caused by incorrect toe on the rear of a front-wheel-drive vehicle.

TECH TIP

SMOOTH IN, TOED-IN; SMOOTH OUT, TOED-OUT

Whenever the toe setting is not zero, a rubbing action occurs that causes a feather-edge-type wear. See Figure 15-35. A quick, easy method to determine if incorrect toe could be causing problems is simply to rub your hand across the tread of the tire. If it feels smoother moving your hand toward the center of the vehicle than when you move your hand toward the outside, then the cause is excessive toe-in. The opposite effect is caused by toe-out. This may be felt on all types of tires, including radial-ply tires where the wear may not be seen as feather edged. Just remember this simple saying: "Smooth in, toed-in; smooth out, toed-out."

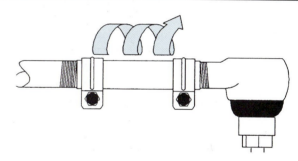

FIGURE 15-34   Toe on the front of most vehicles is adjusted by turning the tire rod sleeve as shown. *(Courtesy of FMC)*

FEATHERED OR SAWTOOTH
TIRE WEAR PATTERN

SHARP EDGES POINT IN THE DIRECTION
OF THE TOE PROBLEM
(IN - TOE IN / OUT TOE OUT)

FIGURE 15-35   While the feathered or sawtooth tire tread wear pattern may not be noticeable to the eye, this wear can usually be felt by rubbing your hand across the tread of the tire. *(Courtesy of FMC)*

STEERING AXIS INCLINATION (SAI)

The steering axis is the angle formed between true vertical and an imaginary line drawn between the upper and lower pivot points of the spindle. See Figure 15-36. **Steering axis inclination (SAI)** is the inward tilt of the steering axis. SAI is also known as **kingpin inclination (KPI)** and is the imaginary line drawn through the kingpin as viewed from the front. SAI is also called **ball joint inclination (BJI),** if SLA-type suspension is used, or **MacPherson strut inclination (MSI).**

The purpose of SAI is to provide an upper suspension pivot location that causes the spindle to travel in an arc when turning, which tends to raise the vehicle, as shown in Figure 15-37.

Vehicle weight tends to keep the front wheels in a straight-ahead position when driving, thereby increasing vehicle stability, directional control, and steering wheel returnability. The greater the SAI, the more stable the vehicle. It also helps center the steering wheel after making a turn and reduces the need for excessive positive caster. The SAI/KPI angle of all vehicles ranges between 2 and 16 degrees. Front-wheel-drive vehicles usually have greater than 9 degrees SAI (typically 12 to 16 degrees) for directional stability, whereas rear-wheel-drive vehicles usually have less than 8 degrees of SAI. The steering axis inclination angle and the camber angle together are called the *included angle.*

INCLUDED ANGLE

The **included angle** is the SAI added to the camber reading of the front wheels only. *The included angle is determined by the design of the steering knuckle, or strut construction.* See Figures 15-38 and 15-39.

Included angle is an important angle to measure for diagnosis of vehicle handling or tire wear problems. For example, if the cradle is out of location due to previous service work or an accident, knowing SAI, camber, and the included angle can help in determining what needs to be done to correct the problem. See Figure 15-40.

If the included angles are equal side-to-side, but the camber is unequal on both sides, then the SAI must be unequal. For best handling, the included angle should be within 1/2 degree of the SAI of the other side of the vehicle.

SCRUB RADIUS

Scrub radius refers to the *distance* between the line through the steering axis and the centerline of the wheel at the contact point with the road surface. See Figure 15-41.

Scrub radius is *not* adjustable and cannot be measured. Scrub radius can be zero, positive, or negative. Zero scrub radius means that the line through the steering axis intersects the centerline of the tire at the road surface. Positive

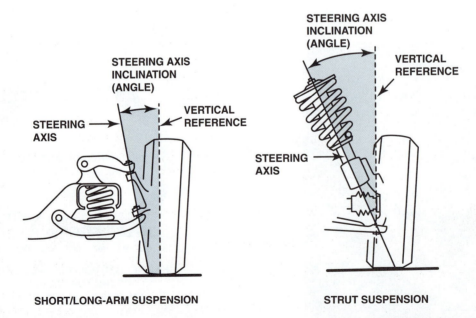

SHORT/LONG-ARM SUSPENSION

STRUT SUSPENSION

FIGURE 15-36 The top illustration shows that the steering axis inclination angle is determined by drawing a line through the center of the upper and lower ball joints. This represents the pivot points of the front wheels when the steering wheel is rotated during cornering. The lower illustration shows that the steering axis inclination angle is determined by drawing a line through the axis of the upper strut bearing mount assembly and the lower ball joint.

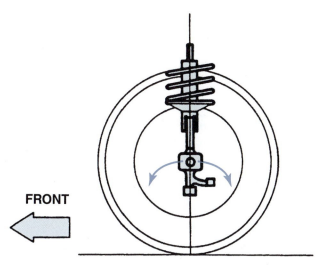

FIGURE 15-37   The SAI causes the spindle to travel in an arc when the wheels are turned. The weight of the vehicle is therefore used to help straighten the front tires after a turn and to help give directional stability. *(Courtesy of Hunter Engineering Company)*

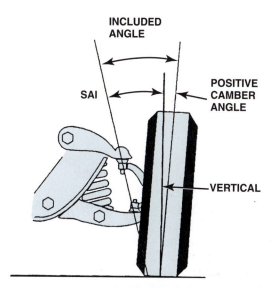

FIGURE 15-39   Included angle on an SLA-type suspension. The included angle is the SAI angle and the camber angle added together. If the camber angle is negative (—) (tire tilted inward at the top), the camber is subtracted from the SAI angle to determine the included angle. *(Courtesy of FMC)*

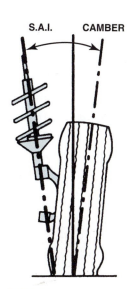

S.A.I. + CAMBER = INCLUDED ANGLE

FIGURE 15-38   Included angle on a MacPherson-strut-type suspension. *(Courtesy of Hunter Engineering Company)*

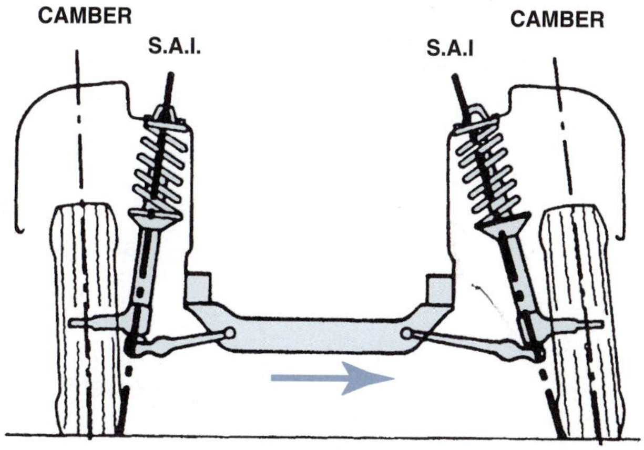

FIGURE 15-40   Cradle placement. If the cradle is not replaced in the exact position after removal for a transmission or clutch replacement, the SAI, camber, and included angle will not be equal side-to-side. *(Courtesy of Hunter Engineering Company)*

scrub radius means that the line intersects the centerline of the tire below the road surface. Negative scrub radius means that the line intersects the centerline of the tire above the road surface. Scrub radius is also called **steering offset** by some vehicle manufacturers. If a wheel is permitted to roll rather than pivot, then steering will be more difficult because a tire can pivot more easily than it can roll while turning the front wheels. If the point of intersection is inside the centerline of the tire and below the road surface, this creates a toe-out force on the front wheels.

Negative scrub radius is required on front-wheel-drive vehicles to provide good steering stability during braking. See Figures 15-42 and 15-43.

Scrub radius is designed into each vehicle to provide acceptable handling and steering control under most conditions. Scrub radius also causes resistance to rolling of the front wheels to exert force on the steering linkage. This tends to dampen the effect of minor movements of the front wheels. Negative scrub radius causes the tire to toe-in during acceleration, braking, or traveling over bumps.

NOTE: It is this tendency to toe-in caused by the negative scrub radius and engine torque that requires many front-wheel-drive vehicles to specify a toe-out setting for the front-drive wheels.

Zero scrub radius is acceptable; positive scrub radius is less desirable because it causes the wheel to toe-out during acceleration, braking, or traveling over bumps and causes instability. Positive scrub radius is commonly used on rear-wheel-drive

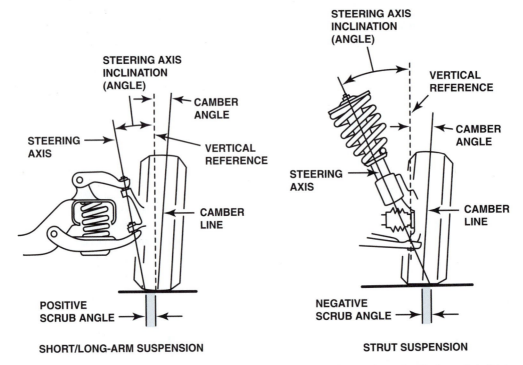

FIGURE 15-41 A positive scrub radius is usually built into most SLA front suspensions, and a negative scrub radius is usually built into most MacPherson-strut-type front suspensions.

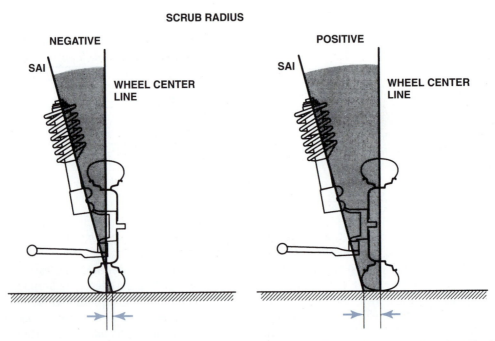

FIGURE 15-42 With negative scrub radius, the imaginary line through the steering axis inclination (SAI) intersects the road outside of the centerline of the tire. With positive scrub radius, the SAI line intersects the road inside the centerline of the tires.

vehicles and requires a toe-in setting to help compensate for the tendency to toe-out.

A bent spindle can cause a change in the scrub radius and could cause hard steering, wander, or pull.

Also, changing tire or wheel sizes can affect the centerline location of the wheel or the height of the tire assembly and will change the scrub radius, which can negatively affect the steering control. When larger-diameter tires and positive-offset wheels are installed, the scrub radius becomes positive and the wheels tend to toe-out, causing wander, poor handling, and tire wear.

TURNING RADIUS (TOE-OUT ON TURNS)

Whenever a vehicle turns a corner, the inside wheel has to turn at a sharper angle than the outside wheel because the inside wheel has a shorter distance to travel. See Figure 15-44.

Turning radius is also called **toe-out on turns,** abbreviated TOT or **TOOT,** and is determined by the angle of the steering knuckle arms. **Turning radius is a nonadjustable angle.** The turning radius can and should be measured as part of an alignment to check if the steering arms are bent or

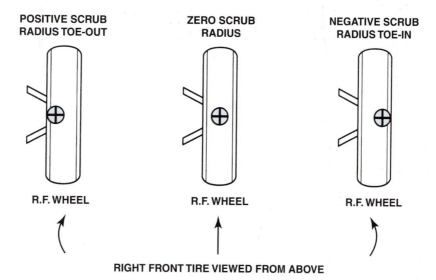

FIGURE 15-43   With a positive scrub radius, the pivot point, marked with a + mark, is inside the centerline of the tire and will cause the wheel to turn toward the outside, especially during braking. Zero scrub radius does not create any force on the tires and is not usually used on vehicles because it does not create an opposing force on the tires, which in turn makes the vehicle more susceptible to minor bumps and dips in the road. Negative scrub radius, as is used with most front-wheel-drive vehicles, generates an inward force on the tires.

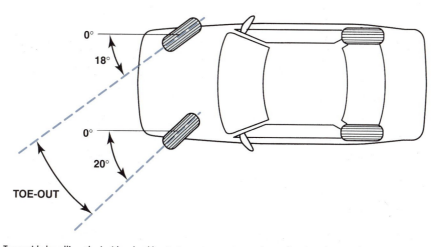

FIGURE 15-44   To provide handling, the inside wheel has to turn at a greater turning radius than the outside wheel.

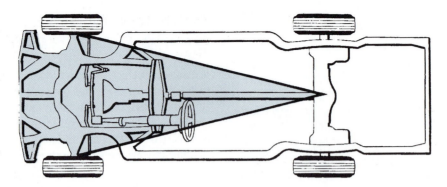

FIGURE 15-45   The proper toe-out on turns is achieved by angling the steering arms. *(Courtesy of Hunter Engineering Company)*

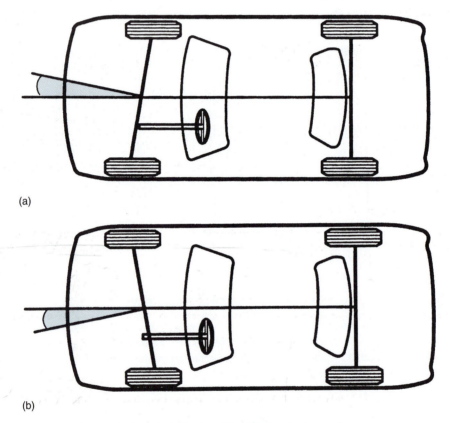

(a)

(b)

FIGURE 15-46   (a) Positive setback. (b) Negative setback. *(Courtesy of Hunter Engineering Company)*

damaged. Symptoms of out-of-specification turning angle include the following:

1. Tire squeal noise during normal cornering, even at low speeds
2. Scuffed tire wear

The proper angle of the steering arms is where imaginary lines drawn from the steering arms should intersect exactly at the center of the rear axle. See Figure 15-45. This angle is called the Ackerman Effect (named for its promoter, an English publisher, Rudolph Ackerman, circa 1898).

SETBACK

Setback is the angle formed by a line drawn perpendicular (at 90 degrees) to the front axles. See Figure 15-46.

Setback is a nonadjustable measurement, even though it may be corrected. Positive setback means the right front wheel is set back farther than the left; negative setback means the left front wheel is set back farther than the right.

Setback can be measured with a four-wheel alignment machine or can be determined by measuring the wheel base on both sides of the vehicle.

The causes of setback include the following:

1. Cradle placement not correct on a front-wheel-drive vehicle. This can be caused by incorrectly installing the cradle after a transmission, clutch, or engine replacement or service. See Figure 15-47.
2. An accident that affected the frame or cradle of the vehicle and was unnoticed or not repaired.

Most vehicle manufacturers do not specify a minimum setback specification. However, a reading of 0.50 degrees or 0.5 in. (13 mm) or less of setback is generally considered to be acceptable.

THRUST ANGLE

Thrust angle is the angle of the rear wheels as determined by the total rear toe. If both rear wheels have zero toe, then the thrust angle is the same as the geometric centerline of the vehicle. The total of the rear toe setting determines the **thrust line,** or the direction the rear wheels are pointed. See Figure 15-48.

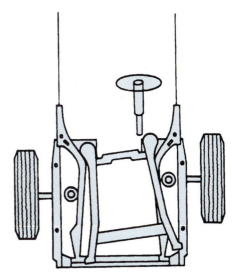

FIGURE 15-47 Cradle placement affects setback. *(Courtesy of Hunter Engineering Company)*

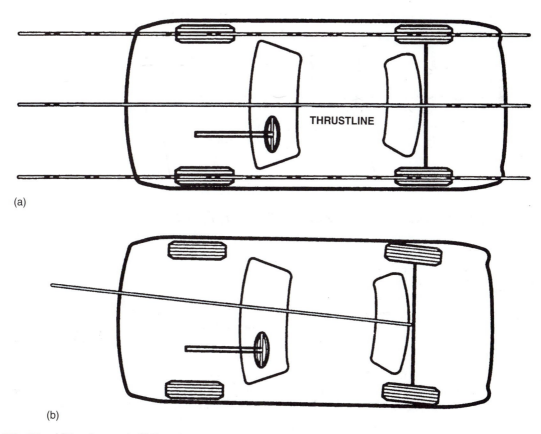

THRUSTLINE

(a)

(b)

FIGURE 15-48 (a) Zero thrust angle. (b) Thrust line to the right. *(Courtesy of Hunter Engineering Company)*

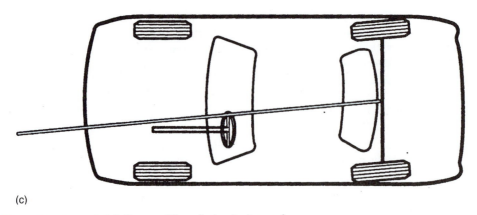

(c)

FIGURE 15-48 (c) Thrust line to the left. *(Courtesy of Hunter Engineering Company)*

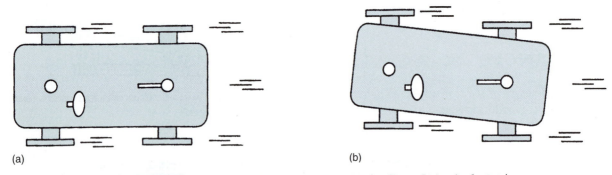

(a) (b)

FIGURE 15-49 (a) Proper tracking. (b) Front wheels steering toward thrust line. *(Courtesy of Hunter Engineering Company)*

On vehicles with an independent rear suspension, if both wheels do not have equal toe, the vehicle will pull in the direction of the side with the most toe-in.

TRACKING

The rear wheels should track directly behind the front wheels. If the vehicle has been involved in an accident, it is possible that the frame or rear axle mounting could cause dog **tracking**.

To check the frame for possible damage, two diagonal measurements of the frame and/or body are required. The diagonal measurements from known points at the front and the rear should be within 1/8 in. (3 mm) of each other. See Figure 15-49.

FOUR-WHEEL ALIGNMENT

Four-wheel alignment refers to the checking and/or adjustment of all four wheels. Four-wheel alignment is important for proper handling and tire wear, to check the camber and the toe of the rear wheels of front-wheel-drive vehicles. Some rear-wheel-drive vehicles equipped with independent rear suspension can be adjusted for camber and toe. Rear-wheel caster cannot be measured or adjusted because to measure caster, the wheels must be turned from straight ahead. Since rear wheels are securely attached, a caster *sweep* (turning the wheels to take a caster reading) is not possible. While rear camber can cause tire wear problems, by far the greatest tire wear occurs due to toe settings. *Unequal* toe in the rear can cause the vehicle to pull or lead. The rear camber and toe are always adjusted first before adjusting the front caster, camber, and toe. This procedure ensures that the thrust line and centerline of the vehicle are the same.

SUMMARY

1. The need for a wheel alignment results from wear or damage to suspension and steering components.

2. Low or unequal tire pressures can often cause symptoms such as wander, pull, and excessive tire wear.

3. Camber is both a pulling angle (if not equal side-to-side) as well as a tire wearing angle (if not set to specifications).

4. Incorrect camber can cause tire wear and pulling if camber is not within 1/2 degree from one side to the other.

5. Toe is the most important alignment angle because toe is usually the first requiring correction. When incorrect, toe causes severe tire wear.

6. Incorrect toe causes excessive tire wear and creates instability if not within specifications.

7. Caster is the basic stability angle, yet it does not cause tire wear (directly) if not correct or equal side-to-side.

8. SAI and included angle (SAI and camber added together) are important diagnostic tools.

9. If the toe-out on turns (TOOT) reading is not within specifications, a bent steering spindle (steering knuckle) is the most likely cause.

10. A four-wheel alignment includes aligning all four wheels of the vehicle; a thrust line alignment sets the front toe equal to the thrust line (total rear toe) of the rear wheels.

REVIEW QUESTIONS

1. Explain the three basic alignment angles of camber, caster, and toe.

2. Describe what happens to tire wear and vehicle handling if toe, camber, and caster are out of specification or *not* equal side-to-side.

3. Explain how knowing SAI, TOOT, and included angle can help in the correct diagnosis of an alignment problem.

4. Explain what thrust angle means.

CHAPTER QUIZ

1. Technician A says that loose tie rod ends can change the camber angle. Technician B says that a defective universal joint between the steering column and the steering gear box stub shaft can cause excessive steering wheel play. Which technician is correct?
   a. Technician A only
   b. Technician B only
   c. Both Technicians A and B
   d. Neither Technician A nor B

2. Technician A says that a vehicle will pull (or lead) to the side with the most camber (or least negative camber). Technician B says that a vehicle will pull (or lead) to the side with the most positive caster. Which technician is correct?
   a. Technician A only
   b. Technician B only
   c. Both Technicians A and B
   d. Neither Technician A nor B

3. Technician A says that the vehicle will pull to the side with the most toe in the rear. Technician B says that the rear toe angle determines the thrust angle. Which technician is correct?
   a. Technician A only
   b. Technician B only
   c. Both Technicians A and B
   d. Neither Technician A nor B

4. Strut rods, if they are adjustable, can be used to adjust which angle?
   a. Toe
   b. Camber
   c. Caster
   d. Toe-out on turns

5. If metal shims are used for alignment adjustment in the front, they adjust _____.

    a. Camber

    b. Caster

    c. Toe

    d. Both a and b

6. Technician A says that as wear occurs, camber usually becomes negative. Technician B says that as steering linkage wear occurs, toe usually becomes toe-out from an original toe-in specification. Which technician is correct?

    a. Technician A only

    b. Technician B only

    c. Both Technicians A and B

    d. Neither Technician A nor B

Use the following information to answer question 7:

Specifications:	Min.	Preferred	Max.
Camber (degree)	0	1.0	1.4
Caster (degree)	.8	1.5	2.1
Toe (inch)	− .10	.06	.15

Results:	L	R
Camber (degree)	− .1	.6
Caster (degree)	1.8	1.6
Toe (inch)	1.12	+ .12

7. The vehicle above will _____.

    a. Pull toward the right and feather-edge both tires

    b. Pull toward the left

    c. Wear the outside of the left tire and the inside of the right tire

    d. None of the above

Use the following information to answer questions 8 and 9:

Specifications:	Min.	Preferred	Max.
Camber (degree)	−1/4	+1/2	1
Caster (degree)	0	+2	+4
Toe (inch)	−1/16	1/16	3/16

Results:	L	R
Camber (degree)	−0.3	−0.1
Caster (degree)	3.6	1.8
Toe (inch)	− .16	+ .32

8. The vehicle above will _____.

    a. Pull toward the left

    b. Pull toward the right

    c. Wander

    d. Lead to the left slightly

9. The vehicle above will _____.

    a. Wander

    b. Wear tires, but will not pull

    c. Will pull, but not wear tires

    d. Pull toward the left and cause feather-edge tire wear

10. Which alignment angle is most likely to need correction and cause the most tire wear?

    a. Toe

    b. Camber

    c. Caster

    d. SAI/KPI

CHAPTER 16

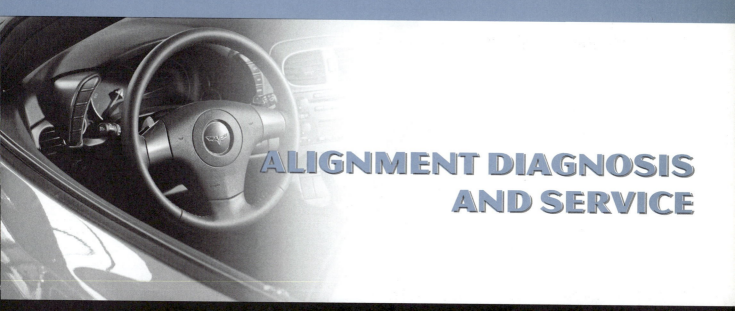

ALIGNMENT DIAGNOSIS AND SERVICE

OBJECTIVES

After studying Chapter 16, the reader should be able to:

1. Prepare for Suspension and Steering (A4) ASE certification test content area "D" (Wheel Alignment Diagnosis, Adjustment, and Repair).
2. List the many checks that should be performed before aligning a vehicle.
3. Describe the proper alignment setup procedure.
4. Explain how to correct for memory steer, torque steer, pull, drift (lead), and wander.
5. Describe the use of unit conversion and diagnostic charts.
6. Discuss tolerance alignment and how to check for accident damage.

Proper wheel alignment of all four wheels is important for the safe handling of any vehicle. When all four wheels are traveling the same path and/or being kept nearly vertical, tire life and fuel economy are maximized and vehicle handling is sure and predictable. A complete wheel alignment is a complex process that includes many detailed steps and the skill of a highly trained technician.

PREALIGNMENT CORRECTION TECHNIQUES

There are four basic steps in the correction of any problem:

1. **Verify.** What, when, where, and to what extent does the problem occur?
2. **Isolate.** Eliminate known good parts and systems. Always start with the simple things first. For example, checking and correcting tire pressure and rotation of the tires should be one of the first things performed whenever trying to isolate the cause of an alignment-related problem.
3. **Repair the problem.** This step involves replacing any worn or damaged components and making sure that the alignment is within factory specifications. See Figure 16-1.
4. **Recheck.** *Always* test drive the vehicle after making a repair. Never allow the customer to be the first to drive the vehicle after any service work.

A thorough inspection of the steering, suspension, and tires should be performed *before* the alignment of the vehicle is begun.

FIGURE 16-1 The owner of this Honda thought that all it needed was an alignment. Obviously, something more serious than an alignment caused this left rear wheel to angle inward at the top.

TECH TIP

ALIGN AND REPLACE AT THE SAME TIME

Magnetic bubble-type camber/caster gauges can be mounted directly on the hub or on an adapter attached to the wheel or spindle nut on front-wheel-drive vehicles. See Figure 16-2. Besides being used as an alignment setting tool, a magnetic alignment head is a great tool to use whenever replacing suspension components.

Any time a suspension component is replaced, the wheel alignment should be checked and corrected as necessary. An easy way to avoid having to make many adjustments is to use a magnetic alignment head on the front wheels to check camber with the vehicle hoisted in the air *before* replacing front components, such as new MacPherson struts. Then, before tightening all of the fasteners, check the front camber readings again to make sure they match the original setting. This is best done when the vehicle is still off the ground. For example, a typical front-wheel-drive vehicle with a MacPherson strut suspension may have a camber reading of +1/4 degree on the ground and +2 degrees while on the hoist with the wheels off the ground. After replacing the struts, simply return the camber reading to +2 degrees and it should return to the same +1/4 degree when lowered to the ground.

Though checking and adjusting camber before and after suspension service work does not guarantee a proper alignment, it does permit the vehicle to be moved around with the alignment fairly accurate until a final alignment can be performed.

PREALIGNMENT CHECKS

Before checking or adjusting the front-end alignment, the following items should be checked and corrected, if necessary, as part of the **prealignment checks:**

1. Check all the tires for proper inflation pressures. Tires should be approximately the same size and tread depth, and the recommended size for the vehicle. See Figure 16-3.

NOTE: Some alignment technicians think that the vehicle must have new tires installed before an accurate alignment can be performed. Excessively worn tires, especially if only one tire is worn, can cause the vehicle to lean slightly. It is this unequal **ride height** that is the important fact to consider. If, for example, all four tires are equally worn, then the vehicle *can* be properly aligned. (Obviously, excessively worn tires should be replaced, and it would be best to align the vehicle with the replacement tires installed to be assured of an accurate alignment.)

2. Check the wheel bearings for proper adjustment.
3. Check for loose ball joints or torn ball joint boots.
4. Check the tie rod ends for damage or looseness.
5. Check the center link or rack bushings for play.
6. Check the pitman arm for any movement.
7. Check for runout of the wheels and the tires.
8. Check for vehicle ride height (should be level front to back as well as side-to-side). Make sure that the factory load-leveling system is functioning correctly, if the vehicle is so equipped. Check height according to the manufacturer's specifications. See Figures 16-4 and 16-5.

NOTE: Manufacturers often have replacement springs or spring spacers that can be installed between the coil spring and the spring seat to restore proper ride level.

9. Check for steering gear looseness at the frame.
10. Check for improperly operating shock absorbers.

FIGURE 16-2   Magnetic bubble-type camber/caster gauge. To help it keep its strong magnetism, it is best to keep it stored stuck to a metal plate as shown here.

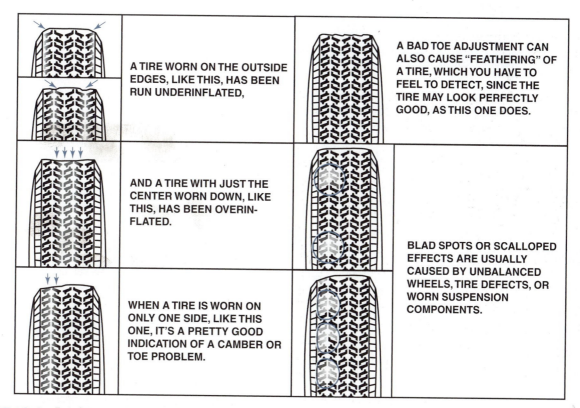

A TIRE WORN ON THE OUTSIDE EDGES, LIKE THIS, HAS BEEN RUN UNDERINFLATED,

AND A TIRE WITH JUST THE CENTER WORN DOWN, LIKE THIS, HAS BEEN OVERINFLATED.

WHEN A TIRE IS WORN ON ONLY ONE SIDE, LIKE THIS ONE, IT'S A PRETTY GOOD INDICATION OF A CAMBER OR TOE PROBLEM.

A BAD TOE ADJUSTMENT CAN ALSO CAUSE "FEATHERING" OF A TIRE, WHICH YOU HAVE TO FEEL TO DETECT, SINCE THE TIRE MAY LOOK PERFECTLY GOOD, AS THIS ONE DOES.

BLAD SPOTS OR SCALLOPED EFFECTS ARE USUALLY CAUSED BY UNBALANCED WHEELS, TIRE DEFECTS, OR WORN SUSPENSION COMPONENTS.

FIGURE 16-3   Typical tire wear chart as found in a service manual. Abnormal tire wear usually indicates a fault in a steering or suspension component that should be corrected or replaced before an alignment is performed.

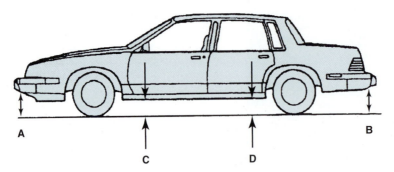

FIGURE 16-4   Measuring points for ride (trim) height vary by manufacturer. *(Courtesy of Hunter Engineering Company)*

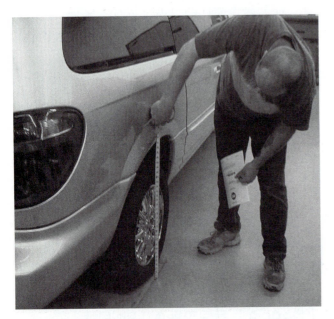

FIGURE 16-5   Measuring to be sure the left and right sides of the vehicle are of equal height. If this measurement is not equal side-to-side by as little as 1/8 in. (3 mm), it can affect the handling of the vehicle.

11. Check for worn control arm bushings.
12. Check for loose or missing stabilizer bar attachments.
13. Check the trunk for excess loads.
14. Check for dragging brakes.

> **NOTE:** Checking for dragging brakes is usually performed when installing alignment heads to the wheels prior to taking an alignment reading. A brake dragging can cause the vehicle to pull or lead toward the side with the dragging brake.

LEAD/PULL

Diagnosis

Many alignment requests come from customers attempting to have a lead or pull condition corrected. Before aligning the

FIGURE 16-6   The bulge in this tire was not noticed until it was removed from the vehicle as part of a routine brake inspection. After replacing this tire, the vehicle stopped pulling and vibrating.

vehicle, verify the customer complaint first, then perform a careful inspection.

1. Inspect all tires for proper inflation. Both tires on the same axle (front and rear) should be the same size and brand. A lead/pull problem could be due to a defect or condition in one or more of the tires, as shown in Figure 16-6. Before attempting to correct the lead/pull condition by changing alignment angles, try rotating the tires front to back or side to side.
2. Road test the vehicle on a straight, level road away from traffic, if possible. Bring the vehicle to about 40 mph (65 km/h), shift into neutral, and feel for a pull in the steering, either to the left or to the right. A lead or drift is less severe than a pull, and may occur only if you momentarily remove your hands from the steering wheel while driving.
3. If the lead/pull problem is sometimes toward the left and other times toward the right, check for a **memory steer** condition. If the lead/pull problem occurs during acceleration and deceleration, check for a **torque steer** condition.

MEMORY STEER

Diagnosis

Memory steer is a term used to describe the lead or pull of a vehicle caused by faults in the steering or suspension system. Often a defective upper strut bearing or steering gear can cause a pulling condition in one direction after making a turn in the same direction. It is as if the vehicle had a memory and pulled in the same direction. To test for memory steer, follow these simple steps during a test drive:

1. With the vehicle stopped at an intersection or in a parking area, turn the steering wheel completely to the left stop and then straighten the wheel without going past the straight-ahead position.
2. Lightly accelerate the vehicle and note any tendency of the vehicle to lead or pull toward the left.
3. Repeat the procedure, turning the steering wheel to the right.

If the vehicle first pulls to the left, then pulls to the right, the vehicle has a memory steer condition.

Correction

A binding suspension or steering component is the most likely cause of memory steer. Disconnect each wheel from its tie rod end and check for free rotation of movement of each wheel. Each front wheel should rotate easily without binding or roughness. Repair or replace components as necessary to eliminate the binding condition.

NOTE: One of the most common causes of memory steer is the installation of steering or suspension components while the front wheels are turned. Most steering and suspension parts contain rubber, which has a memory if moved from its installed position. If the memory steer condition is only in one direction, then this is the most likely cause. The rubber component exerts a force on the suspension or steering that causes the vehicle to pull toward the side that the wheels were turned toward when the part was installed.

TORQUE STEER

Diagnosis

Torque steer occurs in front-wheel-drive vehicles when engine torque causes a front wheel to change its angle from straight ahead. See Figure 16-7. This resulting pulling effect is most noticeable during rapid acceleration, especially whenever upshifting of the transmission creates a sudden change in torque being applied to the front wheels. When turning and

REAL WORLD FIX

THE FIVE-WHEEL ALIGNMENT

The steering wheel should always be straight when driving on a straight, level road. If the steering wheel is not straight, the customer will often think that the wheel alignment is not correct. One such customer complained that the vehicle pulled to the right while driving on a straight road. The service manager test drove the vehicle and everything was perfect, except that the steering wheel was not perfectly straight, even though the toe setting was correct. Whenever driving on a straight road, the customer would "straighten the steering wheel" and, of course, the vehicle went to one side. After adjusting toe with the steering wheel straight, the customer and the service manager were both satisfied. The technician learned that regardless of how accurate the alignment, the steering wheel *must* be straight; it is this "fifth wheel" that the customer notices most. Therefore, a **five-wheel alignment** includes a check of the steering wheel.

NOTE: Many vehicle manufacturers now include the maximum allowable steering wheel angle variation from straight. This specification is commonly ±3 degrees (plus or minus 3 degrees) or less.

accelerating at the same time, torque steer has a tendency to straighten the vehicle, so more steering effort may be required to make the turn. Then, if the accelerator is released, a reversing force is applied to the front wheels. Now the driver must take corrective steering motions to counteract the change in steering effect of engine torque.

To summarize:

Torque to wheel	a toe-in condition
More torque	more toe-in
Unequal torque	unequal toe-in
Unequal drive shaft angles	unequal torque to the wheels

Most manufacturers try to reduce torque steer in the design of their vehicles by keeping drive axle angles low and equal side-to-side. If the engine and transaxle are level and the drive axle shafts are kept level, then the torque from the engine will be divided equally between the front wheels.

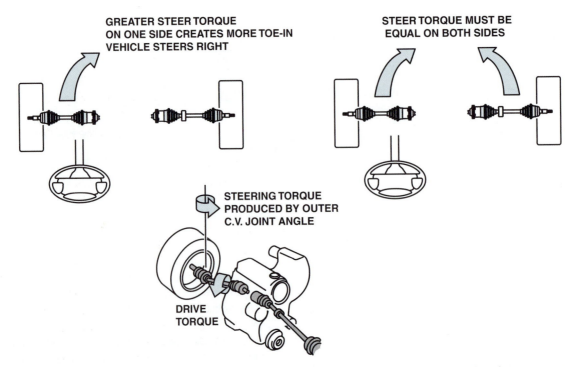

FIGURE 16-7 Equal outer CV joint angles produce equal steer torque (toe-in). If one side receives more engine torque, that side creates more toe-in and the result is a pull toward one side, especially during acceleration.

Correction

The service technician cannot change the design of a vehicle, but the technician can, and should, check and correct problems that often cause torque steer. **Check to be sure that the condition is not normal.** It is normal for front-wheel-drive vehicles to exert a tug on the steering wheel and steer toward one side (usually to the right) during acceleration. This is especially noticeable when the transmission shifts from first to second gear under heavy acceleration. To determine how severe the problem is, place a strip of masking tape at the top of the steering wheel. Drive the vehicle and observe the amount of movement required to steer the vehicle straight during heavy acceleration. Repeat the test with a vehicle of similar make and model. If the torque steer is excessive, determine and correct the cause by carefully following the prealignment inspection steps and checking for a level power train.

A defective engine mount can cause the entire drive train to sag on one end. If the engine and transaxle of any front-wheel-drive vehicle is not level, the drive axle shaft angles will not be equal, as shown in Figure 16-8.

Hold a straightedge along the engine's supporting frame and measure up to points along the transaxle pan rail or the drive axle shaft. Side-to-side distances should be equal. Standard alignment shims can be used to shim the mounts and level the drive train.

If torque steer is still excessive, check all alignment angles, including SAI and included angle. Unequal alignment angles

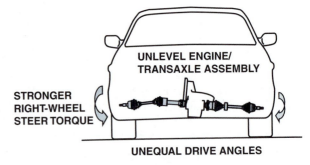

FIGURE 16-8 Broken or defective engine or transaxle mounts can cause the power train to sag, causing unequal drive axle shaft CV joint angles.

can cause a pull or a lead condition. SAI and included angle should be within 1/2 (0.5) degree side-to-side for best results. A vehicle will tend to pull toward the side with the least SAI.

ALIGNMENT SPECIFICATIONS

Before attempting any alignment, consider the following:

1. Determine the make, model, and year of the vehicle.
2. Determine if the vehicle is equipped with power steering or manual steering. (Some older models use lower caster specifications for manual steering to reduce steering effort.)

3. Determine the correct specifications (if possible, check the specifications from two different sources to ensure correct readings).
4. Compensate for the lack of a full gas tank by placing an equal amount of weight in the luggage compartment. (Gasoline weighs 6 lb per gallon [0.7 kg per l]—a 20-gallon gas tank, when full, weighs 120 lb [80 liters weighs 54 kg].)
5. Determine the correct specifications for the *exact* vehicle being checked.

NOTE: Some alignment specifications are published as guidelines for acceptable values for state or local vehicle inspections. Be sure to use the *service* or *set to* specifications.

Reading Alignment Specifications

There are several methods used by vehicle manufacturers and alignment equipment manufacturers to specify alignment angles.

Maximum/Minimum/Preferred Method. This method indicates the preferred setting for each alignment angle and the minimum and maximum allowable value for each. The alignment technician should always attempt to align the vehicle to the preferred setting.

Plus or Minus Method. This method indicates the preferred setting with the lowest and highest allowable value indicated by a negative (−) and positive (+) sign, as in Figure 16-9. For example, if a camber reading is specified as +1/2 degree with a + and − value of 1/2 degree, it could be written as +1/2 degree ±1/2 degree. The minimum value would be 0 degree (1/2° − 1/2° = 0°) and the maximum value would be +1 degree (+1/2° + 1/2° = 1°). The range would be from 0 to 1 degree.

NOTE: The angle is assumed positive unless labeled with a negative (−) sign in front of the number.

KEEP THE DOORS CLOSED, BUT THE WINDOW DOWN

An experienced alignment technician became upset when a beginning technician opened the driver's door to lock the steering wheel in a straight-ahead position on the vehicle being aligned. The weight of the open door caused the vehicle to sag. This disturbed the level position of the vehicle and changed all the alignment angles.

The beginning technician learned an important lesson that day: Keep the window down on the driver's door so that the steering wheel and brakes can be locked without disturbing the vehicle weight balance by opening a door. The brake pedal must be locked with a pedal depressor to prevent the wheels from rolling as the wheels are turned during a caster sweep. The steering must be locked in the straight-ahead position when adjusting toe.

Degrees, Minutes, and Fractions

Specifications are often published in **fractional** or decimal **degrees,** or in degrees and **minutes.** There are 60 minutes (written as 60′) in 1 degree.

Angle-Unit Conversions

Units	Conversions
Fractional degrees	1/4°, 1/2°, 3/4°
Decimal degrees	0.25°, 0.50°, 0.75°
Degrees and minutes	0°15′, 0°30′, 0°45′

WHEEL ALIGNMENT SPECIFICATIONS

	CASTER	CROSS CASTER (LH-RH)	CAMBER	CROSS CAMBER (LH-RH)	TOE (TOTAL IN) DEGREES	STEERING WHEEL ANGLE	THRUST ANGLE
FRONT	+3°±.5°	0°±.75°	+.2° ±.5°	0°±.75°	0°±.3°	0°±3°	- -
REAR	- -	- -	-.3° ±.5°	0°±.75°	+.1° ±.2°	- -	0°±.1°

FIGURE 16-9   This alignment chart indicates the preferred setting with a plus or minus tolerance.

To help visualize the amount of these various units, think of decimal degrees as representing money or cents (100 cents = 1 dollar).

$$0.75 = 75 \text{ cents, or } 3/4 \text{ of a dollar}$$

Minutes can be visualized as minutes in an hour (60' = 1 hour).

$$45' = 3/4 \text{ of an hour}$$

Now which is larger, 35 minutes or 0.40 degrees? The larger angle is 35 minutes because this is slightly greater than 1/2 degree, whereas 0.40 minutes is less than 1/2 degree.

Finding the Midpoint of Specifications

Many manufacturers specify alignment angles within a range. If you are using equipment that requires a midpoint to be entered, use the following method to determine easily the midpoint of specifications.

Example 1.

Specification: 55' to 2° 25'

Step 1   The first step is to determine the specification range or span, which is the total angle value from lowest to highest:

2° 25'
− 55'
1° 30' specification range

Step 2   Dividing the specification range by 2 will give the midpoint of the range:

$$\frac{1° 30'}{2} = \frac{90'}{2'} = 45'$$

Step 3   To find the midpoint of the specifications, add the midpoint of the range to the smaller specification (or subtract from the larger specification):

45' midpoint of range
+55' lowest specification
1° 40' midpoint of specification

Example 2.

Specification: −0.5° to +0.80°

Step 1   The total range of the specification is determined by adding 0.5 (1/2) to 0.80, totaling 1.30°.

NOTE: Since the lower specification is a negative number, we had to *add* the 0.5 degree to bring the lower range of the specification to zero. Then the total is simply the upper range specification added to the number required to bring the lower end of the range to zero.

Step 2   Dividing the specification range by 2 gives the midpoint of the range:

$$\frac{1.30°}{2} = 0.65°$$

Step 3   To find the midpoint of the specification, add the midpoint of the range to the smaller specification:

0.65° midpoint of range
+(−0.50°) lowest specification
+0.15° midpoint of specification

ALIGNMENT SETUP PROCEDURES

After confirming that the tires and all steering and suspension components are serviceable, the vehicle is ready for an alignment. Setup procedures for the equipment being used must always be followed. Typical alignment procedures include the following:

Step 1   Drive onto the alignment rack straight and adjust the ramps and/or turn plates so that they are centered under the tires of the vehicle. See Figure 16-10.

Step 2   Use chocks for the wheels to keep the vehicle from rolling off the alignment rack.

Step 3   Attach and calibrate the wheel sensors to each wheel as specified by the alignment equipment

FIGURE 16-10   Using the alignment rack hydraulic jacks, raise the tires off the rack so that they can be rotated as part of the compensating process.

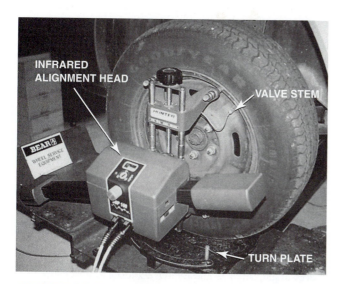

INFRARED
ALIGNMENT HEAD

VALVE STEM

BEAR
WHEEL SERVICE
EQUIPMENT

TURN PLATE

FIGURE 16-11 This wheel sensor has a safety wire that screws to the valve stem to keep the sensor from falling onto the ground if the clamps slip on the wheel lip.

manufacturer. See Figure 16-11. The calibration procedure is required whenever the head of the machine is attached to the wheel of the vehicle. All alignment angles and measurements are taken from the readings of the wheel sensors. Calibration of these wheel sensors is needed for two reasons:

a. *The wheel may be bent.* If the wheel (rim) is bent, even slightly, this small amount of tilt would be read as an angle of the suspension.

NOTE: Compensating or calibrating the wheel sensor for a bent wheel does *not* correct (or repair) the bent wheel! The bent wheel is still present and can result in a shimmy-type vibration.

b. *The sensors may not be identically installed on the wheel.* Most sensors use three or four wheel-mounting locations. It is not possible to install all wheel sensors perfectly at the same depth on the wheel in all locations. If a sensor must be removed during the alignment process and reinstalled, it should be recalibrated. Always follow the manufacturer's recommended procedure for compensating the sensors.

Step 4   Unlock all rack or turn plates.

Step 5   Lower the vehicle and jounce the vehicle by pushing down on the front, then rear, bumper. This motion allows the suspension to become centered.

Step 6   Following the procedures for the alignment equipment, determine all alignment angles.

MEASURING CAMBER, CASTER, SAI, TOE, AND TOOT

Camber

Camber is measured with the wheels in the straight-ahead position on a level platform. Since camber is a vertical reference angle, alignment equipment reads camber directly.

Caster

Caster is measured by moving the front wheels through an arc inward, then outward, from straight ahead. This necessary movement of the front wheels to measure caster is called *caster sweep.* What the alignment measuring equipment is actually doing is measuring the camber at one wheel sweep and measuring the camber again at the other extreme of the caster sweep. *The caster angle itself is the difference between the two camber readings.*

SAI

Steering axis inclination (SAI) is also measured by performing a caster sweep of the front wheels. While this angle can be read at the same time as caster on many alignment machines, most experts recommend that SAI be measured separately from the caster reading. When measuring SAI separately, the usual procedure involves raising the front wheels off the ground and leveling and locking the wheel sensors before performing a caster sweep. The reason for raising the front wheels is to allow the front suspension to extend to its full droop position. When the suspension is extended, the SAI is more accurately determined because the angle itself is expanded.

Toe

Toe is determined by measuring the angle of both front and/or both rear wheels from the straight-ahead (0 degree) position. Most alignment equipment reads the toe angle for each wheel *and* the combined toe angle of both wheels on the same axle. This combined toe is called **total toe.** Toe angle is more accurate than the center-to-center distance, especially if oversize tires are installed on the vehicle. See Figure 16-12.

TOOT

Toe-out on turns (TOOT) is a diagnostic angle and is normally not measured as part of a regular alignment, but it is recommended to be performed as part of a total alignment check.

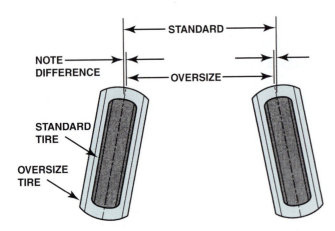

FIGURE 16-12 If toe for an oversize tire is set by distance, the toe angle will be too small. Toe angle is the same regardless of tire size.

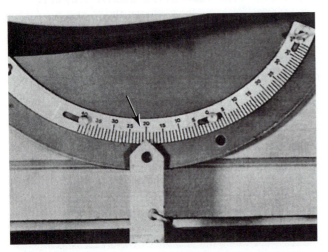

FIGURE 16-13 The protractor scale on the front turn plates allows the technician to test the turning radius by turning one wheel to an angle specified by the manufacturer and observing the angle of the other front wheel. Most newer alignment machines can display turning angle based on sensor readings, and therefore the protractor scale on the turn plate is not needed or used.

TOOT is measured by recording the angle of the front wheels as indicated on the front turn plates. See Figure 16-13.

If, for example, the inside wheel is turned 20 degrees, then the outside wheel should indicate about 18 degrees on the turn plate. The exact angles are usually specified by the vehicle manufacturer. The turning angle should be checked only after the toe is correctly set. *The turning angle for the wheel on the outside of the turn should not vary more than 1 1/2 degrees from specifications.* For example, if the specification calls for the right wheel to be steered into the turn 20 degrees, the outside wheel should measure 18 degrees. This should be within 1 1/2 degrees (16.5 to 19.5 degrees). If the TOOT is not correct, a bent steering arm is the usual cause. If TOOT is not correct, tire squealing noise is usually noticed while cornering and excessive tire wear may occur.

NOTE: Some front-wheel-drive vehicles use a nonsymmetrical (unequal) turning angle design. This design is found on various makes and models of vehicles to assist in controlling torque steer. The test procedure is the same except that the turning angle specifications include left-wheel and right-wheel angles when turned inward and outward.

SPECIFICATIONS VERSUS ALIGNMENT READINGS

Secure both the alignment specifications from the manufacturer and the alignment readings and compare the two. Before starting an alignment, the smart technician checks the SAI, included angle, setback, and toe-out on turns to make sure that there is no hidden damage such as a bent spindle or strut that was not found during the prealignment inspection. *Setback is also a diagnostic angle and should be less than 0.5 in. (13 cm or 1/2 degree).* If setback is greater than 0.5 in. (13 cm or 1/2 degree), check the body, frame, and cradle for accident damage or improper alignment.

NOTE: If the SAI or included angle are unequal, suggesting a possible problem such as a bent strut, check the front and rear toe readings. Some alignment equipment cannot show accurate SAI readings if the front or rear toe readings are not within specifications. If the front and rear toe readings are OK and the alignment readings indicate a bent strut, go ahead with the diagnosis and correction as explained later in this chapter.

CHECKING FOR BENT STRUTS, SPINDLES, OR CONTROL ARMS

Even a minor bump against a curb can bend a spindle or a strut housing.

Before attempting to correct an alignment, check all the angles and use the appropriate diagnostic chart to check for hidden damage that a visual inspection may miss.

The chart in Figure 16-14 can be used to determine what is wrong if the alignment angles are known. Simply use the chart that correctly identifies the type of suspension on the problem vehicle.

At spec	The alignment angle is within specifications.
Over spec	The alignment angle is greater or higher than specified by the manufacturer.
Under spec	The alignment angle is less than or lower than specified by the manufacturer.

DIAGNOSING SAI, CAMBER, AND INCLUDED ANGLE			
SLA AND STRUT/SLA SUSPENSIONS			
SAI	**CAMBER**	**INCLUDED ANGLE**	**DIAGNOSIS**
CORRECT	LESS THAN SPECS	LESS THAN SPECS OR SPINDLE	BENT STEERING KNUCKLE
LESS THAN SPECS	GREATER THAN SPECS	CORRECT	BENT LOWER CONTROL ARM
LESS THAN SPECS	GREATER THAN SPECS	GREATER THAN SPECS	BENT LOWER CONTROL ARM AND STEERING KNUCKLE OR SPINDLE
GREATER THAN SPECS	LESS THAN SPECS	CORRECT	BENT UPPER CONTROL ARM
STRUT SUSPENSIONS			
SAI	**CAMBER**	**INCLUDED ANGLE**	**DIAGNOSIS**
CORRECT	LESS THAN SPECS	LESS THAN SPECS	BENT SPINDLE AND/OR STRUT
CORRECT	GREATER THAN SPECS	GREATER THAN SPECS	BENT SPINDLE AND/OR STRUT
LESS THAN SPECS	GREATER THAN SPECS	CORRECT	BENT CONTROL ARM OR STRUT TOWER OUT AT TOP
LESS THAN SPECS	GREATER THAN SPECS	GREATER THAN SPECS	BENT CONTROL ARM OR STRUT TOWER OUT AT TOP, ALSO BENT SPINDLE AND/OR STRUT
LESS THAN SPECS	LESS THAN SPECS	LESS THAN SPECS	BENT CONTROL ARM OR STRUT TOWER OUT AT TOP, ALSO BENT SPINDLE AND/OR STRUT
GREATER THAN SPECS	LESS THAN SPECS	CORRECT	STRUT TOWER IN AT TOP
GREATER THAN SPECS	GREATER THAN SPECS	GREATER THAN SPECS	STRUT TOWER IN AT TOP AND BENT SPINDLE AND/OR BENT STRUT
KINGPIN TWIN I-BEAM SUSPENSION			
SAI(KPI)	**CAMBER**	**INCLUDED ANGLE**	**DIAGNOSIS**
CORRECT	GREATER THAN SPECS	GREATER THAN SPECS	BENT SPINDLE
LESS THAN SPECS	GREATER THAN SPECS	CORRECT	BENT I-BEAM
LESS THAN SPECS	GREATER THAN SPECS	GREATER THAN SPECS	BENT I-BEAM AND SPINDLE
GREATER THAN SPECS	LESS THAN SPECS	CORRECT	BENT I-BEAM

FIGURE 16-14   By checking the SAI, camber, and included angle, a damaged suspension component can be determined by using this chart.

CHECKING FRAME ALIGNMENT OF FRONT-WHEEL-DRIVE VEHICLES

Many front-wheel-drive vehicles mount the drive train (engine and transaxle) and lower suspension arms to a subframe or cradle. If the frame is shifted either left or right, this can cause differences in SAI, included angle, and camber. See Figures 16-15 and 16-16. Adjust the frame if SAI and camber angles are different left and right side, yet the included angles are equal.

TYPES OF ALIGNMENTS

There are three types of alignment: geometric centerline, thrust line, and total four-wheel alignment.

TECH TIP

ASK YOURSELF THESE THREE QUESTIONS

An older technician told a beginning technician that the key to success in doing a proper alignment is to ask yourself three questions about the alignment angles:

Question 1. **"Is it within specifications?"** For example, if the specification reads 1° ±1/2°, any reading between +1/2° and 1 1/2° is within specifications. All vehicles should be aligned within this range. Individual opinions and experience can assist the technician as to whether the actual setting should be at one extreme or the other or held to the center of the specification range.

Question 2. **"Is it within 1/2° of the other side of the vehicle?"** Not only should the alignment be within specifications, but it should also be as equal as possible from one side to the other. The difference between the camber from one side to the other side is called cross camber. Cross caster is the difference between the caster angle from one side to another. Some manufacturers and technicians recommend that this side-to-side difference be limited to just 1/4 degree!

Question 3. **"If the camber and caster cannot be exactly equal side-to-side in the front, is there more camber on the left and more caster on the right to help compensate for road crown?"** Seldom, if ever, are the alignment angles perfectly equal. Sometimes one side of the vehicle is more difficult to adjust than the other side. Regardless of the reasons, if there *has* to be a difference in front camber and/or caster angle, follow this advice to avoid a possible lead or drift problem even if the answers to the first two questions are "yes."

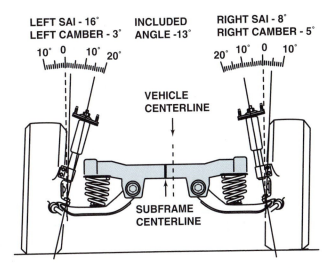

FIGURE 16-15 In this example, both SAI and camber are far from being equal side-to-side. However, both sides have the same included angle, indicating that the frame may be out of alignment. An attempt to align this vehicle by adjusting the camber on both sides with either factory or aftermarket kits would result in a totally incorrect alignment.

Thrust Line

A **thrust line** alignment uses the thrust angle of the rear wheels and sets the front wheels parallel to the thrust line. See Figure 16-18.

The thrust line is the bisector of rear total toe, or the actual direction in which the rear wheels are pointed. The rear wheels of any vehicle *should* be pointing parallel to the geometric centerline of the vehicle. However, if the rear toe angles of the rear wheels do not total exactly zero (perfectly in a line with the centerline of the vehicle), a thrust condition exists. The front wheels will automatically steer to become parallel to that condition. A crooked steering wheel may also result from an improper thrust condition.

NOTE: It has often been said that while the front wheels steer the vehicle, the rear wheels determine the direction in which the vehicle will travel. Think of the rear wheels as a rudder on a boat. If the rudder is turned, the direction of the boat changes due to the angle change at the rear of the boat.

Thrust line alignment is *required* for any vehicle with a nonadjustable rear suspension. If a vehicle has an adjustable rear suspension, then a total four-wheel alignment is necessary to ensure proper tracking.

Total Four-Wheel Alignment

A total **four-wheel alignment** is the most accurate alignment method and is necessary to ensure maximum tire wear and

Geometric Centerline

Until the 1980s, most wheel alignment concerned only the front wheels. Vehicles, such as sports cars, that had independent rear suspensions were often aligned by backing the vehicle onto the alignment rack and adjusting the rear camber and/or toe. This type of alignment is simply an alignment that uses the **geometric centerline** of the vehicle as the basis for all measurements of toe (front or rear). See Figure 16-17.

This method is now considered to be obsolete.

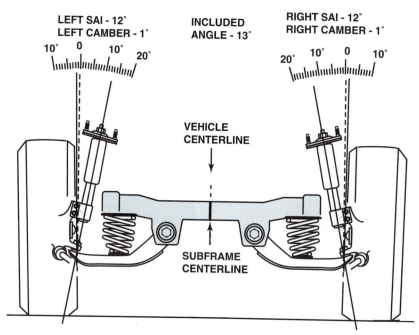

FIGURE 16-16   This is the same vehicle as shown in Figure 16-15, except now the frame (cradle) has been shifted over and correctly positioned. Notice how both the SAI and camber become equal without any other adjustments necessary.

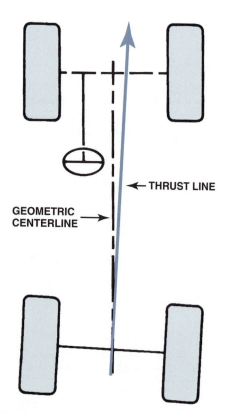

FIGURE 16-17   Geometric-centerline-type alignment sets the front toe readings based on the geometric centerline of the vehicle and does not consider the thrust line of the rear wheel toe angles. *(Courtesy of Hunter Engineering Company)*

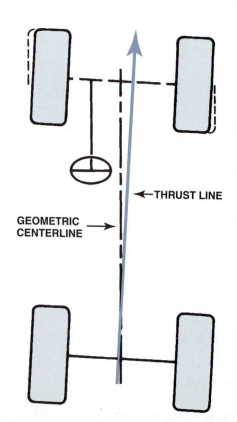

FIGURE 16-18   Thrust-line alignment sets the front toe parallel with the rear-wheel toe. *(Courtesy of Hunter Engineering Company)*

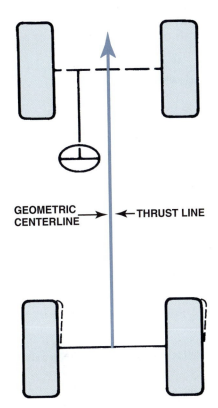

FIGURE 16-19 Four-wheel alignment corrects for any rear-wheel toe to make the thrust line and the geometric centerline of the vehicle both the same. *(Courtesy of Hunter Engineering Company)*

vehicle handling. The biggest difference between a thrust-line alignment and a total four-wheel alignment is that the rear toe is adjusted to bring the thrust line to zero. In other words, the rear toe on both rear wheels is adjusted equally so that the actual direction in which the rear wheels are pointed is the same as the geometric centerline of the vehicle. See Figure 16-19.

The procedure for a total four-wheel alignment includes these steps:

1. Adjust the rear camber (if applicable).
2. Adjust the rear toe (this should reduce the thrust angle to near zero).
3. Adjust the front camber and caster.
4. Adjust the front toe, being sure that the steering wheel is in the straight-ahead position.

SAMPLE ALIGNMENT SPECIFICATIONS AND READINGS

The service technician must know not only all of the alignment angles but also the interrelationship that exists among the angles. As an aid toward understanding these relationships,

two examples are presented: Example 1 gives the front wheel angles that are acceptable when compared with the specifications; Example 2 gives four-wheel alignment and readings of a vehicle that are not within specifications.

Example 1: Wheel Alignment

Alignment Specifications

	Left	Right
Camber =	+1/2° ± 1/2°	+1/2° ± 1/2°
Caster =	+1° ± 1/2°	+1° ± 1/2°
Toe (total) =	1/8 in. ± 1/16 in.	

Actual Reading

	Left	Right
Camber =	+1/4°	0°
Caster =	+1°	+1 1/4°
Toe (total) =	1/8 in.	

Answer

Alignment is perfect:

a. No tire wear
b. No pulling

Explanation

Camber is within specifications.
Camber is within 1/2-degree difference side-to-side.
Camber is not equal, but there is more camber on the left (1/4 degree) than on the right, thereby helping to compensate for the road crown.
Caster is within specifications.
Caster is within 1/2-degree difference side-to-side.
Caster is not equal, but there is more caster on the right (1/4 degree) than on the left, thereby helping (very slightly) to compensate for road crown.
Toe is within specifications.

Example 2: Four-Wheel Alignment

Specifications

	Left	Right
Front camber =	+1/4° ±1/2°	0° ±1/2°
Front caster =	+3° ±1/2°	+1/2° ±1/2°
Front toe (total) =	3/16 in. ±1/16 in.	
Rear camber =	0° ±1/4°	0° ±1/4°
Rear toe =	0 in. ±1/16 in.	

Actual Reading

	Left	Right
Front camber =	−1/2°	−1°
Front caster =	+2 3/4°	+2°
Front toe =	−1/8 in. (toe-out)	
Rear camber =	0°	−1/4°
Rear toe =	+1/2° (toe-in)	

Answer

Alignment is incorrect.

a. Left front tire will wear slightly on the inside edge.
b. Right front tire will wear on the inside edge.
c. Vehicle could tend to pull slightly to the left due to the camber difference (may not pull at all due to the pulling effect of the road crown).
d. Vehicle could tend to pull slightly to the right due to the caster difference (3/4 degree more caster on the left).
e. Overall pull could be slight toward the left because it requires four times the caster difference to have the same pulling forces as camber.
f. Tires could wear slightly on both the inside edges due to toe-out.
g. The negative camber of the present alignment puts a heavy load on the outer wheel bearing, if RWD, because the load is being carried by the smaller outer wheel bearing instead of the larger inner wheel bearing.

Conclusion

The vehicle would wear the inside edges of both front tires.
The vehicle may or may not pull slightly to the left.
The vehicle would not act as stable while driving—possible wander.

ADJUSTING REAR CAMBER

Adjusting rear camber is the first step in the total four-wheel alignment process. Rear camber is rarely made adjustable, but can be corrected by using aftermarket alignment kits or shims. If rear camber is not correct, vehicle handling and tire life are affected. Before attempting to adjust or correct rear camber, carefully check the body and/or frame of the vehicle for accident damage, including the following:

1. Weak springs, torsion bars, or overloading (check ride height)
2. Bowed rear axle, trailing arm, or rear control arm
3. Suspension mount or body dimension not in proper location
4. Incorrectly adjusted camber from a previous repair

The cause of the incorrect rear camber could be accident-related and the body or frame may have to be pulled into correct position. See Figures 16-20 through 16-22 for examples of various methods used to adjust rear camber.

Simple to Use

1. Take alignment readings and determine the change needed.
2. Select proper shims using the easy-to-read chart.
3. Using the template provided, mark and remove tabs to create a proper mounting bolt pattern.
4. Install shim.

ADJUSTING REAR TOE

Many vehicle manufacturers provide adjustment for rear toe on vehicles that use an independent rear suspension. Rear toe

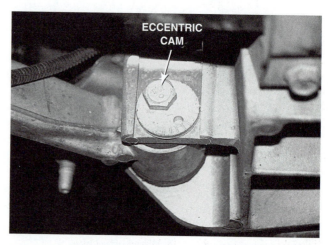

FIGURE 16-20 The rear camber is adjustable on this vehicle by rotating the eccentric cam and watching the alignment machine display.

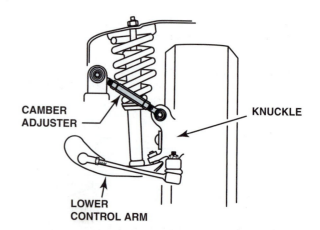

FIGURE 16-21 Some vehicles use a threaded fastener similar to a tie rod to adjust camber on the rear suspension.

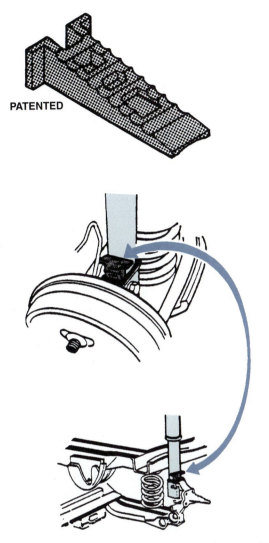

PATENTED

FIGURE 16-22   Aftermarket alignment parts or kits are available to change the rear camber. *(Courtesy of Shimco International, Inc.)*

TECH TIP

THE GRITTY SOLUTION

Many times it is difficult to loosen a Torx bolt, especially those used to hold the backing plate onto the rear axle on many GM vehicles. See Figure 16-23.

A technique that always seems to work is to place some valve grinding compound on the fastener. The gritty compound keeps the Torx socket from slipping up and out of the fastener, and more force can be exerted to break loose a tight bolt. Valve grinding compound can also be used on Phillips head screws as well as other types of bolts, nuts, and sockets.

adjusts the thrust angle. A thrust angle that exceeds 1/2 degree (0.5 degree) on a vehicle with a solid axle is an indication that a component may be damaged or out of place in the rear of the vehicle. Rear toe is often adjusted using an adjustable tie rod end or an eccentric cam on the lower control arm. Check a service manual for the exact method for the vehicle being aligned. Most solid rear axles do not have a method to adjust

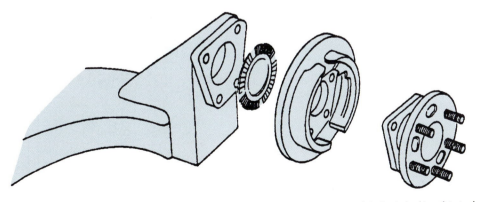

FIGURE 16-23   Full-contact plastic or metal shims can be placed between the axle housing and the brake backing plate to change rear camber, toe, or both. *(Courtesy of Northstar Manufacturing Company, Inc.)*

rear toe except for aftermarket shims or kits. See Figures 16-24 through 16-26.

NOTE: On vehicles equipped with four-wheel steering, refer to the service manual for the exact procedure to follow to lock or hold the rear wheels in position for a proper alignment check.

FIGURE 16-24 The rear toe was easily set on this vehicle. The adjusting nuts were easy to get to and turn. Adjusting rear toe is not this easy on every vehicle.

GUIDELINES FOR ADJUSTING FRONT CAMBER/SAI AND INCLUDED ANGLE

If the camber is adjusted at the base of the MacPherson strut, camber and included angle are changed and SAI remains the same. See Figure 16-27.

If camber is adjusted by moving the upper strut mounting location, included angle remains the same, but SAI and camber change. See Figure 16-28.

This is the reason to use the factory alignment methods before using an aftermarket alignment adjustment kit. SAI and included angle should be within 1/2 degree (0.5 degrees) side-to-side. If these angles differ, check the frame mount location before attempting to correct differences in camber. As the frame is changed, camber and SAI change, but the included angle remains the same. Cross camber/caster is the difference between the camber or caster on one side of the vehicle and the camber or caster on the other side of the vehicle.

Alignment Angle	Recommended Maximum Variation
SAI	Within 1/2° (0.5°) side-to-side
Included angle	Within 1/2° (0.5°) side-to-side
Cross camber	Within 1/2° (0.5°) side-to-side
Cross caster	Within 1/2° (0.5°) side-to-side

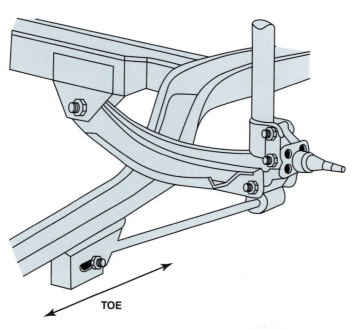

FIGURE 16-25   By moving various rear suspension members, the rear toe can be changed.

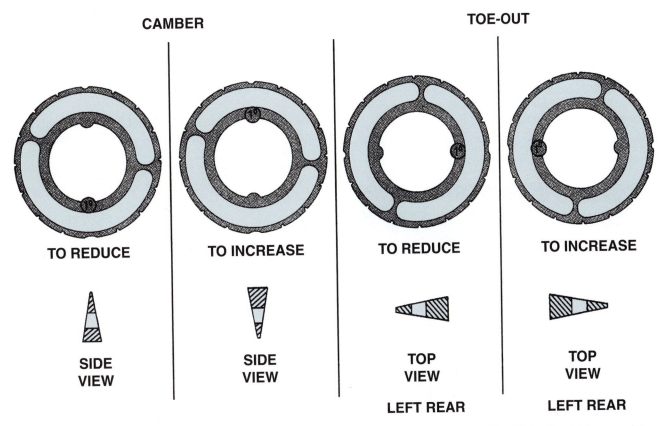

CAMBER

TO REDUCE

SIDE VIEW

TO INCREASE

SIDE VIEW

TOE-OUT

TO REDUCE

TOP VIEW

LEFT REAR

TO INCREASE

TOP VIEW

LEFT REAR

FIGURE 16-26   The use of these plastic or metal shims requires that the rear wheel as well as the hub assembly and/or backing plate be removed. Proper torque during reassembly is critical to avoid damage to the shims. *(Courtesy of Shimco International, Inc.)*

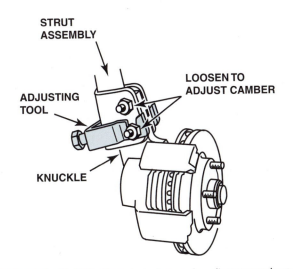

STRUT ASSEMBLY

ADJUSTING TOOL

LOOSEN TO ADJUST CAMBER

KNUCKLE

FIGURE 16-27   Many struts allow camber adjustment at the strut-to-knuckle fasteners. Here a special tool is being used to hold and move the strut into alignment with the fasteners loosened. Once the desired camber angle is achieved, the strut nuts are tightened and the tool is removed.

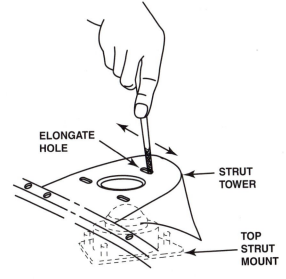

ELONGATE HOLE

STRUT TOWER

TOP STRUT MOUNT

FIGURE 16-28   Some struts require modification of the upper mount for camber adjustment.

FRONT CAMBER/CASTER ADJUSTMENT METHODS

Many vehicles are constructed with only limited camber/caster factory adjustment. See Figure 16-29 for a summary of which adjustments are *generally* possible for various types of vehicles and suspension systems.

ADJUSTING FRONT CAMBER/CASTER

Most SLA-type suspensions can be adjusted for caster and camber. Most manufacturers recommend adjusting caster, then camber, before adjusting the toe. As the caster is changed, such as when the strut rod is adjusted as shown in Figure 16-30, the camber and toe also change.

If the camber is then adjusted, the caster is unaffected. Many technicians adjust caster and camber at the same time using shims (Figures 16-31 and 16-32), slots (Figure 16-33), or **eccentric cams** (Figure 16-34).

Always follow the manufacturer's recommended alignment procedure. For example, many manufacturers include a **shim chart** in their service manual that gives the thickness and location of the shim changes based on the alignment reading. Shim charts are used to set camber and caster at the same time. Shim charts are designed for each model of vehicle. See Figure 16-35.

Regardless of the methods or procedures used, toe is always adjusted after all the angles are set because caster and camber both affect the toe.

SETTING TOE

Front toe is the last angle that should be adjusted and is the most likely to need correction. This has led to many sayings in the alignment field:

TECH TIP

RACE VEHICLE ALIGNMENT

Vehicles used in autocrossing (individual timed runs through cones in a parking lot) or road racing usually perform best if the following alignment steps are followed:

1. *Increase caster (+).* Not only will the caster provide a good solid feel for the driver during high speed on a straight section of the course, but it will also provide some lean into the corners due to the camber change during cornering. A setting of 5 to 9 degrees positive caster is typical depending on the type of vehicle and the type of course.
2. *Adjust for 1 to 2 degrees of negative camber.* As a race vehicle corners, the body and chassis lean. As the chassis leans, the top of the tire also leans outward. By setting the camber to 1 to 2 degrees negative, the tires will be neutral while cornering, thereby having as much rubber contacting the road as possible.

NOTE: Though setting negative camber on a street-driven vehicle will decrease tire life, the negative setting on a race vehicle is used to increase cornering speeds, and tire life is not a primary consideration.

3. *Set toe to a slight toe-out position.* When the front toe is set negative (toe-out), the vehicle is more responsive to steering commands from the driver. With a slight toe-out setting, one wheel is already pointed in the direction of a corner or curve. Set the toe-out to −3/8 to −1/2 degree depending on the type of vehicle and the type of race course.

"Set the toe and let it go."
"Do a toe and go."
"Set the toe and collect the dough."

As wear occurs at each steering joint, the forces exerted on the linkage by the tire tend to cause a toe-out condition.

METHODS OF ADJUSTMENT

TOOLS AND ADJUSTMENT DEVICES MAY BE AVAILABLE FROM AFTERMARKET SUPPLIERS TO PERFORM ADJUSTMENTS IN CASES WHERE MANUFACTURERS DO NOT MAKE SUCH PROVISIONS.

CASTER & CAMBER ADJUSTMENT

SHIMS

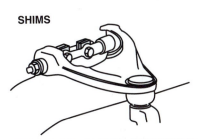

TO INCREASE CASTER, MOVE SHIMS REAR TO FRONT. CAMBER: CHANGE SHIM THICKNESS EQUALLY.

CASTER & CAMBER ADJUSTMENT

SHIMS

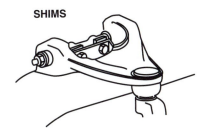

TO INCREASE CASTER, MOVE SHIMS FRONT TO REAR. CAMBER: CHANGE SHIM THICKNESS EQUALLY.

CASTER & CAMBER ADJUSTMENT

SLOTTED HOLES

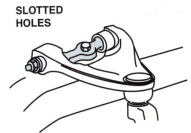

SLACKEN BOLTS, MOVE UPPER ARM SHAFT TO OBTAIN SPECIFIED READINGS. USE SPECIAL TOOL.

CASTER & CAMBER ADJUSTMENT

SHIMS

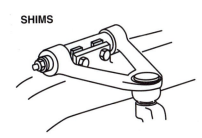

TO INCREASE CASTER, MOVE SHIMS FRONT TO REAR. CAMBER: CHANGE SHIM THICKNESS EQUALLY.

CASTER & CAMBER ADJUSTMENT

CAMS

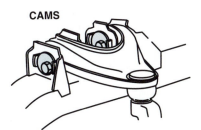

TO ADJUST, ROTATE CAM BOLTS. SET CAMBER FIRST, CHECK/ADJUST CASTER, RECHECK CAMBER.

CAMBER ADJUSTMENT

NUTS

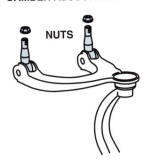

TO ADJUST CAMBER, LOOSEN TWO NUTS ON UPPER ARM AND MOVE WHEEL IN OR OUT.

FRONT CASTER OR REAR TOE ADJUSTMENT

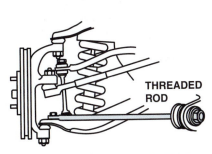

THREADED ROD

TO INCREASE CASTER TO POSITIVE, LENGTHEN STRUT. INCREASE OR DECREASE TOE-IN BY LENGTHENING OR SHORTENING ROD.

CAMBER ADJUSTMENT

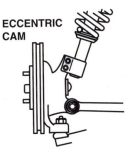

ECCENTRIC CAM

TO INCREASE OR DECREASE CAMBER SETTING, ROTATE CAM BOLT.

CAMBER ADJUSTMENT

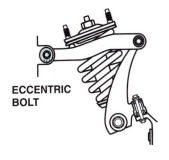

ECCENTRIC BOLT

LOOSEN NUT ON UPPER CONTROL ARM AND ROTATE BOLT TO SET CAMBER.

FIGURE 16-29   An example of the many methods that are commonly used to adjust front caster and camber.

Front-wheel-drive (FWD) vehicles transmit engine power through the front wheels. Many manufacturers of FWD vehicles specify a toe-out setting. This toe-out setting helps compensate for the slight toe-in effect of the engine torque being transferred through the front wheels.

Most newer alignment equipment displays in degrees of toe instead of inches of toe. (See the toe unit conversion chart.) Just remember that positive (+) toe means toe-in and negative (−) toe means toe-out.

Toe Unit Conversions

Units	Conversions			
Fractional inches	1/16 in.	1/8 in.	3/16 in.	1/4 in.
Decimal inches	0.062 in.	0.125 in.	0.188 in.	0.250 in.
Millimeters	1.60 mm	3.18 mm	4.76 mm	6.35 mm
Decimal degrees	0.125°	0.25°	0.375°	0.5°
Degrees and minutes	0°8'	0°15'	0°23'	0°30'
Fractional degrees	1/8°	1/4°	3/8°	1/2°

To make sure the steering wheel is straight after setting toe, the steering wheel *must* be locked in the straight-ahead position while the toe is being adjusted. Another term used to describe steering wheel position is **spoke angle.** To lock the

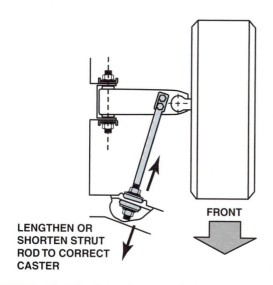

LENGTHEN OR SHORTEN STRUT ROD TO CORRECT CASTER

FRONT

FIGURE 16-30 If there is a nut on both sides of the strut rod bushing, then the length of the rod can be adjusted to change caster.

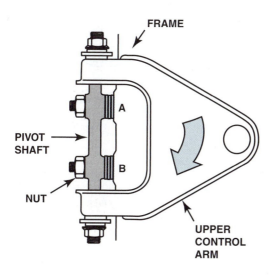

FRAME

A

PIVOT SHAFT

B

NUT

UPPER CONTROL ARM

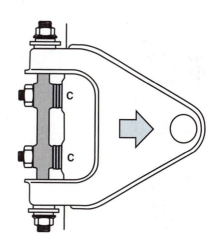

C

C

A SUBTRACT SHIMS TO INCREASE POSITIVE CASTER

B ADD SHIMS TO INCREASE POSITIVE CASTER

C SUBTRACT SHIMS EQUALLY TO INCREASE POSITIVE CAMBER OR ADD SHIMS EQUALLY TO REDUCE POSITIVE CAMBER

FIGURE 16-31 Placing shims between the frame and the upper control arm pivot shaft is a popular method of alignment for many SLA suspensions. Both camber and caster can be easily changed by adding or removing shims.

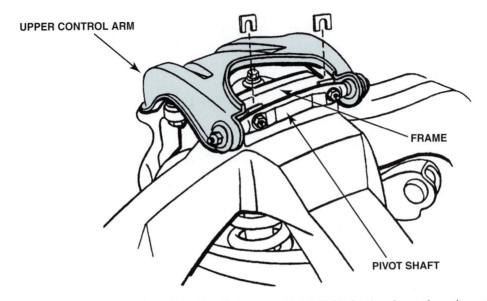

UPPER CONTROL ARM

FRAME

PIVOT SHAFT

FIGURE 16-32   The general rule of thumb is that a 1/8-in. shim added or removed from *both* shim locations changes the camber angle about 1/2 degree. Adding or removing a 1/8-in. shim from *one* shim location changes the caster by about 1/4 degree. *(Courtesy of Hunter Engineering Company)*

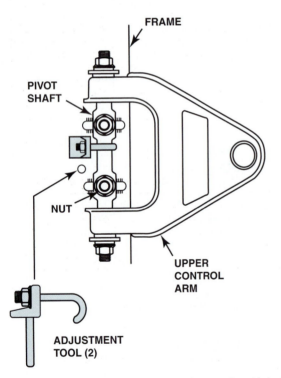

FRAME

PIVOT SHAFT

NUT

ADJUSTMENT TOOL (2)

UPPER CONTROL ARM

FIGURE 16-33   Some SLA-type suspensions use slotted holes for alignment angle adjustments. When the pivot shaft bolts are loosened, the pivot shaft is free to move unless held by special clamps as shown. By turning the threaded portion of the clamps, the camber and caster can be set and checked before tightening the pivot shaft bolts.

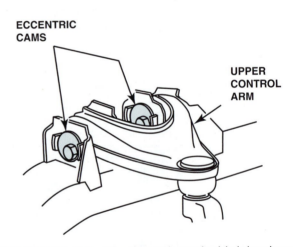

ECCENTRIC CAMS

UPPER CONTROL ARM

FIGURE 16-34   When the nut is loosened and the bolt on the eccentric cam is rotated, the upper control arm moves in and out. By adjusting both eccentric cams, both camber and caster can be adjusted.

steering wheel, always use a steering wheel lock that presses against the seat and the outer rim of the steering wheel. *Do not* use the locking feature of the steering column to hold the steering wheel straight. Always unlock the steering column,

straighten the steering wheel, and install the steering wheel lock. See Figures 16-36 through 16-38.

NOTE: If the vehicle is equipped with power steering, the engine must be started and the steering wheel straightened with the engine running to be assured of a straight steering wheel. Lock the steering wheel with the steering lock tool before stopping the engine.

DEGREES CASTER

DEGREES CAMBER	BOLT	+4.9°	+4.7°	+4.5°	+4.3°	+4.1°	+3.9°	+3.7°	+3.5K	+3.3°	+3.1°	+2.9°	+2.7°	+2.5°	+2.3K	+2.1°
+2.2°	FRONT	+300	+211	+211	+210	+210	+201	+201	+201	+200	+200	+111	+111	+110	+110	+110
	REAR	+101	+101	+110	+110	+111	+200	+200	+201	+210	+210	+201	+211	+300	+301	+301
+2.0°	FRONT	+210	+210	+210	+201	+201	+200	+200	+111	+111	+110	+110	+110	+101	+101	+100
	REAR	+011	+100	+101	+101	+110	+110	+111	+200	+200	+201	+210	+210	+211	+300	+300
+1.8°	FRONT	+201	+201	+200	+200	+111	+111	+110	+110	+110	+101	+101	+100	+100	+100	+011
	REAR	+010	+011	+011	+100	+101	+101	+110	+110	+111	+200	+200	+201	+210	+210	+211
+1.6°	FRONT	+200	+200	+111	+111	+110	+110	+101	+101	+100	+100	+100	+011	+011	+010	+010
	REAR	+001	+001	+010	+011	+011	+100	+100	+101	+110	+110	+111	+200	+200	+201	+210
+1.4°	FRONT	+111	+110	+110	+101	+101	+100	+100	+100	+011	+011	+010	+010	+010	+001	+001
	REAR	+000	+000	+001	+001	+010	+011	+011	+100	+100	+101	+110	+110	+111	+200	+200
+1.2°	FRONT	+110	+101	+101	+100	+100	+011	+011	+010	+010	+010	+001	+001	+000	-000	-000
	REAR	-010	-001	+000	+000	+001	+001	+010	+011	+011	+100	+101	+101	+110	+111	+111
+1.0°	FRONT	+100	+109	+011	+011	+010	+010	+010	+001	+001	+000	-000	-000	-001	-001	-010
	REAR	-011	-010	-010	-001	-000	+000	+001	+001	+010	+011	+011	+100	+101	+101	+110
+0.8°	FRONT	+011	+011	+010	+010	+001	+001	+000	-000	-000	-001	-001	-010	-010	-010	-011
	REAR	-100	-100	-011	-010	-010	-001	-001	+000	+001	+001	+010	+011	+011	+100	+101
+0.6°	FRONT	+010	+001	+001	+001	+000	-000	-001	-001	-010	-010	-010	-011	-011	-100	-100
	REAR	-101	-101	-100	-100	-011	-010	-010	-001	-001	+000	+001	+001	+010	+011	+011
+0.4°	FRONT	+001	+000	+000	-001	-001	-010	-010	-010	-011	-011	-100	-100	-100	-101	-101
	REAR	-111	-110	-101	-101	-100	-100	-011	-010	-010	-001	-000	+000	+001	+010	+010
+0.2°	FRONT	-001	-001	-001	-010	-010	-011	-011	-100	-100	-101	-101	-101	-110	-110	-110
	REAR	-200	-111	-111	-110	-101	-101	-100	-100	-011	-010	-010	-001	-000	+000	+001
+0.0°	FRONT	-010	-010	-011	-011	-100	-100	-100	-101	-101	-110	-110	-111	-111	-111	-200
	REAR	-201	-201	-200	-111	-111	-110	-101	-101	-100	-100	-011	-010	-010	-001	-000
-0.2°	FRONT	-011	-011	-100	-100	-101	-101	-110	-110	-111	-111	-111	-200	-200	-201	-201
	REAR	-210	-210	-201	-201	-200	-111	-111	-110	-101	-101	-100	-100	-011	-010	-010
-0.4°	FRONT	-100	-101	-101	-110	-110	-110	-111	-111	-200	-200	-201	-201	-201	-210	-210
	REAR	-300	-211	-210	-210	-201	-201	-200	-111	-111	-110	-101	-101	-100	-011	-011

1. DETERMINE VEHICLE'S CURRENT CASTER AND CAMBER MEASUREMENTS.
2. USING THE CURRENT CASTER READING, READ DOWN THE APPROPRIATE COLUMN TO THE LINES CORRESPONDING TO THE CURRENT CAMBER READING.
3. CORRECTION VALUES WILL BE GIVEN FOR THE FRONT AND REAR BOLTS.
   EXAMPLE: CURRENT READING +1.6° CASTER +0.4° CAMBER. BY READING DOWN THE CHART FROM +1.6° CASTER TO +0.4° CAMBER YOU WILL FIND THAT THE FRONT BOLT REQUIRES AN ADJUSTMENT OF -101 AND THE REAR BOLT REQUIRES AN ADJUSTMENT OF +010.

FIGURE 16-35 Typical shim alignment chart. As noted, 1/8-in. (0.125) shims can be substituted for the 0.120-in. shims; 1/16-in. (0.0625) shims can be substituted for the 0.060-in. shims; and 1/32-in. (0.03125) shims can be substituted for the 0.030-in. shims.

After straightening the steering wheel, turn the tie rod adjustment until the toe for both wheels is within specifications. See Figure 16-39.

Test drive the vehicle for proper handling and centerline steering. *Centerline steering* is a centered steering wheel with the vehicle traveling a straight course.

CENTERING THE STEERING WHEEL

Centerline steering *should* be accomplished by adjusting the tie rod length on both sides of the vehicle while the toe is set.

CAUTION: Do not attempt to straighten the steering wheel by relocating the wheel on the steering column on a vehicle with two tie rod end adjusters. The steering wheel is positioned at the factory in the center of the steering gear, regardless of type. If the steering wheel is not in the center, then the variable ratio section of the gear will not be in the center as it is designed. Another possible problem with moving the steering wheel from its designed straight-ahead position is that the turning radius may be different for right- and left-hand turns.

STEERING WHEEL REMOVAL

If the steering wheel *must* be removed, first disconnect the airbag wire connector at the base of the steering column. This reduces the chance of personal injury and prevents accidental airbag deployment.

CAUTION: Always follow the manufacturer's recommended procedures whenever working on or around the steering column.

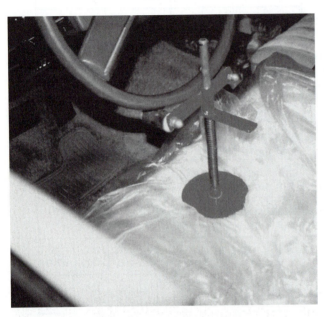

FIGURE 16-36 Many procedures for setting toe specify that the steering wheel be held in the straight-ahead position using a steering wheel lock, as shown. One method recommended by Hunter Engineering sets toe without using a steering wheel lock.

TECH TIP

LOCKING PLIERS TO THE RESCUE

Many vehicles use a jam nut on the tie rod end. This jam nut must be loosened to adjust the toe. Because the end of the tie rod is attached to a tie rod end that is movable, loosening the nut is often difficult. Every time force is applied to the nut, the tie rod end socket moves and prevents the full force of the wrench from being applied to the nut. To prevent this movement, simply attach locking pliers (Vise Grips®) to hold the tie rod. Wedge the pliers against the control arm to prevent any movement of the tie rod. By preventing the tie rod from moving, full force can be put on a wrench to loosen the jam nut without doing any harm to the tie rod end.

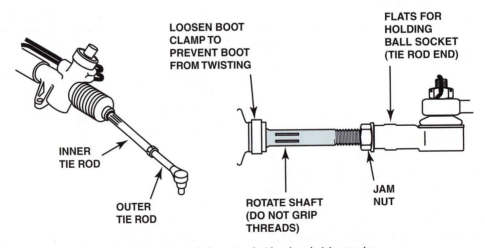

FIGURE 16-37 Adjusting toe by rotating the tie rod on a vehicle equipped with rack-and-pinion steering.

SLEEVE
ROTATING
TOOL

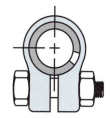

LEFT-HAND SLEEVE

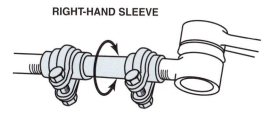

RIGHT-HAND SLEEVE

| TURN DOWNWARD TO DECREASE ROD LENGTH | TURN UPWARD TO INCREASE ROD LENGTH | TURN DOWNWARD TO INCREASE ROD LENGTH | TURN UPWARD TO DECREASE ROD LENGTH |

FIGURE 16-38   Toe is adjusted on a parallelogram-type steering linkage by turning adjustable tie rod sleeves. Special tie rod sleeve adjusting tools should be used that grip the slot in the sleeve and will not crush the sleeve while it is being rotated.

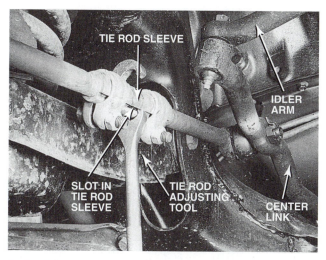

FIGURE 16-39   Special tie rod adjusting tools should be used to rotate the tie rod adjusting sleeves. The tool grips the slot in the sleeve and allows the service technician to rotate the sleeve without squeezing or damaging the sleeve.

Remove the center section of the steering column by removing the retaining screws, including the inflator module on vehicles equipped with an airbag.

After removal of the airbag inflator module, remove the steering wheel retaining nut. Note the locating marks on the steering wheel and steering shaft. See Figure 16-40. These marks indicate the proper position of the steering wheel for centerline steering. This means that the steering wheel spoke angle is straight and in line with the centerline position of the steering gear or rack-and-pinion steering unit.

FIGURE 16-40   Most vehicles have alignment marks made at the factory on the steering shaft and steering wheel to help the service technician keep the steering wheel in the center position.

Most steering wheels are attached to the steering shaft with a spline and a taper. After removing the steering wheel nut, use a steering wheel puller to remove the steering wheel from the steering shaft. See Figure 16-41.

NOTE: Because of the taper, it is easier to remove a steering wheel if the steering wheel puller is struck with a dead-blow hammer. The shock often releases the taper and allows the easy removal of the steering wheel. Some technicians simply use their hands and pound the steering wheel from the taper without using a puller.

To reinstall the steering wheel, align the steering wheel in the desired straight-ahead position and slip it down over the splines. Install and tighten the retaining nut to specifications.

REAL WORLD FIX

LEFT THRUST LINE, BUT A PULL TO THE RIGHT!

A new four-door sport sedan had been aligned several times at the dealership in an attempt to solve a pull to the right. The car had front-wheel-drive and four-wheel independent suspension. The dealer rotated the tires, and it made no difference. The alignment angles of all four wheels were in the center of specifications. The dealer even switched all four tires from another car in an attempt to solve the problem.

In frustration, the owner took the car to an alignment shop. Almost immediately the alignment technician discovered that the right rear wheel was slightly toed-in. This caused a pull to the right. See Figure 16-42.

The alignment technician adjusted the toe on the right rear wheel and reset the front toe. The car drove beautifully.

The owner was puzzled about why the new car dealer was unable to correct the problem. It was later discovered that the alignment machine at the dealership was out of calibration by the exact amount that the right rear wheel was out of specification. The car pulled to the right because the independent suspension created a rear steering force toward the left that caused the front to pull to the right. Alignment equipment manufacturers recommend that alignment equipment be calibrated regularly.

FIGURE 16-41   A puller being used to remove a steering wheel after the steering wheel retaining nut has been removed.

TOLERANCE ADJUSTMENT PROCEDURE

Many vehicles are designed and built without a method to change caster or camber, or both. (All vehicles have an adjustment for toe.) Before trying an aftermarket alignment correction kit, many technicians first attempt to correct the problem by moving the suspension attachment points within the build tolerance. All vehicles are constructed with a slight amount of leeway or tolerance; slight corrections can be made because bolt holes are almost always slightly larger than the bolt diameter, allowing for slight movement. When several fasteners are involved, such as where the power train cradle (subframe) attaches to the body of the front-wheel-drive vehicle, a measurable amount of alignment change (often over 1/2 degree) can be accomplished without special tools or alignment kits. The steps for **tolerance adjustment** include the following:

Step 1   Determine which way the suspension members have to be moved to accomplish the desired alignment— for example, the right front may require more positive camber to correct a pulling or tire wear problem.

Step 2   Locate and loosen the cradle (subframe) bolts about four turns each. DO NOT REMOVE ANY OF THE BOLTS.

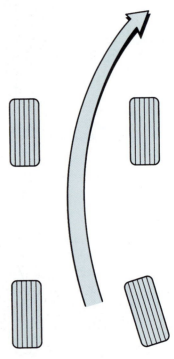

FIGURE 16-42   The toe-in on the right wheel creates a turning force toward the right.

Step 3   Using prybars, move the cradle in the direction that will result in an improvement of the alignment angles. Have an assistant tighten the bolts as pressure is maintained on the cradle.

Step 4   Measure the alignment angles and repeat the procedure if necessary.

AFTERMARKET ALIGNMENT METHODS

Accurate alignments are still possible on vehicles without factory methods of adjustment by using alignment kits or parts. Aftermarket alignment kits are available for most vehicles. Even when there are factory alignment methods, sometimes the range of adjustment is not enough to compensate for sagging frame members or other normal or accident-related faults. See Figures 16-43 and 16-44.

(a)

(b)

FIGURE 16-43   (a) Aftermarket camber kit designed to provide some camber adjustments for a vehicle that does not provide any adjustment. (b) Installation of this kit requires that the upper control arm shaft be removed. Note that the upper control arm was simply rotated out over the wheel pivoting on the upper ball joint.

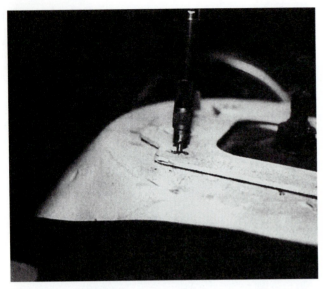

(a)

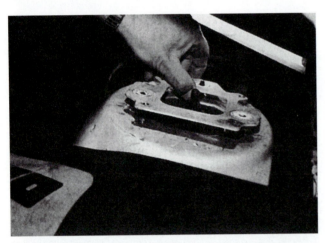

(b)

(c)

FIGURE 16-44 (a) The installation of some aftermarket alignment kits requires the use of special tools such as this cutter being used to drill out spot welds on the original alignment plate on a strut tower. (b) Original plate being removed. (c) Note the amount of movement the upper strut bearing mount has around the square openings in the strut tower. An aftermarket plate can now be installed to allow both camber and caster adjustment.

ALIGNING ELECTRONIC-SUSPENSION VEHICLES

When aligning a vehicle equipped with an electronic suspension, several additional steps may be required. Always check service information and read carefully all on-screen instructions on the alignment machine. Some examples of the steps that may be needed include:

- Verify the exact type of electronic suspension. This step could include checking the regular production order (RPO) code.
- Check that the ride height (suspension height) is within factory specifications.
- The steering wheel angle, as well as the radar cruise control sensor, will often need to be recalibrated using a scan tool. This is needed because the steering wheel may be in a different position after the alignment, and the steering wheel position sensor needs to be reset because the rear toe setting was changed. The rear thrust line could also have been changed. The radar cruise control needs to be calibrated to the revised rear thrust angle using a scan tool.

ALIGNING MODIFIED VEHICLES

If different springs were installed which in turn changes the suspension height or if larger or smaller wheels and tires were installed, many alignment shops would reject doing an alignment. If a shop attempted to align a vehicle, handling and tire wear problems were common. Because the ride height is changed from stock factory setting, the following can occur:

1. The steering axis inclination (SAI) is now incorrect.
2. Because the steering linkage and the control arms are no longer parallel, bump steer can occur. Bump steer cause the vehicle to dart to one side when a wheel hits a bump.
3. Because the ride height changed, camber and toe also changed. The camber change is often enough to prevent it from being able to be adjusted to within specifications.

Alignment alone will not correct these concerns. To allow for proper handling, the following aftermarket kits and part are available:

- Camber kits—These kits usually include a replacement control arm or offset cam, which provides additional camber adjustment.
- Bump steer kits—A bump steer kit can include a modified steering arm or rack-and-pinion steering gear repositioning components.

The kits available can be found listed on the alignment screen of many newer alignment machines, such as the

Hunter Engineering Company's WinAlign Tuner Custom Alignment for Modified Vehicles. During part of this alignment, the technician has to select one of two options:

- Maximum tire wear
- Maximum handling

Therefore, the technician has to determine from the customer which of these two parameters are most important. After the alignment, the instructions often state that the vehicle should be driven and then the temperature of the tires measured and recorded. Using a tire pyrometer, be sure to measure the temperature of each tire at the following locations for each tire:

- Approximately 1.5 inches (38 mm) from the outside edge of the tire in the tread rubber
- In the middle of the tread
- Approximately 1.5 inches (38 mm) from the inside edge of the tire in the tread rubber

The temperatures are then typed into the alignment machine, and the program calculates the final alignment settings. See Figure 16-45.

HIDDEN STRUCTURAL DAMAGE DIAGNOSIS

Many accidents result in hidden structural damage that can cause alignment angles to be out of specification. If alignment angles are out of specification tolerances, then accident damage should be suspected. Look for evidence of newly replaced suspension parts, body work, or repainted areas of the body. While a body and/or frame of a vehicle can be straightened, it must be done by a knowledgeable person using body-measuring equipment.

The first thing that must be done is to determine a *datum plane. Datum* means a basis on which other measurements can be based. The datum plane is the horizontal plane.

However, most alignment technicians do not have access to body/frame alignment equipment. The service technician can use a common steel rule to measure several points of the vehicle to determine if the vehicle is or is not damaged or needs to be sent to a frame shop for repair.

Frame/Body Diagonals

If the frame or body is perfectly square, then the diagonal measurements should be within 1/8 in. (3 mm) of each other. See Figure 16-46.

TECH TIP

TSBs CAN SAVE TIME

Technical service bulletins (TSBs) are issued by vehicle and aftermarket manufacturers to inform technicians of a situation or technical problem and give the corrective steps and a list of parts needed to solve the problem.

TSBs are often released by new vehicle manufacturers to the dealership service department. They usually concern the current-year vehicle of a particular model. While many of these TSBs concern minor problems covering few vehicles, many contain very helpful solutions to hard-to-find problems.

Most TSBs can be purchased directly from the manufacturer, but the cost is usually very high. TSBs can also be purchased through aftermarket companies that are licensed to include TSBs on CD-ROM computer discs. Factory TSBs can often save the technician many hours of troubleshooting.

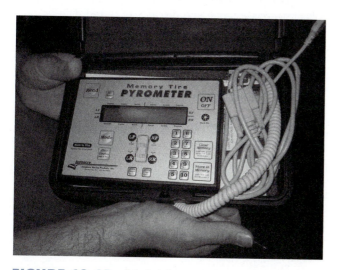

FIGURE 16-45 A typical tire temperature pyrometer. The probe used is a needle that penetrates about 1/4 inch (7 mm) into the tread of the tire for most accurate readings.

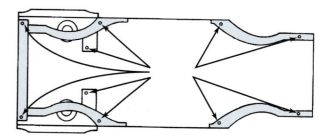

FIGURE 16-46 Jig holes used at the assembly plant to locate suspension and drive train components.

While there are specified measurement points indicated by the manufacturer, the diagonal measurements can be made from almost any point that is repeated exactly on the other side, such as the center of a bolt in the suspension mounting bracket.

ALIGNMENT TROUBLESHOOTING

The following table lists common alignment problems and their probable causes.

Symptom-Based Alignment Guide

Problems	Probable Causes
Pull left/right	Uneven tire pressure, tire conicity, mismatched tires, unequal camber, unequal caster, brake drag, setback, suspension/frame sag, unbalanced power assist, bent spindle, bent strut, worn suspension components (front or rear), rear suspension misalignment.
Incorrect steering wheel position	Incorrect individual or total toe, rear wheel misalignment, excessive suspension or steering component play, worn rack-and-pinion attachment bushings, individual toe adjusters not provided.
Hard steering	Improper tire pressure, binding steering gear or steering linkage, low P/S fluid, excessive positive caster, lack of lubrication, upper strut mount(s), worn power steering pump, worn P/S belt.
Loose steering	Loose wheel bearings, worn steering or suspension components, loose steering gear mount, excessive steering gear play, loose or worn steering coupler.
Excessive road shock	Excessive positive caster, excessive negative camber, improper tire inflation, too wide wheel/tire combination for the vehicle, worn or loose shocks, worn springs.
Poor returnability	Incorrect camber or caster, bent spindle or strut, binding suspension or steering components, improper tire inflation.
Wander/instability	Incorrect alignment, defective or improperly inflated tires, worn steering or suspension parts, bent spindle or strut, worn or loose steering gear, loose wheel bearings.
Squeal/scuff on turns	Defective or improperly inflated tires, incorrect turning angle (TOOT), bent steering arms, excessive wheel setback, poor driving habits (too fast for conditions), worn suspension or steering parts.
Excessive body sway	Loose or broken stabilizer bar links or bushings, worn shocks or mountings, broken or sagging springs, uneven vehicle load, uneven or improper tire pressure.
Memory steer	Binding steering linkage, binding steering gear, binding upper strut mount, ball joint, or kingpin.
Bump steer	Misalignment of steering linkage, bent steering arm or frame, defective or sagged springs, uneven load, bent spindle or strut.
Torque steer	Bent spindle or strut, bent steering arm, misaligned frame, worn torque strut, defective engine or transaxle mounts, drive axle misalignment, mismatched or unequally inflated tires.

ALIGNMENT   Step-by-Step

STEP 1 Begin the alignment procedure by first driving the vehicle onto the alignment rack as straight as possible.

STEP 2 Position the front tires in the center of the turn plates. These turn plates can be moved inward and outward to match a vehicle of any width.

STEP 3 Raise the vehicle and position the alignment rack following the rack manufacturer's instructions.

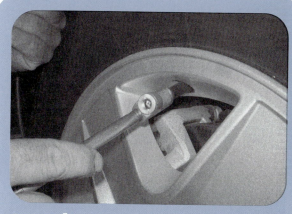

STEP 4 Check and adjust tire pressures and perform the prealignment checks necessary to be assured of proper alignment.

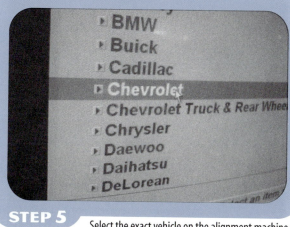

STEP 5 Select the exact vehicle on the alignment machine.

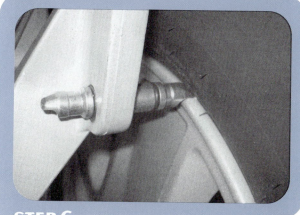

STEP 6 Securely mount the alignment heads or target wheels.

(continued)

ALIGNMENT continued

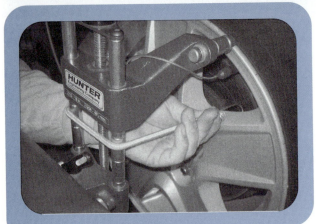

STEP 7   If mounting a transmitter-type alignment head, be sure to attach the retaining wire to the tire valve.

STEP 8   After installation of the heads, follow the specified procedure for compensation, which allows accurate alignment readings.

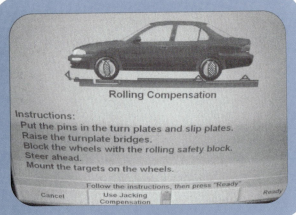

STEP 9   Rolling compensation is used on machines that use lasers and wheel targets.

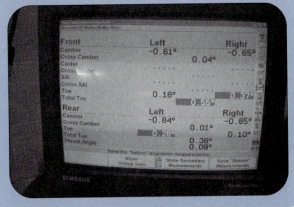

STEP 10   An alignment reading is displayed even though caster has not yet been measured. The readings marked in red indicate that they are not within specifications.

STEP 11   Before performing a caster sweep, install a brake pedal depressor to keep the front wheels from rotating when the steering wheel is turned.

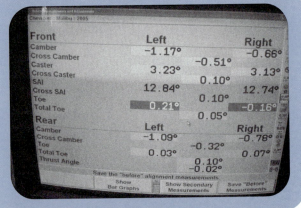

STEP 12   Perform the caster sweep by turning the front wheels inward, and then outward following the instructions on the screen.

ALIGNMENT continued

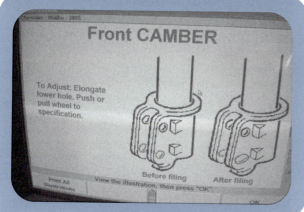

STEP 13

Most alignment machines will display where to make the alignment correction and will often include drawings and live-action videos that show the procedure.

STEP 14

The rear toe is being adjusted by rotating the eccentric cam on the lower control arm while watching the display.

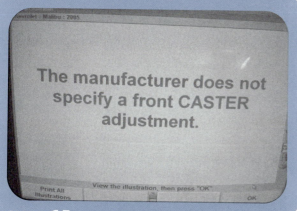

STEP 15

The alignment machine display indicates that front caster is not a factory-adjustable angle.

STEP 16

Adjusting the front toe on this vehicle involves loosening the jam nut (left wrench) and rotating the tie rod using the right wrench.

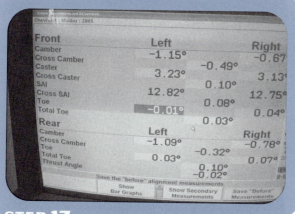

STEP 17

One last adjustment of the left front toe is needed to achieve a perfect alignment. The final alignment reading can be printed and attached to the work order.

STEP 18

After disconnecting all of the attachments, reinstalling the valve caps, and removing the steering wheel holder, the vehicle should be test driven to check for proper alignment before returning it to the customer.

SUMMARY

1. Before attempting to align any vehicle, it must be checked for proper ride height (trim height), tire conditions, and tire pressures. A thorough inspection of all steering and suspension components must also be made.

2. Memory steer is a condition that causes the vehicle to lead or pull to the same direction it was last steered. Binding steering or suspension components are the most frequent causes of memory steer.

3. Torque steer is the pull or lead caused by engine torque being applied to the front wheels unevenly on a front-wheel-drive vehicle. Out-of-level drive train, suspension components, or tires are the most common causes of excessive torque steer.

4. Lead/pull diagnosis involves a thorough road test and careful inspection of all tires.

5. There are three types of alignment: geometric centerline, thrust line, and total four-wheel alignment. Only total four-wheel alignment should be used on a vehicle with an adjustable rear suspension.

6. The proper sequence for a complete four-wheel alignment is rear camber, rear toe, front camber and caster, and front toe.

REVIEW QUESTIONS

1. List 10 prealignment checks that should be performed before the wheel alignment is checked and/or adjusted.

2. Describe the difference between a lead (drift) and a pull.

3. Explain the causes and possible corrections for torque steer.

4. Explain the causes and possible corrections for memory steer.

5. List the necessary steps to follow for a four-wheel alignment.

CHAPTER QUIZ

1. When performing an alignment, which angle is the most important for tire wear?
   a. Toe
   b. Camber
   c. Caster
   d. SAI (KPI)

2. Replacement rubber control arm bushings should be _____.
   a. Tightened while the control arm is held in a vise
   b. Torqued with the vehicle on the ground in normal driving position
   c. Tightened with the control arm resting on the frame
   d. Lubricated with engine oil before tightening

3. Which alignment angle is adjustable on all vehicles?
   a. Camber
   b. Caster
   c. Toe
   d. SAI (KPI)

4. Positive (+) toe is _____.
   a. Toe-in
   b. Toe-out

5. If the top of the steering axis is tilted 2 degrees toward the rear of the vehicle, this is _____.
   a. Positive camber
   b. Negative camber
   c. Negative caster
   d. Positive caster

6. Which angle is largest?
   a. 0.55 degrees
   b. 1/4 degree
   c. 45 minutes
   d. 1/2 degree

7. If the turning radius (toe-out on turns, or TOOT) is out of specification, what part or component is defective?
   a. The strut is bent.
   b. The steering arm is bent.
   c. The spindle is bent.
   d. The control arm is bent.

8. Which angle determines the thrust angle?

    a. Front toe

    b. Rear toe

    c. Rear camber

    d. Front caster, SAI, and included angle

9. The proper order in which to perform a four-wheel alignment is _____.

    a. Front camber, caster toe, rear camber, then rear toe

    b. Rear camber, front camber, caster, front toe, then rear toe

    c. Rear camber and toe, front camber, caster, then front toe

    d. Front toe, camber, front caster, rear camber, then rear toe

10. Centerline steering is achieved by correctly adjusting _____.

    a. Rear and front toe

    b. SAI and included angle

    c. Caster and SAI

    d. Rear camber

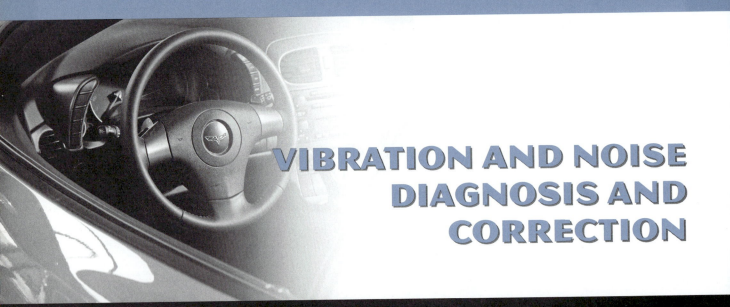

VIBRATION AND NOISE DIAGNOSIS AND CORRECTION

OBJECTIVES

After studying Chapter 17, the reader should be able to:

1. Prepare for Suspension and Steering (A4) ASE certification test content area "C" (Related Suspension and Steering Service).

2. Discuss how to perform a road test for vibration and noise diagnosis.

3. List the possible vehicle components that can cause a vibration or noise.

4. Describe the use of a reed tachometer or electronic vibration analyzer in determining the frequency of the vibration.

5. Discuss the procedures used in measuring and correcting drive shaft angles.

6. List the items that should be checked or adjusted to prevent or repair power steering and/or noise under the vehicle.

KEY TERMS

Companion Flange (p. 411)
Drive Line Angles (p. 411)
Drive Shaft Runout (p. 411)
EVA (p. 408)
Frequency (p. 406)
Hertz (Hz) (p. 406)

Neutral Run-up Test (p. 404)
NVH (p. 403)
Rolling Circumference (p. 406)
Vibration Order (p. 406)
Witness Mark (p. 404)

Vibration and noise are two of the most frequent complaints from vehicle owners and drivers. If something is vibrating, it can move air; changes in air pressure (air movement) are what we call noise. Though anything that moves vibrates, wheels and tires account for the majority of vehicle vibration problems.

CAUSES OF VIBRATION AND NOISE

Vehicles are designed and built to prevent vibrations and to dampen out any vibrations that cannot be eliminated. For example, engines are designed and balanced to provide smooth power at all engine speeds. Some engines, such as large four-cylinder or 90-degree V-6's, require special engine mounts to absorb or dampen any remaining oscillations or vibrations. Dampening weights are also fastened to engines or transmissions in an effort to minimize **noise, vibration,** and **harshness** (called **NVH**).

If a new vehicle has a vibration or noise problem, then the most likely cause is an assembly or parts problem. This is difficult to diagnose because the problem could be almost anything, and a careful analysis procedure should be followed as outlined later in this chapter.

If an older vehicle has a vibration or noise problem, the first step is to question the vehicle owner as to when the problem first appeared. Some problems and possible causes include the following:

Problem	Possible Causes
Vibration at idle	Engine mount could be defective or not reinstalled correctly after an engine or transmission repair.
Noise/vibration	Exhaust system replacement or repair. See Figure 17-1.

NOTE: A typical exhaust system can "grow" or lengthen about 2 in. (1 cm) when warm, as compared with room temperature. Always inspect an exhaust system when warm, if possible, being careful to avoid being burned by the hot exhaust components.

Problem	Possible Causes
Vibration at higher vehicle speeds	Incorrect drive shaft angles could be the result of a change in the U-joints, springs, transmission mounts, or anything else that can cause a change in drive shaft angles.
Noise over rough roads	Exhaust system or parking brake cables are often causes of noise while driving over rough road surfaces. See Figure 17-2. Defective shock absorbers or shock absorber mountings are also a common cause of noise.

TEST DRIVE

The first thing a technician should do when given a vibration or noise problem to solve is to duplicate the condition. This means the technician should drive the vehicle and observe

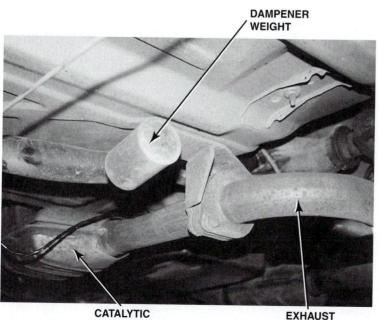

DAMPENER WEIGHT

CATALYTIC CONVERTER

EXHAUST PIPE

FIGURE 17-1 Many vehicles, especially those equipped with four-cylinder engines, use a dampener weight attached to the exhaust system to dampen out certain frequency vibrations.

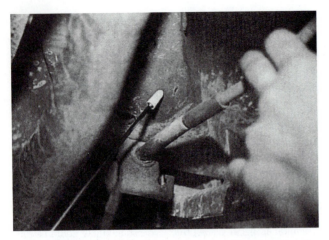

FIGURE 17-2 This parking brake cable was hitting on the underneath of the body. It was found by looking for evidence of **witness marks.**

when and where the vibration is felt or heard. See the chart in Figure 17-3.

Though there are many possible sources of a vibration, some simple observations may help to locate the problem quickly:

1. If the vibration is felt or seen in the steering wheel, dash, or hood of the vehicle, the problem is most likely to be caused by defective or out-of-balance *front* wheels or tires. See Figure 17-4.
2. If the vibration is felt in the seat of the pants or seems to be all over the vehicle, the problem is most likely to be caused by defective or out-of-balance *rear* wheels or tires. In a rear-wheel-drive vehicle, the drive shaft (propeller shaft) and related components might also be the cause.

While on the test drive, try to gather as much information about the vibration or noise complaint as possible.

Step 1   Determine the vehicle speed (mph or km/h) or engine speed (RPM) where the vibration occurs. Drive on a smooth, level road and accelerate up to highway speed, noting the vehicle speed or speeds at which the vibration or noise occurs.

Step 2   To help pin down the exact cause of the vibration, accelerate to a speed slightly above the point of maximum vibration. Shift the vehicle into neutral and allow it to coast down through the speed of maximum vibration. If the vibration still exists, then the cause of the problem could be wheels, tires, or other rotating components, *except* the engine.

If the vibration is eliminated when shifted out of gear, the problem is related to the engine or transmission.

NOTE: If the engine or transmission has been removed from the vehicle, such as during a clutch replacement, carefully observe the location and condition of the mounts. If an engine or transmission mount is defective or out of location, engine and drive line vibrations are often induced and transmitted throughout the vehicle.

NEUTRAL RUN-UP TEST

The **neutral run-up test** is used to determine if the source of the vibration is engine-related. With the transmission in Neutral or Park, slowly increase the engine RPM and with a tachometer observe the RPM at which the vibration occurs. DO NOT EXCEED THE MANUFACTURER'S RECOMMENDED MAXIMUM ENGINE RPM.

VIBRATION DURING BRAKING

A vibration during braking usually indicates out-of-round brake drums, warped disc brake rotors, or other braking system problems. The *front* rotors are the cause of the vibration

TECH TIP

THE DUCT TAPE TRICK

A clicking noise heard at low speeds from the wheels is a common noise complaint. This noise is usually most noticeable while driving with the windows lowered. This type of noise is caused by loose disc brake pads or noisy wheel covers. Wire wheel covers are especially noisy. To confirm exactly what is causing the noise, simply remove the wheel covers and drive the vehicle. If the clicking noise is still present, check the brakes and wheels for faults. If the noise is gone with the wheel covers removed, use duct tape over the inner edge of the wheel covers before installing them onto the wheels. The duct tape will cushion and dampen the wheel cover and help reduce the noise. The sharp prongs of the wheel cover used to grip the wheel will pierce through the duct tape and still help retain the wheel covers.

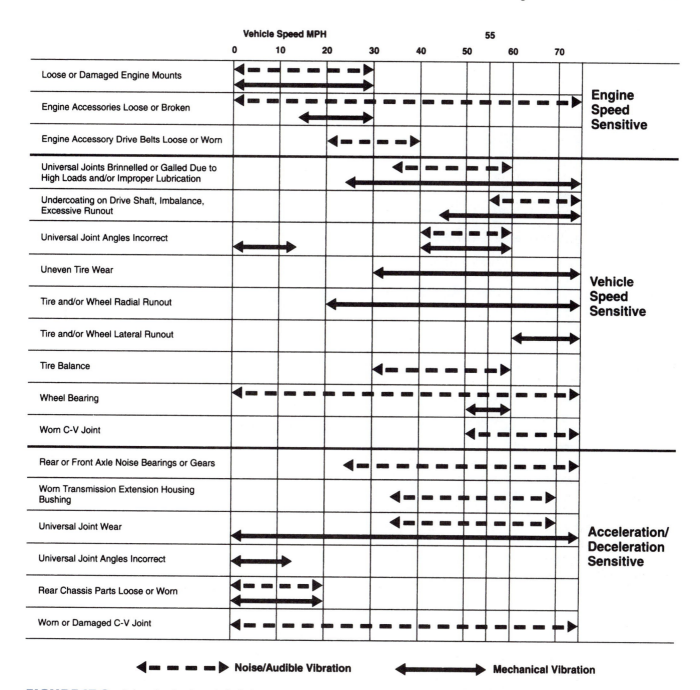

FIGURE 17-3   A chart showing the typical vehicle and engine speeds at which various components will create a noise or vibration and under what conditions. *(Courtesy of Dana Corporation)*

if the steering wheel is also vibrating (moving) during braking. The *rear* drums or rotors are the cause of the vibration if the vibration is felt throughout the vehicle and brake pedal, but *not* the steering wheel. Another way to check if the vibration is due to rear brakes is to use the parking brake to stop the vehicle. If a vibration occurs while using the parking brake, the rear brakes are the cause.

NOTE: Wheels should *never* be installed using an air impact wrench. Even installation torque is almost impossible to control, and overtightening almost always occurs. The use of impact wrenches causes the wheel, hub, and rotor to distort, resulting in vibrations and brake pedal pulsations. Always tighten wheel lugs in the proper sequence and with proper torque value, using a torque wrench or torque-limiting adapter bars.

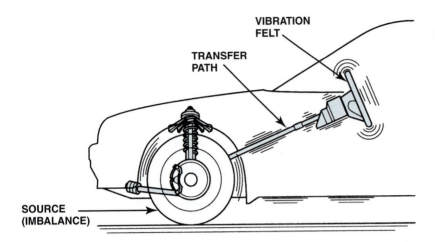

FIGURE 17-4 Vibration created at one point is easily transferred to the passenger compartment. MacPherson strut suspensions are more sensitive to tire imbalance than SLA-type suspensions.

VIBRATION FELT

TRANSFER PATH

SOURCE (IMBALANCE)

REAL WORLD FIX

S-10 PICKUP TRUCK FRAME NOISE

The owner of a Chevrolet S-10 pickup truck complained of a loud squeaking noise, especially when turning left. Several technicians attempted to solve the problem and replaced shock absorbers, ball joints, and control arm bushings without solving the problem. The problem was finally discovered to be the starter motor hitting the frame. A measurement of new vehicles indicated that the clearance between the starter motor and the frame was about 1/8 in. (0.125 in.) (0.3 cm)! The sagging of the engine mount and the weight transfer of the engine during cornering caused the starter motor to rub up against the frame. The noise was transmitted through the frame throughout the vehicle and made the source of the noise difficult to find.

VIBRATION SPEED RANGES

Vibration describes an oscillating motion around a reference position. The number of times a complete motion cycle takes place during a period of 1 second is called **frequency** and is measured in **Hertz (Hz)** (named for Heinrich R. Hertz, a nineteenth-century German physicist). See Figures 17-5 and 17-6.

The unit of measure for frequency was originally cycles per second (CPS). This was changed to Hz in the 1960s.

To help understand frequency, think of the buzzing sound made by some fluorescent light fixtures. That 60-Hz hum is the same frequency as the alternating current. A 400-Hz sound is high-pitched. In fact, most people can only hear sounds

between 20 and 15,000 Hz. Generally, low-frequency oscillations between 1 and 80 Hz are the most disturbing to vehicle occupants.

Vibration Order

Vibration order is the number of vibrations created in one revolution of a component. A single high spot on a tire, for example, will cause one bump per revolution, which is a first-order vibration. If the tire rotates 10 times per second, there are 10 disturbances per second, which is also called a first-order vibration of 10 Hz. If there are two bumps on a tire, a second-order vibration is created that would generate a vibration of 20 Hz if the tire were rotating 10 times per second.

Tire and Wheel Vibrations

Typical vehicle components that can cause vibration in specific frequency ranges at 50 mph (80 km/h) include the following.

Low Frequency (5–20 Hz). This frequency range of vibration is very disturbing to many drivers because this type of vibration can be seen and felt in the steering wheel, seats, mirrors, and other components. Terms used to describe this type of vibration include *nibble, shake, oscillation, shimmy,* and *shudder.*

Tires and wheels are the most common source of vibration in the low-frequency range. To determine the *exact* frequency for the vehicle being checked, the following formula and procedure can be used.

Tire rolling frequency is calculated as follows:

$$Hz = \frac{mph \times 1.47}{tire \; circumference \; in \; ft}$$

This formula works for all vehicles regardless of tire size. The circumference (distance around the tread) can be measured by using a tape measure around the tire. The **rolling**

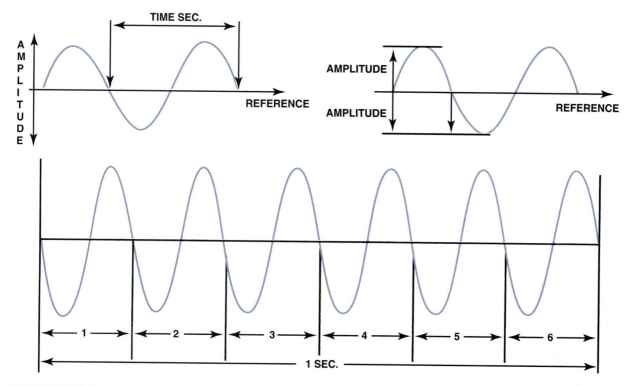

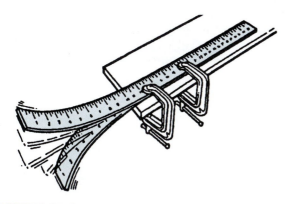

FIGURE 17-5 Hertz means *cycles per second*. If six cycles occur in 1 second, then the frequency is 6 Hz. The amplitude refers to the total movement of the vibrating component. *(Courtesy of Hunter Engineering Company)*

FIGURE 17-6 Every time the end of a clamped yardstick moves up and down, it is one cycle. The number of cycles divided by the time equals the frequency. If the yardstick moves up and down 10 times (10 cycles) in 2 seconds, the frequency is 5 Hertz (10 ÷ 2 = 5). *(Courtesy of Hunter Engineering Company)*

circumference of the tire is usually shorter due to the contact patch. To determine the rolling circumference, follow these easy steps:

Step 1   Inflate the tire(s) to the recommended pressure. Park the vehicle with the valve stem pointing straight down and mark the location on the floor directly below the valve stem.

Step 2   Slowly roll the vehicle forward (or rearward) until the valve stem is again straight down. Mark the floor below the valve stem.

Step 3   Measure the distance between the marks in feet. See Figure 17-7. To change inches to feet, divide by 12 (for example, 77 in. divided by 12 in. = 6.4 ft.). To determine the rolling frequency of this tire at 60 mph, use 6.4 feet as the tire circumference in the formula.

$$\text{Frequency} = \frac{60 \text{ mph} \times 1.47}{6.4 \text{ ft}} = 13.8 \text{ Hz}$$

NOTE: Tire circumference is critical on four-wheel-drive vehicles. The transfer case can be damaged and severe vibration can occur if the rolling circumference is different by more than 0.6 in. (15 mm) on the same axle, or more than 1.2 in. (30 mm) front to rear.

Drive Line Vibrations

Medium Frequency (20–50 Hz). This frequency range of vibrations may also be described as a shake, oscillation, or shimmy. These higher frequencies may also be called *roughness* or *buzz*. **Components become blurred and impossible to focus on above a vibration of 30 Hz.**

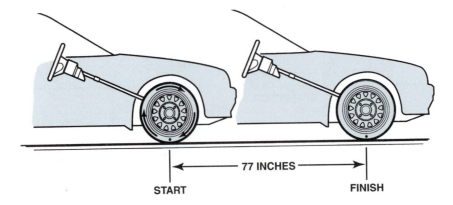

FIGURE 17-7 Determining the rolling circumference of a tire.

REAL WORLD FIX

THE VIBRATING VAN

After the engine was replaced in a rear-wheel-drive van, a vibration that felt like an engine miss was noticed by the driver. Because the vibration was not noticed before the engine was replaced, the problem was thought to be engine-related. Many tests failed to find anything wrong with the engine. Even the ignition distributor was replaced, along with the electronic ignition module, on the suspicion that an ignition misfire was the cause.

After hours of troubleshooting, a collapsed transmission mount was discovered. After replacing the transmission mount, the "engine miss" and the vibration were eliminated. The collapsed mount caused the drive shaft U-joint angles to be unequal, which caused the vibration.

FIGURE 17-8 An electronic vibration analyzer.

For example, if a vibration occurs at 3,000 engine RPM, then the frequency is 50 Hz.

$$Hz = \frac{3000 \text{ RPM}}{60} = 50 \text{ Hz}$$

FREQUENCY

Measuring Frequency

Knowing the frequency of the vibration greatly improves the speed of tracking down the source of the vibration. Vibration can be measured using an **electronic vibration analyzer (EVA).** See Figure 17-8.

A reed tachometer is placed on the dash, console, or other suitable location inside the vehicle. The vehicle is then driven on a smooth, level road at the speed where the vibration is felt the most. The reeds of the reed tachometer vibrate at the frequency of the vibration.

Engine-Related Vibrations

High Frequency (50–100 Hz). Vibrations in this range may also be *heard* as a moan or hum. The vibration is high enough that it may be felt as a numbing sensation that can put the driver's hands or feet to sleep. Engine-related vibrations vary with engine speed, regardless of road speed. Frequency of the vibration from an engine is determined from the engine speed in revolutions per minute (RPM).

$$\text{Frequency in Hz} = \frac{\text{engine RPM}}{60}$$

NOTE: Other types of vibration diagnostic equipment may be available from vehicle or aftermarket manufacturers.

Correcting Low-Frequency Vibrations

A low-frequency vibration (5–20 Hz) is usually due to tire/wheel problems, including the following:

1. Tire and/or wheel imbalance. See Figures 17-9 through 17-11.
2. Tire and/or wheel radial or lateral runout.
3. Radial force variation within the tire itself.
4. If front-wheel drive, a bent or damaged drive axle joint or shaft.

Tires that are out of round or defective will be most noticeable at low speeds, will get better as speed increases, and then will vibrate again at highway speeds.

Tires that are out of balance will tend not to be noticeable at low speeds, and will be most noticeable at highway speeds.

NOTE: High-performance tires are manufactured with different carcass and belt package angles as well as a stiffer, harder tread rubber compound than standard tires. While these construction features produce a tire that allows sporty handling, the tire itself causes a stiff ride, often with increased tire noise. High-performance tires also generate and transmit different frequencies than regular tires. Using replacement high-performance tires on a vehicle not designed for this type of tire may create noise and vibration concerns for the driver/owner that the technician cannot correct.

Correcting Medium-Frequency Vibrations

Medium-frequency vibrations (20–50 Hz) can be caused by imbalances of the drive line as well as such things as the following:

1. Defective U-joints. Sometimes an old or a newly installed U-joint can be binding. This binding of the U-joint can cause a vibration. Often a blow to the joint with a brass hammer can free a binding U-joint. This is often called *relieving the joint*. Hitting the joint using a brass punch and a hammer also works well.
2. Drive shaft imbalance (such as undercoating on the drive shaft) or excessive runout.
3. Incorrect or unequal drive shaft angles.

Drive line vibrations are usually the result of an imbalance in the rotating drive shaft (propeller shaft) assembly.

The drive shaft of a typical rear-wheel-drive (RWD) vehicle rotates at about three times the speed of the drive wheels. The differential gears in the rear end change the direction of the power flow from the engine and drive shaft, as well as provide for a gear reduction. Front-wheel-drive (FWD) vehicles do not have medium-frequency vibration caused by the drive shaft because the differential is inside the transaxle and the drive axle shafts rotate at the same speed as the wheels and tires.

All drive shafts are balanced at the factory, and weights are attached to the drive shaft, if necessary, to achieve proper balance. A drive shaft should be considered one of the items checked if the medium-frequency vibration is felt throughout the vehicle or in the seat of the pants.

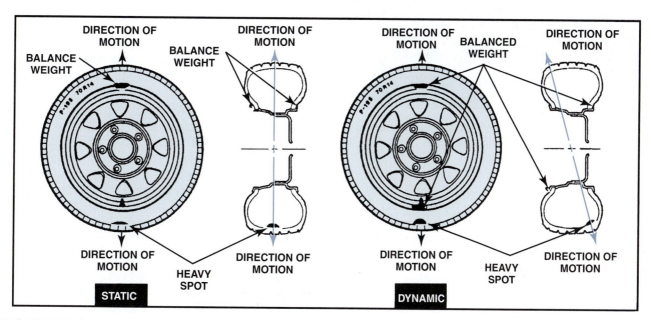

FIGURE 17-9   Properly balancing all wheels and tires solves most low-frequency vibrations.

FIGURE 17-10 An out-of-balance tire showing scallops or bald spots around the tire. Even if correctly balanced, this cupped tire would create a vibration.

FIGURE 17-11 Another cause of a vibration that is often blamed on wheels or tires is a bent bearing hub. Use a dial indicator to check the flange for runout.

NOTE: If a vibration is felt during heavy acceleration at low speeds, a common cause is incorrect universal joint angles. This often happens when the rear of the vehicle is heavily loaded or sagging due to weak springs. If the angles of the U-joints are not correct (excessive or unequal from one end of the drive shaft to the other), a vibration will also be present at higher speeds and is usually torque-sensitive.

Correcting High-Frequency Vibrations

High-frequency vibrations (50–100 Hz) are commonly caused by a fault of the clutch, torque converter, or transmission main shaft that rotates at engine speed; in the engine itself, they can be caused by items such as the following:

1. A defective spark plug wire
2. A burned valve
3. Any other mechanical fault that will prevent any one or more cylinders from firing correctly
4. A defective harmonic balancer

If the engine is the cause, run in Neutral at the same engine speed. If the vibration is present, perform a complete engine condition diagnosis. Some engines only misfire under load and will not vibrate while in Neutral without a load being placed on the engine, even though the engine is being operated at the same speed (RPM).

Exhaust system pulses occur at the following conditions:

4-cylinder engine	$2 \times$ engine RPM
6-cylinder engine	$3 \times$ engine RPM
8-cylinder engine	$4 \times$ engine RPM

If the exhaust system is touching the body, it will transfer these pulses as a vibration. Exhaust system vibrations vary with engine speed and usually increase as the load on the engine increases.

TECH TIP

SQUEAKS AND RATTLES

Many squeaks and rattles commonly heard on any vehicle can be corrected by tightening all bolts and nuts you can see. Raise the hood and tighten all fender bolts. Tighten all radiator support and bumper brackets. Open the doors and tighten all hinge and body bolts.

An even more thorough job can be done by hoisting the vehicle and tightening all under-vehicle fasteners, including inner fender bolts, exhaust hangers, shock mounts, and heat shields. It is amazing how much this quiets the vehicle, especially on older models. It also makes the vehicle feel more solid with far less flex in the body, especially when traveling over railroad crossings or rough roads.

CORRECTING DRIVE LINE ANGLES

Incorrect **drive line angles** are usually caused by one or more of the following:

1. Worn, damaged, or improperly installed U-joints.
2. Worn, collapsed, or defective engine or transmission mount(s).
3. Incorrect vehicle ride height. (As weight is added to the rear of a rear-wheel-drive vehicle, the front of the differential rises and changes the working angle of the rear U-joint.)

CHECKING DRIVE SHAFT RUNOUT

Check to see that the drive shaft is not bent by performing a **drive shaft runout** test using a dial indicator. Runout should be measured at three places along the length of the drive shaft.

The maximum allowable runout is 0.030 in. (0.76 mm). If runout exceeds 0.030 in., remove the drive shaft from the rear end and reindex the drive shaft onto the **companion flange** at 180 degrees from its original location. Remeasure the drive shaft runout. If the runout is still greater than 0.030 in., the drive shaft is bent and needs replacement *or* the companion flange needs replacement.

MEASURING DRIVE SHAFT U-JOINT PHASING

Measuring drive shaft U-joint phasing involves checking to see if the front and rear U-joints are directly in line or parallel with each other. With the vehicle on a drive-on lift, or if using a frame-contact hoist, support the weight of the vehicle on stands placed under the rear axle. Place an inclinometer on the front U-joint bearing cup and rotate the drive shaft until horizontal; note the inclinometer reading. Move the inclinometer to the rear U-joint. The angles should match. If the angles are not equal, the drive shaft is out of phase and should be replaced. Incorrect phasing is usually due to a twisted drive shaft or an incorrectly welded end yoke.

NOTE: Some high-performance General Motors vehicles were built with a slight difference in drive shaft phasing. This was done to counteract the twisting of the drive shaft during rapid acceleration.

COMPANION FLANGE RUNOUT

The companion flange is splined to the rear axle pinion shaft and provides the mounting for the rear U-joint of the drive shaft. Two items should be checked on the companion flange while diagnosing a vibration:

1. The companion flange should have a maximum runout of 0.006 in. (0.15 mm) while being rotated. If the flange was pounded off with a hammer during a previous repair, the deformed flange could cause a vibration.
2. Check the companion flange for a missing balance weight. Many flanges have a balance weight that is spot-welded onto the flange. If the weight is missing, a drive line vibration can result.

BALANCING THE DRIVE SHAFT

If the drive shaft (propeller shaft) is within runout specification and a vibration still exists, the balance of the shaft should be checked and corrected as necessary.

Checking for drive shaft balance is usually done with a strobe balancer. The strobe balancer was commonly used to balance tires on the vehicle and was very popular before the universal use of computer tire balancers. A strobe balancer uses a magnetic sensor that is attached to the pinion housing of the differential. The sensor causes a bright light to flash (strobe) whenever a shock force is exerted on the sensor. The procedure for testing drive shaft balance using a strobe balancer includes the following:

Step 1   Raise the vehicle and mark the drive shaft with four equally spaced marks around its circumference. Label each mark with a 1, 2, 3, and 4. See Figure 17-12.

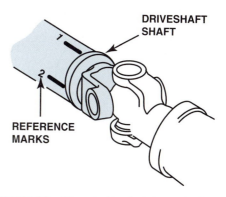

FIGURE 17-12   When checking the balance of a drive shaft, make reference marks around the shaft so that the location of the unbalance may be viewed when using a strobe light.

Step 2   Attach the strobe balancer sensor to the bottom of the differential housing as close to the companion flange as possible. See Figure 17-13.

NOTE: The sensor does not rotate with the drive shaft but picks up the vibration of the drive shaft through the differential housing.

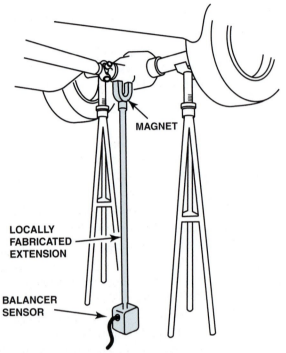

MAGNET

LOCALLY FABRICATED EXTENSION

BALANCER SENSOR

NOTE: LOCALLY FABRICATED EXTENSION FOR BALANCER PICK-UP CONSISTS OF 3/8" TUBE AND COMPRESSION FITTINGS

FIGURE 17-13   Using a strobe balancer to check for drive line vibration requires that an extension be used on the magnetic sensor. Tall safety stands are used to support the rear axle to keep the drive shaft angles the same as when the vehicle is on the road.

Step 3   With the vehicle securely hoisted and the drive wheels off the ground, start the engine and put the transmission into gear to allow the drive wheels to rotate.

Step 4   Hold the strobe light close to the marks on the drive shaft.
  a. If the light does *not* flash, the drive shaft is balanced and no corrective action is necessary.
  b. If the light *does* flash, observe what number mark is shown by the flashing light.

Step 5   Apply hose clamps so that the screw portion of the clamp(s) is *opposite* the number seen with the strobe light. The screw portion of the hose clamp is the corrective weight. Remember, the strobe light sensor was mounted to the *bottom* of the differential housing. The strobe light flashes when the heavy part of the drive shaft is facing *downward*. If the heavy part of the drive shaft is down, then corrective weight must be added to the opposite side of the drive shaft. See Figures 17-14 and 17-15.

NOISE DIAGNOSIS

Noise diagnosis is difficult because a noise is easily transmitted from its source to other places in the vehicle. For example, if a rear shock absorber mount is loose, the noise may be heard as coming from the middle or even the front of the vehicle. As the axle moves up and down, the noise is created where metal touches metal between the shock absorber bolt and the axle shock mount. The noise is then transmitted throughout the frame of the vehicle, and therefore causes the sound to appear to come from "everywhere." To help pin down the exact location of the sound, perform a thorough test drive, including

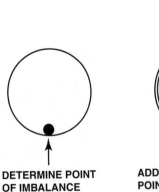

DETERMINE POINT OF IMBALANCE

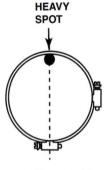

HEAVY SPOT

ADD CLAMPS 180° FROM POINT OF IMBALANCE UNTIL THEY BECOME THE HEAVY SPOT

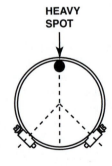

HEAVY SPOT

ROTATE TWO CLAMPS EQUALLY AWAY FROM EACH OTHER UNTIL BEST BALANCE IS ACHIEVED

FIGURE 17-14   Typical procedure to balance a drive shaft using hose clamps.

FIGURE 17-15 Two clamps were required to balance this front drive shaft of a four-wheel-drive vehicle. Be careful when using hose clamps that the ends of the clamps do not interfere with the body or other parts of the vehicle.

REAL WORLD FIX

EVERYTHING IS OK UNTIL I HIT A BUMP

The owner of an eight-year-old vehicle asked that the vibration in the steering wheel be repaired. It seemed that the vehicle drove fine until the front wheels hit a bump in the road—then the steering wheel shimmied for a few seconds.

This problem is typical of a vehicle with excessive steering linkage freeplay. When driving straight, centrifugal (rolling) force on the tires tends to force the front wheels outward (toe-out). When one or both wheels hit a bump, the play in the linkage becomes apparent, causing the steering wheel to shimmy until the rolling force again equalizes the steering.

The service technician performed a test drive and a careful steering system inspection and discovered freeplay in both inner tie rod end sockets of the rack-and-pinion unit. The steering unit also had some power steering leakage at the tie rod bellows. A replacement remanufactured power-rack-and-pinion steering unit was recommended to the customer. The customer approved the replacement rack and authorized the required realignment. A careful test drive confirmed that the problem was corrected.

driving beside parked vehicles or walls with the vehicle windows open. (See the following chart for drive line and bearing-type noise diagnosis.)

Noise	Diagnostic Procedure
Tire noise	Change tire pressure; if no change, then the problem is not tires but bearings, or other components.
	Drive on various road surfaces—smooth asphalt reduces tire noise.
	Rotate the tires front to rear, if possible.
	Various tread designs can cause added noise (see Figure 17-16).
Engine/exhaust noise	Operate the engine at various speeds and loads.
	Drive faster than the speed where the noise occurs, place the transmission in Neutral, and "coast" down through the speed of maximum noise.
	Determine if the engine speed or vehicle speed is the cause of the noise.
Wheel bearing noise (see Figure 17-17)	Drive the vehicle slowly on a smooth road. Make left and right turns with the vehicle. Wheel bearing noise changes as weight is transferred side-to-side.
	If noise occurs when turning to the right, then the left bearing is the cause.
	If the noise occurs when turning to the left, then the right bearing is the cause.
	Hoist the vehicle and rotate the wheel by hand to verify the roughness.
Differential side bearing noise	Drive the vehicle slowly on a smooth road. Differential bearing noise is a low-pitch noise that does not change when turning.
	The noise varies with vehicle speed.
Differential pinion bearing noise	A whine noise increases with the vehicle speed.
	Drive on a smooth road and accelerate, coast, and hold a steady speed (float). A defective front pinion bearing may be louder on acceleration. A defective rear pinion bearing may be louder on deceleration.
	Pinion bearing noise usually peaks in a narrow speed range.
U-joint noise	Drive slowly on a smooth road surface.
	Drive in reverse and forward.
	U-joints usually make a "chirp, chirp, chirp" noise in reverse because of lack of

lubrication and brinelling from driving forward. Driving in reverse changes the force on the needle bearings in the U-joint, and noise is created.

Clutch noise

Transmission input bearing: Start the engine with the transmission in Neutral and the parking brake set. The clutch should be engaged (foot off the clutch pedal). If the bearing noise is heard, the transmission input bearing is the source (see Figure 17-18).

Release (throw-out) bearing: Start the engine with the transmission in Neutral and the parking brake set. Lightly depress the clutch pedal just enough to take up freeplay (usually 1 in. or less). If the noise is now heard, the source is the release (throw-out) bearing as the clutch fingers make contact with the bearing.

Pilot bearing: Start the engine with the transmission in Neutral and the parking brake set. Push the clutch pedal fully to the floor (disengage the clutch). If the bearing noise is heard with the clutch disengaged, it is caused by the pilot bearing.

FIGURE 17-17   This is an outer bearing race (cup) from a vehicle that sat over the winter. This corroded bearing produced a lot of noise and had to be replaced.

FIGURE 17-18   An inner race from an input shaft bearing. This bearing caused the five-speed manual transmission to be noisy in all gears except fourth gear. In fourth gear, the torque is transferred straight through the transmission, whereas in all other gears the torque is applied to the countershaft that exerts a side load to the input bearing.

Some noises may be normal; a similar vehicle should be driven and compared before replacing parts that may not be defective. Noises usually become louder and easier to find as time and mileage increase. An occasional noise usually becomes a constant noise.

NOISE CORRECTION

The proper way to repair a noise is to repair the cause. Other methods that have been used by technicians include the following:

1. Insulating the passenger compartment to keep the noise from the passengers.
2. Turning up the radio!

While these methods are usually inexpensive, the noise is still being generated, and if a noisy bearing or other vehicle component is not corrected, more expensive damage is likely to occur. Always remember: *Almost all vehicle faults*

FIGURE 17-16   Tire wear caused by improper alignment or driving habits, such as high-speed cornering, can create tire noise. Notice the feather-edged outer tread blocks.

TECH TIP

RAP IT

Many technicians who service transmissions and differentials frequently replace *all* bearings in the differential when there is a noise complaint. While this at first may seem to be overkill, these technicians have learned that one defective bearing may put particles in the lubricant, often causing the destruction of all the other bearings. This practice has been called *RAP* (replace all parts), and in the case of differentials, RAP may not be such a bad idea.

REAL WORLD FIX

ENGINE NOISE

An experienced technician was assigned to diagnose a loud engine noise. The noise sounded like a defective connecting rod bearing or other major engine problem. The alternator belt was found to be loose. Knowing that a loose belt can "whip" and cause noise, the belt was inspected and the alternator moved on its adjustment slide to tighten the belt. After tightening the belt, the engine was started and the noise was still heard. After stopping the engine, the technician found that the alternator belt was still loose. The problem was discovered to be a missing bolt that attached the alternator mounting bracket to the engine. The forces on the alternator caused the bracket to hit the engine. This noise was transmitted throughout the entire engine. Replacing the missing bracket bolt solved the loud engine noise and pleased a very relieved owner.

cause noise first—do not ignore the noise because it is the early warning signal of more serious and possibly dangerous problems.

Some of the things that can be done to correct certain vibrations and noise include the following:

1. Check all power steering high-pressure lines, being certain that they do not touch any part of the body, frame, or engine except where they are mounted.
2. Carefully check, tighten, and lubricate the flexible couplings in the exhaust system. Use a drive-on lift to ensure normal suspension positioning to check the exhaust system clearances. Loosen, then tighten, all exhaust clamps and hangers to relieve any built-up stress.
3. Lubricate all rubber bushings with rubber lube and replace any engine or transmission mounts that are collapsed.
4. Replace and/or tighten all engine drive belts and check that all accessory mounting brackets are tight.

SUMMARY

1. Vibration and noise are two of the most frequently heard complaints from vehicle owners. Noise is actually a vibration (vibrations cause the air to move, creating noise).
2. A vibration felt in the steering wheel, dash, or hood is usually due to out-of-balance or defective front tires. A vibration felt in the seat of the pants or throughout the entire vehicle is usually due to out-of-balance or defective rear tires.
3. Defective engine or transmission mounts, warped rotors, and out-of-round brake drums can all cause a vibration.
4. Vibration is measured by an electronic vibration analyzer (EVA) or a reed tachometer and measured in units called Hertz.
5. Low-frequency vibrations (5–20 Hz) are usually due to tires or wheels.
6. Medium-frequency vibrations (20–50 Hz) are usually caused by drive line problems on rear-wheel-drive vehicles.
7. High-frequency vibrations (50–100 Hz) are usually caused by an engine problem.
8. Drive shafts should be inspected for proper U-joint working angles and balance.

REVIEW QUESTIONS

1. Describe how you can tell if the source of a vibration is at the front or the rear of a vehicle during a test drive.

2. Explain the terms *cycle* and *Hertz*.

3. List two types of frequency-measuring instruments.

4. Discuss why the balance of a drive shaft on a rear-wheel-drive vehicle is more important than the balance of a front-wheel-drive axle shaft.

5. Explain how to check and balance a drive shaft on a rear-wheel-drive vehicle.

CHAPTER QUIZ

1. A vibration that is felt in the steering wheel at highway speeds is usually due to _____.
   a. Defective or out-of-balance rear tires
   b. Defective or out-of-balance front tires
   c. Out-of-balance or bent drive shaft on a RWD vehicle
   d. Out-of-balance drive axle shaft or defective outer CV joints on a FWD vehicle

2. A vibration during braking is usually caused by _____.
   a. Out-of-balance tires
   b. Warped front brake rotors
   c. A bent wheel
   d. An out-of-balance or bent drive shaft

3. The rolling circumference of both tires on the same axle of a four-wheel-drive vehicle should be within _____.
   a. 0.1 in. (2.5 mm)
   b. 0.3 in. (7.6 mm)
   c. 0.6 in. (15 mm)
   d. 1.2 in. (30 mm)

4. The maximum allowable drive shaft runout is _____.
   a. 0.030 in. (0.8 mm)
   b. 0.10 in. (2.5 mm)
   c. 0.50 in. (13 mm)
   d. 0.015 in. (0.4 mm)

5. A drive shaft can be checked for proper balance by marking the circumference of the shaft in four places and running the vehicle drive wheels to spot the point of imbalance using a _____.
   a. Reed tachometer
   b. Strobe light
   c. Electronic vibration analyzer (EVA)
   d. Scan tool

6. A defective clutch release (throw-out) bearing is usually heard when the clutch is _____.
   a. Engaged in neutral
   b. Disengaged in a gear
   c. Depressed to take up any freeplay
   d. Engaged in first gear or reverse

7. Wheel-tire imbalance is the most common source of vibrations that occur in what frequency range?
   a. 5–20 Hz
   b. 20–50 Hz
   c. 50–100 Hz
   d. 100–150 Hz

8. Drive line vibrations due to a bent or out-of-balance drive shaft on a rear-wheel-drive vehicle usually produce a vibration that is _____.
   a. Felt in the steering wheel
   b. Seen as a vibrating dash or hood
   c. Felt in the seat or all over the vehicle
   d. Felt by the rear passengers only

9. Rubber is used for exhaust system hangers because the exhaust system gets longer as it gets hot and rubber helps isolate noise and vibration from the passenger compartment.
   a. True
   b. False

10. A vibration is felt in the steering wheel during braking only. A common cause of the vibration is _____.
   a. Worn idler arm
   b. Out-of-balance front tires
   c. Loose or defective wheel bearing(s)
   d. Warped or nonparallel front disc brake rotors

SAMPLE SUSPENSION AND STEERING (A4) ASE CERTIFICATION TEST

1. A customer complains that the steering lacks power assist all the time. Technician A says that the power steering pump drive belt could be slipping or loose. Technician B says that worn outer tie rod ends could be the cause. Which technician is correct?

   a. Technician A only

   b. Technician B only

   c. Both Technician A and B

   d. Neither Technician A nor B

2. A front-wheel-drive vehicle pulls toward the right during hard acceleration. The most likely cause is _____.

   a. Worn or defective tires

   b. Leaking or defective shock absorbers

   c. Normal torque steer

   d. A defective power steering rack-and-pinion steering assembly

3. When replacing a rubber-bonded socket (RBS) tie rod end, the technician should be sure to _____.

   a. Remove the original using a special tool

   b. Install and tighten the replacement with the front wheels in the straight-ahead position

   c. Grease the joint before installing on the vehicle

   d. Install the replacement using a special clamp vise

4. Whenever installing a tire on a rim, do not exceed _____.

   a. 25 psi

   b. 30 psi

   c. 35 psi

   d. 40 psi

5. Two technicians are discussing mounting a tire on a wheel. Technician A says that for best balance, the tire should be match mounted. Technician B says that silicone spray should be used to lubricate the tire bend. Which technician is correct?

   a. Technician A only

   b. Technician B only

   c. Both Technician A and B

   d. Neither Technician A nor B

6. Technician A says that radial tires should *only* be rotated front to rear, never side to side. Technician B says that vehicle manufacturers usually recommend that radial tires should be rotated using the modified X method. Which technician is correct?

   a. Technician A only

   b. Technician B only

   c. Both Technician A and B

   d. Neither Technician A nor B

7. For a tire that has excessive radial runout, Technician A says that it should be broken down on a tire-changing machine and then rotated 180 degrees on the wheel and retested. Technician B says that the tire should be replaced. Which technician is correct?

   a. Technician A only

   b. Technician B only

   c. Both Technician A and B

   d. Neither Technician A nor B

8. Technician A says that overloading a vehicle can cause damage to the wheel bearings. Technician B says that tapered roller bearings used on a nondrive wheel should be adjusted hand tight only after seating. Which technician is correct?
   a. Technician A only
   b. Technician B only
   c. Both Technician A and B
   d. Neither Technician A nor B

9. Defective wheel bearings usually sound like _____.
   a. A growl
   b. A rumble
   c. Snow tires
   d. All of the above

10. Defective outer CV joints usually make a clicking noise _____.
    a. Only when backing
    b. While turning and moving
    c. While turning only
    d. During braking

11. The proper lubricant usually specified for use in a differential is _____.
    a. SAE 15-40 engine oil
    b. SAE 80W-90 GL-5
    c. STF
    d. SAE 80W-140 GL-1

12. A vehicle owner complained that a severe vibration was felt throughout the entire vehicle only during rapid acceleration from a stop and up to about 20 mph (32 km/h). The most likely cause is _____.
    a. Unequal drive shaft working angles
    b. A bent drive shaft
    c. Defective universal joints
    d. A bent rim or a defective tire

13. To remove a C-clip axle, what step does *not* need to be done?
    a. Remove the differential cover
    b. Remove the axle flange bolts/nuts
    c. Remove the pinion shaft
    d. Remove the pinion shaft lock bolt

14. Drive shaft working angles can be changed by _____.
    a. Replacing the U-joints
    b. Using shims or wedges under the transmission or rear axle
    c. Rotating the position of the drive shaft on the yoke
    d. Tightening the differential pinion nut

15. A driver complains that the vehicle darts, or moves first toward one side and then to the other side of the road. Technician A says that bump steer caused by an unlevel steering linkage could be the cause. Technician B says that a worn housing in the spool valve area of the power rack and pinion is the most likely cause. Which technician is correct?
    a. Technician A only
    b. Technician B only
    c. Both Technician A and B
    d. Neither Technician A nor B

16. A vehicle equipped with power rack-and-pinion steering is hard to steer when cold only. After a couple of miles of driving, the steering power assist returns to normal. The most likely cause of this temporary loss of power assist when cold is _____.
    a. A worn power steering pump
    b. Worn grooves in the spool valve area of the rack-and-pinion steering unit
    c. A loose or defective power steering pump drive belt
    d. A defective power steering computer sensor

17. A dry park test is performed _____.
    a. On a frame-type lift with the wheels hanging free
    b. By pulling and pushing on the wheels with the vehicle supported by a frame-type lift
    c. On the ground or on a drive-on lift by moving the steering wheel while observing for looseness
    d. Driving in a figure 8 in a parking lot

18. On a parallelogram-type steering linkage, the part that usually needs replacement first is the _____.
    a. Pitman arm
    b. Outer tie rod end(s)
    c. Center link
    d. Idler arm

19. What parts need to be added to a "short" rack to make a "long" rack-and-pinion steering unit?
    a. Bellows and ball socket assemblies
    b. Bellows and outer tie rod ends
    c. Ball socket assemblies and outer tie rod ends
    d. Outer tie rod ends

20. The adjustment procedure for a typical integral power steering gear is _____.
    a. Overcenter adjustment, then worm thrust bearing preload
    b. Worm thrust bearing preload, then overcenter adjustment

21. A vehicle is sagging at the rear. Technician A says that standard replacement shock absorbers should restore proper ride (trim) height. Technician B says that replacement springs are needed to properly restore ride height. Which technician is correct?
    a. Technician A only
    b. Technician B only
    c. Both Technician A and B
    d. Neither Technician A nor B

22. Technician A says that indicator ball joints should be loaded with the weight of the vehicle on the ground to observe the wear indicator. Technician B says that the nonindicator ball joints should be inspected *unloaded*. Which technician is correct?
    a. Technician A only
    b. Technician B only
    c. Both Technician A and B
    d. Neither Technician A nor B

23. The maximum allowable axial play in a ball joint is usually _____.
    a. 0.001 in. (0.025 mm)
    b. 0.003 in. (0.076 mm)
    c. 0.030 in. (0.76 mm)
    d. 0.050 in. (1.27 mm)

24. The ball joint used on a MacPherson strut suspension is usually load carrying.
    a. True
    b. False

25. Technician A says that tapered parts, such as tie rod ends, should be tightened to specifications, then loosened 1/4 turn before installing the cotter key. Technician B says that the nut used to retain tapered parts should never be loosened after torquing, but rather tightened further, if necessary, to line up the cotter key hole. Which technician is correct?
    a. Technician A only
    b. Technician B only
    c. Both Technician A and B
    d. Neither Technician A nor B

26. When should the strut rod (retainer) nut be removed?
    a. After compressing the coil spring
    b. Before removing the MacPherson strut from the vehicle
    c. After removing the cartridge gland nut
    d. Before removing the brake hose from the strut housing clip

27. "Dog tracking" is often caused by (a) broken or damaged _____.
    a. Stabilizer bar links
    b. Strut rod bushings
    c. Rear leaf springs
    d. Track (panhard) rod

28. A pull toward one side during braking is one symptom of (a) defective or worn _____.
    a. Stabilizer bar links
    b. Strut rod bushings
    c. Rear leaf springs
    d. Track (panhard) rod

29. Oil is added to the MacPherson strut housing before installing a replacement cartridge to _____.
    a. Lubricate the cartridge
    b. Transfer heat from the cartridge to the outside strut housing
    c. Act as a shock dampener
    d. Prevent unwanted vibrations

30. A vehicle will pull toward the side with the _____.
    a. Most camber
    b. Least camber

31. Excessive toe-out will wear the edges of both front tires on the _____.
    a. Inside
    b. Outside

32. A vehicle will pull toward the side with the _____.
    a. Most caster
    b. Least caster

33. If the turning radius (TOOT) is out of specification, what should be replaced?
    a. The outer tie rod ends
    b. The inner tie rod ends
    c. The idler arm
    d. The steering knuckle

34. SAI and camber together form the _____.
    a. Included angle
    b. Turning radius angle
    c. Scrub radius angle
    d. Setback angle

35. The thrust angle is being corrected. The alignment technician should adjust which angle to reduce thrust angle?
    a. Rear camber
    b. Front SAI or included angle and camber
    c. Rear toe
    d. Rear caster

36. Strut rods adjust _____ if there is a nut on both sides of the frame bushings.
    a. Camber
    b. Caster
    c. SAI or included angle, depending on the exact vehicle
    d. Toe

Questions 37 through 40 will use the following specifications:

front camber 0.5° ± 0.3°
front caster 3.5° to 4.5°
toe 0° ± 0.1°
rear camber 0° ± 0.5°
rear toe −0.1° to 0.1°
alignment angles
  front camber left 0.5°
  front camber right −0.1°
  front caster left 3.8°
  front caster right 4.5°
  front toe left −0.2°
  front toe right +0.2°
  total toe 0.0°
  rear camber left 0.15°
  rear camber right −0.11°
  rear toe left 0.04°
  rear toe right 0.14°

37. The first angle corrected should be _____.
   a. Right front camber
   b. Right rear camber
   c. Right rear toe
   d. Left front camber

38. The present alignment will cause excessive tire wear to the inside of both front tires.
   a. True
   b. False

39. The present alignment will cause excessive tire wear to the rear tires.
   a. True
   b. False

40. With the present alignment, the vehicle will _____.
   a. Pull toward the right
   b. Go straight
   c. Pull toward the left

ANSWERS TO THE SAMPLE SUSPENSION AND STEERING (A4) ASE CERTIFICATION TEST

1. a	11. b	21. b	31. a
2. c	12. a	22. a	32. b
3. b	13. b	23. d	33. d
4. d	14. b	24. b	34. a
5. a	15. a	25. b	35. c
6. b	16. b	26. a	36. b
7. a	17. c	27. c	37. b
8. c	18. d	28. b	38. b
9. d	19. a	29. b	39. b
10. b	20. b	30. a	40. a

DOT TIRE CODES

The DOT manufacturer's code on this tire is B9 (always the first two letters or numbers after the DOT lettering).

DOT Tire Codes

Code No.	Tire Manufacturer
AC	General Tire Company Charlotte, NC, USA
AD	General Tire Company Mayfield, KY, USA
AE	General Fabrica Espanola Del Caucho S.A. (General Tire International) Torrelavego, Santander, Spain
AF	Manufactura Nacional De Borracha S.A.R.L. (General Tire International) Porto, Portugal

Code No.	Tire Manufacturer
AH	General Popo S.A. (General Tire International) Mexico City, Mexico
AJ	Uniroyal Tire Company Detroit, MI, USA
AK	Uniroyal Tire Company Chicopee Falls, MA, USA
AL	Uniroyal Goodrich Tire Co. Eau Claire, WI, USA
AM	Uniroyal Tire Company Los Angeles, CA, USA
AN	Uniroyal Goodrich Tire Co. Opelika, AL, USA
AO	Wearwell Tire & Tube Co. Bhopal (MP) India
AP	Uniroyal Goodrich Tire Co. Ardmore, OK, USA
AT	Avon Rubber Co., Ltd. Melksham, Wiltshire, England
AU	Uniroyal Goodrich Tire Co. Kitchener, Ontario, Canada
AV	Seiberling Tire & Rubber Co. Barberton, OH, USA
AW	Samson Tire & Rubber Co., Ltd. Tel Aviv, Israel
AX	Phoenix Gummiwerke, A.G. Hamburg, Germany
AY	Phoenix Gummiwerke, A.G. Reinsdorf, Germany
A1	Pneumatics Michelin Potiers, France
A2	Lee Tire & Rubber Company Sao Paulo, Brazil
A3	General Tire & Rubber Company Mount Vernon, IL, USA

Code No.	Tire Manufacturer
A4	Hung-A Industrial Co., Ltd. Pusan, Korea
A5	Debickie Zaklady Opon Samochodowych Debica, Poland
A6	Apollo Tyres, Ltd. Cochin, India
A7	Thai Bridgestone Tire Co. Ltd. Changwad Patoom-Thani, Thailand
A8	P.T. Bridgestone Tire Indonesia Factory Jawa Barat, Indonesia
A9	General Tire Company Bryan, OH, USA
BA	Uniroyal Goodrich Tire Company Akron, OH, USA
BB	B.F. Goodrich Tire Company Miami, OK, USA
BC	B.F. Goodrich Tire Company Oaks, PA, USA
BD	B.F. Goodrich Tire Company Miami, OK, USA
BE	Uniroyal Goodrich Tire Co. Tuscaloosa, AL, USA
BF	Uniroyal Goodrich Tire Co. Woodburn, IN, USA
BH	Uniroyal Goodrich Tire Co. Kitchener, Ontario, Canada
BK	B.F. Goodrich do Brasil Campinas, Brazil
BL	Industria Colobiana de Liantas S.A. (B.F. Goodrich International) Bogata, Colombia
BM	B.F. Goodrich Australia Pty., Ltd. Campbellfield, Victoria, Australia
BN	B.F. Goodrich Philippines, Inc. Makti, Rizal, Philippines
BO	General Tire Company Casablanca, Morocco
BT	Semperit, A.G. Traiskirehen, Austria
BU	Semperit Ireland Ltd. Dublin, Ireland
BV	International Rubber Industries Jeffersontown, KY, USA
BW	The Gates Rubber Company Denver, CO, USA
BX	The Gates Rubber Company Nashville, TN, USA
BY	The Gates Rubber Company Littleton, CO, USA

Code No.	Tire Manufacturer
B1	Pneumatics Michelin La Rochesur-Yon, France
B2	Dunlop Malaysian Industries Berhad Selongor, Malaysia
B3	Michelin Tire Mfg. Company of Canada, Ltd. Bridgewater, Nova Scotia
B4	Taurus Hungarian Rubber Works Budapest, Hungary
B5	Olsztynskle Zaklady Opon Samochodowych Olsztyn, Poland
B6	Michelin Tire Corporation Spartanburg, SC, USA
B7	Michelin Tire Corporation Dothan, AL, USA
B8	Cia Brasiliera de Pneumaticos Michelin Industria Rio De Janeiro, Brazil
B9	Michelin Tire Corporation Lexington, SC, USA
CA	The Mohawk Rubber Company Akron, OH, USA
CB	The Mohawk Rubber Company Helena, AR, USA
CC	The Mohawk Rubber Company Salem, VA, USA
CD	Alliance Tire & Rubber Co., Ltd. Hadera, Israel
CF	The Armstrong Rubber Company Des Moines, IA, USA
CH	The Armstrong Rubber Company Hanford, CA, USA
CJ	Inque Rubber Company, Ltd. Atsuta-ku, Nagoyo, Japan
CK	The Armstrong Rubber Company Madison, TN, USA
CL	Continental A.C. Hannover, Germany
CM	Continental Gummi-Werke, A.G. Hannover, Germany
CN	Usine Francaise des Pneumatics Sarreguemines, France
CO	Goodyear Lastikleri Tas Adopozare, Turkey
CP	Continental Gummi-Werke, A.G. Korbach, Germany
CT	Continental Gummi-Werke, A.C. Dannenberg, Germany
CU	Continental Gummi-Werke, A.C. Hannover-Stocken, Germany

Code No.	Tire Manufacturer
CV	The Armstrong Rubber Company Natchez, MS, USA
CW	The Toyo Rubber Industry Co., Ltd. Itami, Hyogo, Japan
CX	The Toyo Rubber Industry Co., Ltd. Natori-Gun, Miyagi, Japan
CY	McCreary Tire & Rubber Company Indiana, PA, USA
C1	Michelin (Nigeria) Ltd. Port-Harcourt, Nigeria
C2	Kelly-Springfield Tire Company Americana, Sao Paulo, Brazil
C3	McCreary Tire & Rubber Company Baltimore, MD, USA
C4	Dico Tire, Inc. Clinton, TN, USA
C5	Poznanskie Zaklady Opon Samochodowych Poznan, Poland
C6	MITAS, n.p. Praha Praque, Czechoslovakia
C7	Ironsides Tire & Rubber Company Louisville, KY, USA
C8	Hsin Chu Plant- Bridgestone Hsin Chu, Taiwan
C9	Seven Star Rubber Co., Ltd. Chang-Hua, Taiwan
DA	The Dunlop Tire & Rubber Co. Buffalo, NY, USA
DB	The Dunlop Tire & Rubber Corp. Huntsville, AL, USA
DC	Dunlop Tire Canada, Ltd. Whitby, Ontario, Canada
DD	The Dunlop Company, Ltd. Birmingham, England
DE	The Dunlop Company, Ltd. Washington, Durham, England
DK	Dunlop S.A. Montlucon, France
DL	Dunlop S.A. Amiens, France
DM	Dunlop A.G. Hanau Am Main, Germany
DN	Dunlop A.G. Wittlich, Germany
DO	Kelly-Springfield Lastikleri Tas Adapazari, Turkey
DV	N.V. Nederlandsch-Amerikaansche Enschnede, The Netherlands

Code No.	Tire Manufacturer
DW	Rubberfabriek Vredestein Doetinchem, The Netherlands
DX	N.V. Bataafsche Rubber Ind. Radium Maastricht, The Netherlands
DY	Denman Tire Corporation Leavittsburg, OH, USA
D1	Viking Askim Askim, Norway
D2	Bridgestone/Firestone, Inc. LaVergne, TN, USA
D3	United Tire & Rubber Mfg. Company Cobourg, Ontario, Canada
D4	Dunlop India, Ltd. West Bengal, India
D5	Dunlop India, Ltd. Madras, India
D6	Borovo Borovo, Yugoslavia
D7	Dunlop South Africa Ltd. Natal, Republic of South Africa
D8	Dunlop South Africa Ltd. Natal, Republic of South Africa
D9	United Tire & Rubber Co., Ltd. Rexdale, Ontario, Canada
EA	Metzler, A.G. Munchen, Germany
EB	Metzler, A.G. Zweigwerk Neustadt Neustadt Odenwald, Germany
EC	Metzler, A.G. Hochst, Germany
ED	Michelin—Okamoto Tire Corporation Tokyo, Japan
EE	Nitto Tire Company, Ltd. Kanagawa-ken, Japan
EF	Hung Ah Tire Company, Ltd. Seoul, Korea
EH	Bridgestone Tire Company, Ltd. Fukuoka-ken, Japan
EJ	Bridgestone Tire Company, Ltd. Saga-ken, Japan
EK	Bridgestone Tire Company, Ltd. Fukuoka-ken, Japan
EL	Bridgestone Tire Company, Ltd. Shiga-ken, Japan
EM	Bridgestone Tire Company, Ltd. Tokyo, Japan
EN	Bridgestone Tire Company, Ltd. Tochigi-ken, Japan

Code No.	Tire Manufacturer
EO	Lee Lastikleri Tas Adapazari, Turkey
EP	Bridgestone Tire Company, Ltd. Tochigi-ken, Japan
ET	Sumitomo Rubber Industries Fuklai, Kobe, Japan
EU	Sumitomo Rubber Industries Alchi Prefecture, Japan
EW	Pneumatiques Kleber, S.A. Toul (Meurthe-et-Moselle), France
EX	Pneumatiques Kleber, S.A. La Chapella St. Luc, France
EY	Pneumatiques Kleber, S.A. St. Ingbert (Saar), Germany
E1	Chung Hsing Industrial Co., Ltd. Taichung Hsien, Taiwan
E2	Industria de Pneumaticos Firestone Sao Paulo, Brazil
E3	Seiberling Tire & Rubber Company Lavergne, TN, USA
E4	The Firestone Tire and Rubber Co. of New Zealand, Ltd. Papanui, Christ Church, New Zealand
E5	Firestone South Africa (Pty) Ltd. Port Elizabeth, South Africa
E6	Firestone-Tunisie S.A. Menzel-Bourguiba, Tunisia
E7	Firestone East Africa Ltd. Nairobi, Kenya
E8	Firestone Ghana Ltd. Accra, Ghana
E9	Firestone South Africa (Pty) Ltd. Brits, South Africa
FA	The Yokohama Rubber Company, Ltd. Hiratsuka, Kanagawa-Pref, Japan
FB	The Yokohama Rubber Company, Ltd. Watari-gun, Miye-Pref, Japan
FC	The Yokohama Rubber Company, Ltd. Mishima, Shizuoka-Pref, Japan
FD	The Yokohama Rubber Company, Ltd. Shinsharo, Aichi-Pref, Japan
FE	The Yokohama Rubber Company, Ltd. Ageo, Saitama-Pref, Japan
FF	Manufacture Francaise des Pneumatiques Michelin Clermont-Ferrand, France
FH	Manufacture Francaise des Pneumatics Michelin Clermont-Ferrand, France
FJ	Manufacture Francaise des Pneumatics Michelin Bourges, France
FK	Manufacture Francaise des Pneumatics Michelin Cholet, France

Code No.	Tire Manufacturer
FL	Manufacture Francaise des Pneumatics Michelin Montceau-les-Mines, France
FM	Manufacture Francaise des Pneumatics Michelin Mesmin, Orleans, France
FN	Manufacture Francaise des Pneumatics Michelin Tours, France
FP	Ste. d' Applications Techniques Ind. Algers, Algeria
FT	Michelin Reifenwerke, A.G. Bad Kreuznach, Germany
FU	Michelin Reifenwerke, A.G. Bamberg, Germany
FV	Michelin Reifenwerke, A.G. Homburg, Germany
FW	Michelin Reifenwerke, A.G. Karlsruhe, Germany
FX	S.A. Belge du Pneumatique Michelin Zuen, Belgium
FY	N.V. Nederlandsche Banden, Industries Michelin S'Hertogenbosch, Bois-le-duc, Holland
F1	Michelin Tyre Company, Ltd. Dundee, Scotland
F2	C.A. Firestone Venezolana Valencia, Venezuela
F3	Manufacture Francaise Pneumatiques Michelin Roanne, France
F4	CNB-Companhia Nacional de Borrachas Oporto, Portugal
F5	FATE S.A.I.C.I. Buenos Aires, Argentina
F6	Torrelavega Torrelavega, Spain
F7	Puente San Miguel Firestone Torrelavega, Spain
F8	Vikrant Tyres Ltd. Mysore, Karnataka, India
F9	Dunlop New Zealand, Ltd. Upper Hutt, New Zealand
F0	Fidelity Tire Mfg. Company Natchez, MS, USA
HA	S.A.F.E.N.M. (Michelin) Aranda, Spain
HB	S.A.F.E.N.M. Lasarte (Michelin) Lasarte, Spain
HC	S.A.F.E.N.M. (Michelin) Victoria, Spain
HD	Societa per Azoni, Michelin Cuneo, Italy

Code No.	Tire Manufacturer
HE	Societa per Azoni, S.P.A., Michelin Marengo, Italy
HF	Societa per Azoni, Michelin Turin (Dora), Italy
HH	Societa per Azoni, Michelin Turin (Stura), Italy
HJ	Michelin Tyre Company, Ltd. Ballymena, North Ireland
HK	Michelin (Belfast) Ltd. Belfast, North Ireland
HL	Michelin Tyre Company, Ltd. Burnley, England
HM	Michelin Tyre Company, Ltd. Stoke-on-Trent, England
HN	Michelin Tire Mfg. Co. of Canada New Glasgow, Nova Scotia
HP	Manufacture Saigonnaise des Pneumatiques Michelin Saigon, Vietnam
HT	Ceat, S.P.A. Pneumatici via Leoncavallo Torino, Italy
HU	Ceat 10036 Settimo Torinese, Italy
HV	Gentyre S.P.A. Frosinone, Italy
HW	Barum Tire Co. Otokovice, Czechoslovakia
HX	The Dayton Tire & Rubber Company Dayton, OH, USA
HY	Bridgestone-Firestone Inc. Oklahoma City, OK, USA
H1	DeLa S.A.F.E. Neumaticos Michelin Valladolid, Spain
H2	Kumho & Co., Inc. Tire Division Kwangsan-gun, Chonnam, Korea
H3	Sava Industrija Gumijevih Skofjeloska, Kranj, Yugoslavia
H4	Bridgestone-Houf Yamaguchi-Ken, Japan
H5	Hutchinson-MAPA Chalette Sur Loing, France
H6	Shin Hung Rubber Co. Ltd. Kyung Nam, Korea
H7	Li Hsin Rubber Industrial Co. Chi-Hu, Chang-Hwa, Taiwan
H9	Reifen-Berg Clevischer Ring, Germany
HO	The General Tyre & Rubber Co. Karachi, Pakistan
JA	The Lee Tire & Rubber Co. (Goodyear Co., Plant 1) Akron, OH, USA

Code No.	Tire Manufacturer
JB	The Lee Tire & Rubber Co. (Goodyear Co., Plant 2) Akron, OH, USA
JC	The Lee Tire & Rubber Company Conshohocken, PA, USA
JD	The Lee Tire & Rubber Company (Kelly-Springfield Tire Co.) Cumberland, MD, USA
JE	The Lee Tire & Rubber Company (Goodyear Tire & Rubber Co.) Danville, VA, USA
JF	The Lee Tire & Rubber Company (Goodyear Tire & Rubber Co.) Fayetteville, NC, USA
JH	The Lee Tire & Rubber Company (Goodyear Tire & Rubber Co.) Freeport, IL, USA
JJ	The Lee Tire & Rubber Company (Goodyear Tire & Rubber Co.) Gadsden, AL, USA
JK	The Lee Tire & Rubber Company (Goodyear Tire & Rubber Co.) Jackson, MI, USA
JL	The Lee Tire & Rubber Company (Goodyear Tire & Rubber Co.) Los Angeles, CA, USA
JM	The Lee Tire & Rubber Company (Goodyear Tire & Rubber Co.) New Bedford, MA, USA
JN	The Lee Tire & Rubber Company (Goodyear Tire & Rubber Co.) Topeka, KS, USA
JP	The Lee Tire & Rubber Company (Goodyear Tire & Rubber Co.) Tyler, TX, USA
JT	The Lee Tire & Rubber Company (Goodyear Tire & Rubber Co.) Union City, TN, USA
JU	The Lee Tire & Rubber Company (Goodyear Tire & Rubber Co.) Medicine Hat, AB, Canada
JV	The Lee Tire & Rubber Company (Goodyear Tire & Rubber Co.) Toronto 14, Ontario, Canada
JW	The Lee Tire & Rubber Company (Seiberling Rubber Co. of Canada) Toronto 9, Ontario, Canada
JX	The Lee Tire & Rubber Company (Goodyear Tire & Rubber Co.) Valleyfield, Quebec, Canada
JY	The Lee Tire & Rubber Company (Neumaaticos Goodyear S.A.) Hurlingham, F.C.N.S.M., Argentina

Code No.	Tire Manufacturer
J1	Phillips Petroleum Company Bartlesville, OK, USA
J2	Bridgestone Singapore Company Jurong Town, Singapore
J3	Gumarne 1 Maja Puchov, Czechoslavakia
J4	Rubena, N.P. Nachod, Czechoslavakia
J5	The Lee Tire & Rubber Company Logan, OH, USA
J6	Jaroslavi Tire Company Jaroslavi, USSR
J7	R & J Mfg. Corporation Plymouth, IN, USA
J8	Da Chung Hua Rubber Ind. Co. Shanghai, China
J9	P.T. Intirub Besar, Jakarta, Indonesia
JO	Korea Inocee Kasei Co., Ltd. Masan, Korea
KA	The Lee Tire & Rubber Company (Goodyear Tire & Rubber Co.) Granville, New South Wales, Australia
KB	The Lee Tire & Rubber Company (Goodyear Tire & Rubber Co.) Thomastown, Victoria, Australia
KC	The Lee Tire & Rubber Company (Companhia Goodyear do Brasil) Sao Paulo, Brazil
KD	The Lee Tire & Rubber Company (Goodyear de Colombia S.A.) Cali, Colombia
KE	The Lee Tire & Rubber Company (Goodyear Congo) Republic of the Congo
KF	The Lee Tire & Rubber Company (Compagnie Francaise Goodyear) 80 Amiens-Somme, France
KH	The Lee Tire & Rubber Company (Deut-che Goodyear G.M.B.H.) Phillipsburg Brucksal, Germany
KJ	The Lee Tire & Rubber Company (Goodyear International) 64 Fulda, Germany
KK	The Lee Tire & Rubber Company (Goodyear Hellas S.A.I.C.) Thessaloniki, Greece
KL	The Lee Tire & Rubber Company (Goodyear International) Guatemala City, Guatemala

Code No.	Tire Manufacturer
KM	The Lee Tire & Rubber Company Grand Duchy of Luxembourg
KN	The Lee Tire & Rubber Company (Goodyear India Ltd. Factory) District Gurgaon, India
KP	The Lee Tire & Rubber Company (The Goodyear Tire & Rubber Co.) Bogor, Republic of Indonesia
KT	The Lee Tire & Rubber Company (Goodyear Italiana) Latina, Italy
KU	The Lee Tire & Rubber Company (Goodyear Jamaica Ltd.) Jamaica, West Indies
KV	The Lee Tire & Rubber Company (Compania Hulera Goodyear) Mexico City, Mexico
KW	The Lee Tire & Rubber Company (Compania Goodyear del Peru) Lima, Peru
KX	The Lee Tire & Rubber Company (The Goodyear Tire & Rubber Co.) Las Pinas, Rizal, Philippines
KY	The Lee Tire & Rubber Company (Goodyear Tire & Rubber Co. (GB)) Glasgow, Scotland
K1	Phillips Petroleum Company Stow, OH, USA
K2	The Lee Tire & Rubber Company Madisonville, KY, USA
K2	Kenda Rubber Ind. Co., Ltd. Yualin, Taiwan
K4	Uniroyal S.A. (Uniroyal Goodrich) Queretaro, Mexico
K5	VEB Reifenkombinat Furstenwalde Democratic Republic of Germany
K6	The Lee Tire & Rubber Company Lawton, OK, USA
K7	The Lee Tire & Rubber Company Santiago, Chile
K8	The Kelly-Springfield Tire Co. Selangor, Malaysia
K9	Natier Tire & Rubber Co., Ltd. Shetou, Changhua, Taiwan
KO	Michelin Korea Tire Co., Ltd. San-Kun, Kyungsangnam, Korea
LA	The Lee Tire & Rubber Company (Goodyear Tyre & Rubber Co.) Uitenhage, South Africa
LB	The Lee Tire & Rubber Company (Goodyear Gummi Fabics Aktirbolag) Norrkoping, Sweden

Code No.	Tire Manufacturer
LC	The Lee Tire & Rubber Company (Goodyear International) Bangkok, Thailand
LD	The Lee Tire & Rubber Company (Goodyear International) Kocaeli, Turkey
LE	The Lee Tire & Rubber Company (CA Goodyear de Venezuela) Valencia, Edo Carabobo, Venezuela
LF	The Lee Tire & Rubber Company (Goodyear Tire & Rubber Co. (GB)) Wolverhampton, England
LJ	Uniroyal Englebert Belgique S.A. Herstal-les-Liege, Belgium
LK	Productors Niaconal de Llantas S.A. Cali, Colombia
LL	Uniroyal Englebert France S.A. Compiegne, France
LM	Uniroyal Englebert Deutschland D.A. Aachen, Germany
LN	Uniroyal SA (Uniroyal Goodrich) Mexico City, Mexico
LP	Uniroyal Ltd., Tire & Gen. Products Newbridge, Midlothian, Scotland
LT	Uniroyal Endustri Turk Anonim Adapazari, Turkey
LU	Uniroyal, C.A. Valencia, Venezuela
LV	General Tire Canada Ltd. Barrie, Ontario, Canada
LW	Trelleborg Gummifariks Akiebolag Trelleborg, Sweden
LX	Mitsuboshi Belting Ltd. Kobe, Japan
LY	Mitsuboshi Belting Ltd. Shikoku, Japan
L1	Goodyear Taiwan Ltd. Taipei, Taiwan
L2	WUON Poong Ind. Co., Ltd. Pusan, Korea
L3	Tong Shin Chemical Products Co. Seoul, Korea
L4	Centrala Ind. de Prelucrare Cauciuc Oltentei, Romania
L5	BRISA Bridgestone Sabanci P.K. Izmit, Turkey
L6	MODI Rubber Limited Meerut UP, India
L7	Intreprinderea De Anvelope Zalau Zalau, Judetul Saloj, Romania

Code No.	Tire Manufacturer
L8	Dunlop Zimbabwe Ltd. Domington, Bulawaye, Zimbabwe
L9	Panther Tyres, Ltd. Aintree, Liverpool, United Kingdom
LO	Mfg. Francaise Des Pneumatiques Clermont Ferrand Cedex, France
MA	Goodyear Tire & Rubber Co. (Plant 1) Akron, OH, USA
MB	Goodyear Tire & Rubber Co. (Plant 2) Akron, OH, USA
MC	The Goodyear Tire & Rubber Co. Danville, VA, USA
MD	The Goodyear Tire & Rubber Co. Gadsden, AL, USA
ME	The Goodyear Tire & Rubber Co. Jackson, MI, USA
MF	The Goodyear Tire & Rubber Co. Los Angeles, CA, USA
MH	The Goodyear Tire & Rubber Co. New Bedford, ME, USA
MJ	The Goodyear Tire & Rubber Co. Topeka, KS, USA
MK	The Goodyear Tire & Rubber Co. Union City, TN, USA
ML	The Goodyear Tire & Rubber Co. Cumberland, MD, USA
MM	The Goodyear Tire & Rubber Co. Fayetteville, NC, USA
MN	The Goodyear Tire & Rubber Company Freeport, IL, USA
MO	Neumaticos De Chile S.A. Coquimbo, Chile
MP	The Goodyear Tire & Rubber Company Tyler, TX, USA
MT	The Goodyear Tire & Rubber Co. Conshohocken, PA, USA
MU	Neumaticos Goodyear, S.A. Hurlingham F.C.N.G.S.M., Argentina
MV	The Goodyear Tyre & Rubber Co. Ltd. New South Wales, Australia
MW	The Goodyear Tyre & Rubber Co., Ltd. Thomastown, Victoria, Australia
MX	Companhia Goodyear do Brasil Sao Paulo, Brazil
MY	Goodyear de Colombia, S.A. Cali, Colombia
M1	Goodyear Maroc, S.A. Casablanca, Morocco
M2	The Goodyear Tire & Rubber Co. Madisonville, KY, USA

Code No.	Tire Manufacturer
M3	Michelin Tire Corporation Greenville, SC, USA
M4	The Goodyear Tire & Rubber Co. Logan, OH, USA
M5	Michelin Tire Mfg. Co. of Canada Kentville, Nova Scotia, Canada
M6	Goodyear Tire & Rubber Co. Lawton, OK, USA
M7	Goodyear de Chile, S.A.I.C. Santiago, Chile
M8	Premier Tyres Limited Kerala State, India
M9	Uniroyal Tire Corp. Middlebury, CT, USA
NA	Goodyear Congo Republic of the Congo
NB	The Goodyear Tyre & Rubber Co. Wolverhampton, England
NC	Compagnie Francaise Goodyear Amiens-Somme, France
ND	Deutsche Goodyear G.M.B.H. Phillipsburg Bruchsal, Germany
NE	Gummiwerke Fuida G.M.B.H. Fulda, Germany
NF	Goodyear Hellas S.A.I.C. Thessaloniki, Greece
NH	Gran Industria de Neumatticos Guatemala City, Guatemala
NJ	Goodyear S.A. Grand Duchy of Luxembourge
NK	Goodyear India Ltd. Distric Gurgaon, India
NL	The Goodyear Tire & Rubber Co., Ltd. Bogor, Republic of Indonesia
NM	Goodyear Italiana S.P.A. Latina, Italy
NN	Goodyear Jamaica Ltd. Jamaica, West Indies
NO	South Pacific Tyres Victoria, Australia
NP	Compania Hulera Goodyear Oxo Mexico City, Mexico
NT	Compania Goodyear del Peru Lima, Peru
NU	Goodyear Tire & Rubber Co. Las Pinas, Rizal, Philippines
NV	Goodyear Tyre & Rubber Co. Ltd. Glasgow, Scotland
NW	Goodyear Tyre & Rubber Co. Uitenhage, South Africa

Code No.	Tire Manufacturer
NX	Goodyear Gummi Faabriks Aktirbolag Norrkoping, Sweden
NY	Goodyear (Thailand) Ltd. Bangkok, Thailand
N1	Maloja AG. Pneu-Und Gummiwerke Gelterkinden, Switzerland
N2	Hurtubise Nutread Inc. Tonawanda, NY, USA
N3	Nitto Tire Co., Ltd. Tohin-Cho, Inabe-Gun Mie-Ken, Japan
N4	Centrala Ind. de Prelucrare Cauciue Republic Socialista Romania
N5	Pneumant, VEB Reifenwerk Riesa Riesa, Germany
N6	Pneumant Democratic Republic of Germany
N7	Intreprinderea De Anvelope Caracal Caracal, Judetul Olt., Romania
N8	Lee Tire & Rubber Co. (Goodyear) Selangor, Malaysia
N9	Cla Pneus Tropical Feira de Santana, Bahla, Brazil
PA	Goodyear Lastikleri Tas Kocaeli, Turkey
PB	CA Goodyear de Venezuela Valencia, Edo Carabobo, Venezuela
PC	Goodyear Tire & Rubber Co. Medicine Hat, Alberta, Canada
PD	Goodyear Tire & Rubber Co. Valleyfield, Quebec, Canada
PE	Seiberling Rubber Co. Toronto, Ontario, Canada
PF	The Goodyear Tire & Rubber Co. Toronto, Ontario, Canada
PH	Kelly-Springfield Tire Co. Cumberland, MD, USA
PI	Gislaved Daek AB Gislaved, Sweden
PJ	Kelly-Springfield Tire Co. Fayetteville, NC, USA
PK	Kelly-Springfield Tire Co. Freeport, IL, USA
PL	Kelly-Springfield Tire Co. Tyler, TX, USA
PM	Kelly-Springfield Tire Co. (Goodyear Tire & Rubber Co.) Conshohocken, PA, USA
PN	Kelly-Springfield Tire Co. (Goodyear Tire & Rubber Co.) Akron, OH, USA

Code No.	Tire Manufacturer
PO	South Pacific Tyres New South Wales, Australia
PP	Kelly-Springfield Tire Co. (Goodyear Tire & Rubber Co.) Akron, OH, USA
PT	Kelly-Springfield Tire Co. (Goodyear Tire & Rubber Co.) Danville, VA, USA
PU	Kelly-Springfield Tire Co. (Goodyear Tire & Rubber Co.) Gadsden, AL, USA
PV	Kelly-Springfield Tire Co. (Goodyear Tire & Rubber Co.) Jackson, MI, USA
PW	Kelly-Springfield Tire Co. (Goodyear Tire & Rubber Co.) Los Angeles, CA, USA
PX	Kelly-Springfield Tire Co. (Goodyear Tire & Rubber Co.) New Bedford, ME, USA
PY	Kelly-Springfield Tire Co. (Goodyear Tire & Rubber Co.) Topeka, KS, USA
P1	Gummifabriken Gislaved Aktiebolag Gislaved, Sweden
P2	Kelly-Springfield Tire Co. Madisonville, KY, USA
P3	Skepplanda Gummi, AB Alvangen, Sweden
P4	Kelly-Springfield Tire Co. Logan, OH, USA
P5	General Popo S.A. San Luis Potosi, Mexico
P6	Kelly-Springfield Tire Co. Lawton, OH, USA
P7	Kelly-Springfield Tire Co. Santiago, Chile
P8	No. 2 Rubber Plant Oingdao Quingdao, Shandong, China
P9	MRF, Ltd., PB No. 1 Ponda Goa, India
TA	Kelly-Springfield Tire Co. (Goodyear Tire & Rubber Co.) Union City, TN, USA
TB	Kelly-Springfield Tire Co. Hurlingham F.C.N.G.S.M. Argentina
TC	Kelly-Springfield Tire Co. (Goodyear Tyre & Rubber Co.) New South Wales, Australia
TD	Kelly-Springfield Tire Co. (Goodyear Tyre & Rubber Co.) Thomastown, Victoria, Australia

Code No.	Tire Manufacturer
TE	Kelly-Springfield Tire Co. (Companhia Goodyear do Brasil) Sao Paulo, Brazil
TF	Kelly-Springfield Tire Co. (Goodyear de Colombia, S.A.) Yumbo, Call, Colombia
TH	Kelly-Springfield Tire Co. (Goodyear Congo) Republic of the Congo
TJ	Kelly-Springfield Tire Co. (Goodyear Tyre & Rubber Co.) Wolverhampton, England
TK	Kelly-Springfield Tire Co. (Compagnie Francaise Goodyear S.A.) Amiens-Somme, France
TL	Kelly-Springfield Tire Co. (Deutsche Goodyear G.M.B.H.) Bruchsal, Germany
TM	Kelly-Springfield Tire Co. (Goodyear International) Fulda, Germany
TN	Kelly-Springfield Tire Co. (Goodyear Hellas S.A.I.C .) Thessaloniki, Greece
TO	South Pacific Tyres Campbellfield, Victoria
TP	The Kelly-Springfield Tire Co. (Goodyear International) Guatemala City, Guatemala
TT	The Kelly-Springfield Tire Co. (Goodyear S.A) Grand Duchy of Luxembourg
TU	Kelly-Springfield Tire Co. (Goodyear India Ltd.) District Gurgaon, India
TV	Kelly-Springfield Tire Co. (Goodyear Tire & Rubber Co.) Bogor, Republic of Indonesia
TW	Kelly-Springfield Tire Co. (Goodyear Italiana) Latina, Italy
TX	Kelly-Springfield Tire Co. (Goodyear Jamaica Ltd.) Jamaica, West Indies
TY	Kelly-Springfield Tire Co. (Compania Hulera Goodyear) Mexico City, D.F. Mexico
T1	Hankook Tire Mfg. Co. Ltd. Seoul, Korea
T2	Ozos (Uniroyal) Olsztyn, Poland

Code No.	Tire Manufacturer
T3	Debickle Zattldy Opon Samochodowych (Uniroyal AG) Debica, Poland
T4	S.A. Carideng (Rubberfactory) Lanaken, Belgium
T5	Tigar-Pirot Pirot, Yugoslavia
T6	Hulera Tomel S.A. San Antonia, Mexico, D.F.
T7	Hankook Tire Mfg. Co., Ltd. Daejun, Korea
T8	Goodyear Malaysia Berhad Selangor, Malaysia
T9	MRF, Ltd. Arkonam, India
UA	Kelly-Springfield Tire Co. (Compania Goodyear del Peru) Lima, Peru
UB	Kelly-Springfield Tire Co. (Goodyear Tire & Rubber Co.) Las Pinas, Rizal, Philippines
UC	Kelly-Springfield Tire Co. (Goodyear Tyre & Rubber Co.) Glasgow, Scotland
UD	Kelly-Springfield Tire Co. (Goodyear Tyre & Rubber Co.) Uitenhage, South Africa
UE	Kelly-Springfield Tire Co. (Goodyear Gummi Fabriks Aktiebolag) Norrkoping, Sweden
UF	Kelly-Springfield Tire Co. (Goodyear Thailand Ltd.) Bangkok, Thailand
UH	Kelly-Springfield Tire Co. (Goodyear Lastikleri Tas Pk 2 Izmit) Kocaeli, Turkey
UJ	Kelly-Springfield Tire Co. (CA Goodyear de Venezuela) Edo Carabob, Venezuela
UK	Kelly-Springfield Tire Co. (Goodyear Tire & Rubber Co.) Medicine Hat, Alberta, Canada
UL	Kelly-Springfield Tire Co. (Goodyear Tire & Rubber Co.) Valleyfield, Quebec, Canada
UM	Kelly-Springfield Tire Co. (Seiberling Rubber Co. of Canada) Toronto, Ontario, Canada
UN	Kelly-Springfield Tire Co. (Goodyear Tire & Rubber Co.) Toronto, Ontario, Canada

Code No.	Tire Manufacturer
UO	South Pacific Tyres Thomastown, Vic., Australia
UP	Cooper Tire & Rubber Co. Findlay, OH, USA
UT	Cooper Tire & Rubber Co. Texarkana, AR, USA
UU	Carlisle Tire & Rubber Division Carlisle, PA, USA
UV	Kzowa Rubber Ind. Co., Ltd. Nishinariku, Osaka, Japan
UW	Okada Tire Industry Ltd. Katsushika-ku, Tokyo, Japan
UX	Federal Corporation Taipei, Taiwan
UY	Cheng Shin Rubber Ind. Co. Ltd. Meci Kong, Taipei, Taiwan
U1	Lien Shin Tire Co. Ltd. Taipei, Taiwan
U2	Sumitomo Rubber Industries, Ltd. Shirakawa City Fukushima Prefecture, Japan
U3	Miloje Zakic, Krusevac, Yugoslavia
U4	Geo. Byers Sons, Inc. Columbus, OH, USA
U5	Farbenfabriken Bayer GmBH Leverkusen, Germany
U6	Pneumant Democratic Republic of Germany
U7	Pneumant Democratic Republic of Germany
U8	Hsin-Fung Fac. of Nankang Rubber Co. Taiwan Province, R.O.C.
U9	Cooper Tire & Rubber Co. Tupelo, MS, USA
VA	The Firestone Tire & Rubber Co. Akron, OH, USA
VB	The Firestone Tire & Rubber Co. Akron, OH, USA
VC	The Firestone Tire & Rubber Co. Albany, GA, USA
VD	Bridgestone-Firestone Inc. Decatur, IL, USA
VE	Bridgestone-Firestone Inc. Des Moines, IA, USA
VF	The Firestone Tire & Rubber Co. South Gate, CA, USA
VH	The Firestone Tire & Rubber Co. Memphis, TN, USA
VJ	The Firestone Tire & Rubber Co. Pottstown, PA, USA

Code No.	Tire Manufacturer
VK	The Firestone Tire & Rubber Co. Salinas, CA, USA
VL	The Firestone Tire & Rubber Co. Hamilton, Ontario, Canada
VM	The Firestone Tire & Rubber Co. Calgary, Alberta, Canada
VN	Bridgestone-Firestone Inc. Joliette, Quebec, Canada
VO	South Pacific Tyres Upper Hutt, Wellington, New Zealand
VP	The Firestone Tire & Rubber Co. Bari, Italy
VT	The Firestone Tire & Rubber Co. Bilbao, Spain
VU	Universal Tire Company Lancaster, PA, USA
VV	The Firestone Tire & Rubber Co. Viskafors, Sweden
VW	Ohtsu Tire & Rubber Co. Ltd. Osaka, Japan
VX	Firestone Tyre & Rubber Co., Ltd. Brentford, Middlesex, England
VY	Firestone Tyre & Rubber Co. Ltd. Denbighshire, Wrexhan, Wales
V1	Livingston's Tire Shop Hubbard, OH, USA
V2	Vsesojuznoe Ojedinenic Avtoexport Volzhsk, USSR
V3	TA Hsin Rubber Tire Co. Ltd. Taipei Hsieng, Taiwan
V4	Ohtsu Tire & Rubber Co. Miyazaki Prefecture, Japan
V5	Firestone El Centenario S.A. Mexico City, Mexico
V6	Firestone Cuernavaca Cuenavaca, Mexico
V7	Vsesojuznoe Ojedinenie Avtoexport Voronezh, USSR
V8	Boras Gummifabrik AB Boras, Sweden
V9	M & H Tire Co. Gardner, MA, USA
WA	Firestone—France S.A. Bethune, France
WB	Industria Akron De Costa Rico San Jose, Costa Rica, S.A.
WC	Firestone Australia Pty. Ltd. Sydney, New South Wales, Australia
WD	Fabrik fur Firestone Produkte A.G. Prattlen, Switzerland

Code No.	Tire Manufacturer
WE	Nankang Rubber Tire Corp. West Taipei, Taiwan
WF	The Firestone Tire & Rubber Co. Burgos, Spain
WH	The Firestone Tire & Rubber Co. Boras, Sweden
WM	Dunlop Olympic Tyres W. Footscray, Victoria, Australia
WO	Inocce Rubber Co., Inc. Phatumtani, Thailand
WT	Madras Rubber Factory Ltd. Madras, India
WU	Ceat Tyres of India Ltd. Bhandup, Bombay, India
WV	General Rubber Corporation Taipei, Taiwan
WW	Euzkadi Co. Hulera Euzkadi, S.A. Mexico City, Mexico
WX	Euzkadi Co. Hulera Euzkadi, A.A. La Presa, Edo de, Mexico
WY	Euzkadi, Co. Hulera Euzkadi, S.A. Guadalijara, Jalisco, Mexico
W1	Bridgestone/Firestone, Inc. LaVergne, TN, USA
W2	Bridgestone—Firestone Inc. Wilson, NC, USA
W3	Vredestein Doetinchem B.V. Doetinehem, The Netherlands
W4	Dunlop Olympic Tyres Somerton, Vic., Australia
W5	Firestone de la Argentina Province de Buenos Aires, Argentina
W6	Philtread Tire & Rubber Corp. Makati, Rizal Philippines
W7	Firestone Portuguesa, S.A.R.L. Alcochete, Portugal
W8	Siam Tyre Co., Ltd. Bangkok, Thailand
W9	Ind. de Pneumaticos Firestone S.A. Rio de Janeiro, Brazil
XA	Industrie Pirelli S.p.A., V. le Milan, Italy
XB	Industri Pirelli S.p.A. Settimo, Torinese, Torino, Italy
XC	Industrie Pirelli S.p.A. Tivoil-Roma, Italy
XD	Industrie Pirelli S.p.A. Messina, Italy
XE	Industrie Pirelli S.p.A. Ferrandina, Italy

Code No.	Tire Manufacturer
XF	Productos Pirelli S.A. Barcelona, Spain
XH	Pirelli Hallas, S.A. Patrasso, Greece
XJ	Turk Pirelli Lastilkeri, S.A. Istanbul, Turkey
XK	Pirelli, S.A. Sao Paulo, Brazil
XL	Pirelli, S.A. Campinas, Brazil
XM	Pirelli Co. Platennse de Neumaticos, Merio, Buenos Aires, Argentina
XN	Pirelli, Ltd. Carlisle, England
XP	Pirelli Ltd. Burton-on-Trent, England
XT	Veith-Pirelli, A.G. Sandbach, Germany
XV	Dayton Tire & Rubber Co. (Firestone Tire & Rubber Co.) Hamilton, Ontario, Canada
XW	Dayton Tire & Rubber Co. (Firestone Tire & Rubber Co.) Calgary, Alberta, Canada
XX	Bandag, Inc. Muscatine, IA, USA
XY	Dayton Tire & Rubber Co. (Firestone Tire & Rubber Co.) Joliette, Quebec, Canada
X1	Tong Shin Chemical Prod. Co., Ltd. Seoul, Korea
X2	Hwa Fong Rubber Ind. Co. Ltd. Yualin, Taiwan
X3	Vaesojuznoe Ojedinenic Avtoexport Belaya Tserkov, USSR
X4	Pars Tyre Co. Saveh, Iran
X5	J.K. Industries Ltds. Kankroli, Rajasthan, India
X6	Vsesojuznoe Ojedinenie Avtoexport Bobruysk, USSR
X7	Vsesjuznoe Ojedinenie Avtoexport Chimkentsky, USSR
X8	Vsesojuznoe Ojedimemie Avtoexport Dnepropetrovski, USSR
X9	Vsesojuznoe Ojedinenie Avtoexport Moscow, USSR
X0	Vsesojuznoe Ojedineine Avtoexport Mizhenkamsk, USSR

Code No.	Tire Manufacturer
YA	The Dayton Tire & Rubber Co. (Firestone Tire & Rubber Co.) Akron, OH, USA
YB	The Dayton Tire & Rubber Co. (Firestone Tire & Rubber Co.) Akron, OH, USA
YC	The Dayton Tire & Rubber Co. (Firestone Tire & Rubber Co.) Albany, GA, USA
YD	The Dayton Tire & Rubber Co. (Firestone Tire & Rubber Co.) Decatur, IL, USA
YE	The Dayton Tire & Rubber Co. (Firestone Tire & Rubber Co.) Des Moines, IA, USA
YF	The Dayton Tire & Rubber Co. (Firestone Tire & Rubber Co.) South Gate, CA, USA
YH	The Dayton Tire & Rubber Co. (Firestone Tire & Rubber Co.) Memphis, TN, USA
YJ	The Dayton Tire & Rubber Co. (Firestone Tire & Rubber Co.) Pottstown, PA, USA
YK	The Dayton Tire & Rubber Co. (Firestone Tire & Rubber Co.) Salinas, CA, USA
YL	Oy Nokia A.B. Nokia, Finland
YM	Seiberling Tire & Rubber Co. (Firestone Tire & Rubber Co.) Akron, OH, USA
YN	Seiberling Tire & Rubber Co. (Firestone Tire & Rubber Co.) Akron, OH, USA
YO	Kumho and Co., Inc. Chunnam, Korea
YP	Seiberling Tire & Rubber Co. (Firestone Tire & Rubber Co.) lbany, GA, USA
YT	Seiberling Tire & Rubber Co. (Firestone Tire & Rubber Co.) Decatur, IL, USA
YU	Seiberling Tire & Rubber Co. (Firestone Tire & Rubber Co.) Des Moines, IA, USA
YV	Seiberling Tire & Rubber Co. (Firestone Tire & Rubber Co.) South Gate, CA, USA
YW	Seiberling Tire & Rubber Co. (Firestone Tire & Rubber Co.) Memphis, TN, USA

Code No.	Tire Manufacturer
YX	Seiberling Tire & Rubber Co. (Firestone Tire & Rubber Co.) Pottstown, PA, USA
YY	Seiberling Tire & Rubber Co. (Firestone Tire & Rubber Co.) Salinas, CA, USA
Y1	Companhia Goodyear Du Brasil San Paulo, Brazil
Y2	Dayton Tire & Rubber Co. Wilson, NC, USA
Y3	Seiberling Tire & Rubber Co. Wilson, NC, USA
Y4	Dayton Tire & Rubber Co. Barberton, OH, USA
Y5	Shanghai Tsen Tai Rubber Factory Shanghai, People's Republic of China
Y6	Sime Tyres Inter. Sdn. Bhd. Kedah Darulaman, Malaysia
Y7	Bridgestone/Firestone, Inc. LaVergne, TN, USA
Y8	Bombay Tyres International Ltd. Bombay, India
Y9	P.T. Gadjah Tungual Jawa Barat, Rep. of Indonesia
1A	Union Rubber Ind. Co., Ltd. Taipei, Taiwan, R.O.C.
2A	Jiuh Shuenn Enterprises Co., Ltd. Wufeng, Taichung, Taiwan, R.O.C.
3A	Hualin Rubber Plant People's Republic of China
4A	Vee Rubber Co., Ltd. Samutsakaom Prov., Thailand
5A	Vee Rubber Inter. Co., Ltd. Bangkok, Thailand
6A	Roadstone Tyre & Rubber Co., Ltd. Nontaburi Bangkok, Thailand
7A	Kings Tire Ind. Co., Ltd. Taiwan, R.O.C.
8A	Zapater, Diaz I.C.S.A. Tire Co. Buenos Aires, Argentina
9A	Siemese Rubber Co., Ltd. Bangkok, Thailand
0A	Siam Rubber Ltd. Part. Samutsakhon, Thailand
1B	Neumaticos De Venezuela C.A. Estadro Carabobo, Venezuela
2B	Deestone Limited Samutsakom, Thailand
3B	Tianjin/United Tire & Rubber Tianjin, P.R. China

Code No.	Tire Manufacturer
4B	Goodyear Canada, Inc. Napanee, Ontario, Canada
5B	The Kelly-Springfield Tire Co. Goodyear Canada, Inc. Napanee, Ontario, Canada
6B	Mt. Vernon Plt. of General Tire Mt. Vernon, IL, USA
7B	Bridgestone—Firestone Inc. Decatur, IL, USA
8B	Bridgestone — Firestone Inc. Des Moines, IA, USA
9B	Bridgestone—Firestone, Inc. Joliette, Quebec, Canada
0B	Bridgestone—Firestone Inc. Wilson, NC, USA
1C	Bridgestone—Firestone Inc. Oklahoma City, OK, USA
2C	Bridgestone/Firestone, Inc. Morrison, TN, USA
3C	Mt. Vernon Plt. of General Tire Mt. Vernon, IL, USA
4C	South Pacific Tyres Somerton, Vic., Australia
5C	The Firestone Tire & Rubber Co. Bridgestone Brand Bilbao, Spain
6C	The Firestone Tire & Rubber Co. Bridgestone Brand Burgos, Spain
7C	The Firestone Tire & Rubber Co. Papanui, Christ Church, New Zealand
8C	Firestone—France S.A. Bethune, France
9C	The Firestone Tire & Rubber Co. Bridgestone Brand Bari, Italy
0C	Michelin Siam Co., Ltd. Chonburi, Thailand
1D	Bridgestone Shimonoseki Plant Yamaguchi-ken, Japan
2D	Silverstone Tire & Rubber Co. Taiping, Perak, Malaysia
3D	Cooper Tire and Rubber Co. Albany, GA, USA
4D	Bridgestone/Firestone, Inc. Firestone Brand Morrison, TN, USA
5D	Bridgestone/Firestone, Inc. Dayton Brand Morrison, TN, US

ASE CORRELATION CHART

Automotive Suspension and Steering (A4)

ASE Task List	Textbook Page No.
A. Steering Systems Diagnosis and Repair (10 questions)	
1. Steering Columns (3 questions)	
1. Diagnose steering column noises and steering effort concerns (including manual and electronic tilt and telescoping mechanisms); determine needed repairs.	215–220
2. Inspect and replace steering column, steering shaft U-joint(s), flexible coupling(s), collapsible columns, steering wheels (includes steering wheels and columns equipped with airbags and/or other steering wheel/column-mounted controls, sensors, and components).	216–220
3. Disarm, enable, and properly handle airbag system components during vehicle service following manufacturers' procedures.	215
2. Steering Units (4 questions)	
1. Diagnose steering gear (non-rack-and-pinion type) noises, binding, vibration, freeplay, steering effort, steering pull (lead), and leakage concerns; determine needed repairs.	221–224, 279–286
2. Diagnose rack-and-pinion steering gear noises, binding, vibration, freeplay, steering effort, steering pull (lead), and leakage concerns; determine needed repairs.	226–230
3. Inspect power steering fluid level and condition; determine fluid type and adjust fluid level in accordance with vehicle manufacturers' recommendations.	259–261
4. Inspect, adjust, align, and replace power steering pump belts(s) and tensioners.	279–281
5. Diagnose power steering pump noises, vibration, and fluid leakage; determine needed repairs.	279–286
6. Remove and replace power steering pump; inspect pump mounting and attaching brackets; remove and replace power steering pump pulley.	279–286
7. Inspect and replace power steering pump seals, gaskets, reservoir, and valves.	279–286
8. Perform power steering system pressure and flow tests; determine needed repairs.	279–282
9. Inspect and replace power steering hoses, fittings, O-rings, coolers, and filters.	259–263
10. Remove and replace steering gear (non-rack-and-pinion type).	226–228
11. Remove and replace rack-and-pinion steering gear; inspect and replace mounting bushings and brackets.	226–228
12. Adjust steering gear (non-rack-and-pinion type) worm bearing preload and sector lash.	224
13. Inspect and replace steering gear (non-rack-and-pinion type) seals and gaskets.	263–269

ASE Task List	Textbook Page No.
14. Adjust rack-and-pinion steering gear.	229
15. Inspect and replace rack-and-pinion steering gear bellow/boots.	249–255
16. Flush, fill, and bleed power steering system.	279–286
17. Diagnose, inspect, and repair or replace components of variable-assist steering systems.	270–276
3. Steering Linkage (3 questions)	
1. Inspect and adjust (where applicable) front and rear steering linkage geometry (including parallelism and vehicle ride height).	247–249
2. Inspect and replace pitman arm.	244–245
3. Inspect and replace center link (relay rod/drag link/intermediate rod).	244–245
4. Inspect, adjust (where applicable), and replace idler arm(s) and mountings.	244–245
5. Inspect, replace, and adjust tie rods, tie rod sleeves/adjusters, clamps, and tie rod ends (sockets/bushings).	244–245
6. Inspect and replace steering linkage dampener(s).	249
B. Suspension Systems Diagnosis and Repair (13 questions)	
1. Front Suspensions (6 questions)	
1. Diagnose front suspension system noises, body sway/roll, and ride height concerns; determine needed repairs.	154–157
2. Inspect and replace upper and lower control arms, bushings, and shafts.	174–179
3. Inspect and replace rebound and jounce bumpers.	157
4. Inspect, adjust, and replace strut rods/radius arms (compression/tension) and bushings.	170
5. Inspect and replace upper and lower ball joints (with or without wear indicators).	158–165
6. Inspect nonindependent front axle assembly for bending, warpage, and misalignment.	165
7. Inspect and replace front steering knuckle/spindle assemblies and steering arms.	173
8. Inspect and replace front suspension system coil springs and spring insulators (silencers).	154–157
9. Inspect and replace front suspension system leaf spring(s), leaf spring insulators (silencers), shackles, brackets, bushings, and mounts.	127, 187
10. Inspect, replace, and adjust front suspension system torsion bars and mounts.	174
11. Inspect and replace front stabilizer bar (sway bar) bushings, brackets, and links.	170
12. Inspect and replace front strut cartridge or assembly.	167–169
13. Inspect and replace front strut bearing and mount.	167–169
2. Rear Suspensions (5 questions)	
1. Diagnose rear suspension system noises, body sway/roll, and ride height concerns; determine needed repairs.	154–157
2. Inspect and replace rear suspension system coil springs and spring insulators (silencers).	171–172
3. Inspect and replace rear suspension system lateral links/arms (track bars), control (trailing) arms, stabilizer bars (sway bars), bushings, and mounts.	187–188
4. Inspect and replace rear suspension system leaf spring(s), leaf spring insulators (silencers), shackles, brackets, bushings, and mounts.	184

ASE Task List	Textbook Page No.
5. Inspect and replace rear rebound and jounce bumpers.	187
6. Inspect and replace rear strut cartridge or assembly, and upper mount assembly.	166–169
7. Inspect nonindependent rear axle assembly for bending, warpage, and misalignment.	183, 187
8. Inspect and replace rear ball joints and tie rod/toe link assemblies.	187
9. Inspect and replace rear knuckle/spindle assembly.	187
C. Related Suspension and Steering Service (2 questions)	
1. Inspect and replace shock absorbers, mounts, and bushings.	166, 188
2. Diagnose and service front and/or rear wheel bearings.	294–299
3. Diagnose, inspect, adjust, repair or replace components (including sensors, switches, and actuators) of electronically controlled suspension systems (including primary and supplemental air suspension and ride control systems).	194–211
4. Inspect and repair front and/or rear cradle (crossmember/subframe) mountings, bushings, brackets, and bolts.	187
5. Diagnose, inspect, adjust, repair, or replace components (including sensors, switches, and actuators) of electronically controlled steering systems; initialize system as required.	274, 277–279
6. Diagnose, inspect, repair, or replace components of power steering idle speed compensation systems.	279–286
D. Wheel Alignment Diagnosis, Adjustment, and Repair (12 questions)	
1. Diagnose vehicle wander, drift, pull, hard steering, bump steer (toe curve), memory steer, torque steer, and steering return concerns; determine needed repairs.	370–372
2. Measure vehicle ride height; determine needed repairs.	370–372
3. Measure front and rear wheel camber; determine needed repairs.	375–376
4. Adjust front and/or rear wheel camber on suspension systems with a camber adjustment.	381, 385
5. Measure caster; determine needed repairs.	375–376
6. Adjust caster on suspension systems with a caster adjustment.	385
7. Measure and adjust front wheel toe.	375–376, 385–389
8. Center steering wheel.	389
9. Measure toe-out-on-turns (turning radius/angle); determine needed repairs.	375–376
10. Measure SAI/KPI (steering axis inclination/kingpin inclination); determine needed repairs.	375–377
11. Measure included angle; determine needed repairs.	375–377
12. Measure rear wheel toe; determine needed repairs or adjustments.	375–377
13. Measure thrust angle; determine needed repairs or adjustments.	375–377
14. Measure front wheelbase setback/offset; determine needed repairs or adjustments.	395–396
15. Check front and/or rear cradle (crossmember/subframe) alignment; determine needed repairs or adjustments.	375–377
E. Wheel and Tire Diagnosis and Service (5 questions)	
1. Diagnose tire wear patterns; determine needed repairs.	101–102
2. Inspect tire condition, size, and application (load and speed ratings).	95–96

ASE Task List	*Textbook Page No.*
3. Measure and adjust tire air pressure.	95
4. Diagnose wheel/tire vibration, shimmy, and noise concerns; determine needed repairs.	101–104
5. Rotate tires/wheels and torque fasteners according to manufacturers' recommendations.	100
6. Measure wheel, tire, axle flange, and hub runout (radial and lateral); determine needed repairs.	102–104, 410
7. Diagnose tire pull (lead) problems; determine corrective actions.	370–371
8. Dismount and mount tire on wheel.	96–98
9. Balance wheel and tire assembly.	104–107
10. Test and diagnose tire-pressure monitoring system; determine needed repairs.	79–81, 96

NATEF CORRELATION CHART

NATEF CORRELATION CHART—SUSPENSION AND STEERING (A4)

For every task in suspension and steering diagnosis and repair, the following safety requirement must be strictly enforced:

Comply with personal and environmental safety practices associated with clothing; eye protection; hand tools; power equipment; proper ventilation; and the handling, storage, and disposal of chemicals/materials in accordance with local, state, and federal safety and environmental regulations.

Task	Textbook Page No.	Worktext Page No.
A. General Suspension and Steering Systems Diagnosis		
1. Complete work order to include customer information, vehicle identifying information, customer concern, related service history, cause, and correction. (P-1)	3–4	4, 28
2. Identify and interpret suspension and steering concern; determine necessary action. (P-1)	154–174, 190–191, 244–249	30, 57
3. Research applicable vehicle and service information, such as suspension and steering system operation, vehicle service history, service precautions, and technical service bulletins. (P-1)	2–4	5, 6, 7, 29
4. Locate and interpret vehicle and major component identification numbers (VIN, vehicle certification labels, calibration decals). (P-1)	2–3	8, 9
B. Steering Systems Diagnosis and Repair		
1. Disable and enable supplemental restraint system (SRS). (P-1)	215–216	10, 50
2. Remove and replace steering wheel; center/time supplemental restraint system (SRS) coil (clock spring). (P-1)	215–216	51
3. Diagnose steering column noises, looseness, and binding concerns (including tilt mechanisms); determine necessary action. (P-2)	216–220	52
4. Diagnose power steering gear (non-rack-and-pinion type) binding, uneven turning effort, looseness, hard steering, noise, and fluid leakage concerns; determine necessary action. (P-3)	221–224, 279–286	61, 62
5. Diagnose power steering gear (rack-and-pinion type) binding, uneven turning effort, looseness, hard steering, noise, and fluid leakage concerns; determine necessary action. (P-3)	226–230, 279–286	63
6. Inspect steering shaft universal joint(s), flexible coupling(s), collapsible column, lock cylinder mechanism, and steering wheel; perform necessary action. (P-2)	215–220	53
7. Adjust manual or power non-rack-and-pinion worm bearing preload and sector lash. (P-3)	226–229	54
8. Remove and replace manual or power rack-and-pinion steering gear; inspect mounting bushings and brackets. (P-1)	236, 249	55

Task	Textbook Page No.	Worktext Page No.
9. Inspect and replace manual or power rack-and-pinion steering gear inner tie rod ends (sockets) and bellows boots. (P-1)	236	58
10. Determine proper power steering fluid type; inspect fluid level and condition. (P-1)	259–260	64
11. Flush, fill, and bleed power steering system. (P-2)	277–279	65
12. Diagnose power steering fluid leakage; determine necessary action. (P-2)	279–288	66
13. Remove, inspect, replace, and adjust power steering pump belt. (P-1)	279–288	67
14. Remove and reinstall power steering pump. (P-3)	279–288	68
15. Remove and reinstall power steering pump pulley; check pulley and belt alignment. (P-3)	279–288	69
16. Inspect and replace power steering hoses and fittings. (P-2)	259–263	70
17. Inspect and replace pitman arm, relay (centerlink/intermediate) rod, idler arm and mountings, and steering linkage dampener. (P-2)	244–248	59
18. Inspect, replace, and adjust tie rod ends (sockets), tie rod sleeves, and clamps. (P-1)	249–255	60
19. Test and diagnose components of electronically controlled steering systems using a scan tool; determine necessary action. (P-3)	274–277	71
20. Inspect and test non-hydraulic electric-power-assist steering. (P-3)	274–277	72
21. Identify hybrid vehicle power steering system electrical circuits, and service and safety precautions. (P-3)	274–277	11, 12, 73
C. Suspension Systems Diagnosis and Repair		
1. Front Suspension		
1. Diagnose short- and long-arm suspension system noises, body sway, and uneven riding height concerns; determine necessary action. (P-1)	154–158	31, 32
2. Diagnose strut suspension system noises, body sway, and uneven riding height concerns; determine necessary action. (P-1)	154–158	33
3. Remove, inspect, and install upper and lower control arms, bushings, shafts, and rebound bumpers. (P-3)	171–173	34
4. Remove, inspect, and install strut rods (compression/tension) and bushings. (P-2)	170–171	35
5. Remove, inspect, and install upper and/or lower ball joints. (P-1)	158–164	36
6. Remove, inspect, and install steering knuckle assemblies. (P-2)	173–174	37, 38
7. Remove, inspect, and install short- and long-arm suspension system coil springs and spring insulators. (P-3)	171–173	39
8. Remove, inspect, install, and adjust suspension system torsion bars; inspect mounts. (P-3)	174	40
9. Remove, inspect, and install stabilizer bar bushings, brackets, and links. (P-2)	170	41
10. Remove, inspect, install, and adjust strut cartridge or assembly, strut coil spring, insulators (silencers), and upper strut bearing mount. (P-1)	167–170	42
11. Lubricate suspension and steering systems. (P-2)	154	56
2. Rear Suspension		
1. Remove, inspect, and install coil springs and spring insulators. (P-2)	187–188	44
2. Remove, inspect, and install transverse links, control arms, bushings, and mounts. (P-2)	187–188	45

Task	Textbook Page No.	Worktext Page No.
3. Remove, inspect, and install leaf springs, leaf spring insulators (silencers), shackles, brackets, bushings, and mounts. (P-3)	190–191	46
4. Remove, inspect, and install strut cartridge or assembly, strut coil spring, and insulators (silencers). (P-2)	167–170	47
3. Miscellaneous Service		
1. Inspect, remove, and replace shock absorbers. (P-1)	166–167, 188–190	43, 48
2. Remove, inspect, and service or replace front and rear wheel bearings. (P-1)	293–304	74, 75
3. Test and diagnose components of electronically controlled suspension systems using a scan tool; determine necessary action. (P-3)	194–210	49
D. Wheel Alignment Diagnosis, Adjustment, and Repair		
1. Diagnose vehicle wander, drift, pull, hard steering, bump steer, memory steer, torque steer, and steering return concerns; determine necessary action. (P-1)	346, 370–372	78, 79
2. Perform prealignment inspection; perform necessary action. (P-1)	368–370	83
3. Measure vehicle riding height; determine necessary action.	368–370	84
4. Check and adjust front and rear wheel camber; perform necessary action. (P-1)	375, 381, 385	85
5. Check and adjust caster; perform necessary action. (P-1)	385	86
6. Check and adjust front wheel toe and center steering wheel. (P-1)	385–388	87, 88
7. Check toe-out-on-turns (turning radius); determine necessary action. (P-2)	374–375	89
8. Check SAI (steering axis inclination) and included angle; determine necessary action. (P-2)	375	90
9. Check and adjust rear wheel toe. (P-1)	381	91
10. Check rear wheel thrust angle; determine necessary action. (P-1)	381	92
11. Check for front wheel setback; determine necessary action. (P-2)	376–377	93
12. Check front cradle (subframe) alignment; determine necessary action. (P-3)	376–377	94
E. Wheel and Tire Diagnosis and Repair		
1. Diagnose tire wear patterns; determine necessary action. (P-1)	101–102	16
2. Inspect tires; check and adjust air pressure. (P-1)	95–96	14
3. Diagnose wheel/tire vibration, shimmy, and noise; determine necessary action. (P-2)	102–104	17
4. Rotate tires according to manufacturer's recommendations. (P-1)	100	18
5. Measure wheel, tire, axle, and hub runout; determine necessary action. (P-2)	102–104, 410	19, 20
6. Diagnose tire pull (lead) problem; determine necessary action. (P-2)	370–371	21
7. Balance wheel and tire assembly (static and dynamic). (P-1)	104–108	22
8. Dismount, inspect, and remount tire on wheel. (P-2)	96–98	23
9. Dismount, inspect, and remount tire on wheel equipped with tire-pressure sensor. (P-3)	96	24
10. Reinstall wheel; torque lug nuts. (P-1)	98	25
11. Inspect tire and wheel assembly for air loss; perform necessary action. (P-1)	109–110	26
12. Repair tire using internal patch. (P-1)	110	27
13. Inspect, diagnose, and calibrate tire-pressure monitoring system. (P-3)	79–82	15

ENGLISH GLOSSARY

A-arm   Another name for a control arm because it often looks like the letter A.

Actuator   An electromechanical device that performs mechanical movement as commanded by a controller.

Adjustable wrench   A type of open-ended wrench that is adjustable allowing it to be used on many different sizes of fasteners.

AGST   Above ground storage tank.

Air spring   A rubber-fabric air-filled bag used to replace a spring.

Air suspension   A type of suspension that uses air springs instead of steel springs.

ALC   Automatic level control.

Anti-dive   A term used to describe the geometry of the suspension that controls the movement of the vehicle during braking. It is normal for a vehicle to nosedive slightly during braking, and this feature is designed into most vehicles.

Antifriction bearings   Bearings that use rollers or balls to reduce friction.

Anti-squat   A term used to describe the geometry of the suspension that controls the movement of the vehicle body during acceleration. Anti-squat at 100% means that the body remains level during acceleration. Less than 100% indicates that the body "squats down," or lowers in the rear, during acceleration.

API   American Petroleum Institute.

Armature   The moveable, rotating part of a DC motor used to move a control rod in an air spring to adjust the ride height.

Articulation test   A test specified by some vehicle manufacturers that measures the amount of force necessary to move the inner tie rod end in the ball socket assembly. The usual specification for this test is greater than 1 lb (4 N) and less than 6 lb (26 N) of force.

AS   Air suspension.

Asbestosis   A lung disease that causes shortness of breath and scarring of the lungs.

Aspect ratio   The ratio of height to width of a tire. A tire with an aspect ratio of 60 (a 60-series tire) has a height (from rim to tread) of 60% of its cross-sectional width.

Automatic Level Control (ALC)   A type of electronic suspension that uses air shocks to control the height of the vehicle at the rear.

Axial load   A load applied in the same axis as the centerline of a bearing. Also called *thrust load*.

Axial play   Movement or play in the same axis as the centerline of the ball joint.

Axle windup   The movement during acceleration of the rear axle on a rear-wheel-drive vehicle equipped with a leaf-spring-type suspension.

Back spacing   The distance between the back rim edge and the center section mounting pad of a wheel.

Ball bearings   A type of antifriction bearing that uses ball bearings.

Ball joints   A ball-and-socket joint used in the front suspension to allow up-and-down and turning motion of the front wheel.

Ball socket assembly   An inner tie rod end assembly that contains a ball-and-socket joint at the point where the assembly is threaded onto the end of the steering rack.

BCI   Battery Council International.

Bead   The part of a tire that is made of wire that the body plies are wrapped around.

Belt   A layer of fabric or steel wire under the tread of a tire.

BJI   Ball joint inclination.

Body ply   A layer of cloth that gives a tire its strength.

Bolt circle   The diameter (in inches or millimeters) of a circle drawn through the center of the bolt holes in a wheel.

Bounce test   A test used to check the condition of shock absorbers.

BPP   Brake pedal position.

Breaker bar   A handle used to rotate a socket. Because the handle is longer than a ratchet, it is often used to break loose bolts or nuts.

Breather tube   A tube that connects the left and right bellows of a rack-and-pinion steering gear.

Brinelling   A defective bearing condition where the roller or ball dents the inner and/or outer race. Named after Johann A. Brinell, a Swedish engineer.

Bulkhead   The panel between the engine compartment and the passenger compartment.

Bump cap   A cap worn by a technician that protects the head from harm from overhead objects or vehicle parts.

Bump steer   Used to describe what occurs when the steering linkage is not level, causing the front tires to turn inward or outward as the wheels and suspension move up and down. Automotive chassis engineers call it *roll steer.*

Bump stop   A rubber or urethane stop to limit upward suspension travel. Also called a strikeout bumper, suspension bumper, or compression bumper.

CAA   Clean Air Act.

Cage   The part of an antifriction bearing that holds the balls or rollers.

Calibration codes   The code identification of a particular vehicle and engine calibration.

Camber   The inward or outward tilt of the wheels from true vertical as viewed from the front or rear of the vehicle. Positive camber means the top of the wheel is out from center of the vehicle more than the bottom of the wheel.

Camber roll   The camber angle of the front wheels due to caster.

Campaign   A recall notice sent to owners of vehicles informing them to return to the dealer for a repair.

Cap screw   A name for a bolt that threads into a casting, such as an engine block.

Carcass ply   Plies of fabric in a tire that cover the entire tire from bead to bead.

Cardan joints   A type of universal joint named for a sixteenth-century Italian mathematician.

Caster   The forward or backward tilt of an imaginary line drawn through the steering axis as viewed from the side of the vehicle. Positive caster is where an imaginary line would contact the road surface in front of the contact path of the tire.

Caster sweep   A process used to measure caster during a wheel alignment procedure where the front wheels are rotated first inward, then outward, a specified amount.

Casting number   A series of numbers and/or letters cast into major components, such as engine blocks and cylinder heads.

Castle nut   A type of lock nut that uses a cotter pin to keep it locked in position.

CCR   Computer Command Ride.

CCVRTMR   Abbreviation for chassis continuously variable real-time dampening magneto-rheological. A type of electronic-controlled suspension.

Center bolt   A bolt used to hold the leaves of a leaf spring together in the center. Also called a *centering pin.*

Center link   The center part of a parallelogram-type steering linkage.

Center section   The section of a wheel that attaches to the hub. Also called the *spider.*

Center support bearing   A bearing used to support the center of a long drive shaft on a rear-wheel-drive vehicle. Also called a *steady bearing.*

Center take-off rack   A type of rack-and-pinion steering gear where the tie rods are attached to the center of the rack rather than at the ends of the rack.

Centering pin   See *Center bolt.*

Centerline steering   Used to describe the position of the steering wheel while driving on a straight, level road. The steering wheel should be centered or within plus or minus 3 degrees, as specified by many vehicle manufacturers.

CFR   Code of Federal Regulations.

Chapman strut   A MacPherson-strut-type of suspension used at the rear of the vehicle.

Chassis   The frame, suspension, steering, and machinery of a motor vehicle.

Cheater bar   A length of pipe fitted over the handle of a ratchet or breaker bar to increase the force applied to a fastener. This is not a recommended practice because the socket can shatter due to the extra force applied.

Check ball   A steel ball used to stop the flow of fluid in one direction only.

C-lock axle   A type of rear axle assembly, that uses a C-lock to retain the axles.

Closed-end wrench   A type of wrench that has an open end to enable a bolt or nut to be grasped from the side.

Coefficient of friction   A measure of the amount of friction, usually measured from 0 to 1. A low number (0.3) indicates low friction, and a high number (0.9) indicates high friction.

Coil spring   A spring steel rod wound in a spiral (helix) shape. Used in both front and rear suspension systems.

Cold climate fluid   A typical power steering fluid recommended for use in cold climates.

Collapsible column   A steering column that collapses in the event of a front impact to the vehicle to help prevent injury to the driver.

Combination wrench   A wrench that is open ended at one end and has a box end at the other end.

Companion flange   The part that attaches to the drive shaft at the differential assembly.

Compensation   A process used during a wheel alignment procedure where the sensors are calibrated to eliminate errors in the alignment readings that may be the result of a bent wheel or unequal installation of the sensor on the wheel of the vehicle.

Composite   A term used to describe the combining of individual parts into a larger component. For example, a composite leaf spring is constructed of fiberglass and epoxy; a composite master brake cylinder contains both plastic parts (reservoir) and metal parts (cylinder housing).

Composite leaf spring   A leaf spring made from a composite material, which usually includes fiberglass and epoxy resin.

Computer Command Ride (CCR)   A brand name of a type of electronic suspension system.

Cone   The inner race or ring of a bearing.

Conicity   A fault in a tire that causes it to be shaped like a cone and causes a pull.

Constant velocity joint   Commonly called *CV joints*. CV joints are drive line joints that can transmit engine power through relatively large angles without a change in the velocity, as is usually the case with conventional Cardan-type U-joints.

Control arms   A suspension link that connects a knuckle or wheel flange to the body or frame of the vehicle.

Controller   Commonly used to describe a computer or an electronic control module.

Cotter key   A metal loop used to retain castle nuts by being installed through a hole. Size is measured by diameter and length (for example, 1/8" × 1 1/2"). Also called a *cotter pin*. Named for the old English verb meaning "to close or fasten."

Coupling disc   See *Flexible coupling*.

Cow catcher   A large spring seat used on many General Motors MacPherson strut units. If the coil spring breaks, the cow catcher prevents one end of the spring from moving outward and cutting a tire.

Cradle   A structural support for the engine and transaxle on a front-wheel-drive vehicle.

Crest   The diameter of a bolt measured across the outside of the threads.

Cross camber/caster   The difference of angle from one side of the vehicle to the other. Most manufacturers recommend a maximum difference side to side of 1/2 degree for camber and caster.

Cross-steer linkage   A type of steering linkage commonly used on light and medium trucks.

Cup   The outer race or ring of a bearing.

Cuppy tire wear   Scalloped tire wear usually on the inside or outside edges caused by defective or worn shock absorbers or other faults in the suspension system.

CV joint boot   The covering over a constant velocity joint made from rubber, thermoplastic, or urethane.

CV joints   Constant velocity joints.

Degrees   A degree is 1/360th of a circle.

Desiccant   An ingredient, such as silica gel, used to remove moisture from air. Used in electronic systems that use air shocks or springs.

Diff   Abbreviation for *differential*.

Differential   A mechanical unit containing gears that provides gear reduction and a change of direction of engine power and permits the drive wheels to rotate at different speeds, as required when turning a corner.

Directional stability   Ability of a vehicle to move forward in a straight line with a minimum of driver control. Crosswinds and road irregularities will have little effect if directional stability is good.

Dog tracking   The condition where the rear wheels do not follow directly behind the front wheels. Named for dogs that run with their rear paws offset toward one side so that their rear paws will not hit their front paws.

DOT tire code   The U.S. Department of Transportation's tire coding system.

Double-Cardan joints   A universal joint that uses two conventional Cardan joints together, to allow the joint to operate at greater angles.

Drag link   Used to describe a link in the center of the steering linkage; usually called a *center link*.

Drag rod   See *Strut rod*.

Drift   A mild pull that does not cause a force on the steering wheel that the driver must counteract (also known as *lead*). Also refers to a tapered tool used to center a component in a bolt hole prior to installing the bolt.

Drive axle shaft   The shaft that connects the transaxle or differential to the drive wheels.

Drive line angles   The angles of the drive shaft at the front and rear, which are equal, plus or minus 0.5 degrees.

Drive shaft   A shaft that transfers engine torque from the output of the transmission to the rear axle (differential) assembly.

Drive shaft runout   A measurement of the amount that a drive shaft differs from perfectly round when rotated.

Drive size   The size of a ratchet or breaker bar drive square that is used to rotate a socket. Common drive sizes include 1/4", 3/8" and 1/2".

Driver select switch   A switch that allows the driver to select the harshness of the suspension.

Dropping point   The temperature at which a grease passes from a semisolid to a liquid state under conditions specified by ASTM.

Dry park test   A test of steering and/or suspension components. With the wheels in the straight-ahead position and the vehicle on flat and level ground, have an assistant turn the steering wheel while looking and touching all steering and suspension components, checking for any looseness.

Durometer   The hardness rating of rubber products, named for an instrument used to measure hardness that was developed around 1890.

Dust cap   A functional metal cap that keeps grease in and dirt out of wheel bearings. Also called a *grease cap*.

Dynamic balance   The centerline of weight-mass of a tire/wheel assembly is in the same plane on the centerline of the wheel.

Dynamic seals   Seals used where there is relative movement between the two surfaces being sealed.

EBCM   Electronic Brake Control Module.

Eccentric cam   A plate that has a bolt offset from the center used to change camber and/or caster.

ECU   Electronic control unit.

EHPS   Electro-hydraulic power steering.

Electromagnet   An electromagnet consists of a soft iron core surrounded by a coil of wire. Electrical current flowing through the coiled wire creates a magnetic field around the core.

E-metric tire   A tire designation for electric vehicles, which have low rolling resistance.

Endplay   The movement in line with the centerline of an assembly.

EPA   Environmental Protection Agency.

EPS   Electric power steering.

ESC   Electronic stability control. A system that helps the drive control the vehicle during cornering or under slippery road surface conditions.

ESP   Electronic stability program. Another term used to describe ESC.

EVA   Electronic Vibration Analyzer.

EVO   Electronic variable orifice.

Extension   A round steel bar that connects to a ratchet or breaker bar at one end and a socket at the other end.

Eye wash station   A water-dispensing unit that directs streams of water to the eyes.

Fire blanket   A fireproof wool blanket that is used to smother a fire by wrapping it around a victim.

Fire extinguisher classes   Classification of the types of fires that each specific fire extinguisher is designed to handle.

Five-wheel alignment   An alignment that not only includes the four wheels that are on the ground, but also includes the steering wheel.

Fixed joint   A type of CV joint used at the wheel end of the drive axle shaft.

Flare-nut wrench   A type of wrench used to remove fuel, brake, or air-conditioning lines.

Flexible coupling   A part of the steering mechanism between the steering column and the steering gear or rack-and-pinion assembly. Also called a *rag joint* or *steering coupling disc*. The purpose of the flexible coupling is to keep noise, vibration, and harshness (NVH) from being transmitted from the road and steering to the steering wheel.

Flow control valve   Regulates and controls the flow of power steering pump hydraulic fluids to the steering gear or rack-and-pinion assembly. The flow control valve is usually part of the power steering pump assembly.

Follower ball joint   A ball joint used in a suspension system to provide support and control without having the weight of the vehicle or the action of the springs transferred through the joint itself. Also called a *friction ball joint*.

Forward steer   See *Front steer*.

Force   Energy applied to an object.

4 × 4   The term used to describe a four-wheel-drive vehicle. The first *4* indicates the number of wheels of the vehicle; the second *4* indicates the number of wheels that are driven by the engine.

4 × 2   The term used to describe a two-wheel-drive truck. The *4* indicates the number of wheels of the vehicle; the *2* indicates the number of wheels that are driven by the engine.

Four-wheel alignment   A wheel alignment that checks and adjusts, if necessary, the angles of all four wheels.

Fractions   A measurement in parts of an inch, such as 1/2, 1/4, and 1/8.

Freeplay   The amount that the steering wheel can move without moving the front wheels. The maximum allowable amount of freeplay is less than 2 inches for a parallelogram-type steering system, and 3/8 inch for a rack-and-pinion steering system.

Frequency   The number of times a complete motion cycle takes place during a period of time (usually measured in seconds).

Friction   The resistance to sliding of two bodies in contact with each other.

Friction ball joint   Outer suspension pivot that does not support the weight of the vehicle. Also called a *follower ball joint*.

Front steer   A construction design of a vehicle that places the steering gear and steering linkage in front of the centerline of the front wheels. Also called *forward steer*.

Full-floating   A type of axle assembly where the weight of the vehicle is supported by the axle housing and not the axle itself.

Full frame   A frame of a vehicle that extends the entire length and width of the vehicle.

FWD   Front-wheel drive.

Galvanized steel   Steel with a zinc coating to help protect it from rust and corrosion.

Garter spring   A spring used in a seal to help keep the lip of the seal in contact with the moving part.

GAWR   Gross axle weight rating.

GC-LB   A rating or classification of grease. GC is the highest rating for wheel bearing grease and LB is the highest quality of chassis grease.

Gear lash   Clearance between gears.

Geometric centerline   A type of wheel alignment where all four wheels are aligned parallel to the centerline of the vehicle.

GKN   A company named after its founders, Guest, Keene, and Nettelfolds.

Gland nut   The name commonly used to describe the large nut at the top of a MacPherson strut housing. This gland nut must be removed to replace a strut cartridge.

Grade   The tensile strength rating of a bolt.

Gram   A metric unit of weight equal to 1/1000 kilogram (1 oz × 28 = 1 gram). An American dollar bill or paper clip weighs about 1 gram.

Grease   Oil with a thickening agent.

Grease cap   A functional metal cap that keeps grease in and dirt out of wheel bearings. Also called a *dust cap*.

Grease fitting   A metal replaceable fitting shaped to hold the end of a grease gun in place and equipped with a spring-loaded valve.

Grease retainer   See *Grease seal*.

Grease seal   A seal used to prevent grease from escaping and to prevent dirt and moisture from entering.

Green tire   An uncured assembled tire. After the green tire is placed in a mold under heat and pressure, the rubber changes chemically and comes out of the mold formed and cured.

GVW   Gross vehicle weight. GVW is the weight of the vehicle plus the weight of all passengers and cargo up to the limit specified by the manufacturer.

GVWR   Gross vehicle weight rating.

Half shaft   Drive axles on a front-wheel-drive vehicle or from a stationary differential to the drive wheels.

Halogenated compounds   Chemicals containing chlorine, fluorine, bromine, or iodine. These chemicals are generally considered to be hazardous, and any product containing these chemicals should be disposed of using approved procedures.

Haltenberger linkage   A type of steering linkage commonly used on light trucks.

Handwheel position sensor   A sensor that detects the direction and speed of rotation of the steering wheel.

Hanger bearing   See *Center support bearing*.

HD   Heavy duty.

Height sensor   A height sensor determines the vertical relationship between the suspension component and the body of a vehicle.

Helper springs   Auxiliary or extra springs used in addition to the vehicle's original springs to restore proper ride height or to increase the load-carrying capacity of the vehicle.

HEPA vacuum   A vacuum equipped with a high-efficiency particulate air (HEPA) filter.

Hertz   A unit of measurement of frequency. One Hertz is one cycle per second, abbreviated Hz. Named for Heinrich R. Hertz, a nineteenth-century German physicist.

High-flotation tires   A type of tire that is large in size and holds a large volume of air.

Hooke's Law   The force characteristics of a spring discovered by Robert Hooke (1635–1703), an English physicist. Hooke's Law states that "the deflection (movement or deformation) of a spring is directly proportional to the applied force."

Hotchkiss drive   A type of power transmission for a front engine, rear-drive vehicle where the engine torque reaction is controlled by the suspension, as compared to the use of torque arm or frame-mounted differential.

HSS   High-strength steel. A low-carbon alloy steel that uses various amounts of silicon, phosphorus, and manganese.

Hub cap   A functional and decorative cover over the lug nut portion of the wheel. Also see *Wheel cover*.

Hydraulic   The force exerted by pressurized liquid in a closed system.

Hydrophilic   A term used to describe a type of rubber used in many all-season tires where the rubber has an affinity for water (rather than repelling it).

Hydrophobic   A term used to describe the repelling of water.

Hydroplaning   Condition that occurs when driving too fast on wet roads. The water on the road gets trapped between the tire and the road, forcing the tire onto a layer of water and off the road surface. All traction between the tire and the road is lost.

Hypoid gearset   A type of gearset where the pinion gear is below the centerline of the ring gear.

Hz   An abbreviation for Hertz, cycles per second.

Idler arm   The pivot point and support arm of a parallelogram-type steering linkage located on the passenger side of the vehicle.

Inclinometer   An instrument used to measure angles. Normally used to measure drive shaft angles.

Included angle   SAI angle added to the camber angle of the same wheel.

Independent suspension   A suspension system that allows a wheel to move up and down without undue effect on the opposite side.

Indicator ball joints   A type of ball joint that shows when the joint is worn enough to require replacement.

Inflator module   The part of an airbag that contains the airbag itself, plus the unit that is used to inflate the airbag.

Inner liner   The inner layer of rubber inside a tire.

Input   Information on data from sensors to an electronic controller is called input. Sensors and switches provide the input signals.

Insulators   Thin strips of plastic or hard rubber used to separate the leaves of a leaf spring.

Integral reservoir   A type of power steering pump that includes the pump inside the fluid reservoir.

Iron   Refined metal from iron ore (ferrous oxide) in a furnace. Also see *Steel*.

IRS   Independent rear suspension.

ISO   International Standards Organization.

Isolator bushing   Rubber bushing used between the frame and the stabilizer bar. Also known as a *stabilizer bar bushing*.

Jounce   Used to describe up-and-down movement.

Jounce bumper   A rubber or urethane stop to limit upward suspension travel. Also called a *bump stop, strikeout bumper, suspension bumper,* or *compression bumper*.

JWL   Japan Wheel Light Metal Standard Mark.

Kerf   Large water grooves in the tread of a tire.

Kickback   The movement of the steering wheel when the front wheels strike a curb or bump.

Kingpin   A pivot pin commonly used on solid axles or early model twin I-beam axles that rotates in bushings and allows the front wheels to rotate. The knuckle pivots about the kingpin.

Kingpin inclination   Inclining the tops of the kingpins toward each other creates a force stabilizing to the vehicle.

KPI   Kingpin inclination (also known as *steering axis inclination*, SAI). The angle formed between true vertical and a line drawn between the upper and lower pivot points of the spindle.

Ladder frame   A steel frame for a vehicle that uses cross-braces along the length, similar to the rungs of a ladder.

Lateral accelerometer sensor   A sensor used in many vehicles equipped with electronic suspension and/or traction control systems used to detect sideways movement of the vehicle.

Lateral links   Suspension arms that control the side-to-side movement of the wheels and vehicle. Also called *transverse links*.

Lateral runout   A measure of the amount a tire or wheel is moving side to side while being rotated. Excessive lateral runout can cause a shimmy-type vibration if the wheels are on the front axle.

Lead   A mild pull that does not cause a force on the steering wheel that the driver must counteract (also known as *drift*).

Leaf spring   A spring made of several pieces of flat spring steel.

LED   Light emitting diode.

Live axle   A solid axle used on the drive wheels; it contains the drive axles that propel the vehicle.

LLR   Low rolling resistance.

Load-carrying ball joint   Used in a suspension system to provide support and control. The weight (load) of the vehicle is transferred to the frame through this joint.

Load index   An abbreviated method that uses a number to indicate the load-carrying capabilities of a tire.

LOBRÓ joint   A brand name of CV joint.

Lock nut   See *Prevailing torque nut*.

Lock plate   A plate located in the steering column that is used to lock the steering wheel when the key is removed from the ignition.

Loose   A term used to describe an oversteering condition.

LT   Light truck.

Lug nuts   Nuts used on wheel studs to attach wheels to hubs.

M & S   Mud and snow tires.

MacPherson strut   A type of front suspension with the shock absorber and coil spring in one unit, which rotates when the wheels are turned. Assembly mounts to the vehicle body at the top and to one ball joint and control arm at the lower end. It is named for its inventor, Earle S. MacPherson.

Magnasteer   A type of electronically controlled hydraulic power steering.

Magneto-rheological (MR)   A type of electronic suspension that uses magneto-rheological fluid shocks.

Major splice   A place in a tire where the tread rubber and one or more body plies are spliced during tire construction.

Match mounting   The process of mounting a tire on a wheel and aligning the valve stem with a mark on the tire. The mark on the tire represents the high point of the tire; the valve stem location represents the smallest diameter of the wheel.

Memory steer   A lead or pull of a vehicle caused by faults in the steering or suspension system. If after making a turn the vehicle tends to pull in the same direction as the last turn, then the vehicle has memory steer.

Mercury   A dense liquid metal.

Metric bolts   A bolt that is manufactured and designated in the metric system.

Millisecond   One-thousandth of 1 second (1/1000).

Minutes   A unit of measure of an angle. Sixty minutes equal 1 degree.

Mode select switch   A switch used to select ride comfort settings on a vehicle equipped with electronic suspension.

Modified X   A method of tire rotation.

Moly grease   Grease containing molybdenum disulfide.

Mono leaf   A leaf spring that uses only one leaf.

Morning sickness   A slang term used to describe temporary loss of power steering assist when cold caused by wear in the control valve area of a power rack-and-pinion unit.

Motor   An electromechanical device that converts electrical energy into mechanical movement.

MR   Magneto-rheological.

MRRTD   Magneto-rheological real-time dampening.

MSDS   Material Safety Data Sheet.

MSI   MacPherson Strut Inclination.

Neutral run-up test   A test used to help determine the source of a vibration. Engine speed is increased and vibration is measured with the transmission in Neutral.

NHTSA   National Highway Traffic Safety Administration.

NLGI   National Lubricating Grease Institute. Usually associated with grease. The higher the NLGI number, the firmer the grease. Grease classified as #000 is very fluid, whereas #5 is very firm. The consistency most recommended is NLGI #2 (soft).

Noise   Noise is the vibration of air caused by a body in motion.

Non-load-carrying ball joint   A ball joint used in a front suspension that acts as a pivot joint and does not support the weight of the vehicle.

NVH   Abbreviation for noise, vibration and harshness.

OE   Original equipment.

OEM   Original equipment manufacturer.

Offset   The distance the center section (mounting pad) is offset from the centerline of the wheel.

Open-end Wrench   A type of wrench that allows access to the flats of a bolt or nut from the side.

Opposite-phase steering   A phase used in four wheel steering systems where the rear wheels are moved in the opposite direction of the front wheels.

Orbital steer   See *Bump steer.*

OSHA   Occupational Safety and Health Administration.

Output   The command from an electronic control module.

Overcenter adjustment   An adjustment made to a steering gear while the steering is turned through its center straight-ahead position. Also known as a *sector lash adjustment.*

Overinflation   Used to describe a tire with too much tire pressure (greater than maximum allowable pressure).

Oversteer   A term used to describe the handling of a vehicle where the driver must move the steering wheel in the opposite direction from normal while turning a corner. Oversteer handling is very dangerous. Most vehicle manufacturers design their vehicles to understeer rather than oversteer.

Oz-in.   Measurement of imbalance. A measurement of 3 oz-in. means that an object is out of balance; it would require a 1-oz weight placed 3 inches from the center of the rotating object, a 3-oz weight placed 1 in. from the center, or any other combination that when multiplied equals 3 oz-in.

Panhard rod   A horizontal steel rod or bar attached to the rear axle housing at one end and the frame at the other to keep the center of the body directly above the center of the rear axle during cornering and suspension motions. Also called a *track rod.*

Parallelogram linkage   A parallelogram is a geometric box shape where opposite sides are parallel (equal distance apart). A parallelogram linkage is a type of steering linkage used with a conventional steering gear that uses a pitman arm, center link, idler arm, and tie rods.

Pascal's law   Pascal's law states that pressure on a confined liquid is transmitted equally in all directions. Named after the French scientist Blaise Pascal (1623–1662).

Perform ride mode   A mode of operation for a General Motors vehicle equipped with electronic suspension. In this mode, the suspension is set to a firm setting.

Perimeter frame   A steel structure for a vehicle that supports the body of the vehicle under the sides, as well as the front and rear.

Perimeter frame penetration   A test for grease where a standard cone is dropped into a grease sample and its depth is measured.

Photocell   A type of sensor that uses light-emitting diodes and a phototransistor to detect location.

Phototransistor   An electronic device that can detect light and turn on or off. Used in some suspension height sensors.

Pickle fork   A tapered fork used to separate chassis parts that are held together by a nut and a taper. Hitting the end of the pickle fork forces the wedge portion of the tool between the parts to be separated and "breaks the taper." A pickle fork tool is generally *not* recommended because the tool can tear or rip the grease boot of the part being separated.

Pin bushings   The small roller bearings used in a universal joint.

Pinch bolt   A bolt used to retain a ball joint in some suspension designs.

Pinch weld seam   The place under the vehicle where two body panels are welded together. Often used as a location for placement of the pads when hoisting the vehicle.

Pinion torque   The torque required to rotate the pinion shaft on a rack-and-pinion steering gear.

Pitch   The pitch of a threaded fastener refers to the number of threads per inch.

Pitman arm   A short lever arm that is splined to the steering gear cross-shaft. It transmits the steering force from the cross-shaft to the steering linkage.

Pitman shaft   See *Sector shaft*.

Platform   The platform of a vehicle includes the basic structure (frame and/or major body panels), as well as the basic steering and suspension components. One platform may be the basis for several different brands of vehicles.

Plowing   A term used to describe an understeering condition.

Plunge joint   An inner constant velocity joint that is able to move in and out and transmit torque while the vehicle suspension moves up and down over bumps.

Ply steer   A term used to describe why a tire can cause a pulling condition based on the angle of the cords of the belt layers.

Poppet valve steering gear   A type of power steering gear used on medium trucks that uses a poppet valve to control the direction and amount of assist.

Pound foot   A measurement of torque—1-pound pull, 1 foot from the center of an object.

PPE   Personal protective equipment.

PPM   Parts per million.

Prealignment checks   The checks that should be performed before checking or changing the wheel alignment of a vehicle.

Preload   A term used to describe a tightening of a nut or bolt to provide a force.

Pressure   A force applied to a surface divided by its area.

Pressure-relief valve   A valve located in a power steering pump that uses a check ball, which unseats and allows fluid to return to the reservoir if pressure exceeds a certain volume.

Prevailing torque nut   A special design of nut fastener that is deformed slightly or has other properties that permit the nut to remain attached to the fastener without loosening.

Prop shaft   An abbreviation for *propeller shaft*.

Propeller shaft   A term used by many manufacturers for a drive shaft.

PSCM   Power steering control module.

PSI   Pounds per square inch.

PSP   Power steering pressure.

Pull   Vehicle tends to go left or right while traveling on a straight, level road.

Pulse width   The amount of time electrical current is on compared to the amount of time it is off.

Pulse-width modulation   The control of a device, such as a solenoid, by pulsing the current on and off.

Rack and pinion   A type of lightweight steering unit that connects the front wheels through tie rods to the end of a long shaft called a *rack*. When the driver moves the steering wheel, the force is transferred to the rack-and-pinion assembly. Inside the rack housing is a small pinion gear that meshes with gear teeth, which are cut into the rack.

Rack support   A spring-loaded unit that is used to hold the rack part of a rack-and-pinion steering gear assembly in proper position.

Radial force variation   The variation in force a tire exerts as it rotates and contacts the road surface.

Radial load   A load applied toward the center from all angles.

Radial runout   A measure of the amount that a tire or wheel is out of round. Excessive radial runout can cause a tramp-type vibration.

Radial tire   A tire whose carcass plies run straight across (or almost straight across) from bead to bead.

Radius rod   A suspension component to control longitudinal (front-to-back) support; it is usually attached with rubber bushings to the frame at one end and the axle or control arm at the other end. Also see *Strut rod*.

Rag joint   See *Flexible coupling*.

Ratio   The expression for proportion. For example, in a typical rear axle assembly, the drive shaft rotates three times faster than the rear axles. It is expressed as a ratio of 3:1 and read as "three to one." Power train ratios are always expressed as driving gears divided by driven gears.

RBS Rubber-bonded socket.

RCRA Resource Conservation and Recovery Act.

Real-time dampening (RTD) A type of electronic suspension system used on some General Motors vehicles.

Rear spacing See *Back spacing.*

Rear steer A construction design of a vehicle that places the steering gear and steering linkage behind the centerline of the front wheels.

Rebound clips Clips used around the leaves of a leaf spring.

Rebuilt See *Remanufactured.*

Recall A program where all owners of a vehicle are notified to return to a dealer to have some safety-related fault corrected.

Remanufactured A term used to describe a process in which a component is disassembled, cleaned, inspected, and reassembled using new or reconditioned parts. According to the Automotive Parts Rebuilders Association (APRA), this same procedure is also called *rebuilt.*

Remote reservoir A type of power steering pump where the fluid is in a reservoir separate from the pump.

Retainer-type axles A type of rear drive axle assembly that uses a retainer plate to keep the axles attached to the housing.

Returnability The ability of the steering wheel to return to the straight-ahead position after making a turn.

Ride height The height of the vehicle. Also called the *trim height.*

Right-to-know laws Laws that require businesses to post Material Safety Data Sheets (MSDSs) so that everyone will know what hazardous materials are being used in the building.

RIM Reaction injection molded.

Rim width The width of a wheel as measured between bead sections.

Ring gear The large gear inside a differential assembly, which meshes with the drive pinion gear.

RMP Reaction moldable polymer.

Road crown A roadway condition where the center is higher than the outside edges. Road crown is designed into many roads to drain water off the road surface.

Roll bar See *Stabilizer bar.*

Roll steer See *Bump steer.*

Roller bearings A type of antifriction bearing that uses rollers between the inner and outer races.

Rolling circumference The distance a tire travels when rotated one revolution.

Rotary control valve A power steering valve that operates by rotating an inner valve inside an outer valve to control the amount of steering assist.

RPO Regular Production Order.

RSS Road Sensing Suspension.

RTD Real-time dampening.

Run-flat tires Tires specially designed to operate for reasonable distances and speeds without air inside to support the weight of the vehicle. Run-flat tires usually require the use of special rims designed to prevent the flat tire from coming off the wheel.

RWD Rear-wheel drive.

Rzeppa joint A type of constant velocity (CV) joint named after its inventor, Alfred H. Rzeppa.

SAE Society of Automotive Engineers.

Saginaw Brand name of steering components manufactured in Saginaw, Michigan, USA.

SAI Steering axis inclination (same as KPI).

Same-phase steering A vehicle equipped with four-wheel steering where the front and the rear wheels move in the same direction.

Schrader valve A type of valve used in tires, air-conditioning, and fuel injection systems. Invented in 1844 by August Schrader.

Scrub radius Refers to where an imaginary line drawn through the steering axis intersects the ground compared to the centerline of the tire. *Zero* scrub radius means the line intersects at the centerline of the tire. *Positive* scrub radius means that the line intersects below the road surface. *Negative* scrub radius means the line intersects above the road surface. It is also called *steering offset* by some vehicle manufacturers.

Sector gear A section of a gear inside a steering gear that is attached to the sector shaft. Also called the *pitman shaft.*

Sector lash Refers to clearance (lash) between a section of gear (sector) on the pitman shaft in a steering gear. Also see *Overcenter adjustment.*

Sector shaft The output shaft of a conventional steering gear. It is a part of the sector shaft in a section of a gear that meshes with the worm gear and is rotated by the driver when the steering wheel is turned. It is also called a *pitman shaft.*

Selectable Ride (SR) A brand name for a type of electronic suspension system.

Self-park A system that uses sensors and electric power steering to permit a vehicle to park itself.

SEMA Specialty Equipment Manufacturers Association.

Semi-floating A type of line axle where the inner end of the axle floats and the outer end is supported by a bearing.

Semi-independent suspension A type of rear suspension that allows some transfer of motion to the opposite side.

Semi-trailing arm A type of rear suspension that controls both side-to-side and front-to-rear motion.

Setback The amount the front wheels are set back from true parallel with the rear wheels. Positive setback means the right front wheel is set back farther than the left. Setback can be measured as an angle formed by a line perpendicular (90 degrees) to the front axles.

Shackle A mounting that allows the end of a leaf spring to move forward and backward as the spring moves up and down during normal operation of the suspension.

Shim A thin metal spacer.

Shim chart A chart used to help align a vehicle that uses shims for camber and caster adjustment.

Shimmy A type of vibration that causes the steering wheel to move left and right rapidly.

Shock absorbers A suspension component that links and controls the action and reaction of the springs.

Short/long-arm suspension Abbreviated SLA. A suspension system with a short upper control arm and a long lower control arm. The wheel changes very little in camber with a vertical deflection. Also called *double-wishbone-type suspension.*

Side gears The gears inside a differential that attach to the axles.

Sidewall The side of a tire.

Sipes Small traction-improving slits in the tread of a tire.

SLA Abbreviation for short/long-arm suspension.

Slip angle The angle between the true centerline of the tire and the actual path followed by the tire while turning.

SMC Sheet molding compound.

Socket A hand tool used to grab the flats of a bolt or nut from the top, used with a ratchet or breaker bar.

Socket adaptor A tool that adapts one drive size of socket to be used with a ratchet or breaker bar with another drive size.

Solenoid An electromagnetic device that uses a moveable core that can be connected to a linkage to move a valve or other device.

Solenoid-controlled dampener A shock absorber that is electronically controlled by a solenoid.

Solid axle A solid supporting axle for both front or both rear wheels. Also referred to as a *straight axle* or *nonindependent axle.*

Solvent A liquid that dissolves grease or other substances.

Space frame A type of vehicle construction that uses the structure of the body to support the engine and drive train, as well as the steering and suspension. The outside body panels are nonstructure.

Spalling A term used to describe a type of mechanical failure caused by metal fatigue. Metal cracks break out into small chips, slabs, or scales of metal. This process of breaking up is called spalling.

Speed rating A letter on most tires that indicates the maximum speed at which the tire is designed to perform.

Spider Center part of a wheel. Also known as the *center section.*

Spider gears Another name for the pinion gear used in a differential.

Spindle nut Nut used to retain and adjust the bearing clearance of the hub to the spindle.

Spline bind A condition where the splines on the yoke of a drive shaft bind and then release as a vehicle is first accelerated after a stop.

Spoke angle The angle of the steering wheel.

Spontaneous combustion A condition where a fire starts by itself, such as with improperly stored oily rags.

Spring pocket Also called a spring seat.

Spring rate The spring rate is the amount of weight it takes to compress a spring a certain distance, such as 200 pounds per inch.

Springs Used as a buffer between the suspension and the frame or body and used to absorb wheel movement plus support the weight of the vehicle.

Sprung weight The weight of a vehicle that is supported by the suspension.

SPS Suspension position sensor.

SR Selectable Ride.

SSS Speed Sensitive Steering.

SST Special service tools.

Stabilitrack A brand name of an electronic suspension control system.

Stabilizer bar A hardened steel bar connected to the frame and both lower control arms to prevent excessive body roll. Also called an *anti-sway* or *anti-roll bar.*

Stabilizer links Usually consists of a bolt, spacer, and nut to connect (link) the end of the stabilizer bar to the lower control arm.

Static balance A type of wheel balancer that is in one plane.

Static seal   A type of seal where there is no movement between the parts being sealed.

Steady bearing   See *Center support bearing.*

Steel   Refined iron metal with most of the carbon removed.

Steering arms   Arms bolted to or forged as a part of the steering knuckles. They transmit the steering force from the tie rods to the knuckles, causing the wheels to pivot.

Steering coupling disc   See *Flexible coupling.*

Steering dampener   A shock absorber installed on the steering linkage to reduce the road shock being transferred to the steering wheel.

Steering gear   Gears on the end of the steering column that multiply the driver's force to turn the front wheels.

Steering knuckle   The inner portion of the spindle that pivots on the kingpin or ball joints.

Steering offset   See *Scrub radius.*

Steering shaft   The part of the steering that connects the steering wheel to the steering gear assembly.

Steering stop   The location where the steering linkage stops at the extreme left and right end of travel.

Steering wheel position sensor   A sensor that determines in which direction and how fast the steering wheel is being turned.

Straight axle   See *Solid axle.*

Stress riser   A nick or rust area in a spring that could cause the spring to break.

Strikeout bumper   See *Jounce bumper.*

Strut rod   Suspension member used to control forward/backward support to the control arms. Also called *tension* or *compression rod* (TC rod) or *drag rod.*

Strut rod bushing   A rubber component used to insulate the attachment of the strut rod to the frame on the body of the vehicle.

Strut suspension   A type of suspension system that uses struts.

Struts   A structural part of a suspension that includes the shock absorber.

Stub shaft   A short shaft that is part of the steering gear and attaches to the steering shaft assembly.

Stub-type frame   A type of vehicle frame that only supports the front suspension and engine.

Stud   A short rod with threads on both ends.

Suspension   Parts or linkages by which the wheels are attached to the frame or body of a vehicle. These parts or linkages support the vehicle and keep the wheels in proper alignment.

Suspension bumper   See *Jounce bumper.*

Sway bar   Shortened name for anti-sway bar. See *Stabilizer bar.*

SWPS   Steering wheel position sensor.

Synthetic retainers   A type of retention method for holding together parts of a universal joint.

Tapered roller bearings   A type of antifriction bearing that uses tapered rollers between the inner and outer races.

TC rod   See *Strut rod.*

Telescoping steering column   A steering column that can be adjusted toward and away from the driver.

Tensile strength   The strength of a bolt or other fastener in line with the bolt.

Tension rod   See *Strut rod.*

TFE   Two-Flow Electronic. A type of variable-assist steering.

Three-quarter floating   A type of rear drive axle where some of the weight of the vehicle is supported by the axle shaft.

Thrust angle   The angle between the geometric centerline of the vehicle and the thrust line.

Thrust line   The direction the rear wheels are pointed as determined by the rear wheel toe.

Tie bars   Rubber segments molded between grooves of a tire to help support tread blocks.

Tie rod   A rod connecting the steering arms together.

Tight   A term used to describe an understeering condition.

Tilt steering column   A type of steering column that can be moved upward or downward to fit the driver.

Tire rotation   A term used to describe moving wheel/tire assemblies from one position on a vehicle to another.

Toe   The inward or outward angle of the front or rear wheels as viewed from overhead.

Toe-in   The difference in measurement between the front of the wheels and the back of the wheels (the front are closer than the back).

Toe-out   The back of the tires are closer than the front.

Tolerance adjustment   An alignment method that involves loosening and then retightening all suspension mounting fasteners.

TOOT   Toe-out on turns.

Torque   A twisting force that may or may not result in motion. Measured in lb-ft or Newton-meters.

Torque arm   An arm that attaches the rear differential assembly to the body of the vehicle.

Torque prevailing nut   A type of nut that does not loosen, but rather retains its holding torque.

Torque steer Torque steer occurs in front-wheel-drive vehicles when engine torque causes a front wheel to change its angle (toe) from straight ahead. The resulting pulling effect of the vehicle is most noticeable during rapid acceleration, especially whenever upshifting of the transmission creates a sudden change in torque.

Torsion bar A type of spring in the shape of a straight bar. One end is attached to the frame of the vehicle, and the opposite end is attached to a control arm of the suspension. When the wheels hit a bump, the bar twists and then untwists.

Total toe The total (combined) toe of both wheels, either front or rear.

Touring ride mode A driver-select switch position for an electronic suspension system.

TPC Tire Performance Criteria.

TPD Tire problem detector.

TPMS Tire-pressure monitoring system.

Track rod A horizontal steel rod or bar attached to rear axle housing at one end and the frame at the other to keep the center of the rear axle centered on the body. Also known as a *panhard rod*.

Tracking Used to describe the fact that the rear wheels should track directly behind the front wheels.

Trailing arm A rear suspension arm that attaches to the frame or body in front of the rear axle.

Tramp A vibration usually caused by up-and-down motion of an out-of-balance or out-of-round wheel assembly.

Tread The rubber part of a tire that touches the road.

TREAD Act An act that requires the use of tire-pressure monitoring systems on all new vehicles. TREAD stands for Transportation Recall Enhancement, Accountability, and Documentation.

Trunnions The four arms of a typical universal joint.

TSB Technical service bulletin.

Twin-I beam A type of front suspension used on older Ford pickup trucks and vans.

U-joints Universal joints.

UNC Unified National Coarse.

UNF Unified National Fine.

Unit-body A type of vehicle construction first used by the Budd Company of Troy, Michigan, that does not use a separate frame. The body is built strong enough to support the engine and the power train, as well as the suspension and steering system. The outside body panels are part of the structure. Also see *Space frame*.

Universal joint A joint that allows torque to be transmitted and allows up-and-down movement of the suspension system.

Unsprung weight The parts of a vehicle not supported by the suspension system. Examples of items that are typical unsprung weight include wheels, tires, and brakes.

Used oil Oil that has been used in an engine.

UST Underground storage tank.

UTQGS Uniform Tire Quality Grading System.

Variable ratio A steering gear design that provides a variable steering gear ratio.

VECI Vehicle Emission Control Information.

Vehicle stability enhancement system (VSES) See *VSES*.

VES Variable-Effort Steering.

Vibration An oscillation, shake, or movement that alternates in opposite directions.

Vibration order A description used to help define a vibration.

VIN Vehicle identification number.

Viscous coupling A type of device used to allow a limited difference in the speed of two axles.

VOC Volatile organic compounds.

VS sensor Vehicle speed sensor.

VSES Vehicle Stability Enhancement System is a name used by General Motors to describe an electronic stability system.

Vulcanization A process where heat and pressure combine to change the chemistry of rubber.

Wander A type of handling that requires constant steering wheel correction to keep the vehicle going straight.

Watt's link A type of track rod that uses two horizontal rods pivoting at the center of the rear axle.

Wear bars See *Wear indicators*.

Wear indicators Bald areas across the tread of a tire when 2/32" or less of tread depth remains.

Wear indicator ball joint A ball joint design with a raised area around the grease fitting. If the raised area is flush or recessed with the surrounding area of the ball joint, the joint is worn and must be replaced.

Weight-carrying ball joint See *Load-carrying ball joint*.

Wheel cover A functional and decorative cover over the entire wheel. Also see *Hub cap*.

Wheel mounting torque The amount of torque applied to the lug nuts.

Wheel rate Similar to spring rate, but includes the ratio of wheel travel to spring travel to determine the force-per-inch rate.

Wheelbase The distance between the centerline of the two wheels as viewed from the side.

WHMIS Workplace Hazardous Material Information System.

Witness mark   A mark made by an object that indicates where a noise or vibration could be located.

W/O   Abbreviation for *without*.

Worm and roller   A steering gear that uses a worm gear on the steering shaft. A roller on one end of the cross-shaft engages the worm.

Worm and sector   A steering gear that uses a worm gear that engages a sector gear on the cross-shaft.

Worm gear   A type of gear, most used in an older type of steering gear, that is attached to the steering shaft.

Wrench   A hand tool designed to rotate threaded fasteners, such as bolts and nuts.

Yaw rate sensor   An input sensor usually located in the center of the vehicle that detects yaw as part of an electronic suspension system.

Zerk Fitting   A name commonly used for a grease fitting. Named in 1922 for its developer, Oscar U. Zerk, an employee of the Alamite Corporation. In addition to a Zerk fitting, a grease fitting is also called an *Alamite fitting*.

SPANISH GLOSSARY

4 × 2 El término utilizado para describir un camión con tracción en dos ruedas (4 × 2). El "4" indica el número de ruedas del vehículo; el "2" indica el número de ruedas que son impulsadas por el motor.

4 × 4 El término utilizado para describir un vehículo de tracción en las cuatro ruedas (4 × 4). El primer "4" indica el número de ruedas del vehículo; el segundo "4" indica el número de ruedas que son impulsadas por el motor.

Aceite usado o reciclado Aceite que se ha usado en un motor

Acero de Alta Resistencia Una aleación de acero de bajo contenido carbónico que se compone de diferentes cantidades de silicio, fósforo y manganeso.

Acero galvanizado Acero recubierto con cinc para ayudar a protegerlo del herrumbre y de la corrosión.

Acero Metal de hierro refinado, del cual se ha extraído la mayor parte del carbono.

Acoplador flexible Una parte del mecanismo de dirección entre la columna de dirección y el engranaje de dirección o ensamblaje de cremallera y piñón. También llamada *junta de acople* o *disco acoplador de la dirección*. El propósito del acoplador flexible es la de no transmitir la vibración de ruido y de la dureza del camino desde la dirección hasta el volante de dirección.

Acoplador viscoso Un tipo de instrumento utilizado para otorgar al vehículo una diferencia limitada de velocidades entre dos ejes.

Acoplamiento "cross-steer" Un tipo de varilla de la dirección utilizado comúnmente en camiones livianos y de peso mediano.

Acoplamiento de paralelograma Una caja de forma geométrica de cubo donde los lados opuestos son paralelos (equidistantes). Un tipo de acoplamiento de dirección utilizado en conjunción a una caja de dirección convencional que usa un brazo de conexión (brazo pitman), conector central, rodillo de tensión, y barras de acoplamiento de las ruedas.

Acoplamiento Haltenberger Un tipo de acoplamiento de dirección comúnmente utilizado en camiones livianos.

Actuador Un dispositivo electromecánico que lleva a cabo los movimientos mecánicos que le ordena un controlador.

AGST Siglas en inglés para depósito de almacenamiento no subterráneo.

Aislantes Franjas delgadas de plástico o goma dura utilizadas para separar las placas de un resorte plano.

Ajuste de tolerancia Un método de alineación que comprende el desajuste de todos los fijadores, tuercas y tornillos de la montura de la suspensión y su posterior reajuste.

Ajuste sobre centrado Un ajuste llevado a cabo en un engranaje de la dirección mientras la dirección se gira a través de su posición central y hacia adelante. También conocido como un *ajuste del sector de huelgo*.

ALC Siglas en inglés para sensor automático de suspensión electrónica.

Alineación de cinco ruedas Una alineación que no solamente incluye las cuatro ruedas que están sobre el piso, sino que también incluye el volante de conducir como una quinta rueda.

Alineación de cuatro ruedas Una alineación de ruedas que verifica y ajusta, si fuese necesario, los ángulos de las cuatro ruedas.

Altura de la carrocería La altura del vehículo. También se llama *altura del vehículo.*

Altura de perfil *Véase* distancia de montaje.

Altura del flanco (relación altura/ancho) La proporción de la altura al ancho de un neumático. Un neumático con una relación altura/ancho de 60 (neumático de la serie 60) tiene una altura (medida desde el aro o rin hasta la banda de rodamiento) de un 60% de su ancho en la sección transversal.

Amortiguación en tiempo real, ATR

Amortiguador continuo y variable en tiempo real de chasis magneto reológico Un tipo de suspensión controlada electrónicamente (CCVRTMR por sus siglas en inglés).

Amortiguador de la dirección   Un amortiguador instalado en la varilla de la dirección a fin de que la energía generada en el trayecto se absorba y no se transfiera al volante.

Amortiguador de Solenoide eléctrico   Un amortiguador electrónicamente controlado por un selenoide.

Amortiguadores   Componente de la suspensión que conecta y controla la acción y la reacción de los resortes.

Amplitud del Pulso   El tiempo que una corriente eléctrica está activa o encendida en comparación al tiempo que la misma está apagada o inactiva.

Ancho del aro o rin   La anchura de una rueda, según se mide entre secciones del talón.

Ángulo camber (comba)   Inclinación de las ruedas fuera de la línea vertical, hacia dentro o hacia fuera, como se observa desde enfrente o detrás del vehículo. Un ángulo camber positivo significa que la parte superior de la rueda está alejada del centro del vehículo, más que la parte inferior de la rueda.

Ángulo caster   La inclinación hacia adelante o hacia atrás de una línea imaginaria que pasa por el eje de dirección, según se observa desde el lado del vehículo. Un ángulo caster positivo significa que la línea imaginaria tocaría la superficie del camino delante del punto de contacto del neumático.

Ángulo de convergencia/divergencia total   El ángulo total (combinado) de la divergencia y convergencia de ambas ruedas tanto delanteras como traseras.

Ángulo de convergencia/divergencia   El ángulo de divergencia o convergencia entre los neumáticos delanteros y traseros viendo las ruedas desde arriba.

Ángulo de Convergencia   La diferencia en medida de la distancia entre las partes delanteras de los neumáticos comparado al de las partes traseras de los mismos (la de las ruedas puntas delanteras de los neumáticos están mas próximos entre si que los puntales traseros de las ruedas).

Ángulo de deslizamiento   El ángulo formado por la línea central verdadera de un neumático y el camino que sigue realmente mientras gira.

Ángulo de Divergencia   Las partes posteriores de las llantas están mas cercanas entre si que las partes frontales.

Ángulo de empuje   El ángulo que se encuentra entre la línea geométrica central del vehículo y la dirección de empuje.

Ángulo de giro del volante   El ángulo del volante.

Ángulo de inclinación del eje de pivote   El inclinar las partes superiores de uno de los pivotes hacia el otro, crea una fuerza que estabiliza el vehículo.

Ángulo de inclinación frontal   El ángulo camber de las ruedas frontales debido a la inclinación del montaje de las ruedas (ensamblaje).

Ángulo incluido   Ángulo de inclinación del eje pivote (IEP) añadido al ángulo camber de la misma rueda.

Ángulos de la línea de impulsión   Los ángulos del eje de impulsión en la parte delantera y trasera, los cuales son iguales, más o menos 0, 5 grados.

API   Siglas en inglés de Instituto Estadounidense de Petróleo.

Aquaplaning   Condición que ocurre cuando se maneja demasiado rápido sobre caminos mojados. El agua en el camino se queda atrapada entre el neumático y la superficie del camino, forzando al neumático a avanzar sobre una capa de agua y fuera de la superficie del camino. Se pierde toda la tracción entre el neumático y el camino.

Arcmin   Abreviación de minuto de arco. *Véase* arco minutos.

Arco minutos o arcominutos   Otro nombre para un minuto sexagesimal. *Véase* minutos de arco.

Armazón del perímetro   Una estructura de acero para un vehículo que sostiene el peso del cuerpo del vehículo bajo los lados, así como en las partes delanteras y traseras.

Armazón escalonado   Un armazón de acero para vehículos que utiliza refuerzos horizontales a lo largo de su estructura, los cuales se asemejan a los peldaños de una escalera.

Armazón o carrocería de eje corto   Un tipo de carrocería que solamente soporta y acomoda a la suspensión delantera y al motor.

Articulaciones de rótula   Una articulación de rótula que se utiliza en la suspensión frontal para permitir el movimiento vertical y de viraje de la rueda frontal.

Asbestosis   Condición médica en la que el asbesto produce la formación de cicatrices en los pulmones, lo cual resulta en la falta de aliento.

AS   Siglas en inglés para suspensión de aire.

Balance estático   Un tipo de alineador de ruedas monoplano.

Ballestas   Un resorte hecho de varias láminas u hojas de muelle de acero plano.

Bamboleo   Un tipo de vibración que causa que el volante se mueva rápidamente hacia la izquierda y hacia la derecha.

Banda de rodamiento   La parte neumática de una rueda en contacto con la superficie del camino.

Barra "anti-sway"   Abreviación prestada del idioma inglés de barra anti-balanceo. *Véase* barra estabilizadora.

Barra de acoplamiento de las ruedas   Una barra que conecta los brazos.

Barra de retención.   *Véase* barra de puntal.

Barra de retención   Parte de la suspensión utilizada para controlar la relación de peso delantero / trasero de los brazos de control. También llamada una *barra de tensión o compresión o de arrastre.*

Barra de tensión   Un tipo de resorte en forma de barra recta. Un puntal está unido a la carrocería del vehículo, y su puntal o extremo opuesto esta acoplado a un brazo de control de la suspensión. Cuando las ruedas se encuentran con un bache, la barra se enrosca y se desenrosca.

Barra de tensión   *Véase* barra de retención.

Barra estabilizadora   Una barra de acero conectada a la carrocería y ambos brazos de control inferiores a fin de prevenir un balanceo excesivo del automóvil. También llamada una barra *anti-inclinación* o *anti-vuelcos*.

Barra Panhard   Una barra de acero horizontal acoplada al bastidor del eje trasero en un extremo y a la armazón en el otro, para mantener el centro del cuerpo directamente sobre el centro del eje trasero durante los movimientos vehiculares para doblar esquinas y durante los movimientos de suspensión. También llamada una *barra de acoplamiento*

Barra rodadora.   *Véase* barra estabilizadora.

Barra T.C.   *Véase* barra de retención.

Barra transversal   Una barra de acero horizontal unida por un puntal al eje trasero y a la carrocería en su puntal opuesto a fin de mantener el centro del eje central alineado con la carrocería. También conocido como una barra Panhard.

Barras de Acoplamiento o "tirantes"   Segmentos de goma moldeados y fijados entre los surcos de un neumático para ayudar a sostener los bloques de la banda de rodamiento.

BCI   Siglas en inglés de Consejo Internacional de Baterías.

BJI   Siglas en inglés del grado de inclinación de la rótula

Bobinado del eje   movimiento del eje trasero en un vehículo de propulsión trasera (RWD por sus siglas en inglés) equipado con una suspensión de tipo de muelles planos durante la aceleración.

Bola de retención   Una bola o esfera de acero utilizada para frenar el movimiento de fluidos o líquidos que fluyen en una sola dirección.

Bote   Término utilizado para describir un movimiento de arriba a abajo.

BPP   Siglas en inglés de posición del pedal de freno.

Brazo auxiliar   El punto pivotal y brazo de soporte de una dirección de tipo paralelogramo.

Brazo de la suspensión-A   Otro nombre que recibe el brazo de control porque muchas veces parece una letra A.

Brazo de torción   Un brazo de control que conecta la caja direccional trasera a la carrocería del vehículo.

Brazo pitman   Un brazo de nivel corto que se empalma a la barra transversal de dirección. Este brazo transmite la fuerza de dirección de la barra transversal a la varilla de la dirección.

Brazo reactor   Un brazo de control trasero de la suspensión que se acopla a la carrocería o cuerpo del vehículo delante del eje trasero.

Brazo semi-remolcador   Cierto tipo de suspensión trasera que controla el movimiento tanto lateral como de adelante para atrás.

Brazos de control o muñones   Los cuatro brazos de control de una típica junta de unión universal.

Brazos de control   Una conexión o varillaje de suspensión que conecta una articulación de rótula o acople de rueda al cuerpo o armazón del vehículo.

Brazos de la dirección   Brazos atornillados o soldados como parte integral del muñón de la dirección. Aquellos transmiten la fuerza de la transmisión de las barras de acoplamiento de las ruedas a los muñones, haciendo que las ruedas roten.

Brazos laterales   Brazos de la suspensión que controlan el movimiento lateral de las ruedas del vehículo. También llamados *Brazos transversales*.

Brida de acople   La parte que se fija al árbol o eje de transmisión, en el lugar de ensamblaje del diferencial.

Brinelación   Una condición defectuosa de cojinetes donde las rótulas o bolas abollan el surco interior y/o exterior. Este proceso ha sido nombrado por el ingeniero sueco Johann A. Brinell.

Buje aislador   Buje de goma que opera entre el armazón y la barra estabilizadora. También conocido como *buje de barra estabilizadora.*

Buje de la barra de retensión   Un componente de goma o caucho utilizado para aislar los acoplamientos de la barra de tensión a la carrocería del vehículo.

CAA   Siglas en inglés de la Ley de Aire Limpio.

Cabezal de pistola de grasa   Un cabezal moldeado reemplazable para fijar la posición de la pistola de grasa y equipado con una válvula de retención.

Cabezal de zerk   Un nombre comúnmente utilizado para un cabezal de pistola de grasa. Nombrado por su desarrollador, Oscar U. Zerk, en 1922, un empleado de la Corporación Alamite. Un cabezal de pistola de grasa también se llama *Cabezal Alamite.*

Caja de dirección tipo válvula de alivio de presión   Un tipo de dirección asistida (servodirección) utilizada en camiones medianos que utiliza una válvula de alivio de presión para controlar la dirección y la cantidad de asistencia requerida.

Caja de la dirección o direccional   Los engranajes en el puntal de la columna direccional que multiplican la fuerza aplicada por el conductor al volante para poder girar las ruedas delanteras.

Calza o lámina de relleno   Un espaciador metálico delgado.

Campaña   Un aviso de retiro de circulación de producto que se envía a los dueños de vehículos, para que lleven los mismos a su proveedor para su reparación.

Capa neumática   Una capa de tela que refuerza un neumático y le otorga su resistencia.

Carcasa, refuerzo de la ceja o casco   Capas de telas o lonas en un neumático que cubren todo el neumático de un talón al otro.

Carga axial   Una carga que se aplica en el mismo eje que la línea central de un cojinete. También se llama *carga de empuje*.

Carga radial   Una carga aplicada hacia el centro desde todos los ángulos.

Carrocería   Una armazón de un vehículo que se extiende a todo el largo y el ancho del vehículo.

CCR   Siglas en inglés para designar la marca de un tipo de suspensión activa o inteligente. Véase "Computer Command Ride".

CCVRTMR   *Véase* amortiguador continuo y variable en tiempo real de chasis magneto reológico.

Célula fotoeléctrica   Un tipo de sensor que utiliza diodos fotoemisores y un fototransistor para detectar la ubicación de un objeto.

Cerebro electrónico   Término utilizado comúnmente para describir una computadora o un módulo electrónico de control.

CFR   Siglas en inglés de Código de Reglamento Federal

Chasis   La armazón, suspensión, dirección y maquinaria de un vehículo motorizado.

Círculo de pernos   El diámetro (en pulgadas o milímetros) de un círculo dibujado a través del centro de los orificios para pernos en una rueda.

Circunferencia de rotación   La distancia que un neumático se desplaza cuando se rota una revolución.

Clasificación o código de velocidad   Una letra en la mayoría de los neumáticos que indica el límite o tope de velocidad máximo de desempeño normal de un neumático de acuerdo a su diseño y especificaciones técnicas.

Clips de lámina   Clips utilizados alrededor de las láminas de un resorte plano.

Código DOT de neumáticos   El sistema de codificación de neumáticos del Departamento de Transporte de los Estados Unidos.

Códigos de calibración   Los códigos que identifican a un vehículo en particular y la calibración del motor.

Coeficiente de fricción   Una medida de la cantidad de fricción, que usualmente se mide entre 0 y 1. Una cifra baja (0,3) indica poca fricción, y una cifra elevada (0,9) indica una gran cantidad de fricción.

Cojinete de soporte central   Un cojinete utilizado para soportar el centro de un eje de tracción largo en un vehículo de propulsión trasera (RWD). También conocido como un *cojinete estable*.

Cojinete estable   *Véase* balero de soporte central.

Cojinetes de antifricción   Cojinetes que utilizan rodillos o bolas para reducir la fricción.

Cojinetes de bolas   Un tipo de cojinete antifricción que utiliza bolas de rodamiento.

Columna ajustable   Un tipo de columna ajustable que se puede mover de arriba a abajo a fin de acomodar mejor al conductor.

Columna colapsada   Columna de dirección que colapsa si se produce un choque al frente del vehículo, para prevenir mayores daños al conductor.

Columna de la dirección telescópica   Una columna de la dirección ajustable que se puede ajustar a la medida del conductor.

Combustión espontánea   Un fenómeno por el cual un incendio comienza espontáneamente en trapos llenos de aceite o grasa.

Compensación   Proceso que se utiliza durante un procedimiento para alinear las ruedas, en el cual se calibran los sensores a fin de eliminar errores en las mediciones del alineamiento, los cuales pueden ser el resultado de una rueda torcida o de la instalación desigual del sensor en la rueda del vehículo.

Compuestos halogenados   Químicos que contienen cloro, flúor, bromo o yodo. Estos químicos son por lo general considerados peligrosos, y cualquier producto que contiene estos químicos deberá ser eliminado utilizando procedimientos previamente aprobados.

Compuesto   Término que describe la combinación de partes individuales para formar un componente más grande. Por ejemplo, un resorte plano compuesto está construido de fibra de vidrio y epoxi; un cilindro de freno principal compuesto contiene partes tanto de plástico (el depósito) como de metal (bastidor de cilindros).

"Computer Command Ride"   Un nombre de marca para un tipo de sistema de suspensión activa o inteligente

Conicidad   Una falla en un neumático que le da la forma de un cono y ocasiona una fuerza de resistencia.

Cono   El aro o anillo interior de un cojinete.

Contratuerca   Un tipo de tuerca que no se suelta y mas bien retiene su nivel de torción.

Copa   El aro o anillo exterior de un cojinete.

Corona del camino   Camino cuya parte central se encuentra más alta que los bordes externos. Muchas carreteras tienen el diseño de corona del camino para que el agua drene de la superficie de las mismas.

Corona   La corona dentada o el engranaje dentro del diferencial, la cual encaja con el engranaje del piñón de la dirección.

Correa   Una tira de tela o de alambre de acero que se encuentra bajo la banda de rodamiento de un neumático.

Cremallera de propulsión central   Un tipo de cremallera de dirección donde las barras de acoplamiento de las ruedas se conectan al centro de la cremallera en vez de a sus extremos.

Cresta   El diámetro de un tornillo medido a lo largo del exterior de los pasos.

Cruceta de Cardán (Cuerpo de la cruceta)   Elemento central de un volante. También conocido como la *sección central*.

Cubierta o gomital de junta homocinética   La cubierta que envuelve una junta de velocidad constante hecha de goma, termoplástico o uretano.

Cubrepolvo o antipolvo   Una tapa funcional de metal que mantiene la grasa dentro de los cojinetes de las ruedas y los protege del polvo. También se llama *tapa de grasa*.

Cuerpo de la cruceta   La sección de una rueda que se fija al cubo. También llamada *cruceta de cardán* o *spider* por sus siglas en inglés.

Depósito integral   Un tipo de bomba de dirección hidráulica que incluye la bomba dentro del depósito de fluido.

Depósito separado   Cierto tipo de bomba de fuerza de dirección, donde el fluido se encuentra en un depósito separado de la bomba.

Deriva apretada o estrecha   Término utilizado para describir una condición de subviraje.

Deriva holgada o floja   Un término utilizado para describir una condición de subviraje.

Deriva   Un jalón leve que no resulta en una fuerza en el volante, que el conductor debe contrarrestar (también se conoce como *jaloncito*). También se refiere a una herramienta que acaba en punta y se utiliza para centrar un componente en el hueco de un perno antes de instalar el perno.

Descentrado   La distancia que la sección central (almohadilla de soporte) se encuentra descentrada o desalineada de la línea central de la rueda.

Descentramiento radial   Una medida que mide cuan descentrada se encuentra una rueda o neumático. Un descentramiento radial excesivo pueda causar un bamboleo.

Descuadrado   La condición donde las ruedas traseras no siguen directamente detrás de las ruedas delanteras. El nombre proviene de un término, en inglés, que describe los movimientos que llevan a cabo los perros cuando corren con sus patas traseras ladeadas a un lado para que sus patas traseras no golpeen sus patas delanteras.

Desecador   Un ingrediente, como una gel de sílice, utilizado para retirar la humedad del aire. Se utiliza en sistemas electrónicos que utilizan amortiguadores o resortes neumáticos.

Desgaste de copa de neumáticos   Desgaste cóncavo de neumáticos por lo general en los bordes interiores o exteriores ocasionado por un desgaste en los amortiguadores de choques o por otras fallas en el sistema de suspensión.

Desviación del árbol de transmisión   Una medida que indica la distancia de un árbol de transmisión de ser perfectamente redondo cuando se lo gira o se lo rota.

Desviación lateral   Una medida que refleja la distancia que recorre una rueda, de un lado a otro, mientras ésta está siendo girada. La desviación lateral excesiva puede ocasionar una vibración tipo bamboleo si las ruedas están ubicadas en el eje delantero.

Desviación   El vehículo tiende a irse hacia la izquierda o derecha al recorrer un camino derecho y nivelado.

Dife   Abreviación de diferencial.

Diferencia coaxial de ejes   El grado de desalineación de las ruedas frontales con la línea paralela de las ruedas traseras. Una diferencia positiva coaxial de ejes significa que la rueda frontal a la derecha está detrás de la rueda a la izquierda. La diferencia coaxial de ejes puede medirse como un ángulo formado por una línea perpendicular (90°) con los ejes frontales.

Diferencia de ángulo camber / caster   La diferencia de ángulo de un lado del vehículo al otro. La mayoría de los fabricantes recomiendan una diferencia máxima de un extremo al otro de 1/2° para camber y caster.

Diferencial   Una unidad mecánica que contiene engranajes que permiten un reducción de marcha y un cambio de dirección de la potencia del motor, y permite que las ruedas propulsoras sincronicen o roten a velocidades distintas, tal como se requiere al doblar una esquina.

Dirección adelantada   Un diseño de construcción de un vehículo que coloca el engranaje de dirección y el acoplamiento de dirección en frente de la línea del centro de las ruedas delanteras. También llamada *dirección hacia adelante*.

Dirección de empuje   La dirección hacia la cual apuntan las ruedas traseras en relación al ángulo de convergencia/divergencia trasero.

Dirección de fase opuesta

Dirección hacia adelante   . *Véase* Dirección adelantada.

Dirección mono-fase   Un vehículo equipado con dirección de las cuatro ruedas, donde las ruedas tanto frontales como traseras se orientan en el mismo sentido.

Dirección   *Véase* tope de dirección.

Disco acoplador de la dirección   *Véase* acoplador flexible.

Disco acoplador.   *Véase* Acoplado flexible.

Diseño Monoespacio o Estructura de Armazón Ligero   Un diseño que utiliza la estructura de armazón del vehículo para sostener el motor y su compartimiento así como la dirección y la suspensión. Los paneles externos no son parte integral de la estructura.

Disolvente   Líquido que disuelve grasa u otras sustancias.

Distancia de montaje   La distancia entre el borde del rin o aro trasero de una rueda y la superficie de montaje de la sección central.

Distancia entre ejes de las ruedas   La distancia entre la línea central de las dos ruedas, vista de un lado.

Distancia entre roscas   La distancia de un sujetador enroscado se refiere al número de roscas por pulgada.

Durómetro   La escala de dureza de los productos de goma, nombrado por un instrumento utilizado para medir la dureza, desarrollado alrededor de 1890.

EBCM   Siglas en inglés de Módulo electrónico de control de frenos

ECU   Siglas en inglés de unidad de control electrónico

EHPS   Siglas en inglés de dirección asistida electro-hidráulica

Eje corto   Un eje corto que forma parte de la caja de direcciones y se acopla al eje de la columna de dirección.

Eje de la columna de la dirección   Parte de la dirección que conecta el volante con la caja de la dirección.

Eje de prop.   Una abreviación para eje de propulsión.

Eje de propulsión   El árbol que conecta el eje transversal o diferencial a las ruedas.

Eje de propulsión   Un término utilizado por varios fabricantes para un eje de transmisión.

Eje de seguro-C   Un tipo de ensamblaje del eje trasero que utiliza un seguro en forma de C para retener los ejes.

Eje de transmisión   Un eje o árbol que transfiere la torsión del motor desde el punto de salida de la transmisión al ensamblaje del eje trasero (diferencial).

Eje del sector   El eje de salida de una caja de dirección convencional. Forma parte del eje del sector de un engranaje que encaja con el engranaje helicoidal (engranaje de tornillo sin fin) y es rotado por el conductor al dar vueltas al volante. También se llama *eje pitman.*

Eje flotante Tres Cuartos   Tipo de eje trasero en el cual parte del peso del vehículo es sostenido por el semieje.

Eje flotante   Un tipo de ensamblaje de eje donde el peso del vehículo es sostenido por el bastidor del eje y no por el eje en sí.

Eje pitman.   *Véase* eje del sector.

Eje propulsor   Un eje sólido utilizado en las ruedas de dirección, contiene los ejes de propulsión que impulsan el vehículo.

Eje Rígido   Sistema de suspensión compuesto por un eje rígido que une las ruedas delanteras o traseras de cada lado del vehículo. También conocido como un eje convencional o no independiente.

Eje rígido   *Véase* eje sólido.

Eje semi-flotante   Cierto tipo de eje de línea cuyo extremo interior flota y cuyo extremo exterior es apoyado por un cojinete.

Ejes tipo retenedor   Cierto tipo de eje de propulsión trasero que utiliza una placa de retención para mantener los ejes sujetados al bastidor.

Electroimán   Un electroimán está compuesto de un núcleo de hierro suave envuelto por un cable conductor de forma espiral. La corriente eléctrica que fluye a través del conductor genera un campo magnético alrededor del núcleo.

"E-metric"   Una designación de neumáticos para vehículos eléctricos, los cuales tienen una resistencia de rodaje baja.

Enganche de freno   Un alojamiento de resortes utilizado en varias unidades de puntal MacPherson de General Motors. Si el resorte espiral se rompe, el enganche de freno previene que un extremo del resorte se desplace con un movimiento hacia afuera y corte un neumático.

Engranaje de tornillo helicoidal   Un tipo de engranaje utilizado en un tipo de caja más antigua; se acopla al eje de dirección.

Engranaje del sector   Una sección de un engranaje dentro de la caja de dirección, el cual está sujetado al eje del sector. También se llama el *eje pitman.*

Engranajes del diferencial   Otro nombre para los engranajes del piñón utilizados en un diferencial.

Engranajes laterales   Los engranajes dentro de una diferencial que están sujetados a los ejes.

Enredo de chavetas.   Un fenómeno por el cual las chavetas o lengüetas del cable de un eje de transmisión primero se enredan o aglutinan y enseguida se sueltan durante la primera aceleración de un vehículo después de una parada.

Ensamblaje de receptáculo de rótula   Un ensamblaje interior de la barra de acoplamiento de las ruedas que contiene una articulación de receptáculo de rótula en el punto donde el ensamblaje se conecta al extremo de la cremallera de dirección.

Entrada   Se denomina entrada a la información de datos de los sensores que se transfiere a un controlador electrónico. Los sensores e interruptores proporcionan las señales de entrada.

Entretuerca   Un diseño especial de sujetador de tuerca que se deforma levemente o que tiene otras propiedades que permiten que la tuerca permanezca unida al sujetador sin soltarse.

EPA   Siglas en inglés de Agencia de Protección Ambiental.

EPS   Siglas en inglés de dirección asistida eléctrica.

Equilibrio dinámico   La línea central de la masa del peso del ensamblaje de un neumático/rueda se encuentra en el mismo plano sobre la línea central de la rueda.

Estabilidad direccional   La habilidad de un vehículo para avanzar en línea recta con un mínimo de control por parte del conductor. Los vientos de costado y las irregularidades del camino tendrán muy poco efecto si la estabilidad direccional es buena.

Estación de lavado de ojos   Una unidad dispensadora de agua que dirige chorros de agua hacia los ojos.

EVA   Siglas en inglés de analizador de vibraciones electrónico.

EVO   Siglas en inglés de orificio variable electrónico.

Extinguidor, tipos de incendios   Tipos de incendios que un extinguidor de fuego está diseñado para manejar.

Fatiga de lajas o de metal   Un término utilizado para describir un tipo de desperfecto mecánico causado por la fatiga del metal. Las ranuras en la superficie de metal se convierten en pequeñas astillas, peladuras o escamas de metal. A este proceso de descomposición se lo denomina fatiga de lajas o "spalling" en inglés.

Fluido de climas fríos   Un fluido de uso común en la dirección asistida (servodirección) cuya utilización se recomienda en climas fríos.

Fototransistor   Un dispositivo electrónico que puede detectar la presencia de la luz y encenderse o apagarse como efecto de ello. Se utiliza en algunos sensores de altura de la suspensión.

Fracciones   Una medida en partes de una pulgada, tales como 1/2, 1/4, y 1/8.

Frazada antiincendios   Una frazada de lana a prueba de incendios que se utiliza para apagar el fuego al envolverla alrededor de una víctima.

Frecuencia   El número de veces que un ciclo completo de movimiento se lleva a cabo durante un periodo de tiempo (por lo general medido en segundos).

Fricción   La resistencia de dos cuerpos en contacto el uno con el otro a resbalar.

Fuerza   Energía aplicada a un objeto.

FWD   Siglas en inglés de tracción delantera

GAWR   Siglas en inglés de peso bruto nominal por eje.

GC-LB   Un calificación o clasificación de la grasa. GC es la calificación más alta para grasa de los cojinetes de las ruedas y LB es la calidad más alta de grasa de chasis.

Geometría anti-dive o antihundimiento   Término que describe la geometría de la suspensión que controla el movimiento del vehículo cuando se aplican los frenos. Es normal que el extremo frontal del vehículo sufra un leve descenso al aplicarse los frenos, y la mayoría de los vehículos están diseñados teniendo en cuenta este movimiento.

Geometría anti-squat   Término que describe la geometría de la suspensión que controla el movimiento del cuerpo del vehículo durante la aceleración. 100% anti-squat significa que el cuerpo se mantiene plano durante la aceleración. Menos del 100% anti-squat significa que el cuerpo "se agacha", o sea, la parte trasera desciende o baja durante la aceleración.

GKN   Una compañía nombrada por sus fundadores, Guest, Keene y Nettelfolds.

Golpe de dirección   Utilizado para describir lo que ocurre cuando la varilla de la dirección no está nivelada, lo cual ocasiona que las ruedas delanteras giren hacia adentro o hacia afuera a medida que los neumáticos y la suspensión se mueven hacia arriba o hacia abajo. Los ingenieros de chasis de automóviles lo llaman *rodado de dirección* (*roll steer* en inglés).

Gorra de seguridad   Gorra que usa un técnico que protege la cabeza del daño que puede ser ocasionado por objetos sobresalientes o partes sueltas del vehículo.

Grado   Un grado es uno de las 360 partes iguales que componen un círculo.

Gramo   Una unidad métrica de peso equivalente a 1/1000 kilogramo (1 onza $\times$ 28 = 1 gramo). Un billete de un dólar de los Estados Unidos o un sujetapapeles pesa cerca de 1 gramo.

Grano o mancha de stress   Una pequeña dentadura o área herrumbrada en un resorte que puede causar que dicho resorte eventualmente se quiebre.

Grasa moly   Grasa que contiene bisulfuro de molibdeno.

Grasa   Aceite con un agente espesador.

Grillete   Un soporte que permite que el extremo de un resorte plano se mueva horizontalmente, para adelante y para atrás mientras el resorte se mueve verticalmente, para arriba y para abajo durante la operación normal de la suspensión.

GVWR   Siglas en inglés de nivel de peso total del vehículo.

GVW   Siglas en inglés de peso total del vehículo.

HD   Siglas en inglés de todo terreno

Hertzio   Una unidad de medida de frecuencia. Un Hertzio es un ciclo por segundo, abreviado como Hz. Nombrado en honor al físico alemán del siglo XIX, Heinrich R. Hertz.

Hidrofílico   Un término utilizado para describir un tipo de goma utilizado en varios neumáticos de toda estación donde el neumático tiene una afinidad para el agua (en vez de rechazarla).

Hidrofóbico   Un término utilizado para describir el rechazo del agua.

Hierro   Metal refinado en un horno y extraído de mineral de hierro (óxido ferroso). *Véase también* acero.

HSS   Siglas en inglés de acero de alta resistencia

Huelgo del sector   El huelgo entre la sección (sector) de un engranaje en el eje pitman dentro de una caja de dirección. *Véase también* ajuste sobre centrado.

Hz   Una abreviación para Hertzio, ciclos por segundo.

Inclinómetro   Un instrumento utilizado para medir ángulos. Normalmente utilizado para medir ángulos de ejes de dirección.

Indicador de articulaciones de rótulas   Un tipo de articulación de rótula que indica cuándo una junta se ha desgastado y requiere ser reemplazada.

Indicador de desgaste   Área desnuda o afectada de la banda de rodamiento que retiene menos de 2/32 de pulgadas de su profundidad.

Indicadores de desgaste de cojinete de rótula   Un diseño de rótula que incluye una zona elevada alrededor del cabezal de pistola de grasa. Si la zona elevada se hunde en la rótula, la rótula está desgastada y debe ser reemplazada.

Índice de carga   Un método abreviado que utiliza un número para indicar la capacidad de peso y carga de un neumático.

Inducido o rotor   La pieza movible y rotante de un motor eléctrico de corriente continua cuya función consiste en mover una biela de control en un resorte o muelle de aire a fin de regular la altura del movimiento vehicular.

Instituto Nacional de Grasas Lubricantes   Por lo general asociado con cantidades de grasa. Cuanto mayor sea el número de NLGI, más firme es la grasa. La grasa #000 es muy fluida, mientras que la #5 es muy firme. La consistencia más recomendada es NLGI #2 (suave).

Interruptor de selección de nivel de comodidad   Un interruptor utilizado para seleccionar el nivel de comodidad en un vehículo equipado con un sistema de suspensión electrónica o inteligente.

Interruptor de selección del conductor   Un interruptor que permite que el conductor seleccione el nivel de dureza de la suspensión.

IRS   Siglas en inglés de suspensión independiente trasera

ISO   Organización Internacional para la Estandarización

Jalado de capas   Un término utilizado para describir por qué un neumático puede causar una condición de fuerza en base al ángulo de los cordones de las capas del cinturón.

Jaloncito   Un jalón leve que no ejerce una fuerza en el volante que el conductor debe contrarrestar (también se conoce como *jaloneo*).

Jaula   La parte de un cojinete de anti-fricción que sostiene las bolas o rodillos.

Juego Axial   Movimiento o juego sobre el mismo eje que la línea central de la rótula.

Juego de engranajes hipoidales   Un tipo de juego de engranajes donde el engranaje de piñón se encuentra por debajo de la línea del centro del anillo de engranaje.

Juego del engranaje   Espacio entre los engranajes.

Juego libre (holgura)   La distancia que el volante de dirección se puede mover sin mover las ruedas delanteras. La distancia máxima permitida de holgura o juego libre es menos de 2 pulgadas para un sistema de dirección de tipo paralelogramo, y de 3/8 de pulgada para un sistema de dirección de cremallera y piñón.

Juego longitudinal   El movimiento alineado con la línea central de un ensamblaje.

Junta cardán doble   Una junta universal que utiliza dos juntas Cardán convencionales de forma conjunta, a fin de permitir que dicha unión opere a ángulos mayores.

Junta Cardán   Un tipo de articulación universal nombrada en honor a un matemático italiano del siglo XVI.

Junta de acople.   *Véase* acoplado flexible.

Junta homocinética desplazante   Una junta interior de velocidad constante que puede desplazarse de adentro para afuera y transmitir torsión mientras la suspensión del vehículo se mueve horizontalmente, hacia arriba y abajo, sobre topes o baches.

Junta homocinética fija   Un tipo de junta homocinética utilizada en el extremo de la rueda del eje de propulsión.

Junta homocinética   Comúnmente llamada *junta de velocidad constante* o *Junta VC*. Las juntas homocinéticas son juntas de la línea de propulsión que pueden transmitir el poder del motor a través de ángulos relativamente grandes sin cambiar la velocidad. Esta característica por lo general también se aplica a las juntas universales convencionales de tipo Cardán.

Junta LOBRÓ   La marca de un tipo de junta homocinética.

Junta Rzeppa   Cierto tipo de junta de velocidad constante que lleva el nombre de su inventor, Alfred H. Rzeppa.

Juntas de fricción   Un eje de suspensión externa que no sostiene el peso del vehículo. También llamada una *rótula o junta de apoyo*.

Juntas homocinéticas   Juntas de velocidad constante.

Juntas Universales   Uniones Universales.

JWL   Siglas en inglés del término Marca Estándar de Volante Ligero del Japón

KPI   Ángulo de inclinación del eje del pivote (también conocido como *inclinación del eje pivote*). El ángulo formado entre el vertical natural y una línea dibujada entre los puntos pivotales superior e inferior del huso.

L y N   Lodo y nieve.

Laminilla de calibración   Tabla que se utiliza para alinear un vehículo que usa calzas o láminas de relleno para ajustar los ángulos camber y caster.

Leva excéntrica   Una placa que tiene un perno algo alejado del centro utilizado para cambiar el camber y/o el ángulo caster.

Ley de Hooke   Las características de fuerza de un muelle o resorte, descubiertas por Robert Hooke (1635–1703), un físico inglés. La Ley de Hooke afirma que "la deflexión (movimiento o deformación) de un resorte es directamente proporcional a la fuerza aplicada."

Ley de Pascal   Ley o principio científico que afirma que la presión que se ejerce sobre un líquido confinado se transmite con la misma fuerza en todas las direcciones. Esta ley toma su nombre del científico francés Blaise Pascal (1623–1662).

Leyes del derecho de saber   Leyes que requieren que los negocios exhiban hojas de datos sobre la seguridad de materiales para que todos sepan cuáles materiales peligrosos se utilizan en ese edificio.

Libra por pie   Una medida de torsión. Una fuerza de 1 libra, a 1 pie desde el centro de un objeto.

Línea central geométrica   Un tipo de alineación de ruedas donde todas las ruedas están alineadas paralelas a la línea central del vehículo.

Líneas de desgaste.   *Véase* indicadores de desgaste.

Llave combinada   Llave que tiene un extremo abierto y el otro en forma de estría.

Llave para tuercas cónicas   Un tipo de llave utilizada para retirar líneas de combustible, de frenos o del aire acondicionado.

LLR   Siglas en inglés de resistencia al balanceo agudo.

"Loose"   Termino en inglés para describir una deriva holgada. Una condición que también se la conoce como "Coche suelto" en los círculos automovilísticos.

LT   Siglas en inglés de camión ligero

M&S   Siglas en inglés de "lodo y nieve". Véase L y N.

"Magnasteer"   Un tipo de dirección asistida (servodirección) hidráulica controlada electrónicamente.

Marca destemplada o testigo de ruido   Una marca causada por un objeto que puede indicar la ubicación del ruido o vibración.

"Mareo matutino"   Un término coloquial utilizado para describir la pérdida temporal de dirección asistida (servodirección) cuando el vehículo se encuentra frío, causada por el desgaste en la zona de la válvula de control de una unidad de cremallera y piñón.

Maza de la rueda   Una cubierta funcional y decorativa sobre la porción de las tuercas de la rueda. *También véase* tapa del cubo.

Medición del ángulo caster   Proceso que se utiliza para medir el ángulo caster durante un procedimiento de alineamiento de ruedas, en el cual las ruedas delanteras primero se rotan hacia el centro, y luego hacia afuera, una distancia específica.

Memoria de la dirección   Una guía o tirón del vehículo causado por fallas en la dirección o en el sistema de suspensión. Si luego de hacer un giro, el vehículo tiende a tirar en la misma dirección que en el último giro, entonces el vehículo tiene memoria de dirección.

Mercurio   Un metal denso que se encuentra en forma líquida.

Milisegundo   Una milésima fracción (1/1000) de un segundo.

Minutos de arco   Una unidad de medida de un ángulo. Sesenta minutos de arco o sexagesimales equivalen a un grado.

Modalidad de avance rígido   Una modalidad de operación de un vehículo de General Motors que está equipado con un sistema de suspensión electrónica o inteligente. En esta modalidad la suspensión se fija a un nivel estable pero firme.

Modulación de la amplitud del pulso   El control de un dispositivo, tal como un selenoide, ejercido a través de la activación y desactivación del pulso eléctrico.

Módulo inflable   La parte de una bolsa de aire que contiene la bolsa de aire en sí, además de la unidad utilizada para inflar la bolsa.

Monovolumen   Un tipo de diseño de vehículo utilizado por primera vez por la compañía Budd de Troy, Michigan, EE.UU., que no utiliza un armazón separado para sus diferentes componentes. La carrocería es lo suficientemente fuerte y esta construida de tal manera que soporta tanto al mecanismo de transmisión y al motor, así como a la suspensión y el sistema de dirección. Los paneles externos son fijos y no son partes integrales de la estructura del chasis.

Montado de rueda y alineación de válvula   El proceso de montar un neumático en una rueda y alinear la raíz de la válvula con una marca en el neumático. Esta marca en el neumático representa el punto alto del mismo, y la ubicación de la raíz de la válvula representa el diámetro más pequeño de la rueda.

Motor   Un aparato electromecánico que transforma la energía eléctrica en movimiento mecánico

MR   Magneto reológico(a).

MRRTD   Siglas en inglés de amortiguación magneto reológica en tiempo real

MSDS   Siglas en inglés de hoja de datos de seguridad física

MSI   Siglas en inglés de Inclinación del Puntal McPherson.

Muelle o resorte espiral   Un muelle elaborado de una vara de acero con una forma espiral o helicoidal. Se utiliza en los sistemas de suspensión delanteros y traseros.

Muelle o resorte neumático   Una membrana de caucho llena de aire utilizada para reemplazar un resorte.

Muelle toroidal   Un muelle o resorte utilizado en un sello para ayudar a mantener el borde del sello en contacto con la parte en movimiento.

Muelles o resortes auxiliares   Muelles auxiliares o adicionales utilizados de manera auxiliar a los muelles originales del vehículo para restaurar la altura adecuada de la carrocería o para incrementar la capacidad de carga del vehículo.

Muñón de la dirección   Los elementos que comprenden el interior de un husillo o vástago que gira sobre las rótulas o pivote de la dirección.

Neumático "high flotation"   Un tipo de neumático de gran tamaño y que contiene una gran cantidad de volumen de aire.

Neumático no vulcanizado   Un neumático ensamblado y no vulcanizado. Luego de que este neumático se coloca en un molde bajo calor y presión, la goma cambia químicamente y sale del molde formada y vulcanizada.

Neumático radial   Un neumático cuyas cuerdas de tela o lonas de carcasa lo recubren, en un sentido radial y en línea recta (o casi recta) de talón a talón.

Neumáticos "run-flat"   Neumáticos que se diseñaron especialmente para rodar por distancias razonables, y a velocidades razonables, sin contener aire que sostuviera el peso del vehículo. Los neumáticos "run-flat" usualmente requieren el uso de rines con un diseño especial para impedir que el neumático desinflado se separe de la rueda.

NHTSA   Abreviación de la Oficina Nacional para la Seguridad de Tránsito en las Carreteras (*National Highway Traffic Safety Administration* en inglés).

NLGI   Siglas en inglés de Instituto Nacional de Grasas Lubricantes.

Número de bastidor   Véase VIN.

Número de metal moldeado   Una serie de números y/o letras moldeadas en los componentes principales, tales como el bloque motor o las culatas.

NVH   Siglas en inglés de sonido, vibración y discordancia.

OEM   Siglas en inglés de fabricante original del equipo.

OE   Siglas en inglés de equipos originales.

OPR   Orden de Producción Regular (RPO por sus siglas en inglés).

Orden de vibración   Descripción que se utiliza para definir una vibración.

OSHA   Siglas en inglés de Administración de la Salud y Seguridad Ocupacionales

Oz.-pulgadas   Medida de desequilibrio. 3 onzas por pulgada significa que un objeto se encuentra descentrado; se requiere un peso de 1 onza colocado a 3 pulgadas del centro de un objeto rotante, o un peso de 3 onzas colocado a 1 pulgada del centro, o cualquier otra combinación que multiplicada equivalga a 3 onzas-pulgadas.

Paralelograma De Watt   Un tipo de barra transversal que utiliza dos barras horizontales rotatorias en el centro del eje trasero.

Pared neumática   La porción lateral de un neumático.

Pasador de chaveta   Un circuito de metal utilizado para sostener las tuercas castillo al ser instalado a través de un orificio. Su tamaño se mide por diámetro y largo (por ejemplo, 1/8″ × 1 1/2″). También llamado un *perno de chaveta*. Su nombre proviene de un antiguo vocablo inglés que significaba "cerrar o asegurar".

Perno central   Perno que se utiliza para mantener unidas las láminas de una ballesta en el centro. También se llama *perno de alineación*.

Perno de alineación.   *Véase* perno central.

Perno de pinza   Un perno utilizado para retener una articulación de rótula en algunos diseños de suspensiones.

Perno Métrico   Un perno que se fabrica y diseña en base al sistema métrico.

Perno prisionero o espárrago   Una varilla o barra corta con ranuras en ambos extremos.

Peso no suspendido   Peso de los elementos de un vehículo no soportados por el sistema de suspensión. Un ejemplo de algunos de los elementos típicos de peso no suspendido son los neumáticos, los frenos y las ruedas.

Peso suspendido   El peso total de un vehículo soportado por el sistema de suspensión.

Peso total del vehículo   El peso total del vehículo es el peso del vehículo más el peso de todos sus pasajeros y carga hasta el límite especificado por el fabricante.

Piñón y cremallera   Un tipo de unidad liviana de dirección que conecta las ruedas delanteras a través de barras de acoplamiento al extremo de un eje largo llamado una *cremallera*. Cuando el conductor mueve el volante de dirección, la fuerza se transfiere al ensamblaje del piñón y cremallera. Dentro del bastidor de la cremallera se encuentra una caja de engranajes pequeña de piñón que engrana con los dientes de engranaje, los cuales se encuentran cortados en la cremallera.

Pivote de dirección   Un pivote comúnmente utilizado en ejes convencionales rígidos o en los ejes de los primeros modelos de sistemas de doble viga en I, que rotan en bujes y permiten que las ruedas delanteras roten. El muñón o mangueta gira alrededor del pivote de la dirección.

Placa bloqueadora   Una placa ubicada en la columna de la dirección que se utiliza para bloquear el volante cuando se retira la llave del mecanismo de encendido.

Plataforma   La plataforma de un vehículo incluye la estructura de base (armazón y / o paneles principales del cuerpo), así como los componentes básicos de dirección y suspensión. Una plataforma podría ser la base para varias marcas de vehículos.

Plato del resorte   También llamado *asiento del resorte*.

PPE   Siglas en inglés de equipos de protección personal.

PPM   Partes por millón.

Precarga   Un término utilizado para describir el ajuste de un perno o tuerca para proporcionar una fuerza.

Presión   Cantidad que se obtiene dividiendo la fuerza aplicada sobre una superficie, por el área de la misma.

Propulsión Hotchkiss   Un tipo de transmisión de fuerza para un vehículo de motor delantero y propulsión trasera, donde la reacción de torsión o del motor está controlada por la suspensión, a diferencia del uso del diferencial montado en el brazo o armazón de torción

Prueba de articulación   Una prueba especificada por algunos fabricantes de vehículos, que mide la cantidad de fuerza necesaria para mover el extremo interior de la barra de acoplamiento de las ruedas en el ensamblaje de receptáculo de rótula. La especificación usual para esta prueba es mayor de 1 libra (4 N) y menos de 6 libras (26 N) de fuerza.

Prueba de estacionar en seco   Una prueba de los componentes de viraje y / o de suspensión. Con las ruedas orientadas hacia adelante y cuando el vehículo se encuentra en un terreno plano sin inclinación, un asistente vira el volante mientras se examinan todos los componentes de viraje y de suspensión para verificar si alguno está suelto.

Prueba de fuente de vibración   Una prueba utilizada para ayudar a determinar la fuente de una vibración. La velocidad del motor se incrementa y se mide la vibración con la transmisión en posición neutro.

Prueba de penetración   Una prueba para lubricantes que consiste en introducir un cono estándar a una muestra de grasa para posteriormente proceder a medir la profundidad de dicho desplazamiento.

Prueba de rebote   Prueba que se utiliza para verificar la condición de los amortiguadores de choques.

Pruebas de prealineación   Las pruebas que deberían llevarse a cabo antes de verificar o cambiar la alineación de ruedas de un vehículo.

PSCM   Siglas en inglés de módulo de control de la dirección hidráulica.

PSI   Siglas en inglés de libras por pulgada cuadrada.

PSP   Siglas en inglés de presión de la dirección hidráulica.

Puntal del pivote de la dirección   *Véase* punto pivote de contacto de la rueda.

Puntal McPherson   Un tipo de suspensión frontal con los amortiguadores de choques y resortes en espiral en una sola unidad, la cual rota cuando se giran las ruedas. El ensamblaje se monta al cuerpo del vehículo en la parte superior y en una articulación de bola y en un brazo de control en la parte inferior. Recibe su nombre de su inventor, Earle S. McPherson.

Puntales   Elemento estructural de una suspensión que incluye a los amortiguadores.

Punto pivote de contacto de la rueda   El punto donde una línea imaginaria que atraviesa el eje de dirección cruza el suelo, en comparación con la línea central del neumático. Un punto pivote de contacto de la rueda de *cero* significa que la línea cruza el suelo en la línea central del neumático. Un punto pivote de contacto de la rueda *positivo* significa que la línea cruza por debajo de la superficie del suelo. Un punto pivote de contacto de la rueda *negativo* significa que la línea cruza por encima de la superficie del suelo. Ciertos fabricantes de vehículos también lo llaman *pivote de la dirección*.

Radio   La expresión de proporción. Por ejemplo, en un ensamblaje típico de eje trasero, el eje de transmisión rota tres veces más rápido que los ejes traseros. Se expresa como un radio de 3:1 y se lee como "tres a uno." Los radios correspondientes al mecanismo de transmisión son siempre expresados como engranajes impulsores divididos por engranajes impulsados.

Rango variable   Un diseño de engranaje de la dirección que incluye un rango variable de direccional o de viraje.

Ranura de soldadura de pinza   El lugar bajo el vehículo donde dos paneles del cuerpo se sueldan juntos. A menudo utilizada como una ubicación para la colocación de almohadas cuando se iza un vehículo.

Ranura principal   Un lugar en un neumático donde la goma de la banda de rodamiento y una o más capas neumáticas son empalmadas durante la construcción del neumático.

Ranuras de descargue de agua   Surcos de gran tamaño ubicados en la banda de rodamiento de un neumático.

RBSSG   Siglas en inglés de receptáculo soldado de goma.

RCRA   Siglas en inglés de Ley de Conservación y Recuperación de Recursos.

Rebotar   Una vibración usualmente causada por el movimiento horizontal de un ensamblaje de ruedas no balanceado o desalineado.

Reconstruido.   *Véase* refabricado.

Reculado   La reacción del volante cuando las ruedas delanteras golpean una curva o bache.

Refabricado   Término que describe un proceso donde se desmonta un componente, se limpia, se examina y se vuelve a montar utilizando repuestos nuevos o reparados. Según la Asociación de Refabricadores de Repuestos Automotrices (*Automotive Parts Rebuilders Association* o APRA). El mismo procedimiento se llama también, *reconstruir.*

Relación de la trayectoria del volante   Similar a la relación elástica del resorte pero incluye la relación de la trayectoria de la rueda a fin de determinar la fuerza aplicada por pulgada cuadrada.

Relación elástica del resorte   La relación elástica del resorte es la cantidad de peso que se requiere para comprimir un resorte, tal como por ejemplo una medida de 200 pies por pulgada.

Resistencia a la tracción   La fuerza de un perno u otro ajustador alineado al tornillo o tuerca.

Resistencia   La calificación de fuerza dúctil de una tuerca.

Resorte plano compuesto   Un resorte plano (ballesta) hecho de un material compuesto, el cual por lo general incluye fibra de vidrio y resina epóxica.

Resortes o muelles   Utilizados como elementos amortiguadores entre la suspensión y el armazón o cuerpo así como también para absorber los movimientos de la rueda y soportar el peso del vehículo.

Resortes planos de una sola lámina   Una ballesta que utiliza una sola lámina de acero.

Retenedor de grasa.   *Véase* sello de grasa.

Retenedores sintéticos   Un método dúctil o de retención para mantener juntas ciertas partes de una unión universal.

Retiro   Programa para avisar a todos los dueños de un vehículo para que vuelvan al vendedor del mismo para la corrección de determinado fallo relacionado con la seguridad.

Retornabilidad   La capacidad del volante de volver a la posición delantera después de girar.

RIM   Siglas en inglés de moldeado por inyección de reacción.

RMP   Siglas en inglés de polímero moldeable de reacción.

Rodado de dirección.   *Véase* tope de la dirección.

Rodamiento axial.   *Véase* cojinete de soporte central.

Rodillo cónico   Cierto tipo de cojinete anti-fricción que utiliza rodillos entre las pistas interior y exterior.

Rodillos cónicos del buje   Los rodillos cónicos pequeños utilizados en una articulación universal.

Rodillos cónicos   Un tipo de cojinete antifricción que utiliza rodillos cónicos entre sus extremidades internas y externas.

Rotación de llantas   Término utilizado para describir el movimiento del ensamblaje de las ruedas/neumáticos de una posición vehicular a otra.

Rotula de alta capacidad [de peso o de carga]   *Véase* rótulas de apoyo.

Rótula de apoyo   Utilizada en un sistema de suspensión con la finalidad de proporcionar soporte y control; y a través de la cual el peso (carga) del vehículo se transfiere al armazón.

Rótula o junta de apoyo   Una junta de rótula utilizada en un sistema de suspensión para proporcionar apoyo y control sin que el peso del vehículo o la acción de los resortes sean transferidos a través de la junta misma. También llamada una *junta de fricción.*

RSS   Siglas en inglés de suspensión sensible al camino.

RTD   Siglas en inglés de amortiguación en tiempo real.

Ruido   El ruido es la vibración del aire causada por un objeto que se mueve.

RWD   Tracción trasera (*Rear wheel drive* en inglés).

SAE   Siglas en inglés de Sociedad de Ingenieros Automotrices.

SAEV   Siglas en inglés de sistema de aumento de estabilidad vehicular.

Saginaw   Marca de componentes del sistema de dirección, que se fabrican en Saginaw (Michigan, EE.UU.).

SAI   Siglas en inglés de inclinación del eje de la dirección (es lo mismo que el ángulo de inclinación del eje pivote).

Salida   La orden que emana de un módulo de control electrónico.

Salidas neumáticas   Pequeñas hendiduras en el dibujo de un neumático, las cuales mejoran la tracción.

Seguimiento   Fenómeno que describe el hecho que las ruedas traseras deben seguir a las delanteras en una relación proporcional exacta.

"Selectable Ride" (SR)   Una marca de cierto tipo de sistema electrónico de suspensión.

Selenoide   Dispositivo electromecánico que utiliza un núcleo central movible el cual puede estar conectado a un varillaje a fin de impulsar o mover una válvula u otro aparato.

Sellante   La capa de mezcla impermeable o hule que recubre el interior del neumático.

Sello de grasa   Un sello utilizado para prevenir que la grasa se escape y para prevenir el ingreso de la suciedad y de la humedad.

Sello estático   Un tipo de sellante hermético que no admite movimiento entre las partes selladas.

Sellos dinámicos   Sellos utilizados cuando existe un movimiento relativo entre dos superficies cuando éstas son selladas.

SEMA   Siglas en inglés de Asociación de Fabricantes de Equipos Especializados.

Semieje   Ejes de propulsión en un vehículo de tracción delantera o de un diferencial estacionario a las ruedas de propulsión.

Sensor automático de suspensión electrónica   Un tipo de suspensión electrónica que utiliza amortiguadores de aire para controlar la altura de la parte trasera del vehículo.

Sensor de aceleración lateral   Un sensor utilizado en muchos vehículos con suspensión electrónica y/o sistemas detectores de tracción que se utiliza para detectar el movimiento pendular de un vehículo.

Sensor de Altura   Un sensor de altura determina la relación vertical entre los componentes de la suspensión y el cuerpo del vehículo.

Sensor de Derrapaje o Guiñada   Un sensor por lo general ubicado en el centro del vehículo que detecta el derrape como parte de un sistema de suspensión electrónica.

Sensor de la posición del volante de la dirección   Un sensor que determina cuan rápido y en que dirección se está girando el volante.

Sensor de posicionamiento del volante   Un sensor que detecta la dirección y velocidad de la rotación del volante de dirección.

Separador de rótulas tipo tenedor   Un tenedor de terminación en punta utilizado para separar las partes del chasis que se conectan por un perno y un cono. El dar un golpe al extremo del separador de rótulas fuerza la porción de cuña de la herramienta entre las partes que deben ser separadas y "rompe el cono". Un separador de rótulas tipo tenedor por lo general *no* es recomendado, debido a que esta herramienta puede romper o desgarrar la bota de grasa de la parte que se separa.

Sinfín y engranaje de dirección   Una caja de dirección que utiliza un engranaje sinfín el cual se engrana a un engranaje de sector en la cruceta.

Sinfín y rodillo de dirección   Una caja de dirección que utiliza un engranaje sinfín en el eje de dirección. Un rodillo en un puntal de la cruceta engrana con el sinfín.

Sistemas hidráulicos   La fuerza ejercida por un líquido presurizado al interior de un sistema cerrado.

SMC   Siglas en inglés de compuesto para moldeado de láminas s.

Sobreinflado   Utilizado para describir un neumático con demasiada presión neumática (una presión mayor a la máxima permitida).

Sobreviraje   Un término utilizado para describir el manejo de un vehículo donde el conductor debe mover el volante en la dirección opuesta de lo normal mientras da la vuelta a una esquina. El manejo del sobreviraje es sumamente peligroso. La mayoría de los fabricantes de vehículos diseñan a sus vehículos para subvirar en vez de sobrevirar.

Soporte de la cremallera   Una unidad cargada de resortes utilizada para sostener la parte de la cremallera del ensamblaje de dirección de piñón y cremallera en la posición apropiada.

SPS   Siglas en inglés de sensor de posicionamiento de la suspensión.

SR   Siglas en inglés de sistema de suspensión de selección de altura tipo, "Selectable ride".

SSS   Siglas en inglés de dirección sensible a la velocidad.

SST   Siglas en inglés de herramientas especiales de servicio.

Stabilitrack   El nombre de la marca de un tipo de sistema de control de suspensión electrónica.

Subchasis   Un soporte estructural para el motor y el eje transversal en un vehículo de propulsión delantera (FWD).

Subviraje no intencional   Un término utilizado para describir un tipo de subviraje.

Suspensión Chapman de puntal   Un tipo de suspensión de puntal MacPherson utilizada en la parte trasera del vehículo.

Suspensión de aire   Un tipo de suspensión que utiliza resortes de aire en vez de resortes de acero (AS por sus siglas en inglés).

Suspensión de brazo corto/largo   Se abrevia SLA en inglés. Un sistema de suspensión con un brazo de control superior corto y un brazo de control inferior largo. La rueda cambia muy poco en su ángulo camber con una desviación vertical. También conocida como una suspensión de doble espoleta u horquilla.

Suspensión de puntal   Un tipo de sistema de suspensión a base de puntales.

Suspensión de ruedas tiradas   Un diseño de construcción de un vehículo que coloca la caja de engranaje y la varilla de la dirección detrás de la línea del centro de las ruedas delanteras.

Suspensión delantera independiente   Un sistema de suspensión que permite que una rueda se mueva de arriba a abajo sin tener un efecto mayor en el lado opuesto

Suspensión magneto-reológica   Un tipo de suspensión electrónica que utiliza amortiguadores fluidos magneto-reológicos.

Suspensión semi-independiente   Un tipo de suspensión trasera que permite cierto grado de transferencia de movimiento al lado opuesto.

Suspensión SLA   Abreviación del nombre en inglés de suspensión de brazo corto/largo.

Suspensión   Partes, articulaciones o uniones mediante las cuales las ruedas de un vehículo se sujetan a la carrocería o cuerpo del vehículo. Estos elementos soportan el vehículo y mantienen las ruedas alineadas apropiadamente.

SWPS   Siglas en inglés de sensor del posicionamiento del volante.

Tabica   El panel que se halla entre el compartimiento del motor y el compartimiento de pasajeros.

Talón   La parte de un neumático que está compuesto de alambre, alrededor de la cual se envuelven las capas neumáticas.

Tapa de grasa   Una tapa de metal funcional que mantiene a la grasa dentro y la suciedad fuera de los cojinetes de las ruedas. También llamada *cubrepolvo* o *antipolvo*.

Tapa del Cubo   Una tapa decorativa y funcional que cubre todo el volante. *Véase también* tapa de mazo.

TDP   Siglas en inglés de detector de desperfectos neumáticos.

Temperatura de licuefacción   La temperatura en que una grasa pasa de un estado semisólido a un estado líquido bajo condiciones especificadas por la ASTM.

TFE   Un tipo de dirección asistida variable conocida como "Two flow electronic," o TFE por sus siglas en inglés.

"Tight"   Termino en inglés para describir una deriva apretada.

TOOT/TOT   Siglas en inglés de divergencia al doblar.

Tope [de goma] de la suspensión   Un tope o "stop" de goma o uretano cuya función consiste en limitar el movimiento ascendente de la suspensión. También conocido como *estop, estope, stop de goma, bote del rebote, tope de goma para rebotes, tope del rebote,* o *tope de compresión.*

Tope de bote   *Véase* tope de rebote.

Tope de la suspensión   *Véase* tope del bote o del rebote.

Tope o "stop" de la dirección   El punto donde termina la varilla de la dirección de eje a eje de trayectoria.

Tope o goma de la suspensión   Un tope de goma o uretano que previene el movimiento hacia arriba de la suspensión. También llamado *tope de quiebre, tope de suspensión* o *tope de compresión* (*strikeout bumper, suspension bumper* o *compression bumper* en inglés).

Tornillo de tope   Un nombre para un perno que se coloca en una pieza moldeada, tal como un bloque de motor.

Torque en la dirección   Este cambio autónomo de la dirección ocurre en vehículos con tracción delantera cuando un cambio en el par motor causa que una de las ruedas delanteras cambie su ángulo crítico de alineación. El jaloneo resultante es mucho más notorio durante una aceleración rápida, especialmente cuando los cambios de caja crean una diferencia repentina en la torción o en el par motor.

Torsión del montado de las ruedas   El par motor aplicado a las tuercas de las ruedas.

Torsión del piñón   La torción o par requerido para rotar la barra del piñón en una dirección de piñón y cremallera.

Torsión   Una fuerza que puede o no resultar en un movimiento. Se mide en Pies-Libras (ft.-lbs.) o en Newton-metros (Nm).

TPC   Siglas en inglés de criterio de desempeño neumático.

TPMS   Siglas en inglés de sistema de monitoreo de presión neumática.

TSB   Siglas en inglés de boletín de servicios técnicos.

Tubo respirador   Tubo que conecta el fuelle izquierdo con el fuelle derecho de un engranaje de dirección con cremallera y piñón.

Tuerca castillo   Un tipo de tuerca de seguridad que utiliza un perno de chaveta o clavija hendida para mantenerse en posición.

Tuerca de puntal   El nombre comúnmente utilizado para describir la tuerca de gran tamaño ubicada en la parte superior del bastidor del puntal MacPherson. Esta tuerca hueca debe ser retirada para reemplazar un cartucho de puntal.

Tuerca de seguridad   *Véase* entretuerca.

Tuerca del huso o vástago   Tuerca utilizada para retener y sujetar el reborde de la maza o cubo contra el husillo.

Tuercas de rueda   Tuercas utilizadas en los pernos prisioneros (o espárragos) para acoplar las ruedas a los cubos.

UNC   Siglas en inglés de Estándar Nacional Unificado de Roscas.

UNF   Siglas en inglés de estándar de lámina fina (delgada) del tornillo.

Unión Universal   Una unión o junta que permite que el par motor se transmita y que de esta manera se viabilice el movimiento horizontal del sistema de la suspensión.

UST   Siglas en inglés de depósito de almacenamiento subterráneo.

UTQGS   Siglas en inglés de sistema de medición de calidad neumática uniforme.

Vacío APEE   Un vacío equipado con un filtro de aire particulado de elevada eficiencia (APEF, o HEPA por sus siglas en inglés).

Vagabundeo   Un tipo de conducción o maniobrabilidad que requiere de una corrección constante del viraje del volante a fin de mantener la trayectoria del vehículo en ángulo recto.

Válvula de alivio   Una válvula ubicada en la bomba de fuerza de dirección que utiliza una bola de retención, la cual se desplaza, permitiendo que el fluido vuelva a la reserva si la presión excede un cierto volumen.

Válvula de control giratoria   Una válvula de dirección asistida que funciona al rotar una válvula interior dentro de una válvula exterior para controlar la cantidad de fuerza que se utiliza en asistir la dirección.

Válvula para el control de flujo   Regula y controla el flujo de los fluidos hidráulicos de la bomba de la dirección asistida al engranaje de dirección o ensamblaje de cremallera y piñón. La válvula para el control de flujo es por lo general parte del ensamblaje de la bomba de la dirección asistida.

Válvula Schrader   Cierto tipo de válvula utilizada en neumáticos, sistemas de aire acondicionado y sistemas de inyección de combustible. Fue inventada en 1844 por August Schrader.

Variación de fuerza radial   La variación en la fuerza que ejerce una rueda a medida que rota y se pone en contacto con la superficie del camino.

Varilla central   La parte central de un acoplamiento de dirección tipo paralelogramo.

Varilla de arrastre   Utilizada para describir una conexión en el centro de la varilla de la dirección, por lo general llamada una *conexión central.*

Varilla radial   Un componente de la suspensión para controlar el apoyo longitudinal (de adelante hacia atrás) por lo general se encuentra conectada, a través de bujes de goma, por un extremo a la armazón y en el otro extremo al eje o brazo de control de la suspensión. *También véase* barra de retención.

Varillas estabilizadoras   Por lo general consiste de una tuerca y un tornillo que conectan el puntal de la barra estabilizadora con el brazo de control inferior.

VECI   Siglas en inglés de información de control de emisiones de vehículos.

VES   Siglas en inglés de dirección de esfuerzo variable.

Vibración   Una oscilación, estremecimiento o movimientos laterales en sentidos opuestos (vaivén).

VIN   Siglas en inglés de número de identificación del vehículo.

Viraje de línea central   Describe la posición del volante mientras el vehículo recorre un camino recto y nivelado (plano). El volante debe estar centrado o dentro de más o menos 3 grados del centro, según las especificaciones de los diversos fabricantes de vehículos.

VOC   Siglas en inglés de compuestos orgánicos volátiles.

VSES   Siglas en inglés de sistema de aumento de estabilidad vehicular.

"VS Sensor"   Siglas en inglés de sensor de velocidad del vehículo.

Vulcanización   Proceso que combina el calor y la presión para cambiar la composición química del caucho.

W/O   Abreviación de "without" ("sin" en inglés).

WHMIS   Siglas en inglés de Sistema de Información sobre Materiales Peligrosos en el Lugar de Trabajo.

X modificada   Un método de rotación de neumáticos.

INDEX